# I CHING
## The Oracle

Also by
BENEBELL WEN

*The Tao of Craft*

*Holistic Tarot*

# I CHING
## The Oracle

A Practical Guide to *The Book of Changes*

An updated translation annotated with cultural
and historical references, restoring the
*I Ching* to its shamanic origins

BENEBELL WEN

North Atlantic Books
Huichin, unceded Ohlone land
*aka* Berkeley, California

Copyright © 2023 by Benebell Wen. All rights reserved. No portion of this book, except for brief review, may be reproduced, stored in a retrieval system, or transmitted in any form or by any means—electronic, mechanical, photocopying, recording, or otherwise—without the written permission of the publisher. For information contact North Atlantic Books.

Published by
North Atlantic Books
Huichin, unceded Ohlone land
*aka* Berkeley, California

Cover art: *Studying the I Ching by a Window*
by 陳書 [Chen Shu] (1660–1735)
Cover design by Mimi Bark
Book design by Happenstance Type-O-Rama
Printed in Malaysia

*I Ching, the Oracle: A Practical Guide to* The Book of Changes is sponsored and published by North Atlantic Books, an educational nonprofit based in the unceded Ohlone land Huichin (aka Berkeley, CA) that collaborates with partners to develop cross-cultural perspectives, nurture holistic views of art, science, the humanities, and healing, and seed personal and global transformation by publishing work on the relationship of body, spirit, and nature.

North Atlantic Books' publications are distributed to the US trade and internationally by Penguin Random House Publisher Services. For further information, visit our website at www.northatlanticbooks.com.

Library of Congress Cataloging-in-Publication Data
Names: Wen, Benebell, 1981– translator.
Title: I Ching, the oracle : a practical guide to the book of changes : an updated translation with spells, talisman crafting, and East Asian mysticism and ritual / Benebell Wen.
Other titles: Yi jing. English.
Description: Huichin, unceded Ohlone land aka Berkeley, California : North Atlantic Books, [2023] | Includes bibliographical references and index.
| Summary: "In I Ching, The Oracle, Wen imparts upon readers a foundational understanding of Taoist metaphysics, rooted within the wisdom and knowledge of more than 3,000 years of historical and cultural practice. She specifically draws upon her own experiences to provide readers with a spiritual medium to move through life and connect with our ancestors"— Provided by publisher.
Identifiers: LCCN 2022042286 (print) | LCCN 2022042287 (ebook) | ISBN 9781623178734 (trade paperback) | ISBN 9781623178741 (ebook)
Subjects: LCSH: Yi jing.
Classification: LCC PL2478 .D736 2023 (print) | LCC PL2478 (ebook) | DDC 299.5/1282—dc23/eng/20230210
LC record available at https://lccn.loc.gov/2022042286
LC ebook record available at https://lccn.loc.gov/2022042287

1  2  3  4  5  6  7  8  9  ASIA PACIFIC  28  27  26  25  24  23

This book includes recycled material and material from well-managed forests. North Atlantic Books is committed to the protection of our environment. We print on recycled paper whenever possible and partner with printers who strive to use environmentally responsible practices.

*In honor of my family, near and far,
and to every descendant of the Dragon,
be that in body or soul.*

# CONTENTS

List of Illustrations . . . . . . . . . . . . . . . . . . . . . . . . . . . . xiii
List of Tables . . . . . . . . . . . . . . . . . . . . . . . . . . . . . . . . xvii
List of Practicums . . . . . . . . . . . . . . . . . . . . . . . . . . . . . xx

1. Preface . . . . . . . . . . . . . . . . . . . . . . . . . . . . . . . . . . . 1

2. Myths, Legends, and Cultural Heroes of the I Ching . . . . . 9

3. Yì Xué: An Overview of I Ching Discourse . . . . . . . . . 31
   Before the Common Era . . . . . . . . . . . . . . . . . . . . . . . 33
   New Text Schools vs. Old Text Schools . . . . . . . . . . . . . . . 36
   The Rationalists vs. the Originalists . . . . . . . . . . . . . . . . 38
   Esoteric I Ching: *Yi wei* and the School of Mystery . . . . . . . . 42
   Gua Qi: Theoretical Study of Yin and Yang . . . . . . . . . . . . 45
   A History of Eclectic Influences . . . . . . . . . . . . . . . . . . 57
   Jesuit Missionaries and the I Ching . . . . . . . . . . . . . . . . 61
   Carl Jung and the Theory of Synchronicity . . . . . . . . . . . . 65
   The I Ching in Western Occultism . . . . . . . . . . . . . . . . . 68
   Science, Math, and the Genetic Code . . . . . . . . . . . . . . . 74
   Taoist Mysticism and Magic . . . . . . . . . . . . . . . . . . . . 82
   The Way of the Sages . . . . . . . . . . . . . . . . . . . . . . . . 87

4. Interpreting the Hexagrams . . . . . . . . . . . . . . . . . . . 95
   The Image and Number Tradition (Xiàng Shù) . . . . . . . . . 103
   The Meaning and Principle Tradition (Yì Lǐ) . . . . . . . . . . 112
   The Plum Blossom Methods . . . . . . . . . . . . . . . . . . . . 131
   General Insights, One Fortune-Teller to Another . . . . . . . . 145
   Cultivating Objective Interpretation . . . . . . . . . . . . . . . 150

## 5. The Eight Trigrams (Ba Gua) . . . . . . . . . . . . . . . 153
Yin and Yang Affinities; the Four Faces of God. . . . . . . . . . . . 155
The Book of the River Maps . . . . . . . . . . . . . . . . . . . . . 160
Arrangements of the Eight Trigrams. . . . . . . . . . . . . . . . . 163
Eight Immortals and Archetypes of the Mystic . . . . . . . . . . . 167
Heaven (Qián), Sky: The Virtuoso. . . . . . . . . . . . . . . . . . . 172
Lake (Duì), Exchange: The Warrior . . . . . . . . . . . . . . . . . 179
Fire (Lí), Clarity: The Philosopher. . . . . . . . . . . . . . . . . . . 188
Thunder (Zhèn), Power: The Spellcaster . . . . . . . . . . . . . . 196
Wind (Xùn), Influence: The Shaman . . . . . . . . . . . . . . . . 203
Water (Kǎn), Mysteries: The Healer . . . . . . . . . . . . . . . . . 212
Mountain (Gěn), Knowledge: The Alchemist . . . . . . . . . . . 218
Earth (Kūn), Field: The Enchanter. . . . . . . . . . . . . . . . . . 222
Circling the Square: The I Ching Mandala . . . . . . . . . . . . . 228

## 6. The Five Phases of Change (Wu Xing) . . . . . . . . . 231
Wood (Mù): Sprouting and Cultivating. . . . . . . . . . . . . . . 248
Fire (Huǒ): Blooming and Inspiring. . . . . . . . . . . . . . . . . 250
Earth (Tǔ): Ripening and Maturing. . . . . . . . . . . . . . . . . 252
Metal (Jīn): Culminating and Extinguishing . . . . . . . . . . . 254
Water (Shuǐ): Reflecting and Returning. . . . . . . . . . . . . . . 256

## 7. Divination Methods . . . . . . . . . . . . . . . . . . . . . 267
Preparations before the Divination . . . . . . . . . . . . . . . . . 268
Invoking Divinity and Presenting the Question . . . . . . . . . . 270
Coin Toss Method . . . . . . . . . . . . . . . . . . . . . . . . . . . 298
Divination with Cowrie Shells . . . . . . . . . . . . . . . . . . . . 310
Locked Hexagrams . . . . . . . . . . . . . . . . . . . . . . . . . . 312
Plum Blossom Methods . . . . . . . . . . . . . . . . . . . . . . . 313
    Rice Grain Method . . . . . . . . . . . . . . . . . . . . . . . . 314
    Horary Astrology and I Ching . . . . . . . . . . . . . . . . . . 324
    Numerological Principles and Casting Hexagrams. . . . . . . 339
    Channeled Method of Casting Hexagrams . . . . . . . . . . 341
    I Ching and the Tarot. . . . . . . . . . . . . . . . . . . . . . . 345
Summary Outline of Hexagram Interpretation . . . . . . . . . . 358

8. I Ching: The Book of Changes . . . . . . . . . . . . . . . 373
   Preliminary Notes . . . . . . . . . . . . . . . . . . . . . . . . . . . 373
      The Zhouyi and King Wen's Revealed Sequence . . . . . . . . . . 373
      Auspicious vs. Inauspicious . . . . . . . . . . . . . . . . . . . . . 380
      To Offer Sacrifice and to Divine. . . . . . . . . . . . . . . . . . . 380
      The *Junzi* (Sage), the Eminent One, and the Adversary . . . . . . 382
      "There Is No Blame" . . . . . . . . . . . . . . . . . . . . . . . . . 385
      "Endeavor for Corrective Measures" . . . . . . . . . . . . . . . . 386
      "Crossing the Great Stream". . . . . . . . . . . . . . . . . . . . . 387
   Hexagram 1: Qián. Creative Power. . . . . . . . . . . . . . . . . . 389
   Hexagram 2: Kūn. Supportive Power . . . . . . . . . . . . . . . . 395
   Hexagram 3: Tún. Initial Challenge . . . . . . . . . . . . . . . . . 402
   Hexagram 4: Méng. Naiveté. . . . . . . . . . . . . . . . . . . . . . 407
   Hexagram 5: Xū. Patience. . . . . . . . . . . . . . . . . . . . . . . 414
   Hexagram 6: Sòng. The Trial . . . . . . . . . . . . . . . . . . . . . 419
   Hexagram 7: Shī. The Army . . . . . . . . . . . . . . . . . . . . . 424
   Hexagram 8: Bǐ. Alliance . . . . . . . . . . . . . . . . . . . . . . . 428
   Hexagram 9: Xiǎo Chù. Cultivate Gently. . . . . . . . . . . . . . . 433
   Hexagram 10: Lǚ. Treading. . . . . . . . . . . . . . . . . . . . . . 438
   Hexagram 11: Tài. Harmony . . . . . . . . . . . . . . . . . . . . . 443
   Hexagram 12: Fǒu. Stalemate. . . . . . . . . . . . . . . . . . . . . 449
   Hexagram 13: Tóng Rén. Fellowship . . . . . . . . . . . . . . . . 455
   Hexagram 14: Dà Yǒu. Accolades . . . . . . . . . . . . . . . . . . 460
   Hexagram 15: Qiān. Modesty. . . . . . . . . . . . . . . . . . . . . 464
   Hexagram 16: Yù. Enthusiasm . . . . . . . . . . . . . . . . . . . . 468
   Hexagram 17: Suí. Inspiring Followers . . . . . . . . . . . . . . . 473
   Hexagram 18: Gǔ. Decay . . . . . . . . . . . . . . . . . . . . . . . 478
   Hexagram 19: Lín. Spring Is Coming . . . . . . . . . . . . . . . . 484
   Hexagram 20: Guān. Observation . . . . . . . . . . . . . . . . . . 488
   Hexagram 21: Shih Hé. Bite Through. . . . . . . . . . . . . . . . 493
   Hexagram 22: Bì. Luminosity. . . . . . . . . . . . . . . . . . . . . 499
   Hexagram 23: Bō. Partition . . . . . . . . . . . . . . . . . . . . . . 506
   Hexagram 24: Fù. Repose. . . . . . . . . . . . . . . . . . . . . . . 513
   Hexagram 25: Wú Wàng. Without Folly . . . . . . . . . . . . . . 518
   Hexagram 26: Dà Chù. Cultivate the Supreme . . . . . . . . . . . 523

Hexagram 27: Yí. Receive Nourishment . . . . . . . . . . . . . . . . 526
Hexagram 28: Dà Guò. Undertake the Great. . . . . . . . . . . . . . 532
Hexagram 29: Kǎn. The Abyss . . . . . . . . . . . . . . . . . . . . . 537
Hexagram 30: Lí. The Spark . . . . . . . . . . . . . . . . . . . . . . 542
Hexagram 31: Xián. Mutual Accord. . . . . . . . . . . . . . . . . . . 550
Hexagram 32: Héng. The Eternal . . . . . . . . . . . . . . . . . . . 555
Hexagram 33: Dùn. Withdraw . . . . . . . . . . . . . . . . . . . . . 560
Hexagram 34: Dà Zhuàng. Great Power. . . . . . . . . . . . . . . . . 566
Hexagram 35: Jìn. Advancement. . . . . . . . . . . . . . . . . . . . 571
Hexagram 36: Míng Yí. Darkening of the Light . . . . . . . . . . . 577
Hexagram 37: Jiā Rén. The Family. . . . . . . . . . . . . . . . . . . 586
Hexagram 38: Kuí. Opposition. . . . . . . . . . . . . . . . . . . . . 591
Hexagram 39: Jiǎn. An Impasse . . . . . . . . . . . . . . . . . . . . 597
Hexagram 40: Jiě. Release of Tension . . . . . . . . . . . . . . . . . 602
Hexagram 41: Sǔn. Debilitation . . . . . . . . . . . . . . . . . . . . 607
Hexagram 42: Yì. Burgeoning. . . . . . . . . . . . . . . . . . . . . . 612
Hexagram 43: Guài. Decisive Action . . . . . . . . . . . . . . . . . 617
Hexagram 44: Gòu. Improper Meeting . . . . . . . . . . . . . . . . 622
Hexagram 45: Cuì. Assembly. . . . . . . . . . . . . . . . . . . . . . 628
Hexagram 46: Shēng. Hoist. . . . . . . . . . . . . . . . . . . . . . . 633
Hexagram 47: Kùn. Blockade. . . . . . . . . . . . . . . . . . . . . . 637
Hexagram 48: Jǐng. Fountainhead . . . . . . . . . . . . . . . . . . . 643
Hexagram 49: Gé. Revolution . . . . . . . . . . . . . . . . . . . . . 649
Hexagram 50: Dǐng. The Cauldron . . . . . . . . . . . . . . . . . . 653
Hexagram 51: Zhèn. Jolt. . . . . . . . . . . . . . . . . . . . . . . . . 661
Hexagram 52: Gěn. Listen to the Wind . . . . . . . . . . . . . . . . 666
Hexagram 53: Jiàn. Steadfast . . . . . . . . . . . . . . . . . . . . . . 673
Hexagram 54: Guī Mèi. The Marrying Maiden . . . . . . . . . . . . 680
Hexagram 55: Fēng. Opulence . . . . . . . . . . . . . . . . . . . . . 688
Hexagram 56: Lǚ. The Wanderer. . . . . . . . . . . . . . . . . . . . 695
Hexagram 57: Xùn. Use Gentle Force . . . . . . . . . . . . . . . . . 701
Hexagram 58: Duì. Joyous Exchange . . . . . . . . . . . . . . . . . 706
Hexagram 59: Huàn. Making Waves. . . . . . . . . . . . . . . . . . 710
Hexagram 60: Jié. Boundaries. . . . . . . . . . . . . . . . . . . . . . 718
Hexagram 61: Zhōng Fú. Faith Within . . . . . . . . . . . . . . . . 724

Hexagram 62: Xiǎo Guò. Pay Attention to Details . . . . . . . . . . . 730
Hexagram 63: Jì Jì. After the Ending. . . . . . . . . . . . . . . . . . . . 738
Hexagram 64: Wèi Jì. Toward an End . . . . . . . . . . . . . . . . . . . 745

9. Ancestral Veneration and the I Ching . . . . . . . . . . . 755

10. The *Yì*, the *Wū*, and Shamanism . . . . . . . . . . . . . 773
    Shamanic Origins of the I Ching. . . . . . . . . . . . . . . . . . . . . 773
    The Loanword "Shaman" and the *Wū* . . . . . . . . . . . . . . . . 777
    Shamanistic-Historical Traditions . . . . . . . . . . . . . . . . . . . 780
    The Eight Gods of Shang Shamanism . . . . . . . . . . . . . . . . 792
    Soul Retrieval: Theory and Practice . . . . . . . . . . . . . . . . . 795
    Xī Wáng Mǔ, Goddess of the *Wū* . . . . . . . . . . . . . . . . . . . 804
    Healing the Inner *Shén* . . . . . . . . . . . . . . . . . . . . . . . . . . 817

11. Returning Full Circle . . . . . . . . . . . . . . . . . . . . . . 823

12. Appendices . . . . . . . . . . . . . . . . . . . . . . . . . . . . . 829
    Appendix A: Twenty-Four Solar Terms . . . . . . . . . . . . . . . 831
    Appendix B: Stems, Branches, and Trigrams . . . . . . . . . . . 837
    Appendix C: Trigrams and Feng Shui . . . . . . . . . . . . . . . . 839
    Appendix D: The Eight Bodhisattvas and the Ba Gua . . . . 840
    Appendix E: Map of Shang and Zhou . . . . . . . . . . . . . . . . 843

Bibliography . . . . . . . . . . . . . . . . . . . . . . . . . . . . . . . . . . . . 847
Notes . . . . . . . . . . . . . . . . . . . . . . . . . . . . . . . . . . . . . . . . . 855
Index . . . . . . . . . . . . . . . . . . . . . . . . . . . . . . . . . . . . . . . . . 913
Acknowledgments . . . . . . . . . . . . . . . . . . . . . . . . . . . . . . . 927
About the Author . . . . . . . . . . . . . . . . . . . . . . . . . . . . . . . 929

# LIST OF ILLUSTRATIONS

Figure 1.1 *Studying the I Ching by a Window* by 陳書 [Chen Shu] (1660–1735)

Figure 1.2 Illustration of a *zouyu* 騶虞 (mythic beast referenced in hexagrams 3, 45, and 61)

Figure 2.1 *Yi* in different Chinese scripts

Figure 2.2 *Jīng* in seal script

Figure 2.3 King Wen combines trigrams to form hexagrams

Figure 2.4 *King Wen of Zhou* (1632) by Kanō Sansetsu (1589–1651)

Figure 2.5 *Fuxi and Nǔwā* (eighth century)

Figure 2.6 *Fuxi Creates the Trigrams* (1503) by Guo Xu (1456–1526/32)

Figure 2.7 *The Mystic Tablet* or Lo Shu magic square

Figure 2.8 *Yu the Great* by Ma Lin (1225–1264)

Figure 2.9 *Emperor Yu Controlling the Waters* (Qing dynasty)

Figure 2.10 Shang dynasty oracle bone divination

Figure 2.11 *Tai Ren, Mother of King Wen* by Jiao Bingzhen (1689–1726)

Figure 2.12 *Tai Si, Mother of King Wu of Zhou* by Jiao Bingzhen

Figure 2.13 King Zhou of Shang entering the palace of Nǔwā

Figure 2.14 *Su Daji*

Figure 2.15 King Wen and his son, Wu of Zhou

Figure 2.16 Scene from *The Creation of the Gods* by 許仲琳 [Xu Zhonglin]

Figure 2.17 *Duke of Zhou* (1632) by Kanō Sansetsu

Figure 2.18 Zhou dynasty seal script

Figure 2.19 *King Wen and Four Generations of Beneficence*

Figure 2.20 Frontispiece from *Confucius Sinarum* (Paris, 1687)

Figure 2.21 Scene from the *Ladies' Book of Filial Piety* (1130–1170)

Figure 2.22 Scene from the *Ladies' Book of Filial Piety*

Figure 2.23 The triple gods of Taoism (Qing dynasty) [清無名氏繡三星圖]

Figure 2.24 Detail from *Studying the I Ching by a Window*

Figure 3.1 *Tower on the Xianshan Mountain* by 惲壽平 [Yun Shouping] (1633–1690)

Figure 3.2 Annotated copy of the Book of Rites, 907 AD

Figure 3.3 The changing meaning of *zhen*
Figure 3.4 Portraits of Wang Bi and Zhu Xi
Figure 3.5 Page from the *Interpretations and Incantations of Celestials in the Zhouyi*
Figure 3.6 Gua Qi yin and yang fluctuations
Figure 3.7 Babylonian augury by means of geometrical figures
Figure 3.8 Aleister Crowley's Chinese cosmos and the Tree of Life
Figure 3.9 Diagram of a DNA molecule
Figure 3.10 Diagram of an RNA molecule
Figure 3.11 Classic circular genetic code mandala
Figure 3.12 Square representation of the genetic code
Figure 3.13 Circular I Ching mandala
Figure 3.14 Square representation of the I Ching
Figure 3.15 Fu talismans
Figure 3.16 Seal bonding the coin to the *qi* of the I Ching
Figure 3.17 Mysterious Lady of the Nine Heavens
Figure 3.18 Another detail from *Studying the I Ching by a Window*
Figure 4.1 *Ocean Palace of Increasing Eons* (Ming dynasty)
Figure 4.2 Portrait of Cheng Yi (Qing dynasty)
Figure 4.3 Bronze ritual tripod cauldron, late Shang period (thirteenth–fourteenth century BC)
Figure 4.4 Ritual cauldron belonging to the marquis of Kang (eleventh century BC)
Figure 4.5 Chinese calligraphy brushes and inkstone set
Figure 4.6 The sexagenary cycle
Figure 4.7 Depiction of the Mahayana Buddhist Pure Land
Figure 4.8 Inscription on the mural tomb of Du Jiyuan (AD 940)
Figure 5.1 Fu Xi's sequence of the eight trigrams
Figure 5.2 Taijitu and the ouroboros
Figure 5.3 The Hé Tú 河圖 square
Figure 5.4 The Luò Shū (Lo Shu) 洛書 square
Figure 5.5 The River Maps, as printed in Zhu Xi's *Zhouyi benyi*
Figure 5.6 Han Xiangzi: The Virtuoso
Figure 5.7 Depiction of astral projection
Figure 5.8 Queen Mother of the West 西王母 (1772) by Gu Quan 顧銓
Figure 5.9 Zhong Li Quan: The Warrior
Figure 5.10 Prosperity Lake talisman

Figure 5.11 The mystic's Dharma Fan
Figure 5.12 Lü Dong Bin: The Philosopher
Figure 5.13 Receiving the sacred powers of fire
Figure 5.14 Cao Guo Jiu: The Spellcaster
Figure 5.15 Jing Guang hand mudra
Figure 5.16 Cao Guo Jiu's name in calligraphy
Figure 5.17 He Xian Gu: The Shamaness
Figure 5.18 Crystal lotus vessel for bottling the Wind spirit
Figure 5.19 Li Tie Guai: The Healer
Figure 5.20 Calabash or bottle gourd (*húlu*)
Figure 5.21 Zhang Guo Lao: The Alchemist
Figure 5.22 Lan Cai He: The Enchanter
Figure 5.23 *Bhumisparsha* hand mudra
Figure 5.24 *Assembly of the Eight Immortals* (Song dynasty)
Figure 5.25 Squaring the circle of changes
Figure 5.26 *Om yamantaka hum phat: Vajrabhairava* mandala (1332)
Figure 6.1 Guo Kuntao's 1858 seal script excerpt I of the Book of Documents
Figure 6.2 Wu Xing cycles of creation and destruction
Figure 6.3 The five changing phases and eight trigrams
Figure 6.4 Guo Kuntao's 1858 seal script excerpt II of the Book of Documents
Figure 7.1 I Ching divination methods
Figure 7.2 The divination table
Figure 7.3 *Lady of the Nine Heavens* (1829) by Katsushika Hokusai
Figure 7.4 Yarrow stalks for divination
Figure 7.5 Handpicked yarrow stalks
Figure 7.6 Copper alloy coins from the Qing dynasty (1645–1911)
Figure 7.7 Using round pieces of wood for coins
Figure 7.8 Divination with cowrie shells
Figure 7.9 Reference for the cowrie shell toss method
Figure 7.10 Rice grain divination
Figure 7.11 Anointing your rice grains
Figure 7.12 Seal of Jiǔ Tiān Xuán Nǚ with hexagrams, stems, and branches
Figure 7.13a The ninth Gua, for marking the spirit helpers
Figure 7.13b *The Rider-Waite-Smith Tarot* (1911) by A. E. Waite and Pamela Colman Smith

Figure 7.13c *La Grande Tarot Belline* (1863) by Magus Edmond

Figure 7.14 Sample two-card reading

Figure 8.1 The six maidens of Jiu Tian Xuan Nu 六丁神女 (1493)

Figure 8.2 Oracle bone (twelfth century BC)

Figure 8.3 Scanned page of Hexagram 1, Zhouyi in the *Siku Quanshu* (四庫全書)

Figure 8.4 Jade Emperor and the heavenly kings (1545)

Figure 8.5 Protection amulet to ward against poison magic

Figure 8.6 Script for "Yue" in bird script 鳥書 as inscribed on the sword of Goujian

Figure 8.7 *Chang-Er Flees to the Moon* (1868–1892) by Yoshitoshi Taiso

Figure 9.1 Nine-headed phoenix 九鳳

Figure 9.2 *A Child Worshipping the Sage*

Figure 9.3 Shrine and altar

Figure 9.4 Cowrie shell divination

Figure 9.5 Cowrie shell correspondences

Figure 9.6 Cowrie shell casting for Hexagram 2

Figure 10.1 Oracle bone script for *wū* 巫

Figure 10.2 Illustration of Jiahu turtle shells

Figure 10.3 Kuan Yin from the Heart Sutra by Zhao Mengfu 趙孟頫 (AD 1254–1322)

Figure 10.4 Knotted red string bracelet of protection

Figure 10.5 Hangonkō 返魂香 (1780) by Toriyama Sekien

Figure 10.6 Queen Mother of the West 西王母 (Qing dynasty) by 金廷標

Figure 10.7 The Banquet of Seowangmo (Joseon, 1392–1910)

Figure 10.8 Seiōbo, Queen of the West

Figure 10.9 Short-form method for yarrow stalk divination

Figure 10.10 Bridging the worlds

Figure 10.11 Combining yarrow stalk and rice grain methods

Figure 11.1 A cyclical Book of Changes

Figure 11.2 Summary of divination methods

Figure 11.3 The Queen Mother's Shòu Yān 獸焉

Figure 12.1 Leaf 2 from the *Landscapes* 山水 by Jiao Bingzhen 焦秉貞 (1689–1726)

Figure 12.2 *Immortals Gathering around the Buddha* (Qing dynasty)

Figure 12.3 Map of the Shang and Zhou dynasties

# LIST OF TABLES

Table 1.1 Trigram Cross-References for Hexagram Construction

Table 3.1 The Twelve Hexagrams of the Son of Heaven 天子卦 (*Tiānzǐ Guà*)

Table 3.2 The Four Perfected Hexagrams (四正卦, *Sì Zhèng Guà*) and the Twenty-Four Solar Terms

Table 3.3 Gua Qi Diagram Attributed to Confucius

Table 3.4 The Thaumaturgical Order of Trigrams Relative to the Directions and Seasons

Table 3.5 King Wen Order vs. Mawangdui Order of Hexagrams

Table 3.6 Huang's and Crowley's Translations of Hexagram 7

Table 3.7 The Qabalistic Four Worlds and the Trigrams

Table 3.8 Crowley's Tarot and Yi King Correspondences

Table 3.9 Leibniz's Binary Calculus and the Ba Gua

Table 3.10 The Four Bases of DNA

Table 3.11 Yin and Yang in the Four Nucleotides of DNA

Table 3.12 The Eight Spirit Helpers

Table 3.13 Order of Incantations in a Hexagram Spell

Table 4.1 Lo Shu Magic Square Numerology and the Trigrams

Table 4.2 Comparing Innate *Qi* with Hexagram Lines

Table 4.3 Five Ranks of Nobility and Hexagram Rulers

Table 4.4 Feudal Hierarchies of the Hexagram Lines

Table 4.5 Narrative Arc of Changes

Table 4.6 Comparison of English Translations of Hexagram 62

Table 4.7 Hexagram Line Designations

Table 4.8 Buddhist Interpretation of the Hexagram Lines Narrative

Table 4.9 Numerical Assignments for the Eight Trigrams

Table 4.10 Numerical Assignments for the Five Phases of Change

Table 4.11 Written Figures Designating Yin and Yang Lines of the Trigrams

Table 4.12 The Plum Blossom Ba Gua, Following Fuxi's Early Heaven Ba Gua

Table 4.13 Shao Yong's Nine Categories of Time

Table 5.1 Eight Trigrams, Four Western Elements, and Five Phases
Table 5.2 The Yin and Yang Binary
Table 5.3 Principles of Yin and Yang
Table 5.4 The Four Combinations of Yin and Yang
Table 5.5 Fuxi's Sequence of the Eight Trigrams
Table 5.6 Fuxi's and King Wen's Ba Gua Arrangements
Table 5.7 Taiji and Lo Shu Numerology in the Trigrams
Table 5.8 Two Rules Governing King Wen's Arrangement
Table 5.9 Correspondences for Creation and Completion Numbers
Table 5.10 Comparison of Differing Ba Gua and Eight Immortals Correspondences
Table 5.11 Eight Trigrams and the Eight Immortals
Table 5.12 Seal Script (Zhou Dynasty) for the Eight Trigrams and Wū Xing Correspondences
Table 5.13 Zodiac Wheel and King Wen's Eight Trigrams
Table 5.14 Spirit Helpers for Your Zodiac Animal
Table 5.15 *Fēng Jiǎo* Wind Divination Directional Correspondences
Table 5.16 James Legge's Simplified Coin Toss Method (1899)
Table 6.1 Phase Changes of Yin: Metal and Water
Table 6.2 Phase Changes of Yang: Wood and Fire
Table 6.3 Yin and Yang at Equilibrium: Earth
Table 6.4 Five Turning Points in the Human Narrative Cycle
Table 6.5 Five Phase Changes and the Four Faces of God
Table 6.6 Wu Xing and Human Functions
Table 6.7 The Five State Functions and Wu Xing
Table 6.8 The Five Mystical Arts and Wu Xing
Table 6.9 The Five Mystical Arts and the Eight Archetypes of the Mystic
Table 6.10 Eight Guiding Principles for Mystical Studies
Table 6.11 Wu Xing, the Zodiac, and the Lo Shu Eight Trigrams
Table 7.1 Yarrow Stalk Line Construction Reference Table
Table 7.2 Quick Reference Chart for Yarrow Stalk Counting
Table 7.3 Image and Number vs. Meaning and Principle Coin Toss Methods
Table 7.4 Coin Toss Reference Table
Table 7.5 Numerical Assignments for the Eight Trigrams
Table 7.6 Solar Terms and Lunar Months of Spring
Table 7.7 Plum Blossom Calendar Numerology Formulas

Table 7.8 Numerology of the Year (Stems and Branches)
Table 7.9 Numerology of the Hour (Earthly Branches)
Table 7.10 Numerology of Zodiac Signs (Ascendant Hour)
Table 7.11 Tarot and Trigram Correspondences
Table 7.12 The Xuan Hexagram Revealed in the Tarot Major Arcana
Table 7.13 The Ninth Trigram Revealed (the Phantom "Xuán" Gua)
Table 7.14 Comparing the Cosmological Trinities in Alchemy
Table 7.15 The Eight Spirit Helpers
Table 7.16 The Six Alchemical Keys of Eudoxus
Table 7.17 The Science and Magic of the Six ※ Spirit Helper Cards
Table 7.18 Tarot and I Ching Trigram Correspondences
Table 7.19 Changing Lines Position Correspondences
Table 7.20 Four Affinities and the Alchemical Stages
Table 7.21 Dr. Michael McDonald's Personality Profile Model
Table 8.1 Interpreting Hexagram 4 as Guiding Principles for Mystical Cultivation
Table 9.1 Ancestral Spirit Communications through Hexagrams
Table 10.1 Eight Trigrams and Five Mystical Arts Correspondences
Table 10.2 Eight Gods of the *Wū* Shamans and the Ba Gua
Table 10.3 Eight Trigrams and Corresponding Gods
Table 10.4 *Shou Jing* Incantation for an Exorcism and Soul Retrieval
Table 11.1 Revealing the Secret Hexagram
Table 12.1 Solar Terms to Solar Longitude and Lunar Months
Table 12.2 Solar Terms, Eight Trigrams, and the Lo Shu
Table 12.3 Solar Terms and Taiji Trigram Systems, Part 1
Table 12.4 Solar Terms and Taiji Trigram Systems, Part 2
Table 12.5 Heavenly Stems, Trigrams, and Wu Xing
Table 12.6 Earthly Branches, Trigrams, and Wu Xing
Table 12.7 Trigrams and Feng Shui Correspondences
Table 12.8 Eight Bodhisattvas and the Ba Gua

# LIST OF PRACTICUMS

3.1 The Hexagrams Ruling Your Birth Month
3.2 First Reading with the I Ching
4.1 Oracle Reading by Comparative Study of Three I Ching Texts
4.2 Bibliomancy and Plum Blossom Numerology
4.3 Divining the Wu Xing Ruler of a Book
4.4 Applying a Buddhist Interpretation to an I Ching Reading
5.1 Ascent to Heaven: Spirit Body Journeying
5.2 A Jade Amulet for Power and Protection
5.3 Growing Prosperity and Business Success Talisman
5.4 Crafting a Dharma Fan
5.5 Nine-Day Fire Ritual for Clarity and Advancement
5.6 New Moon Purification Ritual with the Pavamāna Mantra
5.7 Bottling Thunder Magic
5.8 Retributive Justice Magic
5.9 Petitioning the Patron Immortal of Witches
5.10 The Healing Wind Spirit in a Crystal Lotus
5.11 Wind Divination and the I Ching
5.12 Healing Gourd Feng Shui Cure for Good Health (and James Legge's Coin Toss Method)
5.13 Inner Alchemy: Visualization Technique for Spiritual Cultivation
5.14 Calling upon the Earth Goddess to Remove Your Pain
6.1 Journaling and Reflection Prompt on the Five Mystical Arts
6.2 Mystical Art Associated with Your Date of Birth
6.3 Guarding of the One Meditation (37 – 32 BC)
6.4 Psychic Health Readings with the I Ching
7.1 Handpicking Your Divination Stalks
7.2 An I Ching Reading by the Yarrow Stalk Method
7.3 An I Ching Reading by the Coin Toss Method
7.4 Trying Aleister Crowley's Coin Toss Method

7.5 A State of the Union Prophecy

7.6 An I Ching Reading by the Cowrie Shell Toss Method

7.7 An I Ching Reading by the Rice Grains Method

7.8 A General Forecast for Your Year to Come

7.9 Plum Blossom Numerology and I Ching

7.10 Channeling a Hexagram from the Lady of the Nine Heavens

7.11 An I Ching and Tarot Card Reading

7.12 Using the I Ching to Find Lost Objects

7.13 Answering the Question "Who Am I?" with a Personality Profile

8.1 Reflections on the Oracle's Lesson to the Shaman-Medium

8.2 Small Victories, Gain by Gain Mantra

8.3 Poison Magic and Defenses to Ward Off Poison Magic

8.4 A Mantra to Reverse Misfortune

9.1 Setting Up a Basic Ancestor Shrine or Altar

9.2 Cowrie Shell Divination and Invoking a Twelfth-Generation Ancestor

10.1 I Ching Divination by Dance

10.2 An Ancestral Shaman Spirit's Blessing

10.3 Soul Retrieval Ritual Invoking Kuan Yin

10.4 Invoking the Queen Mother of the West

10.5 Healing Your Spiritual Center

11.1 Where Do I Go from Here?

**TABLE 1.1** Trigram Cross-References for Hexagram Construction

| Upper Trigram ▶<br><br>Lower Trigram ▼ | **Qián**<br>Heaven | **Duì**<br>Lake | **Lí**<br>Fire | **Zhèn**<br>Thunder |
|---|---|---|---|---|
| **Qián**<br>Heaven | 1 Qián<br>Creative Power | 43 Guài<br>Decisive Action | 14 Dà Yǒu<br>Accolades | 34 Dà Zhuàng<br>Great Power |
| **Duì**<br>Lake | 10 Lǚ<br>Treading | 58 Duì<br>Joyous Exchange | 38 Kuí<br>Opposition | 54 Guī Mèi<br>The Marrying Maiden |
| **Lí**<br>Fire | 13 Tóng Rén<br>Fellowship | 49 Gé<br>Revolution | 30 Lí<br>The Spark | 55 Fēng<br>Opulence |
| **Zhèn**<br>Thunder | 25 Wú Wàng<br>Without Folly | 17 Suí<br>Inspiring Followers | 21 Shih Hé<br>Bite Through | 51 Zhèn<br>Jolt |
| **Xùn**<br>Wind | 44 Gòu<br>Improper Meeting | 28 Dà Guò<br>Undertake the Great | 50 Dǐng<br>The Cauldron | 32 Héng<br>The Eternal |
| **Kǎn**<br>Water | 6 Sòng<br>The Trial | 47 Kùn<br>Blockade | 64 Wèi Jì<br>Toward an End | 40 Jiě<br>Release of Tension |
| **Gěn**<br>Mountain | 33 Dùn<br>Withdraw | 31 Xián<br>Mutual Accord | 56 Lǚ<br>The Wanderer | 62 Xiǎo Guò<br>Pay Attention to Details |
| **Kūn**<br>Earth | 12 Fǒu<br>Stalemate | 45 Cuì<br>Assembly | 35 Jìn<br>Advancement | 16 Yù<br>Enthusiasm |

| | | | | |
|---|---|---|---|---|
| **Xùn** Wind | **Kǎn** Water | **Gèn** Mountain | **Kūn** Earth | ◀ Upper Trigram  Lower Trigram ▼ |
| **9 Xiǎo Chù** Cultivate Gently | **5 Xū** Patience | **26 Dà Chù** Cultivate the Supreme | **11 Tài** Harmony | **Qián** Heaven |
| **61 Zhōng Fú** Faith Within | **60 Jié** Boundaries | **41 Sǔn** Debilitation | **19 Lín** Spring Is Coming | **Duì** Lake |
| **37 Jiā Rén** The Family | **63 Jì Jì** After the Ending | **22 Bì** Luminosity | **36 Míng Yí** Darkening of the Light | **Lí** Fire |
| **42 Yì** Burgeoning | **3 Tún** Initial Challenge | **27 Yí** Receive Nourishment | **24 Fù** Repose | **Zhèn** Thunder |
| **57 Xùn** Use Gentle Force | **48 Jǐng** Fountainhead | **18 Gǔ** Decay | **46 Shēng** Hoist | **Xùn** Wind |
| **59 Huàn** Making Waves | **29 Kǎn** The Abyss | **4 Méng** Naiveté | **7 Shī** The Army | **Kǎn** Water |
| **53 Jiàn** Steadfast | **39 Jiǎn** An Impasse | **52 Gèn** Listen to the Wind | **15 Qiān** Modesty | **Gèn** Mountain |
| **20 Guān** Observation | **8 Bǐ** Alliance | **23 Bō** Partition | **2 Kūn** Supportive Power | **Kūn** Earth |

# 1

# Preface

THE BOOK OF CHANGES is both a compass and an atlas for finding your path. Just as a path is found by walking it,[1] to know the Tao, you practice the Way. This is a guidebook for how to practice the Way, putting wisdom into action.

The I Ching entered my life one summer in Taiwan when I was around eleven years old. My parents took my sisters and me into a sprawling bookstore in Taipei and told us we could each buy one book, any book of our choosing. I chose Kerson Huang's *I Ching: The Oracle.* Each two-page spread consisted of the traditional Chinese text on one side and the English translation on the other.

Of course, the text was light-years beyond my comprehension. I didn't even know what it was and initially presumed that perhaps I had acquired a book of poetry. I lacked the life experience, the maturity, and the wisdom to understand even one page of the Oracle.

Yet that did not deter me from trying.

A pivotal moment in my relationship with the Book came when my grandmother passed away. I was in my twenties and did not fully understand mortality. That I'd had a finite number of years with my grandmother was not something I grasped until it was too late. My grandmother's death hit me harder than I thought it would because in my head I had this running checklist of questions to ask her, and I kept telling myself I still had plenty of time . . . until I had no time at all.

No one told me I could use the I Ching as a device to communicate with the dead. It was something I dabbled with intuitively. Late at night, alone, I burned incense and offerings, lit candles, recited mantras in prayer, and thought of my grandmother. I clutched my last memento of her and begged her to show up for me.

**FIGURE 1.1** *Studying the I Ching by a Window* by 陳書 [Chen Shu] (1660–1735)[2]
SOURCE: National Palace Museum, Taipei.

I hadn't been a very good granddaughter. There were countless instances from my childhood when I was purely awful to her. Communication was a challenge between us because she only spoke the Taiwanese dialect, in which I only knew cuss words. She showered me with love, gifts of candy, clothes, and gold (it's an Asian thing), and in return I would play pranks on her and mope at the sight of dishes she laboriously cooked, pouting and puttering as I nudged the food with my chopsticks. "I'm not hungry," I'd say, only to scarf down a burger and fries in front of her half an hour later.

As a young adult, I finally came to a newfound commitment to learning Taiwanese so I might converse with her. I ignited an interest in my own heritage. As for that list of questions to ask her, I planned on asking them myself, in Taiwanese. I also had a lot to atone for. I needed opportunities to demonstrate my filial piety.

When I was in college, during finals week at the end of a semester, I got the call from Mom. She forbade me from pausing school and said no, I could not go back to Taiwan for Grandma's funeral. I'd just have to live with missing it.

My imagination convinced me I could use the I Ching to communicate with my grandmother, like a spirit talking board.

My imagination also convinced me I had succeeded.

I now work with the I Ching in my regular practice of ancestor veneration. As an Asian American, this practice is what keeps me connected to my family roots. My maternal grandfather died before I was born, and the I Ching has become a medium through which I can remain in contact with his spirit. The Book breaks barriers of communication that once existed between the motherland and me in the living world; through the veil, there is now this alternative mode of language.

The I Ching is the divinatory tool I reach for when I need career or relationship advice, direction in life, and sage counsel. It doesn't just give me guidance on how best to proceed when I'm feeling lost; it inspires me to live virtuously. When geopolitics and the world around me are in turmoil, I seek clarity from the Book to ground and center me. It offers practical advice. It consoles me in my darkest hour.

For the last decade I've given thousands of professional I Ching divinatory readings that have foretold marriages, breakups, pregnancies, career advancements, financial recessions, and momentous life changes. In the same way the Book has opened a channel of communication with my ancestors, it's helped many diasporic Asians bond with theirs.

Deeper and more sentimental than mediumship or divination, the I Ching is a fundamental cornerstone of Asian philosophy. The history, culture, and development of civilizations across East Asia evolved from the ethos of the I Ching. Whether you study Eastern rationalism or Taoist occultism, the most essential text in both is the Book of Changes.

China's imperial examinations for determining who would hold the most prestigious positions in government required knowledge of the I Ching and writing an academic commentary on it.[3] The literati of Imperial China would spend their lives refining their understanding of the I Ching, one of the Five Classics,[4] because their discourses on these texts were the testaments of their intellect and erudition.

Records of the I Ching in Japan date back to 539 AD, when it was studied by Buddhist monks and high-ranking warriors in addition to scholars.[5] Similar cultural and spiritual developments in Vietnam syncretized the I Ching with Zen and Mahayana Buddhism during the Ly dynasty (AD 1010–1225).[6] During the Tokugawa or Edo period of Japan (AD 1603–1867), thousands of pieces of scholarship on the I Ching were published, including 659 books of commentaries and criticisms expounding upon the textual interpretation of the I Ching, 146 books on just the symbolism and numerology of the hexagrams, and 223 books on divination with the I Ching, with the total rivaling the output of Chinese texts during the corresponding Qing dynasty.[7]

The eighteenth-century Vietnamese statesman, philosopher, and scholar Lê Quý Đôn (Lí Guì Dūn, 1726–1784),[8] a prodigy said to have mastered the Five Classics by the age of fourteen, wrote seminal commentaries on the I Ching, the Tao Te Ching, and the Buddhist Diamond Sutra.[9] Robust I Ching scholarship thrived in Vietnam during the Nguyễn dynasty (1802–1945).[10]

The I Ching was formative during the Joseon period (1392–1897) of Korea's dynastic history, as evinced in the trigrams featured on the present-day Korean flag, and had been a part of the peninsula's philosophical and spiritual development since the fourth century.[11] The Indigenous religion of Tibet—Bön, a system of magical practices and religious ritualism—integrates the I Ching, with correspondences to the trigrams and hexagrams found in Tibetan mythology, folk religions, medicine, and geomancy.[12]

The *Zuo zhuan* (左傳), a primary text narrating Chinese history dating back to the fourth century BC, noted early versions of the I Ching written by a historical ethnic group called the Qiang (羌), the ancestors of the Tibetan and Burmese people.[13] The Qiang influence promulgated the I Ching throughout Southeast Asia in both the mainland and the maritime civilizations,[14] where I Ching cosmology was assimilated with animism and the Indigenous folk religions of Vietnam,

Thailand, the Malay Kingdom, and Java. The testament of that is found today in the streets of these nations, where fortune-tellers and shamans utilize the hexagrams in their soothsaying and trigrams in spell-crafting and ritual magic.

The notion that a formally written personal commentary on the Book of Changes was a rite of passage for a scholar of the East as well as being integral to the occult knowledge of an Asian mystic planted an aspiration in me. I would undertake translation and annotations of the I Ching for myself,[15] as a cultural and spiritual rite of passage.

Many insecurities inhibited me from publishing this book. I've been separated from the motherland for so long; what entitlement do I have to comment on this culture? I hold exactly zero university degrees in philosophy, metaphysics, classical Chinese, or Chinese history. What are my qualifications for undertaking I Ching scholarship (易學, Yì Xué)? Can my work that contextualizes the I Ching within Taoist mysticism, occultism, mediumship, and shamanistic practices even be called "scholarship"?

I nursed this manuscript for another decade before I could finally release my inhibitions. In that time, I continued my research, synthesized my ruminations, and explored the Book of Changes to greater depths. I found solace in the perspective that there is no one absolute and determinative interpretation of the sixty-four hexagrams; their meanings have been heartily debated over the centuries, for thousands of years.

There have been two mutually exclusive ways that books in English have presented the I Ching—either as unverified personal gnosis by a practitioner of the craft, or as a scholarly treatise authored by a professor with impressive schooling on the topic but who is not a practitioner of the craft. Undertones in the latter often suggest a contempt for mysticism.

I hope as a practicing occultist I might bridge these two worlds. This book will not shy away from the mystical. Embedded in this primer on the I Ching is a Taoist grimoire.

The Book of Changes is a mirror that will reflect the changes that have transpired in you, and it is a mirror that talks back. You'll see the future through this looking glass. The Book will speak words of advice you need to hear. You'll wonder if it's alive, a living oracle. The wisdom and insight into the universe and the human condition that you seek to attain can be found here.

As you embark on a personal journey with the I Ching, I hope I might be one of your guides, a companion in spirit at this juncture of your path. No matter where you go from here, the I Ching will be a map that gets you there. You'll be guided chapter by chapter through the building blocks of the Oracle, and you'll come to a rich, multifaceted understanding of the very DNA—the fundamental genetic instructions—of Taoist metaphysics.

The I Ching isn't Taoist; it inspired Taoism. It isn't Confucian; it inspired Confucianism. There is a universality of sacred wisdom to be found here that transcends culture and history, so no matter who you are, where you come from, or where you're going, I hope this book inspires you.

**FIGURE 1.2** Illustration of a *zouyu* 騶虞 (mythic beast referenced in hexagrams 3, 45, and 61). From the *Book of Mountain and Seas* 山海經 (originally pre-Qin, before 221 BC); Qing dynasty edition, 1644–1911.

# ETYMOLOGY OF I CHING (YIJING)[1]

**FIGURE 2.1** *Yi* in different Chinese scripts. 1: Shang dynasty oracle bone script. 2: Zhou dynasty bronze inscription. 3: Seal script. 4: Regular script.

*Yi* (易) holds multiple layers of meaning. It means "to change" or "interchange," which is to cause a turn of events in succession, and it also means "to bestow" and "to reveal," "to exchange hands from one to the other." "Change" in the context of this book holds a dual nature: it denotes the changes that take place in the natural course of events, and it simultaneously denotes the changes that will now go into effect as a direct result of having divined on the matter. The *yi* signifies an exchange. The Oracle is as much a book of exchanges as it is a book of change.

**FIGURE 2.2** *Jīng* in seal script. 1: Seal script (1000 BC–1 BC). 2: Regular script.

*Jīng* (經) is translated as "classics" or "scripture," though in the context of the I Ching it is more commonly translated as "book," for Book of Changes. The term is indicative of an authoritative doctrine, that which has been designated as canon and is a text with ethical, moral, philosophical, or religious implications. Texts described as *jīng* are often revelatory and can signify a book of transcendental revelation. The Heart Sutra in Mahayana Buddhism, for instance, is translated as Xīn Jīng (心經). The Tao Te Ching, the classic attributed to Lao Tzu and surfacing later in the Zhou dynasty, is translated to Dào Dé Jīng (道德經). The Abrahamic Bible is called the Shèng Jīng (聖經); the Koran is the Gǔlán Jīng (古蘭經).

# 2

# Myths, Legends, and Cultural Heroes of the I Ching

A REVOLUTION BIRTHS THE I CHING. It's the Bronze Age. Around 1050 BC, King Wen is imprisoned by King Zhou of Shang for seven years,[2] and during his imprisonment, Wen stacks the eight trigrams of the Ba Gua in combinations for a total of sixty-four hexagrams. A divination

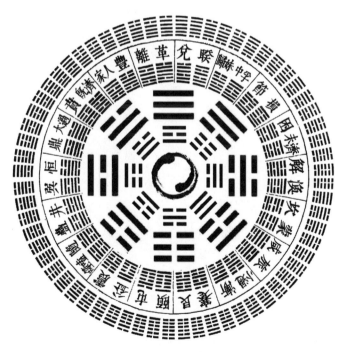

**FIGURE 2.3** King Wen combines trigrams to form hexagrams

system—the Book of Changes—reveals itself to King Wen, empowering the people with knowledge of the Divine Will. The Oracle's first prophecy: the coming of a new age.

**FIGURE 2.4** *King Wen of Zhou* (1632) by Kanō Sansetsu (1589–1651).[3] SOURCE: Tokyo National Museum.

The eight trigrams that King Wen uses in paired combinations are said to date back to the prior millennium, around 2600 BC, created by Fuxi and Nǚwā, the mythic sole survivors of an apocalyptic Great Flood.[4] Fuxi and Nǚwā are depicted with serpent bodies intertwined,[5] likened to a caduceus.[6] According to myth, a people existed on earth before Fuxi and Nǚwā.[7] The God of Fire and the God of Water battled, causing a Great Flood that wiped out that people. Nǚwā remade people from clay, and they are our ancestors.

**FIGURE 2.5** *Fuxi and Nǚwā* (eighth century). Colored ink on silk scroll. SOURCE: Xinjiang Uighur Autonomous Region Museum.

Fuxi then harnesses the power to connect Earth (☷) and Heaven (☰), the duality of yin and yang, and as a result, the gods gift him with knowledge of the trigrams. Yin is the receptive, occulted, and dark force of nature, represented by a broken line, while yang is the assertive, exoteric, and light force of nature, represented by a solid line.

These eight trigrams become an early form of writing so that those on Earth can communicate with the spirits in Heaven.[8] Fuxi's arrangement of the eight trigrams is called Fuxi's Ba Gua, or the Early Heaven arrangement.

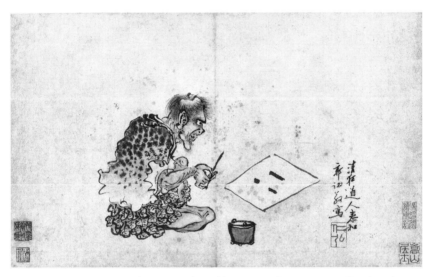

**FIGURE 2.6** *Fuxi Creates the Trigrams* (1503) by Guo Xu (1456–1526/32)[9]. Ink and watercolor on album leaf. SOURCE: Shanghai Museum.

Five hundred years after Fuxi, the Great Floods return, and when Yu the Great[10] enters a cave seeking divine guidance on how to control the waters so as to save humanity, a celestial manifestation of Fuxi gives him jade tablets (玉簡, *yùjiǎn*) with the secrets of sciences and magic revealed. At first, he fails. The earth goddess Houtu comes to his assistance and helps redirect Yu's canals.[11]

Houtu sends a tortoise messenger to Yu the Great. Upon the tortoise is inscribed the Book of the River Maps 河圖洛書 (Hé Tú Luò Shū), a nine-sector square we now refer to as the Lo Shu magic square.[12] With the Lo Shu magic square, Yu successfully controls the floods and saves China. Inspired by the Lo Shu, he subdivides the kingdom into nine regions and forges the mythic Nine Tripod Cauldrons (九鼎, Jiǔ Dǐng) passed from king to king in ancient China as a symbol of the Mandate of Heaven,[13] which in turn is symbolic of Divine Will.

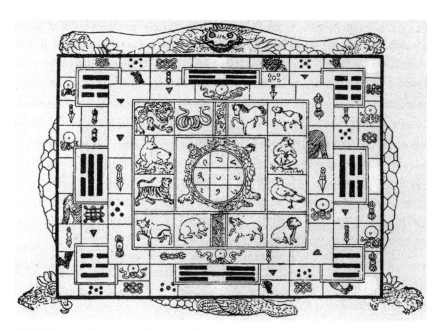

**FIGURE 2.7** *The Mystic Tablet* or Lo Shu magic square. From *Chinese Thought* (1907) by Dr. Paul Carus.[14]

The flood myths of both Fuxi and Yu the Great express early Taoist cosmogony, espousing that creation begins with chaos, and only through a process of division can chaos be tamed into order.[15] Fuxi extracts the binary essences of yin and yang from a singular yin, and the binary in singular yang, then subdivides the binaries further into trinities;[16] and through that process of division, one is revealed to be two, two as three, three as the four directions, dividing until there are eight trigrams, the Ba Gua.[17] It is through the subdivisions of eight that humankind achieves order. Likewise, Yu divides the kingdom into regions to unite it.

**FIGURE 2.8** *Yu the Great* by Ma Lin (1225–1264). Color on silk, hanging scroll. SOURCE: National Palace Museum, Taipei.

## Myths, Legends, and Cultural Heroes of the I Ching  15

**FIGURE 2.9** *Emperor Yu Controlling the Waters* (Qing dynasty). SOURCE: National Palace Museum, Taipei.

Five hundred years after Yu the Great, the Xia dynasty falls, and one clan, the Shang, rises to power.[18] During the Shang, kings and gentry seek answers from diviners who crack pieces of ox bone or tortoise shell with a hot iron rod and read the lines in the bone, using the Lo Shu and the eight trigrams. The oldest known form of Chinese writing is found on these bones, now referred to as oracle bone script. Oracle bone divination is a clear forerunner of the I Ching, as many bones were found with three-line trigrams and six-line hexagrams.[19] The lines indicate yin or yang, and the combinations of yin and yang energies are interpreted.

**FIGURE 2.10** Shang dynasty oracle bone divination

Another cycle of five hundred years completes, and a great new philosopher-sage comes into prominence. King Wen is the son of a wise and kind woman, Tai Ren (太任, Tàirèn), whom later historians would credit as one of the great influences on the founding men of the Zhou dynasty. It is her virtue, beneficence, and intelligence that nurture the great sage King Wen. While pregnant with the future king, Tai Ren "beheld nothing evil with her eyes, heard no lascivious sounds with her ears, and did not let a single haughty word pass from her lips,"[20] thus ensuring that King Wen is born a paragon of virtue.

As oral tradition tells it, King Wen brings together Fuxi's Early Heaven Ba Gua and Yu the Great's Lo Shu magic square to rearrange the trigrams into the Later Heaven Ba Gua, also known as King Wen's Ba Gua. He then combines the dualities of trigram pairs to form a system of hexagrams. The I Ching is formed from a process of division to show that inherent in the eight is sixty-four, and by dividing the chaos, humans can wield control over it, and through control, unite the divisions to create order. This act of connecting Earth and Heaven, yin and yang, dividing it, then uniting it, produces a divination system that guides the Zhou clan to power.

**FIGURE 2.11** *Tai Ren, Mother of King Wen* by Jiao Bingzhen (1689–1726).[21] From the series "The Story of the Dynasties and Empresses [歷朝賢後故事圖冊]." Ink on silk.
SOURCE: National Palace Museum, Taipei.

Wen assigns a name (卦名, *guàmíng*) and a pithy oracle (卦辭, *guàcí*) to each hexagram and uses the revealed hexagrams to prophesy the passing of the Mandate of Heaven from the corrupt ruler King Zhou of Shang to the rebellion that would be led by his son, King Wu of Zhou (周武王, Zhōu Wǔ Wáng). Wu is King Wen's second son through his marriage to Tai Si (太姒, Tàisì), a descendant of Yu the Great.

Tai Si is described as a model wife and mother and is given the epithet Wén Mǔ (文母), or Accomplished Mother.[22] Her beauty is so captivating that when King Wen first sees her from across a lake, he connects boats together to build a bridge so he can cross the lake just to meet her.[23] Tai Si is

**FIGURE 2.12** *Tai Si, Mother of King Wu of Zhou* by Jiao Bingzhen. From the series "The Story of the Dynasties and Empresses [歷朝賢後故事圖冊]." Ink on silk. SOURCE: National Palace Museum, Taipei.

lauded as having been kind and gentle. Modest, prudent, diligent in her work ethic, and celebrated for being a devoted mother, the good queen raises her ten sons to be virtuous and strong.[24] Her son, the first reigning king of the Zhou dynasty, declares that he has ten capable ministers, and among them he counts his mother, Tai Si.[25] She and Tai Ren would be known as the Mothers of the House of Zhou. Much later in China's history during the Tang dynasty, Empress Wu Zetian will name King Wen and his wife Tai Si as China's Founding Ancestors (始祖, Shǐzǔ).

Earlier in his reign, the corrupt King Zhou of Shang had been a formidable sovereign: clever, charismatic, and so tough that he hunted wild beasts with his bare hands. But soon he neglects the welfare of his kingdom in favor of extravagant excess. According to popular legend, he falls under the evil spell of a concubine, Su Daji (蘇妲己).

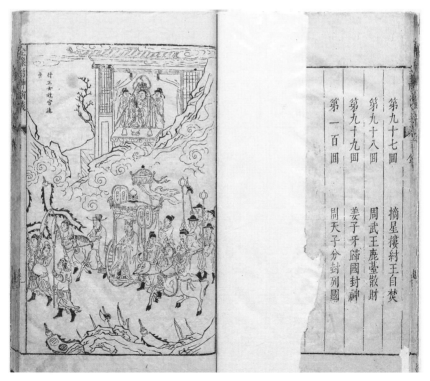

**FIGURE 2.13** King Zhou of Shang entering the palace of Nüwa. From *The Creation of the Gods* by 許仲琳 [Xu Zhonglin] (1573–1620).

In the sixteenth-century novel *The Creation of the Gods* (封神演義, Fēng Shén Yǎnyì),[26] a fictionalized account of the Shang and Zhou, the concubine Daji is portrayed as a demonic fox spirit who possesses the concubine's body. Under the possessed concubine's enchantment, King Zhou becomes so infatuated with her that, at her behest, he abandons state affairs to indulge in decadence.

Figure 2.13 depicts a scene from the novel when King Zhou of Shang is urged by his advisors to pay a visit to Nǚwā's temple on the goddess's birthday.[27] When the wanton king sees the beautiful image of the goddess, he lusts after her and vandalizes the wall of the temple with a suggestive poem. Angered, the goddess summons a fox spirit and two attendant demons. The goddess instructs the three demons to transform into beautiful women, seduce the king, and bring about his downfall.

When King Zhou hears that the daughter Daji of the marquis of Jizhou resembles the beautiful Nǚwā, he arranges for Daji to be brought to court. On her way to the imperial court, the fox spirit possesses Daji's body. The king becomes enraptured by Daji. When the king's first wife, the empress, tries to intervene, the king, under Daji's demonic influence, has the empress executed and her eyes plucked out.

**FIGURE 2.14** *Su Daji.* From a Qing dynasty picture book of *The Creation of the Gods.*
SOURCE: National Library of Taiwan.

Daji convinces King Zhou to torture King Wen's firstborn son. The son, Bo Yikao (伯邑考), is sliced apart piece by piece, flesh and limbs, then ground up and baked into a meat pastry. The corrupt king then forces King Wen to eat his own firstborn. These stories and more depict the Shang as the embodiment of all vices and the Zhou of all virtues.

**FIGURE 2.15** King Wen and his son, Wu of Zhou. From *The Creation of the Gods* by 許仲琳 [Xu Zhonglin]. In this illustration from a seventeeth-century copy of *The Creation of the Gods,* King Wen is on his deathbed. His beloved son and heir apparent, Wu of Zhou, is kneeling by the bed. King Wen calls forth the Eight Immortals to ask that they look after his son.

Shortly after he is freed from imprisonment, King Wen dies. At the Battle of Muye (牧野之戰, Mùyě zhī Zhàn) in 1046 BC, King Zhou of Shang is defeated by King Wen's son, Wu of Zhou. The battle takes place near the Shang capital, Chaoge. According to legend, Wu delays his attack on advice of the Oracle, because the timing is not yet right. Dutifully, he waits until the Oracle confirms that he has the Mandate of Heaven, and only then does he launch his revolt.

**FIGURE 2.16** Scene from *The Creation of the Gods* by 許仲琳 [Xu Zhonglin]

Wu of Zhou's rebel forces are the underdog, outnumbered, with fewer resources, and fighting on foreign land, whereas in every respect, the Shang hold the advantage. The rebel army of 50,000 men fight against King Zhou of Shang's 170,000, but on the battlefield, many of the Shang soldiers defect to Wu's side.[28] Thus, Wu is the clear victor.

The Battle of Muye is considered one of the most decisive watershed battles fought in Chinese history, marking a moment that becomes indelibly formative to the Chinese identity. It's often used to exemplify both a just war and the transfer of the Mandate of Heaven.

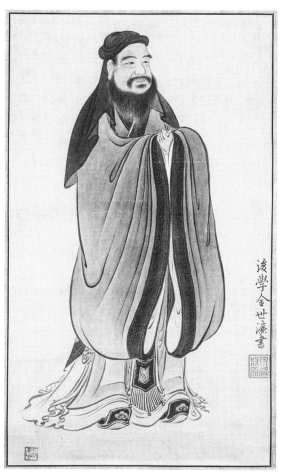

**FIGURE 2.17** *Duke of Zhou* (1632) by Kanō Sansetsu. SOURCE: Tokyo National Museum.

These narrative accounts of founding kings; their mothers, wives, and concubines; the eastern region of Shang; the western region of Zhou; and the Battle of Muye are alluded to in the lines of the I Ching. A story set during the court of Yu the Great is found in Hexagram 8. The Battle of Muye is referenced in Hexagram 36. Hexagram 17 conveys the founding of the Zhou dynasty after King Wu of Zhou is granted the Mandate of Heaven. Tai Si is referenced in Hexagrams 11 and 54. The roles that various court officials, princes, and consorts played in the House of Zhou are told throughout the Oracle. Hence, King Wen's original iteration of the I Ching is called the Zhouyi 周易, the Changes of Zhou.

The Duke of Zhou is the one credited for memorializing these storied chronicles in the I Ching. He is the younger brother of King Wu, fourth son of King Wen and Tai Si. The duke continues adding to the Zhouyi and writes the oracles for each of the six lines in the hexagrams (the 爻辭, Yáocí). King Wu dies three years after taking the throne, so the Duke of Zhou, acting as regent to King Wu's young son, stabilizes the newfound Zhou dynasty. He is later canonized as the Chinese god of dreams, with the oldest and most well-known Chinese text on dream interpretation named in his honor.[29]

The Zhou dynasty marked another historic and enduring change to Chinese society. The Xia and early generations of the Shang were matriarchal.[30] Women could ascend to prestigious positions of leadership. They were mystics, shamans, mediums, priestesses with a direct channel to the Divine, and they were instrumental in shaping government and politics.[31] In burial sites dated to the Shang, women were given equal treatment with men, compared to the subsequent dynasties of imperial China. Fu Hao, who lived around 1200 BC, was the wife of King Wu Ding of Shang. She served as a celebrated military general, commanding a force of thirteen thousand warriors,[32] and was a strategist and a high priestess. She

**FIGURE 2.18** Zhou dynasty seal script

owned land, divined with oracle bones, counseled the king, and led ancestral ceremonial rites.³³

The Neolithic Yellow River civilizations were matriarchal, with patrilineal kinship developing much later in Chinese history.³⁴ Sometime in the late years of the Shang and early years of the Zhou, matrilineal succession was replaced by a patriarchal society.³⁵ Although the transition to patrilineal kinship likely took place well before the Zhou,³⁶ in cultural lore the Duke of Zhou is credited for the transformation of China from a matriarchy to a patriarchy. A key point of criticism that the Zhou dynasty launched against the incumbent Shang was that the corrupt Shang emperor was "taking counsel from a woman" (his concubine Daji).

Yet this particular critique of women influencing politics seems to originate from the Duke of Zhou specifically, rather than being reflective of the founding kings of Zhou. King Wu of Zhou never hides his welcomed reliance on his mother, Tai Si, for counsel. His own wife, the queen Yi Jiang 邑姜, is also a government minister who joins the ranks of Fu Hao as one of the most politically influential women in Chinese history.³⁷

**FIGURE 2.19** *King Wen and Four Generations of Beneficence* Illustration titled 文王四世累善 *(Wén wáng sì shì lèi shàn)* depicting King Wen; his mother, Tai Ren; his wife, Tai Si; and his son, King Wu of Zhou. From 清代版新刊古列女傳 *(Qīng dài bǎn xīnkān gǔ liè nǚ chuán)* (Qing dynasty).

Another shift credited to the Zhou is in how gods were honored. The Shang were documented as engaging in human sacrifice to please their gods.[38] The warrior queen Fu Hao led ceremonial rites involving human sacrifices and offerings of tiger heads.[39] It is the Duke of Zhou who shifts the culture to a society of ritual and religious ceremony. Rather than using human sacrifice as the means to appeal to gods, the Zhou dynasty establishes the precedent of using rites, poetry, and songs.[40]

During the Zhou, the I Ching replaces oracle bone divination as the method for priests, kings, and gentry to prognosticate turning tides and events to come.[41] Milfoil or yarrow stalks are cast to divine numbers that then correspond with hexagram lines. King Wen's oracle attributions for the hexagrams are then interpreted as the answer to the question.

The second century BC historian Sima Qian forecasted that every five hundred years, or about eight cycles of the lunisolar sexagenary calendar,[42] a great philosopher-sage will rise to mark a change and transition into a new era. Five hundred years after King Wen is the arrival of Confucius (551–479 BC).[43] A series of appendices that serve as commentary on King Wen's Zhouyi are credited to Confucius (though they were more likely authored by Confucian scholars[44]). These appendices come to be called the Ten Wings (十翼, Shíyì).

**FIGURE 2.20** Frontispiece from *Confucius Sinarum* (Paris, 1687)[45]

It is impossible to overstate the influence of Confucianism on how the I Ching hexagrams have been interpreted over the centuries.[46] Confucius criticized the government corruption and materialism of his time and what he saw as a lack of virtue, so his interpretation of the Oracle emphasizes the cultivation of morality.[47] His teachings were centered on interpersonal relationships, social contracts, loyalty, and filial piety. Confucius reiterates the Duke of Zhou's emphasis on feudal patriarchy, noting that women should not participate in politics, because if and when they do, disaster will befall the state.[48] Augmenting the Duke of Zhou's perspective of the Zhouyi, he will set the tone of I Ching discourse for the next two thousand years.

Confucius espoused the universal aspiration of embodying the *junzi* (君子, *jūnzǐ*), commonly translated as "gentleman." The *junzi* is an archetype of one with noble and perfected virtuous character. The present text will translate *junzi* as "the sage." The translation of "君子" to "sage" isn't precise from a literal standpoint. Conceptually, however, it achieves the purpose of conveying one who is prudent, judicious, profoundly wise, and venerated by society for embodying those traits.

By the Song dynasty (AD 960–1279), the four cultural heroes credited for writing the Book of Changes were cemented:

- Fuxi for devising the eight trigrams;
- King Wen for devising the sixty-four hexagrams;
- his son, the Duke of Zhou, for composing the text for each line of the hexagrams;
- Confucius for writing the Ten Wings, the appendices to the I Ching.[49]

**FIGURE 2.21** Scene from the *Ladies' Book of Filial Piety* (1130–1170) by 馬和之 [Ma Hezhi].[50] SOURCE: National Palace Museum, Taipei.

**FIGURE 2.22** Scene from the *Ladies' Book of Filial Piety* by 馬和之 [Ma Hezhi].
SOURCE: National Palace Museum, Taipei.

**FIGURE 2.23** The triple gods of Taoism (Qing dynasty) (清無名氏繡三星圖).
SOURCE: National Palace Museum, Taipei.

## Myths, Legends, and Cultural Heroes of the I Ching

A revolution births the I Ching. King Zhou of Shang, purportedly manipulated by the evil fox spirit–possessed concubine Daji, loses the Mandate of Heaven when he neglects civil duties, inflicts cruelty and poverty upon the people, and abuses his power and privileges. The Mandate of Heaven is a political philosophy integral to imperial China and implied throughout the text of the I Ching. It ordains the legitimacy of a sovereign ruler and reveals whom the gods have favored under Heaven's Will. It also instructs on how a sovereign can maintain that Mandate.

The political philosophy of the Mandate includes the right of rebellion against a ruler who isn't taking care of the kingdom. The moral duty to dissent is expressed in hexagrams such as 36 and 49. Counsel on how to rebel is found among the lines of Hexagrams 2 and 12. Nevertheless, equally advocated in the text is how to quash a rebellion. Hexagrams 30 and 35 each contain lines of advice to a leader on how to deal with insurgents.

These legends contextualize the I Ching. Historical and cultural figures are referenced by the Oracle as parables to learn from. To understand the Book of Changes, the mythos is as important as the philosophy. To know these myths, legends, and cultural heroes is to know the heart of the I Ching.

**FIGURE 2.24** Detail from *Studying the I Ching by a Window*[51] by 陳書 [Chen Shu].
SOURCE: National Palace Museum, Taipei.

From the lore of its origins, then its migration from the Yellow River Valley across the Asian continent and westward to Europe, where Jesuit priests saw biblical myths within the pages of the Oracle, and into the present day, the Book of Changes has been a mirror in which every society sees itself reflected. Every generation, every school of political philosophy, and every path of thought—from the varied shamanistic and animistic traditions indigenous to the Asian continent, to Christianity, Marxism, and Jungian psychology—people find their own truths within the lines of this sacred text.

For thousands of years, the Book of Changes has served as both practical and spiritual counsel among the royal families of Asia. Aristocracies across the continent have divined with the I Ching on state affairs, wars, military expeditions, marriages, alliances, and their ancestors.[52]

Intrinsic to the I Ching is the encouragement that you can override any negative circumstance you are dealt. When you read the text as literature, you'll deepen your knowledge of the world. When you divine with the text, you'll excavate knowledge of yourself and be empowered. When you study the text with discipline and reason, you'll become the sage. Once you become the sage, the esoteric meaning of the Book will reveal itself to you. Reflecting the depths of Taoist alchemy, the Oracle is a master key for ascending to the domain of the immortals.

# 3

# Yì Xué: An Overview of I Ching Discourse

THE STUDY OF THE I CHING has its own name: Yì Xué (易學), meaning "I Ching scholarship." In the Taoist scriptural tradition, the I Ching is ranked first among three major texts known as the Three Mysteries (三玄, Sān Xuán).[1] The text was appended to and amended many times throughout the Han dynasty (206 BC–AD 8), then systematized during the Tang (AD 618–907), giving rise to a host of different schools of thought.

With over three thousand years of Yì Xué, a diversity of opinions and interpretations have emerged. From prophetic apocalyptic and messianic predictions to scholarship that is heavily critical of divination, or reading the Book through a Legalist lens in stark contrast to aligning it with Buddhism, the field of I Ching studies has historically been eclectic. This sets a precedent for inviting the present-day reader to radically explore original approaches to the Book.

The most important takeaway from this chapter is an understanding of the long-standing thesis that the I Ching and Taoism espouse: this world belongs to all (天下為公, Tiān xià wèi gōng). The maxim comes from the Book of Rites (禮記, Lǐjì)[2] and is more fully expressed this way: "The Path of the Tao and all that is of this world belongs to all—all who are worthy and capable, all who are trustworthy and in harmony with nature."

Sovereignty isn't inherited; sovereignty is earned. You earn sovereignty by demonstrating your virtues. Likewise, spiritual awakening is not destined; it's cultivated, and anyone who earns the merit can achieve it.

**FIGURE 3.1** *Tower on the Xianshan Mountain* by 惲壽平 [Yun Shouping] (1633–1690).³
SOURCE: National Palace Museum, Taipei.

Over the millennia, the Book of Changes has remained fluid, ever changing, in constant evolution, consistent with the evolving consciousness of the people. The spirit of the Tao is bound to no one place, nor the Book to any one form.⁴ The Book is a shape-shifter, becoming the image you need to see in order for you to recognize the truth. Europeans saw biblical values in the I Ching as well as its concordance with the Hermetic Qabalah and Western ceremonial magic.

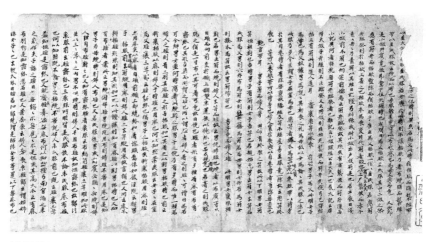

**FIGURE 3.2** Annotated copy of the Book of Rites, 907 AD

Carl Gustav Jung applied the I Ching to expound upon his theories of synchronicity and archetypal psychology. Groundbreaking integrative studies comparing the sixty-four hexagrams to the sixty-four triplets of paired codons in DNA are currently being explored. Since its canonization in 136 BC, the Book of Changes has become a handbook both for governing feudal states and for spiritual self-cultivation. It holds value for the imperial scholar writing an exegesis on neo-Confucian ethics and equally for the peasant psychic-medium using it to spell-craft talismans for love and good fortune.

This chapter will cover key areas of intersectional study in Yì Xué. Influential commentaries and commentators on the I Ching will also be discussed to showcase the many fields that the Book of Changes has branched out into, from the practical and the academic to alchemy and the occult.

## Before the Common Era

The I Ching was first used for divining on matters of political importance, the outcome of battles, and marriage prospects. These early forms of divination utilized yarrow stalks, which were counted and arranged in numerologically significant groupings. Both the predecessor Shang dynasty oracle bone divination and the I Ching began with prayers to the spirits.[5] The request would be purposefully stated in the prayer. Then a sacrifice or offering was often presented to the spirit, though not always. Finally, the oracle reading was performed.

Elucidating the cryptic oracle messages was a challenge then as it is a challenge today. For hundreds of years after the I Ching's inception, scholar-diviners and court intelligentsia (士, *shì*) struggled with interpreting the lines of the Oracle. The presumption was that it took a divinely gifted *shì* to interpret the message from Heaven. Naturally, disagreements erupted among the *shì* on meanings and interpretations.

Disagreements produced discourse. Many philosophical commentaries on the I Ching authored by scholar-diviners emerge during the Warring States period (403–221 BC), along with ongoing edits and revisions to the text itself. The Ten Wings are added to the Zhouyi during this period and are credited to Confucius's authorship. The Ten Wings in effect transform the Zhouyi, the basic classic of the I Ching, into a handbook on cosmology and ethics.

Even the question of whether the I Ching is a morality book or a morally ambiguous one is subject to debate. Perhaps due to the culture it sprang from, the undertone of morality is inevitable. Both Taoism and Confucianism, the two belief systems that the I Ching has become most closely tied to, contend with ethics and morality, each in slightly different ways. That itself complicates the matter even more. A strict Taoist reading of the text for ethics will yield a different conclusion from a strict Confucian reading of the text for ethics.

With the Oracle born out of politics, its early uses were for statecraft and governance. During the Zhou and into the Spring and Autumn period (771–476 BC), the I Ching was syncretized with Legalism. Legalism is not so much a definitive school of thought as it is a body of methods for how to govern a state, both administrative and sociopolitical. Confucianism idealizes humanity as fundamentally good, and all we need to do is appeal to our inner goodness to behave virtuously. In stark contrast, Legalism assumes the worst in people and dictates that a code of rewards and punishments must be implemented to keep the people in line. Thus, the very consideration that the I Ching could be either Confucianist or Legalist, used by either or both, conveys the essential fluidity of the text itself.

Legalism was adopted as the official state philosophy during the Qin dynasty (221–207 BC). A historic book-burning took place around 213 BC called the Burning of Books and Burying of Confucian Scholars (焚書坑儒, fén shū kēng rú). Due to the anti-Confucianist sentiments during the Qin,

Emperor Qin Shi Huang ordered the burning of the works of one hundred schools of philosophical thought, and according to lore, killed 460 Confucian scholars by live burial. Books of poems, historical documents, discourses, and philosophical treatises "from one hundred lineages of thought" were burned. I Ching texts that espoused Confucianist philosophy were summarily destroyed, though the emperor allowed texts on divination to remain.

Whether the historical event actually took place as recorded (our only written record of the event is from a century later) or has been embellished remains unverified,[6] but it's frequently cited to explain the glaring absence of certain records left over from the Zhou, which had been a golden age of literature, the arts, and philosophy.

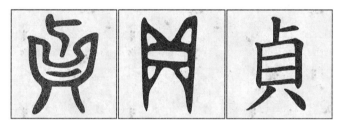

**FIGURE 3.3** The changing meaning of *zhēn*

The answer to the question of whether the I Ching is a book of morality or is morally neutral is ever changing, as exemplified in the changing meaning of the word "貞" (*zhēn*). The earliest oracle bone script of the word is seen in the leftmost cell of figure 3.3, resembling a cauldron with smoke rising from its interior. Cauldrons were used for holding ritual offerings to the gods and ancestors. The center cell is the oracle bone script character for "divination," and during the Zhou dynasty this character unequivocally meant "to divine, holding ritual offerings to the gods and ancestors."[7]

By 206 BC, the I Ching is well recognized as a Confucian classic and therefore is predominantly interpreted through the Confucian moral lens.[8] It becomes canonical around 136 BC,[9] and by then, interpretation of the text is inextricable from Confucian principles. Governed by Confucian ethics, the meaning of "貞" (*zhēn*) changes to mean "purity, perseverance, chastity, loyalty." The word "貞" (*zhēn*) is changed to instruct on virtue and morality.

Likewise, during the dynasty of its origins, the word "亨" (*hēng*) meant ritual sacrifice and divination—first a sacrifice as an offering to the gods, then the divination to obtain an answer from the gods. By the Han dynasty (202 BC–AD 220), the word was used in the context of the Confucian four virtues—元亨利貞 (*yuán hēng lì zhēn*)—to be perfected, to be accomplished, to always advance, and to always persevere. In one sense, the I Ching expresses the East Asian ethos of connecting magic with morals.[10]

These are but a few examples of shifting definitions. Many of the words have fluctuated in meaning over time. Different versions of the I Ching bear different wording; which one should be given authority? While the ordering of the sixty-four hexagrams found in most present-day versions of the book is presumed to be King Wen's order, several conflicting orders have surfaced that date to before the Common Era. Are we so sure we as a global collective have been working off King Wen's actual order? All of this compounds the difficulties with interpreting the I Ching.

## New Text Schools vs. Old Text Schools

Which version of the I Ching to use has been a point of contention throughout history. A schism between the New Text (今文經學, Jīn Wén Jīngxué) Confucianist school, which was considered orthodox during the Han dynasty, and the Old Text (古文經, Gǔwén Jīng) school of interpretation characterized first-century Yì Xué.

Around AD 100–200, ancient pre-Qin versions of the I Ching surfaced, written before 221 BC and in *gǔwén* (古文), an archaic Chinese script. These ancient texts were believed to be dated before the Burning of Books and Burying of Confucian Scholars.

The Old Text school placed authority on these resurfaced archaic versions of the I Ching (specifically, the commentaries to the Zhouyi), believed to have escaped the Qin dynasty book-burning. The New Text Confucianist school placed authority on the evolved and amended texts that had been passed down through oral transmission over the centuries and that had survived the Burning of Books by remaining in the Qin emperor's imperial library.[11]

New Text I Ching commentaries characterized Confucius as a messianic figure and an uncrowned king—a prophetic leader who should have been given the Mandate of Heaven. The classics, which were all credited as having been written personally by Confucius, were treated as sacred religious texts. The New Text school also promoted new and evolving methods of divination with the Oracle.

Old Text commentaries, which challenged the incumbent New Text dominance, approached Confucianism more as a philosophy. Confucius was characterized as a philosopher-sage, not as a religious prophet. The New Text school tended to be more theist, while the Old Text school was viewed as atheist (though that generalization isn't entirely accurate, due to the fundamentally different perspectives that Eastern and Western philosophy have on theism).

The New Text vs. Old Text conflict applied to the corpus of Confucian classics, such as the Spring and Autumn Annals, a chronicle of Chinese history from 722 to 481 BC. Commentaries to the Annals can offer cultural and historic context for how to approach interpretation of the I Ching. The New Text school interprets the Annals as concluding that if a lord unjustly sentences a subject to death, then the lord's son has the divine right to seek vengeance and to attack and overthrow that corrupt lord. However, the Old Text school would interpret the same material as meaning that the lord holds the Mandate of Heaven, and therefore what the lord does is by its very nature just; no son is permitted to seek blood vengeance.[12] In later sections of this chapter, this distinction between the two schools can help to explain how, when two equally reputed Yì Xué scholars read the same hexagram lines, one can interpret it as pro-revolution and anti-nationalism while the other interprets it as anti-revolution and pro-nationalism.

After AD 200, Old Text came to prominence, and over the next few centuries, New Text fell out of favor. By the 1600s, during the Qing, the New Text school swung back into favor and became the orthodox. To throw another wrench in the debate, Han dynasty librarian Liu Xin 劉歆 (50 BC–AD 23) was alleged to have produced counterfeit versions—or, to put it in a kinder way, heavily edited versions—of the I Ching for the imperial library.[13] In the 1900s, Old Text was blamed for everything wrong with China, and New Text swung back into favor.[14]

Since the Han (202 BC–AD 220), the Old Text vs. New Text controversy remained an impassioned point of contention among Yì Xué scholars.[15] Which one came into authority was more politically motivated than a matter of philosophical discourse.

# The Rationalists vs. the Originalists

Two contrasting approaches to interpreting the hexagrams are exemplified by Wang Bi, a Rationalist who emphasized the practical use of the I Ching to solve immediate worldly affairs, and Zhu Xi, an Originalist who emphasized the experience of divination as an experience of the Divine itself, and divination as a journey in self-cultivation.

An early school of thought established by Confucian philosopher and statesman Wang Bi 王弼 (AD 226–249) became canon for much of Yì Xué's early history.[16] Wang Bi served in the court of Wei during the Three Kingdoms era (AD 220–266).[17] This was a time of political turmoil and civil unrest.

In the Han dynasty prior to Wang Bi, King Wen's prescribed order of the hexagrams was considered authoritative, but Wang Bi didn't see it as important. According to Wang Bi, the order of hexagrams as presented in the Zhouyi was not cosmologically significant. Instead, each hexagram should be considered as freestanding and independent. Whereas the later Zhu Xi separated analysis of the Zhouyi and the Ten Wings, Wang Bi treated the Ten Wings as determinative of how the Zhouyi should be interpreted. To him, there was an inherent system of metaphysical correspondences between the two, which could be

**FIGURE 3.4** Portraits of Wang Bi (left) and Zhu Xi (right). SOURCE: National Palace Museum, Taipei.

understood through Taoist philosophy and therefore by applying principles found in the Tao Te Ching.

The Wang Bi school of thought studies the totality of the text for any given hexagram as a fluid field. In his commentaries, Wang Bi interprets the I Ching through the Tao Te Ching. Furthermore, an I Ching reading is approached as a form of practical problem-solving.

Wang Bi was also one of the early proponents of not imposing moral judgments on external events. Rather, he advocated seeing events as the natural course of the Tao. To understand his point, consider the meaning of *te* (or *de* 德) in Tao Te Ching 道德經, a word that will be found dozens of times over in the I Ching. A Confucianist understanding of *te* 德 is virtue, to be virtuous and moral, to be of superior character, sound mind, and to demonstrate faith. A Taoist understanding of *te* 德 is what you embody when you are in alignment with the Tao, and to be in alignment with the Tao (the Tao being the natural flow of *qi* through the universe) doesn't necessarily involve morality or character.

This again brings up the interesting question of how to translate the I Ching. If, for instance, the word "德" appears, is the counsel to be moral and virtuous, or is the counsel to go with the natural flow of the Tao? Do you interpret the Confucianist and Taoist views as being congruous or incongruous? For the wisdom of the I Ching to be written down, it must pass through the ideologies of the one who is writing, which is the reason for the famous Taoist tenet: the Tao that can be spoken is not the true Tao.

Wang Bi did not ascribe sentience to the Tao, who, per Taoist cosmology, created the myriad things in the beginning. In his interpretation of Taoist cosmology, the Tao, unlike humans, has no agency and is a nonbeing. The Tao that an I Ching divination detects and gives a reading on is just "where things come from."

In contemplation of the question of *how* I Ching divination works, Wang Bi notes that the six-line code for each hexagram is an analogous diagram or microcosmic model of a certain change or transformation occurring in the cosmos. Divination is a calculation method for detecting what change or transformation is occurring, and the detected result is given to the sage-scholar (士, *shì*) as a six-line coded diagram.[18] The yarrow stalks respond to the questioner as echoes of the spirits that were governing that change.[19] Finally, at no time should divination with the I Ching be construed as removing human agency or an individual's agency.

Prior to Wang Bi, Han dynasty scholars held a more romanticized outlook of the Oracle, seeing it as revelatory of divine mysteries, whereas Wang Bi advocated for a more rational focus on human affairs and on how the I Ching could be used to solve immediate, pressing concerns rather than using it as an aid for cogitation of poetics on metaphysics and cosmology.

Wang Bi's Rationalist approach was the standard through the Tang and Song dynasties, spanning AD 618–1279. The imperial examinations for civil service during that time tested applicants for their knowledge of the Wang Bi commentaries in I Ching scholarship.

The Originalist approach—valuing divination for the experience of divination itself, in contrast to the Rationalists—was exemplified by Zhu Xi 朱熹 (AD 1130–1200), a neo-Confucianist I Ching scholar.[20] The Originalists sought to restore interpretation of the I Ching to how it would have been and should have been interpreted by its four forefathers, in light of their contributions to the discourse: Fuxi's eight trigrams; King Wen's order of the hexagrams, often referred to as the received order; the text for each line of the hexagrams, attributed to King Wen's son, the Duke of Zhou; and most important of all, Confucius and his Ten Wings.

For Zhu Xi, divination is not a superstitious act of seeking guidance from a supernatural power. Rather, it is an enriching experience of encountering the unknown and unfathomable. In the process of divination, one faces the multiple forces that shape human life, and thereby becomes aware of the opportunities and resources for improving one's situation. For the Originalists, the purpose of divination was to walk the path of self-knowledge.

Benyi (本義), meaning the Originalist approach, was set forth in Zhu Xi's seminal I Ching commentaries, *Zhouyi benyi* (周易本義). While the Rationalist would look for patterns, correspondences, and metaphysical connections, the Originalist approach was not to connect hexagrams to each other or to draw associations between them. Each hexagram should be considered on its own independent merits. Case in point: some of my approach to annotating the hexagram meanings diverges from a Zhu Xi school of thought, because I draw comparisons and associations between different hexagrams.

Zhu Xi's main contention was that the infusion of Taoism into I Ching studies has diluted its original meaning. Originalists like Zhu Xi were critical of Rationalists like Wang Bi. Originalists hold that metaphysical correspondences aren't as important as Rationalists think, and divination is a means for cultivating self-knowledge that is meant for everyone. (The laborious, exclusive study of metaphysical correspondences could only be reserved for the privileged, whereas an intuitive approach to divination for cultivating self-knowledge could be for everyone and anyone.)

That last sentiment is what sets Zhu Xi apart from Wang Bi. Wang Bi focused on the political value of the I Ching, which meant it was the scholar-sages who had the requisite capabilities to comprehend the Book of Changes. Prior to establishment of the Originalist schools, study of the I Ching was reserved for elite scholars and court ministers only.

In contrast, Zhu Xi believed that the I Ching was originally created for the people. It wasn't just for the literati; it was for the farmers, artisans, merchants, and peasants alike, though each person will use the Book slightly differently from the others, and that was the original intent of the Oracle.

In an AD 1175 letter, Zhu Xi writes: "When the sages created the I Ching, it originally was to cause people to engage in divination, in order to decide what was permissible or not in their behavior, and thereby to teach people to be good."[21] Zhu Xi's approach is nothing short of monumental in its influence. It sought to make the I Ching accessible and the wisdom it has to offer attainable by anyone.

By the seventeenth century and for most of China's history, the Originalist neo-Confucian approach is the accepted paradigm.[22] The Originalist approach studies the sixty-four hexagrams of the Zhouyi separate from the Ten Wings. The Zhouyi should then be interpreted based on the original understanding of it from the Zhou dynasty.

To the Originalists, the most profound value of divination was as a standard method for self-cultivation. Rather than working through metaphysical questions by complex deductive reasoning to produce practical answers (i.e., the Rationalists), the personal experience of divination would reveal innate knowledge of philosophy, ethics, and morality. Answers are naturally received, not logically deduced.

These generalizations of the two schools are imperfect, and the mere statement of the generalizations runs the risk of great error, because within each school there was a spectrum of opinions. Few philosophers were either/or. Most cherry-picked doctrinal morsels from both. The commentaries of certain scholars from certain schools at various times of imperial China came into prominence and were held as orthodox, but the actual range of beliefs was still diffuse and complex.

Comparing the Wang Bi and Zhu Xi schools of I Ching scholarship is just one demonstration of how divergent historical opinions have been. Furthermore, what's seen as authoritative in terms of I Ching scholarship waxes and wanes. By the Yuan dynasty (1279–1368), over seven hundred different schools of Yì Xué could be catalogued.[23] Thus, as you, the reader, develop your own interpretative approach to the I Ching, there is no right or wrong. There may be orthodox versus unorthodox, but your guiding principle should be this: do not dismiss the context of your own perspective when interpreting the Oracle.

# Esoteric I Ching: *Yi wei* and the School of Mystery

The *Yì wěi* 易緯[24] is an apocryphal text on the I Ching consisting of eight texts, though only seven remain intact today, dated AD 127–200 AD during the Han dynasty, then annotated and amended later during the thirteenth century in the Ming dynasty.[25] The word *wěi* 緯 in the title suggests occult Confucian literature, or esoteric Confucianism—knowledge and wisdom that are veiled. The *yì* (易) is in reference to the I Ching. Greater importance was given to the text in the thirteenth century, as scholars at the time felt that those who authored the *Yì wěi* must have understood the original meaning and intent of the I Ching better than contemporary scholars would have. As study of the I Ching moved in the direction of philosophy, texts like the *Yì wěi* fell out of favor and into obscurity.

One of the eight texts in the Yì Wěi, *Interpretations and Incantations of the Celestial Spirits* (乾坤鑿度, *Qián kūn záo dù*), discusses the four gates of the four directions and how the hexagrams are used in geomancy and feng shui. Another, the *Diagrams and Overview of the* Yì wěi (易緯稽覽圖, Yì wěi *jī lǎn tú*), assigns the Four Perfected Hexagrams (四正卦, Sì Zhèng Guà) to the four directions.

In the *Common Book of Hexagram Study* (通卦驗, *Tōng guà yàn*), the twenty-four solar terms of the lunisolar calendar are further subdivided and governed by three princely rulers per term, for a total of seventy-two princes (24 × 3 = 72). Conceptually, the seventy-two princes are not unlike the thirty-six decanate rulers in Hellenistic astrology, where three are assigned to each of the twelve zodiac signs. Here, the increments are three princely rulers to each of the twenty-four terms.

These seventy-two princes create, or have the power to create, the manifold disasters that can befall Earth and Man. This principle was called the Way (or the Tao) of Heaven and Man (天人之道, *Tiān rén zhī Dào*). A ceremonial magician trained in the Way of Heaven and Man could learn to control these seventy-two princes and thus control the manifold disasters.

In line with first-century BC texts on timing and seasonal correspondences in the I Ching, the *Yì wěi* gives instruction on how to use the Book for predictions relating to time. The *Divination Compendium* (筮類謀, *Shì lèi móu*) was an encyclopedia on how to ensure that auspicious prognostications with the I Ching would come true and was, in general, a handbook written for and to be studied by diviners.

Among mystics, the *Interpretations and Incantations of Celestials in the Zhouyi* (周易乾鑿度, *Zhōuyì qián záo dù*) is one of the more frequently cited and commented-on texts from the *Yì wěi* collection. The text addresses the three divine powers, four directional deities, spirits of the underworld, and spirits of the hexagrams. The Lo Shu magic square is also explained.

All numerical values in the Lo Shu equal the number fifteen, which this text will explain is the number of the Tao. (In chapter 5, we'll discuss the Lo Shu in greater detail.) Furthermore, each trigram combines with every trigram (including itself) in fifteen combinations. That each trigram combines with the eight to form fifteen hexagrams further underscores the Taoist numerological principle that the number fifteen represents the harmony of life and the order of the universe.[26]

In arcane, mystifying language, *Interpretations and Incantations* uses mathematics to explain how the nine palaces of the Lo Shu magic square, with the sums of fifteen, move through the yin and yang of the four directions and four seasons to produce the sixty-four hexagrams. Heaven and Earth communicate through yin and yang, which is why Heaven and Earth communicate to humanity through the sixty-four hexagrams.[27] One passage instructs on using Hexagram 63, Jì Jì, to subdue ghosts and demons.

**FIGURE 3.5** Page from the *Interpretations and Incantations of Celestials in the Zhouyi*

A recurring topic covered in these esoteric texts is the *qi* life force of the trigrams and hexagrams. Every hexagram emanates with a particular *qi* life force (卦氣, *guà qì*), and it is this *qi* life force of the hexagram that influences the human condition. Like acupuncture, where particular points connect to certain channels of *qi* in the body that affect the body's circulation of that *qi* (and therefore affects physical health), I Ching divination connects to certain channels of hexagram *qi* in the universe that affect the universe's circulation of that hexagram *qi* (and therefore affect those dwelling within that universe).

The texts espouse cosmological tenets such as the creation of all physical matter in this universe sourcing from the eight spirits of the Ba Gua (the trigrams). After the eight trigrams were created, the Wu Xing (five phases of change) were established. The five phases of change are five universal constants. They move the changes of the hexagrams through the trigrams.

Another, more esoteric approach to the I Ching is found among adherents of the School of Mystery, who combine the school's metaphysical emphasis with the I Ching. Han Kangbo is an example of that school. During the Eastern Jin period, Han Kangbo 韓康伯 (AD 332–380) was an I Ching metaphysician who rose to prominence from the poor peasant class.[28] He was an adept within the Xuan Xue (玄學), or School of Mystery, a Taoist school of esoteric philosophical thought followed by a small intellectual elite.[29]

The School of Mystery ran against Confucianism, though it's often considered an esoteric branch of Confucianism. Whereas Confucianism emphasized rules of conduct and ethics for social order, the School of Mystery emphasized that humans should live intuitively in accordance with their natural inclinations, free from and unhindered by social rules, propriety, or etiquette. Confucianism sought to establish rules of conduct to inspire beneficence and righteousness, but the School of Mystery wanted people to naturally find that inspiration themselves, without established rules of conduct.

Wang Bi, who has come to represent the Rationalist approach to I Ching studies, was a member of the School of Mystery. This school of thought advocated rationalism and analytical rigor in pursuit of understanding the universal Mysteries. It was esoteric, and yet it was about using logic, rationalism, the dialectic, and rigorous scholarship to unveil those Mysteries.

## Gua Qi: Theoretical Study of Yin and Yang

When we say Gua (卦), we can be referring to either the eight trigrams or the sixty-four hexagrams. Both are described as Gua 卦. The eight Gua, or trigrams, are the most essential units of substance, whereas the sixty-four Gua, or hexagrams of the I Ching, are the most essential units of change. Each of the sixty-four units of change comprises a pair of trigrams, a binary of units of substance. The units of substance comprise the essential units of *qi*, yin, and yang. The hexagrams themselves represent static properties of yin and yang combinations (specific patterns or codes of *qi*), but then the anatomy of every hexagram represents the dynamic properties of ebb and flow.

That is the fundamental principle in the Gua Qi school (卦氣學, *Guà Qì xué*) of theoretical study, which rose in prominence during the Western Han (202 BC–AD 9).[30] Inspired by the *Yi wěi* (易緯),[31] Gua Qi blended older preexisting metaphysical principles in Yì Xué with the works of Meng Xi 孟喜, one of the most influential I Ching scholars of the Former Han (206 BC–AD 8), and of his student Jing Fang 京房 (77–37 BC), a mathematician and astrologer.

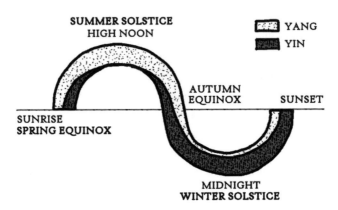

**FIGURE 3.6** Gua Qi yin and yang fluctuations

Meng Xi proposed a system of fortune-telling using the hexagrams, whereby yang lines mark warmer weather and the day, while yin lines mark cooler weather and the night. Jing Fang, a New Text school adherent, expanded on his teacher's theories and proposed that the sixty-four hexagrams mark the progression of the seasons, hours, and changes in weather; and since human behavior mirrors Heaven's movements, changes in time and space can predict human personality traits and lucks. That became the basis of Gua Qi.

Under Gua Qi theory, yin and yang qualities of *qi* form combinations. These combinations are characterized by certain correspondences to physical and natural laws. How dark or how light, how hot or cold, shape and size, numerical values, sounds, all of it relates to its specific pattern of *qi*. Nature, being both a schema of space and a schema of time, is represented in the sixty-four hexagrams as units of space and also as units of time.

Thus, seasonal cycles are expressed in the functions of the hexagrams. After the winter solstice is the first break of warm *qi*, marked by a single yang line rising from the bottom. In table 3.1, you can see the progression of the yang line as the months get progressively warmer. As we peak toward the summer solstice, all six lines in the hexagram function are yang. As the weather cools toward autumn, cold *qi* or yin lines rise from the bottom up.

The twelve hexagrams in the I Ching that correspond with the functions of the twelve lunar months in the lunisolar calendar system are called the Twelve Hexagrams of the Son of Heaven 天子卦 (Tiānzǐ Guà), also known as the Twelve Sovereign Hexagrams (the Bi Gua, 辟卦).[32] Jing Fang proposed that these twelve ruling hexagrams (君卦, *jūn guà*) correspond with the lunar months based on their patterns of yin and yang fluctuations.

**TABLE 3.1** The Twelve Hexagrams of the Son of Heaven 天子卦 (*Tiānzǐ Guà*)[33]

| MONTH 11 Dec.–Jan. | MONTH 12 Jan.–Feb. | MONTH 1 Feb.–Mar. | MONTH 2 Mar.–Apr. | MONTH 3 Apr.–May | MONTH 4 May–June |
|---|---|---|---|---|---|
| Hexagram 24 | Hexagram 19 | Hexagram 11 | Hexagram 34 | Hexagram 43 | Hexagram 1 |
| 子 *Zi* Rat Water | 丑 *Chou* Ox Earth | 寅 *Yin* Tiger Wood | 卯 *Mao* Rabbit Water | 辰 *Chen* Dragon Earth | 巳 *Si* Snake Fire |
| **MONTH 5** June–July | **MONTH 6** July–Aug. | **MONTH 7** Aug.–Sept. | **MONTH 8** Sept.–Oct. | **MONTH 9** Oct.–Nov. | **MONTH 10** Nov.–Dec. |
| Hexagram 44 | Hexagram 33 | Hexagram 12 | Hexagram 20 | Hexagram 23 | Hexagram 2 |
| 午 *Wu* Horse Fire | 未 *Wei* Goat Earth | 申 *Shen* Monkey Metal | 酉 *You* Rooster Metal | 戌 *Xu* Dog Earth | 亥 *Hai* Boar Water |

*Note:* Month 11 always corresponds with the winter solstice. Beneath each hexagram correspondence is the lunar month's earthly branch, zodiac animal ruler for the month, and governing Wu Xing phase of change.

Jing Fang 京房 also proposed that the hexagrams have solar correspondences in addition to the lunar ones, and specifically with the Huang Tao (黃道), the Yellow Path. The Huang Tao is the path of the sun in the celestial sphere. The Four Perfected Hexagrams and the six lines each one has equal twenty-four terms (4 × 6 = 24), which corresponds with the lunisolar calendar.

After removing the twenty-four lines from the Four Perfected Hexagrams for the twenty-four solar terms, you're left with exactly 360 lines in the I Ching (64 hexagrams × 6 lines = 384 lines − 24 lines of the Four Perfected Hexagrams = 360). Accounting for leap years, the hexagrams correspond precisely with the seasonal arc of the sun.

With sixty hexagrams remaining (less the Four Perfected) and 360 days to account for, each hexagram represents approximately six days to six days and seven minutes of the calendar year, meaning each of the six lines of every hexagram represents approximately one minute of the year. The sixty hexagrams are plotted in between the Four Perfected Hexagrams per the seasonal cycles. Mapped out, a diviner could then in theory predict the timing of events with great specificity.

Jing Fang proposed that when the *qi* of natural forces is conducive to human well-being, humans embodying that same *qi* will be good; when such *qi* from Heaven is destructive toward human well-being, humans embodying that same *qi* will be evil and will encounter disaster. Furthermore, the influence went both ways, so that when people in power were evil, their evildoing caused destructive *qi* in the environment, resulting in natural disasters. Only when people in power are good, producing positive *qi* in the world, will there be prosperity. Thus, Jing Fang concluded, the natural disasters the kingdom faced at the time were the direct result of evil rulers and failings of government officials. Ultimately, Jing Fang's theories got him convicted of treason and executed.[34]

Table 3.2 shows the Four Perfected Hexagrams (四正卦, Sì Zhèng Guà) per the Gua Qi school canon from the Western Han.[35] The Four Perfected Hexagrams mark the four quadrants of space and time, i.e., the four seasons and the four directions. Furthermore, each line of the four hexagrams corresponds with the equinoxes, the solstices, and the twenty-four solar terms of the lunisolar calendar. Corresponding Western zodiac sign correspondences have been added to the table.

**TABLE 3.2** The Four Perfected Hexagrams (四正卦, Sì Zhèng Guà) and the Twenty-Four Solar Terms[36]

| 四正卦<br>Sì Zhèng Guà<br>Four Perfected Hexagrams | 震榆<br>Zhèn mìng<br>Thunder<br>**Hexagram 51**<br>Zhèn | 離梓<br>Lí zuó<br>Fire<br>**Hexagram 30**<br>Lí | 兌橢<br>Duì duǒ<br>Lake<br>**Hexagram 58**<br>Duì | 坎棄<br>Kǎn chéng<br>Water<br>**Hexagram 29**<br>Kǎn |
|---|---|---|---|---|
| 主四時<br>Zhǔ sì shí<br>Four seasons | 春 Chūn<br>Spring | 夏 Xià<br>Summer | 秋 Qiū<br>Autumn | 冬 Dōng<br>Winter |
| 主四方<br>Zhǔ sì fāng<br>Four directions | 東 Dōng<br>East | 南 Nán<br>South | 西 Xī<br>West | 北 Běi<br>North |
| 上爻.<br>Shàng yáo<br>**Line 6** | 芒種<br>Mángzhòng<br>Blossoms form<br>June 5–7<br>Gemini | 白露<br>Báilù<br>White dew<br>Sept. 7–9<br>Virgo | 大雪<br>Dàxuě<br>Heavy snow<br>Dec. 6–8<br>Sagittarius | 驚蟄<br>Jīngzhé<br>Insects awaken<br>Mar. 5–7<br>Pisces |
| 五爻.<br>Wǔ yáo<br>**Line 5** | 小滿<br>Xiǎomǎn<br>Green buds form<br>May 20–22<br>Gemini | 處暑<br>Chùshǔ<br>Dissipating heat<br>Aug. 22–24<br>Virgo | 小雪<br>Xiǎoxuě<br>Light snow<br>Nov. 22–23<br>Sagittarius | 雨水<br>Yǔshuǐ<br>Spring showers<br>Feb. 18–20<br>Pisces |
| 四爻.<br>Sì yáo<br>**Line 4** | 立夏<br>Lìxià<br>Start of summer<br>May 5–7<br>Taurus | 立秋<br>Lìqiū<br>Start of autumn<br>Aug. 7–9<br>Leo | 立冬<br>Lìdōng<br>Start of winter<br>Nov. 7–8<br>Scorpio | 立春<br>Lìchūn<br>Start of spring<br>Feb. 3–5<br>Aquarius |
| 三爻.<br>Sān yáo<br>**Line 3** | 穀雨<br>Gǔyǔ<br>Gathering rain<br>Apr. 19–21<br>Taurus | 大暑<br>Dàshǔ<br>Great heat<br>July 22–24<br>Leo | 霜降<br>Shuāngjiàng<br>The first frost<br>Oct. 23–24<br>Scorpio | 大寒<br>Dàhán<br>Great cold<br>Jan. 20–21<br>Aquarius |

**TABLE 3.2** The Four Perfected Hexagrams (四正卦, Sì Zhèng Guà) and the Twenty-Four Solar Terms[36] *(continued)*

| 二爻.<br>*Èr yáo*<br>**Line 2** | 清明<br>*Qīngmíng*<br>Bright and clear<br>Apr. 4–6<br>Aries | 小暑<br>*Xiǎoshǔ*<br>Coming heat<br>July 6–8<br>Cancer | 寒露<br>*Hánlù*<br>Cold dew<br>Oct. 8–9<br>Libra | 小寒<br>*Xiǎohán*<br>Coming cold<br>Jan. 5–7<br>Capricorn |
|---|---|---|---|---|
| 初爻.<br>*Chū yáo*<br>**Line 1** | 春分<br>*Chūnfēn*<br>Vernal equinox<br>Mar. 20–22<br>Aries | 夏至<br>*Xiàzhì*<br>Summer solstice<br>June 21–22<br>Cancer | 秋分<br>*Qiūfēn*<br>Autumn equinox<br>Sept. 22–24<br>Libra | 冬至<br>*Dōngzhì*<br>Winter solstice<br>Dec. 21–23<br>Capricorn |

According to Gua Qi theory, at the precise moment of, say, the spring equinox, marked by when the solar longitude (a measure of time) is at 0°, yin and yang values of *qi* lock into place per the code that we've identified as Hexagram 51 to mark the solar influence but also Hexagram 11 to mark the lunar influence (lunar month 1). Effective at that moment in time, spatially designated by where the Han dynasty would have been located, or mainland China, the fixed, static properties of Hexagram 51 define the solar longitude at 0°, the vernal equinox.

That's the Huang Tao, or Yellow Path of the sun's ecliptic longitude, rectified with the I Ching. Meanwhile, Hexagram 11 defines the lunar influences leading up to the vernal equinox, and Hexagram 34 defines the period of the vernal equinox. Contemporaneously, Hexagram 51 continues to govern April through early June, due to the solar influences at that time. Under the umbrella influence of Hexagram 51 are the lunar influences from Hexagrams 34, 43, and 1, corresponding with that vernal equinox (line 1 of Hexagram 51) through early June (line 6).

Every date in time has a lunar hexagram correspondence from one of the Twelve Hexagrams of the Son of Heaven per table 3.1 and, in addition, a solar terms hexagram correspondence per the Four Perfected Hexagrams referenced in table 3.2.

The Gua Qi diagram attributed to Confucius (孔子卦氣圖, Kǒngzǐ Guà Qì Tú) shows the correspondences between the hexagrams, lunar months, and twelve earthly branches.[37] Although the diagram is referred to as the Gua Qi Diagram of Confucius, it is unlikely that it has anything at all to do with Confucius. The attribution is more likely due to the correspondences in the Gua Qi diagram coming from the Ten Wings.[38]

Under the following schema, the hexagrams at the four cardinal points (forming the square) each designate two of the twelve lunar months. The arrangement of the eight hexagrams is based on the arrangement of trigrams in King Wen's Ba Gua, also known as the Later Heaven Ba Gua.

**TABLE 3.3** Gua Qi Diagram Attributed to Confucius[39]

| | 巳 (Sì) | 午 (Wǔ) SOUTH | 未 (Wèi) | |
|---|---|---|---|---|
| 辰 (Chén) | 57 | 30 | 2 | 申 (Shēn) |
| 卯 (Mǎo) EAST | 51 | Lunar Month 3 & 4 / Lunar Month 2 / Lunar Month 1 & 12 | Lunar Month 5 / ※ / Lunar Month 11 | Lunar Month 6 & 7 / Lunar Month 8 / Lunar Month 9 & 10 | 58 | 酉 (Yǒu) WEST |
| 寅 (Yín) | 52 | 29 | 1 | 戌 (Xū) |
| | 丑 (Chǒu) | 子 (Zǐ) NORTH | 亥 (Hài) | |

Gua Qi is, in brief, a branch of East Asian alchemy, with crossovers into using the I Ching for fortune-telling—in other words, it's both. Gua Qi approaches to the I Ching are practiced in Vietnam, Korea, Japan, and throughout the diaspora of Taoist alchemists across the Pacific, with varying schools branching off from the historical tenets.

Such theories were readily adopted by alchemists because the principles meant that if an alchemist can master control over patterns of *qi,* then the alchemist can master control over nature. The same principles that help us in predictive fortune-telling because it tracks yin and yang are the same principles that can be turned around and used in ceremonial magic to transmute natural yin and yang and conform them to the magician's will. Thus, trigrams and hexagrams become periodic tables for Taoist mystics to override natural cycles.

## PRACTICUM 3.1:
## The Hexagrams Ruling Your Birth Month

Use table 3.2 to find the two hexagram lines that correspond with your horoscope sun sign. For example, I am a Libra, so the two lines that correspond with my sun sign Libra are lines 1 and 2 of Hexagram 58.

Find the entry in this book for the hexagram corresponding with your sun sign. Read "The Oracle" section for that hexagram. Then continue into the hexagram entry until you reach the two lines corresponding with your horoscope (sun) sign. In the example of Capricorn, after turning to the section of this book on Hexagram 29, Kǎn, the Abyss, continue past "The Oracle" section to the "First Line" section and the "Second Line" section. Read the two sections together.

These lines express the prevailing *qi* energy in the environment during the time of the year when you were born. So what's being expressed in those lines won't pertain to your life path specifically; rather, it's a general projection of the nature of *qi* influence at your moment of birth, which inevitably will have an impact on the very start of influences of nurture in your life.

To interpret the line text specific to this exercise, "auspicious" is going to mean that the environment you were born into was generally stable and prosperous, whereas "ominous" or "inauspicious" simply refers to environments that were harsher and less stable. The latter can indicate one born into uncertain times, and they have no bearing on your personal luck. Rather, it's an indication that the society around you at your moment of birth was going through challenges or upheaval. References such as "there is no blame" or "blameless" are neutral, with some aspects prosperous and some aspects unstable.

Let's take a look at Cancer to demonstrate. Cancers will turn to Hexagram 30 and read the text for the first and second lines. Broadly speaking, during this time of year that Cancerians were born into, there are more unpredictable, vacillating forces at play ("footprints show a trail faltering between right and wrong, a confused path"), so to optimize success, Cancerians will want to "honor with offerings," meaning to be more mindful of cultivating personal spirituality. Continuing on to the second line, we see closer ties with ancestors. Cancers are more likely to directly inherit and embody strikingly similar traits to their ancestors. (This can mean grandparents or even deceased aunts and uncles whose passing happened prior to your birth.)

## SUMMARY OF STEPS

1. **What is the hexagram associated with your Western astrological horoscope sign?** Refer to table 3.2. For the astrologers among us wrinkling their noses at sun signs, you are free to complicate this exercise by adding in analysis of your moon and rising signs alongside the sun. Why stop there? Check for the midheaven as well. **Read "The Oracle" message for that hexagram.** *Example:* Pisces corresponds with Hexagram 29. "The Oracle" section opens with a summary judgment of the hexagram. Lines in bold are the translations from the original, the riddles for you to solve.

2. **Which two lines of that hexagram correspond with your horoscope sign?** Refer again to table 3.2. Read the two line sections from that hexagram entry. *Example:* Note how Hexagram 29 covers Capricorn, Aquarius, and Pisces. Of the six lines, line 5 and line 6 are specific to Pisces. For line 5, turn to the section in Hexagram 29 noted as the "Fifth Line." The text in bold is a translation of the original Zhouyi. Subsequent to that are supplemental annotations.

## OPTIONAL LUNAR MONTH ANALYSIS

If you know which lunar month you were born in, then take a look at table 3.1 as well and look up the hexagram corresponding to your lunar birth month. Read "The Oracle" section of that hexagram. In terms of an astrological equivalence to the Western astrological system, this Son of Heaven hexagram will correspond with both your sun and moon signs combined.

For example, my September birthday corresponds with lunar month 8, so I'd look up Hexagram 20 and read "The Oracle" section as a synopsis of my sun sign Libra plus my moon sign Leo. I interpret "see and also be seen" from the passage as very Leo, while "restate for yourself what your motivations are" feels very Libra.

Alternatively, I might look at the month 8 Hexagram correspondence in table 3.3 for another point of view. Per the Gua Qi diagram attributed to Confucius, lunar month 8 corresponds with Hexagram 58.

Table 3.4 sets forth a contrasting approach to the preceding one, seeking to reconcile the inherent contradiction that arose in the lunar and solar hexagram correspondences. For example, someone born in late September (lunar month 8) would look at Hexagram 58 if following the Four Perfected Hexagrams, and narrowly, only two lines from Hexagram 58; but then in theory, those lunar influences would also be characterized by Hexagram 20 per the Twelve Hexagrams of the Son of Heaven. These table references can work in tandem for natal astrology, but a more cohesive approach might be in order for alchemical operations, spell-crafting, and ritual magic.

Thus, the correspondences in table 3.4 are formulated for the purposes of thaumaturgy, or being able to control the natural order in a way that induces what resembles miracle-working. The thaumaturgical approach continues to account for the Huang Tao, the path of the sun throughout the hours of the day. However, in addition to the Huang Tao, now it's also based on the positioning of the sun marked by the Tropic of Cancer and the Tropic of Capricorn. By doing so, it can account for the Western zodiac wheel Aries through Pisces.

**TABLE 3.4** The Thaumaturgical Order of Trigrams Relative to the Directions and Seasons

| | | *(Tropic of Capricorn)*<br>SOUTH | | |
|---|---|---|---|---|
| EAST | **Xun**<br>WIND | **Li**<br>FIRE | **Kun**<br>EARTH | WEST |
| | **Zhen**<br>THUNDER | Cardinal Spring / **Spring Equinox** / Cardinal Summer ☯ **Winter Solstice** / **Summer Solstice** / Cardinal Winter / **Autumn Equinox** / Cardinal Autumn | **Dui**<br>LAKE | |
| | **Gen**<br>MOUNTAIN | **Kan**<br>WATER | **Qian**<br>HEAVEN | |
| | | NORTH<br>*(Tropic of Cancer)* | | |

In the northern hemisphere, at the Tropic of Cancer, the sun is directly overhead at the zenith at high noon on the summer solstice. Thus, I align the summer solstice with the north sector. When King Wen's Ba Gua is superimposed over the eight directions, Water corresponds with north. The arrangement is the same as the Gua Qi diagram attributed to Confucius, except the former featured hexagrams, while the latter features trigrams.

At the Tropic of Capricorn, the sun is directly overhead at high noon on the winter solstice. In a tropical horoscopic wheel chart, the high noon is marked at the south position of the tropical chart. South corresponds with Fire. Thus, I align the winter solstice with the Tropic of Capricorn as charted in the Lo Shu magic square, which corresponds with the trigram Fire.

On the spring equinox in the northern hemisphere (around March 20), the sun is directly overhead at high noon on the equator, corresponding with the first point of Aries, and likewise again on the autumn equinox (around September 22), corresponding with the first point of Libra. Outside these tropic zones, the sun is never directly overhead at the high noon zenith.

The cardinal directions remain the same whether you are in the northern hemisphere or southern hemisphere, as they are derived from your point of view, wherever you are. Thus, in both hemispheres, Thunder and Wind correspond with the period of tracking solar longitude from February 3–5 to March 20–22. That's four of the twenty-four solar terms in the lunisolar calendar, irrespective of whether it is spring (northern hemisphere) or autumn (southern hemisphere). Lake and Heaven correspond with the four solar terms from August 7–9 to September 22–24, or in the lunisolar calendar system, from the start of autumn (立秋, *lìqiū*) through the autumnal equinox (秋分, *qiūfēn*).

The table 3.4 approach thus reconciles alchemical principles in Gua Qi, the eight directions, eight seasonal points, and the Huang Tao path of the sun with the Babylonian and Hellenistic zodiac wheel (incidentally, due to the alignment with the Tropic of Cancer and Tropic of Capricorn). Appendix A features a side-by-side comparison of the natural cycle of trigram and seasonal correspondences with the thaumaturge's trigram and seasonal correspondences.

As the alchemist seeking to control or even override nature in a manner that supports personal prosperity, this approach makes more sense because in the cold winter, to stay warm, the mystic will seek to raise Fire; whereas in the hot summer, to prevent droughts and stay hydrated, the mystic will seek to raise Water. Springs are more likely to bring thunderstorms, which is when the ceremonial magician will want to harvest thunder *qi* for use in Thunder Rites.

The trigrams rectified with the tropical zodiac now present a system of I Ching correspondences that empower the spellcaster, the alchemist, the healer, and the archetypes of the mystic that we'll cover later in chapter 5.

When you read I Ching commentaries where hexagram explanations are heavily reliant on discussions of how yin and yang interact with one another among the lines, you're looking at the influence of Gua Qi theories. Gua Qi is the set of principles that seek to explain the ebb and flow of yin and yang across spacetime and how the trigrams and hexagrams, which are codes of yin and yang, are sympathetically connected to that cosmic ebb and flow. Fortune-tellers apply Gua Qi to predict timing. Alchemists and ceremonial magicians use it to control that ebb and flow. Both acknowledge it has principles that reveal the interplay of relationships between gods, nature spirits, ancestors, and humans.

## A History of Eclectic Influences

Each transformation of I Ching interpretation is a testament to how the Book is an ever-evolving Oracle, remaining in constant motion throughout human history and still in motion today.

Confucian classics like the I Ching gained favor in Vietnam around the tenth century.[40] During the Lý dynasty (AD 1009–1225), I Ching diviners were appointed to court positions to advise the reigning monarchs on statecraft, elevating the Book to a place of prominence among the ruling class. By the fifteenth century under the Hậu Lê dynasty, Confucianism gained a strong foothold and further popularized the I Ching.[41] Neo-Confucianism in China was antagonistic toward Taoism and Buddhism, whereas Vietnamese scholars advanced scholarship at the intersection of Yì Xué and Buddhism, and also contributed greatly to the I Ching's magical applications in Taoist mysticism. Neo-Confucianism, in brief, is the revival movement of Confucianist political philosophy that took place in the AD 850s and peaked in the eleventh century during the Northern Song dynasty.[42]

Over the centuries, the Oracle has been integrated into shamanistic practices that served the subject class of these Southeast Asian dynasties. Metaphysics arising from the Oracle heavily influenced the precursor mysticism in esoteric traditions such as Caodaism in thirteenth-century Vietnam.[43] Caodaism[44] is an Indigenous Vietnamese religion syncretizing Buddhism, Confucianism, and Taoism that emerged during the Trần dynasty (AD 1225–1400).[45] I Ching divination became part of local mediumship practices, revealing prophecies from the spirit realm.

In spite of the polarizing discourses of New Text vs. Old Text or Rationalist vs. Originalist, Korean and Japanese philosophers found middle ground, giving rise to new, syncretized schools of thought. Yi Hwang 이황 (1501–1570) was a Korean Confucian philosopher and part of the Joseon dynasty literati. A child prodigy, he mastered most of the Confucian classics by the age of twelve, and at the age of twenty, he undertook intense pursuit of Yì Xué, following the Zhu Xi school of thought. Yi went on to be one of the leading neo-Confucian scholars of the sixteenth century. His work spearheaded an advancement in Zhu Xi's school, resulting in Eclecticism, an approach that was better tailored to the specific statecraft needs of the Joseon.[46]

Historically the I Ching was used to support liberal politics. Huang Zongxi 黃宗羲 (1610–1695)[47] was a political philosopher and soldier during the late part of the Ming dynasty. He advocated for constitutional law and the right of the people to criticize the emperor, and he found authority for those positions in the I Ching. When he was eighteen, his father was executed for expressing controversial political ideologies, but the dead man became a martyr to the people. With the collapse of the Ming and rise of the Qing, a warrant was issued for Huang Zongxi's capture, but he was never found. It's believed that he fled to Japan by that time. In addition to commentaries on the I Ching, Huang's most notable works were in political philosophy, advocating for the rights of the individual and the consent of the governed.

Yet Huang also observed that the I Ching itself is neutral and apolitical; people, with their political agendas, imbue it with morality. He writes: "The nine traditions of philosophy and the hundred schools of thought have all used the I Ching to promote their own theories."[48]

It is equally well documented in history that the I Ching has been used to support conservative politics. The Yì Xué scholar Nemoto Michiaki (1822–1906) advanced an interpretation of the I Ching as supportive of nationalism.[49] He critiqued past Chinese scholars for interpreting the I Ching as a text advocating revolution, and instead viewed the Oracle as being anti-revolution and pro-nationalism.[50] This perspective found support among schools of Chinese thought as well, such as among Old Text scholars in the imperial court of Qing, who disagreed with the revolutionary implications.

New approaches to divinatory methods and the syncretizing of the Oracle with other religions emerge over the centuries as it migrates out of the mainland. In Tokugawa Japan, the I Ching was interpreted through a Shinto paradigm, notably advanced by scholars such as Hirata Atsutane (1776–1843), a Shinto theologian who received visionary knowledge that the I Ching had been authored by a Shinto deity who had traveled to ancient China to cultivate the Chinese.[51] New schools of thought emerged that departed from Confucianist readings of the text and syncretized it with Shinto. In 1897, Nemoto Michiaki published a seminal text on I Ching divination, *Restoring the Ancient Divination Method of Zhouyi*, where he revised the divination method from using forty-nine yarrow stalks and popularized a method that used forty-five.[52]

In its passage through the course of world history, I Ching scholarship—and even divinatory methods—have shown themselves to be varied. When two different yet equally venerated philosophers look at the same verse from the Oracle, two contrasting and even contradicting interpretations will often emerge. Every culture that encounters the Oracle integrates what works for them and modifies what doesn't.

Look no further than interpretations for Hexagram 1 to validate that point. Historian and mystic Gan Bao 干寶,[53] who lived during the Jin dynasty, was most notable for both his I Ching scholarship and his book that compiled spirit encounters and supernatural events. Gan Bao saw Hexagram 1 as a justification for revolution and reformation. Meanwhile, Nemoto Michiaki examined the same text and saw it as justification for imperial succession and unconditional loyalty to the emperor.[54]

In the seventeenth and eighteenth centuries, Vietnamese, Korean, and Japanese scholars were developing new schools of Yì Xué commentary, which tended to be critical of Zhu Xi and Song dynasty Originalists. While I Ching scholars in China placed great importance on the Ten Wings, I Ching scholars from the latter Tokugawa period, for instance, were moving away from reliance on it. Japanese Confucianist scholar Inoue Kinga (1732–1784) founded a new school of thought, the Eclectic school, which shared similarities to the Korean I Ching school of Eclecticism, but also differed in certain respects. Japanese Eclecticism synthesized various selected Han and Song dynasty commentaries.[55]

An Oracle school also emerged during this period, gaining such momentum across the villages of Japan that, by the eighteenth century, there was at least one I Ching diviner in every village.[56] The Oracle school of Yì Xué was less about producing philosopher-sages or scholars for the literati, and more about producing professional I Ching diviners. These I Ching professionals from the Oracle school ranged from the commoner with a *tachimi* street stall to renowned diviners with *sayauchi* academies. The Oracle school produced intersectional studies in Yì Xué that combined I Ching with medicine, military strategy, business, agriculture, and meteorology, just to name a few examples.[57] The Oracle school greatly expanded the breadth and scope of Yì Xué.

After the modernization of China in the twentieth century, however, interest in and regard for the I Ching declined dramatically. Three landmark events in Chinese history dismantled the authority that the I Ching had once held. The first was the 1905 abolition of the civil service examinations. The second was the 1911 Revolution ending imperial rule. And the third was the New Culture Movement that took place between 1915 and 1925, promoting Western ideology in China.[58] European culture and thought were perceived as superior to traditional and historical Chinese culture and thought. Antiquated texts such as the Zhouyi receded into obscurity, and only after the Book of Changes gained popularity in the West did it reappear in China with renewed interest; and even then, that interest was reliant on Western perspectives on the I Ching.

Interestingly, Yì Xué didn't exactly disappear during the Cultural Revolution either. In his speeches, Mao Zedong often quoted from the I Ching,[59] and Marxist philosophers in China found the I Ching to be consistent with communism. There was an equivalence drawn between yin and yang polarity and Hegelian dialectical thinking.[60] Hexagram 13 was interpreted as advocating for a communist society and social ownership of property. Hexagram 49 was interpreted as supportive of a proletarian cultural revolution.

Just as one vantage point concludes that the I Ching supports Marxism, a different vantage point on that very same text concludes that it supports capitalism. In early twentieth-century Japan, business tycoons such as Takashima Donsho attributed their wealth and success to the I Ching, and economic scholars interpreted the Book's philosophies as advocating for a free-market economy.[61]

New discoveries and Yì Xué scholarship continue to advance and evolve in modern times. In 1973, archaeologists in the Hunan province found a copy of the I Ching dated to around 168 BC buried in a tomb with a feudal lord. This silk document is referred to as the Mawangdui manuscript. The text was written on silk and contains the entirety of the Zhouyi intact, along with some commentaries on the text similar to the Ten Wings.[62] However, the ordering of the sixty-four hexagrams differed from the more commonly established King Wen's order.[63] The remarkable discovery renewed an interest in the I Ching among modern-day scholars.

The King Wen order of the hexagrams is cryptic, and a systematic order isn't easily deciphered, beyond grouping polarities together, which we'll cover in chapter 8. Meanwhile, the Mawangdui manuscript arranges the hexagrams in a systematic order by trigrams. In the Mawangdui order, the first eight hexagrams in the text all bear Heaven as the upper trigram, while the lower trigrams from 1 to 8 are in a fixed sequential order.[64] See table 3.5 to compare the King Wen order (the current orthodox sequence) with the Mawangdui order.[65]

**TABLE 3.5** King Wen Order vs. Mawangdui Order of Hexagrams

| KING WEN'S ORDER OF HEXAGRAMS 1–8 |||||||||
|---|---|---|---|---|---|---|---|
| 1 | 2 | 3 | 4 | 5 | 6 | 7 | 8 |
| ䷀ | ䷁ | ䷂ | ䷃ | ䷄ | ䷅ | ䷆ | ䷇ |
| THE MAWANGDUI ORDER OF HEXAGRAMS 1–8 |||||||||
| 1 | 2 | 3 | 4 | 5 | 6 | 7 | 8 |
| ䷀ | ䷋ | ䷠ | ䷓ | ䷅ | ䷌ | ䷘ | ䷤ |
| *Equivalent in King Wen's Order* |||||||||
| 1 | 12 | 33 | 10 | 6 | 13 | 25 | 44 |

Having covered over three thousand years of history and culture that have moved the direction of I Ching scholarship across Asia, let's now consider Western perspectives on Yì Xué.

## Jesuit Missionaries and the I Ching

By the late sixteenth century, during the Qing dynasty (AD 1644–1912), the Book of Changes is pervasive across most of the Asian continent and has arrived in Europe.[66] Its westward migration began with the eastward imperialist movement of the West.[67] Christian missionaries from Europe traveled to China, as they had to other parts of the world, with the intent of proselytizing. Jesuits in China were determined to reconcile Confucianism and Christianity as a means to persuade the Chinese to convert.[68]

Shangdi 上帝, a supreme god in Heaven venerated since the Shang dynasty and inscribed on Bronze Age oracle bones, was equated to the Christian God.[69] Jesuit priest Matteo Ricci (1552–1610) proposed that the "Tao that produced the myriad things"[70] found in Taoist and Confucian cosmogony was the same as the Abrahamic God that produced the myriad things. Ricci asserted that, in fact, the ancient Chinese worshipped a monotheistic God.[71]

Early on there were Christians who didn't see the I Ching as magical or religious. Charles Porterfield Krauth (1823–1883), a Lutheran pastor and theologian, considered the text to be one of philosophy, not magic. In an 1879 treatise, Krauth defined the I Ching as follows: "**Y-KING,** in Chinese Philosophy, 'the book of changes,' one of the most ancient books of China; a sort of encyclopedia, embracing physics, ethics, and metaphysics."[72]

Not all Western Europeans were in agreement, however. Many Christian missionaries and biblical scholars came to view the I Ching as witchcraft and heretical.[73] When the Kangxi emperor commissioned French Jesuit priest Joachim Bouvet (1656–1730) to compile an annotated edition and translation of the I Ching in 1715, the undertaking received backlash from both the Christian community and the Chinese scholarly community. Ultimately the Vatican condemned the idea that a pagan text like the I Ching was in alignment with Christian values.[74] By the way, remember that name—Bouvet—because we'll return to him when we cover the I Ching and the sciences.

One of the early English translations of the I Ching was a version by Reverend Canon Thomas McClatchie (1812–1885), who interpreted the text through a Christianized lens, but also criticized it as being un-Christian.[75] McClatchie's approach to I Ching study was comparative; he saw some Catholic implications in the Taoist cosmogony of a Great Father in Heaven being a triplicated Mystery, or a Holy Trinity, but also saw the text as inferior and a gross distortion of biblical truths.

The Great Father of the I Ching is a hermaphroditic monad, noted McClatchie.[76] He also compared I Ching philosophy to the philosophy of the Greeks. For instance, in his translation of Hexagram 1, McClatchie likened the dragon references to the Roman god Neptune, and the concept of the *junzi* (君子, *jūnzǐ*) to the hero-sage *sapiens* of the Stoics.[77] For McClatchie, the Shangdi that Matteo Ricci connected to the Abrahamic God was more in line with Jupiter, Zeus, and Bel of ancient Babylon,[78] Bel being the Mesopotamian god of order and destiny.[79]

McClatchie went a step beyond Bouvet, maintaining that the I Ching was pagan, representing a form of phallic worship and heathenry.[80] Shangdi (spelled "Shang-te" in McClatchie's text) is a representation of the "indecent symbols" of the "male portion . . . the *membrum virile*" and Kun (Hexagram 2), which

McClatchie correlates with a goddess, is the "female portion . . . the *pudendum muliebre*" (the vulva).⁸¹

McClatchie writes: "The Universe was supposed to have originated from their mystic union,"⁸² a "Bestial Transmutation of the Great Father and Mother."⁸³ The "obscene picture" of pagan thought, be that from the East or the West in Jupiter and Juno, was an early heathen interpretation of "matter having received the spermatic reasons of God . . . and that Juno, in this picture in Samos, signifies matter, and Jupiter god."⁸⁴ And so Christians should not mistake these heathen interpretations of a monad for the Christian God and must "take care not to defile divine things with impure names." The reverend then included a footnote citing an article on phallic worship.⁸⁵

Both Bouvet and McClatchie advanced a proposition that the I Ching was brought to China by one of the sons of Noah after the biblical Great Flood.⁸⁶ Other European Orientalists of the time saw a resemblance between Chinese ideograms and "Babylonian hieroglyphs" (cuneiform), setting forth a theory that the people of the Xia dynasty were Mesopotamians. One proponent of that theory was French scholar Albert Étienne Terrien de LaCouperie (1844–1894), who asserted that the I Ching originated from the Akkadian Empire (2234–2154 BC).⁸⁷

Babylonian-origins-of-China theorists saw a resemblance between the eight trigrams (which Europeans observed the Chinese using in magical charms⁸⁸) and the I Ching, on the one hand, and a form of ancient Near East divination and talisman-crafting that used geometrical figures not unlike I Ching trigrams and hexagrams, on the other. A theory was advanced—and became popular—that the I Ching originated from Chaldea.⁸⁹ Figure 3.7 is an example of the

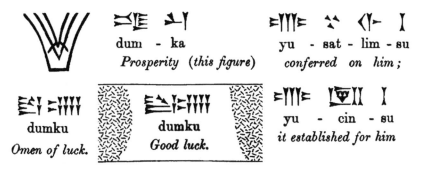

**FIGURE 3.7** Babylonian augury by means of geometrical figures. SOURCE: *Transactions of the Society of Biblical Archaeology* (1876).⁹⁰

Babylonian augury by geometrical figures that late nineteenth-century biblical scholars saw as related to the I Ching.

After McClatchie came the two most well-known translations of the I Ching in the West: one by James Legge (1815–1897) and the other by Richard Wilhelm (1873–1930). Both were Christian missionaries who saw their God in the pages of the Oracle, though Legge's work tended to show disdain for the Chinese people and culture.[91] Where Legge was singularly focused on converting the Chinese to Christianity, Wilhelm seemed more open to counting Taoist priests among his friends.[92]

Legge described the divinatory uses of the I Ching as "vain" and "absurd,"[93] asserting that the historical King Wen and Duke of Zhou weren't using the I Ching for divination, and therefore millennia of Chinese scholars have been wrong in their interpretations of the text. He made it his mission to reform Confucianism, drawing upon what is good within the existing Chinese classics—i.e., what is consistent with Christianity—and removing what he saw as deficient.[94] Ultimately, he becomes representative of the Victorian Orientalist movements in Europe, adopting the mentality that his missionary work was "the one-sided encounter of a so-called progressive West with a r——d Orient."[95]

To his credit, Legge broke down language barriers so that a wealth of ancient texts of the East are now accessible to the Western world. His contributions add greatly to the global corpus of I Ching scholarship by interpreting the text through a biblical exegetical tradition. He doesn't reject the I Ching or Confucianism as heretical, but rather as merely defective[96] and therefore reparable. Legge emphasizes that Shangdi is "God—our God—the true God"[97] and that the tenets espoused in the I Ching were merely inferior, less evolved iterations of Abrahamic monotheism.

Therefore, he concludes, the I Ching proves that the pagans of the East had the potential for accepting Christianity. Thus, he made it his personal mission to save China, one baptism at a time. The recurring theme in his diaries was how many Chinese he converted, characterized as victories, and how many were in attendance at his sermons.[98]

Wilhelm, in contrast, expressed a sincere love for China's people and culture. He saw the mysteries of Christ within the pages of the I Ching, asserting that the Book of Changes and the Holy Bible were in alignment, and that the I Ching, in its own right, held great value to humanity. Wilhelm presents the text as universal, for instance by drawing parallels to Kantian ethics.[99] And while Wilhelm was also a Christian missionary, he succeeds at applying a secular and impartial view in his translations. His granddaughter, Bettina Wilhelm, said of the man, "instead of baptizing a Chinese congregation, he delved deep into Chinese wisdom."[100]

Through his friendship with Carl Gustav Jung, Richard Wilhelm deepens an interest in the sciences of the mind, and with the popularity of his translations, he will have a lasting impact on interpretations of the I Ching in the West. Rather than assuming the involvement of spirits, Wilhelm interprets the power of the Oracle as coming from a connection between the human unconscious and the cosmic order.[101] He notes that "the manipulation of the yarrow stalks makes it possible for the unconscious in man to become active."[102]

It is worth considering who assisted Wilhelm with the translations, a person often described in the West as an I Ching master. Perhaps Lao Naixuan 勞乃宣 (1843–1921) was well schooled in the I Ching, but among the Chinese, he is better known as a Qing dynasty politician who opposed the Boxer Rebellion. The Boxer Rebellion was an anticolonialism, anti-Christian uprising that broke out across China between 1899 and 1901. Lao despised the Taoist/Buddhist secret societies that drove those rebellions. One such prominent secret society at the time was the White Lotus (白蓮教, Báilián jiào),[103] which syncretized Pure Land Mahayana Buddhism with Taoist ritual magic. The White Lotus organized many of the rebellions against the Ming and later the Qing dynasty.[104] Lao Naixuan welcomed colonial rule and Christian influence, unlike the Boxer rebels who were insurrectionists trying to rid their homeland of the foreigners. Lao's relationship with Wilhelm and his interpretation of the I Ching would have been informed by that perspective.

In sum, the contributions of European missionaries to Yì Xué paved the way for its entrance into the world of psychology.

## Carl Jung and the Theory of Synchronicity

"It is a curious fact that such a gifted and intelligent people as the Chinese has never developed what we call science,"[105] writes Carl G. Jung in his foreword for his friend Richard Wilhelm's translations of the I Ching. However, Jung does go on to clarify that Western science has always been "based upon the principle of causality,"[106] which he challenges with his theory of synchronicity, and which Eastern philosophy supports. Thus, he predicts that "a great change in our standpoint is setting in,"[107] and he seeks inspiration from both the I Ching and Taoist alchemy[108] to support his developing theories.

In the I Ching, Jung believes he has found testamentary evidence for synchronicity, a phenomenon of nonlogical and nonscientific events yielding meaning and value in human life.[109] Synchronicity postulates acausal connections between what happens in a divinatory experience with the Book of Changes and what happens in the physical world.[110]

Jung then overturns his earlier point and describes the Book of Changes as comparable to that of modern physics.[111] In his studies and work with the I Ching, he comes to value it as instrumental for advancing the sciences of the mind, such as psychology.[112]

When Jung observes that the Chinese "never developed what we call science," he is referring to the I Ching's challenge to the scientific method. "While the Western mind carefully sifts, weighs, selects, classifies, isolates," he writes, "the Chinese picture of the moment encompasses everything down to the minutest nonsensical detail, because all of the ingredients make up the observed moment."[113]

The act of sifting, weighing, selecting, classifying, and isolating is done through the conscious mind, whereas the "picture of the moment" that an I Ching reading encompasses, including that most "minutest nonsensical detail," is a work product of the unconscious part of the mind. "If the I Ching is not accepted by the conscious, at least the unconscious meets it halfway, and the I Ching is more closely connected with the unconscious than with the rational attitude of consciousness."[114] For Jung, the divine and the unconscious mind were inextricable from each other,[115] a concept he found present in the Oracle.[116]

By the twentieth century, I Ching discourse is presenting questions about what relation, if any, the Oracle has to psychology. Depth psychology, inspired by Jung's work, is psychological and psychoanalytic therapy that explores the unconscious aspects of the human experience.[117] Techniques in that modality of therapy include dream interpretation, free association, and methods in archetypal psychology.

Reflecting on an I Ching reading is similar to dream interpretation, whereby the content of the Oracle's message can reveal latent issues. What the reading means to you can be profoundly revelatory of what's going on in your subconscious mind. Since an I Ching reading is cast by a randomized process and the divinatory result itself is a combination of symbolic lines and metaphors, the effort to interpret the meaning is essentially a form of free association. Moreover, the foundational structure of the I Ching as eight trigrams that build upon each other to form a fixed set of hexagram arrangements is in line with Jung's archetypal theory. Jung himself acknowledges the Book of Changes as one of the most significant contributions to his study of archetypal theory and the unconscious.[118]

In turn, he has contributed to the evolution of Yì Xué. In summary, here is Jung's explanation for the Oracle's efficacy: The casting of yarrow stalks or coins is representative of the inquirer's present space and moment in time. The I Ching is then likened to a clock or calendar: the way the ticking hands on a clock represent the present moment in time, or the divisions on a calendar mark the passage of that time, the Oracle contains an algorithmic wisdom that is able to forecast what is to come.[119]

"My argument as outlined above has of course never entered a Chinese mind,"[120] he points out. Yet take, for instance, the writings of third-century philosopher Wang Bi, who addresses the question of how divination works, or the apocryphal texts from the Western Han. In the subsequent chapter, we'll cover Shao Yong (AD 1011–1077), who devoted a great deal of written commentary to philosophizing on how and why divination works, arriving at a conclusion similar to what Jung writes about nine hundred years later: human experiences can be reduced to mathematical ratios and archetypes (the sixty-four hexagrams of the I Ching). Shao reached similar conclusions to Jung about God and the collective unconscious, though Shao used the terms "the Tao" and "accessing the Tao from our heart-minds."

Nevertheless, Jung wasn't wrong. In the nineteenth century, the accepted explanation for the "Chinese mind" on how divination works was *qi*. Hexagrams emanate with *qi*, and the sixty-four I Ching hexagrams represent every channel of *qi* in the universe, based on mathematics that represent the creation process of the universe. The Oracle provides a diagnosis of what *qi* is affecting the situation at hand. Where Western scholars were skeptical, questioning how and why divination works and thus devoting more time writing about it, Chinese scholars took it as an easy given and thus focused their writings on interpretation.

*Qi* is an intangible force or energy that emits an electromagnetic frequency wave. Every object has *qi*, though different characteristics will emit different frequencies of *qi*. The hexagrams are archetypes of *qi,* and divination reveals the core archetype of *qi* at play in a situation. Arguably, the *qi* theory found in that I Ching commentary from 200 BC sounds like Jung's archetypal theory.

Beyond that, admittedly, scholars in the East did not focus their scholarship on answering the questions of *how* or *why* I Ching divination works, because among East Asians, those issues weren't points of contention. Jung is correct in that Eastern philosophy often took the functioning of the I Ching as a given, and not as a point of controversy. The point of controversy for Eastern philosophers was that of interpretation.

Thus, Jung advances global Yì Xué by focusing on the *how* and the *why,* while Eastern I Ching philosophers continued to focus on the *what.* Jung maintains that study of the I Ching is consistent with psychological objectives and therefore is science, not superstition. The Oracle insists upon self-knowledge, and Jung assures the reader that nothing "occult" is inferred from how the I Ching operates.[121]

## The I Ching in Western Occultism

Ironically, despite Jung's assurance that there is nothing "occult" about the I Ching, the connecting link between the Book of Changes and the postwar Western occultism that describes the I Ching as a sentient spirit—is Jung.

By way of Wilhelm, and the missionary's friendship with Jung, whose writings often referenced a coming "new aeon" (with Jung thus being credited as the father of the term "New Age"),[122] Jung introduces the three-thousand-year-old Oracle into the Age of Aquarius counterculture. Jung's thought explorations on synchronicity and the unconscious gain traction with that particular crowd, and through Jung, the Beat Generation finds Wilhelm.

It's true that long before Jung, translations of the I Ching had already been circulating across Europe, and the text found itself in the hands of interested ceremonial magicians. By the mid- to late 1800s, the "Yi King" or "Yih-king," as it was often spelled at the time, had already been absorbed into spiritualist movements such as Theosophy and Western ceremonial magic.[123] In *Dogme et rituel de la haute magie*—a book originally published as two separate volumes, *Dogme* in 1854 and *Rituel* in 1856—author Eliphas Levi makes several references to "the trigrams of Fohi" (Fuxi)[124] and draws equivalences between Taoist metaphysics and Western occultism.

Rosicrucian occultist Reuben Swinburne Clymer (1878–1966) describes the power that the uneven number of three imparts to magic, especially the trilogy of unity as expressed by "the trigrams of Fohi"[125] (the trigrams of Fuxi, or the Ba Gua). Moreover, Western occultists such as Clymer proposed that the trigrams Heaven and Earth combined are an equivalent to the hexagram that is the Seal of Solomon.[126]

The most controversial Western occult figure at the turn of the twentieth century, Aleister Crowley, devoted a substantial portion of his magical work to the I Ching. While Crowley relied on Legge's English translations of the Book, he derided Legge's work by calling it "pitiable pedantic imbecility."[127] Crowley constantly referred to Legge as an "ass," and on the title page of his personal copy of Legge's translations, he rewrote Legge's byline as "Wood'n Legge," mocking Legge's stiff writing style.[128]

Crowley regularly consulted the I Ching and wrote about his readings.[129] According to his journal entries, he consulted the Oracle frequently, and relied upon the divinations to make major decisions. In describing the I Ching, Crowley writes that it is "in some ways the most perfect hieroglyph ever constructed. It is austere and sublime, yet withal so adaptable to every possible emergency that its figures may be interpreted to suit all classes of questions. One may resolve the most obscure spiritual difficulties no less than the most mundane dilemmas…. The Master Therion [Crowley refers to himself in the third person as Master Therion] has found the Yi King entirely satisfactory in every respect."[130]

Like Wilhelm and Jung, Crowley asks the questions *how* and *why*. Whereas Jung concludes that the efficacy of an I Ching divination comes from operations of the unconscious and acausal synchronicity, Crowley concludes that divinatory systems are animated by spirit intelligences. It is the spirit intelligence that gives information to the diviner through these divination systems.

In Crowley's *Magick in Theory and Practice* (1929), he asserts that the spirit intelligences that the diviner interacts with in geomancy are gnomes.[131] In tarot divination, the spirit intelligence operating the system is Mercury (Hermes).[132] These spirit intelligences have the tendency to be erratic and cannot always be trusted; they often have ulterior motives.

But the "Yi King is served by beings free from these defects. The intense purity of the symbols prevent them from being usurped by intelligences with an axe of their own to grind,"[133] suggesting that gnomes and the god Hermes are far more temperamental than whatever spirits seem to be animating the Book of Changes.[134]

Crowley, writing as the Master Therion, undertakes his own translations of the I Ching in his work titled *Liber 216*. He opens his text with this introductory statement: "The Yi King is mathematical and philosophical in form. Its structure is cognate with that of the Qabalah."[135] Crowley's version reinterprets the lines of the Zhouyi in rhyming poems. Table 3.6 provides a comparison between the late Professor Kerson Huang's more literal translation of Hexagram 7 and Crowley's poetic verse.

Crowley's contribution to Yì Xué is the correspondence work he does between the I Ching trigrams and the Qabalistic Tree of Life.[136] Figure 3.8 is a redrawing of a Tree of Life diagram from Crowley's *The Equinox* originally titled "The Chinese Cosmos." The diagram sets forth his correspondences between the trigrams of the Ba Gua, I Ching cosmology, the *sefirot* of Jewish mysticism, and the four alchemical elements (Fire, Water, Air, and Earth).

**TABLE 3.6** Huang's and Crowley's Translations of Hexagram 7

| HEXAGRAM 7 | | | |
|---|---|---|---|
| Kerson Huang's *I Ching: The Oracle* | | Aleister Crowley's *Liber 216* | |
| Earth *over* Water | | Yoni *of* Moon | |
| THE ARMY. Auspicious for the great personage. No troubles. | | SZE: Armies; all depends upon the sage, His ripe experience, and his wisdom's age. | |
| -- 1 | A marching army must have discipline. Otherwise disaster will befall, Even if it had strength. | -- 1 | Mark well the rules of martial strategy. |
| -- 2 | Flourishing in the ranks. Safe and sound. The King thrice bestows titles. | -- 2 | Chief of the host, thy king confers the post. |
| -- 3 | The army might be carrying corpses. Misfortune. | -- 3 | Divided counsel—inefficiency! |
| -- 4 | The army camps on the left. Safe and sound. | -- 4 | Retreat is not an error if need be. |

**TABLE 3.6** Huang's and Crowley's Translations of Hexagram 7 *(continued)*

| HEXAGRAM 7 ||
|---|---|
| Kerson Huang's *I Ching: The Oracle* | Aleister Crowley's *Liber 216* |
| Earth *over* Water | Yoni *of* Moon |
| THE ARMY. Auspicious for the great personage. No troubles. | SZE: Armies; all depends upon the sage, His ripe experience, and his wisdom's age. |

| | | | |
|---|---|---|---|
| -- 5 | Bagging games in a hunt. Favorable omen for catching an escapee. No troubles. The elder son commands the army. The younger brother hauls corpses. Omen of misfortune. | -- 5 | Seek and destroy bad faith and mutiny! |
| -- 6 | The king bestows titles. To found a state, head a clan, Use not common people. | -- 6 | But find good men for posts of dignity. |

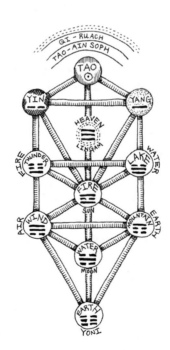

**FIGURE 3.8** Aleister Crowley's Chinese cosmos and the Tree of Life[137]

Crowley renames the trigrams. Heaven (Qian) becomes Lingam, Earth (Kun) is Yoni, Fire (Li) is the Sun, Water (Kan) is the Moon, and the remaining four trigrams correspond with the four Western Aristotelian elements. Thus, Hexagram 1, which is traditionally read as Heaven over Heaven, becomes Lingam of Lingam under Crowley's approach. Hexagram 3, which would traditionally be described as Water over Thunder, is now Moon of Fire. Hexagram 41, comprising the trigrams Mountain over Lake, is now Earth of Water.

The renaming of the trigrams is a form of computation to a common denominator between the I Ching and the Qabalah.[138] Now the renamed trigrams under Crowley's system correspond directly with the Western elemental correspondences to the Qabalistic Four Worlds and the Tetragrammaton.

**TABLE 3.7** The Qabalistic Four Worlds and the Trigrams

| Kabbalistic World | Assiah | Yetzirah | Briah | Atziluh |
|---|---|---|---|---|
| Divine name (Tetragrammaton) | He ה | Vau ו | He ה | Yod י |
| Element | Earth | Air | Water | Fire |
| Tarot suit | Pentacles/disks | Swords | Cups | Wands |
| Trigram | | | | |
| Traditional name | Mountain | Wind | Lake | Thunder |
| Crowley's name | Earth | Air | Water | Fire |

Under the system of metaphysical correspondences established by the Hermetic Order of the Golden Dawn—an occult order of which Crowley was a member, before he left to found his own occult movement, called Thelema—the Qabalistic World Atziluth corresponds with the suit of Wands, which then corresponds with the element (and now trigram) Fire. Using the Queen of Wands for demonstration, the suit corresponds with Fire, and the Queen corresponds with the first He in the Tetragrammaton, which corresponds with the element Water. Thus, the Queen of Wands would be the Water part of Fire. Crowley reconfigures the trigram Lake (Dui) to Water and the trigram Thunder (Zhen) to Fire. Thus, the Water of Fire that is the Queen of Wands through its Qabalistic associations is the trigram combination of Water (Lake) over Fire (Thunder). Lake over Thunder (which Crowley would call Water of Fire) is Hexagram 17. Under his system, the Queen of Wands in tarot corresponds with Hexagram 17 in the I Ching.

There are also five additional cards among the pips assigned hexagrams, which are the five cards ruled by the decanate the Sun. When the decan ruler is the Sun, a hexagram is assigned. Table 3.8 sets forth Crowley's tarot to hexagram correspondences, a total of twenty-one of the sixty-four hexagrams.

TABLE 3.8 Crowley's Tarot and Yi King Correspondences[139]

| CROWLEY-HARRIS THOTH TAROT | I CHING HEXAGRAM # | CROWLEY-HARRIS THOTH TAROT | I CHING HEXAGRAM # |
|---|---|---|---|
| Knight of Wands (Fire of Fire) | Hexagram 51 | Prince of Wands (Air of Fire) | Hexagram 42 |
| Queen of Wands (Water of Fire) | Hexagram 17 | Princess of Wands (Earth of Fire) | Hexagram 27 |
| Knight of Cups (Fire of Water) | Hexagram 54 | Prince of Cups (Air of Water) | Hexagram 61 |
| Queen of Cups (Water of Water) | Hexagram 58 | Princess of Cups (Earth of Water) | Hexagram 41 |
| Knight of Swords (Fire of Air) | Hexagram 32 | Prince of Swords (Air of Air) | Hexagram 57 |
| Queen of Swords (Water of Air) | Hexagram 28 | Princess of Swords (Earth of Air) | Hexagram 18 |
| Knight of Disks (Fire of Earth) | Hexagram 62 | Prince of Disks (Air of Earth) | Hexagram 53 |
| Queen of Disks (Water of Earth) | Hexagram 31 | Princess of Disks (Earth of Earth) | Hexagram 52 |
| Three of Wands (Sol in Aries) | Hexagram 11 | Six of Cups (Sol in Scorpio) | Hexagram 20 |
| Ten of Swords (Sol in Gemini) | Hexagram 43 | Four of Disks (Sol in Capricornus) | Hexagram 2 |
| Eight of Disks (Sol in Virgo) | Hexagram 33 | | |

Although I don't work with Crowley's approach, historically he establishes a groundbreaking precedent in the Western occult world for how the I Ching is interpreted. Thus, it's worth the reader's time to understand his approach.

His Thelemic writings have also addressed the concept of the *junzi* (君子, *jūnzǐ*) found throughout the I Ching. Crowley's *Liber LVIII, The Qabalah* or *The Temple of Solomon the King*,[140] explores comparative study of the *junzi* principle (where *junzi* is translated as "the Great Person") and likens it to concepts found in other esoteric traditions, such as:

- The Higher Self, Silent Watcher, or Great Master (Theosophy)
- The Genius (Hermetic Order of the Golden Dawn)
- Logos (Gnosticism)
- Jechidah (Kabbalah/Qabalah)
- Holy Guardian Angel (Abramelin)

I Ching divination enjoyed a resurgence of popularity in the West through the counterculture movement of the 1960s, largely made possible by the Wilhelm-Baynes translation of the Oracle, with Carl Jung's foreword.[141] Postwar counterculture youths who were fatigued by the standard Abrahamic fare of spirituality took interest in an obscure text from three millennia ago, suddenly making it an international bestseller.[142] Although this "I Ching used by theosophists"[143] gets swept up in the New Age movement, on a coextending path, it captivates the attention of mathematicians and scientists.

## Science, Math, and the Genetic Code

The driving theme in the creation myth narrating the origins of the I Ching hexagrams is the process of division to unite what had been chaos. The division-to-unite process produces an intelligently designed order. In every beginning, the Tao is chaos, and it is through a subdivision process of that Tao that the Tao becomes an intelligent design of order and structure. That design of order and structure becomes the creation of all things. A similar theme is found in chaos theory, which could explain the epigenetic processes for human behavioral development.[144]

The last century witnessed an increasing interest in the intersection of the I Ching and science, but first, let's return to the eighteenth century. The French Jesuit priest Joachim Bouvet, who had initially been tasked by the emperor of

China to translate the Book of Changes, writes a letter about the I Ching to Gottfried Wilhelm von Leibniz (1646–1716),[145] describing it as "the oldest work of China and perhaps the world."[146] Setting him apart from his contemporaries, and earning him hostile criticism, was Bouvet's contention that the I Ching is a source of science and philosophy "perhaps superior to that of contemporary Europe."[147] At the time, Leibniz is working on binary calculus using zeroes and ones, and Bouvet is convinced that Lebiniz's numerical calculus will benefit his religious cause.[148]

Bouvet and Leibniz are convinced that there is a metaphysical foundation to calculus and that the I Ching might offer insight into that foundation. Leibniz becomes convinced that the trigrams follow an arithmetical progression and are an operation of Boolean algebra.[149] Likewise, Bouvet is insistent that there is a Pythagorean wisdom to the I Ching, where the diagrams represent the perfected state of science, math, music, astronomy, medicine, and physics, and he likens Fuxi to Hermes Trismegistus.[150] Meanwhile, during the Edo period of Japan, scientists with an interest in Confucian metaphysics, such as Shizuki Tadao (1760–1806) were studying the intersection of I Ching cosmology and Newtonian physics.[151]

While the Western occult world credits Aleister Crowley for connecting the I Ching and Qabalah, the first to do so was probably Bouvet in the 1700s. Bouvet writes to Leibniz describing his belief that the Jewish Kabbalah and the I Ching share the double geometrical system Leibniz is working on, and therefore calculus might connect the two mystical traditions to prove a universal truth.[152] Furthermore, Bouvet relates the eight trigrams to Aristotelian elements.[153]

**TABLE 3.9** Leibniz's Binary Calculus and the Ba Gua

| Yin–0 | | | | Yang–1 | | | |
|---|---|---|---|---|---|---|---|
| 00 | | 01 | | 10 | | 11 | |
| Earth | Mountain | Water | Wind | Thunder | Fire | Lake | Heaven |
| 000 | 100 | 010 | 110 | 001 | 101 | 011 | 111 |
| 0 | 1 | 10 | 11 | 100 | 101 | 110 | 111 |

SOURCE: *"Explication de l'arithmétique binaire"* (1703)

Then, in Leibniz's 1703 "Explication de l'arithmétique binaire" published in *Mémoires de l'Académie des sciences,* he presents dyadic or binary mathematics as double geometrical progression following the progression of trigrams in exactly the manner Bouvet had described them in his letters to Leibniz.[154]

The correspondence between the binary code of computer processor instructions (bit strings of zeroes and ones) and the base components of DNA has led to comparisons between the two. Both a computer hard drive and the DNA complex serve dual purposes of (1) being a centralized information storage system and (2) being a processing system, with functional equivalents.[155] DNA—deoxyribonucleic acid, the molecule that carries genetic information for life—is like the software program that runs the body's hardware. That functional comparison provides a new framework for considering DNA as a dynamic—a changing—system of biological information.

A DNA molecule carries genetic information necessary for the development and function of organisms. It comprises two linked strands that wind around each other, resembling a twisted ladder called a double helix. These strands are categorized into four bases: adenine (A), cytosine (C), guanine (G), and thymine (T).[156]

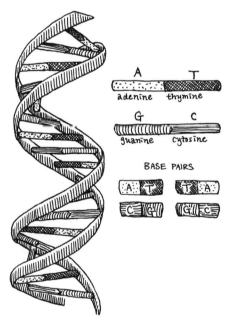

**FIGURE 3.9** Diagram of a DNA molecule

Adenine (A) bonds with thymine (T), and cytosine (C) bonds with guanine (G).[157] The sequence of the paired bases is the code for biological information, such as the instructions for making an RNA molecule. Ribonucleic acid (RNA) is the single-stranded nucleic acid present in all living cells, similar to DNA. The four bases of RNA molecules are similar to DNA—adenine (A), cytosine (C), and guanine (G), but instead of thymine, in RNA it's uracil (U).[158] RNA is the actual functional form of nucleic acids that the body uses—they are the messengers and builders.

**TABLE 3.10** The Four Bases of DNA

| A (adenine) | T (thymine) | C (cystosine) | G (guanine) |
|---|---|---|---|
|  |  |  |  |

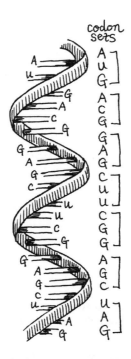

**FIGURE 3.10** Diagram of an RNA molecule

78    I Ching, the Oracle

Three of the four bases then group together to form triplet codon sets for protein synthesis, not unlike how combination pairs of the binary yin and yang group together to form the eight trigrams that are the foundational building blocks of the I Ching hexagrams. In short, nature communicates through a binary code, as does the virtual world, as does the living soul of the I Ching. Here, DNA molecules and the I Ching begin to look strikingly similar in structure. The four bases of DNA correlate with the four combination expressions of yin and yang.

In 1991, polymer scientist Dr. Johnson F. Yan publishes groundbreaking literature on the intersection of interpreting the I Ching and interpreting DNA and protein sequences. He proposes that adenine and thymine (or uracil in RNA) correspond with "elder yin" and "younger yin" respectively, while cytosine and guanine correspond with "younger yang" and "elder yang."[159] When either yin or yang forms a pairing with itself, creating two yin lines or two yang lines, the resulting pairs are described as *elder*. When yin pairs with yang as permutations of opposites, the pairs are described as *younger*. The principles of elder and younger yin and yang will be discussed in more detail in chapter 5.

Then in 1998, scientific writer Yang Li examines the intersection of the I Ching and genetics and proposes a different set of correspondences for the four bases.[160] The two approaches are provided side by side for comparison in table 3.11.

I'm not a scientist, so my lay opinion doesn't mean much here, but intuitively Dr. Johnson F. Yan's correspondences appear to make more sense to me; or at least there is more congruity in which molecules are assigned to the elders and which molecules are assigned to the youngers.

**TABLE 3.11** Yin and Yang in the Four Nucleotides of DNA

| JOHNSON F. YAN (1991) | | | |
|---|---|---|---|
| A (adenine) | T (thymine) | C (cystosine) | G (guanine) |
| 太陰 Elder Yin | 少陰 Younger Yin | 少陽 Younger Yang | 太陽 Elder Yang |

**TABLE 3.11** Yin and Yang in the Four Nucleotides of DNA *(continued)*

| YANG LI (1998) | | | |
|---|---|---|---|
| **A (adenine)** | **T (thymine)** | **C (cystosine)** | **G (guanine)** |
| 少陰<br>Younger Yin | 少陽<br>Younger Yang | 太陽<br>Elder Yang | 太陰<br>Elder Yin |

The binary and quaternary code that the DNA molecule is based on generates a system of sixty-four triplet combinations.[161] Likewise, the I Ching diagrams are based on a binary (yin and yang) and quarternary code (the elder and younger yin and yang combinations) that generates a system of sixty-four hexagrams.

Hexagrams are but triplet paired combinations of yin and yang lines. Both DNA codons and I Ching hexagrams are groupings of six—hexagrams are groupings of six lines, while DNA codons are groupings of six amino acids.

The mathematical process for both DNA and the I Ching operates from four to eight to sixteen to sixty-four, as expressed in figure 3.11, a mandala diagram of the genetic code, and figure 3.13, a mandala diagram of the equivalent mathematical process in the I Ching. Just as DNA processes are at their essence processes of change, the I Ching at its essence is about processes of change.

Figure 3.12 is derived from Dr. Marshall Nirenberg's 1954 handwritten laboratory notes on the sixty-four triplet combinations of codons.[162] In 1968 Nirenberg won the Nobel Prize in Physiology and Medicine for his work in DNA codes and the sixty-four nucleotide codons, or the specific segments of DNA that code for amino acids. Combinations of the four bases—As, Cs, Gs, and Us (or Ts)—can encode all twenty amino acids in RNA in triplet codes, forming a total of sixty-four triplet combinations that can be mapped out on an eight-by-eight square.[163] This eight-by-eight square of combinations corresponds rather succinctly with the eight-by-eight square of sixty-four hexagrams pictured in figure 3.14.

80  I Ching, the Oracle

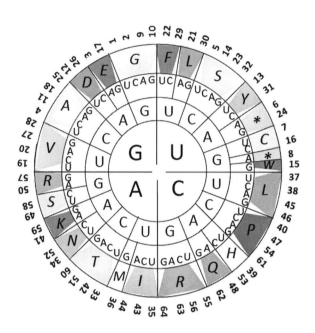

**FIGURE 3.11** Classic circular genetic code mandala. From Fernando Castro-Chavez's "A Tetrahedral Representation of the Genetic Code Emphasizing Aspects of Symmetry" (2012).[164]

| 1<br>GGU<br>G | 2<br>GGC<br>G | 3<br>GAA<br>E | 4<br>GCU<br>A | 5<br>UCU<br>S | 6<br>UAA<br>* | 7<br>UGU<br>C | 8<br>UGA<br>* |
|---|---|---|---|---|---|---|---|
| 9<br>GGA<br>G | 10<br>GGG<br>G | 11<br>GCC<br>A | 12<br>GAU<br>D | 13<br>UAU<br>Y | 14<br>UCC<br>S | 15<br>UGG<br>W | 16<br>UGC<br>C |
| 17<br>GAG<br>E | 18<br>GCA<br>A | 19<br>GUU<br>V | 20<br>GUC<br>V | 21<br>UUA<br>L | 22<br>UUU<br>F | 23<br>UCA<br>S | 24<br>UAG<br>* |
| 25<br>GCG<br>A | 26<br>GAC<br>D | 27<br>GUA<br>V | 28<br>GUG<br>V | 29<br>UUC<br>F | 30<br>UUG<br>L | 31<br>UAC<br>Y | 32<br>UCG<br>S |
| 33<br>ACU<br>T | 34<br>AAU<br>N | 35<br>AUU<br>I | 36<br>AUG<br>M | 37<br>CUU<br>L | 38<br>CUC<br>L | 39<br>CAU<br>H | 40<br>CCU<br>P |
| 41<br>AAA<br>K | 42<br>ACC<br>T | 43<br>AUC<br>I | 44<br>AUA<br>I | 45<br>CUA<br>L | 46<br>CUG<br>L | 47<br>CCC<br>P | 48<br>CAA<br>Q |
| 49<br>AGU<br>S | 50<br>AGA<br>R | 51<br>ACA<br>T | 52<br>AAC<br>N | 53<br>CAC<br>H | 54<br>CCA<br>P | 55<br>CGU<br>R | 56<br>CGC<br>R |
| 57<br>AGG<br>R | 58<br>AGC<br>S | 59<br>AAG<br>K | 60<br>ACG<br>T | 61<br>CCG<br>P | 62<br>CAG<br>Q | 63<br>CGA<br>R | 64<br>CGG<br>R |

**FIGURE 3.12** Square representation of the genetic code. From Fernando Castro-Chavez's "A Tetrahedral Representation of the Genetic Code Emphasizing Aspects of Symmetry" (2012).[165]

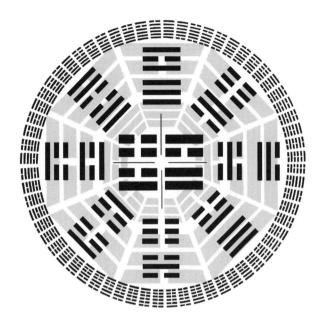

**FIGURE 3.13** Circular I Ching mandala

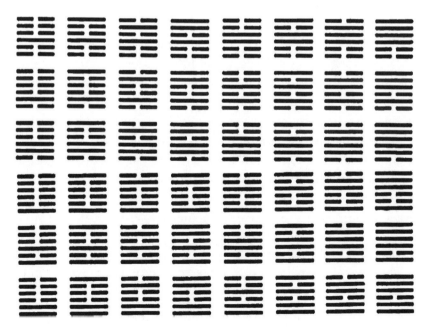

**FIGURE 3.14** Square representation of the I Ching

A gene map is essentially permutations of G, T, A, and C. Our DNA molecules make us who we are, and the more understanding of DNA that science can advance, the more we'll come to know ourselves. When we understand how the four bases—these pairs of A with T(U) and C with G—combine and interact, we'll arrive at deeper understanding of the diseases that plague the body.

Perhaps likewise, the sequence of codes produced by the hexagrams of the I Ching make this universe what it is, and make us who we are; therefore, the more we understand the Oracle as a science of the mind, the more we'll come to know ourselves. Dr. Yan muses that perhaps divination is "the main connection of the *I Ching* to combinatorial and probabilistic mathematics."[166]

## Taoist Mysticism and Magic

It would be remiss to not consider the night market fortune-teller's I Ching. This is the I Ching where trigrams and hexagrams are drawn on paper talismans sold from a makeshift shrine one block from the red-light district. Smoke fills the nostrils, whether from cigarettes or incense. Whatever contempt the literati want to show for mysticism, magic, and sorcery with the Book of Changes, there is no denying the longstanding subculture of using the I Ching to communicate with and petition spiritual beings.[167] These fortune-tellers, psychic-mediums, and shamanic witch doctors can be found in alleyways across the South Pacific.

There is precedent within the original Zhouyi for interpreting the text as instructions for ritual, rites, and incantations. The sixth yin line of Hexagram 54 makes reference to the ritual bloodletting of a sacrificial sheep for determining whether the gods will endow the blessing of a good harvest. If the sheep bleeds, the gods are pleased. If the sheep does not bleed, then the gods are displeased, and misfortune will befall. The fifth yang line of Hexagram 10 affirms a fork in the path: one is an ascent to the throne, and the other is a divergence to discovering new territory. Either path will prove risky. Thus, the line advises conducting rites to summon protection magic. The sixth yang line of Hexagram 53 refers to goose feathers used in rites and rituals.

Hexagram 18 is titled "蠱," the same "蠱" used for a tradition of Taoist baneful magic called Poison Magic (蠱道, Gǔ Dào). That's "蠱" (Gǔ) for "poison" and "道" (Dào) for "path" or "way"—the same character in the word for Taoism. Seen in English as Ku, Gu, or Gu Shu (蠱術), the full name of the tradition is typically written out as 蠱道巫術 (Gǔ Dào Wūshù).

The historical and etymological origin of the word "蠱" is a vessel filled with poisonous insects or reptiles. Confined and without food, the animals will eat each other, the strong eating the weak, until only the strongest of them all survives, having in effect eaten every other insect in the vessel. The poison extracted from that lone survivor is said to not only be the strongest poison possible, but is also used in malevolent sorcery. While contemporary forms of Poison Magic are not quite as dramatic, the focus is still on poisons, be that from plants or animals, use of noxious fumes and insects that grow on rotted food, vermin, curses, and petitions to demons or hungry ghosts.

Hexagram 51, consisting of the trigrams Thunder over Thunder, corresponds with the Taoist tradition of Thunder Magic (雷法, Léi Fǎ). The modality of Taoist sorcery is also translated to Thunder Rites. Thunder magic consists of invocations or evocations of a thunder god, often expressed as Lei Gong, and harnessing the potent force or *qi* of thunder and lightning. It was popularized during the Song dynasty (AD 960–1279) and is considered an advanced modality of esoteric cultivation. Methodologies are premised on the belief that thunder is the divine command of Heaven, and a practitioner can harvest the power of thunder to absorb powers from Heaven and use those powers to both exorcise demons and heal sickness. A practice of Thunder Rites commonly consists of routine meditations to cultivate thunder and lighting *qi*, aligning with a thunder deity, giving daily offerings, and developing a working relationship with that thunder deity, which entails rites and rituals that involve mudras, pacing the Lo Shu magic square, and mastering exorcisms.[168] Magical spells within Thunder Rites are often used to combat Poison Magic. You can probably assume that a practitioner of Thunder Rites is also a Taoist exorcist.

Fu talismans commonly include sigils of the trigrams, the hexagrams, or glyphs inspired by the hexagram names. To tap into the *qi* in this universe to gain prosperity, win great victories, and rise to leadership, use the coding of Hexagram 14. The Fu pictured to the right in figure 3.15 is a talisman for career success utilizing Hexagram 14. To the left is a talisman featuring Hexagram 42 to increase wealth and prosperity, and to channel universal *qi* that will move you toward increase and material gains. Use the coding of Hexagram 22 for love, beauty, and attraction spells.

If the 圖 *(tú)* or diagram of the hexagram is the code for its corresponding universal *qi* energy, then drawing it while setting intentions through each line is a form of mystical programming. The belief that writing influences physical reality is deeply embedded in the consciousness of Taoist mystics. By ritually drawing a hexagram, you're programming the *qi* around you with that hexagram code and your intentions—your thoughts.

**FIGURE 3.15** Fu talismans

The eight double hexagrams pictured in table 3.12 are referred to as the Eight Spirit Helpers, per the Eighth Wing of the Ten Wings. These Eight Spirit Helper hexagrams are the most powerful for harnessing the fundamental building blocks of Fuxi's Ba Gua as coded into the sixty-four hexagrams. Shamans, spirit mediums, and Taoist priests build their magical practices around the Eight Spirit Helpers. The table provides a brief description of the *qi* associated with the eight hexagrams. In the following instructions for a simple magical spell, choose one of the hexagrams as the base code for programming your specific spell-crafting intentions.

**TABLE 3.12** The Eight Spirit Helpers

| Heaven \| Heaven | Lake \| Lake | Fire \| Fire | Thunder \| Thunder |
|---|---|---|---|
| **1 Qián** | **58 Dui** | **30 Li** | **51 Zhen** |
| Summons the initiatory directive power of Heaven; makes contact with yang celestial beings | Inner peace, happiness, and contentment; success in business deals; career or social advancement | Casting out a fishing line to hook an objective and reel it in toward you; to tether to an object | To absorb the powers of thunder *qi* and amplify the magus's personal power |
| Wind \| Wind | Water \| Water | Mountain \| Mountain | Earth \| Earth |
| **57 Sun** | **29 Kan** | **52 Gen** | **2 Kun** |
| Steady flow of profit and gains channeled toward you; financial security; prosperity | Successful and effective shamanic journeying through the underworld or spirit realms | To help facilitate insights, psychic visions, or spiritual awakening; improves meditation | Fertility spells; amplifies mediumship; facilitates ghost and yin spirit communications |

To use one of the hexagrams from table 3.12 to program a specific result into your life, begin by choosing one of the eight that is a base code most supportive of your intention. Thoroughly clean the table you will be working on. It should be free of debris and well sanitized. Taking inspiration from Zhu Xi's divination ritual instructions, arrange the table so you will have to walk toward it from the south, and when channeling the hexagram *qi*, you will be facing north.

To draw the hexagram, use an inkstone and traditional calligraphy brush. Have all materials prepared ahead of time—shallow water dish, inkstone, brush, brush stand, a lacquered board to place the paper on, and your paper. Traditionally, you'd have a stone seal stamp with your signature seal carved into it, and that would be stamped onto any talisman you craft to conclude the ritual.

Light incense and place the materials to the east of the incense holder. Approach the table from the south, and as you sit, face north. Draw the lines of the hexagram bottom up, so the first line you draw will be the bottommost line, then the second one from the bottom, then third, until the final one you draw is the topmost line.

The odd line positions of all hexagrams are assigned yang. Thus, the first line, third line, and fifth line are yang. Even line positions are assigned yin. That's the second, fourth, and sixth lines. As you draw an odd position line, assert hardness and feel yourself thrusting out your *qi* energy to meet the *qi* of the universe around you. As you draw an even position line, be soft and receptive, and feel yourself receiving empowering, beneficent, and stronger *qi* from the universe. In response to each of the six prompts in table 3.13, think the response or state it aloud.

**TABLE 3.13** Order of Incantations in a Hexagram Spell

| 6 | ▬▬ ▬▬ | Express gratitude to the Divine for changing the path of *qi*. |
|---|---|---|
| 5 | ▬▬▬▬▬ | Declare affirmatively that the problem will be resolved. |
| 4 | ▬▬ ▬▬ | State a secondary concern related to the problem at hand. |
| 3 | ▬▬▬▬▬ | Declare affirmatively the outcome you desire. |
| 2 | ▬▬ ▬▬ | State with specificity the problem you would like to solve. |
| 1 | ▬▬▬▬▬ | Recite an invocation prayer to call upon the Divine. |

Traditionally, a Taoist practitioner will then stamp the hexagram with their personal seal while reciting *"Jí jí rú lǜ lìng"* (急急如律令), an incantation equivalent to "So mote it be" or "Amen."

# The Way of the Sages

Confucius described the I Ching as one of the most important texts for sages and scholars, both for moral cultivation and for achieving a deeper understanding of cosmology. In Sima Qian's Shiji (史記, Shǐjì) annals, or "Records of the Grand Historian" dated to the Western Han (109–91 BC),[169] the Confucian approach to the I Ching, described as the Way of the Sages, consists of four levels of study:

1. The first level of study is to read the text and honor it as a literary work.

2. The second level of study is to reconcile our conduct and actions with the counsel that the divinatory text gives. How do you interpret the Oracle to improve yourself and cultivate personal wisdom? How do you improve the conditions of your life?

3. Third, after the scholar's diligent study of the text and authoritative commentaries, the scholar will attain knowledge of the I Ching's exoteric values. How do you interpret the Oracle to give counsel to the state and to your community? How do you improve the conditions of your society?

4. Finally, the fourth level, which is achieved after one has become the sage—the *junzi*—is to attain knowledge of the I Ching's esoteric values. This is spiritual transcendence.

The Way of the Sages becomes a core paradigm for the scholar-diviner to strive for.

Yì Xué will deepen your understanding and solidify the foundations of any study you pursue in Eastern metaphysics. The sixty-four hexagrams represent a rule book for how *qi* flows in nature, which is essential in astrology and feng shui. It gives context to the theoretics you learn in martial arts and qigong.

A common aphorism among practitioners of traditional Chinese Medicine is, "Medicine cannot be approached without studying the Book of Changes."[170] The basic theories of internal medicine and inner alchemy are the same undercurrent theories of the I Ching.[171] The *Yellow Emperor's Classic of Internal Medicine* 黃帝內經 *(Huángdì nèi jīng)* from the early Han (202 BC–AD 9)[172] is one of the most important treatises on premodern internal medicine as rooted in Taoist cosmology, and the text is based on the I Ching.[173]

Assuming that you've been reading these chapters in order from the first page, your undertaking of Yì Xué has begun. Now we'll conduct a first reading exercise; with the intention of introducing ourselves to the Book of Changes; not so much for the sake of divination, but just for a first impression. The exercise will yield one hexagram result. Reading the selected sections of the hexagram entry as instructed in the first reading exercise will be your first level of study—a reading of the text as a literary work.

You'll then proceed to the second level of study, which is to consider what counsel is given through a divinatory approach to what you've just read. Consider the response from the Oracle and how it might or can be applied to your perspective on the inquired situation.

The third and fourth aspects of the Way of the Sages will unfold through the progression of readings herein.

## PRACTICUM 3.2:
## First Reading with the I Ching

In Carl Jung's foreword to Wilhelm's translations of the I Ching, he characterizes one school of thought on what's powering the divinatory accuracy of the Oracle—spiritual agencies. "These powers form, as it were, the living soul of the book," Jung writes.[174] Despite his skepticism toward that school of thought, he ventures to ask a question of the Oracle, as if they were a friend of his: "Why not venture a dialogue with an ancient book that purports to be animated?"[175]

Jung then shares his interpretation of the I Ching's guidance. He had inquired about how to proceed with writing that foreword for Wilhelm and what value the Wilhelm text would contribute to I Ching studies.[176]

The aspiration toward knowledge and conversation with your Holy Guardian Angel, as found in Western ceremonial magic, is not too different a psychic exercise from Jung's venture to hold a conversation with the I Ching as if they were a personal friend.

Divination, at its most secular expression, is a conversation between you and a randomized set of symbols. You commence a dialectical discourse with yourself in an effort to interpret those symbols.

For this exercise, and in the interest of keeping it simple, we'll be working with a nontraditional divinatory method, though one inspired by twelfth-century ritual techniques.

Place a coin on the square sigil below. Then speak aloud, addressing the Book as if they were a friend. "I have a question for you," you'll say. Meanwhile your coin is on the square sigil below. Then ask your question.

**FIGURE 3.16** Seal bonding the coin to the *qi* of the I Ching[177]

The side of the coin designated "heads" shall be yang.

| | |
|---|---|
| The side of the coin designated "heads" shall be yang. | ▬▬▬▬▬ |
| The side of the coin designated "tails" shall be yin. | ▬▬  ▬▬ |

Toss the coin once. In the table cell below designated for line 1, draw the corresponding yang or yin line based on whether your coin turned up heads or tails.

Toss the coin a second time. Draw the corresponding yang or yin coding in the cell for line 2. Toss the coin a third time. Draw the corresponding yang or yin coding in the cell for line 3. Continue for a total of six tosses until all lines are filled with your results.

| Line 6 | |
|---|---|
| Line 5 | |
| Line 4 | |
| Line 3 | |
| Line 2 | |
| Line 1 | |

Refer to table 1.1 in this book. Lines 1–3 form the lower trigram, which you'll look up along the outer-edge column of the table. Lines 4–6 form the upper trigram, which you'll look up along the top row of the table. Cross-reference the two and identify the resulting six-line hexagram. Use the table of contents to look up that hexagram in this book.

Read the Oracle section for the Oracle's direct response to your inquiry. Then skip to line 5 and read the corresponding text to reveal the forecasted outcome or climax of the situational circumstances of your inquiry. The fifth line of the hexagram is the position of the Ruler.

If your closest and dearest of friends had, in full candor, given you that same or similar response to your question, how would you react toward your friend? Lean in to those emotions and direct that back to the Oracle, responding emotionally just as you would to your friend.

Conclude your reading, closing this book, and seek out a different activity for now. Return when you've had sufficient time to reflect on the Oracle's answer. When ready, proceed onward to study the next chapter.

There will be several more chapters of study before we get to instructions on traditional long-form divination methods.

**About the Mysterious Lady of the Nine Heavens:** Also referred to as the Lady of the Nine Heavens (or Lady of the Ninth Heaven), 九天玄女 (Jiǔ Tiān Xuán Nǚ) is a celestial spirit of the esoteric arts, martial arts, and ceremonial magic. She is often invoked for dispelling evil, subduing violence, thwarting harm, providing protection magic, and most important of all, enacting justice. She is strongly associated with justice. Records of her predate the Qin dynasty (221 BC), and she is often linked to the matriarchal societies of the Shang (1600–1046 BC).

According to myth, the Yellow Emperor loses nine battles, and upon that last defeat, he prays for three days and three nights to the Queen Mother of the West (西王母, Xī Wáng Mǔ) for help. After the third day, the Queen Mother sends the Mysterious Lady of the Nine Heavens to assist him.[178]

**FIGURE 3.17** Mysterious Lady of the Nine Heavens

The *Seven Signs of Yunji* (云笈七签, *Yún jí qī qiān*) (AD 1017–1021), a multivolume Taoist grimoire from the Northern Song dynasty, notes that the Lady of the Nine Heavens teaches the Yellow Emperor to craft a powerful protection Fu (符) talisman, the 陰陽術 *(Yīnyáng shù)* or the yin and yang technique.[179] The jade-green talisman was approximately 3.5 inches across and 12 inches tall (converting "三寸" and "一尺").[180] The *Yellow Emperor's Classics of the Hidden Talisman* (黃帝陰符經, *Huángdì yīn fú jīng*) was a magical text that the Lady of the Nine Heavens gave to the Yellow Emperor.[181] The *Seven Signs* is an alchemical text and book of spells, providing instruction about various spirit realms.

The Mysterious Lady of the Nine Heavens is often depicted with a sword to symbolize martial arts and with a gourd to symbolize healing magic. The Han and Song dynasty texts describe her as a celestial with the head of a woman and the body of a bird, with the bright, luminescent blue plumage of a kingfisher. Myths from Taiwan reveal that Nǚwā was an incarnation of the Lady of the Nine Heavens. When the Lady descends from Heaven to Earth, she often does so taking the form of a magnificent bird; once on Earth, to get from place to place undetected, she takes on the form of a fox.

There's also a legend that the Lady of the Nine Heavens invented incense. She had reincarnated as a human, and when her father was too ill to take medicine, she ground the herbal medicine into a fine powder, pressed it into a stick with rice flour and water, and then burned it. The medicinal incense smoke healed her father. Thus, burning fragrant incense when petitioning or honoring the Lady of the Nine Heaven is, arguably, required.

**FIGURE 3.18** Another detail from *Studying the I Ching by a Window*.[182] Artist: 陳書 [Chen Shu]. SOURCE: National Palace Museum, Taipei.

A legend of a skilled martial artist and swordswoman known as Yuenü, or Maiden of the Southern Forest, was described as an emanation or reincarnation of the Lady of the Nine Heavens. The celestial took the human form of Yuenü to help King Goujian 句踐 of Yue (496–465 BC) in the same way she descended from the heavens to help the Yellow Emperor in 2600 BC. The legend of Goujian is alluded to in the fifth line of Hexagram 30.

In antiquity she was beloved by soldiers and martial artists, who invoked her for mentorship in training. When invoked, she'll descend to Earth and impart secrets of magical spells, talismans, and strategy to the worthy.

**FIGURE 4.1** *Ocean Palace of Increasing Eons* (Ming dynasty). Reference map for an astral journey to the Ocean Palace. Embroidered tapestry. SOURCE: National Palace Museum, Taipei.

# 4

# Interpreting the Hexagrams

YÌ XUÉ HERMENEUTICS—theories and methodologies for interpreting ancient, sacred, or philosophical texts—are generally classified into two main traditions: The Image and Number tradition of interpretation and the Meaning and Principle tradition. The distinctions between the Image and Number tradition and the Meaning and Principle covered in this chapter are more of a conceptual exercise than a distinction grounded in practical reality.

Zhu Xi criticized both traditions, and he saw merits in both. Renowned I Ching scholars such as Cai Yuanding 蔡元定 (AD 1135-1198)[1] sought to reconcile the two traditions,[2] and the farther the Oracle has migrated out of the Yellow River valley, the more integrative and eclectic the interpretive approaches have become. This chapter will supply you with some materials so that you might formulate your own school of thought.

Under I Ching cosmology, every function of the universe is a particular combination of yin and yang energies, and that particular combination of yin and yang make up an object's *qi,* or life force.

The two fundamental components of this binary mathematically combine with each other to form four patterns. When the combination is of yin and yang polarities coming to a union, it's in motion, moving toward growth, and is therefore "younger." Once it has changed, past tense, into a plenary status of itself, it has matured and is therefore the "elder."³

| 太陰 | 少陽 | 少陰 | 太陽 |
| --- | --- | --- | --- |
| *Tài yīn* | *Shǎo yang* | *Shǎo yīn* | *Tài yáng* |
| Elder yin | Younger yang | Younger yin | Elder yang |

Since all functions in the universe are composed of yin and yang, all *qi* is a pattern of yin and yang. Mathematically speaking, elder and younger yin and yang, when encountering functions of yin and yang, produce a total of eight fundamental building blocks, where each building block is a triplicity. These eight triplicities are the eight trigrams of the Ba Gua.

| 坤 | 艮 | 坎 | 巽 |
| --- | --- | --- | --- |
| **Kūn** | **Gěn** | **Kǎn** | **Xùn** |
| Earth | Mountain | Water | Wind |
| 震 | 離 | 兌 | 乾 |
| **Zhèn** | **Lí** | **Duì** | **Qián** |
| Thunder | Fire | Lake | Heaven |

Every hexagram in the I Ching is a paired combination of two of the eight trigrams. As triplicities of yin and yang combine with triplicities, mathematically they form a total of sixty-four combinations, and so these sixty-four combinations represent the totality of universal functions.

At the most fundamental level, when you endeavor to interpret a hexagram, you are assessing the alchemical functions of the yin and yang lines—that is, how the different combinations of yin and yang forces in nature are being transmuted. The operational result of the yin and yang combination forms a deduced meaning. That's how you ascertain the *qi* of a hexagram.

The hexagrams (卦, Guà) are diagrams representing the binary code of materialized reality. It's similar to how letters of the Latin alphabet are produced by a binary code of eight 0s and 1s. Computing systems exchange text through a string of 0s and 1s, and the materialized output is the letter.

| LETTER | BINARY CODE | LETTER | BINARY CODE |
|---|---|---|---|
| A | 01000001 | a | 01100001 |
| B | 01000010 | b | 01100010 |
| C | 01000011 | c | 01100011 |

In I Ching cosmology, the universe materializes output through a string of yin and yang and codes of six yin and yang values, which fundamentally are the equivalent to a pair of trigrams. Some more theist schools of thought believe that King Wen divinely received the correct order of hexagrams to represent the order of universal functions, and so in that school of thought, the order of the trigrams and hexagrams is included in your interpretation. Other schools of thought, however, see the diagram of six yin and yang lines as a field, and therefore interpretation can and ought to be nonlinear, not unlike relativity and nonlocality in quantum mechanics.

During the Spring and Autumn period of the Eastern Zhou (770–221 BC), we find early accounts of divination methods. Divination methods were also appended to the Ten Wings sometime during the Warring States period (403–221 BC), which is the basis for divinatory methods utilized to this day, with minimal change.

The Ten Wings address how the Book is used in divination—with the casting of yarrow stalks—assigning the value 3 to Heaven and the value 2 to Earth to reveal the mysterious Light of the gods.[4] Numbers help the diviner to contemplate the changes in the dark and the light, the yin and the yang, to establish the hexagrams in accordance with Heaven's Will.

Changes in the dark and the light are expressed in the trinity of Heaven, Earth, and Humanity, whereby Heaven brings the light, Earth brings the dark, and Humanity brings the beneficence. The trinitarian force of *qi* gathered is what powers the divination. The divination will then reveal what is in accordance with the Tao.[5] Such are the explanatory commentaries found in the Ten Wings.

It's in the Ten Wings that we are given greater clarity on the structure and purpose of the Zhouyi. The six-line hexagrams are figurative or coded representations of material movements on earth. In totality, the sixty-four hexagrams illuminate the past and reveal the future. They hold the power to open what was closed and to shed light on what was concealed by the darkness of ignorance.

To demonstrate the interpretation of a hexagram, consider the sequential combination of yin and yang in this specific order: yin, yin, yang; yin, yang, yang. As the building blocks of *qi* move through the universe, when they combine into a triplicity, they form a trigram. Yin, yin, and yang in that order form Mountain. We construct from the bottom up.

Then energy continues its movement of change until yin and yang form the second trigram. Yin, yang, and yang in that order form Wind. Two trigrams combined form the hexagram. The resulting hexagram, like the eight-string binary code forming a letter of the alphabet, forms Jian. In King Wen's received order, this is Hexagram 53.

The Image and Number tradition of interpretation, which we'll discuss in this chapter, would say that the numerology of 53 matters, the hexagram that came before and the hexagram that comes after matter, and how this hexagram might relate to other hexagrams (such as per changing lines, or per metaphysical correspondences) with shared qualities all matter in how you interpret Jian. In esoteric schools, astrology and astronomy—such as working with heavenly stems and earthly branches—would be woven into the interpretation.

The Meaning and Principle tradition would say no, don't dwell on the numerology of 53 or what relates to what; focus on the essential meaning and the guiding principles espoused by this image and by the text channeled by our ancestors, the Zhou, and given to us. Any lines of the hexagram designated as ruling, changing, or significant in any capacity help you to better understand the core principle of the hexagram. Instead of focusing on astrology, feng shui, geomancy, or magical spirits, focus on what the Oracle is trying to say to you to support your path to self-knowledge. Consider what commentaries or translations of the I Ching you find authoritative, and rely on those books to help you determine meaning.

| 巽上艮下 | 風山漸 | 第五十三卦： | 利貞 | 女歸吉 | 漸： | 君子以居賢德善俗 | 漸山上有木 | 象曰： | 53 ䷴ 漸 Jiàn |
|---|---|---|---|---|---|---|---|---|---|

Returning to Mountain over Wind, or Hexagram 53, the first part of each hexagram's text in the I Ching is often translated as "the Judgment" (象, Tuàn). In this book, I'll be calling this section of each hexagram's entry "the Oracle." These are expository comments describing the name of the hexagram and the trigrams they comprise.

The Image and Number tradition would focus on that six-line bit string of yin and yang data structured as a diagram that represents the archetypal change at hand, and like a scientist or mathematician, the diviner would approach the diagram as if it were a formula or algorithm to solve.

The Meaning and Principle tradition would look to the text in the Zhouyi accompanying Jian, which, according to legend, was written by our ancestor, King Wen. To interpret the divination, you extract the meaning and the principles, the values and the espoused virtues, revealed in that text.

Each line (爻, yáo) of the hexagram also holds meaning. The revelatory text added by the Duke of Zhou for each of the six lines (爻辭, yáo cí) is referred to as line statements. Once a hexagram is formed in the universe, every yin and yang line assumes a meaning, status, rank, and role in the greater narrative of the archetype that the hexagram represents. How you approach these lines depends on the divination method employed.

| Xùn  |||  Gěn  |||
| Wind |||  Mountain |||
| Line 6 | Line 5 | Line 4 | Line 3 | Line 2 | Line 1 |
| 上九：鴻漸于陸其羽可用為儀吉 | 九五：鴻漸于陵婦三歲不孕終莫之勝吉 | 六四：鴻漸于木或得其桷無咎 | 九三：鴻漸于陸夫征不復婦孕不育凶利禦寇 | 六二：鴻漸于磐飲食衎衎吉 | 初六：鴻漸于干小子厲有言無咎 |

Following Wang Bi's Rationalist approach, the sequential order of the Duke of Zhou's text within each line is not determinative. Instead, approach it in a nonlinear manner, as if the totality of the text was a field. Then seek out the core principle of the hexagram, and therefore the solution to your problem, based on the essential meaning.

Following Zhu Xi's Originalist approach, we assume the Duke of Zhou knew what he was doing and that the order of text within each line is intentional, sequentially representative of an order in the universe. The Originalist would also not feel compelled to consider relativity or to bring in implied meanings from other hexagrams or other commentaries.

Each line in the six-line code is assigned a role. Some read the progression from line 1 to line 6 as a chronological narrative arc of events. Others read each line separately, occupying one particular position, much like different appointed court positions at the imperial palace. Each position can be read as holding the title of a different rank, with line 1 as the lowest rank, line 5 as the highest rank on Earth, and line 6 relating to Heaven.

According to the Confucian commentaries in the Ten Wings, line 1 of every hexagram is difficult to understand, while line 6 should be easy to understand. Generally, if the inquiry pertains to practical matters, such as questions about relationships or career, and the divinatory method does not account for changing lines or fluctuating hexagrams, then I'll read the oracular message for line 5 as a prognostication of what is to come. That's because line 5 is assigned as the hexagram ruler.

For example, if the question was, "Will my business venture be profitable enough to financially sustain my livelihood?" and the resulting locked (single) hexagram is Hexagram 53, I would interpret the message in the "Oracle" section as the direct response to my question. After that, one approach is to read all text in totality for the six lines, and then, through self-reflection, intuit an answer or divinatory insight to your inquiry. Another approach is to read the fifth line, given its assigned ranking.

*Fifth Line*

**The wild goose dawdles slowly toward the summit. For three years the one who conceives cannot conceive. Yet all will be well—good auspices.**

That reads like the answer is that the business venture will not be profitable enough to sustain the questioner's livelihood for another three years; but take heart, because the long-term outcome is very promising.

If the nature of my inquiry is spiritual or religious, then I'll read the oracular message for the sixth line, the hexagram ruler over mystical matters. When using the Oracle as a medium for communicating with the spirit world, for example, then I'll read the sixth line text as the spirit's reply.

*Sixth Line*

**The wild goose dawdles slowly toward the highlands. Its feathers can be used for the sacred rites. Good auspices.**

The philosopher-student will want to study the first line of every hexagram reading, if we're following the Ten Wings commentary that the first line is always the hardest to comprehend; but if you can understand the first line, you'll deepen your pool of wisdom.

*First Line*

**The wild goose dawdles slowly toward the shore. Ominous for the young offspring. There is talk, but there is no blame.**

I tend to interpret a hexagram divination as going beyond prediction to offer counsel. There are always calls to action associated with the revelation. The Oracle does not permit the recipient of the divination to remain passive or complacent. Even advice to do nothing is a call to certain action. And ironically, when the Oracle's advice is to do nothing, it happens in situations when you are most tempted to do something rash.

Whether you find yourself partial to the Image and Number tradition or the Meaning and Principle tradition, or if you reconcile the two for an integrative approach, there is a uniting principle: the Three Meanings of Change. This uniting principle is the undercurrent of every divination you seek from the Oracle.

Since at least 200 BC, the varying schools seem in agreement about the philosophical Three Meanings of Change (易有三義, Yì Yǒu Sān Yì) governing interpretation of the hexagrams. The Three Meanings of Change are as follows:

1. **Biànyì** 變易: The universe is self-generative and self-transformative. Therefore, the First Meaning of Change is that humanity lives in a universe of ceaseless change.

2. **Yìjiǎn** 易簡: The universe changes in an orderly, reasoned pattern, so the Second Meaning of Change is that humanity can anticipate and control the ceaseless change when we understand those patterns of change.

3. **Bùyì** 不易: The universe's patterns of change are knowable. Therefore, the Third Meaning of Change is to know those patterns through divination so that humanity might find peace and contentment in life.

An oft-quoted line from the Ten Wings: whosoever knows the Tao of Change, or the Way of Transformation, knows Heaven's Will. The guiding principle behind consulting the I Ching is to be open to change, and if you are open to changing, then the Oracle will guide you to change in the ways you want, to achieve your own stated goals.

What does it mean to be "open to change"?

The First Meaning of Change asks you to acknowledge that you don't and can't stay the same in terms of your personal identity, your fate doesn't and won't stay fixed, and no matter what your luck is right now, "this, too, shall pass." Intellectually we all can acknowledge the truth in that principle, but in terms of actual practice, most people behave in a manner that is resistant to it. Letting go of that resistance is the First Meaning.

The Second Meaning of Change asks that you take ownership of and accountability for the changes that transpire. The changes that happen to you are not arbitrary or irrational; rather, they are orderly and reasoned. That means you are capable of knowing how changes transpire, and if you can know how changes transpire, then you can control the course of those changes for yourself. The Second Meaning asks that you never cease with your education and never limit what you learn. I tend to interpret the Second Meaning as implying that divination is a knowable science.

The Third Meaning of Change relates to life purpose. One's life purpose is to perpetuate a constant state of transformation, and in doing so, to move progressively toward transcendence. When you come to the Oracle for divination, know your purpose. Every change should be purposeful, meaning the changes are within your control. In a way, this restates the principle of taking ownership of and accountability for the changes that transpire in your life.

This is in no way saying that you shouldn't come to the I Ching for trivial matters. You can—as long as you know that your purpose is a trivial matter. Your purpose for knowing what you would not otherwise be able to know through the exercise of divination should be, on some level and to some degree, to help you or humanity find peace, and to help you or your loved ones (your family or your subjects, if you're a figurative sovereign over others) find contentment.

The Three Meanings guide the underlying motivation for approaching the I Ching.

## The Image and Number Tradition (Xiàng Shù)

Rising in prominence in 200 BC around the time of the Western Han, the Image and Number tradition (象數派, Xiàng Shù Pài)[6] of interpretation is all about the metaphysical correspondences, and it treats the abstract six-line diagram as a code to be deciphered. Numerology matters. Trigram correspondences matter. Gather as many correspondence tables as you can. The *tu* (圖) or diagrams matter, because they're symbolic. Focus your reading at that graphic level. The esoteric significance of how the yin and yang lines are arranged determines your reading of the hexagram. So pretend like looking at the combination of six abstract broken and solid lines means something to you.

At least that is my unscholarly layman's way to explain the Image and Number tradition of interpreting hexagrams. Oftentimes Rationalists were also proponents of the Image and Number tradition, as were many literati from the School of Mystery (玄學, Xuan Xue). Even the group name of the tradition's biggest proponent belies some of the pretension of the Image and Number sect. This approach is an investigative process. Look for clues by way of correspondences, follow those clues, arrive at conclusions, and keep going until you solve the mystery of your divinatory reading.

To be fair, the Image and Number approach is liberating. The diviner is given a great deal of freedom in how the I Ching reading is interpreted. By not focusing on the literary text, which can be confining, and focusing on the abstract diagrams, the divinatory exercise might very well be more psychic, which is a fascinating paradox, given that those of the Image and Number tradition tend to be Rationalists who emphasize the importance of logical reasoning and practical analysis. This again goes to show that fundamentally, paradigms differ widely between East and West, right down to how we conceptualize science versus art, or how we define philosophy or religion.

There's also a great variance in correspondence tables in the Image and Number tradition, given that its origin dates back to 100 BC at the latest. The collective of its adherents can agree that numerology matters, and the number correspondences for the eight trigrams determine the direction of your interpretation of the hexagram result. However, that's pretty much where the agreement ends. There are so many different correspondence tables for numbers to trigrams that it's dizzying to keep straight.

**TABLE 4.1** Lo Shu Magic Square Numerology and the Trigrams

| | | | |
|---|---|---|---|
| 1 | Water (Kan) | 2 | Earth (Kun) |
| 3 | Thunder (Zhen) | 4 | Wind (Xun) |
| 7 | Lake (Dui) | 6 | Heaven (Qian) |
| 9 | Fire (Li) | 8 | Mountain (Gen) |

The numerology-to-trigram correspondence that will be presented here is based on the Lo Shu magic square and the number configuration in the Lo Shu superimposed with the Later Heaven Ba Gua, or King Wen's Ba Gua (as opposed to Fuxi's Early Heaven Ba Gua). The number 5 is not assigned to a trigram because it represents the center.

The significance of numbers is paramount in the Image and Number tradition. Proponents of this tradition believe that all things in this universe are mathematical functions, and numbers reveal the divine.[7] If you can fully understand the calculus of life, then nothing in this life is fated or out of your control, because it is but a mere function of calculation to achieve what you seek.

Let's say the hexagram you've drawn, bottom line upward, yields the lower trigram Fire and the upper trigram Mountain. You would read this as Mountain over Fire.

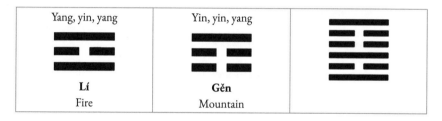

The metaphysical correspondences for yin and yang combine in the triplicities to produce an alchemical reaction. A subsequent chapter will cover popular correspondences, which you'd assemble in your mind like pieces of the puzzle. The two triplicities, Fire in the lower position and Mountain in the upper position, also produce an alchemical reaction. A divination yielding this hexagram is telling you that this is the alchemical reaction at play.

Based on what you know as a learned scholar about this type of alchemical reaction, you can forecast what is to come and offer advice on the situation at hand. Under the Image and Number tradition, a divinatory reading is approached as if it were alchemy, and therefore a certain scientific rigor is applied to your analysis.

To consider the hexagram in totality first, look at the alchemical reactions produced between each line (yin or yang) compared to the natural line position *qi*. By taking an accounting of the six alchemical reactions produced between the line of the hexagram in question and the natural line position *qi*, you'll start to get a high-level understanding of the hexagram's intrinsic energy.

Recall earlier when we affirmed that the line positions for 1, 3, and 5 (the odd numbers) are yang and the line positions for 2, 4, and 6 (the even numbers) are yin. Compare the yin or yang nature of the innate line position with the yin or yang output of the resulting hexagram.

**TABLE 4.2** Comparing Innate *Qi* with Hexagram Lines

|   | A. | Innate Qi | B. | Hexagram 22 | Trigrams in Hexagram 22 | C. | Binary |
|---|----|-----------|----|-------------|-------------------------|----|--------|
| 6 |    | ▬▬ ▬▬     |    | ▬▬▬▬▬       | *Upper trigram*         |    | Younger yang |
| 5 |    | ▬▬▬▬▬     |    | ▬▬ ▬▬       |                         |    | Younger yin |
| 4 |    | ▬▬ ▬▬     |    | ▬▬ ▬▬       | Mountain                |    | Elder yin |
| 3 |    | ▬▬▬▬▬     |    | ▬▬▬▬▬       | *Lower trigram*         |    | Elder yang |
| 2 |    | ▬▬ ▬▬     |    | ▬▬ ▬▬       |                         |    | Elder yin |
| 1 |    | ▬▬▬▬▬     |    | ▬▬▬▬▬       | Fire                    |    | Elder yang |

| B. | Hexagram 22 | ▬▬ ▬▬ | ▬▬▬▬▬ | ▬▬ ▬▬ | ▬▬▬▬▬ |
|----|-------------|-------|-------|-------|-------|
| A. | Innate Qi   | ▬▬ ▬▬ | ▬▬ ▬▬ | ▬▬▬▬▬ | ▬▬▬▬▬ |
| C. | Binary      | **Elder yin** | **Younger yang** | **Younger yin** | **Elder yang** |

In the example of Mountain over Fire, or Hexagram 22, the lower trigram for Hexagram 22 is in perfect alignment energetically with the innate *qi* of the lower three positions (1, 2, and 3). Table 4.2 compares the yin and yang values of each line of Hexagram 22 with the innate *qi* of those line positions. All three of the lower trigram lines are elder, or matured, so there is a stabilizing energy present. The beginning phases of this alchemical reaction were strong and in alignment with the natural flow of *qi* (yin and yang combination); therefore, there are no measurable changes to the onset of the natural flow.

The line positions of the upper trigram (4, 5, and 6) show transformations happening, or shifting energy at the fifth and sixth lines. Younger, meaning growing and changing energy, dominates. (See table 4.2 for reference.) While the initiating energy is stable at line 4, because the innate *qi* is yin and the hexagram line is yin, it's exacerbated with a slight tension as time progresses. For instance, the innate *qi* of line 4 is yang, but in Hexagram 22, the fifth line is yin. This starts to show the energy of change that Hexagram 22 produces in the natural flow of *qi* through the universe.

You'll also want to consider whether a given hexagram is yin dominant or yang dominant. In a tally of the total yin lines compared to yang, it's three yin lines and three yang lines, so there's an innate symmetry within, even if there isn't graphic symmetry.

Let's turn our attention to the binary qualities of Hexagram 22. You'll see that elder or matured energy dominates (lines 1, 2, 3, and 4 in Hexagram 22 are all elder), and among the elders, there is yin and yang balance (two elder yin and two elder yang).

This is going to be a preview of a subsequent chapter on the five changing phases, Wu Xing, but suffice it to know for now that elder yin corresponds with the changing phase Water, and elder yang to Fire. That the lower *trigram* is Fire and one of the prevailing alchemical *phases* is Fire amplifies this quality. There is a luminosity here, which happens to be the English translation for the hexagram title: "with beauty and grace; luminosity."

Even though the *trigram* that dominates in Hexagram 22 is Fire (離), we have to account for the alchemical reaction between the *phase* Fire (火) and the *phase* Water (水). Water dominates over Fire, and Fire is weakened by Water.

| HEXAGRAM 22 CORRESPONDENCES ||||
|---|---|---|---|
| Heavenly Stems | Earthly Branch | Gregorian Calendar | Western Zodiac Sign |
| 癸 *Guǐ* | 壬 *Rén* | 寅 *Yín* | February 18–20 | Pisces |

| | Elder yin | | | Elder yang | |
|---|---|---|---|---|---|
| 水 Water *Shuǐ* | **Direction:** | North | 火 Fire *Huo* | **Direction:** | South |
| | **Planet:** | Mercury | | **Planet:** | Mars |
| | **Action:** | Contract, retreat | | **Action:** | Expand, assert |
| | **Signs:** | Boar, Rat | | **Signs:** | Snake, Horse |

That means if your style of divination includes predictions, then correspondences of Fire try to challenge that of Water, but Water prevails. A diviner might read this as prognosticating a battle between an army coming from the north and an army coming from the south, and the north will be the victor.

If we revisit the trigrams composition, the lower trigram Fire corresponds with ambitions, honor, and social status. It refers to gaining recognition for your accomplishments. Here, all three *yao* or lines are in stable positions and matured. So this is someone who enjoys positive social standing, someone with charisma who attracts people (the "clinging" energy of Fire). You are a light . . . though as we continue this analysis, perhaps a light that attracts moths.

The upper trigram Mountain corresponds with knowledge, education, and academia, but the last two lines (lines 5 and 6) are young and shifting. The Mountain that should be stable is unstable in this context. Due to that instability, the advice might be to hold back and not advance forward because the path up ahead is shaky ground.

The Duke of Zhou's text for these six lines of Hexagram 22 make reference to the image of adornments on different parts of a noble. The image for line 1 is adornments on the feet. The image for line 2 is adornments in a man's hair. Both instances are indicative of a high-ranking official during the Zhou. The first sign of challenge enters at line 4, when trespassers are mistaken for robbers, though their intention was only to take a wife, a cultural reference to the practice of marriage by wife abduction. These would be part of the puzzle pieces of images that the Image and Number diviner would focus on demystifying.

|   | Hexagram 22 |   | Trigram Quality |
|---|---|---|---|
| 6 | ▬▬▬▬ | ▬▬▬▬<br>▬▬ ▬▬<br>▬▬ ▬▬<br>**Mountain:**<br>Stabilizing, block | Learning. Knowledge, education, academia. Seeking stability. Inner reflection. Conservation. Long-term business matters. |
| 5 | ▬▬ ▬▬ | | |
| 4 | ▬▬ ▬▬ | | |
| 3 | ▬▬▬▬ | ▬▬▬▬<br>▬▬ ▬▬<br>▬▬▬▬<br>**Fire:** Clinging, expanding up | Glory. Ambitions, honor, social status. Upward mobility. Passion. Innovation. Leadership. Politics. Progress. To increase and advance. |
| 2 | ▬▬ ▬▬ | | |
| 1 | ▬▬▬▬ | | |

The Image and Number scholar would be knowledgeable on all the correspondences as set forth in the subsequent chapters. You would then read, cross-reference, and cross-reference again the various diagrams or *tu* (圖) and deductively arrive at your interpretation of the divinatory reading.

A crucial point in this tradition of interpretation is to consider the correlations of the trigrams. The trigram Fire is connected to the 9 position in the Lo Shu magic square, the changing phase (Wu Xing) of Fire, and all that these elements of the whole correspond to. Map it all out and deduce a meaning.

The second point of analysis emphasized in the Image and Number tradition is the hexagram ruler (卦主, *guà zhǔ*). A hexagram ruler is the line in the hexagram that embodies the significance and main theme of the entire hexagram, so it is given greater emphasis in the interpretation of the reading.[8] As it is with correspondence tables, within this tradition there are myriad opinions on how to designate the hexagram ruler. That's why practicum 3.2, "First Reading with the I Ching," focused on reading the fifth line.

As a broad general rule, line 5 is the hexagram ruler, which Legge's translation refers to as the "lord of judgment" or the "place of honor." Returning to table 4.3, the fifth line is weak, because the innate *qi* of the fifth line (yang) paired with the fifth line of Hexagram 22 (yin) produces younger yin. It's this line causing the instability in the entire diagram. The topmost sixth line of Hexagram 22 also shows instability, as younger yang, but it is more promising in terms of prognostications than a younger yin result.

**TABLE 4.3** Five Ranks of Nobility and Hexagram Rulers

|        | INNATE *QI* | THE KING AND FIVE RANKS OF NOBILITY (五爵, WǓ JUÉ) | | |
|--------|-------------|------|--------|------|
| Line 6 | — —         | 王 Wáng | King    | Ruler of the person's destiny or karma |
| Line 5 | ———         | 公 Gōng | Duke    | Ruler of immediately pressing affairs |
| Line 4 | — —         | 侯 Hóu  | Marquis | Ruler of romantic matters and marriage |
| Line 3 | ———         | 伯 Bó   | Earl    | Ruler of legal matters and social affairs |
| Line 2 | — —         | 子 Zi   | Viscount| Ruler of medical matters |
| Line 1 | ———         | 男 Nán  | Baron   | Ruler of short-term money matters |

The Wǔ Jué, or Five Ranks of Nobility, dates back to the pre-Qin dynasty periods during the Zhou, before 221 BC. Such titles could be either inherited or earned by merit. The rank for line 6 would be the king, or the Son of Heaven, the ruler of the dynasty. Table 4.3 provides a reference for the inquiry themes assigned to each line position. Thus, if the question was relating to a short-term money matter, for instance, then in addition to reading the Oracle (or Judgment) section of the hexagram entry in the Book, you would also read the oracular text for line 1. If the resulting hexagram was 22, you would read the following:

*First Line*

**Beautiful adornments on the feet, yet abandoning the carriage to walk as a humble apprentice. Going forth plainly on foot.**

For a question relating to short-term money matters, the first line prophetic message indicates that there may be a slight downturn in earnings, but nothing that will hurt your overall livelihood. You'll need to make some adjustments to your expenditures.

Now let's say the question was about a romantic prospect and your result was Hexagram 22. After reading the Oracle section for the general message, turn to the fourth line, corresponding with the marquis, because per the preceding table 4.3 reference, the marquis is the ruler of romantic matters and marriage.

*Fourth Line*

**To wear the adornments that purify, purge, and refine—a white horse gallops so gallantly it appears to have wings. Bandits trespass, arriving like thieves, but they do not come to plunder; they come to escort the bride.**

As synchronicity would have it, there is a direct reference here to marriage, or to be more specific, the tradition of marriage by bride kidnapping. In the Image and Number tradition, what does "marriage by bride kidnapping" symbolize as a metaphor? What does "white horse gallops . . . appears to have wings" symbolize as a metaphor? Deconstruct the symbolic elements of the text and determine, one by one, what they represent in terms of correspondences.

In answer to the hypothetical romantic prospect question, I might interpret such a reading as indicative of a commitment you enter into reluctantly, perhaps because you don't think you have better options, along with a warning that nothing is as it seems. The white horse is probably not actually flying, but something in the manner gives you the false impression that it is. Thus, I would interpret the answer as "yes, the relationship will happen, *but ...*" and the Oracle is cautioning you of a big "but."

Third and most important of all in the Image and Number tradition is ascertaining the changing lines, and considering how hexagrams fluctuate and transform based on their alchemical relationships with other hexagrams. If you can calculate these points of transformation and understand them, then you can calculate and forecast every change in the universe with precision, or so goes the Image and Number theory.

Hexagram transformation by way of changing lines is called Guà Biàn (卦變). Guà Biàn, or hexagram transformations, happen when the result from the divination method you've employed yields younger yang or younger yin, the fluctuating binary pairs. Note that this is specific to divination methods under the Image and Number tradition. For example, the attributions for coin toss methods under the Meaning and Principle tradition are the exact opposite. (This will be explained in detail later in chapter 7, as summarized in table 7.1.)

| 少陽 *Shǎo yang* | 少陰 *Shǎo yīn* |
| Younger yáng | Younger yin |

Under Image and Number, anytime there is a merger of yin and yang to form a complementary binary, the interaction of these opposites produces change. Whereas elder yin and elder yang are mergers of the same, so they remain matured and unchanged.

|   | A. | Innate *Qi* | B. | Hexagram 22 | Transformation | Hexagram 63 |
|---|----|----|----|----|----|----|
| 6 |   | ▬▬ ▬▬ |   | ▬▬▬▬▬ | → | ▬▬ ▬▬ | ▬▬ ▬▬ |
| 5 |   | ▬▬▬▬▬ |   | ▬▬ ▬▬ | → | ▬▬▬▬▬ | **Water:** Abyss, chasm, darken, deepening |
| 4 |   | ▬▬ ▬▬ |   | ▬▬ ▬▬ |   | ▬▬ ▬▬ |
| 3 |   | ▬▬▬▬▬ |   | ▬▬▬▬▬ |   | ▬▬▬▬▬ |
| 2 |   | ▬▬ ▬▬ |   | ▬▬ ▬▬ |   | ▬▬ ▬▬ | **Fire:** Clinging, expanding up |
| 1 |   | ▬▬▬▬▬ |   | ▬▬▬▬▬ |   | ▬▬▬▬▬ |

Where only a single hexagram is being read, the hexagram transformations happen, if they happen at all, where the pairing of the innate *qi* line with the line from the hexagram produces younger yang or younger yin. In the case of Hexagram 22, that's lines 5 and 6. After changing these lines, the result is Water over Fire, which is Hexagram 63. Thus, in the I Ching, according to Image and Number scholars, Hexagram 22 is alchemically related to Hexagram 63. Even if Hexagram 63 does not literally show up in your divination, if there is Hexagram 22, then there is an implied prediction of change to Hexagram 63.

Think of this concept as a known physics or algebra formula. Every time you run a computation by applying that known formula, you'll get a reliable result. That's the rationale behind divination under the Image and Number interpretive school.

## The Meaning and Principle Tradition (Yì Lǐ)

Scholars like the Originalist Zhu Xi, whom we covered in the previous chapter, criticized the esoteric Rationalists with their Image and Number approach. He saw the Image and Number diviners as getting carried away with all those excessive tables of correspondences and arithmetical changing lines, which weren't even in the original text. Around AD 100 to 200,[9] scholars challenged the Image and Number tradition, though the Meaning and Principle school wouldn't formalize until the Song dynasty (AD 960–1279). These scholars sought to return to the text itself and to stay grounded in the text to derive meaning.

Recall how hexagram transformations and changing lines define the Image and Number tradition, emphasizing the concept that hexagrams relate to each other and those relations should be considered part of the divination. In contrast, the Originalists advancing the Meaning and Principle tradition emphasized that each hexagram should be considered on its own independent merits.

The Meaning and Principle tradition (義理派, Yi Li Pai) of interpretation tends to be the more popularized tradition seen in the West. It is a more literary mental exercise than an Image and Number approach, which is more analytical. The Image and Number tradition is considered more esoteric, whereas the Meaning and Principle tradition is philosophical.

However, there are still analytical elements to Meaning and Principle. Case in point: the importance of etymology. The etymological origins of every word and what the original intentions of its author were matter a lot under Meaning and Principle and are often determinative of how you would interpret the text.

Relevant philology also matters a great deal under Meaning and Principle, which in this case refers to the study of literary texts and commentaries associated with the I Ching.[10] You would read as many commentaries and critiques by authoritative figures as possible to supplement your understanding of the hexagrams. Compare different historical texts. Critique past commentaries. Make historical inquiries about the authenticity of texts. These are all imperative to the Meaning and Principle school.

In summary, the Meaning and Principle tradition stipulates that you study as many past commentaries on the I Ching as you can, preferably the authentic ones, and discern for yourself what works for you and what doesn't; and that should be your paradigm for interpreting the hexagrams. Which are the "authentic" ones? If you're a true Yì Xué scholar, you'll debate that passionately and disagree with other fellow Yì Xué scholars.

Also, treating the text as poetry to study the rhythms and speech patterns when the words are spoken is another aspect of Meaning and Principle interpretation. The music of the words conveys an emotional value, and that emotional value conveys the meaning of the lines.

While the Image and Number tradition believed that human affairs could be deduced algorithmically from the correspondences and symbolic value of the images, the Meaning and Principle tradition criticized that point, arguing that images and their numerological significance are human-made structures. As constructs we've created, there is nothing divine to them. Moreover, many of the purported mathematical methods of the Image and Number school felt arbitrary and forced to the Meaning and Principle proponents.[11]

The Meaning and Principles school of interpretation focuses on moral principles, teaching virtue, and the literary value of the written text that accompanies the hexagrams. Read the text first and foremost. Nothing is more important than the text. The text—assuming you're working from the "right" text—is authoritative. The question of which text is the "right" text goes back to New Text vs. Old Text schisms, and there isn't a unanimous consensus within the Meaning and Principle tradition on which are the "right" texts. Nevertheless, from dynasty to dynasty, different texts will come and go as the established orthodoxy.

A representative proponent of the Meaning and Principle tradition is Cheng Yi.

**FIGURE 4.2** Portrait of Cheng Yi (Qing dynasty). SOURCE: Palace Museum, Beijing.

Cheng Yi 程頤 (1033–1107) was a Song dynasty neo-Confucian philosopher and politician whose political advocacy work defined his I Ching commentaries. Cheng Yi completed his volumes of commentary, titled the *Yi River Commentary on the Book of Changes,* during periods of political exile. The reference to the Yi River is a sobriquet he adopted, in tribute to a river that flows through his hometown of Luoyang.[12]

Under the Meaning and Principle interpretative approach, Yi distanced himself from using the Book for fortune-telling. His annotations and commentaries reflect a conscious distancing from predictive language. Later, the Originalist philosopher Zhu Xi would credit Cheng Yi as having been the one who moves Yi Xué away from Taoist mysticism and more toward political and philosophical discourse.

While the Image and Number school ascribes esoteric and symbolic meaning to the number associated with each hexagram and the numbers of the two trigrams, under Cheng Yi's approach, there is no numerological significance to these numbers. If Image and Number sought meaning in the mathematics of cosmology, then Meaning and Principle sought meaning in moral philosophy.

Heavily influenced by Confucian values, reading the I Ching for moral philosophy meant insisting on defined hierarchies. A core principle in the Meaning and Principle tradition is Lèi (類), translated as "kind, class, genus, category, or order," but which is culturally understood to mean "to know": one must divide, subdivide, and categorize to know the holistic meaning and principle at hand. The concept of Lèi is essential to Cheng Yi's approach.[13] What defines a *junzi* (君子) is the ability to discern Lèi—to know how to put everything in its place, in its right order and category.

Thus, under such a theory of Lèi as a constitutive principle in Confucian wisdom, a divinatory reading will in its natural course be ordered in a set hierarchy. Furthermore, knowing how to divine with the I Ching to advise on state or political matters was essential to the livelihoods of early I Ching diviner-sages: "Only someone with a cultivated awareness of *lèi* will be able to apply such a hexagram to an actual state. It requires seeing what position in the actual state corresponds with the fifth position in the hexagram"[14] (the fifth position being generally designated as the hexagram ruler).

**TABLE 4.4** Feudal Hierarchies of the Hexagram Lines

|        | Innate *Qi* | Cheng Yi's Class Hierarchy | | | Confucian Social Order | | |
|--------|---|---|---|---|---|---|---|
| Line 6 |   | 神 | *Shén* | Divine Spirit | | | |
| Line 5 |   | 君 | *Jūn* | Lord, ruler | 士 | *Shì* | Scholar |
| Line 4 |   | 大臣 | *Dàchén* | Minister | 商 | *Shāng* | Merchant |
| Line 3 |   | 侯爵 | *Hóujué* | Marquis | 工 | *Gōng* | Artisan |
| Line 2 |   | 臣 | *Chén* | Vassal | 農 | *Nóng* | Farmer |
| Line 1 |   | 農民 | *Nóngmín* | Commoner | | | |

The position of the hexagram ruler is envisioned as being perched atop the *yao* lines below it, and therefore from the vantage point of line 5, you can see the full context and landscape of the situation at hand. It is at the line 5 position that you can best decide how to proceed.

In a Meaning and Principle approach, where wisdom is derived from the text irrespective of the divination method, read lines 1 through 4 for situational insight and then line 5, the hexagram ruler, for the direct advice from the Oracle on what decision to make, though at all times stay mindful of the point

Wang Bi made: the Oracle never takes away your agency. You alone control the narrative.

The principle (理, *lǐ*) of a hexagram—that is, its essential meaning—is encapsulated in one of its six lines. Once the principle is identified among the six lines, the other five lines become supporting cast and secondary themes to the principle. The six lines together convey a set meaning, but only one of those six lines contains the hexagram's core principle, its ruling judgment.

When hexagrams are used in fortune-telling, the feudal hierarchy assignments to the line positions become more relevant. The yin or yang line in each position and its corresponding phase per the Wu Xing five phases or astrological correspondences are interpreted as occupying the six palaces (the six lines of the hexagram). The hierarchical assignment informs how the fortune-teller reads the correspondences per the themes associated with each palace.

Consider a hypothetical divination result of Fire over Wind, Hexagram 50, where lines 2 and 4 are changing, thus producing a secondary transformed Hexagram 52. One divination method would read lines 2 and 4 as containing the principle meaning or *lǐ* of the situation inquired about, while another approach would be to continue focus on line 5, because it's the hexagram ruler, though the changing lines would still be accounted for as part of the oracle message, just not as the principle meaning.

I read a tension between fate and free will, where the changing lines reveal free will and the practical advice being given, while the fifth line, the lord or scholar per the feudal hierarchies, reveals the esoteric universal truth of situations like the matter being inquired about.

|        | Primary Hexagram | Changing Lines | Transformed Hexagram |
|--------|------------------|----------------|----------------------|
| Line 6 | ▅▅▅▅▅ |  | ▅▅▅▅▅ |
| Line 5 | ▅▅ ▅▅ |  | ▅▅ ▅▅ |
| Line 4 | ▅▅▅▅▅ | X → | ▅▅ ▅▅ |
| Line 3 | ▅▅▅▅▅ |  | ▅▅▅▅▅ |
| Line 2 | ▅▅▅▅▅ | X → | ▅▅ ▅▅ |
| Line 1 | ▅▅ ▅▅ |  | ▅▅ ▅▅ |
|        | *Fire* over *Wind* **Hexagram 50** |  | *Mountain* over *Mountain* **Hexagram 52** |

Wang Bi's Rationalist approach to reading these hexagrams in the Meaning and Principle tradition would be to see the totality of the divination result as a field. Apply reasoning to assess what *li* or principle meaning arises from that field. Zhu Xi and Originalists would warn not to impose a Taoist view of the text, and to reflect on what the original author of the text meant by these words. Getting esoteric, reflect on what the original author of the universe meant by this hexagram code.

Returning to the hypothetical where the result is Hexagram 50, the Cauldron, with the second and fourth as the changing lines, let's consider the second line of Hexagram 50 to assess whether the matter inquired about is auspicious or inauspicious.

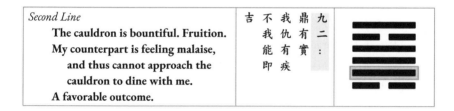

*Second Line*
**The cauldron is bountiful. Fruition. My counterpart is feeling malaise, and thus cannot approach the cauldron to dine with me. A favorable outcome.**

九二：鼎有實　我仇有疾　不我能即　吉

The short answer is yes, the undertaking inquired about is auspicious, but there is counsel being provided as well. "九二" lets you know that this is the second (二) line of the hexagram, and it's a yang line (九). The Oracle speaks in the first person, using "I" (我) twice.

To understand the core meaning and principles of a given hexagram, I like to consider the progressing lines or *yao* to be a narrative arc. Approach the diagram as a story, tell the story to yourself, and then consider what the themes of the story are.

**TABLE 4.5** Narrative Arc of Changes

| Line 6 | Denouement | Closing remarks; untying the knot; transitioning onward. |
|---|---|---|
| Line 5 | Climax | The judgment. How to navigate the peak of the conflict. |
| Line 4 | Resolution | Decisive action to resolve the thickening plot. |
| Line 3 | Complication | The plot thickens. |
| Line 2 | Dawn: The Rise | The actual start of the journey. |
| Line 1 | Orientation | Setting up the initiation of events. |

In the Hexagram 50 hypothetical with lines 2 and 4 changing, the inherent plot point of line 2 tells me this prognostication is for the start of the journey. Chronologically, there is a second prognostication for the changing line 4 position. This is another yang line, hence the designation "九." The "四" denotes that this is the text for the fourth line.

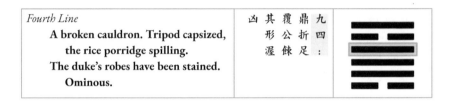

| Fourth Line | | |
|---|---|---|
| A broken cauldron. Tripod capsized, the rice porridge spilling. The duke's robes have been stained. Ominous. | 九四：鼎折足，覆公餗，其形渥，凶 | |

The second line and fourth line prognostications contradict each other, or so it would seem; but if read as a narrative arc, then the rising action of the event starts off well. The Oracle affirms that intentions are in the right place, but there's an implied forecast that something will happen between point A (line 2) and point B (line 4) that causes the resolution not to turn out not quite as hoped for.

**FIGURE 4.3** Bronze ritual tripod cauldron, late Shang period (thirteenth–fourteenth century BC). Carvings represent Thunder. SOURCE: National Palace Museum, Taipei.

Reading the two lines together as a story, the cauldron started off bountiful, with the potential of yielding a great amount of nourishment to all. The undertaking is one for the greater good that is going to solve a societal malaise. But then the tripod legs of the bountiful cauldron are broken off and its contents spill out, staining the duke's clothes.

Why does the story end like that?

Also, in the Meaning and Principle tradition, we might look at etymology to derive deeper or secondary meaning from the text. "折" *(zhé)* is a pictograph of a person with an axe cutting down a tree. In what circumstances and for what motivations would someone take up an axe and cut down a tree? Our answers to these thought explorations inspire insights on what the Oracle means.

In the case of a reading where there are changing lines, the resulting hexagram will transform into a second hexagram. It transforms through the

**FIGURE 4.4** Ritual cauldron belonging to the marquis of Kang. The marquis of Kang was the ninth son of King Wen, younger brother to King Wu. The inscription shows the seal of the marquis. Western Zhou dynasty (eleventh century BC). SOURCE: National Palace Museum, Taipei.

changing lines. The final ending to the story about the cauldron and the duke's stained clothes can still be changed, and the outcome is mutable.

If changing lines are at the line 2 and line 4 positions of Hexagram 50, then it transforms into Hexagram 52. The purpose of this chapter is to discuss interpretation of hexagrams, so for now, the divinatory method for arriving at that result is unimportant. If you recall from table 3.12 in chapter 3, Hexagram 52, Mountain over Mountain, is one of the Eight Spirit Helpers per Taoist mysticism. This Spirit Helper can facilitate psychic visions and spiritual awakenings, or help improve one's meditation practice.

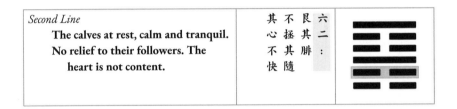

The "二" designation in the section title tells you that this is the text for the second line of the hexagram, and "六" tells you that line is yin.

So how do we prevent the ominous outcome of line 4 from the previous Hexagram 50?

This second line from transformed Hexagram 52 is giving advice. Calf muscles support you when you stand, enable movement of your feet, and propel you forward when you walk or run. The Oracle is saying to you, "You have the tendency to go too far," and even continues with the anticipatory remark: "*Sigh, you're probably not going to listen to what I say, and that's your problem.*"

You'll also see that one of the classical Chinese characters is "心," directly translated to "heart." In antiquity during the times of Zhou, the heart was believed to be the center of your thoughts and ideas. The passage "其心不快" *(qí xīn bù kuài)* is often translated to "unhappy," suggesting an emotion, which is culturally associated with the heart "心." Yet this passage is reminiscent of the opposite meaning to another phrase, "心直口快" *(xīn zhí kǒu kuài)*, meaning to be outspoken, to be direct with your words so that your speech is an unfiltered reflection of your thoughts.

Continuing on to the fourth line of Hexagram 52:

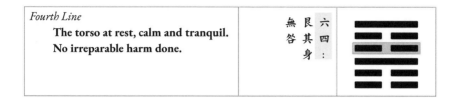

| *Fourth Line* | | |
|---|---|---|
| **The torso at rest, calm and tranquil.** **No irreparable harm done.** | 無 艮 六<br>咎 其 四<br>  身 ：| |

The torso is our anatomical center. It's where the chest is (and where the heart "心" is, a reference back to the second line's message) and where most of our organs are located. The torso also includes our backbone. The solution to diverting the forecast of misfortune in Hexagram 50 is found here in the fourth line of Hexagram 52. Change the path of fate by showing restraint. Even when you are well within your rights to act, hold yourself back. Keep your composure. As noted in the annotations, "If you remain still, calamity will pass you by."

Taking into account the added commentaries for these lines found not just in my annotations to the I Ching, but the commentaries from contemporary scholars of the I Ching, you can begin to formulate your interpretation of the Oracle's message to you. To me, these lines narrate the story of a hero with big ambitions who possesses the strengths needed to achieve those ambitions. But when faced with criticism and opposition, our hero unwisely shoots first and asks questions later. This only intensifies the opposition. In the name of retaliation, you are more than happy to hurt yourself if it means you'll be inflicting hurt on your adversary. This ends badly. Instead, when the criticisms come, show restraint. When you stay calm and don't act at all while your adversary acts badly, you come out looking good and will gain supporters. By increasing your support, you avert the crisis and silence the naysayers.

If you were to adopt a Meaning and Principle approach, then you can't limit your study of the I Ching to this book. You'll need to consider which voices and perspectives on Yì Xué you find authoritative and consider their commentaries when you try to discern meaning. Let's consider the introductory lines to Hexagram 62, Xiao Guo.

The Meaning and Principle proponent will consider etymology and historical meaning. Xiǎo (小) means small, with the ideogram depicting three grains of rice or three grains of sand. This word can indicate someone who is young or a stage of action that is still premature. This is the condition of being physically small in stature or socially lower rank in terms of status. It can mean the minor and that which is lesser in intensity. Guò (過) means to pass. The radical, or the glyph you see on the left, is the pictographic image of a foot walking. The pictographic image atop it to the right suggests a gateway. The word means to pass through a gateway.

In your efforts to interpret Hexagram 62's opening lines, consider how it's been worded in various seminal English translations of the I Ching, provided in table 4.6. Whether you are a Rationalist or an Originalist, applying a Meaning and Principle approach means textual analysis.

My translations of the Zhouyi given here are inescapably filtered through my perspective, culture, and lived experiences. Even if you are culturally Chinese and a native speaker of the language, fully literate, you would still have a difficult time interpreting the text. So every published work of it, even the Zhouyi in Chinese, is effectively a translation, and it represents little more than one author's interpretation of the Book. A Taoist author will interpret the cryptic and often archaic words one way, a Confucianist another, a Buddhist yet a third. An author who maintains that the I Ching is secular and just a work of philosophy will phrase the translations to keep it secular, while my background in occultism and ritual magic means I am not going to shy away from theistic language. There are times when I interpret the Oracle, which often addresses themselves in the first person, as giving the advice of prayer, offerings, ritual, rites, and conveying spirit contacts. I'm convinced that's the original intention of the Oracle, but the current majority view would likely disagree. So it's important to collect multiple texts and use your own perspective, culture, and lived experience to reconcile that diversity of voices. That's how you find meaning.

**TABLE 4.6** Comparison of English Translations of Hexagram 62

| TRANSLATOR | TITLE | OPENING LINES OF HEXAGRAM 62 |
|---|---|---|
| M. A. Canon McClatchie[15] | The Sëaou-Kwo Diagram | The Sëaou-Kwo Diagram prognosticates Luxuriance; profit is derived from the preservation of moral rectitude; small matters may be undertaken but not great ones; the flying bird sends its notes downwards, so, remaining below when it is improper to ascend; bring great good luck. [That is practicing humility. The bird ascends, it is said, to seek a resting place, but the higher it goes, the farther it is from attaining the object of its search.] |
| James Legge[16] | The Hsiao Kwo Hexagram | Hsiao Kwo indicates that (in the circumstances which it implies) there will be progress and attainment. But it will be advantageous to be firm and correct. (What the name denotes) may be done in small affairs, but not in great affairs. (It is like) the notes that come down from a bird on the wing—to descend is better than to ascend. There will (in this way) be great fortune. |
| Richard Wilhelm[17] | Preponderance of the Small | Success.<br>Perseverance furthers. Small things may be done; great things should not be done.<br>The flying bird brings the message:<br>It is not well to strive upward,<br>It is well to remain below.<br>Great good fortune. |
| Aleister Crowley[18] | The Hsiao Kwo Hexagram | Exceeding in small things I've heard to soar too high is risky for the bird. |
| Kerson Huang[19] | Small Excess | Sign of the Sacrifice.<br>Auspicious omen.<br>Attempt the small, not the big.<br>A flying bird leaves a message:<br>Go not high, but low.<br>Great fortune. |
| L. Michael Harrington[20] *Translating Cheng Yi* | Small Excess | There is progress, and profit in purity. There should be a small affair; there should not be a great affair. The sound of the flying bird is distant. It is not fitting to ascend, it is fitting to descend. There is great good fortune. |

**TABLE 4.6** Comparison of English Translations of Hexagram 62 *(continued)*

| TRANSLATOR | TITLE | OPENING LINES OF HEXAGRAM 62 |
|---|---|---|
| Joseph Adler[21] *Translating Zhu Xi* | Small Surpassing | Success; appropriate and correct. One can engage in small matters, but cannot engage in great matters. The flying bird lets go his cry. Not fitting to ascend; fitting to descend: greatly auspicious. |
| Alfred Huang[22] | Xiao Guo— Little Exceeding | The flying bird leaves a message: Not appropriate to ascend, Appropriate to descend. Great good fortune! |
| Thomas Cleary[23] | Predominance of the Small | When the small predominates, it gets through successfully, beneficial if correct. It is sustainable for small matters, but not for great matters. The call left by a flying bird should not rise but descend; that is very auspicious. |
| My translations | Pay Attention to Detail | A bird in flight delivers a message: it is not the proper time to strive upward; instead, strive downward. Seek not from the Heavens, but seek from the Underworld. Great prosperity and fortune if you heed the message. It is not a time for expanding; it is a time for refining. |

# PRACTICUM 4.1:
# Oracle Reading by Comparative Study of Three I Ching Texts

*Applying the Meaning and Principle Interpretive Approach*

Several of the aforementioned English translations of the I Ching are now in the public domain and freely accessible, although those who can should consider adding a few of the other mentioned texts to your home library of I Ching sources. In this exercise, you'll be casting a hexagram, yielding a single hexagram line oracle message, and then consulting this text plus two more for a total of three sources to study.

For this divinatory method, you will be imagining yourself invoking the Lady of the Nine Heavens 九天玄女 (Jiǔ Tiān Xuán Nǚ), and with her divine hand guiding yours, you will "channel" the hexagram. You'll also want to try this exercise at a late hour, preferably between midnight and three a.m.

Have pen and paper ready at hand. If you'd like to be fancy, get out your Chinese calligraphy set and prepare the ink from the inkstone, with the water and your calligraphy brush. As an aside, given the arm form required in Chinese calligraphy and the way you hold the brush, automatic writing, or channeled spirit writing, is a lot easier with a traditional Chinese calligraphy brush than with a modern-day pen.

**FIGURE 4.5** Chinese calligraphy brushes and inkstone set

Begin by lighting incense. Select your personal favorite and the most prized incense you have. Turn off all electrical lighting and then light a candle. You'll want to cast this hexagram by candlelight only. As you light the candle, recite aloud the following:

VENERABLE LADY OF THE NINE HEAVENS, master teacher of the mystic arts, I light this flame in petition for your presence. I seek to be guided by your hand. By your hand taking hold of mine, show me the Way.

If you are new to such methods, you may need to repeat the recitation several more times before you feel the shift. It's perfectly permissible to read the text aloud from your notes, though just like musical performance, it's more powerful when you can recite it from the heart.

The candle flame will flicker in an inordinate way. You will naturally sit up straighter and taller. You suddenly feel more empowered, taking deeper breaths and feeling a surge of confidence.

Detach from any and all knowledge you believe you have of the I Ching, and yield to the mystical experience. Detach from any concentration or thought about what trigrams are being formed from your lines. Do not second-guess yourself. Whatever line, broken or solid, you feel being drawn by your hand as if automatically, let it come.

Upon feeling the shift in consciousness and a powerful, potent, pressured hand taking hold of your own, ask aloud, "What is the first line?" Let that line, be it yin or yang, flow from you. You are not drawing a line; rather, the Lady of the Nine Heavens is moving your hand to draw.

"What is the second line?" you ask. Let that line flow from you, above the first. "Venerable One, what is the third line?" And continue constructing the hexagram from the bottom up until your hand has been guided to draw all six lines.

After the six lines are drawn, acting as compulsively as you can—feeling as if another is in control, driving the movements of your arm—mark one of the six lines as the changing line to read.

When the guided message is complete, on your own you are going to feel an immediate lurch or reversion back to your ordinary self, and that sense of divinity will have left you. You'll know that the divination is complete and the Venerable One has returned to Heaven.

At this time, snuff out the candle and turn on the lights. In this divination exercise, you did not present a specific question to be answered. Rather, you channeled a divine presence and asked to receive a revelation. Consider this revelation of six lines a complete book of six chapters. However, for the time being, you are being guided toward one of those six lines in particular. Table 4.7 shows you the indications for the line you had spontaneously marked during the channeling session.

Consult the oracle passage for the marked line only. Do so first from this text; then seek out two more versions of I Ching translations and take note of the same line in those texts.

**TABLE 4.7** Hexagram Line Designations

|        | SIX CHAPTERS WITH SIX REVELATIONS |
|--------|-----------------------------------|
| Line 6 | Forecast of the long-term future to come |
| Line 5 | Forecast of the short-term future to come |
| Line 4 | Practical advice on the next step to take |
| Line 3 | For seeking clarity when you feel lost |
| Line 2 | How to prepare for the journey ahead |
| Line 1 | For seeking a new direction in life |

To apply a Meaning and Principle interpretive approach, you'll want to consider the moral principle that the living Oracle is imparting to you. There is a double meaning to how the name of the Meaning and Principle tradition is pronounced in Mandarin: Yi Li 義理 is the name of the tradition, "Meaning and Principle," and Yi Li 義理 also means "righteousness" and "reason."

*Yi* 義 means to conduct yourself in a righteous manner that serves a greater collective good, to only fight just wars, and to always be magnanimous in your actions.

*Li* 理 means to cut and refine jade, or to refine your understanding of a principle. The word also means logic, science, and truth-seeking.

Meditate on the value of righteousness the Oracle is conveying to you, and what core logical or rational principle is driving that message.

To demonstrate the Meaning and Principle tradition of interpreting a hexagram, let's consider an example. Using the ritualized channeled approach and invoking the Lady of the Nine Heavens, the result is Hexagram 10, Lu.

I've translated the fourth line of Hexagram 10 as follows:

| | |
|---|---|
| *Fourth Line*<br>**Treading on the tiger's tail. Remain cautious. Show resolve. A purpose fulfilled. The mission is a success.** | 九四：履虎尾愬愬終吉 |

The hexagram I channeled was Heaven over Lake, and I was pulled to mark line 4. This suggests to me that Divinity is a bit fearful that my next step could be a misstep, so it's warning me to be careful and more alert than usual, because I've treaded dangerously close to the "tiger's tail." Hence, the spirit guide pushed me toward line 4 to give me practical advice on next steps and the immediate course of action to take.

For this exercise, you'll now want to consult two more versions of interpretation for your chosen line. Here are Wilhelm's and K. Huang's:

| | Hexagram 10, Line 4 (Yang) |
|---|---|
| Richard Wilhelm | He treads on the tail of the tiger.<br>Caution and circumspection lead ultimately to good fortune. |
| Kerson Huang | Treading on the tiger's tail: Fearful situation.<br>All ends well. |

After reading your selected line, cast a transformed hexagram. To do so, return to the line you marked. If it was a yang line, change it to yin. If it was a yin line, change it to yang. Then look up what this new transformed hexagram is.

In my case, line 4 was a yang line, so I changed it to a yin. The result was as follows:

| | | | |
|---|---|---|---|
| Line 6 | ▬▬▬ | | ▬▬▬ |
| Line 5 | ▬▬▬ | ▶ | ▬▬▬ |
| Line 4 | ▬▬▬ | | ▬▬ ▬▬ |

| | | | |
|---|---|---|---|
| Line 3 | ▬▬ ▬▬ | | ▬▬ ▬▬ |
| Line 2 | ▬▬▬▬▬ | | ▬▬▬▬▬ |
| Line 1 | ▬▬▬▬▬ | | ▬▬▬▬▬ |
| | 10 | | 61 |

My previous upper trigram of Heaven is now changed to Wind. Instead of the previous Heaven over Lake, now it's Wind over Lake. Wind over Lake is Hexagram 61. I now look up line 4 (the marked line, which identifies the changing line) for Hexagram 61.

| | |
|---|---|
| *Fourth Line*<br>A waxing moon is near full. A herd of horses perish. There is no blame. | 六四：月幾望 馬匹亡 終吉 無咎 |

For fun, this time around I've consulted two different translators for the changed hexagram line. Since I'm most familiar with K. Huang's translations, I've included that as a third for continuity of reference.

| Hexagram 61, Line 4 (Yin) | |
|---|---|
| L. Michael Harrington | The moon is almost full. The horse's mate vanishes. There is no blame. |
| Thomas Cleary | With the moon almost full, the loss of teammates is not blamed. (The loss of teammates means parting with peers to rise higher.) |
| Kerson Huang | After the full moon, horses go astray. No fault. |

I interpret the changed fourth line as a forecast. Since the changed line 4 yields a rather specific reference to the moon phase, I will take a look at my calendar to see the timing of the next full moon. From the date that the divination took place, it will be in less than two weeks' time, and I happened to have done the reading close to the new moon. A mystic is going to read this as prophetic, and therefore in two weeks' time, a "herd of horses" could perish, but because this is a changing line, the phase of change has not yet completed. I still have time to turn this around and prevent the "herd of horses" from perishing before the next full moon.

Now take some time to consider the moral of the story the Oracle has told, and the core principle or reasoning of that moral. That is, apply a Meaning and Principle approach to understanding the hexagram. In my example, Hexagram 10 warns: do not unnecessarily provoke sleeping tigers just to appease your ego or pride. Hexagram 61 advises not to rush judgment of another before you've diligently considered all factors and perspectives. Keep your heart-mind open. Your reactions to another's transgression should always be responsive, not reactionary. The core principle here is: if you're going to put yourself at risk and in harm's way, then make sure you're doing so to fulfill a profound purpose, and not just to assuage a bruised ego.

In your reading, feel free to wander and read the oracular message for any line you like in your channeled divinatory result, any Oracle or Judgment for either of the two hexagrams. Consider the totality of the result as a complete book of revelation you've received, with each segment representative of a chapter or subthought. The totality of the result is a world map, and you are free to visit any province on that map.

In this reading example, I've opted to take the route from the primary hexagram's fourth line to the transformed hexagram's fourth line, but after following the exercise for the purposes of working with multiple perspectives, feel free to wander at will. Table 4.7 is like your tourist pamphlet to let you know what's located at each of the local regions. From there, choose which regions you'd like to visit and which specific revelatory insight you'd like to receive.

The channeled approach you've just worked through is in line with the Plum Blossom method circa AD 1011–1077.

# The Plum Blossom Methods

Shao Yong 邵雍 (AD 1011–1077), one of the five great Confucian scholars of the Northern Song period,[24] is credited with devising a method of divination with the I Ching that integrates numerology and Ba Zi cosmological astrology. Shao Yong's original text (梅花易數, *Méihuā yì shù*) relied on mathematics, applying many of the techniques from the Image and Number tradition.[25]

What distinguished him from his Confucian contemporaries was a well-documented ability he possessed that was widely acknowledged among his literati peers: Shao Yong seemed to have the gift of foreknowledge. He could use the I Ching to predict the future, with remarkable accuracy. Beyond moral self-cultivation with the I Ching, which at the time was considered the more refined approach to Yì Xué, Shao seemed to wield the types of powers more common among shamans and mediums.[26]

The school of divination methods arising from Shao Yong's work is referred to as Mei Hua Yi (梅花易), or Plum Blossom I Ching. Plum Blossom methods were popularized during the Song dynasty, inspired by and endeavoring to reconstruct mathematics-oriented divination methods from the *Han yi* 漢易, a collection of texts dated to the Western Han (202 BC–AD 9). Several different methodologies are referred to as Plum Blossom methods, ranging from mathematical calculations that require long division to free-flowing channeled intuitive methods.

The methods are united by their reliance on an established order of numerological associations for the Ba Gua trigrams and the Wu Xing five phases. Those numerological associations are set forth in table 4.8 and table 4.9 respectively. These numerical order assignments predate Shao Yong's time by centuries, though they became more cohesively systemized under the Plum Blossom methods of divination.

**TABLE 4.8** Numerical Assignments for the Eight Trigrams

| 一 1 | 二 2 | 三 3 | 四 4 | 五 5 | 六 6 | 七 7 | 八 8 |
|---|---|---|---|---|---|---|---|
| 乾 Qián Heaven | 兌 Duì Lake | 離 Lí Fire | 震 Zhèn Tthunder | 巽 Xùn Wind | 坎 Kǎn Water | 艮 Gěn Mountain | 坤 Kūn Earth |

**TABLE 4.9** Numerical Assignments for the Five Phases of Change

| 一 1 | 二 2 | 三 3 | 四 4 | 五 5 |
|---|---|---|---|---|
| 水 Shuǐ Water | 火 Huǒ Fire | 木 Mù Wood | 金 Jīn Metal | 土 Tǔ Earth |

Table 4.10 shows a popular approach to rendering the eight trigrams, which you'll find among native I Ching practitioners in East Asia. I've found this to be prevalent among contemporary practitioners in Taiwan, for instance. The figures more clearly delineate the functions of yin and yang. Thunder, per these figures, is the image of an upright teacup, receiving from beyond; while Mountain, in contrast, is the image of a reversed teacup, more stable in its positioning than the teacup upright and signifying a teacup not in use.

Note the ninth column (九, 9) with the symbol of the Taiji (太極), a key cosmological concept that Shao Yong emphasized. Under Plum Blossom, the ninth Gua (卦) can be added to the Ba Gua to designate the reunification of all eight trigrams and the return to the Tao. The ninth Gua as a binary reminds us that what appears as a trinity is inherently a binary, and what appears as a binary is inherently a trinity.

Another key principle of the Plum Blossom methods is use of the lunar calendar over the Gregorian calendar. This divination method integrates numerology, often working with the numerology of calendar dates, but those dates need to be converted from the Gregorian calendar currently in use to the sexagenary or sixty-year lunar calendar.

**TABLE 4.10** Written Figures Designating Yin and Yang Lines of the Trigrams

| 一 | 1 | 二 | 2 | 三 | 3 | 四 | 4 | 五 | 5 |
|---|---|---|---|---|---|---|---|---|---|
| ☰ | | ☱ | | ☲ | | ☳ | | ☴ | |
| 乾 Qián Heaven | | 兌 Duì Lake | | 離 Lí Fire | | 震 Zhèn Thunder | | 巽 Xùn Wind | |
| 六 | 6 | 七 | 7 | 八 | 8 | 九 | 9 | | |
| ☵ | | ☶ | | ☷ | | ☯ | | | |
| 坎 Kǎn Water | | 艮 Gěn Mountain | | 坤 Kūn Earth | | 太極 無極 八卦 | | | |

The sexagenary calendar, which is observed in China, Vietnam, Korea, and Japan, is based on ten heavenly stems and twelve earthly branches that cycle through the five changing phases. The twelve earthly branches correspond with the twelve zodiac signs, or constellations. A system of combinations of stems and branches results in a total of sixty terms that repeat as sixty-year cycles.

**FIGURE 4.6** The sexagenary cycle

Plum Blossom methods of uniting numerology and the I Ching are premised on the philosophy that every movement in the cosmos produces a sound that has a pitch. Every pitch can be expressed through mathematical ratios. Thus, all human experiences can be reduced to mathematics in ratios.

Shao Yong then proposed that the universe operated in orders of three ($n = 3$) or ternary operations, whereby any self-contained set of elements in this universe—*everything*—consisted fundamentally of three elements combined. In other words, the eight trigrams. Even the celestial bodies in the skies produced pitches of sound, noted Shao Yong. This is reminiscent of the Pythagorean expression of the harmony of the spheres, further refined by Johannes Kepler as the principle of *musical universalis*.[27]

The movements of celestial bodies, having sounds that can be mathematically expressed by numbers, can therefore be calculated by way of numbers, and one method of determining those numbers and reading the movements of the celestial bodies was through the I Ching hexagrams, which are based on ternary operations, or orders of three.

Per Shao Yong's philosophy, the myriad things (萬物 *wànwù*) are determined by numbers and archetypes that predate the Taiji (太極), meaning numbers and archetypes that predate the Creation of the universe.

Even before the Tao split itself to produce Heaven and Earth, there were numbers and archetypes. The archetypes are the sixty-four hexagrams. These numbers and archetypes carry on in humanity's heart (心, *xīn*). The Chinese of antiquity believed that thoughts, logic, reasoning, and calculations came from the heart, or what's often designated as the heart-mind.[28]

An unconscious understanding of divine truths lay buried deep within every human's heart-mind, a residue left over from pre-Creation times, and we reconnect with that understanding through numbers and archetypes. This focus on innate knowledge of pre-Creation times deep within the human heart-mind leads the Plum Blossom school to work primarily with the Fuxi's Early Heaven Ba Gua rather than the more popular King Wen's Later Heaven Ba Gua.

**TABLE 4.11** The Plum Blossom Ba Gua, Following Fuxi's Early Heaven Ba Gua

| 2. Lake | 1. Heaven | 5. Wind |
|---|---|---|
| 3. Fire | | 6. Water |
| 4. Thunder | 8. Earth | 7. Mountain |

Shao Yong devised a system of mathematical operations and numerology for divining those orders of thee and interpreting what those orders signify through the Book of Changes. The work that Gottfried Wilhelm von Leibniz (1646–1716) did with the I Ching was based on Shao Yong's writings.

In many ways, Shao Yong's theories read like a precursor to Carl Jung's. In writing about the correlation of events, Shao wrote that something happening in the universe, for instance, is detected and mimicked through micromotions upon your hand; and if you can learn to read the signs of those micromotions upon your hand, you can know the unknowable about the universe.

The concept of cyclical patterns of the Tao was a great point of emphasis for Shao Yong. These cyclical patterns were what reconciled space, time, numerology, and astrology, all of which he believed was accounted for in the sixty-four hexagrams. Per Shao Yong, time can be categorized into nine periods. The ancient word *fen*, though translated to "minute," was closer to the equivalent of four of our current minutes. *Chen*, the ascendant hour, is an astrological measure of approximately two hours.

**TABLE 4.12** Shao Yong's Nine Categories of Time

| 1. | 分 | *Fēn*  | 4-minute unit   | 129,600 *fen* in 1 year |
|----|---|--------|-----------------|--------------------------|
| 2. | 辰 | *Chén* | Ascendant hour  | 4,320 *chen* in 1 year   |
| 3. | 日 | *Rì*   | Solar day       | 360 days in 1 year       |
| 4. | 月 | *Yuè*  | Lunar month     | 12 months in 1 year      |
| 5. | 年 | *Nián* | Year            |                          |
| 6. | 世 | *Shì*  | Generation      | 30 years                 |
| 7. | 運 | *Yùn*  | Revolution      | 12 generations, 360 years |
| 8. | 會 | *Huì*  | Epoch           | 30 revolutions, 360 generations, 10,800 years |
| 9. | 元 | *Yuán* | Cycle           | 12 epochs, 360 revolutions, 4,320 generations, 129,600 years |

Every 360 years, humanity will undergo a revolution that overturns the status quo. At any given point in time, 360 years prior to your current year was the year geopolitical events set a causal wave rippling into the current year's resulting events. What is occurring in the current year sets a causal wave rippling into the future by 360 years. Moreover, after a revolution (time unit 7 in table 4.12), everything that transpires over the next 360 years will conclude, cease, and reset itself before the next revolution, similar to how every day resets itself sunrise to sunset to sunrise again.

Astrology is premised on these theories of cycles. Everyone sharing the same ascendant hour, for example, will inherit certain traits characteristic of that ascendant sign, simply by reason of having been born at that hour. Everyone born in the same lunar month will inherit certain traits characteristic of the signs or terms associated with that month. Likewise with every zodiac year. Taken in combination and assessed by an astrologer who knows how to balance the measures of traits, one's personality and most likely life path can be ascertained.

Shao Yong believed that humanity was in its seventh epoch, which he prophesied in the eleventh century. The seventh epoch began after the Great Flood wiped out the previous form of humanity from earth and Nǔwā had to create new humans. At the conclusion of this 129,600-year period, humanity as we know it will end, and a new cycle of life will begin, without us.

Shao Yong's ideas were likely borrowed from Buddhism, which espouses the concept of *kalpas,* world cycles. A *kalpa* is a span of 4.32 billion years.

While the cyclical patterns of the Tao are not generally perceivable through our five physical senses, our heart-mind—that sixth sense—can calculate the Tao through the numbers of the Tao. Thus, Shao's approach to hexagram interpretation, and the Plum Blossom school of thought that modeled itself after his work, focus heavily on mathematics and the numerical implications of cycles.

Chapter 7 will cover several of the divinatory methods from the Plum Blossom school.

## PRACTICUM 4.2:
## Bibliomancy and Plum Blossom Numerology

Focus on the question you'd like the Oracle to answer through a form of bibliomancy and Plum Blossom numerology. Close your eyes and continue to stay focused on the inquiry. With your eyes still closed, turn to a random page in this book, with a general intention to select a page number over 100. Anchor your pointing finger onto the selected page. Open your eyes to see the page number.

Divide the page number by 8. Note the remainder. (The quotient is the number of times the dividend can be evenly divided by the divisor. The remainder is the amount left over in the dividend that does not divide evenly into the divisor.)

To demonstrate with an example, I closed my eyes and opened this book to a random page, and placed my index finger onto page 222. That number, 222, is the dividend. I divide that number by 8, which is the divisor.

$$222 \div 8$$

The long division results in a quotient of 27—the dividend 222 can be evenly divided into the divisor 8 a total of 27 times—and a remainder of 6.

Your remainder is the numerical assignment of a trigram per table 4.9. This is the lower trigram. In the example of a remainder of 6, the number 6 is assigned to the trigram Water. The resulting trigram from the bibliomancy exercise is Water. Had the page number divided evenly into 8, your trigram result would be 8, which is assigned to Earth.

Close this book again, close your eyes, focus on the question, and open the book and anchor your pointing finger to a page. Note the page number. Again, divide the page number by 8 and note the remainder. The numerical assignment, which will be somewhere in 1 through 8, is the resulting hexagram. If your page number divides evenly into 8, then the numerical assignment is 8, and the trigram result is Earth.

In my reading, the second time I opened to a random page, the page number was 140.

$$140 \div 8 = 17 \text{ with a remainder of } 4.$$

The remainder from the long division of 140 divided by 8 is 4. (The quotient is 17.) Per table 4.9, the number 4 corresponds with Thunder. The upper trigram of my hexagram result is Thunder.

The resulting hexagram is Thunder over Water, or Hexagram 40.

Close the book a third time, open to a random page, and for the third and final time, note the page number. However, for this third page number, divide by 6 to yield the changing line.

For my example, I turned to page 214 the third time. I divide that page number by 6 and note the remainder. If the page number divides evenly into 6, then the changing line is line 6.

$$214 \div 6 = 35 \text{ with a remainder of } 4.$$

The remainder from $214 \div 6$ is 4. (The quotient is 35.) Thus, after reading the "Oracle" section of Hexagram 40, I'll turn and read the text for the fourth line.

# PRACTICUM 4.3:
## Divining the Wu Xing Ruler of a Book

As a fun exercise with numerology, note the total page count of any book from your home bookshelf. For this exercise, do not count unnumbered pages. Thus, turn to the back of the book and look for the final printed page count in that text.

Divide that last printed page count by 5. Note the remainder. If the page count divides evenly into 5, then the numerical assignment is 5, and the corresponding Wu Xing or ruling agent of change that governs the book is Earth.

The numerical assignments for the Five Phases of Change, or ruling agents of changing, are provided in table 4.9.

My book *The Tao of Craft* shows a total page count of 586, not counting unnumbered pages. $586 \div 5 = 117$ with a remainder of 1. Per table 4.9, the numerical assignment of the value 1 is the phase change Water. Thus, the *Tao of Craft* is governed by the Wu Xing agent of change Water. Turn in chapter 6 to the section "Water (Shuǐ): Reflecting and Returning" to consider the corresponding characteristics of the book. Water is the Abyss, which characterizes the book's esoteric and occult topics. The virtue it seeks to impart, per Wu Xing correspondences, is wisdom.

Funnily enough, the phrase "be like water" or "上善若水 *(shàng shàn ruò shuǐ)*" from chapter 8 of the Tao Te Ching is often used to express the whole of the Tao: supreme beneficence is to be like water. Water benefits all things without trying to benefit all things; it dwells in a way that is loathed and unwanted, and thus Water is the perfect exemplification of the Tao.

My book *Holistic Tarot* shows a printed last page count of 874. $874 \div 5$ equals a quotient of 174 and a remainder of 4. The number 4 corresponds with the Wu Xing phase of change Metal. Thus, per this divinatory exercise, *Holistic Tarot* is governed by Metal. Metal corresponds with logic, reason, and more analytic methods. Per Wu Xing correspondences for Metal, the virtue that *Holistic Tarot* tries to impart is incorruptibility. Some of its negative traits are being cold, aloof, or insensitive, though in the positive, it's cerebral and urbane. In terms of state function per Dong Zhongshu (179–104 BC), Metal corresponds with the Minister of Education, which resonates with *Holistic Tarot*'s intent of being a reference manual.

Try this numerology and bibliomancy exercise on several books, determining their ruling phase change per the Wu Xing, and consider the metaphysical implications such an exercise reveals about those books. Turn to chapter 6 and scan the metaphysical correspondences for each Wu Xing phase to see what resonates and what general insights you can gain about the soul of that book based on its Wu Xing ruler.

After running this exercise on several books from your shelf, you'll have gained proficiency with the Plum Blossom numerology method.

# PRACTICUM 4.4:
# Applying a Buddhist Interpretation to an I Ching Reading

**FIGURE 4.7** Depiction of the Mahayana Buddhist Pure Land. Qing dynasty (1636–1912).

Ouyi Zhi-xu 蕅益智旭 (1599–1655), one of the four great Buddhist masters of the Ming dynasty, was an I Ching scholar who applied Pure Land Mahayana Buddhism to I Ching interpretation.[29] We'll be exploring the field of a hexagram (i.e., the implications of each of the six lines, one by one) through a Mahayana Buddhist perspective to impart the thematic wisdom of that hexagram.

The method of divination for this practicum will be an adaptation of the Rice Grains Method, which will be covered in chapter 7. You'll need about a bowl full of uncooked rice grains or small dry beans, such as mung (or green) beans, lentils, peas, or adzuki red beans. Dry, uncooked quinoa would also work. You will also need a clean spoon.

An optional initiating step is to press your palms together in a prayer mudra and, per Mahayana tradition, recite Amitofuo 阿彌陀佛 once before proceeding with the divination. (The Korean equivalent is Amitabul 아미타불; Amidabutsu あみだぶつ in Japanese; and A Di Đà Phật in Vietnamese.)

To start, scoop up a spoonful of the uncooked grains or beans. As you do so, focus on the question you're seeking an answer to, and seek insight that will facilitate your success and yet keep you aligned with your spiritual path.

Count the number of grains or beans in that spoonful.

Divide that total count by 8.

Sharing my own reading to demonstrate, before commencing the divination, I recited the sacred name Amitofuo and asked for divine insight on how best to navigate my career path at this particular juncture of my life.

I started with about half a teacup full of dried, uncooked mung beans, and I used a regular kitchen spoon. My first spoonful yielded 221 beans.

If your total count divides evenly into 8 with no remainder, then your lower trigram assignment is 8, Earth. Otherwise, after the long division, note the remainder, which should be a value between 1 and 8. The remainder number will correspond with one of the eight trigrams, as follows:

| 1 | 2 | 3 | 4 | 5 | 6 | 7 | 8 |
|---|---|---|---|---|---|---|---|
| Qián | Duì | Lí | Zhèn | Xùn | Kǎn | Gěn | Kūn |
| Heaven | Lake | Fire | Thunder | Wind | Water | Mountain | Earth |

For my reading, 221 ÷ 8 equals a quotient of 27 and a remainder of 5. The trigram assigned to the number 5 is Wind, which is my lower trigram result.

|  |  | **HEXAGRAM** |
|---|---|---|
| Upper trigram (*second count*) | Line 6 |  |
|  | Line 5 |  |
|  | Line 4 |  |
| Lower trigram (*first count*) | Line 3 |  |
|  | Line 2 |  |
|  | Line 1 |  |

Set that spoonful of counted grains aside. Scoop up another spoonful of grains and proceed with the counting process again. Divide the total count of this second spoonful by 8. Again, if the total count divides evenly, then your upper trigram is Earth. Otherwise, note the remainder number's trigram correspondence.

For my own reading, the second spoonful's total count was 133 beans. 133 ÷ 8 equals a quotient of 16 and a remainder of 5 again, so again my trigram result is Wind. Wind over Wind is Hexagram 57.

|  | HEXAGRAM | |
|---|---|---|
| Upper trigram (*second count*) | Line 6 | |
| | Line 5 | |
| | Line 4 | |
| Lower trigram (*first count*) | Line 3 | |
| | Line 2 | |
| | Line 1 | |

Read the "Oracle" section of your hexagram result. This is the Oracle's response to your question, expressed so as to impart the advice and insight you need.

Table 4.13 summarizes the Buddhist narrative arc of the hexagram lines. In this exercise, we'll be applying a Buddhist interpretation to an I Ching reading. Each line of a hexagram reveals one key principle in Buddhist spirituality, and the six lines linked together form a narrative arc of the Buddhist's path.

The divination method selected for this exercise yields a locked hexagram with no changing lines. Thus, we are going to read all six lines as a narrative arc, a field for us to scry into, explore, and navigate.

**TABLE 4.13** Buddhist Interpretation of the Hexagram Lines Narrative

| Line 6 | **Insight: Realize the true nature of a thing; discernment and mental clarity. Seeking the inner character or underlying truth.** The transformation that occurs during or after achieving realization; lesson learned or wisdom attained. After realization comes the release of all prior tensions. To shed intellectual or spiritual light upon the matter at hand. Enlightenment. Achieving pure and unqualified knowledge. |
|---|---|
| Line 5 | **Results of the process; realization.** Achieving realization; greater comprehension; deeper understanding of the situation at hand and its implications. This is causing what had been conceptualized, designed, or planned to become materialized. The results of your process. Coming into perceptible existence; appearing. That which had been ideal becomes corporeal. |

**TABLE 4.13** Buddhist Interpretation of the Hexagram Lines Narrative *(continued)*

| Line 4 | Show fortitude. Catalyst and first light of realization; effects of the action initiated; thematic energy of the situation at hand; vibrational frequency of the situation. If you are assured that your purpose is righteous, your plan is rationale and reasonable, and you have shown virtuous dedication, then at this time be resolved and confident. Do not let anyone challenge your strength or cause your conviction to waver. Show that your position is defensible. |
|---|---|
| Line 3 | Be persistent and resilient; persevere. Meditation on ideal or potential, initiation of action; developing a process for negotiating and navigating the situation at hand. Execution is always harder than planning; this is the arduous path of walking what has been mapped out. The destination is always a little farther than we think it is. Be patient with yourself, and with the process. |
| Line 2 | Be disciplined in your methods. Intellectual understanding of ideal or potential; establishing a strategic plan for self-discipline. Focus on the plan of action. Think through exactly what needs to be done before you do anything. |
| Line 1 | Exemplify beneficence. Ideal or potential; formulating a conception or set of standards to apply to the situation at hand; setting or fine-tuning intentions; defining purpose. Know your purpose before you start the journey. |

Begin with the bottommost line, line 1. Read the first line of your hexagram entry. Reading the I Ching through a Buddhist lens, line 1 of the hexagram always imparts moral or ethical instructions. What is the moral or ethical instruction the Oracle is conveying to you at this time, to help you navigate your situation? Take a moment to free-write in a journal and reflect on the message.

Line 2 of the hexagram gives you practical advice. This is an actionable next step to get you where you want to go with regard to the matter inquired about. Read the second line of your hexagram entry and take note of what constructive prescription is being offered. Consider what you can do immediately following this divination to move toward success and achievement of your objective.

Line 3 offers prophetic advice on some of the challenges (or good auspices) along the current path in the long term. This is what to expect or what could come your way. These are future possibilities assessed by the Oracle at this time based on your present accounting of karma. Line 3 is often a premonition of a reckoning, the effect that comes after events you've caused, regardless of your intentionality.

Line 4 forecasts what comes after the events prognosticated in line 3, continuing the calculation and accounting of karmic factors at play. This line can also offer spiritual advice on how to change those karmic factors and thus change the course of fate. Pay attention to whether your fourth line tells you to stay the course (and how to stay the course) or change course.

Line 5 is climactic. Meditate on the divinatory message given here. Be patient and take your time reflecting on what the Oracle wants you to realize about the situation you've inquired about. The fifth line is the key to fully understanding the situation, why it's happening, what's happening, and how to be fully empowered so that you navigate it with success. However cryptic the message may initially seem, motivate yourself to analytically and intuitively process it.

Finally, Line 6 is interpreted as spiritual wisdom that the Oracle seeks to convey to you, a greater universal message about the life lesson to learn here. Here, there's also a reminder of impermanence, that life is a continual cycle of peaks and troughs.

To conclude the reading, I clasp my hands in a prayer mudra and recite Amitofuo in closing. Alternatively, you can simply clasp your hands in gratitude and whisper a heartfelt thanks to the universe for sharing these words of wisdom.

## General Insights, One Fortune-Teller to Another

"I'm not a fortune-teller!" I grit my teeth and grumble in protest, shaking my fists under the table.

I'm at a dinner get-together with Mom and her friends, whom I call aunties. Mom just told the aunties, "Ask my daughter—she can answer that for you. She's a fortune-teller."

I don't perceive what I do as fortune-telling, and at every turn, I'll disclaim the title of fortune-teller. Maybe what I think doesn't matter; nevertheless, for my own sake, I draw a distinction between divination and fortune-telling.

Divination is subservience to a higher power, acknowledgement of and reverence for that higher power, with the intention that the prognostication to follow is limited by what the Divine, in its profound wisdom, will grant me to know at this time. Divination assumes there is a higher power and I am nothing more than a vessel in receipt of that wisdom. I must embody Hexagram 2, the sacred receptive power, to become such a vessel. And like the cauldron of Hexagram 50, that vessel needs to be properly maintained and kept clean.

Fortune-telling is psychic ability and does not require acknowledgement of or reverence for a higher power. It's secular. Prognostications by fortune-telling are only limited by the fortune-teller's abilities. Other than that, there are no guardrails in place for how much foreknowledge can be attained. Accurate fortune-telling is entirely dependent on personal ability. The fortune-teller embodies Hexagram 1, the sacred directive power, to project into the numinous void of the Tao and retrieve the exact fiber of knowledge being sought.

Mediumship and channeling fall somewhere in between. Divination and fortune-telling are methods of assessing *qi* and interpreting the results, though fortune-telling presumes that you're the calculator, while divination invokes divinity to provide the calculation for you. In mediumship and channeling, a third-party spirit force is called upon and asked what it might know. It's a conversation with that spirit.

As a tool for divination, fortune-telling, or spirit contacts, the Book of Changes proves itself to be one of the most reliable providers of foreknowledge and answers, although it presents as a living oracle, with a fully formed personality, and thus will often make you work for it. If metaphors are difficult for you, then interpreting the I Ching is going to be a challenge. If, however, you've got a gift for metaphors, then the Book will be your playground.

The more interactions you have with the Book, the deeper the relationship develops, and the more distinct a voice of the Oracle emerges. Those who have developed a working relationship with the Oracle often comment that the I Ching seems to have a very distinct personality. The Oracle can be a little too blunt for comfort, and at times can even resort to name-calling. However, I find that when the Oracle takes a curt tone with me, it is exactly what was needed at the time to kick me in the right direction.

If the Oracle knows you can take it, then truth comes as a bitter pill. And yet in the great mystery, just when you need comfort and have no one else to lean on, the Oracle softens and is there to nurture you. Even a Western occultist like Aleister Crowley credits the I Ching as having a steady, reliable, and beneficent voice, which he didn't attribute to the tarot.

Truly, the living Oracle will only support your highest purpose. The sentience operating the voice of the Book has a vested interest in your success and spiritual cultivation. Its methods for achieving that, however, may come across as a bit too brusque.

I've even found that the Oracle will take on a different tone for different individuals. This became especially noticeable when I offered professional I Ching readings. For the more sensitive and vulnerable, the Oracle is gentle; when there is greatness needing to be forged, the Oracle will push and challenge you to refine that greatness. The Oracle won't sugarcoat and won't speak to you in euphemisms.

Rather, what is of note is how the Oracle speaks in metaphor. Parables, figures of speech, allusions, and symbolism speak to the truths in your life. "Marrying the maiden as a concubine" does not literally mean that someone in your life who can be described as a maiden will be a concubine. Especially in the modern context, the two designations are more likely metaphorical designations of your inner self, entirely unrelated to gender.

When "bird in flight meets with misfortune" comes up, reflect on who or what is being represented by that bird. "A fox's tail gets wet," as pithy and vague as the statement may be, is a forecast of what's to come. To decipher it, you'll need to figure out who or what is represented by the fox, what anatomical aspect of that who or what is represented by the tail, and where that moisture or the metaphysical implications of water are coming from.

Furthermore, consider the line position and what's ruling that line position in the hexagram. All of that is then filtered through those preliminary statements, which this book will refer to as "the Oracle." The trigram formed from that line is telling. Look up the metaphysical correspondences for that trigram. Line 1 is closer in time to your point of reference, and line 6 is further away in time.

Hexagram 47 narrates different facets of oppression. I have known line 2 to come up to indicate a substance use disorder. Line 3 of Hexagram 52 predicted a miscarriage. Curiously, line 3 of Hexagram 33 came up often in 2020 and 2021 during the global shutdowns and quarantines for the COVID-19 pandemic.

You can present any sort of question for divination, but how you approach interpretation of the hexagram will determine whether you can make sense of the result. I've asked silly questions before, such as, "What should we eat for dinner tonight?" I asked this question just the other day, using a method that yields a single hexagram (no changing lines). I got Hexagram 3, which I interpreted as going vegetarian for dinner. Read through Hexagram 3's line statements and consider the Wu Xing correspondences to see how I arrived at that conclusion.

When a divinatory result doesn't make sense, before you give up, consider the trigram and Wu Xing correspondences for the hexagram result. For instance, for the line statement "a fox's tail gets wet," to help you decipher that divinatory message, look to the trigram that the line is part of. Turn to chapter 5 and then to chapter 6 and create bullet-point lists of correspondences for the trigram and its corresponding phase.

| TRIGRAM: FIRE (LÍ) | | PHASE: FIRE (HUǑ) | |
|---|---|---|---|
| • South<br>• New moon<br>• Logical reasoning<br>• Applied sciences | • Technical know-how<br>• Prepare to travel soon<br>• Fast tempo<br>• Higher pitch | • Summer<br>• Heat<br>• Heart<br>• Small intestines<br>• Nervous system | • Cardiovascular<br>• Circulatory<br>• Lipids<br>• Blood vessels |

Combine deductive and inductive reasoning with intuition. Scry into the bullet-point lists. What spontaneous realizations come to you? Conceptualize these correspondences as trigger points that can cause a reflex in your psychic muscles.

Hexagrams are but binary codes for certain characterizations of $qi$ in this universe. They are not confined to the received text in any literal sense. As we discussed in the previous chapter, whether you place more emphasis on the received text (as translated here into English) or more emphasis on the correspondences and essential $qi$ of the hexagram lines is a matter of interpretative approach.

To demonstrate, let's look at a love forecast reading. As you'll find happening in your own readings, the hexagram result is topical. In the case of a love forecast reading, Hexagram 31, one of the four hexagrams that directly address love and civil unions, was the primary hexagram. It changed into the transformed Hexagram 38, and coincidentally the inquirer was born in the year of the Rooster, corresponding with Hexagram 38's lower trigram Lake. Looking at the upper trigram Fire, the Rooster is going to be pairing up with a Horse. It's one of those relationships where opposites attract, and that will be both what they love most about each other, and what fuels most of the couple's arguments.

When you see Fire pushing into Earth in Hexagram 36 in a reading about the geopolitical tensions between two countries, it predicts war brought on by self-serving leaders. The nation represented by Earth is acting in response to the actions of the nation represented by Fire, because per the alchemical principles of Wu Xing, Fire creates Earth.

The subtext of Hexagram 4 offers food for thought to the mystic: as I read it, psychics, mediums, witches, shamans, and magi are not born, they're made. We have to first prove ourselves worthy, and then we get tapped to initiate and train. Though an even more profound question is raised: is there any meaningful difference between fate and free will, nature versus nurture?

Hexagram 56 in modernity tells the story of immigrants and refugees. It also tells the story of one who feels like an outsider within a social group. Hexagram 6 talks about a legal or civil dispute. In a health reading, it might be telling you that two different parts of your body seem to be at war with each other. The Eminent One can mean retaining legal counsel or getting a referral to a specialty physician. Hexagram 47 in a career reading could signify barriers to entry that need to be overcome. In a love and romance reading, it's probably a sign for you to reevaluate the relationship.

The Oracle statements often read like riddles. Take, for instance, the fourth line of Hexagram 29. While an argument can be made to take it literally and set out some offerings of food and wine for the gods or ancestors, more likely it's intended as a riddle. With a rare first-person reference, the line sure gives the impression of Spirit challenging you to solve the riddle.

Most important of all, ask and answer this question: "What is the Oracle really trying to tell me?"

Be patient. It's okay if the meaning isn't clear to you immediately. The Book of Changes is a method of spiritual cultivation. Working with it refines your wisdom.

Every line represents multiple layers of meaning. The Oracle expects you to work for the answer. The purpose is to give you just enough, then compel you to achieve the realizations on your own. When someone spells out sage advice and simply tells you what to do, you're less likely to listen. When you believe you've come up with the idea all on your own, you're far more motivated to take action on your own idea.

The Book will only ever help you to help yourself.

## Cultivating Objective Interpretation

The historical account conveyed in the fifth line of Hexagram 11 is instructive on the importance of being impartial and farsighted. When we fail to be objective, we risk grave misinterpretation of the Oracle.

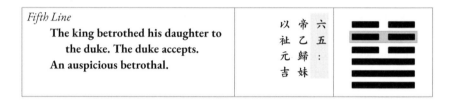

*Fifth Line*
**The king betrothed his daughter to the duke. The duke accepts. An auspicious betrothal.**

The king referenced in the fifth line is Emperor Di Yi of the Shang dynasty, father to the corrupt last emperor of Shang. Tensions between the kingdoms of Shang and Zhou were growing. Emperor Di Yi, in his wisdom and hope for peace, betrothed his beloved daughter to a Duke of Zhou in hopes that doing so would nurture good faith between the rival kingdoms.

That duke was a prince who would later become known as King Wen. That beloved daughter was Tai Si. Tai Si is of the Shang clan, though after the wedding, she'd join the Zhou. Her roots are still Shang.

Imagine, if you will, Emperor Di Yi consulting the I Ching, asking whether the marriage of Tai Si to this Duke of Zhou will be favorable. Remember that his sole purpose for marrying his precious Tai Si off to Zhou is to ensure peace and keep war from breaking out.

First lesson: the phrasing of your question matters, and it matters a lot. If you want to ensure a coherent response, then devote a great deal of thought to how you phrase your question.

Next, imagine that the Oracle's response to the emperor's inquiry is this fifth line. Di Yi would probably assume that the betrothal will appease Zhou and avert war between the kingdoms. It wouldn't be a stretch to assume that the Oracle is confirming that the marriage will successfully broker peace. He would probably interpret the augury of "auspicious" as favorable to the Shang. Partially true to Di Yi's hopes, there is no war between Shang and Zhou for the remainder of his lifetime.

However, after Di Yi's death and his son takes the throne, the last king of Shang becomes corrupt. Zhou revolts and war breaks out in spite of Di Yi's hopes. Di Yi's sole purpose for the marriage is not fulfilled. From Emperor Di Yi's perspective, the outcome is not favorable to him at all. Marrying his daughter off to the Zhou results in the birth of the very man who would topple the Shang dynasty.

The Oracle, at least per history and legend, would have accurately predicted the outcome. It was favorable toward the greater good. The betrothal results in the birth of several cultural heroes that would be remembered for millennia in the Chinese consciousness. The stories of King Wen and his kind, virtuous wife, Tai Si, would go on to inspire not just a nation, but through the I Ching, the world.

Second lesson: the mystery of the universe is so much bigger and more profound than any one of us has the capacity to comprehend. If you were Emperor Di Yi, you can empathize with how easy it would have been to misinterpret the divinatory message.

How can we avoid personal bias and misinterpretation of the Oracle's wisdom? Is it possible for us to expand our perspective broadly enough to truly see beyond ourselves?

Sages from nearly every major religion warn against fortune-telling and divination. I understand their reasoning. Without wisdom and humility, misinterpretations of and addictive dependency on such readings can result in more personal harm than good. Only with wisdom and humility do these practices become sacred and spiritual.

To cultivate objective interpretation of divinations, first cultivate wisdom. When you study the Book of Changes, you'll cultivate wisdom. There is an inexplicable instructive power to the Book. Read it in consecutive order from Hexagram 1, through every line of text, to the last line of Hexagram 64.

Studying the philosophy of the I Ching will bring enlightening perspectives that assure greater impartiality and objectivity. Then when you do decide to approach the Oracle for divination or fortunetelling, you'll have a more judicious view of what is truly being communicated to you.

The Divine does not impart foreknowledge and prophetic revelations to us without reason. There is always a greater purpose. Understanding why we are receiving the revelation ensures that the greater purpose is achieved.

Thus, always ask and answer the question: "What is the Oracle really trying to tell me?"

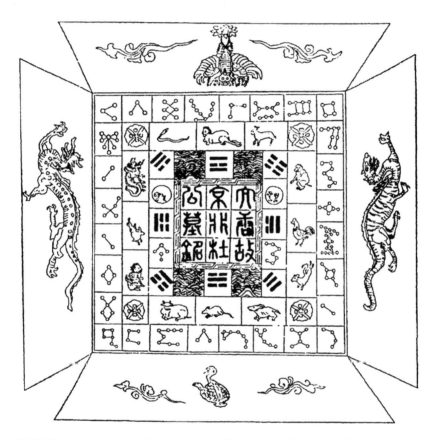

**FIGURE 4.8** Inscription on the mural tomb of Du Jiyuan (AD 940). Northern Song dynasty, Nanjing.[30]

# 5

# The Eight Trigrams (Ba Gua)

THE EIGHT TRIGRAMS (八卦, Ba Gua) are the eight classical elements of Taoist metaphysics, which has been adopted into Confucian cosmology and Mahayana Buddhism. The eight trigrams explain the fundamental nature of all matter. They're comparable to the Platonic concept of the four classical elements Fire, Water, Air, and Earth.

Both the Platonic four elements and the Taoist eight trigrams are the basic theoretical principles of matter and form, and the alchemical reactions between these elemental principles are the source of all physical transformations. Both form the basic building blocks of every metaphysical correspondence system within their esoteric traditions, the traditions undertaking to explain how unseen energies influence human fate.

**TABLE 5.1** Eight Trigrams, Four Western Elements, and Five Phases

| Four Western elements | Fire<br>*Active* | Water<br>*Passive* | Air<br>*Active* | Earth<br>*Passive* |
|---|---|---|---|---|
| Four images (or faces) of God | 少陽<br>*Shǎo yáng*<br>Younger yang | 少陰<br>*Shǎo yīn*<br>Younger yin | 太陽<br>*Tài yáng*<br>Elder yang | 太陰<br>*Tài yīn*<br>Elder yin |

**TABLE 5.1** Eight Trigrams, Four Western Elements, and Five Phases *(continued)*

| Ba Gua trigrams | | | | |
|---|---|---|---|---|
| | 離 Lí<br>Fire<br>火 Huǒ<br>Fire | 坎 Kǎn<br>Water<br>水 Shuǐ<br>Water | 乾 Qián<br>Heaven<br>金 Jīn<br>Metal | 坤 Kūn<br>Earth<br>土 Tǔ<br>Earth |
| *Key*<br>Yin | 震 Zhèn<br>Thunder<br>木 Mù<br>Wood | 巽 Xùn<br>Wind<br>木 Mù<br>Wood | 兌 Duì<br>Lake<br>金 Jīn<br>Metal | 艮 Gěn<br>Mountain<br>土 Tǔ<br>Earth |

Heaven and Earth are the forces of push and pull in this universe. Thus, Hexagram 1 is characterized as divine yang, a directive power, while Hexagram 2 is characterized as divine yin, a receptive power. Combined, Heaven and Earth produce either harmony as we see in Hexagram 11 or stasis as we see in Hexagram 12.

The Ten Wings describes the trigram Heaven as corresponding with the circle:

> The trigram Heaven 乾 corresponds with the skies and celestials, with the circle and with cycles... with jade, with metal... with a sublime red.[1]

乾為天，為圜... 為玉，為金... 為大赤.[2]

Lake and Mountain together represent the matron and patron forces of all nature spirits. Thus, Hexagram 31, Lake over Mountain, is the power to attract and amplify, the alchemical phase of multiplication, while Hexagram 41, Mountain over Lake, is the power to repel, the alchemical phase of putrefaction.

Thunder and Wind give momentum. Thunder is the vehicle through which Shangdi, the high god of the ancients, produces work; Thunder is the hand of God.[3] Thunder over Wind, Hexagram 32, is momentum in the face of forceful opposition, and thus it is endurance. Wind over Thunder, Hexagram 42, is the momentum that overpowers the opposition, and thus it is change toward increase, gain, and escalation.

Fire and Water are in opposition. Combined, they form the last two hexagrams of King Wen's received order, Hexagrams 63 and 64. In pure form, both swallow all that is in their wake—Fire over Fire clings then consumes; Water over Water is the abyss that engulfs then consumes.

Each trigram is also associated with one of the Eight Immortals from Taoist mythology. Occult practitioners seek to "bottle" pure-form powers of the Eight Immortals to use in their craft, and one way to do so is through the trigrams that the Immortals are associated with.

## Yin and Yang Affinities; the Four Faces of God

The eight trigrams represent the eight triplicities from which all matter is constructed. Those triplicities are composed of the smallest of metaphysical units in Taoist cosmology, yin (陰) and yang (陽), like atoms being composed of the positive charge of protons and the negative charge of electrons. When we get casual with our descriptive terminology, we're prone to describing yin and yang as energy. That's not wrong—they're charges of *qi*, though it might be more helpful to describe them as subatomic particles where yin is a negative charge and yang is a positive charge.

The Tao (likened to a numinous void) gave birth to the One, and the One gave birth to the Two. Yin and yang are the first generation of self-contained matter (or energy). I say self-contained because it can exist independently on its own and, on its own, transform to create. Both are self-creating.

**TABLE 5.2** The Yin and Yang Binary

| 陰 Yin | | | 陽 Yang | | |
|---|---|---|---|---|---|
| Northern, shaded side of the hill | | | Southern, sunny side of the hill | | |
| Dark | Curved | Spirit realm | Light | Straight | Sentient realm |
| Night | Wet | Underworld | Day | Dry | Celestial kingdom |

**TABLE 5.2** The Yin and Yang Binary *(continued)*

| ▬ ▬ 陰 Yin | | | ▬▬▬ 陽 Yang | | |
|---|---|---|---|---|---|
| Northern, shaded side of the hill | | | Southern, sunny side of the hill | | |
| Moon | Cold | Occult | Sun | Hot | Canonical |
| Restraint | Even numbers | Intuition | Action | Odd numbers | Logic |
| Contracting | Electron | Diplomatic | Expanding | Proton | Authoritarian |
| Yielding | Estrogen | Mercy | Forceful | Androgen | Justice |
| Passive | Autumn | Esoteric | Active | Spring | Exoteric |
| Responsive | Winter | Receiving hand | Assertive | Summer | Giving hand |

**TABLE 5.3** Principles of Yin and Yang

| 1. | Yin is the opposite of yang. Yang is the opposite of yin. |
|---|---|
| 2. | Yin cannot exist without yang. Yang cannot exist without yin. |
| 3. | Yin can be furher subdivided into elder yin (yin) and younger yin (yang). Yang can be further subdivided into elder yang (yang) and younger yang (yin). |
| 4. | Yin holds the potential to become yang because within yin, there is innate yang. Yang holds the potential to become yin because within yang, there is innate yin. |

Considering the core principles and operational capacity of yin and yang does not, however, assign strict gender values to the two forms of *qi*. While historically there are I Ching scholars who ascribe the feminine to yin and masculine to yang in an absolutist manner,[4] Meaning and Principle scholars such as Cheng Yi did not. Any gender has the capacity to emanate with either yin or yang.

A particular proportion of yin and yang results in the manifested character traits of the personality in a particular given situation. Even the same person will fluctuate between different proportions of yin and yang, with changing *qi*, depending on the circumstances of spacetime. Someone yin-dominant will demonstrate softer, more receptive personality traits, whereas someone yang-dominant will demonstrate more assertive traits.

| LETTER | BINARY CODE | LETTER | BINARY CODE |
|---|---|---|---|
| A | 01000001 | a | 01100001 |
| B | 01000010 | b | 01100010 |
| C | 01000011 | c | 01100011 |

Returning to the table of binary codes that computing systems read, the letter *A* isn't either yin or yang, just as a person, irrespective of gender identity, isn't absolutely yin or absolutely yang. The binary code for the letter *A* is a string of 0s and 1s, just as the yin and yang composition of a person is a unique composite of yin and yang.

Yin and yang are complementary and mutually formative, never inert, always in a state of transformation. The reciprocal interaction of yin and yang is called the Tao.[5]

The next phase of evolution for the atomic-level building blocks of yin and yang is for them to combine with each other. Since yin contains within itself the potential to become yang, and yang holds within itself the potential to become yin (see table 5.3 listing the four principles), they can self-create into four possible combinations.

**TABLE 5.4** The Four Combinations of Yin and Yang

| The Four Faces of God | | | |
|---|---|---|---|
| ⚎ | ⚎ | ⚎ | ⚌ |
| 太陰 | 少陽 | 少陰 | 太陽 |
| **Elder yin** | **Younger yang** | **Younger yin** | **Elder yang** |

When yin outwardly manifests its inner potential to become yang and combines with it, it forms a pairing of yin and yang called younger yang, shown in table 5.3. When yang outwardly manifests its inner potential to become yin and combines with what it has manifested, the pairing is called younger yin. When either manifests itself again, its quality matures and becomes more fixed, which we call elder yin and elder yang. The four combinations of yin and yang are called the Four Faces of God (四象生八卦, Sì Xiàng). The word "象" *(xiàng)* is more commonly translated as "images." The cultural implication is that of an image or emanation, such as of a deity. Thus, the word "像" can also be used to denote the statue of a god.

Each of the Four Faces of God can self-generate with yin and yang to produce trinities. Elder yin mates with yin to form the triplicity Earth. When it mates with yang, it forms the triplicity Mountain. When younger yin mates with yin, it forms the triplicity Water, and with yang, it forms the triplicity Wind. Elder yang mates in the same combinations, and mathematically eight combinations of three are possible, producing the eight trigrams, the Ba Gua. Etymologically, Gua (卦) holds connotations of divination, to divine, or to reveal divine messages—revelations. Thus, I'd argue one ought to translate Ba Gua to the Eight Revelations.

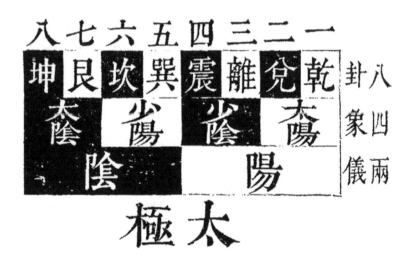

**FIGURE 5.1** Fu Xi's sequence of the eight trigrams. SOURCE: Zhu Xi's *The Original Meaning of the* Zhouyi (周易本義, *Zhōuyì běnyì*)[6].

**TABLE 5.5** Fuxi's Sequence of the Eight Trigrams

| Wuji 無極<br>Numinous Nothingness | ⇌ | Taiji 太極<br>Numinous Omnipresence | | | | | |
|---|---|---|---|---|---|---|---|
| The Pair of Affinities 兩義 ||||||||
| ⚋<br>陰<br>Yin ||||| ⚊<br>陽<br>Yang |||
| The Four Faces of God 四象 ||||||||
| ⚏<br>太陰<br>Elder yin || ⚎<br>少陽<br>Younger yang || ⚍<br>少陰<br>Younger yin || ⚌<br>太陽<br>Elder yang ||
| The Eight Trigrams 八卦 (Eight Divine Revelations) ||||||||
| 8 | 7 | 6 | 5 | 4 | 3 | 2 | 1 |
| ☷ | ☶ | ☵ | ☴ | ☳ | ☲ | ☱ | ☰ |
| 坤<br>Kūn<br>Earth | 艮<br>Gěn<br>Mountain | 坎<br>Kǎn<br>Water | 巽<br>Xùn<br>Wind | 震<br>Zhèn<br>Thunder | 離<br>Lí<br>Fire | 兌<br>Duì<br>Lake | 乾<br>Qián<br>Heaven |

*Note:* Table 5.5 is a translation of figure 4.8, though the order of the rows is reversed.

Taiji 太極 produces the pair of affinities, yin and yang. From the Taiji, creation of the universe unfolds by the order diagrammed in table 5.5. Yin and yang form four compounds, or affinities, which I express as the Four Faces of God. They're often personified as four directional deities or four guardian animal spirits. The four form the eight trinities, or eight divine revelations, which in Taoism are personified as the Eight Immortals. Taiji is the Way, the Tao, and the force that drives change.

The Taiji is a numinous omnipresence. It represents the dual nature philosophy at the heart of Asia's shamanistic practices, Taoism, Buddhism, and Confucianism. In Taoist philosophy, Taiji is created from and equivalent to Wuji (無極), or numinous nothingness, a numinous void. What does that mean exactly? Chinese philosophers have been debating that point and writing dense treatises on just that topic for the last three thousand years.

In Taoist cosmology, the Taijitu 太極圖 yin–yang symbol is likened to a dragon, with yang as its head and yin as its tail. The one dragon evolves into twin dragons of contrasting colors, chasing one another's tails. The yin dragon's eye is yang, and the yang dragon's eye is yin. Thus, the Taijitu is reminiscent of the ouroboros dragon eating its own tail. The ouroboros is a symbol of life, death, and rebirth, of the cycles of change. It is a symbol of infinity, as the Tao is infinity.

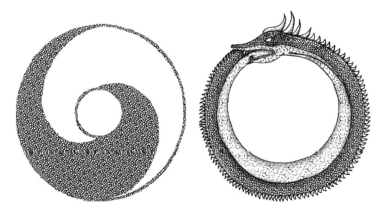

**FIGURE 5.2** Taijitu and the ouroboros. Left: the Taiji River Map of Confucian philosopher Lai Zhide 來知德 (1525–1604).[7] Right: the ouroboros dragon eating its own tail.

## The Book of the River Maps

The Book of the River Maps 河圖洛書 (Hé Tú Luò Shū), from which we get the Lo Shu magic square, forms the pattern of squares. A tortoise messenger sent by the gods transmits the Hé Tú Luò Shū to Yu the Great. With the Book of the River Maps, Yu stops the Great Flood, saves his people, and earns the title of king.

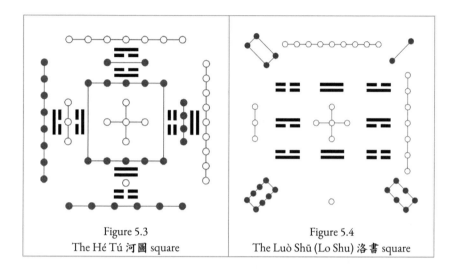

Figure 5.3
The Hé Tú 河圖 square

Figure 5.4
The Luò Shū (Lo Shu) 洛書 square

The River Maps are the essential foundation of the Book of Changes.[8] As described in the Xi Ci, Great Treatise I 繫辭上 of the Ten Wings: "From the River came the Maps. The Luo produced the Book. The sages follow the Book of the River Maps."[9]

The Hé Tú depicts the natural or innate flow of the four affinities of yin and yang. The Hé Tú forms Fuxi's Early Heaven Ba Gua. This is the map designed by Fuxi, which he gave to Yu the Great as jade tablets (玉簡, *yù jiǎn*) on which the secrets of sciences and magic were revealed. The changing younger yang and younger yin flow together along the south axis and the east. The matured elder yang and elder yin flow together along the north and the west axis.[10]

From the myth of Yu the Great, we often assume the river is the Yellow River, when the Hé Tú map is really a depiction of the constellations. The "river" in question is the Milky Way. This is a map of Heaven for the sages on Earth to follow. Align Heaven and Earth by following this map, and you will know all the secrets of sciences and magic. Or so goes the myth.

The Luò Shū demarcates the key patterns of change for the yin and yang affinities, and by understanding the Luò Shū, a sage will wield control over space and time, the four directions, and the four seasons. If the Hé Tú depicts the innate flow, the Luò Shū depicts the applied sciences for controlling that flow. The yin and yang affinities in this second map produce the nine-sector square 九宮格 *(jiǔ gōng gé)* that became the Lo Shu magic square. Taoist ritual magic, astrology, and feng shui are based on the Lo Shu magic square. In the Lo Shu, the sum of the three numbers along any row, column, or diagonal is fifteen, which in Taoist numerology signifies balance of the trinities.[11]

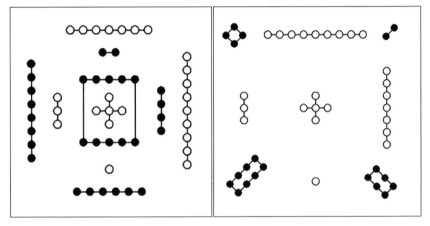

**FIGURE 5.5** The River Maps, as printed in Zhu Xi's *Zhouyi benyi*

The earliest record we have explaining the River Maps is in Zhu Xi's *Original Meaning of the* Zhouyi (I Ching) 周易本義 *(Zhōuyì běnyì)* from around the twelfth century, as diagrammed in figure 5.5. The cross of five at the center of both the Hé Tú and the Luò Shū represents the Wu Xing five changing phases of yin and yang flow. What moves the yin and yang affinities to form arrangements of the Ba Gua eight trigrams is the Wu Xing. The power of five drives every action and nonaction in the Book of Changes.

The importance of these River Maps cannot be overstated. They form the basis of Taoist cosmology, are referenced in the Ten Wings as the basis of the I Ching, and have become valued as the essential formulas that birthed East Asian philosophy and mysticism.

# Arrangements of the Eight Trigrams

The Early Heaven sequence is mythologized as the arrangement of the eight trigrams that Heaven revealed to Fuxi. Fuxi's Ba Gua reveals the natural cosmic cycles of creation and destruction. By understanding the flow of nature (Heaven and Earth), humanity can predict the cycles of change and accommodate those natural cycles.

**TABLE 5.6** Fuxi's and King Wen's Ba Gua Arrangements

| Xian Tian, or Early Heaven<br>**Fuxi's Ba Gua**<br>Corresponding with the Hé Tú | Hou Tian, or Later Heaven<br>**King Wen's Ba Gua**<br>Corresponding with the Luò Shū |
|---|---|
| Lake, Heaven, Wind / Fire, Yang–Yin, Water / Thunder, Earth, Mountain | Wind, Fire, Earth / Thunder, +, Lake / Mountain, Water, Heaven |

The Later Heaven sequence is the diagram that was revealed to King Wen. King Wen's Ba Gua reveals the secrets of controlling those natural cosmic cycles. The Later Heaven arrangement reveals how humanity can self-determine its own fate and override the natural cycles. The Later Heaven, in a sense, represents science and technology.

Fuxi's Early Heaven Ba Gua is a representation of the spiral sequence of Creation—the Hé Tú 河圖 sequence, or River Pattern. King Wen's Later Heaven Ba Gua is a representation of alchemical functions for the operations of magic and divination. It is a methodical rearrangement of Fuxi's Early Heaven, inspired by the Lo Shu magic square.

**TABLE 5.7** Taiji and Lo Shu Numerology in the Trigrams

| Fuxi's Ba Gua | King Wen's Ba Gua |
|---|---|
| Xian Tian, or Early Heaven | Hou Tian, or Later Heaven |

Note how in Fuxi's Ba Gua, the bottommost line in 1 Heaven, 2 Lake, 3 Fire, and 4 Thunder is yang, while the bottommost line in 5 Wind, 6 Water, 7 Mountain, and 8 Earth is yin. The Ba Gua is a representation of the Taijitu yin–yang symbol.

1 Heaven is a yang-dominant trigram, and notice its position in relation to the Taijitu symbol, where the form of the shape is enlarged. We also see the small dot of yin in this area of the Taijitu, reminding us that even in the trigram Heaven, there is the innate potential of yin. When you get to 4 Thunder, yin dominates, and we're now at the tail of the Taijitu's yang part.

In the top right corner where the Taijitu's yin part is just its tail, yang lines are dominant in 5 Wind, where we only have a single line of yin. Then we get to 8 Earth, the enlarged head part of the yin portion. Again, we're reminded that even though Earth is three yin lines, it contains the innate potential for yang, as depicted in the white dot of yang within the yin segment.

Compare that to the arrangement of trigrams in King Wen's Ba Gua. This Later Heaven arrangement is governed by two rules. First, if there is symmetry to the trigrams, then the yin line in one trigram changes to yang in its polarity (the trigram positioned at its direct 180° opposite point). For example, in King Wen's Ba Gua, locate any symmetrical trigram. Take, for instance, 9 Fire. The trigram positioned at the direct 180° opposite position from Fire is Water. If the bottom and top yang lines of Fire became yin and its center yin line became yang, you'd get Water. Same with Heaven and Earth, which are positioned directly 180° opposite one another and are each other's polar opposites in terms of symmetry.

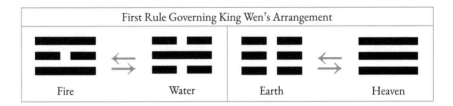

The second rule governs the 2 + 1 triplicities. When there are two lines of the same plus one line that's different, *first* the trigram flips on itself; *second*, yang lines becomes yin and yin lines become yang, to transform into the trigram at its direct 180° opposite position.

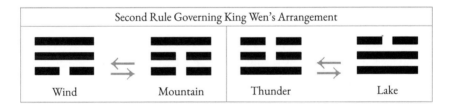

Reading the trigram from the bottom up, Wind is yin, yang, yang. The diagram flips on itself, then the two yang lines become two yin, and the single yin line becomes yang to form Mountain. Same with Thunder, which is a 2 + 1 triplicity, so *first* it flips on itself; *second*, its single yang line becomes yin, and its two yin lines become two yang lines to form Lake.

The four trigrams that form a cross and the four trigrams along the "four corners of the universe" each contain one pair of trigrams following the first rule and one pair of trigrams following the second rule. See the shaded-in formations of trigram sets in table 5.8. The cross configuration has one set of trigrams from the first rule (Fire ⇌ Water) and one set from the second rule (Thunder ⇌ Lake). The four corners configuration has one set from the first rule (Earth ⇌ Heaven) and one set from the second rule (Wind ⇌ Mountain).

**TABLE 5.8** Two Rules Governing King Wen's Arrangement

| Cross Configuration | | | Four Corners Configuration | | |
|---|---|---|---|---|---|
| 4 Wind | 9 Fire | 2 Earth | 4 Wind | 9 Fire | 2 Earth |
| 3 Thunder | 4 9 2 / 3 5 7 / 8 1 6 | 7 Lake | 3 Thunder | 4 9 2 / 3 5 7 / 8 1 6 | 7 Lake |
| 8 Mountain | 1 Water | 6 Heaven | 8 Mountain | 1 Water | 6 Heaven |

In the Image and Number tradition, the numerology of the hexagram's order number matters. The presumption is that the numerological order in the Zhouyi is King Wen's received (divinely channeled) order of the hexagrams to represent a certain sequential order of creation in the universe.

That the diagram of Fire over Water is Hexagram 64 would be interpreted as numerologically significant because that was the last and sixty-fourth diagram received by King Wen. 6 + 4 = 10, which is the final completion number. See table 5.9. Notice how the completion number 10, per the Lo Shu arrangement, which is also King Wen's arrangement, transcends directionality.

Hexagram 1, where the creation of the universe begins, corresponds with the direction of north. Interestingly, *jí* 極—from Taiji (太極) and Wuji (無極), the numinous omnipresence and the numinous void that produced yin and yang, which produced the Four Faces of God, and so on to the eight trigrams—is also the North Star. The North Star 極星 (Jí Xīng), or pole star, is the mythical center of the universe and the place where the universe originated.

The subsequent pages provide the standardized correspondences for the eight trigrams. In the Image and Number tradition, these correspondences are consulted for more predictive, fortune-telling uses of the I Ching.

**TABLE 5.9** Correspondences for Creation and Completion Numbers

| | NUMBER | BINARY | WU XING | FUXI'S BA GUA (HÉ TÚ) | KING WEN'S BA GUA (LO SHU) |
|---|---|---|---|---|---|
| Creation number | 1 | Yang | Heaven | Water | North | North |
| | 2 | Yin | Earth | Fire | South | Southwest |
| | 3 | Yang | Heaven | Wood | East | East |
| | 4 | Yin | Earth | Metal | West | Southeast |
| | 5 | Yang | Heaven | Earth | Center | Center |
| Completion number | 6 | Yin | Earth | Water | North | Northwest |
| | 7 | Yang | Heaven | Fire | South | West |
| | 8 | Yin | Earth | Wood | East | Northeast |
| | 9 | Yang | Heaven | Metal | West | South |
| | 10 | Yin | Earth | Earth | Center | — |

# Eight Immortals and Archetypes of the Mystic

I've assigned eight archetypal facets of the Taoist mystic to the eight trigrams: the Virtuoso, the Warrior, the Philosopher, the Spellcaster, the Shaman, the Healer, the Alchemist, and the Enchanter. These archetype assignments are inspired by the Eight Immortals 八仙 (Bā Xiān)[12] of Taoist folklore. A Taoist mystic will strive to embody all eight and seek to cultivate the abilities that correspond with the Eight Immortals' powers.

The Eight Immortals, which in cultural practice have long been linked to the eight trigrams, are the ascended masters that guide a Taoist mystic's training. Each corresponds with a particular ritual tool for the mystic to master. Each also corresponds with skills, technical knowledge, and models of morality to guide you along the Way of the Sages. Foundational understanding of the Eight Immortals is essential to Taoist mystical study.

It's worth noting that there are countless differing approaches to corresponding the eight trigrams to the Eight Immortals. Table 5.10 compares several of the more popular correspondences you'll find. One assignment that seems to recur as a dominating majority view in the Chinese language is to assign Lü Dong Bin, the leader of the Eight Immortals, as Heaven (pure yang) and He Xian Gu, the only unequivocally identified woman in the group, as Earth, giving the explanation that women are yin. For example, the Zou treatise on Yì Xué (I Ching studies) cites the reason for assigning He Xian Gu to Earth: "She corresponds with Earth because she is the only female among the Eight Immortals."[13]

In my personal approach, I prefer assigning He Xian Gu to Wind,[14] and the subsequent pages for the Wind entry will offer my reasoning. Since my background is in feng shui, the correspondences I'm working with are perhaps what's more commonly observed in that particular mode of metaphysics.

The subsequent pages will provide briefs on each of the Eight Immortals and discuss how to tap in to their teachings and powers through the trigrams. After actually using these correspondences in various modalities of ritual work and spell-crafting, the correspondences in table 5.11 make the most sense to me.

**TABLE 5.10** Comparison of Differing Ba Gua and Eight Immortals Correspondences

| TRI-GRAM | WU AND MCBRIDE[15] | CHIA AND DAO[16] | ANYANG I CHING ASSOCIATION[17] | ZOU'S TREATISE ON I CHING STUDIES IN MEDICINE[18] | MY APPROACH (ORAL TRADITION) |
|---|---|---|---|---|---|
| Heaven | Zhong Li Quan | Lan Tsai-Ho (Lan Cai He) | Lü Dong Bin | Lü Dong Bin | Han Xiangzi |
| Lake | Zhang Guo Lao | Lu Tung-Pin (Lü Dong Bin) | Zhang Guo Lao | Li Tie Guai | Zhong Li Quan |
| Fire | Li Tie Guai | Li Tieh-Kuai (Li Tie Guai) | Zhong Li Quan | Zhong Li Quan | Lü Dong Bin |
| Thunder | Cao Guo Jiu | Chuan Chung-Li (Zhong Li Quan) | Cao Guo Jiu | Zhang Guo Lao | Cao Guo Jiu |
| Wind | Han Xiangzi | Han Hsien-Ku (Han Xiangzi) | Han Xiangzi | Lan Cai He | He Xian Gu |
| Water | Lü Dong Bin | Chang Kuo-Lao (Zhang Guo Lao) | Li Tie Guai | Han Xiangzi | Li Tie Guai |
| Mountain | Lan Cai He | Tsao Kuo-Chiu (Cao Guo Jiu) | Lan Cai He | Cao Guo Jiu | Zhang Guo Lao |
| Earth | He Xian Gu | Ho Hsien-Ku (He Xian Gu) | He Xian Gu | He Xian Gu | Lan Cai He |

However, the varied correspondences you'll find means there is no immutable authority on the topic, only differing perspectives. Decide for yourself what works best. As the Meaning and Principle tradition would say about correspondences, all of it is human-conceived and filtered through our subjective frameworks anyway. The Eight Immortals would be wielding full mastery over all eight trigrams regardless of what we assign to them. Their *qi* as immortals would be balanced among the Ba Gua and would transcend any single trigram.

**TABLE 5.11** The Eight Trigrams and the Eight Immortals

| TRIGRAM | | WU XING | IMMORTAL | MAGICAL WEAPON | DIRECTION |
|---|---|---|---|---|---|
| ☰ | Heaven 乾 *Qián* | Metal 金 | Han Xiangzi 韓湘子 | Flute 笛子 *Dí zi* | Northwest |
| ☱ | Lake 兌 *Duì* | Metal 金 | Zhong Li Quan 鍾離權 | Fan 葵扇 *Kuí shàn* | West |
| ☲ | Fire 離 *Lí* | Fire 火 | Lü Dong Bin 呂洞賓 | Sword 寶劍 *Bǎo jiàn* | South |
| ☳ | Thunder 震 *Zhèn* | Wood 木 | Cao Guo Jiu 曹國舅 | Clappers 雲陽板 *Yún yáng bǎn* | East |
| ☴ | Wind 巽 *Xùn* | Wood 木 | He Xian Gu 何仙姑 | Lotus 蓮 *Lián* | Southeast |
| ☵ | Water 坎 *Kǎn* | Water 水 | Li Tie Guai 李鐵拐 | Gourd 葫芦 *Hú lu* | North |
| ☶ | Mountain 艮 *Gěn* | Earth 土 | Zhang Guo Lao 張果老 | Drum 鱼鼓 *Yú gǔ* | Northeast |
| ☷ | Earth 坤 *Kūn* | Earth 土 | Lan Cai He 藍采和 | Flowers 花籃 *Huā lán* | Southwest |

**TABLE 5.12** Seal Script (Zhou Dynasty) for the Eight Trigrams and Wu Xing Correspondences

Thus, the exercise of correspondences is more about discerning which trigram best enables us, the mortals, to connect with them and learn from these ascended masters. The presentation of these differing perspectives on correspondences also challenges you to not blindly follow any table given to you, but rather to think for yourself.

For those preferring to follow the orthodox majority view, Zou's treatise on I Ching studies provided in table 5.10 is the most frequently accepted standard, though it is not the one observed herein.

**TABLE 5.13** Zodiac Wheel and King Wen's Eight Trigrams

| | 蛇 Snake | 馬 Horse | 羊 Sheep | |
|---|---|---|---|---|
| 龍 Dragon | Southeast ☴ Wind Cardinal Spring | South ☲ Fire Winter Solstice | Southwest ☷ Earth Cardinal Winter | 猴 Monkey |
| 兔 Rabbit | East ☳ Thunder Spring Equinox | | West ☱ Lake Autumn Equinox | 雞 Rooster |
| 虎 Tiger | Northeast ☶ Mountain Cardinal Summer | North ☵ Water Summer Solstice | Northwest ☰ Heaven Cardinal Autumn | 狗 Dog |
| | 牛 Ox | 鼠 Rat | 豬 Boar | |

*Note:* The zodiac animal correspondences for the trigrams provided herein are based on the overlay of the zodiac wheel and King Wen's arrangement of the eight trigrams, based on the Lo Shu magic square. The correspondences are summarized in table 5.13 and mirror the Lo Shu, eight trigrams, and zodiac wheel design in figure 4.8, circa 940 AD, which appeared at the beginning of this chapter. The center nine ideograms are the numbers of the Lo Shu square in archaic oracle bone script.

# Heaven (Qián), Sky: The Virtuoso

| Trigram Name | | Oracle Bone Script | Nature | Oracle Bone Script |
|---|---|---|---|---|
| Heaven ☰ | 乾 Qián | 𩫖 | 天 Tiān | 𠕁 |

| Wu Xing | Qi Quality | Direction | Ritual Tool | Planet | Zodiac Animals |
|---|---|---|---|---|---|
| 金 Metal | Naturally occurring creative force that asserts itself. Innovation. Ingenuity. Divine inspiration. Petitioning a god or goddess. Increasing personal *shen*. Attunement to the celestial realm. | 西北 Northwest | 笛子 Flute | 金星 Metal star Venus | 狗 Dog |
| | | Moon Phase | | Qi in Nature | 豬 Boar |
| | | Full moon | | 天 Sky | |

| | |
|---|---|
| Key Associations | A circle; jade; metal; the fruit of trees |
| Part of the Body | The head |
| Traits You'll Notice | Tall, regal, shows integrity, ethereal, decisive, exudes power and prestige, clarity of mind |
| Personages | Elders, seniors, leader, celebrity, aristocracy, positions of authority |
| Materials | Gold, jade, precious stones, mirrors |
| Land Forms | Verdant meadows, gardens, lush landscapes, the capital city |
| Building Structures | Public or government buildings |
| Weather | Clear and bright skies; ice and cold |
| Travel Forecast | Prepare to travel soon |
| Hour(s) | 7 p.m.–11 p.m. |
| Sound | Steadily paced rhythms, a slow drumbeat |
| Totemic Animal[19] | Horse |

## Han Xiangzi
## 韓湘子

As a boy, Han Xiangzi climbed onto a sacred peach tree and fell asleep while daydreaming. When he fell out of the tree, one of its branches saved him, and Han achieved immortality. He was a talented flute player, and thus as an immortal is venerated by musicians. His innate gifts are in transmutation and music, and his flute playing can tame wild animals. Given the association with a sacred peach tree, the implication is that Han is divinely blessed by the Queen Mother of the West.

Han was born into a prominent aristocratic family, but he chose to live the life of a commoner, cultivating inner alchemy. Stories of Han Xiangzi often involve him giving prophecies, like the story of his attendance at his

**FIGURE 5.6** Han Xiangzi: The Virtuoso. Qing dynasty woodblock prints (1844–1899).[20]

great-uncle's birthday, where he places a clump of dirt into an earthenware pot and uses his powers to instantly grow peonies. Then, etched in gold upon the peony petals were these words: *Snow piles upon the Blue Pass, and my horse will not push on.* Years later, the great-uncle is dismissed from the emperor's court and banished from the capital. On his way out, the road along Blue Pass gets blocked by snowfall. The prophecy illuminated the darkest moment of the great-uncle's life.

The tragic romance between the immortal Han Xiangzi and Longnu, the Dragon Maiden, seventh daughter of the Dragon King, is popular folklore in China. Han Xiangzi was playing his flute by the shores when the Dragon Maiden heard him play. She swam to the surface of the seas, and when he saw her, the two fell instantly in love. But her father, the Dragon King, forbade the romance and imprisoned his daughter under the ocean to keep the lovers apart. Her last gift to Han Xiangzi was a rod of magical gold bamboo, which the immortal turned into a flute. In one account, crops were failing across the provinces and the people were starving due to a severe drought. Han Xiangzi plays his magical flute and soon it begins to rain down from the heavens, and the crops are magically restored.

Corresponding with the trigram Heaven is the archetype of the Virtuoso, like Han Xiangzi, who achieves spiritual awakening by way of a divine endowment. In Chinese, we'd call him a 天才 *(tiāncái)*, meaning the blessing of a talent or ability from Heaven.

# PRACTICUM 5.1:
## Ascent to Heaven:
## Spirit Body Journeying

*Encountering the Mysterious Lady of the Nine Heavens*

The Ascent to Heaven spirit body journeying technique was foremost a children's game, though it seems to also have rather esoteric and spiritual undertones.

For the game, on the full moon eve of the Harvest Moon Festival in autumn, children would spin clockwise in circles as fast as they could while reciting certain Chinese nursery rhymes invoking Chang-Er, the moon goddess. The premise of the game is if you spin fast enough, your spirit will become so light it will instantaneously float up to the moon and you can catch a glimpse of the goddess; then it will immediately descend back to earth into your physical body.

For the spirit body journeying technique, a similar approach to the child's game is used. The technique sends your astral body, or an aspect of your consciousness, to astrally project to Heaven. For a brief moment, your astral body (that aspect of your consciousness) will be close to the celestial palace of Queen Mother of the West, and perhaps you will encounter her protégé, the Mysterious Lady of the Nine Heavens.

Start by fasting from sunrise to sunset. (Still continue to hydrate your body with water, however.) At the hour of sunset, as solar light begins its descent in the west, light nine sticks of incense. Traditional options for incense are sandalwood, cedar wood, frankincense, or pine. My preferred incense is either sandalwood or cedar wood. Arrange the incense sticks in three rows of three, replicating a Lo Shu magic square.

Take great care ahead of time to ensure you have ample space for this exercise and that the space is sufficiently cleared to be safe. As the aroma of the incense smoke fills your space and the sun begins its descent, invoke the Lady of the Nine Heavens by steadily holding a mental vision of her in your thoughts. Endeavor to call out to her. A traditional method is simply a chant, reciting her name rhythmically. Alternatively, visualize your mind sending a cord upward, much like casting a fishing line, and envision that an anchor at its end hits the base of Heaven and latches on.

Continue the visualization and proceed to spin clockwise in circles until you feel your astral body lightening. When you feel a noticeable shift and lightening of your consciousness, sit down in meditation position and close your eyes.

You will then feel your astral body ascending upward from the crown of your head and floating into the heavens for just a moment. As you alight upon Heaven, you will find yourself landing somewhere along the outskirts of the celestial palace or, if you're lucky, one if its outer courtyards. Take in the vision and move around to the extent you feel you can.

**FIGURE 5.7** Depiction of astral projection. SOURCE: *The Secret of the Golden Flower,* translated by Richard Wilhelm.

In your vision, does anyone see you? Does anyone speak to you? Because you called upon the Lady of the Nine Heavens, she'll probably be the one waiting for you. Since you've succeeded at journeying to Heaven, she'll have a prophetic message for you.

Listen closely, remember it, and be sure to thank her reverently. Also, do not forget to request that she convey your respects to the Queen Mother. You've alighted upon her palace grounds, after all, so it is only proper to acknowledge her.

Your astral body will then return to your physical body by taking the same path downward. When you feel the shift of your astral body realigning with your physical body, open your eyes and take a deep breath to reactivate ordinary respiration and circulation in your body.

For the unpracticed, astral journeying can be a bit like dreams—it's hard to remember it clearly upon waking. It may take concerted effort to write down the vision immediately upon your return, before the recall slips away. Other times, you may have some impression that you went somewhere but cannot remember any details of it at all. After some practice, you'll learn to retain more of the memories and be able to recall the accounts with greater precision. In particular, strive to remember the prophetic message you received. That part you'll definitely want to write down and remember.

After the journeying, especially since you fasted all day, treat yourself to a filling and satisfying evening meal.

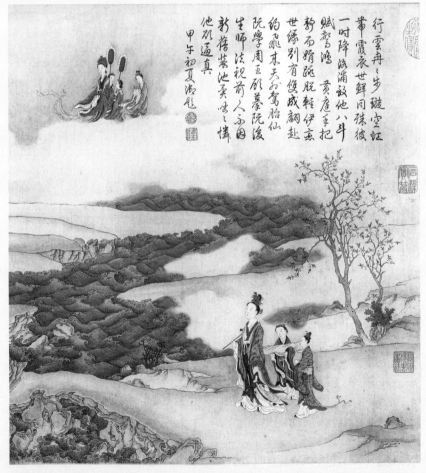

**FIGURE 5.8** Queen Mother of the West 西王母 (1772) by Gu Quan 顧銓. SOURCE: National Palace Museum, Taipei.

**About the Queen Mother of the West:** The Queen Mother of the West (西王母, Xīwángmǔ) was invoked as the Western Mother on Shang dynasty oracle bones dating to the fifteenth century BC.[21] She is a mother goddess associated with love, marriage, and fertility, as well as safe transition in death, funeral rites, necromancy, and the spirits of our ancestors. She is also the beloved mother goddess of religious Taoists who seek her guidance in the quest for immortality. Thus, she's also associated with alchemy.

# PRACTICUM 5.2:
# A Jade Amulet for Power and Protection

The *wū* 巫 shaman uses jade to petition the spirits. From *Shuowen jiezi* 說文解字 (AD 100) by Xu Shen 許慎 (AD 58–148): 巫以玉事神 *(wū yǐ yù shì shén)*.

When the Yellow Emperor prayed to the Queen Mother of the West for divine guidance, the Queen Mother sent the Lady of the Nine Heavens, who taught the emperor how to craft a powerful talisman made of jade. The magical tablets of knowledge that the ancestral spirit Fuxi gave to Yu the Great, with the secrets of sciences and magic revealed, were the *yùjiǎn* 玉簡 jade tablets. The jade stone contains within it the *qi* resonant with the Jade Maidens of heaven, the spirit gatekeepers at the liminal points of the cosmos.

The recurring word "吉" *(ji)* in the Zhouyi means good fortune, happiness, and contentment, an omen of success; the ideogram depicts a jade tablet to express that Heaven's Will is aligned in your favor. Jade absorbs negative energy. When it breaks or when you lose it, that's because it has taken the hit for you. It has absorbed so much toxic and malefic energy that it breaks from you so it won't affect you.

Many Asian and Pacific Islander cultures believe that as you pass jade stone from one generation on to the next, the heirloom will increase in power. The *bi*, or jade carved into a circular medallion with a circular cutout in the center, has been a part of Chinese history since the Neolithic era, before 3000 BC.

If you only invest in one amulet for protection, prosperity, and ensuring good health, then invest in a piece of jade. The highest-quality jade will be found by riverbeds. Untreated jadeite jade is optimal and will become an heirloom, though nephrite is perfectly fine for use as a protection amulet. Serpentine is a great stone for connecting with the Queen Mother of the West.

Just by wearing jade while you perform rituals, divination, and invocations of the divine, the stone will absorb the celestial light from the divine presence and grow in power. The stone is believed to be a natural connection between Heaven and Earth, the celestial realm and the human, so it also amplifies the efficacy of your divination rituals. The stone doesn't need to be consecrated or treated in any particular way; just wear it, and you are what activates its magical properties.

## Lake (Duì), Exchange: The Warrior

| Trigram Name | | Oracle Bone Script | Nature | Oracle Bone Script |
|---|---|---|---|---|
| Lake ☱ | 兑 Duì | (glyph) | 澤 Zé | (glyph) |

| Wu Xing | Qi Quality | Direction | Ritual Tool | Planet | Zodiac Animal |
|---|---|---|---|---|---|
| 金 Metal | Nourishing, sustaining force. Creating a servitor. Business success. Law. Exchange of energy; one reflects the other in an equal and opposite manner; mutual joy. Winning legal matters and/or negotiations. Clear and shallow waters, fertile environment for growth. | 西 West | 葵扇 Fan | 金星 Metal Star Venus | 雞 Rooster |
| | | Moon Phase | Qi in Nature | | |
| | | Waxing gibbous | 澤 Marshes | | |

| | |
|---|---|
| **Key Associations** | The sorceress,[22] harvest, salt |
| **Part of the Body** | The mouth |
| **Traits You'll Notice** | Happy, charismatic, expressive, a good writer or orator, likes to gossip, does not take criticism well |
| **Personages** | Young children, hospitality service occupations, writers, researchers; law |
| **Materials** | Silver, light metals, ornamentals, metal instruments |
| **Land Forms** | Riverbanks, marshes, wetlands, valleys |
| **Building Structures** | Walls, metal-heavy urban areas, fences |
| **Weather** | Rainy and cloudy |
| **Travel Forecast** | Difficult personalities while traveling |
| **Hour(s)** | 5 p.m.–7 p.m. |
| **Sound** | Chimes, sound of bells, clanging |
| **Totemic Animal** | Sheep; also Tiger |

## *Zhong Li Quan*
## 鍾離權 (*also: Jidao* 寂道)

Zhong Li Quan was a necromancer with the ability to resurrect the dead. He possessed a magical fan that could change stone into gold and silver. Zhong was a warrior general who fought the northern Huns, but after a brutal defeat in battle, he lost his way. Directionless, Zhong abandoned his military life to study alchemy. Through his studies, Zhong achieves immortality.

He then returns to the lay world, defeating monsters with his flying daggers and transforming stones into gold and silver to enrich the commoners. Spiritually awakened, he goes back to military service as a warrior general.

Zhong also possesses the ability to ward off floods and pandemics. In one legend, he uses his magical fan as a dam to stop a flood from destroying a province. In another, he comes upon a village ravaged by a plague and sees dead parents and orphaned children strewn across the streets. Zhong resurrects the parents and reunites the families. Another story recounts a time when Zhong fights off a demon python who was attacking innocent villagers.

**FIGURE 5.9** Zhong Li Quan: The Warrior. Qing dynasty woodblock prints.[23]

Zhong Li Quan is the patron divinity of ceremonial magicians, necromancers, shamans, and alchemists. His most notable power is his alchemical ability to transform stones into gold, which he does to save commoners from poverty and to bless people with prosperity when they call upon him. He endows generously with funds when you are in need. Thus, among mystics he's associated with prosperity or money magic, with spell-crafting for the purposes of transforming what you already have into what will bring you more wealth and gains.

Although the trigram Lake is associated with a more placid, joyous, and calm state, the archetype of the Warrior is attributed to Lake through Zhong Li Quan. The strongest of warriors will have cultivated the demeanor of Lake, not of the more commonly associated Fire or Thunder, despite Zhong Li Quan being known for his fiery, fierce temperament. As an immortal, however, what enables him to be a fearsome warrior isn't his fiery temperament, but the calm and the control he commands underneath the surface, so the *qi* is still Lake. True mastery over martial arts requires the sustaining, mindful, and calm state of Lake, while the changing phase of Metal arms and propels the warrior's movements.

The Metal Wu Xing phase that propels the state of Lake is manifested in Zhong Li Quan's flying daggers. Lake is also associated with material prosperity, and Zhong Li Quan can be petitioned for prosperity magic, supported by Lake.

Like the progression of lines in Lake, Zhong Li Quan evolves from the aggression of the double yang lines to the calmer state in the end. Zhong's association with Lake is also a testament that the Warrior archetype and the greatest of martial artists are not belligerent or combative.

# PRACTICUM 5.3:
# Growing Prosperity and Business Success Talisman

The trigram Lake is the core component that produces joy and exchange. Harmonious exchanges beget joy; hence the two are connected. Lake is the image of a shallow but fertile medium for culturing blessings, work products, and growth. This is a talisman imbued with the *qi* of Lake to help you grow a business to achieve success or steadily cultivate prosperity by ensuring the fertility of the *qi* in your environment.

Taking inspiration from Zhong Li Quan's abilities, you'll be figuratively transmuting a "stone" in your possession into "gold" by using the Lake trigram. There is no need to take the stone reference too literally. For example, my preference is to use a tiny porcelain bottle for crafting this prosperity talisman.

**FIGURE 5.10** Prosperity Lake talisman

The first step is to energetically clear the object you will be charging into a talisman. Sandalwood, cedar wood, and frankincense are examples of woods and resins that are historically associated with purification. Thus, passing the object through the smoke of such incense will clear it.

If the selected medium won't be harmed by it, then cleansing it with alcohol also works. Other methods of energy clearing include placing it under direct sunlight or for a bath under moonlight, selecting either the yang sun or yin moon based on the metaphysical correspondences of your object.

A more solar object such as an object of the color red or yellow or composed of metal will do better with energy purification under the sun. A more lunar object in the color white or the opposite, black and very dark colors or composed of a yin material such as a pale, subtle-colored jade (intense green and brightly toned jade is yang) would do better under the moon.

The best time for crafting this talisman is the full moon, given its correspondence to the trigram Lake.

After the object has been energetically cleared, light seven sticks of incense (the numerology of seven corresponds with Lake, per the Lo Shu). The incense will protect your ritual space while you work.

Charge the object with the *qi* of Lake by inscribing it with either the trigram lines or the oracle bone script for "Lake." Paint it onto the object with permanent ink. Personally, I don't mind using permanent marker, but that may be too nontraditional for purists. If you're opting for a tiny bottle, paint Lake onto parchment, roll it up into a scroll, and tuck it inside the bottle. You can add in sprinkles of gold dust, cinnamon bark, cowrie shells, or well-cleaned fish bone. The word for fish, "魚" *(yú)*, is a homophone for abundance, affluence, plenitude, and riches, "裕" *(yù)*. The intentional synchronicity connects their *qi*.

Critical to this working is your mindset while you craft. You must set aside all thoughts or emotions that can challenge or block the flow of prosperity *qi* toward you, such as pessimism, negativity, self-doubt, self-criticism, skepticism, and so on. The *qi* of these thoughts and emotions blocks and challenges the *qi* of the goals you're intending to achieve. Visualization of your prosperity and business success, on the other hand, helps to increase the momentum of the *qi* you seek to harness. Incantations work because they ensure that your thoughts and emotions give momentum to the right kind of *qi*.

Thus, repeating an affirmation or short poetic spell you've drafted will significantly increase the efficacy of this work. The intention should be around the theme of prosperity, business or financial success, and security of your livelihood to ensure perpetual abundance.

Once you've completed inscription of the Lake trigram, recite words in closing, such as *"Jí jí rú lü ling"* (急急如律令), a Taoist magical incantation equivalent to "So mote it be" or "Amen." Alternatively, conclude your thoughts in a deliberate way, ending with a convincing and confident affirmation to yourself that the talisman you've crafted will multiply your financial gains manifold, that this talisman shall keep you financially secure at all times and ensure your material prosperity.

All of the foregoing should be complete before the seven sticks of incense have extinguished. Let the energy workings settle within the talisman by keeping it on your altar, close to the incense. When all seven sticks of incense have extinguished in the natural course, your talisman is fully charged.

The talisman can be kept on your person at all times, if you prefer that, or stored in a location related to your source of financial income. This can be the top drawer of your office desk, near your work computer, in a cash register if you own a storefront, or in a feng shui prosperity bowl in your home.

## PRACTICUM 5.4:
## Crafting a Dharma Fan

Inspired by Zhong Li Quan, the Dharma Fan (法扇) is a ritual folding fan crafted by Taoist ceremonial magicians. Historically the fans would have been made from bird feathers, hand-woven leaves, or silk. Zhong Li Quan's magical fan is traditionally depicted as being made out of banana leaf. In the present day, paper fans are more common. The folding fan consists of ribs made from bamboo or animal bone. Iron fans were also used in warfare, and in a beloved sixteenth-century Chinese novel, *Journey to the West*, about the Monkey King and an entourage of misfits, there's a story of an encounter between the Monkey King and a Princess Iron Fan, a demoness in possession of a powerful magical fan.

The mystic's Dharma Fan is a form of magical and psychic protection. You can use it as a form of defensive or protection magic, especially while traveling.

**FIGURE 5.11** The mystic's Dharma Fan

The folding Dharma Fan resembles a bat wing. In Chinese symbolism, bats represent good health, longevity, peace, and prosperity. Typically, one side of the fan represents the exoteric, which will be decorated with an ornamental design or artwork, while the other side of the fan represents the esoteric, where Fu talismanic sigils will be inscribed. Most mystics might be willing to show you the exoteric side of their ritual fan, but they are unlikely to show you the esoteric side that is empowered with their custom sigils.

To craft your own Dharma Fan, acquire a paper folding fan. Every region of Asia has their own culturally specific version of the folding fan (which doesn't necessarily need to fold; for instance, the banana leaf fan isn't technically a folding fan). Opt for one that attunes you to the cultural heritage you're seeking to connect to.

Blank paper folding fans with just the parchment can be purchased and painted upon. Alternatively, purchase one with ornate décor on one side, which will be the side of your ritual fan corresponding to the exoteric, and then hand-paint your own talismanic sigils on the other side, which will correspond with the esoteric.

Each lineage of Taoist mystery tradition will have its own proprietary method of crafting a ritual Dharma Fan, and individual practitioners will have their own personalized processes. Thus, there isn't any "right" or "wrong" to this craft. In an initiated setting, for instance, you would ignore any instructions given here and adhere strictly to the traditions within your lineage.

The following instructions offer a generic crafting method. It will work sufficiently for you until you are able to independently craft your own method. A personally tailored Dharma Fan will always be more powerful than generic instructions.

To start, you'll need to know the Chinese zodiac animal corresponding to your birth year (based on the lunar calendar). For example, I was born in September of 1981 per the Gregorian calendar, which corresponds with the Rooster.

TABLE 5.14 Spirit Helpers for Your Zodiac Animal

| Heaven: 1 Qián | | Lake: 58 Duì | Fire: 30 Lí | Thunder: 51 Zhèn | |
|---|---|---|---|---|---|
| Dog | Boar | Rooster | Horse | Rabbit | |
| Protection of the Celestial Father | | Career Success and Inner Peace | Commanding the Power of Attraction | Thunder Magic, Control of Elements | |
| Wind: 57 Xùn | | Water: 29 Kǎn | Mountain: 52 Gěn | Earth: 2 Kūn | |
| Dragon | Snake | Rat | Ox | Tiger | Sheep | Monkey |
| Prosperity and Abundance | | Safe Journeys and Power to Heal | Spiritual Awakening and Mastery of Alchemy | Protection of the Earth Goddess | |

Recall the Eight Spirit Helpers covered in chapter 3 on Taoist Mysticism and Magic. You'll be inscribing the Spirit Helper that is the double of the trigram corresponding with your zodiac animal. In my case, since I'm the Rooster, and Rooster corresponds with the trigram Lake, my Spirit Helper would be Lake over Lake, or Hexagram 58.

Bear in mind that these correspondences aren't always accurate; you might be the exception, not the rule, especially since the zodiac sign corresponds with everyone born in your year. The other metrics of your natal chart could very well mean that you don't conform with the typical traits of your zodiac sign. So discretionary judgment calls are needed here. You may have to override the generic instruction and manually select one of the eight Spirit Helper hexagrams.

Locate the hexagram entry in the I Ching. Take your time reading it and reflecting on your mind's response to it, then your body's response, and your spirit's response. Colors, a landscape (whether realistic or conceptual), shapes, formations, and flows of lines will begin to form in your mind in response to your connection to that hexagram.

If you are working with a fan that already has art on both sides that you don't want to interfere with, then leave it as is physically, but psychically "paint" the artwork you're seeing through your mind's eye onto the esoteric side of your Dharma Fan. Harness as much personal *qi* as you can and use it to psychically project the art you see in your mind onto the canvas of the fan.

If you are working with a blank canvas for the esoteric side of your fan and you're interested in painting it, use ink and watercolors as your medium. Replicate what you saw in your mind's eye onto the esoteric side of the Dharma Fan.

When complete, add the hexagram lines, which you will draw from the bottom up, and the oracle bone script of the word associated with that hexagram onto the painting. If you had "painted" it psychically in a virtual manner, you'll want to actually and physically paint the hexagram lines and oracle bone script onto the fan.

Note the thematic correspondences to your Spirit Helper hexagram. For example, mine would be "Career Success and Inner Peace" because that is the thematic correspondence to Rooster. Recite the themes as a form of energetic intention setting while you draw the hexagram lines and oracle bone script.

It is then common in Taoist magical traditions to stamp the work with your signature practitioner's seal. In initiatory traditions, you might be given one that represents your lineage, so you would stamp such workings with both the lineage seal and your own practitioner's seal. Among solitary practitioners, you might have various preset seal stamps petitioning patron deities or seals you've worked with over long periods of time that now have their own empowered *qi*. These would all get stamped onto your Dharma Fan.

Light seven sticks of incense on your altar and place your completed fan on the altar. When the incense sticks extinguish in their natural course, the charging of your Dharma Fan is done.

The fan can be kept on your altar when not in use and taken with you when you travel abroad. The Dharma Fan will serve as a personal talisman of protection while away from home. Alternatively, it can simply stay at home and be used in rituals as a means to control the flow of *qi* around your work space during the rite. Another use for the Dharma Fan is to "fan" away malefic or poisonous *qi*.

## Fire (Lí), Clarity: The Philosopher

| Trigram Name | | Oracle Bone Script | Nature | Oracle Bone Script |
|---|---|---|---|---|
| Fire ☲ | 離 Lí | 離 | 火 Huǒ | 火 |

| Trigram | *Qi* Quality | Direction | Ritual Tool | Planet | Zodiac Animal |
|---|---|---|---|---|---|
| ☲ 火 Fire | The Sun: Solar forces. Per the Ten Wings, Fire is also associated with lightning. | 南 South | 寶劍 Sword | 火星 Fire Star Mars | 馬 Horse |
| | Radiate; attract, cling, enliven, inspire. Illuminate. Clarity. Rapid movement. Logical reasoning. Promotion, public recognition. Applied sciences. Technical know-how. Accolades. | Moon Phase First quarter | | *Qi* in Nature 火 Blaze | |

| | |
|---|---|
| Key Associations | The helmet, the sword, the spear |
| Part of the Body | The eyes |
| Traits You'll Notice | Ambitious, active, assertive, extroverted, quick to agitate, intelligent, quick learner |
| Personages | Intellectuals, students, soldiers, a wise person, leader, manager, sales |
| Materials | That which heats or gives light |
| Land Forms | Deserts, arid plains; can also indicate lushly fertile land still black with ash (i.e., recent volcanic eruption or storm of some nature that causes devastation but renews the land for future growth potential) |
| Building Structures | Kitchen, library, cultural centers |
| Weather | Sunny and clear, risk of drought |
| Travel Forecast | Prepare to travel soon |
| Hour(s) | 11 a.m.–1 p.m. |
| Sound | Fast tempo and higher-pitched |
| Totemic Animal | Phoenix/Pheasant |

## *Lü Dong Bin*
## 呂洞賓

Considered the leader of the Eight Immortals, Lü Dong Bin was a Jinshi (進士), the most exclusive and elite title that can be conferred upon scholars. A Buddhist, he achieved immortality by reciting sutras under a willow tree, and his legacy is revered by Taoists, Buddhists, and Confucians alike. Lu was a master of thunder magic (雷法, *Léi Fǎ*), known for crafting Fu talismans and casting spells. Due to his renowned benevolence and compassion, gods of the celestial world and nature spirits were always willing to support him.

A master of both inner and outer alchemy, like Zhong Li Quan, Lü Dong Bin can change stone into gold, but the gold will change back to stone in three thousand years. He is called upon to illuminate the path for those who've lost their way. His light and powers can defeat the darkness of demons.

**FIGURE 5.12** Lü Dong Bin: The Philosopher. Qing dynasty woodblock prints.[24]

Though he traveled with a sword, which became his signature, he was a pacifist. When asked when it was permissible to use a sword, he replied, "Only to cut away your anger, hate, and ignorance." Thus, although Fire corresponds with Mars and the sword, here they are forces wielded for the purpose of enlightening. The sword cuts away what was obscuring one's clarity. Correspondences to war here are more in line with Sun Tzu's *Art of War*—the aspect of it that is intellect and reason.

Inspired by a legend of Lü Dong Bin protecting a brothel and healing the prostitutes from diseases, he also became a patron divinity of sex workers. Lu is associated with the cryptic phrase "濟世度人須用指南針" *(Jì shì duó rén xū yòng zhǐ nán zhēn),* which translates to: "To save the world, people must use a compass."

The trigram Fire evokes a state of illumination and clarity, corresponding with the archetype of the Philosopher, one associated with the logical reasoning and insights of Fire. The scholarly Lü Dong Bin embodies that archetype of the Philosopher. Also, the Fire trigram is often associated with sovereignty, given its correspondence with the sun and solar forces. That the leader among the Eight Immortals is best characterized as embodying the *qi* of Fire makes sense.

## PRACTICUM 5.5: Nine-Day Fire Ritual for Clarity and Advancement

Fire has long been associated with clarity, illuminated insight, and purification, where the light of flames chases away ghosts and demons. In feng shui, Fire corresponds with professional and career advancements, promotions, achieving honors, and increases in social status. Per the *qi* quality of the trigram Fire, this is achieving clarity, personal sovereignty, and enhancing your power to attract toward you what you seek. Fire also corresponds with leadership and innovation in the applied sciences. Per the Lo Shu, the numerology of nine corresponds with Fire.

This nine-day ritual fortifies your personal *qi* and aura with greater Fire *qi* so you can amplify your ability to problem-solve (thus gaining clarity) and enhance your ability to magnetically attract toward you the social gains you seek.

Source a red candle that is large enough to burn for about nine minutes per day for nine consecutive days. You will be burning the candle daily during that period to clarify and amplify your personal *qi* in such a way that you empower yourself for greater likelihood of social gains and professional advancements.

You'll also need a lighter. A modern-day lighter will work just fine. In ancient times, producing fire called for a flint stone and a piece of steel, which were struck together to produce the spark. Early North and Central Asian shamanism conceptualized the flint stone as a mother spirit and the steel as a father spirit, which, when struck together, consummated to produce a sacred fire that could then be used in ceremonial rites. The practice is still found in Mongolian Tengrist traditions today. Producing a flame in the modern-day home hasn't changed much. Your lighter operates by a spark wheel that strikes a stone to light a fuel-soaked wick that produces the flame. You can also use matches, where the materials on the striking surface are the metaphysical equivalent of the flint stone and the head of the matchstick is the equivalent of steel.

Select a late evening hour and work in a dimly lit room. This allows total focus on the candle you will be lighting. The metaphor you're invoking is illumination to see despite the darkness.

As you light incense to set your sacred space, take the moment to gather your thoughts and intentions. What exactly is it you want in terms of personal advancement? What are you confused about? What matter or issue are you seeking clarity for? Can you state that matter or issue clearly in your mind? In terms of your burden of responsibility here, you must bring forth clarity as to what you don't know or what it is you seek. Spirit will then reciprocate and provide clarity with an answer.

The incense is now lit. Turn your attention to the candle. As you strike your lighter (or matches), recite the following incantation:

> Spirit of Fire, born to a flint stone mother and a blue steel father, rise and come forth. Imbue me with your sacred powers.

If you prefer, you can write your own equivalent. Repeat the incantation as many times as needed to feel the shift of personal consciousness. Maintain your gaze on the candle flame. At a turning point, you'll suddenly feel much larger than your usual self, more confident; you'll naturally sit up taller, you'll feel powerful, and that's when you know it's taken effect.

In this state enhanced by the Fire spirit, reflect on the matter you are seeking clarity on. As you consider the matter, feel as if your intelligence, reasoning abilities, and knowledge of the universe have been enhanced, and through that state of mind, reconsider the issue. Feel two states, one exalted and one ordinary, occupying your body simultaneously, and both are facets of yourself. You are and always have been both, but ordinarily, that exalted state of self isn't accessible.

From your ordinary state, present the issue to the exalted state. Then in the exalted state, empowered by the Fire spirit, know that you know what the solution is. It is only a matter of having to unpack it, and that might take the full nine days.

**FIGURE 5.13** Receiving the sacred powers of fire

If your purpose is to achieve a promotion or career advancement, use the time in the empowered state to visualize yourself achieving the objective. Recite prayers to the Fire spirit, such as, "Fire spirit, lend me your strength so that I radiate with your power and compel . . ." and complete the sentence with the individuals you intend your increased magnetism and power of attraction to influence and what you would like those individuals to do for you so you attain your advancement.

As you recite the prayer, place your hands around the flame as shown in figure 5.13. Be sure to maintain a safe distance away from the candle. Feel yourself siphoning the Fire spirit from the flame through the hand mudra. Through your palms, you're more effectively collecting and conducting that Fire energy and routing it toward you.

Aim to stay in this meditative state contemplating your objectives, clinging to those energies, for about nine minutes. When you feel you've been sufficiently enriched by the Fire *qi,* use a candle snuffer to put out the flame. Repeat every day for a consistent consecutive nine days to fully fortify your personal *qi* and aura with greater Fire *qi*.

The metaphysical theory behind such an exercise is not unlike increasing intake of a certain nutrient supplement because the specific constitution of your body lacks it. Here, the reason you haven't achieved your desired goal of advancement is, fundamentally, a lack of Fire *qi*. By fortifying your personal *qi* with greater Fire, you're readjusting your psychic constitution. Lighting the flame for nine consecutive days is also a form of path clearing, to remove any blockages of *qi* that have been obstructing your advancement.

# PRACTICUM 5.6:
# New Moon Purification Ritual
# with the Pavamāna Mantra

The *jhākri* are the shamans of Nepal. Both the *wū* 巫 shamans in regions of East and Southeast Asia and the *jhākri* of Nepal integrate Buddhism and/or Hinduism into their practice.[25] Spellcasting that utilizes Buddhist or Hindu sacred texts is common in the folk magical practices of Burma, Thailand, Cambodia, Laos, Vietnam, Malaysia, Singapore, and the ethnic groups along the South China Sea.

One example is the recitation of mantras. Mantras are magical formulas or a magically charged sequence of words that a *jhākri* or *wū* commits to memory and recites as an incantation for healing, blessings, protection, or warding off evil.[26]

Recitations from sacred texts are used during ritual for blessing ritual tools, counteracting another sorcerer's baneful magic, healing ailments, and petitioning spirits. In the shamanic traditions of the Indochinese Peninsula and southwest China, especially where influences of Hinduism are strong, many of the passages from the Upanishads are recited with magical intentions as mantras.

The recitation known as the Pavamāna Mantra comes from verse 1.3.28 of the Brihadaranyaka Upanishad (the Upanishad of the Great Forests), the tenth scripture in the canon of 108 Upanishads, written sometime between the seventh and sixth centuries BC, before Buddhism. Historically it was an opening recitation for Vedic fire rituals and libations.

| from untruth lead us to truth<br>from darkness lead us to light<br>from death lead us to immortality | asatō mā sadgamaya<br>tamasō mā jyōtirgamaya<br>mṛtyōrmā amṛtaṁ gamaya | असतो मा सद्गमय<br>तमसो मा ज्योतिर्गमय<br>मृत्योर्मा अमृतं गमय |
|---|---|---|

On the evening of a new moon, go outside barefoot so your feet touch the earth. Light incense and a candle. Sit or kneel before the candle flame and take a few deep calming, centering breaths.

Pour a teacup of rice wine or clear liquor to be offered to the god of fire. Face southeast-ward if you'll be invoking Agni, the Hindu/Vedic deity of fire. Agni is also venerated in Buddhist canon, so many who identify as Buddhist still honor Agni. In Japan, the deva of Fire is Katen (火天), one of the eight protectors of the heavens, considered an equivalent to Agni अग्नि.

Hold the filled cup of libations high above your head and recite the Pavamāna Mantra. Pour out the drink reverently onto the earth in front of you as an offering. Pour another cup, this time for yourself. Hold the filled cup above your head again and once more, recite the mantra. This time, drink. The drink has been blessed and will purify you of last month's anxieties, stress, pain, and difficulties. You begin the new lunar month rejuvenated. Close by snuffing out the candle flame and recite *om* ॐ or simply "So may it be" as a form of closing affirmation.

The new moon purification ritual would be powerful in a group setting, while still being simple enough for all to follow. The libations can be performed in front of a campfire or bonfire. Unlike snuffing out the candle at the close of the mantra recitation, you would let the fire continue to burn and continue on with the mundane festivities. It's perfectly fine to recite in English. The lead will recite one line, and the group will repeat in chorus. Same with the second and third lines.

## Thunder (Zhèn), Power: The Spellcaster

| Trigram Name | | Oracle Bone Script | Nature | Oracle Bone Script |
|---|---|---|---|---|
| Thunder | 震 Zhèn | | 雷 Léi | |

| Wu Xing | *Qi* Quality | Direction | Ritual Tool | Planet | Zodiac Animal |
|---|---|---|---|---|---|
| Wood 木 Wood | Arouse; shake, jolt; incite. Divisive force with the intent to unite. To awaken a sense of purpose or cause. To stir up. Stimulate. | 東 East | 雲陽板 Clappers | 木星 Wood Star Jupiter | 兔 Rabbit |
| | Defensive magic. Protecting the home. Agitate *qi*. Revolution, division. Agitate. Electrify. Galvanize. To supply with an electric charge that will generate forceful activity or a powerful field (from which spellcasters draw upon to empower their craft). | Moon Phase | *Qi* in Nature | | |
| | | Waxing crescent | 雷 Thunder and Lightning | | |

| | |
|---|---|
| Key Associations | Roadways, road openers, bamboo, vengeance and vehemence, hand of God |
| Part of the Body | The feet |
| Traits You'll Notice | Proud, good-looking, successful, anxious, musicianship, quick-tempered, talented |
| Personages | Age thirty to forty; fast-paced business personnel, corporate, entertainers; artisans; research and development |
| Materials | Wood, wooden instruments, drums |
| Land Forms | Forests, dense woods, parched but grassy areas, dried grass (if combined with Mountain, could indicate volcano) |
| Building Structures | Highways and busy streets; skyscrapers, tall buildings; buildings that rattle with movement |
| Weather | Thunder and lightning |
| Travel Forecast | Long-distance travel |
| Hour(s) | 5 a.m.–7 a.m. |
| Sound | Clamorous, boisterous, cries of protest, jolly noises, rowdy |
| Totemic Animal | Dragon (union of the azure and the yellow dragons) |

## Cao Guo Jiu
## 曹國舅

Cao Guo Jiu was the younger brother to the empress, and he objected to the corruption he saw in the imperial palace. He thus renounced his royal title, donated the entirety of his wealth to the poor, and became a monk. By dueling with demons, performing exorcisms, and defeating evil, Cao attained enlightenment.

Cao's objections to imperial corruption knew no bounds. In one story, his brother assaults a scholar's wife, then to keep her from testifying in court, murders her. Since the brother was part of the imperial family, he gets away with his crime. After the brother's death, Cao sends his own brother's soul to hell as eternal punishment, preventing the brother from attaining rebirth.

**FIGURE 5.14** Cao Guo Jiu: The Spellcaster. Qing dynasty woodblock prints.[27]

Many of the legends about Cao Guo Jiu involve him fighting demons and defeating evil with his magic. This is not unlike the exorcistic rites associated with thunder magic. Of note are Cao Guo Jiu's powerful jade clappers 雲陽板 *(yún yáng bǎn)*, which can be used to summon thunder, lightning, wind, and rain, and which have also become ritual tools that exorcists use to chase away unwanted ghosts and malevolent spirits.

In a mythic battle between the Eight Immortals and the Dragon King of the East China Sea, the Dragon King took Lan Cai He prisoner in the Dragon Palace. Angered, the Immortals went to save their friend and waged war against the Dragon King's armies. It was Cao Guo Jiu's powerful clappers that parted the seas. Just as the Dragon King was about to send the full force of his army to attack, Kuan Yin, the bodhisattva of mercy, appears and mediates between the two sides. The bodhisattva convinces the Dragon King to release Lan Cai He.

Admittedly, it's a bit counterintuitive for Lü Dong Bin, who was said to be a master of thunder magic, to be associated with the trigram Fire, while Cao Guo Jiu is associated with Thunder (though Fire is necessary for effective thunder rites). The appearance of a paradox is representative of I Ching philosophy; not everything is literal, and innate meaning matters more.

Over the centuries, Taoist ceremonial magicians themselves associated Lü Dong Bin with thunder magic and sought to petition him in thunder rites. That isn't to say that Cao Guo Jiu wasn't himself also a master of thunder magic. Considering his representative magical tool, the clappers, it would make sense that Cao Guo Jiu's *qi* is characterized by the trigram Thunder.

## PRACTICUM 5.7:
## Bottling Thunder Magic

This exercise is a method of collecting and storing thunder *qi* in objects, transforming them into fuel or battery packs for magic. However, it will require you to wait until a thunderstorm. Have all the materials on hand well ahead of time so when thunder hits, you'll be ready.

To bottle thunder magic, you'll need vessels you can seal, and the more durable the vessel material, the better. Traditional gourds or glass bottles with cork stoppers work well. I prefer to use quartz crystals and charge them into battery packs for thunder magic. Clear quartz crystals are considered a *qi* conductor. Once the crystals are charged with thunder *qi,* you keep them wrapped in black silk to retain that *qi*.

Theoretically, the ceremonial magician would want to be as exposed to the inclement weather as possible, such as in an open field, but realistically, you want to stay safe. Safety first.

Set out as many vessels or quartz crystals as you would like charged into thunder magic fuel or battery packs. Make sure they are placed so they are directly exposed to the thunderstorm. The vessels will also fill with rain, though the crystals will only be absorbing the thunder-charged *qi* of the rainwater.

Stand before the spirit of Thunder. Forming the Jing Guang hand mudra illustrated in figure 5.15 can facilitate greater control over the flow of the thunder *qi*. The spirit of Thunder has many facets that go by many different names. Some names may work better for you than others in invocations, depending on your culture and tradition.

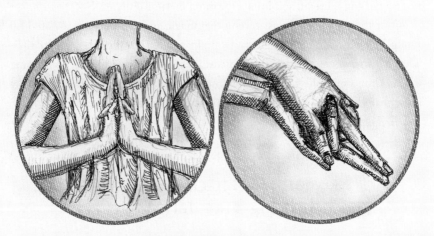

**FIGURE 5.15** Jing Guang hand mudra

In Taoist magic, Lei Gong (雷公) is the god of thunder often invoked by practitioners of thunder rites. You can also call upon the immortal Cao Guo Jiu for an assist. Certain lineages of thunder magic will invoke Zhang Dao Ling. In Taoist cosmological theory, these personified aspects are produced by a mathematical binary code, so if you prefer to work with the abstract concept of thunder as a code rather than invoke a personification of it in the form of a god, animate a drawing of the Thunder trigram—from the bottom line upward, beginning with the solid yang line and then two broken yin lines—in your mind's eye as your method for harnessing that force.

Make your request to the thunder god (or divinity of thunder you're invoking) in the form of a prayer. Invoke by name and then, in your own sincere words, request the gift of the thunder god's magic to be placed into the vessels or crystals you've set out. State your intentions, what you plan on using the thunder *qi* for. Typically, you'll state your name in the petition. Consider it good manners. For example:

> Lei Gong, Lord of Thunder, destroyer of evil, god who vanquishes demons, lord of unlimited power, I seek a few of your thunder bolts and ask that you

send them down into the vessels I've gathered here tonight. I pledge that the powers you bless me with shall never be used to maliciously harm, only to defend, in service of the good, protection of the innocent, and always with beneficent intentions. I, [*state your name*], declare all this to be true and come to you with reverent heart. *Ji ji ru lu ling.*

Repeat the incantation three times. Under the Lo Shu correspondences, the numerological assignment for Thunder is three. Leave the items out overnight through the full course of the thunderstorm. When the thunderstorm subsides, return to collect your charged objects. Gently wipe them dry, and store them covered in black silk. The black silk is believed to keep the *qi*-empowered objects from draining unnecessarily. You can also store them in a consecrated hardwood box (such as sandalwood or rosewood).

The water collected in the vessels can be used to charge talismans for protection, such as charms that ward off evil. Numismatic charms, such as coins inscribed with Taoist magical writing, or red string that will then be knotted or braided into jade jewelry for protection, can first be soaked in this thunder-charged water.

Conceptualize the crystals as fully charged batteries. They can be placed anywhere you would like the *qi* in that environment to be invigorated and to circulate in an active, electrified manner. A Taoist magician's work space would be ideally charged with such thunder *qi* to generally amplify any magical working done in that space.

# PRACTICUM 5.8:
## Retributive Justice Magic

Cao Guo Jiu personally collected his own brother's soul and imprisoned him in hell as punishment for the egregious crimes the brother had committed against a scholar's wife—and worse yet, for which he had evaded justice in the courts of man. Cao fights evil. It was the particular path to spiritual awakening he took, and he shows great determination and strength when he is seeking justice, as he had done when the Dragon King imprisoned his fellow immortal, Lan Cai He.

At the midnight hour, write out Cao Guo Jiu (曹國舅)'s name in traditional oracle bone script onto paper with a calligraphy brush. Though black ink can be used, if you can, it's more ideal to use red in this specific case, given the intentions in the matter. Write the characters out slowly and deliberately, while thinking intently on the injustice you've experienced. This is a means of communicating the facts of the situation to the Immortal.

If you are eager to try this spell out but are apprehensive about your calligraphy, it won't detrimentally influence the craft if you print out a copy of figure 5.16 and trace over the template with your ink. In fact, if doing so alleviates your worry over your calligraphy skills and liberates you to focus your intentions entirely on the spell-crafting, then it might very well be the better option to simply trace.

As the paper dries, assemble as many personal identifiers of the perpetrator as you can, which will be shown to Cao Guo Jiu so the perpetrator can be identified. When your calligraphy ink has fully dried, fold the parchment over to wrap any of the personal identifiers you'll be sending to Cao Guo Jiu, such as printed papers with the perpetrator's name, photographs, any objects that might still have a trace of the perpetrator's *qi*, and the like. Tie the bundle together with red string.

FIGURE 5.16
Cao Guo Jiu's name in calligraphy.

Go somewhere far from where you live to bury this in the earth and plant a seedling tree directly above it. The seedling tree will help to fortify your bundle with Wood *qi* per the Wu Xing five changing phases.

Afterward, take a bath or rinse yourself with salt water. You can do this by way of a washcloth soaked in a homemade solution of one cup water to three spoonfuls of sea salt. Boil the water and sea salt together for about fifteen minutes, then remove from heat and let cool. Once the water reaches room temperature, use it to rinse yourself. If you're taking a bath, pour the salt solution into the bathwater.

Part of having unwavering faith is to fully leave this matter behind you. You've put it in the immortal's hands, and you must rest assured that he will make sure the perpetrator gets the correctly measured retributive penalty for how you were wronged. You may or may not see it, and it may be beyond your capability to recognize how the perpetrator has been punished, so you have to detach, let go, and hold that faith. Perform the retributive justice spell, put it in the hands of the immortal, and let go, move on.

## Wind (Xùn), Influence: The Shaman

| Trigram Name | Oracle Bone Script | Nature | Oracle Bone Script |
|---|---|---|---|
| Wind ☴ 巽 Xùn | 巽 | 風 Fēng | 亯 |

| Wu Xing | Qi Quality | Direction | Ritual Tool | Planet | Zodiac Animals |
|---|---|---|---|---|---|
| 木 Wood | Gentle influence; a soft force. Diffusion. Genial. Humane. Agreeable. Pleasing. Pliable. Cultivated. Adaptable, flexible. | 西南 Southeast | 蓮 Lotus | 木星 Wood Star Jupiter | 龍 Dragon |
| | Clearing to increase *qi* flow. Mental acuteness. Discernment. To permeate and diffuse throughout. To reach. To pass through. The Ten Wings describes Wind as the Trigram of Decision. | Moon Phase | *Qi* in Nature | | 蛇 Snake |
| | | Waning gibbous | 風 Wind | | |

| | |
|---|---|
| **Key Associations** | Tools of the architect and the carpenter; the color white; pursuit of gains |
| **Part of the Body** | Lower limbs |
| **Traits You'll Notice** | Tall, slim, graceful, refined, elegant, fastidious, pays attention to details, restless, cares about appearances |
| **Personages** | Corporate, legal professions; teachers, educators; innovators; "ideas" people, but who may not be equipped to execute those ideas; dissemination of ideas; journalism |
| **Materials** | Telephones and cables, wood |
| **Land Forms** | Forests, woods, marketplaces, business centers, skyscrapers |
| **Building Structures** | Religious buildings or sacred sites; art displays |
| **Weather** | Windy; monsoons |
| **Travel Forecast** | Long-distance travel |
| **Hour(s)** | 7 a.m.–11 a.m. |
| **Sound** | Arias, chamber music, birdsongs |
| **Totemic Animal** | Swan |

# *He Xian Gu*
# 何仙姑

A beautiful young maiden, He Xian Gu has a vision of a fairy (仙女, xiān nǚ) who instructs her on how to find a mystical powdered mica. When she awakens, she heeds the vision, finds the mystical powder, and ingests the mica, achieving immortality. She becomes a fairy herself.

She takes a vow of chastity and, now a fairy, no longer needs to eat, so she grows lighter and lighter, able to float from village to village as she uses her powers to save and heal the people.

He Xian Gu is also described as a Taoist priestess (道姑, *Dào gū*) and a shamaness (女巫, *nǚ wū*). Her powers include the gift of prophecy and the gift of healing. He Xian Gu possesses mastery over herbs. She uses her magical white lotus to heal any illness, mental or physical.

Her animal companion is a *fenghuang* (鳳凰), or a flying phoenix. After mastering occult arts from Li Tie Guai and Lan Cai He's tutelage, she transforms a sparrow into the phoenix.

**FIGURE 5.17** He Xian Gu: The Shamaness. Qing dynasty woodblock prints.[28]

The trigram Wind is gentle influence and soft power, which He Xian Gu exemplifies through the many legends told of her compassion and gentle nature, and how storytellers have lauded her for her classically feminine traits, which are encapsulated in the gentle influence of Wind.

Wind also better memorializes her quality of *qi*, given that her companion animal is the *fenghuang* (鳳凰), aligning with the nature of Wind, *feng* (鳳).

The Wind spirit is the most influential of the nature spirits. When it wants to, it can take and deliver your message anywhere, to the top of a mountain, down into the depths of a cave, to any realm, the heavens or the underworld, or to the realm of the ancestors. The Wind spirit has a particular affinity with He Xian Gu, so if you can win her support, you'll have the Wind spirit's support as well. The Wind listens to the immortal shamaness, so appeal to He Xian Gu.

When the Ba Gua is superimposed over the Lo Shu, the trigram Wind links to the energies that influence matters relating to wealth, finances, assets, and your access to resources. For prosperity magic, Wind or the trigram Lake are optimal *qi* to be working with. Where Lake helps to produce a fertile environment for cultivating growth and prosperity, Wind clears any atrophic or harmful *qi* blocking your way. Wind gently pushes the status quo and changes it so you can achieve prosperity.

In the way that wind scatters seeds from a blossom in a process called dispersal, which is how the plant kingdom reproduces, the essence of Wind is associated symbolically with sending out your investments into the world and reaping abundance in return. While it does so, it also pushes aside and scatters what had been obstacles.

# PRACTICUM 5.9:
# Petitioning the Patron Immortal of Witches

He Xian Gu is often referred to as a "巫" *(wū)*, which can be translated as *shamaness*, but culturally is the equivalent to a witch. She is a natural patron divinity or ascended master to work with among those who identify as witches.

On an inordinately windy day, stand or sit in stillness, facing the wind, eyes closed, and petition He Xian Gu. Repeat her name several times, like a mantra. Typically, an honorific is used, such as "the Venerable He Xian Gu" or "Great Healer, Powerful and Mighty Priestess."

On each slow, drawn-out exhale, whisper her name into the wind: *huh—shen—goo*. The "huh" is a soft, breathy "h" like "hello."

In a state of calm, recite the immortal's name again: "Great Healer, Great Priestess, the Benevolent and Gentle Shamaness, He Xian Gu."

Close your eyes and let your emotions move you to find your own words of prayer. Persist, calmly and patiently, with the recitations of the immortal's name. When you can sense that she has arrived and you have her attention, speak.

Introduce yourself. Summarize your family heritage, cultural background, livelihood, and level of knowledge in the mystical arts or the level you seek to attain, and ask her to train you.

Divinities communicate with us through synchronicities. Upon your first request, she might say no or respond with silence if she finds that you are not yet ready. Do not feel dismayed—you're in great company. The Eight Immortals themselves experienced rejection from master teachers many times over. When they were still human and seeking to learn the Tao, only when they were ready did their masters finally agree to teach them. Likewise, you must be patient and persistent, and be mindful of what's in your heart, because certainly the gods already know.

# PRACTICUM 5.10:
# The Healing Wind Spirit in a Crystal Lotus

A faceted crystal lotus is commonly used as a feng shui cure. Here, you'll be using one to "bottle the Wind spirit." The efforts of your *qi* as a mystic will pull the *qi* of the Wind spirit into a vessel that can contain it, which in this case is a faceted crystal lotus.

On an inordinately windy day, sit in stillness outdoors in the direct path of the wind, and listen to the Wind spirit. Although I use the term "listen," implying hearing, the more accurate term is "sense" the wind. Quoting Confucius as characterized in the *Zhuangzi* (300 BC):

"Listen not with your ears but with your mind. Listen not with your mind but with your primal breath."[29]

The wind is poetic and expressive and is always singing, dancing, always creating art, using the world around us as its medium and canvas. And like every artist, the wind is most content when its art is appreciated. Listening to—or sensing—the wind and acknowledging its handiwork with awe and admiration will get its attention. But take care; wind is perceptive, and will detect insincerity.

Experiencing the wind while the spirit is active and appreciating its every expression is how you communicate with the Wind spirit. As you appreciate, form thoughts and send those thoughts into the wind through exhales of breath. That's how you hold a conversation—through that primal breath.

**FIGURE 5.18** Crystal lotus vessel for bottling the Wind spirit

Take in deep, steady breaths, and before you exhale, form a thought you would like to communicate to the Wind spirit. Conceptualize yourself converting that thought into energy and placing that energy atop your breath. Then exhale.

After the exhale (having completed your "train of thought"), close your mouth and breathe through your nose. Listen, sense, follow the movements and expressions of the Wind spirit. Appreciate it as being alive and sentient. The subjective act of treating another as alive and sentient, with feelings and fully formed ideas, will naturally cause you to be more respectful and compassionate. That's why you want to shift your paradigm into perceiving the Wind as, first and foremost, a spirit, and second, as sentient. The state of empathy you achieve from showing respect and compassion will be crucial for this exercise to work.

When you can sense that a certain affinity and rapport has been established with the Wind spirit, be candid and share your issue with Wind. What are you bottling the Wind spirit's $qi$ for?

The Wind spirit's $qi$ heals and can help reshape and therefore reform what has accumulated in the past, just as it reshapes land formations through its gentle influence, and can thus push and carve away what was causing harm to health. Wind is sentient, and if you receive its $qi$ with the spirit's blessing, the *qi* of Wind will have the intelligence to precisely remove what is harmful and preserve what is good.

Once you have fully relayed why you need to bottle Wind's *qi* and you've stated your request, wait patiently for a sign. An omen will come and you will know in your heart, by the way the wind communicates to you through the expressions you've now attuned yourself to understanding, that Wind seeks to bless you and is ready.

At that time, hold up the crystal lotus, open blossom side facing the wind, and wait for the intensity of the wind to pick up. Keeping the lotus open like a net catching the *qi*, close your eyes so you can concentrate on attuning your personal *qi* to that of the Wind spirit. By tempering and balancing until both are at the same wavelength, you create a closed circuit of sorts, allowing concentrated Wind *qi* to flow into your crystal lotus and charge it like a battery. Let the Tao of Wind and your Tao within become one. This is the mystic living and practicing the wisdom of the I Ching.

You'll know when the crystal lotus is as filled as it will get. At that time, you can set it down and resume your light conversation with Wind. Express your gratitude.

You can feel the charged crystal lotus vibrating differently in your hands now. A crystal lotus charged with the Wind spirit is a powerful healing talisman. Place it on the bedstand of one who is ill. The talisman will emit a gentle calming and healing energy. Inside a home that has too much stagnant energy, causing lethargy, fatigue, and even compromised immune systems among its occupants, those conditions can be alleviated somewhat with a Wind spirit–charged crystal lotus.

# PRACTICUM 5.11:
# Wind Divination and the I Ching

Wind divination, called *fēng jiǎo* 風角, is a traditional method of divination dating back to the Han dynasty. *Fēng* 風 is wind and *jiǎo* 角 is a horn, in reference to the music and cadences of the sound of wind. Sounds of the wind are categorized into five tones, corresponding with the Wu Xing. King Wen's Later Heaven arrangement of trigrams is superimposed over the Lo Shu magic square so that each trigram corresponds with one of the eight directions.

On a windy day, sit outside with compass in hand and feel the wind. Which direction is it blowing from, and which direction is it blowing toward? Adjust your position until the wind is blowing directly on your face, and note the directionality.

If you are facing due north and the wind is blowing on your face from the north, then it is a north wind. A north wind corresponds with the trigram Water, generally considered ominous. A north wind signifies a "chilling" of luck. In contrast, if you are facing due south with the wind blowing on your face from the south, since that direction corresponds with Fire, it's considered fortuitous. A south wind signifies a "warming" of luck. An east wind (you are facing due east and the wind is blowing on your face) corresponds with Thunder, and the Wu Xing phase of Wood, so great change is coming. A west wind, corresponding with Lake, brings advancement after a productive gestation phase.

**TABLE 5.15** *Fēng Jiǎo* Wind Divination Directional Correspondences

| TRIGRAMS | HEXAGRAM # | WIND | FORECAST |
| --- | --- | --- | --- |
| Wind over Heaven | 9 | Northwest | Storm is brewing. Unseen influences. Make preparations: conserve and preserve. |
| Heaven over Wind | 44 | Southeast | What had been suppressed now reemerges with a vengeance. Negotiate compromises. |
| Fire over Water | 64 | North | After a peak comes a decline. Waning period to come. Pray and seek divine guidance. |
| Water over Fire | 63 | South | Auspicious omen for minor affairs. The gods are pleased. Chaos becomes order. |

**TABLE 5.15** *Fēng Jiǎo* Wind Divination Directional Correspondences *(continued)*

| TRIGRAMS | HEXAGRAM # | WIND | FORECAST |
|---|---|---|---|
| Earth over Mountain | 15 | Northeast | Cull away excess. Do not take major risks at this time. Favorable outcome despite obstacles. |
| Mountain over Earth | 23 | Southwest | Turbulence. Move slowly and methodically. Brewing political strife. Social conflicts. |
| Thunder over Lake | 54 | West | Alliances bring prosperity. Wet conditions bring a delayed harvest season. |
| Lake over Thunder | 17 | East | Supreme good auspices. Advantageous timing and positioning. Progressive movement. |

For the five tones, this will call for some intuition. A quick tempo, higher-pitched wind corresponds with Wood. The phases change in the order of Wood, Fire, Earth, Metal, and Water. At the opposite end of the range, a slow tempo, lower-pitched wind corresponds with Water. Listen intuitively to whether the wind sounds cheerful or ominous.

Astrological considerations for the date and time of the wind are also accounted for, and historically, the sexagenary calendar of heavenly stems and earthly branches were used. Thus, a southeast wind in the winter would be interpreted differently from a southeast wind in spring. Geomancy, or feng shui, was also considered. The land formations at the site where the wind is heard and their feng shui correspondences were factored in as well.

Wind divination is an invaluable technique to cultivate, no matter what tradition of mysticism, shamanism, or witchcraft you practice. It teaches you to listen to the land. In turn, among society you learn to listen to the voices that aren't shouting, but rather those who have important, truthful messages to convey. At the end of the day, a shaman is someone who possesses a deep understanding of people. An incidental result of mastering wind divination is a skill for listening to and understanding people.

# Water (Kǎn), Mysteries: The Healer

| Trigram Name | | Oracle Bone Script | Nature | Oracle Bone Script |
|---|---|---|---|---|
| ☵ Water | 坎 Kǎn | (graph) | 水 Shuǐ | (graph) |

| Wu Xing | Qi Quality | Direction | Ritual Tool | Planet | Zodiac Animal |
|---|---|---|---|---|---|
| 水 Water | The moon; lunar forces. Abyss, the darkest of depths. Danger. Risk. Rushing rivers. Depths. Waters deep and dark. The arcane and the occult. Career success. Professional development. Flowing, fluent, shifting, indefinite force. Trigram of the shape-shifter. The Ten Wings describes Water as the trigram of the blood. | 北 North | 葫蘆 Gourd | 水星 Water Star Mercury | 鼠 Rat |
| | | Moon Phase | | Qi in Nature | |
| | | Third quarter | | 水 Water | |

| | |
|---|---|
| Key Associations | Channels and ditches (that which is hidden and concealed); the wheel; thieves |
| Part of the Body | The ears |
| Traits You'll Notice | Emotional, intense, headstrong, pensive, melancholic, prone to depression, inclination toward esoteric knowledge, soft features |
| Personages | Persons in their twenties or thirties; medical professionals, nurses, health care, diplomats, cosmopolitan international relations; underhanded statecraft; cunning; sleight of hand |
| Materials | Medicines, healing soups, dark mirrors |
| Land Forms | Bodies of water, coastal terrain, rivers, the sea |

| | |
|---|---|
| **Building Structures** | Hospitals, restaurants and bars, cafes, fisherman's wharf |
| **Weather** | Heavy rains, snow, gloomy, dew, frost |
| **Travel Forecast** | Challenges encountered while traveling |
| **Hour(s)** | 11 p.m.–1 a.m. |
| **Sound** | Mantra recitations, prayers, minor keys, lamentations, nocturnes |
| **Totemic Animal** | Boar |

## *Li Tie Guai*
## 李鐵拐

Li Tie Guai achieved immortality through merit and perseverance, and he sought out many different masters to study under them. He renounced materialism, becoming a beggar, and is thus often depicted holding onto an iron crutch or rod, which can transform into a dragon. Li retreats into a cave to cultivate, isolated for forty years as an ascetic hermit until he finally awakens.

In one mythical telling, Li Tie Guai was a young, handsome man born into wealth and privilege who then retreats into a cave to cultivate himself. While deep in meditation and astral journeying, his astral spirit leaves his body for seven days, causing a passerby to assume that Li had died. His body is cremated. When Li's astral spirit returns, he finds his body in ashes. The spirit searches for a body to occupy and finds a beggar. Li occupies the body of that beggar and thus loses his previous handsome form, thereafter appearing in a rotund body with a disheveled face, and having to walk with a crutch.

During his civilian life, he was an herbalist (or pharmacologist). Thus he became a patron divinity of physicians and those in the medical profession. In addition to the iron crutch, his symbol is a medicine gourd (葫蘆), or *húlu*, filled with magical medicine pills.

Li is also associated with advocacy against social injustices and oppression. Legendary accounts of him center around the theme of helping ease the suffering of the sick, the poor, and the downtrodden.

Considering Li's animal companion, the dragon, and the Chinese dragon's association with water, especially the deep seas (the realm of the Dragon King), Li Tie Guai's powers and *qi* corresponding with the trigram Water makes sense to me. Water possesses strong metaphysical shape-shifting qualities, and given

Li Tie Guai's origin story of losing his former body while astrally journeying and having to occupy a new one, there is a lot of Water *qi* to his powers. That he is a pharmacologist by trade, where water is the vehicle for most medicinal preparations, also lends to the correspondence with the trigram Water.

Water's connection to the immortal Li Tie Guai connects it to healing magic and medicine, but also to forms of vengeance magic to rectify harms and restore justice.

**FIGURE 5.19** Li Tie Guai: The Healer. Qing dynasty woodblock prints.[30]

## PRACTICUM 5.12:
## Healing Gourd Feng Shui Cure for Good Health (and James Legge's Coin Toss Method)

Inspired by Li Tie Guai's *húlu* 葫芦, or magical gourd, fill a dried, hollowed-out calabash or bottle gourd, a traditional vessel for healing potions, with pulses, or uncooked dry legumes. It's also common to simply use a vase or container shaped like a gourd.

Per the *Yellow Emperor's Classic of Internal Medicine* (黄帝內徑, Huángdì Nèi Jìng), dated to 475–221 BC, the Wu Xing phase Water corresponds with legumes. These can be broad beans, dried green beans, dried peas, chickpeas, lentils, or the like.

After filling the gourd with the selected legumes, pass it through the smoke of incense to clear its *qi*. Typically, the crafted talisman would be placed on an altar to be blessed by a patron divinity. Set it on the altar for a full day and over the course of a full night.

**FIGURE 5.20** Calabash or bottle gourd *(húlu)*

An I Ching reading the next day will determine whether the talisman has been adequately charged and blessed for your intended purposes. When crafting your healing gourd feng shui cure talisman for sincere purposes, you'll want to utilize your tried-and-true go-to I Ching divination method. Ask, in your own words, whether the healing gourd you've crafted has been adequately blessed with healing *qi* to serve as a home feng shui cure.

However, for this exercise, we will take the opportunity to learn the simplified coin toss method that James Legge conveys in his 1899 text.

Take three pennies and throw them together a total of six times. Interpret the coin toss results as noted in table 5.16.

**TABLE 5.16** James Legge's Simplified Coin Toss Method (1899)

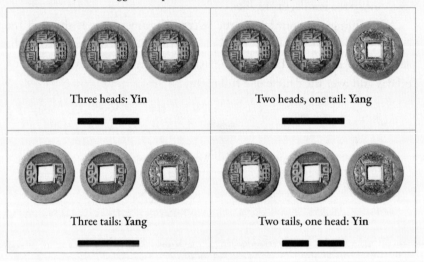

Construct the six lines from the bottom up, so that line 1 is the bottom-most line result from your first coin toss. Line 2 is the line immediately above line 1, resulting from your second coin toss. Continue until the sixth and final coin toss to construct line 6, the topmost line of your revealed hexagram.

Look up your hexagram result, and only read the oracle message for line 5 of the hexagram. Thematically, does that line indicate a positive response of yes, or a negative response of no? If yes, then you're done. If no, you may want to recalibrate. Reflect on where you may have made a misstep or how you can improve upon what you had done.

For example, I used a white porcelain vase shaped like a gourd to craft a health and healing feng shui cure. I've opted to use red beans, also known as adzuki beans. They symbolize love, marriage, and a promise to be loyal and true, but more than that, they represent longevity. The adzuki bean's red color is considered auspicious for all things related to health, wealth, and longevity.

I then used James Legge's simplified coin toss method, and my result was Earth over Heaven, or Hexagram 11. I then turned to the fifth line to read the bold-faced text. The subsequent paragraphs beneath it offered supplemental insight. The references to peace and prosperity here let me know that my healing-*qi*-endowed gourd talisman is ready to go. By the way, in the Book, any time you see "吉" *(ji)* the answer is indicative of good auspices and prosperity. The ideogram is the image of a jade tablet and is thus a symbol of good luck and divine authority granted.

Place the filled bottle gourd in your kitchen, and integrate it into your décor in that area of the home. In feng shui, this bottle gourd is a symbol of health, wellness, and longevity. As a magical talisman, it's believed to help ward against illness and generally bless the occupants of the home with good health and longevity.

Alternatively, if you aren't able to source a gourd, a copper water vessel works just as well.

# Mountain (Gěn), Knowledge: The Alchemist

| Trigram Name | | Oracle Bone Script | Nature | Oracle Bone Script |
|---|---|---|---|---|
| Mountain ☶ | Gěn 艮 | (script) | Shān 山 | (script) |

| Wu Xing | Qi Quality | Direction | Ritual Tool | Planet | Zodiac Animals |
|---|---|---|---|---|---|
| 土 Earth | Stillness, to stop, to halt. Serenity, tranquility. Inactivity. Quietude. Lull. Standstill. Preserving, stabilizing, balancing force. Cultivating knowledge. Excelling in ceremonial magic (方術, fāng shù, or 藝術, yìshù). | 東北 Northeast | 魚鼓 Fish drum | 土星 Earth star Saturn | 牛 Ox |
| | | Moon Phase | Qi in Nature | | 虎 Tiger |
| | | Waning crescent | 山 Mountain | | |

| | |
|---|---|
| **Key Associations** | Gateways, vines, tall and strong trees |
| **Part of the Body** | The hands |
| **Traits You'll Notice** | Skillful, clever, introverted, stubborn, stagnant, quiet unless spoken to, resistant to change, pensive, philosophical |
| **Personages** | Peak of life; someone self-assured and independent-thinking; builder, architect, geologist, historian, archaeologist |
| **Materials** | Clay, stone, earthy materials |
| **Land Forms** | Hills and mountains, forests, small paths not often traveled, rocky terrain; caves or dark caverns within the mountain (if combined with Fire or Thunder, could indicate volcano) |
| **Building Structures** | Industrial buildings or complexes; religious buildings |
| **Weather** | Unpredictable |
| **Travel Forecast** | Travel delays |

| | |
|---|---|
| **Hour(s)** | 1 a.m.–5 a.m. |
| **Sound** | Dark, rounded timbres, precise pitches |
| **Totemic Animal** | Wolf/Dog[31] |

## *Zhang Guo Lao*
## 張果老

According to legend, Zhang Guo Lao was a peasant boy, and one day on his way to market with his donkey, he made a detour to a mysterious abandoned monastery where he found a bubbling cauldron of stew. Starving, he ate from the cauldron and fed some of the stew to his donkey. Little did he realize that the cauldron contained an alchemical elixir of immortality. After he became

**FIGURE 5.21** Zhang Guo Lao: The Alchemist Qing dynasty woodblock prints.[32]

immortal, he became a recluse hermit to master inner and outer alchemy, cultivate magical powers, and practice Taoist magic. Zhang became one of the most renowned *fangshi* 方士 or masters of the occult arts.[33]

Mundane or exoteric powers associated with Zhang Guo Lao include the birthing of sons; blessings of healthy, happy baby boys; wine; and wine-making. Magical or esoteric powers associated with the immortal are far ranging, as he is *the* immortal patron of occultists, alchemists, necromancers, and healers, given the legend associated with *how* he became an immortal.

He is associated with the fish drum (魚鼓) or *yúgǔ* often found on a Taoist ceremonial magician's altar. The fish drum is hit while reciting scriptures, mantras, or incantations. The sound of the fish drum removes obstacles and awakens consciousness. Taoist ceremonial magicians use the fish drum in rituals to amplify the power of incantations and to bring spirits under their control.

Zhang's animal companion, the donkey, is adept at scaling mountains. Considering the plethora of legends involving alchemists or alchemy happening in seclusion atop high mountains, the connection between that archetypal facet of the mystic and Mountain works. The stillness and serenity of Mountain is what the Alchemist's heart must be to succeed at turning stone (or lead) into gold.

Mountain, expressed in the neutral Earth phase of change, corresponds with cultivation of the magical arts (方術, *fāng shù*, or 藝術, *yìshù*), such as geomancy (堪輿, *kānyú*), ceremonial magic, and crafting talismans that activate powers petitioned from spirits. Mastery over the magical arts and true power requires the personal *qi* to be like Mountain, in stillness and unmoved; and through that state of Mountain, the practitioner can execute the magical methods. The state of the most powerful alchemists is expressed by Mountain.

# PRACTICUM 5.13:
# Inner Alchemy: Visualization
# Technique for Spiritual Cultivation

When the Ba Gua is superimposed over the Lo Shu magic square used in feng shui, Mountain as a metaphysical essence links to the energies that influence matters relating to knowledge and education. Working with the trigram Mountain, you'll practice a form of astral projection that will lead you to a divinatory insight into which area of study to cultivate or which practice to deepen and advance in further.

Practices of astral projection were popular in Tang dynasty grimoires dating to AD 618–907. These instructions would typically consist of meditation or breathing techniques along with visualization of a symbolic narrative. Astral projection was also taught as a method for meeting and conferring with the gods.

Start by focusing a meditative gaze on the trigram Mountain and either beat a drum (traditionally you might opt for the Taoist fish drum) or listen to an audio recording of drumming to 220 beats per minute (bpm) to best induce theta waves in the brain. You can find a metronome application and set it to 220 bpm to figure out what that rhythm is. Visualize the solid nature of a mountain, and impose that visualization over yourself, sitting so as to imitate a mountain—sitting tall, back and spine straight, chin up, head facing forward, and securely rooted in your seat.

Immersed in this meditation, let the sound of the drumbeats shift your consciousness. Strive to connect to a sense of a collective unconscious, or the universe on an astral plane.

Close your eyes and let your astral body float up and out of your body through the crown of your head. Your astral body ascends into the clouds of the heavens, and beyond the clouds, your vision clears as you see yourself landing just outside the entranceway to an abandoned Buddhist-style monastery. Enter the monastery, and in the clearing just before the temple, you see a cauldron just as the peasant boy Zhang Guo Lao had seen before becoming an immortal.

Gaze into the cauldron, which appears filled with a golden broth, and see your own face reflected back at you. This reflection is you, but it is also not exactly you; this is your Higher Self, an ascended version of you. Speak to this reflection of you as the Higher Self. Ask for a sign or omen regarding which area of study to cultivate next, which one will advance your destined path, or which one will best serve your higher purpose.

Hear yourself saying aloud a statement of what knowledge you seek or what spiritual practice you would like mastery over.

When you feel ready, visualize yourself cupping your hands in the reflective waters, watching the reflection of your own face ripple, and drink from the golden broth in that cauldron.

Take your time making your way out to exit the monastery grounds, and leap through the clouds, feeling your astral body descend back into your physical body. When you feel your astral body realign within your body, open your eyes.

Be patient and take a few deep breaths to reorient in the waking state. Know that a sign or omen will be presented to you in the next seven days revealing to you which path of study to take on next, to deepen, to advance, which will lead to greater personal empowerment.

## Earth (Kūn), Field: The Enchanter

| Trigram Name | | Oracle Bone Script | Nature | Oracle Bone Script |
|---|---|---|---|---|
| Earth ☷ | 坤 Kūn | 〔glyph〕 | 地 Dì | 〔glyph〕 |

| Wu Xing | Qi Quality | Direction | Ritual Tool | Planet | Zodiac Animals |
|---|---|---|---|---|---|
| 土 Earth | Naturally occurring receptive force; receiving; absorbing and then nurturing or cultivating; the fertile field for growth. | 西南 Southwest | 花籃 Flower basket | 土星 Earth star Saturn | 羊 Sheep |
| | Per its Lo Shu correspondence, Earth blesses with healthy, loving romantic relationships. Yet this is also the trigram that can connect us to the underworld, guided there by the earth goddess. | Moon Phase | Qi in Nature | | 猴 Monkey |
| | | New moon | 地 Soil Field | | |

| | |
|---|---|
| **Key Associations** | The cauldron, a wagon, black soil, woven textiles, variety and multitudes |
| **Part of the Body** | Torso or trunk of the body |
| **Traits You'll Notice** | Open and receptive, devoted, faithful, loyal, nurturing, easygoing, passive, frail, moderate, temperate, patient, calm; larger belly or thicker torso; square |
| **Personages** | Queen, mother, farmer, artisan, the masses; manufacturing, fashion, retail, marketing |
| **Materials** | Clay, silk, grains, cotton, fabrics |
| **Land Forms** | Open fields, rural, country, small town |
| **Building Structures** | Basement, smaller houses, earth tones |
| **Weather** | Misty, light rain, cloudy, dank or dark |
| **Travel Forecast** | Travel delays |
| **Hour(s)** | 1 p.m.–5 p.m. |
| **Sound** | Silence; or night sounds, crickets chirping late at night |
| **Totemic Animal** | Bull |

# Lan Cai He
# 藍采和

An immortal who embodies a trickster archetype, Lan Cai He is gender fluid and is often depicted as androgynous. Depictions range from feminine presenting wearing feminine clothes with a masculine voice, to masculine clothes with a feminine voice, to intentionally ambiguous. Ultimately, gender presentation of Lan Cai He gets left up to the authors who write the stories, so throughout the centuries, characterizations have ranged widely. As noted by British sinologist Walter Perceval Yetts, "Legend relating to this *hsien* [immortal] is so uncertain that even the question of sex seems to be left to the fancy of the artist."[34]

Lan carries a basket of magical fruits and flowers with varying purposes, including magical mushrooms, healing herbs, orchids, and enchanting chrysanthemums, and thus is often considered a patron divinity to florists and gardeners.

**FIGURE 5.22** Lan Cai He: The Enchanter. Qing dynasty woodblock prints.[35]

Lan was renowned for being a talented entertainer, dancer, and musician, someone who wandered drunk from town to town, singing lyrics that seemed nonsensical, but always revealed the deepest secrets of the Tao. Lan Cai He's great power is mastery over the physical body's responses to the elements. The immortal was often depicted as not dressing for the weather, meaning it would snow or rain, and Lan would be dressed as if it were summer, or it would be sunny and warm, and Lan would be dressed in winter clothes.

Lan achieved such mastery over the body that Lan did not feel excess heat or cold, did not grow sick or old, and did not feel pain, as represented by the immortal's innocent smile and happy, sprightly demeanor.

A common characterization would be Lan begging on the streets for money or singing and dancing for tips, then letting the money dangle from broken cords so that the coins fell back on to the streets as Lan walked.

Lan did not visibly age, and as the decades advanced, retained the gift of youth. Lan achieved immortality by living a carefree, worry-free lifestyle. By transcending the drudgery of routine labor and not caring about money or wealth, Lan achieved spiritual awakening and cultivated the power to be impervious to discomfort and physical pain.

While the other immortals are associated with having studied alchemy or dedicated hard work to spiritual cultivation, it's not entirely clear how Lan Cai He achieves awakening, other than through natural joie de vivre and disinterest in materialism.

The archetype for the mystic to embody through the trigram Earth is that of the Enchanter. This is the ability to hold magical influence over others, as Lan possesses. The trigram Earth is a force of receptivity and nurturance, which are emanations of empathy. To truly charm others, one must be empathetic and empathic. Lan's association with a magical cornucopia of fruits and flowers connects the immortal to the *qi* of Earth—that of the soil, and that of one who is truly receptive of others' needs and feelings.

## PRACTICUM 5.14:
## Calling upon the Earth Goddess to Remove Your Pain

According to Buddhist lore, three lesser demons—Desire, Fulfillment, and Regret—attempt to lure the Gautama Buddha away from the path of enlightenment. He resists. After they fail, Mara, the Demon King, brings his army to challenge the Buddha. Mara transforms himself into illusory dharma, appealing to Gautama by contending that Gautama still owes a moral duty to those on earth. Enlightenment would disrupt the natural order and bring harm to the earthly realm. Gautama reaches down to the ground with his right hand, forming the *bhumisparsha* mudra, and calls upon the Earth Goddess as witness. The Earth Goddess appears and affirms that Gautama Buddha has complied with all true dharma and gives her blessing for his enlightenment. Thereafter, the Buddha attains nirvana.

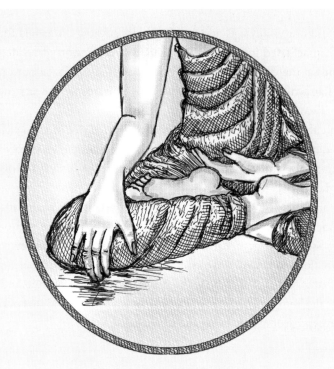

FIGURE 5.23 *Bhumisparsha* hand mudra

Before he ascends, and with the Earth Goddess's blessing, the Buddha proclaims that the *bhumisparsha* (earth touching) mudra is a consecrated gesture that anyone may use to call upon the Earth Goddess to confess any pain, shame, or guilt, or any failure of duty, violation of law or order, any transgression to dharma, and when their right hand touches the earth, the Goddess will draw out their pain and alleviate them of the impurities the pain has caused. The Buddha leaves behind this blessing for the people.

The following meditation exercise will help calm, center, and ground you when you most need it. In times when your heart is unstill or you are feeling unsettled by your past, or when you seek to call upon the powerful nurturing maternal force of the Earth Goddess to bear witness to you and to affirm your destiny, sit upon the earth and connect to the Earth Goddess through this mudra.

Find a quiet place outdoors where you can be in solitude. Sit in meditation position or in a manner that is comfortable for you. Close your eyes and feel how your foundation connects to the earth, how the earth supports you, how safe and secure you feel with that support.

Reach down to the ground and place your right hand upon the soil. Call upon the Earth Goddess. Ask her to bear witness. When you feel her nurturing presence, convert all the pain, anxiety, and suffering you are feeling into a dark, viscous, tar-like *qi*, and then feel it drain out of you through your hand and into the ground. Then feel the Earth Goddess taking that pain away from you. Feel the catharsis that happens.

When your desires or regrets disempower you, this simple release-and-purification exercise will restore your inner balance. When you are unclear as to how you can reconcile dharma with your past acts and contemplated future acts, call upon the Earth Goddess to bear witness, and she will send you omens of guidance.

**FIGURE 5.24** *Assembly of the Eight Immortals* (Song dynasty). Embroidered tapestry.
SOURCE: National Palace Museum, Taipei.

## Circling the Square: The I Ching Mandala

In a passage from the Book of Documents 書經 (Shūjīng), the Duke of Zhou asks his brother Ji Shi 姬奭, "Where do numbers come from?"

Ji Shi replies that numbers come from the circle and the square.[36]

The square is the double of two right-angled triangles, which are formed from 90-degree angles. This is the Pythagorean triple of 3, 4, 5 that is the basis of trigonometry.

Explains Ji Shi, "The square pertains to Earth, and the circle pertains to Heaven."

The metaphor of Earth being square dates back to the Xia dynasty, predating the Shang.[37] Sacrificial altars built by the clans of the Xia had one feature in common: the platforms were square, with a circular enclosure built around the

**FIGURE 5.25** Squaring the circle of changes

square. The consecrated site for worshipping gods and ancestors consisted of the circular enclosure, while the shaman stood upon the square platform to perform the rites. Thus, circling the square creates the shaman's sacred space, just as ritualized representations of circling the square are integral to I Ching divination.

The templates from which our world was created are numbers and archetypes. That's what we learned from Shao Yong's eleventh-century mathematical universe philosophy.

When King Wen's arrangement of the eight trigrams (archetypes) and the Hé Tú Luò Shū (numbers) are placed within the circle of sixty-four hexagrams, we square the circle, and circle the square—a symbol of the Great Work. In Western alchemy, circling the square is a metaphor for the philosopher's stone. The philosopher's stone, in turn, is a metaphor for turning lead to gold, achieving immortality, and completing one's magnum opus.

That is the purpose of studying the I Ching. The mandala is both the compass and the atlas for finding your Way and realizing Heaven's Will 天命 for you. When we circle the square, we achieve knowledge and conversation with the Tao. The shaman perceives the Tao as gods, ancestors, and spirits—*shén* 神.

To circle the square is to go through the gateways of the four alchemical phases: *nigredo, albedo, citrinitas,* and *rubedo*.[38] In Eastern alchemy, that's Wood (sprouting and cultivating), Fire (blooming and inspiring), Earth (ripening and maturing), Metal (culminating and extinguishing), and Water (reflecting and returning) of the Wu Xing.

From the center point of the circle, you are able to see in the four directions and know every moment in the cycles of time, thus achieving transcendence. The four directions and the four seasons represent four gates.

The I Ching is a mandala of the universe. Sacred in Hinduism, Buddhism, and Shinto, mandalas contain a square with four gates within a circle; from there, unique geometric forms and symbols express the spiritual journey of circling the square. In Shinto, mandalas are maps transmitted to us by the *kami*. A shaman uses these maps to navigate the astral spaces of the spirits. When you are the shaman who connects Heaven and Earth, you circle the square.

Mandalas represent impermanence, resonant with the I Ching's theme of change. The four affinities of yin and yang establish the gateways of the I Ching mandala. When the four affinities combine and multiply, they produce the eight trigrams, and by a mathematical process they then form the circle of sixty-four hexagrams. They also form an eight-by-eight square grid.

**FIGURE 5.26** *Om Yamantaka hum phat: Vajrabhairava* mandala (1332)[39]. 大威德金剛 *(Dà wēi dé jīn gāng)*. Yuan dynasty *kesi* tapestry 緙絲, or woven silk textile art. SOURCE: Metropolitan Museum of Art.

Thus, innate to the function of the hexagrams is circling the square. Study of the I Ching and putting its wisdom into action for yourself is a form of inner alchemical work. It is inner alchemy that materializes physical results of greater self-awareness and heightened achievement. The Oracle doesn't teach you a particular set of doctrines. Rather, the Oracle reveals to you what you've believed all along. It clarifies your Truth, and it does so by compelling you to solve its riddles. Thus, I emphasize that the I Ching is universal, transcending culture and history, available for anyone and everyone to access.

# 6

# The Five Phases of Change (Wu Xing)

WHAT ACCELERATES ALCHEMICAL reactions between the eight trigrams? The catalyst for the transformations that result from changing lines (the *yao*) or trigrams (the *gua*) pairing off to become hexagrams is categorized into five different phases, or the Wu Xing (五行).

*Wŭ* (五) means "five" and *xíng* (行) means "movement," so a direct translation might be the Five Movements. You might also hear the Wu Xing referred to as the Five Agents. I opt for the five phases of change.

The five phases of change express the five basic transformations forming the physical concept of mass-energy equivalence—the concept that, on some fundamental level, anything of physical matter is equivalent to energy. It's the scientific concept that mass is a measure of energy content, reliant on the speed of light. While $E = mc^2$ is in the realm of physics, in the realm of Eastern metaphysics Wu Xing expresses the five phases of energy as it transforms into matter. Through certain agents of change, mass can become energy, and energy becomes mass.

What drives the changing lines? What propels movement from one hexagram to another? The answer is *qi*, and there are two characters of *qi*—yin and yang—but fueling the changes of yin and yang *qi* are the Wu Xing.

These five agents or phases of change are expressed as follows:

1. **Wood** (木, Mù): The energy of sprouting; generating vitality. Wood motivates the myriad things to grow.
2. **Fire** (火, Huǒ): The energy of blooming and expansion with heat. Fire expands the myriad things and spreads them all over the world.

3. **Earth** (土, Tǔ): The energy of ripening. This is a stable, damp transition period. Earth swallows the myriad things.

4. **Metal** (金, Jīn): The energy of extinguishing. This is also harvesting, collecting, and dryness. Metal destroys the myriad things.

5. **Water** (水, Shuǐ): The energy of returning. This is stillness, contracting, and coldness. Water nourishes the myriad things.

The earliest reference to the Wu Xing is sourced from the Book of Documents,[1] dating to the Shang and Zhou dynasties:

一、五行：一曰水，二曰火，三曰木，四曰金，五曰土。

"First, the Five Agents of Change: The first is Water, the second is Fire, the third is Wood, the fourth is Metal, the fifth is Earth."

水曰潤下，火曰炎上，木曰曲直，金曰從革，土爰稼穡。

"Water is the dampness moving downward, Fire is the rising flame, Wood is the straight column, Metal will reform and expel, Earth is the sowing, the labor, and the harvest of the grains."

The annals of the philosopher Zhuang Zhi, circa fifth century BC, described *qi* as giving "rise to the Five Tastes; display themselves as the Five Colors, and are evidenced by the Five Sounds."[2] However, it isn't until 350–270 BC that the Wu Xing as it is systemized today becomes fully developed into the "Five Powers" of Wood, Fire, Earth, Metal, and Water.[3] Zou Yan (305–240 BC), an alchemist and magician, noted that these Five Powers caused, influenced, and could even predict the rise and fall of natural phenomena and of governments and civilizations.[4]

Yin (陰) changes through the phases (or alchemical agents) Metal (Jīn) and Water (Shuǐ). Metal corresponds with the western direction, where the sun sets, and Water corresponds with the north, where it's cold. Metal is autumn and Water is winter.

Note how Heaven, which is three yang lines, is created when the agent of change Metal governs yin. I interpret that as answering the philosophical question of which came first, yin or yang; since Metal acting upon yin results in Heaven, a rather dominant form of yang, I would say that in the order of Creation, yin came first.

**TABLE 6.1** Phase Changes of Yin: Metal and Water

| 陰 Yin | 少陰 Younger yin | 金 Metal | 乾 Heaven | 兌 Lake | ▲ Analytic ▼ Overwrought |  |
|---|---|---|---|---|---|---|
| | | | | | Direction | West |
| | | | | | Season | Autumn |
| | | | | | Planet | Venus |
| | | | | | Action | Harvest, gather |
| | 太陰 Elder yin | 水 Water | 坎 Water | | ▲ Compassionate ▼ Callous | |
| | | | | | Direction | North |
| | | | | | Season | Winter |
| | | | | | Planet | Mercury |
| | | | | | Action | Contract, retreat |

**TABLE 6.2** Phase Changes of Yang: Wood and Fire

| 陽 Yang | 少陽 Younger yang | 木 Wood | 震 Thunder | 巽 Wind | ▲ Resilient ▼ Stiff | |
|---|---|---|---|---|---|---|
| | | | | | Direction | East |
| | | | | | Season | Spring |
| | | | | | Planet | Jupiter |
| | | | | | Action | Growth, sprout |
| | 太陽 Elder yang | 火 Fire | 離 Fire | | ▲ Passion ▼ Hatred | |
| | | | | | Direction | South |
| | | | | | Season | Summer |
| | | | | | Planet | Mars |
| | | | | | Action | Expand, assert |

Yang (陽) changes alchemically through the phases of Wood (Mù) and Fire (Huǒ). Wood corresponds with the eastern direction, where the sun rises, and Fire corresponds with the south, where it's hot. Wood is spring, the season of growth, and Fire is summer.

**TABLE 6.3** Yin and Yang at Equilibrium: Earth

| Yin and yang in balance | 土 Earth | 坤 Earth | 艮 Mountain | ▲ Contentment ▼ Distress | |
|---|---|---|---|---|---|
| | | | | Direction | Center |
| | | | | Season | |
| | | | | Planet | Saturn |
| | | | | Action | Equilibrium |

**TABLE 6.4** Five Turning Points in the Human Narrative Cycle

| First turning | 木<br>Wood | Optimism. Curiosity. Growth spurts. Skills development. Tillage. |
|---|---|---|
| Second turning | 火<br>Fire | Awakening. Expansion. Pushing boundaries. Enthusiasm for life. |
| Third turning | 土<br>Earth | Seeking balance and purpose. Stability in relationships. Aspiring for harmony. |
| Fourth turning | 金<br>Metal | Defending what you've attained. Standing your ground. Unraveling. Dismantling. |
| Fifth turning | 水<br>Water | Calm in the face of crisis. Experiences of mortality bring wisdom. |

Equilibrium between yin and yang is the fifth changing phase, Earth (Tǔ). Earth is still flux, meaning *qi* energy is still flowing, but it is doing so internally such that the inherent binary of energy is of equal forces in opposition. The "change" of two forces opposing one another creates a surface of stillness, producing matter such as the trigram Mountain.

Further underscoring my theory that in the order of Creation yin came first, to produce the state of Earth (the trigram), yin and yang need to be in balance. Dominant yin (the trigram Earth) is not produced from any presence of yang, whereas dominant yang (the trigram Heaven) can only be produced with the elemental presence of yin.

**TABLE 6.5** Five Phase Changes and the Four Faces of God

| 木<br>Wood | 火<br>Fire | 土<br>Earth | 金<br>Metal | 水<br>Water |
|---|---|---|---|---|
| 少陽<br>Younger yang | 太陽<br>Elder yang | Yin and yang in balance | 少陰<br>Younger yin | 太陰<br>Elder yin |

The Wu Xing correspond with the four combinations of yin and yang, or the Four Faces of God (四象, sì xiàng) as noted in table 6.5. When yin progresses into yang, that face is called "younger yang." The agent of change causing this particular order is Wood. When yang progresses into more yang, that face is called "elder yang," and its agent of change is Fire (the Wu Xing Fire 火, not to be confused with the trigram Fire 離).

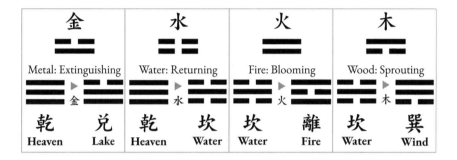

Under I Ching cosmological theory, the trigram Heaven changes into Lake when the agent of change is Metal. Heaven changes into Water when the agent of change is Water. Water becomes Fire if there is the presence of the Xing (行), or driving force of Fire (not to be confused with the trigram Fire).

The Wu Xing is the basis of East Asian philosophy, metaphysics, medicine, martial arts, and every aspect of culture in between. The Sacred Seven of traditional astrology—the sun, moon, Mercury, Venus, Mars, Jupiter, and Saturn—are connected to the Wu Xing, and the seven-day week is named after them: Tuesday is Fire, Wednesday Water, Thursday Wood, Friday Metal, and Saturday Earth, with Sunday and Monday the sun and moon respectively.

At the intersection of traditional Chinese medicine and natal astrology, the phase change dominant in a person's birth chart is used to consider which physical health complications they are more likely to experience in life due to their innate *qi*. The dominating phase in the chart is interpreted as showing what *qi* tends to be overactive in that person's physical constitution, and which may, if left unchecked or imbalanced, cause the organs and systems corresponding to that phase change to weaken due to the excess strain on that *qi*. Ba Zi (八字), which literally translates to the Eight Terms, is one traditional method for assessing dominant and weak phases in a body constitution. The eight terms, calculated based on date, time, and location of birth, create Four Pillars of Destiny that are used to assess fate.

For example, if someone's chart is Metal dominant, then in theory, that person's body tends to put undue strain on Metal *qi*. They'll want to keep their body well supplied with Metal *qi* to stay balanced. To the Taoist mystic, that means eating a diet that supports Metal *qi*. Otherwise there could be greater vulnerability to lung and respiratory conditions, such as asthma.

People who are Fire dominant tend to exhaust more Fire *qi*, so if their regular diet does not support that excess use of Fire *qi*, the predicted result under Wu Xing theory would be heart or circulatory issues. A chart that is Water dominant can indicate a person being more prone to kidney and urinary tract conditions. Earth dominance in the chart of a person who isn't then adequately supported with Earth *qi* to maintain its balance can result in tendencies to experience stomach and digestive issues. Wood-dominant charts are seen as being more prone to liver and metabolic issues.

**TABLE 6.6** Wu Xing and Human Functions

|  | WOOD | FIRE | EARTH | METAL | WATER |
|---|---|---|---|---|---|
| Heavenly stem (yang) | 甲 *Jiǎ* | 丙 *Bǐng* | 戊 *Wù* | 庚 *Gēng* | 壬 *Rén* |
| Heavenly stem (yin) | 乙 *Yǐ* | 丁 *Dīng* | 己 *Jǐ* | 辛 *Xīn* | 癸 *Guǐ* |
| Sense | Sight | Touch | Taste | Smell | Hearing |
| Organs | Liver, gallbladder | Heart, small intestine | Stomach, spleen, pancreas | Lungs, large intestine | Kidney, bladder |
| Organ systems or functions | Endocrine, metabolism, reproductive | Nervous, cardiovascular, circulatory | Muscular, lymphatic, digestive | Respiratory, integumentary, skin and hair | Skeletal, urinary, detoxifying |
| Chemical composition | Carbohydrates | Lipids | Proteins | Nucleic acids | Water |
| Brain function | Language | Voluntary movement | Judgment | Memory | Involuntary movement |

**TABLE 6.6** Wu Xing and Human Functions *(continued)*

|  | WOOD | FIRE | EARTH | METAL | WATER |
|---|---|---|---|---|---|
| **Body part** | Tendons | Blood vessels | Muscles | Skin | Bones |
| **Finger** | Index | Middle | Thumb | Ring | Little |
| **Taste** | Sour | Bitter | Sweet | Pungent | Salty |
| **Color** | Green | Red | Yellow | White | Blue |
| **Mental** | Sensitivity | Motivation | Clarity | Intuition | Empathy |
| **Personality** | Charity, benevolence, generosity, openness | Leadership, passion, sensuality, avarice, greed | Confidence, diligence, patience, perseverance | Courageousness, independence, communication, rationalism | Diplomacy, congeniality, sociability, mercurial |
| **Life phase** | Early childhood | Prepuberty | Adolescence | Adulthood | Old age and conception |

In Eastern philosophy, Wu Xing is used to help curate a diet that will, in the long term, alleviate certain health conditions. For example, if someone tends to have digestive problems, sweet foods will sit better with the body constitution (e.g., cooking with honey and adding honey to your drinks; steamed rice is considered "sweet"), as will yellow squash, yellow bell peppers (applying color theory to diet), golden potatoes, and foods rich in yellow tones. One with a weak liver will find that sour foods and cooking with a little more vinegar will help to keep their Wood-dominant *qi* in balance, along with eating more greens. Those with weak kidneys might do well to add more eggplant, purple cabbage, black currants, blueberries, and plums.[5]

There is no scientific data to back up these claims, however. Thus, while integrating Wu Xing into a balanced and healthy diet could have some benefits, it should not be relied upon at the surrender of common sense.

Also, under the theories of traditional Chinese medicine, our body constitutions do not necessarily stay the same from cradle to grave. The *qi* of one of these five agents might be dominant during your early childhood, and then you may change to a different dominating phase in adulthood. If two phases are of equal impact in your birth chart, then your environment and life choices determine which of those two phases end up causing more issues. Per some natal charts, a child could experience severe respiratory issues in youth, and then those issues seem to disappear on their own in adulthood, only to be replaced by digestive issues or cardiovascular issues. Moreover, your lifestyle has the potential to irreversibly alter your innate body constitution. There are always many factors at play.

There is one final food-as-medicine principle with the Wu Xing that I personally do *not* give credence to and do not follow, but let's mention it anyway, just to be thorough. There is a traditional belief among the Chinese that if a particular organ in your body is suffering, you should eat more of that organ in other animals, or eat animal organs corresponding to the Wu Xing phase you're looking to balance. So if you have kidney issues, you would literally eat the kidneys of animals. Applied across the Wu Xing correspondence table, if you have a calcium density issue in your bones (Water), eat more cartilage and bone marrow (Water). Eating animal skin is believed to improve your hair, skin, and nails because of the Metal connection. If you're dealing with metabolic or reproductive issues, eat more animal liver (Wood).

The five agents of change also correspond with how a functioning government should be structured. In the *Treatise on the Five Elements,* Dong Zhongshu 董仲舒 (179–104 BC), a Han dynasty philosopher and politician, connected the Wu Xing to the five heads of state in imperial China.

**TABLE 6.7** The Five State Functions and Wu Xing

| WU XING | | | THE FIVE HEADS OF STATE | | |
|---|---|---|---|---|---|
| 木 | Mù | Wood | Minister of agriculture | 司農 | Sī nóng |
| 火 | Huǒ | Fire | Minister of war | 司馬 | Sī mǎ |
| 土 | Tǔ | Earth | Sovereign (agent of Heaven) | 君之官 | Jūn zhī guān |
| 金 | Jīn | Metal | Minister of education | 司徒 | Sī tú |
| 水 | Shuǐ | Water | Minister of justice | 司寇 | Sī kòu |

We can also conceptualize the Five Mystical Arts through the framework of the five changing phases, as the five modalities of the mystic's craft are contingent on change and transformation. The Five Mystical Arts (五術, Wǔ Shù) are also known as the Five Arts of Taoist Metaphysics. These are the five techniques that the mystic will aspire to master.

**TABLE 6.8** The Five Mystical Arts and Wu Xing

| WU XING | | | THE FIVE MYSTICAL ARTS | | |
|---|---|---|---|---|---|
| 木 | Mù | Wood | Spiritual Cultivation | 仙學 | Xiān Xué |
| 火 | Huǒ | Fire | Divinatory Arts | 卜筮 | Bǔ Shì |
| 土 | Tǔ | Earth | Study of Appearances | 相學 | Xiàng Xué |
| 金 | Jīn | Metal | Study of Fate | 命學 | Mìng Xué |
| 水 | Shuǐ | Water | Study of Healing Arts | 醫學 | Yī Xué |

Spiritual Cultivation (仙學, Xiān Xué) covers the modalities of meditation and related practices that facilitate spiritual transcendence. In Taoist mysticism, that transcendence is expressed as immortality, with the Eight Immortals role-modeling as our aspirations. In Buddhism, it's nirvana. In Confucianism (and Taoism), these are the religious rites and rituals to ensure that we are at all times in alignment with Heaven. I connect Spiritual Cultivation with Wood, symbolic of growth and development. When contemplated for its philosophical value, study of the I Ching is a form of Spiritual Cultivation.

The Study of Divinatory Arts (卜筮, Bǔshì) is assigned to Fire, honoring our ancestral history of Shang oracle bone divination, which used fire to crack the bones. Also, pyromancy is one of the earliest forms of divination across all cultures, given fire's association with deity and divine presence. The subsequent chapter will cover several historically significant methods of divination with the Oracle.

The Study of Appearances (相學, Xiàng Xué) is the practice of assessing a person, a place, or an object based on its physical appearance, which I associate with Earth. The practices of studying appearance operate on the theory that the superficial appearance of a person or land formation will reveal its innate character. Feng shui and geomancy, the study of land formations and how they influence our luck, is covered here. Historically, this study included physiognomy, or face reading. I would also include palmistry here. When the mystic assesses the metaphysical correspondences of a gemstone, crystal, or herb by considering its color, shape, and other physical attributes, that's the Study of Appearances.

The Study of Fate (命學, Mìng Xué), which I assign to the changing phase Metal for Metal's association with the trigram Heaven, is the study of destiny. Destiny is determined by Heaven. The premise behind this mode of study is that divine forces at play, which Buddhists express as past-life karma, determine when and where you are born. Heaven's Will is written in the stars, and so looking at what the stars had to say at the exact moment of your birth will reveal a profile of your fate. These are essentially a composite of cause-and-effect statements relating to an individual's life path, where causes sourced back to a past life, or even to arbitrary Divine Will, are recorded in movements of the universe.

The Study of Appearances, in terms of land formations and geomancy, and the Study of Fate, specifically astrology, are considered imperative background knowledge for advanced work with the I Ching. According to the Ten Wings, if you want to align with Heaven and Earth, look up to study astrology and look down to study geomancy.[6] References to lunisolar astrology and patterns in land formations abound in the Zhouyi. Thus, to deepen your understanding of the Oracle, endeavor for a basic understanding of the lunisolar calendar and feng shui.

The Study of Fate and the Study of Divinatory Arts are distinguished by the point in time that the mystic is basing the calculation on. In metaphysical theory, you study fate and destiny by casting someone's natal chart. The variables used for calculating fate are based on what happened before your birth, leading to you being born at that exact date, time, and location. Studying that date, time, and location can reveal those prebirth variables.

In contrast, general divination seeks answers to specific questions you have at a given point in time. Natal astrology, or the study of your birth chart, is the Study of Fate. Horary astrology, which are methods used to answer specific questions by casting a horoscopic chart, would be the Divinatory Arts. Determining what your innate personality traits are and what occupational paths you're more prone to succeed in would be the study of destiny. Determining whether you will get into your top-choice university or what unseen forces are at play in a given situation would be the study of divination.

The fifth art for the mystic to master is the Study of Healing Arts, or medicine (醫學, yī xué). I associate this with Water for Water's association with the immortal Li Tie Guai, the patron of physicians. To be more precise here in light of the modern era, this is the study of holistic health practices, such as traditional

Chinese medicine or Ayurveda. This is herbal medicine, understanding how to work with the medicinal properties of plants or animal parts, and also the framework of the Wu Xing for improvement of physical and mental health. Water as the defining agent for the Healing Arts is also a metaphor for what this craft is at its heart: after the death of one thing, such as an animal or plant, it is repurposed to bring life to another, and that concept of *returning* is the core theme of Water.

Profound guiding principles for the mystic emerge here. For example, two archetypal facets of the mystic—the Enchanter (Earth) and the Alchemist (Mountain)—correspond with the agent of change Earth, which corresponds with the Study of Appearances. Consider how the Enchanter, embodied by the immortal Lan Cai He and Lan's magical basket of flowers, herbs, and fruits, uses the Study of Appearances to mirror and establish empathy with someone in an enchantment, or how the Alchemist uses the study to determine correspondences. The Spellcaster (Thunder) corresponds with Spiritual Cultivation, because the level of power you cultivate so you can control *qi* determines how effective of a spellcaster you are. As a guiding principle, meditation and practices of qigong (learning how to control *qi*) are more important in spell-crafting than knowing which herbs and ingredients do what.

**TABLE 6.9** The Five Mystical Arts and the Eight Archetypes of the Mystic

| STUDY OF FATE | | DIVINATORY ARTS | HEALING ARTS |
|---|---|---|---|
| 金 Metal | 金 Metal | 火 Fire | 水 Water |
| Heaven | Lake | Fire | Water |
| The Virtuoso | The Warrior | The Philosopher | The Healer |
| **SPIRITUAL CULTIVATION** | | **STUDY OF APPEARANCES** | |
| 木 Wood | 木 Wood | 土 Earth | 土 Earth |
| Wind | Thunder | Mountain | Earth |
| The Shaman | The Spellcaster | The Alchemist | The Enchanter |

# PRACTICUM 6.1:
# Journaling and Reflection Prompt on the Five Mystical Arts

Take time writing down your reflections, thoughts, and commentaries on what the correspondences between the Five Mystical Arts and the eight archetypal facets of the Mystic reveal to you. What insights emerge from your understanding of table 6.10?

**TABLE 6.10** Eight Guiding Principles for Mystical Studies

| BA GUA | | GUIDING PRINCIPLES FOR MYSTICAL STUDIES | | | WU XING |
|---|---|---|---|---|---|
| Heaven | 1 | To be | the Virtuoso | I master | the Study of Fate. | Metal |
| Lake | 2 | To be | the Warrior | I master | the Study of Fate. | Metal |
| Fire | 3 | To be | the Philosopher | I master | the Divinatory Arts. | Fire |
| Thunder | 4 | To be | the Spellcaster | I master | Spiritual Cultivation. | Wood |
| Wind | 5 | To be | the Shaman | I master | Spiritual Cultivation. | Wood |
| Water | 6 | To be | the Healer | I master | the Study of Healing Arts. | Water |
| Mountain | 7 | To be | the Alchemist | I master | the Study of Appearances. | Earth |
| Earth | 8 | To be | the Enchanter | I master | the Study of Appearances. | Earth |

Start with principle 1: "To be the Virtuoso, I master the Study of Fate." To me, this means mastering knowledge of my birth chart so I can understand what my innate talents are. By knowing my innate talents, I can better develop them to embody the Virtuoso in those particular fields. Then I would ask myself: do I know my birth chart—and the study of at least one system of astrology—well enough so I can become the Virtuoso? If not, what goals and resolutions can I set for myself so that I follow guiding principle 1? Moving on to principle 2, the Warrior is somebody who confronts battles by fighting to their strengths and learning to overcome their weaknesses. Ask yourself how the Study of Fate helps you to embody the Warrior, which is the second archetypal facet of the well-rounded mystic.

To be the Shaman, per guiding principle 5, under Ba Gua to Wu Xing correspondences, the most important mystical study for empowerment of the Shaman is Spiritual Cultivation. Free-write in your journal what that means to you. The shaman is one whose consciousness can journey through different worlds and experience different spirit encounters. To do that requires the fluid ability to change states of consciousness, which is achieved through spiritual cultivation techniques such as meditation, or per some traditions, initiatory rites and rituals.

Consider what the Ba Gua–Wu Xing correspondences reveal about Eastern cultural perspectives, such as the prerequisite of mastering divinatory arts to be the Philosopher. Contemplation of these eight guiding principles will help you to formulate your own systematized understanding of Taoist metaphysics and to develop your own answers to these fundamental questions.

## PRACTICUM 6.2:
## Mystical Art Associated with Your Date of Birth

Applying Plum Blossom numerology methods, consider which of the Five Mystical Arts corresponds with your date of birth. Note, however, that after study of the Plum Blossom methods discussed in chapter 7, you may want to return to this practicum and try it again with the lunar calendar date equivalent for your Gregorian calendar date of birth. For now, let's just have fun and try this method out with the birth date numbers you're probably most familiar with.

| Month | + | Day | + | Year |
|---|---|---|---|---|
| 7 | + | 15 | + | 1985 |
| = | 2007 | | | |

Let's demonstrate with the example of July 15, 1985. Add the three numbers together as is, meaning do not do any further numerological operations to any of the double-digit numbers or to the year. Add the three whole numbers together, and in the example, the sum is 2007.

Divide that number by 5 to get the remainder.

2007 ÷ 5

Quotient = 401

Remainder = 3

The remainder after the sum 2007 is divided into 5 is 2.

|   | WU XING | | | THE FIVE MYSTICAL ARTS | | |
|---|---|---|---|---|---|---|
| 1 | 水 | Shuǐ | Water | Study of Healing Arts | 醫學 | Yī Xué |
| 2 | 火 | Huǒ | Fire | Divinatory Arts | 卜筮 | Bǔ Shì |
| 3 | 木 | Mù | Wood | Spiritual Cultivation | 仙學 | Xiān Xué |
| 4 | 金 | Jīn | Metal | Study of Fate | 命學 | Mìng Xué |
| 5 | 土 | Tǔ | Earth | Study of Appearances | 相學 | Xiàng Xué |

The number 2 corresponds with Fire. The Wu Xing phase Fire corresponds with Divinatory Arts. A person with this date of birth, per this Plum Blossom numerology and Wu Xing exercise, is going to be best served in their path of personal spirituality by pursuing Divinatory Arts.

Here's a second example. Let's take the date of birth December 26, 1978. Add the three calendar numbers together: 12 + 26 + 1978 = 2016. Divide by 5: 2016 ÷ 5 = a quotient of 403 and a remainder of 1. The number 1 corresponds with Water. Water corresponds with the Study of Healing Arts. Thus, someone born on December 26, 1978, will be best served, in terms of personal spiritual development, by the Study of the Healing Arts.

Try this calculation on your date of birth to see which of the Five Mystical Arts, per the Wu Xing and Plum Blossom numerology, is the path that will most elevate your personal spirituality and the art that you're innately most gifted in.

The Five Phases of Change (Wu Xing)    245

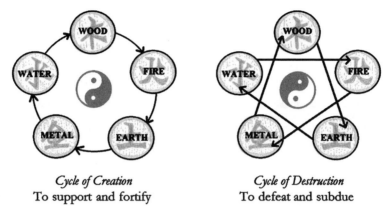

Cycle of Creation
To support and fortify

Cycle of Destruction
To defeat and subdue

**FIGURE 6.2:** Wu Xing cycles of creation and destruction

Having covered what the five phases of change are, let's consider the two cycles governing the alchemy of the changing phases.

The first is a cycle of creation (相生, *xiāng shēng*). The cycle is depicted as a circle where Wood creates Fire, Fire creates Earth, Earth creates Metal, Metal creates Water, and Water creates Wood, and the cycle repeats. The second is a cycle of destruction (相克, *xiāng kè*). This cycle is depicted as a pentagram where Wood breaks down Earth, Earth breaks down Water, Water breaks down Fire, Fire breaks down Metal, and Metal breaks down Wood. These two cycles are the foundational rules governing Taoist alchemy.

For instance, Wood breaks down or subdues Earth. Therefore, a social or political order that is Earth dominant can be conquered by a force that is Wood, because Wood subdues Earth. If you are Earth and you are faced with an oppositional force that is Wood, you can defeat Wood by changing into Metal, because Metal defeats Wood. If you have an ally or someone in your inner circle who is Water, be careful, because those of Water are more likely to turn against you and support Wood. The Wu Xing even govern traditional concepts in the art of war.

The remainder of this chapter will set forth these foundational rules. I've structured the reference tables to first present three main rules of alchemy and then five key rules on alchemical reactions with that agent of change. Let's walk through an example using Metal.

Consider (1) what strengthens the power of Metal, (2) what power Metal controls, and (3) what weakens the power of Metal. These three main rules of Wu Xing alchemy are then presented in tandem with their Ba Gua correspondences so you can see the interplay between the trigrams.

| | | | | | | |
|---|---|---|---|---|---|---|
| ☷ Earth Enchanter | ☶ Mountain Alchemist | 土 Earth | Nourishes | 金 Metal | ☰ Heaven Virtuoso | ☱ Lake Warrior |
| ☳ Thunder Spellcaster | ☴ Wind Shaman | 木 Wood | Yields to | 金 Metal | ☰ Heaven Virtuoso | ☱ Lake Warrior |
| | ☲ Fire Philosopher | 火 Fire | Weakens | 金 Metal | ☰ Heaven Virtuoso | ☱ Lake Warrior |

The philosopher Mozi 墨子 (470–391 BC)[7] noted in the Mohist Canons that a caveat to the cycles of creation and destruction is the effect of quantity and mass. While Wood creates Fire, the quantity and mass of the Wood versus the Fire determines whether the input of Wood will have any effect on that Fire. Sure, Fire destroys Metal per the cycle of destruction, but a minimal quantity and mass of Fire compared to the Metal it's interacting with might not doom the Metal to destruction.

In more practical terms, if a social movement corresponding with Fire is attempting to overthrow a government that is characterized by Metal, as long as the Metal is still much larger in force and size than the Fire, it can quash Fire. Metal can defeat Fire if its quantity and mass are large enough, in spite of the Cycle of Destruction rules.

To further clarify the distinction between how to conceptualize the Ba Gua and the Wu Xing, I use the analogy of spell-crafting. The eight trigrams (Ba Gua) represent the elements you consider in assembling the ingredients that will go in to your spell. The five phases of change (Wu Xing) are not elements; rather, they are characterizations of your method of spell-crafting—your incantation, your rituals, the *agents* of change are categorized into these five movements of energy to produce the mass equivalents that are represented by the trigrams.

# The Five Phases of Change (Wu Xing)

**TABLE 6.11** Wu Xing, the Zodiac, and the Lo Shu Eight Trigrams

| | 蛇<br>Snake | 馬<br>Horse | 羊<br>Sheep | |
|---|---|---|---|---|
| 龍<br>Dragon | Southeast<br>☴<br>Wind<br>Cardinal spring | South<br>☲<br>Fire<br>Winter solstice | Southwest<br>☷<br>Earth<br>Cardinal winter | 猴<br>Monkey |
| 兔<br>Rabbit | East<br>☳<br>Thunder<br>Spring equinox | 木 火 土<br>木 ※ 金<br>土 水 金 | West<br>☱<br>Lake<br>Autumn equinox | 雞<br>Rooster |
| 虎<br>Tiger | Northeast<br>☶<br>Mountain<br>Cardinal summer | North<br>☵<br>Water<br>Summer solstice | Northwest<br>☰<br>Heaven<br>Cardinal autumn | 狗<br>Dog |
| | 牛<br>Ox | 鼠<br>Rat | 豬<br>Boar | |

**FIGURE 6.3** The five changing phases and eight trigrams[8]

Now what does this all have to do with I Ching hexagrams?

A lot, actually, especially for the mystic seeking to integrate I Ching divination into the Five Arts of Taoist metaphysics. For starters, the Image and Number tradition of interpreting the hexagrams would probably rely heavily on the Wu Xing correspondences to understand the pair of trigrams that make up the hexagram. We've established that to understand the six-line hexagrams, we need to understand the pair of three-line trigrams. And to understand the trigrams, we need to understand the five phases of change that govern the movements of the trigrams.

## Wood (Mù): Sprouting and Cultivating

*Wood sprouts. Water is essential to Wood.*

| | | | | | | | |
|---|---|---|---|---|---|---|---|
| | Water<br>Healer | 水<br>Water | Nourishes | 木<br>Wood | Thunder<br>Spellcaster | Wind<br>Shaman |
| Earth<br>Enchanter | Mountain<br>Alchemist | 土<br>Earth | Yields to | 木<br>Wood | Thunder<br>Spellcaster | Wind<br>Shaman |
| Heaven<br>Virtuoso | Lake<br>Warrior | 金<br>Metal | Weakens | 木<br>Wood | Thunder<br>Spellcaster | Wind<br>Shaman |

| WOOD | Livelihood. Innovation. Personal Growth. | |
|---|---|---|
| Is created by | Water | Rain produces plant life. Growth of Wood is dependent on the energy of Water. |
| Exhausts | Water | Wood consumes Water and enriches itself with it. Wood depletes Water. |
| Yields to | Metal | A metal blade will cut down a tree. |
| Creates | Fire | Wood supports Fire. Wood empowers Fire. |
| Subdues | Earth | Wood and Earth conflict. Wood dominates Earth. Wood depletes Earth of its nutrients. |

State function, per Dong Zhongshu 董仲舒: Minister of agriculture (司農, *sī nóng*).

**Wood traits in people:** A dominance of Wood in the personal *qi* will result in a golden undertone to the complexion and one who is thinner or has a thin pulse. They tend to be active, nimble, curious, and sensitive. They flourish under open sky.[9] Wood-dominant personalities are curious and fearless when it comes to trial and error. Their *qi* is more empowered and productive during the spring and summer, and less productive during the autumn and winter.[10]

| | 木 **Wood** Mù Azure Dragon | The Bamboo Altar Table | |
|---|---|---|---|
| | | Number | 3 |
| | | Heavenly stem (yang) | 甲 *Jiǎ* |
| | | Heavenly stem (yin) | 乙 *Yǐ* |
| Action | Grow, germinate | Mental | Sensitivity |
| Planet | Jupiter 木星 | Virtue | Kindness |
| Direction | East | Personality | Charitable, benevolent, generous spirit, open, humane |
| Season | Spring | | |
| Weather | Wind | | |
| Time of day | Morning | Positive traits | Artistic, idealistic, visionary, curious, altruistic |
| Color | Green | | |
| Mystical practice | Spiritual Cultivation | Negative traits | Demanding, inflexible, unyielding, acrimonious |
| Alchemical processes | Purifying, chrysalis stage, origination | Grains | Oats, wheat |
| | | Foods | Vegetables, chicken, sour fruits |
| Sense | Sight | | |
| Organ yin | Liver | Altar or shrine offering | Plum, flowers, crab apples, pickled vegetables |
| Organ yang | Gallbladder | | |
| Organ systems or functions | Endocrine, metabolism, reproductive | Gemstones | Turritella agate, petrified wood |
| Chemical composition | Carbohydrates | Metal | Iron |
| | | Feng shui and geomancy | Trees, plants, wooden decks, columns, paper, books, bamboo, resin |
| Brain function | Language | | |
| Tissue | Tendons | | |
| Finger | Index | Life phase | Early childhood |
| Taste | Sour | Life phase (alternate) | Childhood |
| Livestock | Chicken | Confucian five relations 五倫 | Ruler ≈ subject 君 ≈ 臣 |

# Fire (Huǒ): Blooming and Inspiring

*Fire blooms. Wood is essential to Fire.*

| | | | | | | |
|---|---|---|---|---|---|---|
| Thunder Spellcaster | Wind Shaman | 木 Wood | Nourishes | 火 Fire | | Fire Philosopher |
| Heaven Virtuoso | Lake Warrior | 金 Metal | Yields to | 火 Fire | | Fire Philosopher |
| | Water Healer | 水 Water | Weakens | 火 Fire | | Fire Philosopher |

| FIRE | | Expansion of dominion. "Go higher, burn brighter." |
|---|---|---|
| Is created by | Wood | The activated energy of Wood produces Fire. Fire is born from Wood energy. |
| Exhausts | Wood | Fire heats Wood until the bonds in Wood break down. |
| Yields to | Water | Water extinguishes Fire. Water will weaken Fire. |
| Creates | Earth | Fire fortifies Earth, and Earth fortified by Fire becomes fertile and able to support life. When Fire is extinguished, it becomes Earth. |
| Subdues | Metal | Fire and Metal conflict. Fire dominates Metal. Fire will vaporize and weaken Metal. |

State function, per Dong Zhongshu 董仲舒: Minister of war (司馬, *sīmǎ*).

**Fire traits in people:** Those with a dominance of Fire in the personal *qi* are comfortable around fire and are empowered by it. The sun energizes them. These individuals may have a ruddier complexion. They're identified by a solid, strong, quick-beating pulse. A Fire disposition enables one to withstand the cold better than average. Heart disease can be a bigger risk when there is Fire dominance.[11] They are more prone to being active in the spring and summer, while they tend to feel lethargic and uninspired through autumn and winter.[12]

| | | | |
|---|---|---|---|
| | 火 **Fire** Huǒ Vermilion Phoenix | | Ceramic and Porcelain Figurines |
| | | Number | 2 |
| | | Heavenly stem (yang) | 丙 *Bǐng* |
| | | Heavenly stem (yin) | 丁 *Dīng* |
| Action | Expand, assert upward | Mental | Motivation |
| | | Virtue | Discipline |
| Planet | Mars 火星 | Personality | Motivational leader, intense, sensual, assertive, passionate |
| Direction | South | | |
| Season | Summer | | |
| Weather | Heat | Positive traits | Innovative, loving, blissful, festive |
| Time of day | Noon | | |
| Color | Red | Negative traits | Irascible, reckless, vengeful, spiteful |
| Mystical practice | Divination | | |
| Alchemical processes | Synthesis, integration, assimilation, illumination | Grains | Corn, amaranth |
| | | Foods | Dried or fried meats, barbecue, pheasant, deep-fried foods in general |
| Sense | Touch | | |
| Organ yin | Heart | Altar or shrine offering | Apricot, dragon fruit, sweet potatoes, goji berries, alfalfa |
| Organ yang | Small intestine | | |
| Organ systems or functions | Nervous, cardiovascular, circulatory | | |
| | | Gemstones | Cinnabar, carnelian |
| | | Metal | Copper |
| Chemical composition | Lipids | Feng shui and geomancy | Triangular forms, amber, sunstone, bright lighting, fireplace, stove, red and orange |
| Brain function | Voluntary movement | | |
| Tissue | Blood vessels | | |
| Finger | Middle | Life phase | Prepuberty |
| Taste | Bitter | Life phase (alternate) | Young adulthood |
| Livestock | Goat | Confucian five relations 五倫 | Father = son 父 = 子 |

# Earth (Tǔ): Ripening and Maturing

*Earth ripens. Fire is essential to Earth.*

| | | | | | | |
|---|---|---|---|---|---|---|
| | ☲ Fire Philosopher | 火 Fire | Yields to | 土 Earth | ☷ Earth Enchanter | ☶ Mountain Alchemist |
| | ☵ Water Healer | 水 Water | Yields to | 土 Earth | ☷ Earth Enchanter | ☶ Mountain Alchemist |
| ☳ Thunder Spellcaster | ☴ Wind Shaman | 木 Wood | Weakens | 土 Earth | ☷ Earth Enchanter | ☶ Mountain Alchemist |

| EARTH | | Seeking purpose. Love, family, security, stability. |
|---|---|---|
| Is created by | Fire | Fire reduces all that it burns to ash, which creates Earth. Earth is dependent on the energy of Fire. |
| Exhausts | Fire | Earth will smother the embers of Fire. Earth extinguishes Fire. |
| Yields to | Wood | Trees push into Earth and extract their nourishment from the Earth, depleting Earth. |
| Creates | Metal | Earth supports Metal. Metal empowers Earth. From the womb of Earth, Metal is born. |
| Subdues | Water | Earth and Water conflict. Earth dominates Water by blocking its flow. |

State function, per Dong Zhongshu 董仲舒: Sovereign (君之官, *jūn zhī guān*), agent of Heaven.

**Earth traits in people:** Those with a dominance of Earth in the personal *qi* are the children closest to the mother goddess of the earth. Their physiques tend to show closeness to the ground, and a more solid build, with earthy undertones in the skin. They may tend toward introversion or take longer to arrive at decisions or growth, as they tend to be risk-averse. Earth dominance blesses the individual with longevity and stability. Root causes of illness or weakness tend to come from the spleen.[13] Those who are Earth dominant are more empowered by the *qi* in nature during autumn and winter, and they feel more productive during those seasons and less productive over the spring and summer.[14]

| | | | |
|---|---|---|---|
| | 土 **Earth** Tǔ Ocher *Qilin (Kirin)* | | Jade and Marble Snuff Bottle |
| **Action** | Equilibrium, stability | **Number** | 5 |
| | | **Heavenly stem (yang)** | 戊 *Wù* |
| **Planet** | Saturn 土星 | **Heavenly stem (yin)** | 己 *Jǐ* |
| **Direction** | Center | **Mental** | Clarity |
| **Season** | Late summer | **Virtue** | Dignity |
| **Weather** | Humid (moist) | **Personality** | Confident, diligent, patient, persevering |
| **Time of day** | Afternoon | **Positive traits** | Loyal, reliable, patient, philanthrope |
| **Color** | Yellow | | |
| **Mystical practice** | Physiognomy, palmistry | **Negative traits** | Misanthrope, dull, materialistic, insecure |
| **Alchemical processes** | Manifesting, fulfillment, materialization | **Grains** | Barley, millet |
| | | **Foods** | Potatoes, mushrooms, beef, cereals, roots |
| **Sense** | Taste | **Altar or shrine offering** | Pumpkin, honey, candies, jujubes, walnuts, peanuts, soybean products |
| **Organ yin** | Spleen, pancreas | | |
| **Organ yang** | Stomach | **Gemstones** | Lodestone, yellow zircon |
| **Organ systems or functions** | Muscular, lymphatic, digestive | **Metal** | Gold |
| | | **Feng shui and geomancy** | Clay, terra-cotta, stone, ceramic, marble, granite, mountains, square forms, neutral tones |
| **Chemical composition** | Proteins | | |
| **Brain function** | Judgment | **Life phase** | Adolescence |
| **Tissue** | Muscles | **Life phase (alternate)** | Adulthood |
| **Finger** | Thumb | **Confucian five relations** 五倫 | Husband ⇆ wife 夫 ⇆ 婦 *Alternate:* Spouse ⇆ spouse |
| **Taste** | Sweet | | |
| **Livestock** | Cattle | | |

# Metal (Jīn): Culminating and Extinguishing

*Metal destroys. Earth is essential to Metal.*

| Earth Enchanter | Mountain Alchemist | 土 Earth | Nourishes | 金 Metal | Heaven Virtuoso | Lake Warrior |
| Thunder Spellcaster | Wind Shaman | 木 Wood | Yields to | 金 Metal | Heaven Virtuoso | Lake Warrior |
| | Fire Philosopher | 火 Fire | Weakens | 金 Metal | Heaven Virtuoso | Lake Warrior |

| METAL | | The sciences. Accumulated knowledge. Machines. |
|---|---|---|
| Is created by | Earth | Metal is produced deep within the Earth. Metal is born from Earth energy. |
| Exhausts | Earth | Metal depletes the Earth of its innate qualities. Metal siphons *qi* and matter from Earth. |
| Yields to | Fire | Fire melts and softens Metal, causing Metal to yield to Fire's control. |
| Creates | Water | Metal fortifies Water with minerals. Ocean chemistry is made up of trace metals that influence the productivity of the seas. Metal in Water allows Water to give life. |
| Subdues | Wood | Metal and Wood conflict. Metal dominates Wood. Metal cuts down and destroys Wood. |

State function, per Dong Zhongshu 董仲舒: Minister of education (司徒, *sītú*).

**Metal traits in people:** Those who have a dominance of Metal in the personal *qi* will be paler in complexion, with cool undertones in the skin, and will have lighter bone density. Lung and respiratory issues can be of higher concern.

Metal dominance brings innovation and a methodical way of thinking. They will thrive in government, institutions, law, and politics. Wu Xing Metal corresponds with metal-tinged gases discharged into the galaxy, or galactic metal. These people are attuned to the essential metals in the universe.[15] Those who are Metal dominant are more likely to be productive through the autumn and winter seasons, and they tend to feel less productive during the spring and summer.[16]

| | | | |
|---|---|---|---|
| | 金 **Metal** Jīn White Tiger | | The Bronze Cauldron |
| **Action** | Harvest, gather | **Number** | 4 |
| **Planet** | Venus 金星 | **Heavenly stem (yang)** | 庚 Gēng |
| **Direction** | West | **Heavenly stem (yin)** | 辛 Xīn |
| **Season** | Autumn | **Mental** | Intuition |
| **Weather** | Dry | **Virtue** | Incorruptibility |
| **Time of day** | Evening | **Personality** | Courageous, independent, rational, methodical, objective, dispassionate |
| **Color** | White | | |
| **Mystical practice** | Study of Fate/Destiny | | |
| **Alchemical processes** | Dissolution, division, severance | **Positive traits** | Independent, valiant, intrepid, equitable, cerebral, urbane |
| **Sense** | Smell | **Negative traits** | Cold, aloof, destructive, melancholic, insensitive |
| **Organ yin** | Lungs | **Grains** | Rice |
| **Organ yang** | Large intestine | **Foods** | Freshwater seafood, spicy foods, duck |
| **Organ systems or functions** | Respiratory, integumentary, skin and hair | **Altar or shrine offering** | Peach, white sesame, bananas, Asian pears, winter melon, daikon, cumin, gardenia |
| **Chemical composition** | Nucleic acids | | |
| **Brain function** | Memory | **Gemstones** | Malachite, pyrite |
| **Tissue** | Skin | **Metal** | Silver (also gold) |
| **Finger** | Ring | **Feng shui and geomancy** | Clocks, metals, electronics, wind instruments, weaponry, metal jewelry |
| **Taste** | Pungent | | |
| **Livestock** | Horse | | |
| | | **Life phase** | Adulthood |
| | | **Life phase (alternate)** | Middle age–old age |
| | | **Confucian five relations** 五倫 | Elder brother ⇋ younger brother 兄 ⇋ 弟 |

# Water (Shuǐ): Reflecting and Returning

*Water is resting. Metal is essential to Water.*

| | | | | | | | Metal and minerals fortify Water. Remember that Water 水 is the phase change. It implies that Water 坎 the trigram is strengthened (and grows) via Heaven and Lake. |
|---|---|---|---|---|---|---|---|
| ☰ Heaven Virtuoso | ☱ Lake Warrior | 金 Metal | Nourishes | 水 Water | ☵ Water Healer | | |
| | ☲ Fire Philosopher | 火 Fire | Yields to | 水 Water | ☵ Water Healer | | |
| ☷ Earth Enchanter | ☶ Mountain Alchemist | 土 Earth | Weakens | 水 Water | ☵ Water Healer | | |

| WATER | Diplomacy. International relations. Cunning statecraft. | |
|---|---|---|
| Is created by | Metal | Water aggregates because of Metal. As Metal matures, it transmutes into Water. |
| Exhausts | Metal | Water will break down Metal. Water corrodes Metal. |
| Yields to | Earth | Earth forces the flow of Water. Earth absorbs nourishment from Water and depletes it. |
| Creates | Wood | Water nourishes Wood. Water supports the growth of Wood. Through Water, Wood can multiply. |
| Subdues | Fire | Water and Fire conflict. Water dominates Fire. Water can extinguish Fire. |

State function, per Dong Zhongshu 董仲舒: Minister of justice (司寇, *sīkòu*).

**Water traits in people:** A dominance of Water in the personal *qi* will result in a darker undertone to the complexion and slower pulses. These people are deeply pensive, introverted, and highly intelligent to the point of cunning, and thus are also more prone to melancholy. They are at greater risk of illnesses originating or having root causes in the kidneys, though they are often blessed with long lives. They are empowered by Water, and their *qi* is energized by the moon.[17] Those with Water-dominant constitutions will tend to feel more empowered and productive over the autumn and winter, and less productive during the spring and summer.[18]

| | | | |
|---|---|---|---|
| | 水 **Water** *Shuǐ* Black Tortoise | | Calligraphy Art |
| | | **Number** | 1 |
| | | **Heavenly stem (yang)** | 壬 *Rén* |
| | | **Heavenly stem (yin)** | 癸 *Guǐ* |
| **Action** | Contract, retreat | **Mental** | Empathy |
| **Planet** | Mercury 水星 | **Virtue** | Wisdom |
| **Direction** | North | **Personality** | Diplomatic, congenial, sociable, mercurial |
| **Season** | Winter | | |
| **Weather** | Cold | **Positive traits** | Composed, willful, high-browed, cultured |
| **Time of day** | Midnight | | |
| **Color** | Blue, black | **Negative traits** | Volatile, fickle, anxious, cynical |
| **Mystical practice** | Study of Healing Arts, medicine | | |
| | | **Grains** | Beans |
| **Alchemical processes** | Purging, decomposition, catharsis | **Foods** | Soups, seafood, cool drinks, wine |
| **Sense** | Hearing | **Altar or shrine offering** | Water chestnut, raisins, tea, seaweed, jasmine |
| **Organ yin** | Kidneys | | |
| **Organ yang** | Bladder, urinary | **Gemstones** | Fluorite, selenite |
| **Organ systems or functions** | Skeletal, urinary, detoxifying | **Metal** | Tin |
| | | **Feng shui and geomancy** | Rivers, lakes, mirrors, glass, fountains, aquariums, blue tones |
| **Chemical composition** | Water | | |
| **Brain function** | Involuntary movement | **Life phase** | Old age and conception |
| | | **Life phase (alternate)** | Twilight years |
| **Tissue** | Bones | **Confucian five relations** 五倫 | Friend ⇌ friend 朋 ⇌ 友 |
| **Finger** | Little | | |
| **Taste** | Salty | | |
| **Livestock** | Pig, boar | | |

# PRACTICUM 6.3:
# Guarding of the One Meditation

*From the Scriptures of the Great Peace (37–32 BC)*

The Scriptures of the Great Peace (太平經, Tàipíng jīng or 太平清領書, Tàipíng qīng lǐng shū)[19] date back to the Han dynasty (202 BC–AD 220). An early intact copy of the text dates to around 37–32 BC. The scriptures refer to a set of Taoist sacred texts preserved in the *Daozang* (道藏), or Taoist canon, consisting of 170 volumes. The volumes cover the cosmology of Heaven and Earth, the Wu Xing, and cultivation methods for invoking and learning from the Immortals. They include grimoires with instructions on how to cure diseases and exorcise demons. The stated purpose of the scriptures was to reveal esoteric methods for ushering in an era of Great Peace.

Most notable in the Scriptures of the Great Peace is the Guarding of the One meditation (守一冥想, Shǒu Yī *míng xiǎng*), the "One" a reference to the Tao. The meditation reunites the individual spirit with the Tao. According to the text, after the One divided into the Two, then Three and into the myriad things per Lao Tzu's Tao Te Ching, the myriad things, which includes us, become more matter than spirit (which is sourced from the One). The more matter we become and the less spirit we are as bodies, the more prone to illness, pain, and suffering we are. Thus, the Taoist mystic's objective is to reunite their matter with the spirit of the One. By reuniting with the One, which is the Tao, we can transcend mortality, suffering, and misfortune.

The purpose of the Guarding of the One meditation is to improve physical health and longevity. That objective is achieved through visualization of yourself integrating the Light of the five changing phases, which in turn fortifies and increases the power of your personal *qi*.

To start, you'll need a room dedicated as your sacred space for spiritual cultivation. The space should be set up such that entering the room will be akin to entering a different realm or dimension. To achieve that, the space needs a fortified entrance (門戶, *mén hù*). Conceptualize this like a *torii*, a traditional Shinto gate found at the entrance of a shrine that symbolically marks the threshold between a mundane space and a sacred space. You'll need to construct a threshold from a physical door so that it separates your sacred space from mundane space.

Then meditate in that space daily. Perform all of your rites and rituals there. The routine performance of meditation and rites in that space further empowers it.

Instructions for the actual process of the Guarding of the One meditation begin with projecting a mirror image of yourself out of your physical body and being able to see that projected image of you as if looking at your own reflection in a mirror.

To achieve this, sit comfortably in meditation position with a neutral hand mudra, or hand positioning. Close your eyes and focus on your breathing. When you feel grounded and centered, you are ready to project that mirror reflection of yourself—your astral body—out of your physical body.

Once your astral body is outside your physical body, keep your gaze and focus on this astral body, this reflection of yourself. The text notes that in the beginning, this reflection may be hard to hold still in your mind's eye, and it might come in and out of view, so you must guard it, like tending to a fire that has just started so as not to let the flames disappear. Likewise, stay razor-focused on that astral body reflection so it doesn't flicker or vanish.

Visualize a numinous, colorless, yet brilliant light suddenly flashing from above and illuminating the room to the point of blinding. Once the flash subsides, the vision of your astral body, that reflection you are looking at, is red as the burning sun. The *qi* of Fire is imbuing your astral body with fortified powers of blooming and expanding, and your own Fire *qi* is amplified.

The red light around your astral body will then begin to turn white. The *qi* of Metal is imbuing your astral body with fortified powers of Metal *qi*. You are now increased in the power to destroy, the power of invincibility, and the power to conquer.

This white is also the yang of Heaven. Now visualize your astral body floating upward, climbing above and beyond the constellations and piercing through the veil into Heaven, where it is all white. At all times you are seeing your astral body as if it were a reflection. Keep your focus anchored and strongly connected to that reflection.

Once your astral body reaches a white Heaven, the *qi* of divine yang is imbuing your astral body with fortified powers of Heaven. Then your body begins its descent. It returns to that room with you and then continues below the floor into the ground, able to move through the soil of the Earth, where it is all black. Continue to keep your focus anchored and strongly connected to your reflection.

Once your astral body is deep below in the belly of the black Earth, the *qi* of divine yin imbues your astral body with the fortified powers of Earth. Then your body begins its ascend and return to your room.

You are now looking straight ahead at your astral body, this reflection. The reflection you are looking at shimmers blue like the clearest oceans. The *qi* of Water is fortifying your astral body, and you feel your own Water *qi* amplified.

The blue light shifts to azure green. The green light blazes. You are being strengthened by the *qi* of Wood. The azure-green light is also called the Light of Central Harmony, and it is the most potent healing energy, able to repair the Tao and guard the Light of the One. Feel your astral body growing stronger and increasing in vitality from the azure-green light.

The green light drives the hundred diseases out of your body. It is all-encompassing and omnipresent, expanding beyond the astral body, enveloping your physical body and everywhere within the walls of your sacred space.

Draw the astral body back in toward you so it reunites with your physical body. Then open your eyes. The Guarding of the One meditation is complete.

Over the centuries, different lineages of Taoist traditions have developed their own variations of the Guarding of the One meditation. The Zheng Yi lineage during the Wei and Jin dynasties had a name for the god who guards the body. A Taoist practitioner of that lineage would connect to that god during the Guarding the One meditation. The Zheng Yi method also included having to fast for a hundred days and daily meditations of visualizing yourself reincarnating into different bodies and astrally traveling through a palace of mirrors.

The Tian Shi and Ling Bao traditions during the Eastern Jin would integrate their astral bodies with the *qi* of the sun, moon, and the five planets corresponding with the Wu Xing, "eating the *qi*" of these planets during meditation. And the Shangqing school of Taoist mystical practice believed there were twenty-four inner gods within the body ruled over by a holy trinity of sovereign gods. Their Guarding of the One meditation involved integration with each of the twenty-four inner gods.

## PRACTICUM 6.4:
## Psychic Health Readings with the I Ching

Historically, a predictive health reading could be done through fortune-telling with the I Ching by referencing the Wu Xing correspondences. According to this wholly unscientific and irrational premise, you can do a psychic divinatory reading on the root cause of a physical ailment.

I share this practicum with a great bit of trepidation because it's controversial, and it runs the risk of people misinterpreting my point in sharing it. No one is saying a psychic health reading can replace the diagnosis of a medical professional. You should never, under any circumstances, rely on a psychic reading over the expert advice of your physician.

This practicum is a tribute to what I know has been historically a part of my culture and how Taoist mystics in Asia use the I Ching. For cultural reasons, it would seem remiss to leave this out. I'm presenting this section as a practicum in hopes that it might offer enjoyable entertainment as you experiment with it for yourself. Do not rely on your I Ching reading results in lieu of getting qualified medical treatment. Everything your doctor says should always override your experimental fortune-telling.

With that said, if there is a physical health condition you've been grappling with and some aspect of it stumps you, try a psychic I Ching reading on your health condition.

Apply any divination method of your choosing, selected from any of the methods from this text. If the reading is for yourself, take a moment before you start to focus on the health condition, feel its presence in your body, and pinpoint your focus on the *qi* of that health condition. If someone has asked you to do this reading for them, and if, in a case-specific assessment, you've determined it's ethical for you to proceed, set up some photographs and images of the health condition and visualize your concentration perforating through spacetime to connect to the *qi* of that person's health condition. The sympathy generated from focusing on the images can really help facilitate this.

Proceed with the divination. The Oracle message or Judgment will give a general prognosis and summary characterizing the situation. The changing lines will give practical advice and psychic predictions. If there are no changing lines, then look to the hexagram ruler, or line 5.

To demonstrate, I'll give an example. A friend of mine, let's call her Jane, was dealing with a hair loss and balding issue. Her dermatologist hadn't been able to identify a root cause, beyond a general theory of stress. Jane wanted to see whether a psychic reading might bear any interesting insights into the problem.

The reading result was as follows:

|   | PRIMARY: HEXAGRAM 54 | | WU XING | | TRANSFORMED: HEXAGRAM 16 |
|---|---|---|---|---|---|
| 6 | ▬▬ ▬▬ | ▬▬ ▬▬ | 木 Wood | | ▬▬▬▬▬ |
| 5 | ▬▬ ▬▬ | ▬▬ ▬▬ | | | ▬▬ ▬▬ |
| 4 | ▬▬▬▬▬ | Thunder | | | ▬▬▬▬▬ |
| 3 | ▬▬ ▬▬ | ▬▬ ▬▬ | 金 Metal | | ▬▬ ▬▬ |
| 2 | ▬▬▬▬▬ | ▬▬▬▬▬ | | → | ▬▬ ▬▬ |
| 1 | ▬▬▬▬▬ | Lake | | → | ▬▬ ▬▬ |

As soon as the Lake formed, I saw a womb. I filed that thought away and continued. The Metal correspondence of Lake offers a confirmation through synchronicity that we are dealing with a skin and hair problem. For reference, consult table 6.6 on Wu Xing and Human Functions.

If you're doing an I Ching reading on a health matter, apply an Image and Number approach and look at the Wu Xing correspondences for the trigrams. Then look at the health correspondences for the Wu Xing. Scry through the table entries and try to formulate a holistic, composite sense of what could be going on, using one part psychic intuition and one part rational induction.

| CORRESPONDENCES | WOOD | METAL |
|---|---|---|
| Sense | Sight | Smell |
| Organs | Liver<br>Gallbladder | Lungs<br>Large intestine |

| CORRESPONDENCES | WOOD | METAL |
|---|---|---|
| Organ systems or functions | Endocrine, metabolism, reproductive | Respiratory, integumentary, skin and hair |
| Chemical composition | Carbohydrates | Nucleic acids |
| Brain function | Language | Memory |
| Body part | Tendons | Skin |
| Finger | Index | Ring |
| Taste | Sour | Pungent |
| Color | Green | White |

The synchronicities in the reading startled Jane. Hexagram 54, the Marrying Maiden, is one of four hexagrams in the I Ching that addresses romantic love and civil unions. Jane had recently married. She had also been undergoing treatment for in vitro fertilization (IVF) and taking medications on that account, though she had not connected that to her hair loss and balding issue. Her physician had also said that the two were most likely not connected.

Continuing with the reading, the results yielded two changing lines, 1 and 2, which, upon reading the oracle messages, also seemed to validate that extraordinary technological measures have been taken. There are other indications here that, in the long term, Jane will be successful in her IVF endeavors.

Per the alchemical rules, Metal subdues Wood, so we see something in that Lake overpowering and thus causing imbalances in the reproductive, metabolic, or endocrine systems of the body. These deductions are based on the correspondence tables for Metal and Wood, the governing agents of change for the pair of trigrams forming the primary hexagram.

Since Metal is overpowering Wood, the source of the problem, at least from a psychic health reading perspective, is to be found in the correspondences of Metal. This reading seems to be pointing at an origin point in the lungs or large intestine. Rudimentary knowledge of the functions of each organ helps here. The large intestine's functions are to absorb water, electrolytes, and vitamins. A malfunction at this point is what's causing the symptom of hair loss and balding.

In short, while Jane continues receiving treatment from her dermatologist for the hair loss and balding, one small lifestyle adjustment she can make to help herself is to eat more sour and pungent foods. Examples of this might be adding more vinegar to her cooking, leeks, pickled vegetables, sour fruits, and sourdough bread. Garlic, turnips, and daikon radishes are the types of white foods that will help as well, corresponding with Metal. Jane might also want to add a lot more dark, leafy greens to her regular diet.

The point isn't for these foods to be a cure, but rather that eating more of these foods will help her body to regulate its own *qi* and rebalance it. After it rebalances itself, it might begin to absorb more vitamins and minerals and thus reduce the hair loss and minimize balding.

If the dermatologist remains stumped about the root cause of the balding, Jane could take it upon herself to request testing to at least consider and either rule out or confirm an issue in her large intestines. Getting blood work done to assess her vitamin levels could be a starting point.

By the way, the first and second lines of the transformed hexagram, Hexagram 16, could be interpreted as the Oracle showing its exasperation at the expert physician's inability to diagnose the problem. The second line and the final thesis of this reading assures Jane not to worry too much about the problem, as it is cosmetic and, unless her physician tells her otherwise, this is a condition she will absolutely be able to overcome and get through.

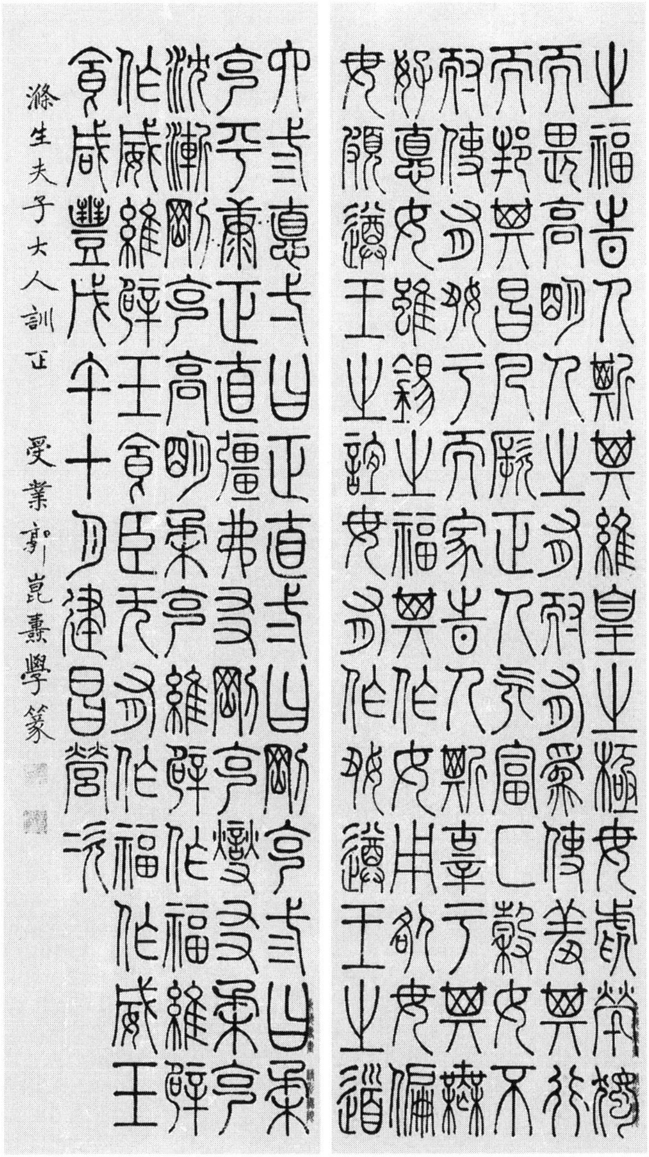

**FIGURE 6.4** Guo Kuntao's 1858 seal script excerpt II of the Book of Documents

**FIGURE 7.1** I Ching divination methods

# 7

# Divination Methods

THE ORIGINAL CASTING METHOD for the I Ching was with yarrow stalks, though the underlying means for divining is numerology. Thus, the method can vary, so long as the mathematical basis does not.

Records of using coins in I Ching divination surface around AD 200 during the Three Kingdoms era, though it may have originated earlier than that. The method of tossing three coins six times gains in popularity by the Tang dynasty, circa AD 618.

Shao Yong 邵雍 (1011–1077), also known by the pen name Shao Kangjie 邵康節, was a polymath in both mathematics and mysticism. His work was heavily influenced by Buddhism. He proposed a mathematics and numerology-based system of divination with the I Ching under the Image and Number tradition, which became known as the Plum Blossom methods. In the twenty-first century, Shao Yong's Plum Blossom methods reemerged, contributing to an I Ching renaissance in East Asia.

In Western occultism, efforts to reconcile the I Ching with European divination systems such as tarot cards have produced several different systems of correspondences. We covered Crowley's associations connected through the Qabalistic Tree of Life back in chapter 3. This chapter will conclude with a proposition on how the seventy-eight cards of the tarot and the sixty-four hexagrams of the I Ching might be reconciled, and in doing so, how it reveals six points of Divinity that also impart six principles of magic.

# Preparations before the Divination

**FIGURE 7.2** The divination table

The Ten Wings commentaries place as much emphasis on preparations prior to divination and the setting of the work as they do on the actual casting methodology itself. Nearly all of the Yì Xué scholars we've covered in this text have talked about the importance of spiritual cultivation as a prerequisite for successful divination. Shao Yong, who was both a highly reputed scholar and a mystic—acknowledged by his literati contemporaries in Yì Xué as having possessed shamanic and mediumship abilities—stated that what makes one a powerful and accurate diviner is the ability to spot patterns. To effectively spot patterns, you need to be observant and studious. The prerequisite to successful divination is a dedication to study.

The *junzi* 君子 will want a room in the home dedicated to divination and spiritual cultivation. Following general feng shui principles, the ideal divination and home ritual room would be along the north side with an entrance facing the south. Assuming there is already a dedicated space for divination and ritual, make it a habit to approach your divination table from the east and leave toward the west. This is in acknowledgement of the sun's path (the Huang Tao, or Yellow Path), rising in the east and setting in the west.

Upon deciding you would like to consult the I Ching, prepare the table. Wash it down and tidy it so it's clean. Burn three sticks of incense to their ends so that the space is cleansed. Set out all the tools you'll need—paper, writing utensils, any books, incense holder, lighter, a divination mat,[1] candles (optional)—anything and everything you can think of. Arrange the area and then leave it be for a while.

A few hours later or the next day—whatever you intuit is right for you in that moment—return to the prepared space. Wash your hands before commencing the divination ritual. Following Shinto *harae* ritual purification traditions, wash your hands and rinse your mouth before entering the space. Salt is also often used in cleansing rituals. Following Buddhist traditions, read sutras prior to divination work. Better yet, read sutras or meditate regularly so that your default setting is already attuned to Heaven.

When you are ready to begin the divination ritual, approach the table from the east. Light the incense and sit in stillness for a moment. Contemplate the matter you will be inquiring about. Why are you coming to the I Ching for a reading? What is it about the situation that makes it difficult for you to problem-solve it yourself? If you'll be petitioning a particular divinity or using the I Ching as a form of mediumship, take this time to "dial in" to the divine being or to the departed. If your intentions are highly specialized and have to do with the mystical realm, then perhaps a more specialized ritual is called for.

Traditionally, there are predetermined ceremonial robes a Taoist priest would wear for divination rituals. There's a lot of practical value to considering what to wear for divination. What you wear has such an impact on how you feel, especially how much power and confidence you exude. Thus, it isn't so much that dressing the part is a requirement; rather, it's about how dressing the part is a tried-and-true method for ensuring that you're in the optimal state of mind.

While I don't personally wear ceremonial robes for divinatory work, I do make sure I'm dressed respectfully. I'll dress in a neat and tidy manner, and I'll pay attention to my posture. Assume someone's watching.

Fastidious care devoted to the divination space and to what you wear motivates you to take the divination seriously. In doing so, you'll give the answers from the Oracle deeper thought and spend more time contemplating their meaning. When you do that, you're more likely to arrive at a complete understanding of the revelation conveyed.

## Invoking Divinity and Presenting the Question

In the traditional yarrow stalk casting method, certain steps call for invoking Divinity, or at the very least, formally stating your inquiry for the divination. Approaching an I Ching reading with heartfelt intention and sincerity isn't so much for the sake of a magical reaction; rather, it's for our sake, to ensure that we are adjusted to an open and receptive state of mind for the answers to come. Otherwise, what's the point?

However, invocation or opening statements can be secular, so in lieu of invoking "Divinity," take a moment to be earnest, sincere with yourself, and humble. It's perfectly okay to vocalize your uncertainty as to whether anyone is even listening to you. In fact, that's exactly the right attitude—humility— acknowledging that you don't know, and you're not sure, but you're ready and willing to experience.

As you walk through the instructions for the original yarrow stalk divination method, you'll observe how every step of the process is about replicating and acknowledging Taoist cosmological principles. Thus, the invocation or petition prior to commencing an I Ching divination will include a restatement of those cosmological principles. The following is a rewording of one often used:

> I call upon the Taiji, the numinous Light, the Wuji, the numinous stillness of Being. I call upon the affinity of the sun and the moon, and the four faces of the holy Spirit, and who, through the five mysteries of change, produce the eight divine revelations. I seek the Spirit's guidance. I seek the Tao. [*State your inquiry for divination.*]

"Taiji" is an abstract term signifying the divine monad, the omnipresent Light of creation. The Taiji is the Wuji, and the Wuji is the Taiji. Yet the Wuji is a polarity to the Taiji—it's nothingness, the numinous void. The reference to the sun and the moon is a metaphor for yin and yang. The four faces of the holy Spirit are the changing and unchanging lines of yin and yang, the elders and the youngers. The five mysteries refer to the Wu Xing five phases of change, and the eight divine revelations are the Ba Gua.

These terms are conceptual and abstract, though certain folk traditions might personify them into deities just to make them easier to understand. The petition simply restates Taoist cosmology: the one, which we call the Tao, is also the Taiji, which means Tao is everything, and is also the Wuji, which means Tao is nothingness and void; and the interplay between the two creates the myriad things.

You don't have to use those words precisely. The best option is to use your own words, words that mean something to you, that genuinely reflect your state of mind, and to use the text provided here for reference only.

A Mahayana Pure Land Buddhist approach would be to precede the divination with a mantra recitation of the name Amitabha (阿彌陀佛, Amítuófó [Chinese]; Amidabutsu [Japanese]; Amitabul [Korean]; A Di Đà Phật [Vietnamese]). Commence the divination operations, and when completed, close with the same mantra. Reading Buddhist or Taoist scriptures prior to commencing is another method of empowering the divinatory work to come.

For I Ching divination rituals, I invoke the Mysterious Lady of the Nine Heavens (九天玄女, Jiǔ Tiān Xuán Nǚ), a beloved divinity in Taoist mysticism.[2] In English, she's often described as a goddess, an immortal, or a fairy. Long before Fuxi and King Wen, the Lady descended from the heavens in answer to the Yellow Emperor's prayer, to help him defeat a formidable adversary and teach him the art of magic and the art of war.

The invocation I use goes as follows:

Jiǔ Tiān Xuán Nǚ, Lady of the Nine Heavens, Lady of the Mysteries: lend me the spirit and power of your sword, and the spirit and power of your gourd. I seek answers, I seek knowledge. I seek guidance on the auspices of my present Path . . .

Then state your inquiry for divination.

Jiǔ Tiān Xuán Nǚ is a protégé of the Queen Mother of the West (西王母, Xī Wáng Mǔ), a goddess venerated since the Shang dynasty (1766–1122 BC), and in popular myths, she pays homage to Kuan Yin, the Buddhist bodhisattva of mercy and compassion. Thus, invocations and petitions of the Lady will often include references to the Queen Mother or Kuan Yin.

Taoist mystics connect the Lady of the Nine Heavens to the Zhouyi, the Book of Changes, through the magical techniques she imparted to the Yellow Emperor. She brought to Earth the secret yin and yang technique (陰陽術, *yīn yáng shù*) and the Scripture for the Esoteric Talisman (黃帝陰符經, Huángdì yīn fú jīng), a text instructing on methods in Taoist magic. According to myths

**FIGURE 7.3** *Lady of the Nine Heavens* (1829) by Katsushika Hokusai. *Ukiyo-e* woodblock print, ink on paper.

popular in Taiwan, Nǔwā was an incarnation of the Lady. Thus, not only is the Lady of the Nine Heavens part of the origin story of the I Ching; the Book of Changes is a synthesis of ancient knowledge made possible by her.

For those reasons, she is ever present in this text on the I Ching, and every few chapters, including a handful of expository endnotes, we circle back to discussions of her.

To pronounce Jiǔ Tiān Xuán Nǔ in Mandarin, here's an informal pronunciation guide:

| | | | | | |
|---|---|---|---|---|---|
| 吅 | 圼 | 九 | Jiǔ | Nine (or ninth) | Pronounced "joe." |
| 巫 | 而 | 天 | Tiān | Sky/heaven | The "ā" sound here is more like "Tien" or "Tyen." It rhymes with "wen." |
| 吉 | 吉 | 玄 | Xuán | Black, deep, mysterious (also: night sky) | Pronounced "shwen"—"sshh" followed by "wen." |
| 虎 | 爻 | 女 | Nǔ | Lady, woman, maiden | Unless you go all-in to learn Mandarin, this is going to be a hard one. Pronounce "n" like "noon," purse your lips, and try to say "nee-yu" through slightly pursed lips. |

The leftmost column above features one style of oracle bone or seal script for writing Jiǔ Tiān Xuán Nǔ's name; the next column to the right features an alternative style.

## *Yarrow Stalk Method*

The Xici (繫辭傳, Xìcí chuán), comprising two of the appendices in the Ten Wings, sets forth the yarrow stalk divination method. It dates back to around 221 BC, per historians' estimation.³ The original text was vague and was thus recreated by Zhu Xi in AD 1188. Remarkably, the way the yarrow stalk method of divination is done today remains relatively unchanged from how it was taught in 221 BC.

**FIGURE 7.4** Yarrow stalks for divination

The divinatory method is performed with fifty stalks of yarrow cut to similar height, width, and shape. The Ten Wings explains why we use fifty stalks: they represent a balanced proportion of yin and yang, where odd numbers 1, 3, 5, 7, and 9 are Heaven, or yang, while even numbers 2, 4, 6, 8, and 10 are Earth, or yin. Thus, there are five heavenly numbers and five earthly numbers. The sum of the odd numbers is 25 (1 + 3 + 5 + 7 + 9), while the sum of the even numbers is 30 (2 + 4 + 6 + 8 + 10). Their sum, 25 + 30, is 55, representing a balance of "gods and demons in movement."[4]

These cardinal numbers correspond with the ten heavenly stems marking the ten days of the week and the culture of ten-day cycles used during the Shang dynasty (1600–1046 BC). The ten ordinals of heavenly stems are still used today in astrological and divination systems throughout East Asia. With

10 ordinals (the heavenly stems) multiplied by 5 designations of yin and yang affinity, with 5 signifying the five agents of change per the Wu Xing, we get 50.

Of these fifty stalks, only forty-nine are used. Wang Bi views the group of forty-nine stalks as the universe of the diviner or questioner, representing the Taoist cosmological concept of Being. The single unused stalk represents *wu* (無), or Nonbeing, from the Taoist and Confucian principle of *wu wei* (無為).

When a divination commences, the stalks are divided into two portions to represent the separation into two binary forces. This replicates the Creation myth. From the One singularity of a numinous omnipresence (太極, Tàijí) that is also a numinous nothingness (無極, Wújí) came the pair and duality of affinities yin and yang, the two primal forces.

One portion is set apart to represent the next step of Creation into the three powers and the holy trinity that governs all of the cosmos. They are then counted in fours, with four representing the four seasons.

The arrangements of the stalks as you count them are methods of sympathetic magic, using gestures at the microcosmic individual level to tap in to the movements of *qi* at the macrocosmic universal level. Groupings of stalks will be arranged to signify Heaven and to signify Earth, which will then be connected by a single stalk to represent the diviner who is operating this technology to connect Heaven and Earth and thus reveal movements in the universe through the coded language of the hexagrams.

When not in use, these sacred yarrow stalk divination sticks should be wrapped in scented silk and kept inside a pouch made from black or very dark cloth.[5] Black is symbolic of *wu wei* and of the One from which the myriad things arose. When divination stalks are in use, the diviner calls upon the light to active the tool. Thus, when not in use, they are shrouded in the darkness of the heavens and the earth in stillness. Moreover, black is the color that results from complete absence or complete absorption of visible light, thus symbolic of the numinous omnipresence and numinous void of the Tao.

The black pouch should then be kept in a cylindrical bamboo or wooden tube. This tube should then always be placed along the north side of your divination table or altar. Even when you are not actively divining with the yarrow stalks, burn a stick of incense daily at your divination table or altar. Doing so maintains the healthy level of forceful *qi* it needs for performing accurate divinations.

# PRACTICUM 7.1:
## Handpicking Your Divination Stalks

The most powerful divination tool you can craft is one for which the fifty stalks have been collected, dried, and prepared by your own hand. When the Chinese texts of antiquity instruct on using yarrow, a plant native to the continent of Asia and commonly found everywhere, the underlying principle was to collect the stalks from your local region, which would contain the *qi* of nature in such a way that would best empower the diviner. In Asia, yarrow would have been easily sourced by the would-be diviner.

If you live in a region of the world where yarrow is *not* easily sourced and not part of your local ecosystem, then my recommendation is to consider what would be a yarrow equivalent in your region. Go out into nature on the day of a full moon, the moon phase of harvest, and handpick fifty carefully selected stalks that you will be able to smooth out, cut, and dry to equal lengths and shape.

**FIGURE 7.5** Handpicked yarrow stalks

Before picking the stalks, take a look around at the environment the stalks are growing in. Generally speaking, opt for locations that are fertile, verdant, and getting plenty of sunlight, where you can intuit harmony and a cheerful, peaceful atmosphere. The stalks here are enriched with healthier *qi*.

That being said, a certain style of occultist might very well intentionally go for stalks growing resiliently somewhere dark, cold, and difficult. Plants that are prevailing in challenging environments show strength and perseverance, and while the *qi* of such stalks may be a little more volatile than most are prepared to deal with, in the hands of the occultist who knows how to work with that energy, they prove to be spectacularly potent.

Once you've collected your fifty stalks, lay them out under direct sunlight to dry them.

The original texts are silent on the point of whether a deliberate consecration ritual is necessary to prepare the stalks as a divinatory tool. However, there are clear mentions of routine incense offerings at the divination table, and it's implied—or well understood by those who would be reading the texts—that the dedicated daily ritual of incense offerings is what empowers the tool.

Within its cultural and historical context, anyone with the level of know-how to be performing I Ching divinations would already have a dedicated practice of veneration or spiritual cultivation and would be doing so in a dedicated room, imbuing that room and its contents with a *qi* that transcends the mundane. To have to spell that out explicitly in a philosophical text written for them would have been absurd.

Also, invocations and prayers right before a divination begins will empower the tool. In short, whether consecration of the tool is necessary will be left up to your personal discretion.

In assembling a new set of divination stalks, however, I do like to perform an intentional consecration ritual on the freshly picked and dried stalks. Wash the stalks with water gathered during thunder rites, per the practicum from chapter 5. Create a charging grid with the crystals charged by thunder magic. Placing it at a centralized point of a crystal charging grid, where the crystals are vessels containing thunder *qi,* infuses even more power into the tool. Or pass each stalk, one by one, through the smoke of sacred incense, such as sandalwood or frankincense.

## The Ten Wings Divination Method (221 BC)

| | | |
|---|---|---|
|  |  |  |
| **1.** Set down 1 vertical stalk, and as you do so, invoke Divinity and/or state your inquiry for divination. | **2.** Divide the bundle in your hands in two, and place one bundle atop the vertical stalk. You are connecting to Heaven. | **3.** Set down the remaining bundle along the bottom, to signify Earth. You've now connected Heaven and Earth. |
|  |  |  |
| **4.** Pick up 1 stalk from the bottom Earth bundle and place it between your pinky and ring finger. This represents your *qi*. | **5.** Pick up the bottom Earth bundle. You'll be counting these stalks in groups of 4. Hold the stalks in your hand as shown. | **6.** Count and group the stalks in bundles of 4, and set them out. This symbolizes the four directions and four seasons (space and time). |
|  |  |  |
| **7.** Count and group until you have **4 or fewer stalks remaining.** Place this group of 4, 3, 2, or 1 stalk(s) between your ring and middle finger. | **8.** Pick up the top Heaven bundle. Count these stalks in groups of 4. Hold the stalks in your hand as shown. | **9.** Just a reminder: 1 stalk for your *qi* is between your pinky and ring fingers. The remainder (4 or fewer) stalks from **Step 7** are between your ring and middle fingers. |

| 10. Count and group the stalks from the top Heaven bundle until you have **4 or fewer stalks remaining**. | 11. In your hands you *must* have *either* **5 or 9 stalks in your hand**. If 5, the *qi* is Earth. If 9, the *qi* is Heaven. | 12. Set the **5** *or* **9 stalks** from this COUNT 1 off to the side. Mathematically, if counted correctly, you will get 5 or 9. |
|---|---|---|

Write down your result for COUNT 1.

| If you had **5 stalks** remaining from Count 1: |
|---|
| At the initiation of what became the matter at hand you're inquiring about, terrestrial influences were at play. The number 5 here represents the Wu Xing, the five phases of change. Which of the five phases are at play is governed by the Trinity of Lucks 福祿壽 (Fú Lù Shòu), also known as the Three Celestial Stars 三星 (Sānxīng): Jupiter, Ursa Major, and Canis Major. To reenact the Creation myth, 5 converts to 3, because in the Beginning, the Wu Xing five agents of change create the Three Celestial Stars that govern fate and destiny. |
| If your result was **5 stalks**   →   assign it the number:      **3** |

| If you had **9 stalks** remaining from Count 1: |
|---|
| At the initiation of what became the matter at hand you're inquiring about, celestial influences were at play. The number 9 here represents the nine heavenly kingdoms (the Nine Heavens). The Nine Heavens dispense of yin and yang throughout the universe to create matter. To reenact the Creation myth, 9 converts to 2, because in the Beginning, the Nine Heavens dispense of the divine binary principle to produce changes. |
| If your result was **9 stalks**   →   assign it the number:      **2** |

| | | |
|---|---|---|
|  |  |  |
| **13.** Setting aside the stalks from Count 1, continue with the remainder bundle. | **14.** Set down 1 stalk and refocus on the question for divination. | **15.** Split the bundle in your hands in two and place one bundle on top for Heaven. |
| 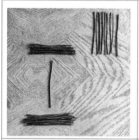 |  |  |
| **16.** Place the remaining bundle at the bottom to signify Earth. | **17.** Pick up 1 stalk from the bottom bundle and place it between your pinky and ring fingers to signify your *qi*. | **18.** Count the bottom Earth pile in groups of 4 until you have **4 or fewer stalks remaining.** |
|  |  |  |
| **19.** Place that remainder between your ring and middle fingers. Pick up the top Heaven bundle and count in groups of 4. | **20.** You will be left with a remainder of **4 or fewer** stalks like before. Place them between your middle and index fingers. | **21.** Set the **4 or 8 stalks** from this COUNT 2 next to the 5 or 9 stalks from Count 1. You now have two bundles of remainder counted stalks. |

Write down your result for COUNT 2.

| If you had 4 stalks remaining from Count 2: |
|---|
| At a crucial midpoint of the matter at hand you're inquiring about, terrestrial influences were dominant. The number 4 here represents the four seasons and four directions for the quaternary cycles of change in nature. The four seasons and four directions are governed by the Trinity of Lucks. Thus, 4 converts to 3 to acknowledge the lordship of the 3 over the 4. |
| If your result was **4** stalks →　　assign it the number:　　3 |

| If you had 8 stalks remaining from Count 2: |
|---|
| At the crucial midpoint of the matter at hand you're inquiring about, celestial influences were dominant. The number 8 here represents the eight trigrams of the Ba Gua. The eight trigrams are constructed of yin and yang to create matter. Thus, 8 converts to 2 to acknowledge the lordship of the 2 over the 8. |
| If your result was **8** stalks →　　assign it the number:　　2 |

22. You now have the Count 1 and Count 2 bundles off to one side. Gather up the remaining bundle to count.

23. Set down 1 vertical stalk, and as you do, refocus on the question presented for the divination.

24. Split the bundle in hand in two. Place one bundle atop the vertical stalk to signify invocation of Heaven.

|  |  |  |
|---|---|---|
| 25. Set down the other half below to signify connection to Earth. Pick up 1 stalk from the bottom Earth bundle. | 26. The 1 stalk goes between your pinky and ring fingers. Count the bottom Earth bundle in groups of 4. | 27. Like before, you should be left with a remainder of **4 or fewer** stalks. |

|  |  | |
|---|---|---|
| 28. After counting the Earth and Heaven bundles, the total remainder stalks in your hand **is 4 or 8**. | 29. Set the **4 or 8 stalks** from this COUNT 3 next to the bundles from Counts 1 and 2. You now have three bundles of remainder counted stalks. | 30. Count 1 (above right) yielded a remainder of either 5 or 9 stalks. Count 2 (above center) yielded 4 or 8, and Count 3 (above left) yielded 4 or 8. |

Write down your result for COUNT 3.

| If you had 4 stalks remaining from Count 3: |
|---|
| At the last turning point of the matter at hand, terrestrial influences were dominant. The 4, symbolic of the cycles of space and time, converts to 3 to acknowledge the lordship of the 3 over the cycles of the 4. |
| If your result was 4 stalks → assign it the number: **3** |

| If you had **8** stalks remaining from Count 3: |
|---|
| At the last turning point of the matter at hand, celestial or spirit influences were dominant. The 8, symbolic of the eight trigrams, converts to 2 to acknowledge the lordship of the 2 over the creation of the 8. |
| If your result was **8** stalks　　→　　assign it the number:　　2 |

The assigned numbers for the three counts will have yielded line 1 of your hexagram.

Each count yielded an assigned number of 2 or 3.

Add these three digits together. Thus, 2 + 2 + 2 for 6; 2 + 2 + 3 for 7; 2 + 3 + 3 for 8; or 3 + 3 + 3 for 9. Follow the prompts in the subsequent table to tally up the total sum.

| | | | |
|---|---|---|---|
| COUNT 1 | If 9 stalks → write 2 in box | If 5 stalks → write 3 in box | |
| COUNT 2 | If 8 stalks → write 2 in box | If 4 stalks → write 3 in box | + |
| COUNT 3 | If 8 stalks → write 2 in box | If 4 stalks → write 3 in box | + |
| | | Total Sum: | |

The total sums correspond to the yin and yang affinities, or the Four Faces of God as noted in table 7.1. This produces the result for line 1, the bottom-most line.

**TABLE 7.1** Yarrow Stalk Line Construction Reference Table

| Total Sum | Resulting Line | | | |
|---|---|---|---|---|
| 6 | ▬▬　▬▬ | X | Changing yin line | Younger yin |
| 7 | ▬▬▬▬▬ | | Unchanging yang line | Elder yang |
| 8 | ▬▬　▬▬ | | Unchanging yin line | Elder yin |
| 9 | ▬▬▬▬▬ | X | Changing yang line | Younger yang |

|  |  |  |
|---|---|---|
| **31.** Gather up all 50 stalks again and start anew. | **32.** Set down 1 vertical stalk and focus on the question. | **33.** Call upon Heaven and set down the top bundle. Call upon Earth and set down the bottom bundle. |
|  |  |  |
| **34.** From the bottom Earth bundle, pick up 1 stalk and place it between your pinky and ring fingers. | **35.** Gather the bottom Earth bundle and count out groups of 4 until you have a remainder of **4 stalks or fewer.** | **36.** Tuck the 4 or fewer stalks between your ring and middle fingers. Take the top Heaven bundle and count out groups of 4 until **4 or fewer remain.** |

|  |  |  |
|---|---|---|
| 37. The remainder count from Earth and Heaven should be 5 stalks total or 9 stalks total. Set it aside. Note whether an assigned 2 or 3 is yielded from step 37. | 38. Repeat: 1 vertical stalk, focus on the question. Call Heaven, top bundle; call Earth, bottom bundle. Take 1 from Earth and place it between your pinky and ring fingers. | 39. Pick up the bottom Earth bundle and count out groups of 4 until you have a remainder of 4 or fewer. Place it between your ring and middle fingers. |

Write down your result for COUNT 1.

| 37. | COUNT 1 | If 9 stalks → write 2 in box | If 5 stalks → write 3 in box | |
|---|---|---|---|---|
| | COUNT 2 | If 8 stalks → write 2 in box | If 4 stalks → write 3 in box | + |
| | COUNT 3 | If 8 stalks → write 2 in box | If 4 stalks → write 3 in box | + |
| | | | Total Sum: | |

|  |  |  |
|---|---|---|
| 40. Pick up the top Heaven bundle and count out groups of 4 until you have a remainder of **4 or fewer**. | 41. The count from Earth and Heaven should be **4 stalks total or 8 stalks total**. Set it aside. Note whether an assigned 2 or 3 is yielded from step 41. | 42. We now proceed with the final Count 3. Set down 1 stalk and reorient yourself by thinking about your question again. |

Write down your result for COUNT 2.

| 37. | COUNT 1 | If 9 stalks → write 2 in box | If 5 stalks → write 3 in box | |
|---|---|---|---|---|
| 41. | COUNT 2 | If 8 stalks → write 2 in box | If 4 stalks → write 3 in box | + |
| | COUNT 3 | If 8 stalks → write 2 in box | If 4 stalks → write 3 in box | + |
| | | | Total Sum: | |

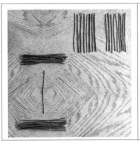

**43.** Set one part of the bundle up top for Heaven. Set the remainder at the bottom for Earth. As above, so below. Your prayer connects Heaven and Earth.

**44.** From the bottom Earth pile, pick up 1 stalk to place between your pinky and ring fingers. This represents you, the questioner and diviner, integrating your *qi*.

**45.** Count and group the bottom Earth bundle in groups of 4 until you get a remainder of **4 or fewer stalks.**

**46.** Count and group the top Heaven bundle in groups of 4 until you get a remainder of **4 or fewer stalks.**

**47.** Set the **4 or 8 stalks** from this COUNT 3 next to the bundles from Counts 1 and 2. You now have three bundles of remainder counted stalks.

**48.** Count 1 (above right) yielded a remainder of either 5 or 9 stalks. Count 2 (above center) yielded 4 or 8, and Count 3 (above left) was 4 or 8.

Write down your result for COUNT 3.

| | | | |
|---|---|---|---|
| 37. | COUNT 1 | If 9 stalks → write 2 in box | If 5 stalks → write 3 in box |
| 41. | COUNT 2 | If 8 stalks → write 2 in box | If 4 stalks → write 3 in box   + |
| 47. | COUNT 3 | If 8 stalks → write 2 in box | If 4 stalks → write 3 in box   + |
| | | | Total Sum: |

The total sums correspond to the yin and yang affinities, or the Four Faces of God as noted in table 7.1. This produces the result for line 2. The reading demonstrated in the photographs yielded 2 (9 stalks) + 3 (4 stalks) + 3 (4 stalks) = 8 for line 1, producing an unchanging yin line, or elder yin.

The next casting yielded 2 (9 stalks) + 2 (8 stalks) + 3 (4 stalks) = 7 for line 2, producing an unchanging yang line, or elder yang.

| | PRIMARY HEXAGRAM | | TRANSFORMED HEXAGRAM | |
|---|---|---|---|---|
| Line 6 | | | | |
| Line 5 | | | | |
| Line 4 | | | | |
| Line 3 | | | | |
| Line 2 | ▬▬▬▬▬ | | | |
| Line 1 | ▬▬  ▬▬ | | | |

| **49.** Gather up all 50 yarrow stalks again and repeat the process. | **50.** Set down 1 vertical, focus on the question. Divide the bundle in two: as above, so below. Pick 1 from the bottom and hold it. | **51.** Count and group the bottom bundle in 4s until you have a remainder of **4 stalks or fewer** in hand. |
|---|---|---|

| | | |
|---|---|---|
|  52. Hold that remainder from Count 1 between your ring and middle fingers. |  53. Now pick up the top Heaven bundle. | 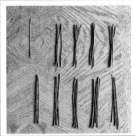 54. Count and group the Heaven bundle of stalks in groups of 4. |
|  55. You will have a remainder of **4 stalks or fewer** from this second count. |  56. Replicate **steps 11 and 12** to yield Count 1. That's the rightmost bundle pictured in the photograph. |  57. Replicate **steps 13 through 21** to yield Count 2. Pick up the remaining bundle and cast for Count 3. |
|  58. Begin with the bottom bundle, counting and grouping in groups of 4 until you have a remainder of 4 or fewer. |  59. You will now have either 4 stalks or 8 stalks in hand after the third count. |  60. Up to this point, you have completed casting of the lower trigram. Repeat the entire process to cast for the upper trigram. |

From the photographs demonstrating the steps, you'll see that for the third line, the results were 3 (from 5 stalks in the rightmost pile pictured) + 2 (from 8 stalks in the center pile) + 2 (from 8 stalks in the leftmost pile) = 7, which corresponds with unchanging yang.

The lower trigram of my yarrow stalk reading so far is Wind.

|        | **PRIMARY HEXAGRAM** | **TRANSFORMED HEXAGRAM** |
|--------|----------------------|--------------------------|
| Line 6 |                      |                          |
| Line 5 |                      |                          |
| Line 4 |                      |                          |
| Line 3 | ▬▬▬▬▬               |                          |
| Line 2 | ▬▬▬▬▬               |                          |
| Line 1 | ▬▬  ▬▬              |                          |

From the photographs demonstrating the steps, you'll see that for the third line, the results were 3 (from 5 stalks in the rightmost pile pictured) + 2 (from 8 stalks in the center pile) + 2 (from 8 stalks in the leftmost pile) = 7, which corresponds with unchanging yang.

Table 7.2 is a quick reference chart for the number assignments for stalk counts. Every three counts (First Count, Second Count, and Third Count) yields one of the six *yao* or hexagram lines. One of the four possible results is yielded by the total sum of the three counts being 6, 7, 8, or 9, as noted. Changing lines are marked by an X next to the line.

**TABLE 7.2** Quick Reference Chart for Yarrow Stalk Counting

| SUM OF EACH OF THREE COUNTS | | | | SUM OF THREE COUNTS | | | |
|---|---|---|---|---|---|---|---|
| First count | → | 5 stalks = 3 | | 6 ▬▬ ▬▬ | X | Changing yin | |
| | | 9 stalks = 2 | | 7 ▬▬▬▬▬ | | Unchanging yang | |
| Second count | → | 4 stalks = 3 | | 8 ▬▬ ▬▬ | | Unchanging yin | |
| | | 8 stalks = 2 | | 9 ▬▬▬▬▬ | X | Changing yang | |
| Third count | → | 4 stalks = 3 | | | | | |
| | | 8 stalks = 2 | | | | | |
| **6** | | **7** | | **8** | | **9** | |
| ▬▬ ▬▬<br>▬▬▬▬▬<br>少陰<br>**Younger yin** | | ▬▬▬▬▬<br>▬▬▬▬▬<br>太陽<br>**Elder yang** | | ▬▬ ▬▬<br>▬▬ ▬▬<br>太陰<br>**Elder yin** | | ▬▬▬▬▬<br>▬▬ ▬▬<br>少陽<br>**Younger yang** | |

Once you've completed casting the three counts six times, producing the six lines of the hexagram from the bottom up, note which of the lines were changing lines. You'll have marked the changing lines with an X.

| | **PRIMARY HEXAGRAM** | | **TRANSFORMED HEXAGRAM** |
|---|---|---|---|
| Line 6 | ▬▬ ▬▬ | X | ▬▬▬▬▬ |
| Line 5 | ▬▬▬▬▬ | | ▬▬ ▬▬ |
| Line 4 | ▬▬▬▬▬ | X | ▬▬ ▬▬ |
| Line 3 | ▬▬▬▬▬ | | ▬▬▬▬▬ |
| Line 2 | ▬▬▬▬▬ | | ▬▬▬▬▬ |
| Line 1 | ▬▬ ▬▬ | | ▬▬ ▬▬ |
| | Thunder over Wind | | Mountain over Wind |
| | 32 | | 18 |

The changing lines will produce a transformed hexagram.

Where there are changing lines in the hexagram you've cast, that line will transform into its polar opposite. For example, line 4 in the primary hexagram was changing yang, so as a changing line, it becomes a yin line in the transformed hexagram. Line 6 in the primary hexagram is changing yin, so it grows into a yang line.

You will now have produced two hexagrams with their point(s) of connection—the changing lines—marked by an X. In the example provided, the primary hexagram is composed of the trigrams Thunder over Wind, which is Hexagram 32.

Your divinatory reading results consist of the following:

- The Oracle abstract or summary judgment for the primary hexagram
- Line statements of the primary hexagram for the changing lines
- The Oracle abstract or summary judgment for the transformed hexagram
- Corresponding line statements in the transformed hexagram, per the changing lines

Which of the listed aspects you read and how you interpret the various aspects is a matter of personal preference. What distinguishes the artistry of a diviner is in the developed approach, which only arises from experience. Thus, get creative and intuitive.

Here's how I read the aspects. Start with the Oracle section of the primary hexagram. In this book, the Oracle section consists of a summary of the hexagram's divinatory meaning, followed by the translations and commentaries. I interpret this as a concise briefing of the answer. It will denote a general prognostication of auspicious versus inauspicious, take action or do not take action.

Next, read the changing lines. The changing lines convey the thesis, and the concrete points of advice from the Oracle. Changing lines are action items. It's your to-do list. Changing lines give advice on how to navigate the situation and how to turn the tides in your favor.

When there are changing lines, it means you still have the opportunity to turn things around. The more changing lines there are, the more volatile the situation. This could be positive, because it means there is still ample time to create the change you seek. It is also a warning to tread with care, because every decision, every action matters and could become decisive.

Since forces that can influence the situation at hand are still in movement, and you have the opportunity to control those forces, the transformed hexagram reveals more insight into how those forces can change. Both the Oracle section and the corresponding text for the changing lines are read. The transformed hexagram reveals the "what if."

Notwithstanding those basic points, chapter 4 demonstrated that once the casting process for the hexagram is done, how it's interpreted depends on which school and tradition you subscribe to and is often a combination of both Image and Number and Meaning and Principle techniques.

Divination is an art. As an artist, you'll probably begin by mimicking those you admire, but as you grow, you'll formulate your own style. Likewise, the best I Ching practitioners are ones who have established their own style. How you move among the six Lines of text, how you approach the Oracle or Judgement section, and to what extent you consider trigram meanings and Wu Xing are all parts of curating your own style.

In the section "Summary Outline of Hexagram Interpretation" at the end of this chapter, there will be a step-by-step guide recommending how to apply the interpretive principles from chapter 4 and navigate your divinatory reading result. As a beginner, work with that step-by-step guide until you develop your own unique approach.

If, however, your divination result yielded *no* changing lines, then you've produced what I call a locked hexagram. A subsequent section in this chapter will cover how to approach interpreting locked hexagrams.

## PRACTICUM 7.2:
## An I Ching Reading by the
## Yarrow Stalk Method

Assuming the myths are true, then King Wen was imprisoned when he conceived of this divination method—so he had time on his hands. These days, for those without the patience of a Buddha, the traditional yarrow stalk method can be overwhelming. It's no wonder the coin toss approach was popularized over this one.

Yet something can be said about the power of this casting method. If I'm coming to the Oracle for an everyday mundane problem, I'll probably skip this option and go for one of the easier methods. But if I need an answer to one of life's Big Questions, then the yarrow stalk method is the one I'll go for.

When working with the I Ching to channel spirit entities or achieve spirit contact, I find that the lengthiness of the process itself gives me the time I need to truly immerse in the altered state of consciousness. The ritualism of the process and the collective psychic power it's enriched with from millennia of use by the most powerful diviners of Asia enable me to feel the motions of my hands interacting with the sacred stalks as activating sympathetic magic. It's like plucking the strings of an instrument and creating music that I'll then interpret. When you take this method seriously, and approach it sincerely, you will feel the progression of the counts amplifying your personal power, and your *qi* intensifying.

Do not simply take my word for it—try it out for yourself. Record your first attempt with the traditional yarrow stalks method in the space below. Consider what it means to you in the present, but then revisit it years from now and see if your added life experiences have changed its meaning to you.

| | | Total Sum of the Three Counts | | |
|---|---|---|---|---|
| 6 | ▬▬ ▬▬ | ☒ | Changing yin | Younger yin |
| 7 | ▬▬▬▬ | | Fixed yang | Elder yang |
| 8 | ▬▬ ▬▬ | | Fixed yin | Elder yin |
| 9 | ▬▬▬▬ | ☒ | Changing yang | Younger yang |

| Line 1 | Count 1 | ☐ 5 stalks = 3 | ☐ 9 stalks = 2 |
|---|---|---|---|
| | Count 2 | ☐ 4 stalks = 3 | ☐ 8 stalks = 2 |
| | Count 3 | ☐ 4 stalks = 3 | ☐ 8 stalks = 2 |
| | Total sum, adding the 3s and 2s: | | |
| | **Resulting Line:** | | ☐ |

| Line 2 | Count 1 | ☐ 5 stalks = 3 | ☐ 9 stalks = 2 |
| --- | --- | --- | --- |
| | Count 2 | ☐ 4 stalks = 3 | ☐ 8 stalks = 2 |
| | Count 3 | ☐ 4 stalks = 3 | ☐ 8 stalks = 2 |
| | Total sum, adding the 3s and 2s: | | |
| | Resulting Line: | | ☐ |

| Line 3 | Count 1 | ☐ 5 stalks = 3 | ☐ 9 stalks = 2 |
| --- | --- | --- | --- |
| | Count 2 | ☐ 4 stalks = 3 | ☐ 8 stalks = 2 |
| | Count 3 | ☐ 4 stalks = 3 | ☐ 8 stalks = 2 |
| | Total sum, adding the 3s and 2s: | | |
| | Resulting Line: | | ☐ |

| Line 4 | Count 1 | ☐ 5 stalks = 3 | ☐ 9 stalks = 2 |
| --- | --- | --- | --- |
| | Count 2 | ☐ 4 stalks = 3 | ☐ 8 stalks = 2 |
| | Count 3 | ☐ 4 stalks = 3 | ☐ 8 stalks = 2 |
| | Total sum, adding the 3s and 2s: | | |
| | Resulting Line: | | ☐ |

| Line 5 | Count 1 | ☐ 5 stalks = 3 | ☐ 9 stalks = 2 |
| --- | --- | --- | --- |
| | Count 2 | ☐ 4 stalks = 3 | ☐ 8 stalks = 2 |
| | Count 3 | ☐ 4 stalks = 3 | ☐ 8 stalks = 2 |
| | Total sum, adding the 3s and 2s: | | |
| | Resulting Line: | | ☐ |

| Line 6 | Count 1 | ☐ 5 stalks = 3 | ☐ 9 stalks = 2 |
|---|---|---|---|
| | Count 2 | ☐ 4 stalks = 3 | ☐ 8 stalks = 2 |
| | Count 3 | ☐ 4 stalks = 3 | ☐ 8 stalks = 2 |
| | Total sum, adding the 3s and 2s: | | |
| | Resulting Line: | | ☐ |

| | PRIMARY HEXAGRAM | TRANSFORMED HEXAGRAM |
|---|---|---|
| Line 6 | | |
| Line 5 | | |
| Line 4 | | |
| Line 3 | | |
| Line 2 | | |
| Line 1 | | |
| Upper trigram: | | |
| Lower trigram: | | |
| Hexagram: | | |

For a reference on how to fill in the tables, the below would be a record of the first line casting results from the photographed demonstration. See steps 29 and 30.

| Line 1 | Count 1 | ☐ 5 stalks = 3 | ☒ 9 stalks = 2 |
|---|---|---|---|
| | Count 2 | ☒ 4 stalks = 3 | ☐ 8 stalks = 2 |
| | Count 3 | ☒ 4 stalks = 3 | ☐ 8 stalks = 2 |
| | Total sum, adding the 3s and 2s: | | 8 |
| | Resulting Line: | ▬▬ ▬▬ | ☐ |

**TABLE 7.3 Image and Number vs. Meaning and Principle Coin Toss Methods**

| IMAGE AND NUMBER TRADITION | | | | MEANING AND PRINCIPLE TRADITION | | | |
|---|---|---|---|---|---|---|---|
| 陰 Yin | | 陽 Yang | | 陰 Yin | | 陽 Yang | |
| 太陰 Elder yin | 少陰 Younger yin | 少陽 Younger yang | 太陽 Elder yang | 太陰 Elder yin | 少陰 Younger yin | 少陽 Younger yang | 太陽 Elder yang |
| 3 tails | 2 tails 1 head | 2 heads 1 tail | 3 heads | 3 tails | 2 tails 1 head | 2 heads 1 tail | 3 heads |
| ↓ | ↓ | ↓ | ↓ | ↓ | ↓ | ↓ | ↓ |
| Fixed line | Changing line | Changing line | Fixed line | Changing line | Fixed line | Fixed line | Changing line |

| **Rationale:** The Image and Number school emphasizes the importance of metaphysical correspondences. The symbolism of younger yin and younger yang as fluctuating, shifting energy means they produce the changing lines. When the result is elder yin or elder yang, these are matured and therefore fixed lines. | **Rationale:** The probability of getting 3 heads *or* 3 tails is 1 out of 7. However, the probability of getting 1 tail and 2 heads *or* 2 tails and 1 head is 3 out of 7. Since you're more likely to get 1 or 2 than 3, the 1–2 is assigned a fixed line to isolate a narrower focus on what changes, which is only when the result is all 3. |
|---|---|

The Meaning and Principle assignments of coin toss results to yin and yang affinities is the majority view and my personal approach. However, you'll also find texts that instruct the coin toss method under the Image and Tradition assignments. Thus, both are presented to you so you are aware that they coexist.

**TABLE 7.4** Coin Toss Reference Table

| IMAGE AND NUMBER TRADITION | | MEANING AND PRINCIPLE TRADITION | |
|---|---|---|---|
| 3 tails → Elder yin | | 3 tails → Elder yin | |
| Fixed yin line | ▬▬  ▬▬ | Changing yin line | ▬▬  ▬▬    X |
| 1 heads 2 tails → Younger yin | | 1 heads 2 tails → Younger yin | |
| Changing yin line | ▬▬  ▬▬    X | Fixed yin line | ▬▬  ▬▬ |
| 2 heads 1 tails → Younger yang | | 2 heads 1 tails → Younger yang | |
| Changing yang line | ▬▬▬▬▬ | Fixed yang line | ▬▬▬▬▬ |
| 3 heads → Elder yang | | 3 heads → Elder yang | |
| Fixed yang line | ▬▬▬▬▬    X | Changing yang line | ▬▬▬▬▬    X |

# Coin Toss Method

Heads. Chinese script 乾隆通寶. Qianlong emperor (1736–1795)

Tails. Mint marks in Manchu script. Minted by Board of Works, Beijing.

**FIGURE 7.6** Copper alloy coins from the Qing dynasty (1645–1911)

Records of using coins in I Ching divination date to well before AD 200, the Three Kingdoms era. Wang Bi 王弼 (AD 226–249) wrote several commentaries on using coins for I Ching divination.[6] The three-coins-tossed-six-times method of I Ching divination was also popular during the Tang dynasty (AD 618–690, 705–907).[7] In premodern Chinese coinage (the traditional coins used for I Ching divination), there is a square cutout at the center. The circular form of the coin represents Heaven, and the square represents Earth. Embedded into the coin itself is the expression of circling the square.

There are two conflicting approaches to how the coin toss results are interpreted. Under the Image and Number tradition, presented in the left-hand columns of table 7.3 and table 7.4, three heads or three tails indicate fixed lines, while two heads and one tail or two tails and one head indicate changing lines. The Meaning and Principle tradition is the reverse, as shown in the right-hand columns of tables 7.3 and 7.4. Three heads or three tails indicate changing lines, while two heads and one tail or two tails and one head are the fixed lines.

I follow the Meaning and Principle tradition. The following instructions for the coin toss method will be per the Meaning and Principle tradition.

Begin by formulating the question in your mind, and envision yourself having a conversation with the Book. Toss three coins together in your hands, and as you shake the coins, focus on your inquiry. When you're ready, let the coins land on a flat surface, and read your results.

| COIN TOSS RESULT | PRIMARY HEXAGRAM | | YIN AND YANG AFFINITY |
|---|---|---|---|
| 3 tails | ▬▬ ▬▬ | X | Changing yin line |
| 2 tails 1 head | ▬▬ ▬▬ | | Fixed yin line |
| 2 heads 1 tail | ▬▬▬▬▬ | | Fixed yang |
| 3 heads | ▬▬▬▬▬ | X | Changing yang line |

If either three heads or three tails lands, then that line is a changing line. I mark the changing lines with an "X" to the side of the line.

| | PRIMARY HEXAGRAM | TRANSFORMED HEXAGRAM |
|---|---|---|
| Line 6 | | |
| Line 5 | | |
| Line 4 | | |
| Line 3 | | |
| Line 2 | | |
| Line 1 | ▬▬▬▬▬ | |

Your first coin toss (tossing all three coins simultaneously) will yield the result for line 1. Construct the hexagrams from the bottom up. To demonstrate, let's say the first toss yielded 2 heads and 1 tails. The resulting line is yang.

| | PRIMARY HEXAGRAM | | | TRANSFORMED HEXAGRAM |
|---|---|---|---|---|
| Line 6 | | | | |
| Line 5 | | | | |
| Line 4 | | | | |
| Line 3 | | | | |
| Line 2 | ▬▬ ▬▬ | X | → | ▬▬▬▬▬ |
| Line 1 | ▬▬▬▬▬ | | | |

Gather the three coins again, shake, and toss. Continuing the example, the second toss yields 3 tails. That will be a changing yin line marked with an X. A changing line means that whatever it was in the primary hexagram, yin or yang, change the line to its opposite in the transformed hexagram. In the example of line 2, since it was a changing yin line in the primary hexagram, it changes to a yang line in line 2 of the transformed hexagram.

Toss the three coins again and let's say the result was 2 tails 1 head, and the fourth toss yielded 3 heads. Line 3 will thus be a fixed yin line, and line 4 will be a changing yang line.

|  | PRIMARY HEXAGRAM |  |  | TRANSFORMED HEXAGRAM |
|---|---|---|---|---|
| Line 6 |  |  |  |  |
| Line 5 |  |  |  |  |
| Line 4 | ▬▬▬ | X | → | ▬ ▬ |
| Line 3 | ▬ ▬ |  |  |  |
| Line 2 | ▬ ▬ | X | → | ▬▬▬ |
| Line 1 | ▬▬▬ |  |  |  |

When you have tossed the three coins together a total of six times, you'll have constructed the six lines of the hexagram.

|  | PRIMARY HEXAGRAM |  |  | TRANSFORMED HEXAGRAM |
|---|---|---|---|---|
| Line 6 | ▬ ▬ |  |  | ▬ ▬ |
| Line 5 | ▬▬▬ |  |  | ▬▬▬ |
| Line 4 | ▬▬▬ | X | → | ▬ ▬ |
| Line 3 | ▬ ▬ |  |  | ▬ ▬ |
| Line 2 | ▬ ▬ | X | → | ▬▬▬ |
| Line 1 | ▬▬▬ |  |  | ▬▬▬ |

For the transformed hexagram, move all fixed lines from the primary hexagram over unchanged. They remain *fixed*. Meanwhile, all changing lines marked by the X (i.e., either 3 heads or 3 tails) will change to the line's opposite—yin broken lines in the primary hexagram become yang solid lines in the transformed hexagram, and yang solid lines become yin broken lines.

You now have the defined scope and field you'll be reading from:

- The Oracle message for the primary hexagram
- The changed lines of the primary hexagram (e.g., lines 2 and 4)
- *Optional:* The text for any or all of the six lines of the primary hexagram
- The Oracle message for the transformed hexagram
- The changed lines of the transformed hexagram

How you navigate within the defined scope or field is at the diviner's discretion and is part of the art form. In the specific context of the question asked, it's up to you to decide which sections of this field you'll focus on. What the Oracle has presented to you is an organized case file on the matter you've asked about. Which sections you want to highlight, which sections feel like secondary, supporting insight, what feels immutable, and what is just conditional and still within your control to change, is a matter of subjective—and creative—interpretation. This is where you actively exercise critical reasoning, induction, and deduction.

|  | **PRIMARY HEXAGRAM** |  |  | **TRANSFORMED HEXAGRAM** |
|---|---|---|---|---|
| Line 6 | ▬▬ ▬▬ |  |  | ▬▬ ▬▬ |
| Line 5 | ▬▬▬▬▬ |  |  | ▬▬▬▬▬ |
| Line 4 | ▬▬▬▬▬ | X | → | ▬▬ ▬▬ |
| Line 3 | ▬▬ ▬▬ |  |  | ▬▬ ▬▬ |
| Line 2 | ▬▬ ▬▬ | X | → | ▬▬▬▬▬ |
| Line 1 | ▬▬▬▬▬ |  |  | ▬▬▬▬▬ |
|  | Lake over Thunder |  |  | Water over Lake |
|  | **17 Suí**<br>Inspiring Followers |  |  | **60 Jié**<br>Boundaries |

My personal go-to approach is to interpret the cast field as follows:

1. The Oracle message from the primary hexagram is a summary of the situation. This is also the thesis, a bit like the abstract of a written article.
2. The changing lines from the primary hexagram give practical advice or are forecasts based on current variables in play.

3. The transformed hexagram reads like an if-then statement. It's revealing to me what *could* happen if I do not heed the advice of the Oracle. That advice will have been contained within the primary hexagram.

4. The changing lines in the transformed hexagram give the parting words—some final thoughts on the situation at hand.

If there were no changing lines during the casting of the primary hexagram, meaning none of your coin tosses yielded three tails or three heads, then you have a locked hexagram.

|  | COIN TOSS RESULTS | LOCKED HEXAGRAM |
|---|---|---|
| Line 6 | 2 heads 1 tails | ▬▬▬▬▬ |
| Line 5 | 2 heads 1 tails | ▬▬▬▬▬ |
| Line 4 | 2 heads 1 tails | ▬▬▬▬▬ |
| Line 3 | 1 head 2 tails | ▬▬  ▬▬ |
| Line 2 | 2 heads 1 tails | ▬▬▬▬▬ |
| Line 1 | 2 heads 1 tails | ▬▬▬▬▬ |
|  |  | Heaven over Lake |
|  |  | **10 Lu** Treading |

I interpret a locked hexagram as indicating that all possible variables that would have been factored into determining the outcome of the situation have already revealed themselves, and so, in a certain sense, the outcome is immutable. It's the expression of an algebra problem where every $x$ in the equation is already known now, so there are no if-then statements to follow. That's why the result is a locked hexagram with no changing lines.

Another way to read the locked hexagram is as internal energies in flux, causing stasis. This is an internalized stalemate. Something within must be unblocked first. Due to that inner blockage, no actions are being taken to move the situation along.

Recall from chapter 4 the various historical approaches to interpreting the innate meaning or position assignments of each line. Those can be applied here as well, regardless of whether there are changing lines or your result is a locked hexagram. Even with a locked hexagram, you can navigate between the segments of text for each line.

# PRACTICUM 7.3:
## An I Ching Reading by the Coin Toss Method

Light incense and sit comfortably in stillness for a moment. Take a few slow, deep breaths, and hold a copy of the Book of Changes in your hands. Close your eyes and bow your head slightly. In whatever way you visualize Deity—be that as a particular image, by particular cultural or pantheon specific iconography, or as pure luminescence—see Deity in your mind's eye and continue to feel calm and in the moment. If you are not invoking a specific Divinity by name and you prefer to keep this mental exercise secular, then make sure to strongly anchor yourself in positive, optimistic emotions that are warm, loving, and beneficent. Maintain a pastoral calm at all times throughout.

Present your question to the Oracle. As you formulate the inquiry, merge your thought of Deity (or light) with the thought of the Book in your hands. The Book will become the common language used for conversations between Deity and you.

Place the book down and set it aside. Pick up the three coins and proceed with the six tosses as this section has instructed. As you shake the coins in your hands, focus on the question presented. After each coin toss, note the results in the following format:

|        | PRIMARY HEXAGRAM | | TRANSFORMED HEXAGRAM |
|--------|------------------|---|----------------------|
| Line 6 |                  |   |                      |
| Line 5 |                  |   |                      |
| Line 4 |                  |   |                      |
| Line 3 |                  |   |                      |
| Line 2 |                  |   |                      |
| Line 1 |                  |   |                      |

Mark any changing lines with an (X) in that narrow column between the primary hexagram cells and the transformed hexagram cells. When complete, use the trigrams cross-reference table to determine the hexagram results.

**Read the Oracle message.** Begin by reading the Oracle message for your primary hexagram. After reading, set the Book down and reflect on your impressions of the message. Does it resonate? Did something not make sense? If you're still confused, read the Oracle again, this time more slowly, much more slowly than you would ordinarily read text. Deliberately slow down, and consider the symbolism, phrase by phrase.

Create a two-column table for yourself. In the left column, list any short phrasing from the Oracle that you immediately understood the meaning of, especially anything that jumps out at you and takes hold of your attention. For any phrases that continue to stump you, write them down in the right column under "I do not understand."

| I understand. | I do not understand. |
|---|---|
| 1. | 1. |
| 2. | 2. |
| 3. | 3. |

**Read the lines.** If you had no changing lines and you're working with a locked hexagram, skip this part. Otherwise, at this time, turn to the text corresponding with each changing line and read those sections. As you had done with the Oracle message, write down any phrasing that you immediately understand and resonate with in the left column, and any that are stumping you in the right column.

**Consider the Ba Gua trigram and Wu Xing correspondences.** Turn to the section in this book on correspondences to the Ba Gua eight trigrams and to the Wu Xing five changing phases. Skim through the tables and, without putting in too much deliberate thought, pluck out any keywords that leap out at you from those entries and jot them down in a form of mind map or brainstorm table in your notes.

The subsequent table shows an example of how I jotted down notes on the trigram and Wu Xing correspondences as I skimmed across the pages on Lake, Wind, Metal, and Wood. Once you've assembled enough keywords from the correspondence tables, scan the notes you took to see what leaps out at you. Think of these keywords as puzzle pieces that could fit into the Oracle and line messages, and help fill in any gaps of understanding from that right column under "I do not understand."

You can also cross-reference the correspondence tables with the passages from the Oracle that you weren't understanding. Perhaps keywords from the correspondence tables will trigger insight.

| | | PRIMARY HEXAGRAM | TRIGRAM COR-RESPONDENCES | WU XING CORRESPONDENCES | |
|---|---|---|---|---|---|
| Line 6 | ▬▬ ▬▬ | LAKE | Nourishing, sustaining force. Creating a servitor. Business success. Full moon. Energy exchange. | METAL | Metal weakens wood. Memory. Respiratory. Dry. Autumn. |
| Line 5 | ▬▬▬▬▬ | | | | |
| Line 4 | ▬▬▬▬▬ | | | | |
| Line 3 | ▬▬▬▬▬ | WIND | Gentle influence. Diffuse. To pass through. Waxing moon. Jupiter. | WOOD | Unyielding. Green. Purifying. Spiritual cultivation. East. |
| Line 2 | ▬▬▬▬▬ | | | | |
| Line 1 | ▬▬ ▬▬ | | | | |

Repeat the reasoning and reflection process for the transformed hexagram. If you had changing lines, repeat these steps for analysis of the transformed hexagram.

## PRACTICUM 7.4:
## Trying Aleister Crowley's Coin Toss Method

In his book *Liber 216,* Aleister Crowley gives his personal method of I Ching divination. He advises to obtain "6 Chinese coins," where five shall be of one type of metal and one of another. One approach here is to use five coins of one denomination and a sixth coin of a different value, and preferably one made of a different alloy; for example, five of a copper alloy and the sixth one of silver. Crowley recommends that the coins should be wrapped in black cloth when not in use and "no other should lay his hand upon them. For they swell with thine aura when used with sincerity and repetition."

If you cannot source six Chinese coins, he recommends using six flat stalks, one side painted with a solid line and one side painted with a broken line, with one of those six stalks marked in a special way. "Care for thine stalks as though they were coins." In lieu of stalks, I recommend using six round wooden pieces, about one inch in diameter, and painting the yin and yang lines on each side. Then mark one of the six round wooden pieces differently from the other five.

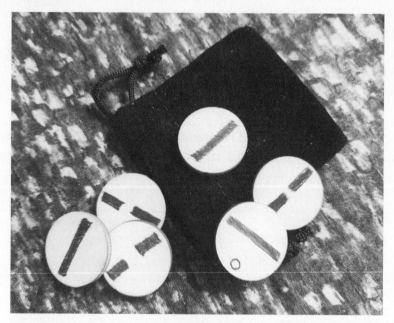

**FIGURE 7.7** Using round pieces of wood for coins

Face east, clear your mind, and "call upon what god ye will." Visualize yourself filling with pure light. Keep the coins in your black cloth bag. Extract them one by one for each toss. That way you are drawing the coins at random.

Toss the first closer to you to form the bottom line of the hexagram. Toss the second a little beyond the first so it forms the second line, and so on until the sixth and final toss is the farthest from you, forming the top line.

Where the different coin or stalk lands is going to designate the changing line. For example, if your third toss was with the randomly drawn different coin, then the changing line of your primary hexagram is line 3. The changing line will designate the direct answer to the situation, an answer from the Tao.

# PRACTICUM 7.5:
## A State of the Union Prophecy

Combine your strengthening divinatory prowess with the I Ching to prophesy what is to come in the next three years in the country where you reside or the country you call home. Divining on statecraft was one of the most oft-used purposes of the I Ching, right from its inception. Now it's your turn.

Derived from the Ranks of Nobility hierarchy that was covered in chapter 4, the six lines of the cast hexagram will be read as follows:

| Line 6 | Diplomatic and international affairs |
| --- | --- |
| Line 5 | Arts and culture |
| Line 4 | Education, family, personal rights |
| Line 3 | Law and policy, civil institutions |
| Line 2 | Public health and technology |
| Line 1 | Finance and economy |

Use three coins of the same denomination from the currency system used in the country you'll be divining on, minted within the last five years. Don't work with coins earlier than that. Keep the coins recent. And no need to consecrate or bless—use them as is. The coins will contain a rich deposit of the nation's current *qi*, which is what you and the Oracle will be picking up on during the divination.

Prepare the table you will be divining upon. Tidy it up, and burn three sticks of incense to their end so that the space is cleansed. Set out all of your tools, including this book. When the three sticks of incense have extinguished in their natural course, you may begin.

Dress wearing what you would typically wear to work for your particular occupation. Approach the table solemnly. Recite a simple invocation, once. You can call upon the names of your country's founders or work in the founding of the nation in a meaningful way. You can keep it entirely secular, albeit ceremonial.

Then state your inquiry as you shake the three coins in your hands: "Show me what's in store for [the country you're divining on] these next three years." Recite the inquiry once each time you toss the coins, for a total of six tosses as instructed in the preceding sections of this chapter.

|        | PRIMARY HEXAGRAM | TRANSFORMED HEXAGRAM |
|--------|------------------|----------------------|
| Line 6 |                  |                      |
| Line 5 |                  |                      |
| Line 4 |                  |                      |
| Line 3 |                  |                      |
| Line 2 |                  |                      |
| Line 1 |                  |                      |

Changing lines (where the result was three heads or three tails) mark the areas in national affairs that will incur the greatest shifts and flux.

|        | PRIMARY HEXAGRAM | | TRANSFORMED HEXAGRAM |
|--------|------------------|---|----------------------|
| Line 6 | ▬▬  ▬▬ |   | ▬▬  ▬▬ |
| Line 5 | ▬▬  ▬▬ |   | ▬▬  ▬▬ |
| Line 4 | ▬▬▬▬▬ | X | ▬▬  ▬▬ |
| Line 3 | ▬▬▬▬▬ | X | ▬▬  ▬▬ |
| Line 2 | ▬▬▬▬▬ |   | ▬▬▬▬▬ |
| Line 1 | ▬▬  ▬▬ | X | ▬▬▬▬▬ |
|        | Thunder over Wind | | Earth over Lake |
|        | Hexagram 32 | | Hexagram 19 |

In the example of Hexagram 32 changing into the transformed Hexagram 19, the economy (line 1), law and policy or civil institutions (line 3), and family or matters of personal rights (line 4) will be most volatile and incur the greatest changes.

The Oracle message for the primary hexagram would be the statecrafting advice on how the country should navigate the trajectory it's on. This is a general prediction of what's to come.

If your reading result was a locked hexagram, read all six lines of the single hexagram, and each line will forecast what's to come in the corresponding area of governance. So, for example, the fifth line of your locked hexagram would give a forecast on arts and culture, including pop culture; the sixth line would reveal matters of international affairs and how your country interacts with other nations; and so on.

If your result produces changing lines, read those changing lines. In the example given, the first changing line is line 1, which means in the coming three years, finance and economy will be volatile. Major law or policy changes that affect civil institutions in the country will be another volatile area in the next three years. I'd then read line 3 for Hexagram 32. Line 4, the final changing line in the example, forecasts that matters relating to education, family, and individual rights will also be disproportionately in flux.

In the case of a presidential or major election in the coming three years for which you're doing the forecast, look to the transformed hexagram to see whether the incumbent or a challenger will win, or how politics in general will play out. Interpret affairs relating to leadership in the transformed hexagram.

| 1 | 2 | 3 | 4 | 5 | 6 | 7 | 8 |
|---|---|---|---|---|---|---|---|
| ☰ | ☱ | ☲ | ☳ | ☴ | ☵ | ☶ | ☷ |
| Heaven | Lake | Fire | Thunder | Wind | Water | Mountain | Earth |

Compare the lower trigram of your primary hexagram to the upper trigram of your transformed hexagram. If you received a locked result, then simply compare the lower to the upper.

Locate the numerical value of the lower trigram of the primary. In the example, that would be Wind, number 5. Locate the numerical value of the upper trigram. In the example, that would be Earth from the transformed hexagram, number 8. Did the numerical value increase or decrease? If it went from 8 to 1, then the country is entering a new cycle, hence the return to 1. When the numbers increase, as it does in the example, going from 5 to 8, we interpret that as measurable improvement in the state of affairs. If the numbers decrease, then there may be some regression and a downturn when it comes to the state of affairs.

## Divination with Cowrie Shells

Since the Shang (1600–1046 BC) and through the Zhou (1046–256 BC), cowrie shells were a prized commodity, perhaps even an early form of currency.[8] While it's unclear whether cowries were used as currency during the Shang and Zhou, we are fairly certain they held religious meaning.[9]

Cowries migrated to the prehistoric mainland from the South China Sea and Indus Valley, and they were traded as prized commodities among the elites. The shells were placed in the mouths of the dead, similar to ritual jade, and symbolized power, prestige, and wealth.[10]

Oracle bone inscriptions made references to cowries, and the legendary Lady Fu Hao's tomb included over six thousand cowrie shells contained in bronze vessels. Cowrie pieces fashioned from bronze were popular during both the Shang and the Zhou.

In lieu of coins, cowrie shells can be used, applying the same method instructed in the previous section. The convex, rounded side of the cowrie corresponds with yang, or heads on a coin. The hollowed, concave side corresponds with yin, or tails. In chapter 9, we'll cover a divination method using cowries for contacting the spirits of your ancestors.

**FIGURE 7.8** Divination with cowrie shells

# PRACTICUM 7.6:
## An I Ching Reading by the Cowrie Shell Toss Method

Wash your hands and three cowrie shells. As you do so, envision a white light beaming down from above the crown of your head, creating a current that runs down your arms and out your hands to illuminate the shells and consecrate the waters that are cleansing them. Thoroughly dry your hands and the three shells.

Light incense and sit comfortably in stillness for a moment. Take a few slow, deep breaths, and set this book to the right side of your work space. Hold the three cowrie shells in your dominant hand, the hand you tend to rely on the most for the occupational work you do. If you are ambidextrous or the nature of your work calls for equal reliance on both hands, cup the cowrie shells with both.

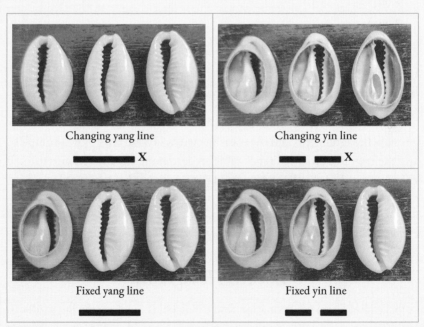

FIGURE 7.9 Reference for the cowrie shell toss method

Recite: "I call upon the Eternal Tao to open the door of Mysteries to me. Show me my path to greatest prosperity. I seek abundance so that neither I nor those who rely on me will ever be without. Reveal what it is I most need to know right now."

Exchange and pass the cowries back and forth from one hand to the next, and repeat the recitation two more times. You will now have recited the invocation prayer three times.

Toss the three cowries together as you would with the coins. I follow the Meaning and Principle tradition of heads and tails assignment.

Proceed with the six tosses. Between each toss, pass and exchange the cowries back and forth between your hands before tossing. Note the results in the following format:

|        | **PRIMARY HEXAGRAM** | **TRANSFORMED HEXAGRAM** |
|--------|----------------------|--------------------------|
| Line 6 |                      |                          |
| Line 5 |                      |                          |
| Line 4 |                      |                          |
| Line 3 |                      |                          |
| Line 2 |                      |                          |
| Line 1 |                      |                          |

Mark any changing lines with an (X) in that narrow column between the primary hexagram cells and the transformed hexagram cells. When complete, use the trigrams cross-reference table to determine the hexagram results. If there are no changing lines, then read the single cast hexagram as locked.

## Locked Hexagrams

A locked hexagram is a divination result that yields no changing lines. All cast lines are either elder yin or elder yang. How a locked hexagram is interpreted will vary, so really, the only way to understand the implications of one is to become an experienced I Ching practitioner and, through trial and error, figure out what works for you. Nevertheless, here are some of my thoughts.

Since a locked hexagram means all lines cast were matured elder states of yin and yang, I interpret it as confirming that all factors relevant to the matter at hand have long been in play and have matured. It's not so much that this is a point of no return; rather, it's just an indication that forces affecting the situation have been simmering for a very long time.

It thus implies that the matter may be a lot more complicated than you realize, involving more moving parts than you're aware of. You may *feel* like it's a point of no return only because the forces at play are so locked in that it would take an extraordinary feat of opposition and counteraction to unlock those influencing forces.

One way to optimize your reading of a locked hexagram is to navigate the six lines based on their inherent indications. In chapter 4, we covered the inherent values assigned to the six positions. For example, in table 4.3, Five Ranks of Nobility and Hexagram Rulers, take a closer look at line 4 of your locked hexagram if you had asked a love and romance question. If your question was health related, take a closer look at line 2 instead. For money matters, you would focus on line 1, though I would look to line 3 for career-related questions. If you had asked a very specific inquiry not covered by any of the listed categories, then go with an emphasis on line 5.

Table 4.4, Feudal Hierarchies of the Hexagram Lines, is inspired by the Confucian social order. Line 4 of a locked hexagram is more applicable to business questions or to those who would categorize themselves as part of the merchant class. If you consider yourself part of the artisan class or equivalent, then go with reading line 3.

A single hexagram is characterized as locked only if the divination method employed accounts for changing lines and transforming hexagrams. There are methods of divination where the entire purpose is to yield a single hexagram and then move within the six lines or choose which of the six lines to read. In those instances, a single hexagram would not be treated as being locked.

# Plum Blossom Methods

In chapter 4 we covered the Plum Blossom school of I Ching divination following the works of Shao Yong. This section will instruct on the more prevalent divination methods under the Plum Blossom school.

## Rice Grain Method

For this method, you will need about one cup of uncooked rice. Be sure to discard any broken grains. All grains you'll be using for divination should be whole and intact.

Find your center, exhale slowly, then take a deep breath, and as you do, concentrate intently on the inquiry at hand. While focused on your question, scoop out a small handful of rice grains. For reference, scoop up an amount of between one teaspoon and one tablespoon, though it doesn't need to be exact. Lean in to your intuition.

Per Shao Yong's eleventh-century mathematical universe philosophy, where all of the cosmos is a book of math that can be represented as a book of archetypes, which is the I Ching, numbers make up the fabric of our reality. If you can tap into a given moment, pierce beyond the matter we experience through our physical senses, and intuit the number associated with that moment, you can reveal that number's archetype through the I Ching and thus answer questions about that moment, allowing you to know things about that moment that you couldn't otherwise know.

The act of intentional concentration and the deliberate motion of scooping up that bit of rice grains is a physical mimicking of a much deeper unconscious process in your brain that is able to compute the numerology of that moment. The physical motions of scooping rice grains and counting are instructing your mind to replicate the equivalent process within, which then manifests itself

**FIGURE 7.10** Rice grain divination

physically as the exact number of rice grains counted. "The universe is in my hand," wrote Shao Yong. "The myriad things are in my body."[11]

Count the number of rice grains in that handful.

Next, divide the total number of rice grains you counted by 8.

You will get a quotient and a remainder.

The remainder will be a number less than 8. Note the trigram that corresponds with the numerical value of your remainder. This is provided in table 7.5.

**TABLE 7.5** Numerical Assignments for the Eight Trigrams

| 一 1 | 二 2 | 三 3 | 四 4 | 五 5 | 六 6 | 七 7 | 八 8 |
|---|---|---|---|---|---|---|---|
| ☰ | ☱ | ☲ | ☳ | ☴ | ☵ | ☶ | ☷ |
| 乾 Qián Heaven | 兌 Duì Lake | 離 Lí Fire | 震 Zhèn Thunder | 巽 Xùn Wind | 坎 Kǎn Water | 艮 Gěn Mountain | 坤 Kūn Earth |

If there is no remainder and the total number of rice grains divides evenly into 8, then the number assigned will be 8, or the trigram Earth.

The trigram result will be your lower trigram.

To illustrate the instructions with a hypothetical, assume a counted total of 224 grains of rice from that first handful. Divide the total number of grains by 8.

224 ÷ 8 = 28. There is no remainder.

Thus, the number assigned is 8.

The number 8 corresponds with the trigram Earth.

If there is a remainder from the division, then the remainder is the assigned number. For example, let's say there were 225 grains of rice counted.

225 ÷ 8 = 28.125

To determine the exact number of rice grains in the remainder, multiply the whole number result (e.g., 28 from 28.125) by 8:

8 × 28 = 224

Next, subtract that value (e.g., 224) from the total number of rice grains (e.g., 225):

225 − 224 = 1

If there had been 225 rice grains in the first handful of rice, the remainder would be 1, and thus the result would be the Heaven trigram.

After the first count of rice grains, we've produced the lower trigram.

|        | PRIMARY HEXAGRAM |   |
| ------ | ---------------- | - |
| Line 6 |                  |   |
| Line 5 |                  |   |
| Line 4 |                  |   |
| Line 3 | ▬▬  ▬▬<br>▬▬▬▬▬▬<br>▬▬  ▬▬ |   |
| Line 2 |                  |   |
| Line 1 |                  |   |

Set aside the first pile of counted rice grains and scoop up a second pile of rice grains. Aim for more than one teaspoon but a bit under one tablespoon.

Count the number of rice grains in the second handful. Your heart-mind should be singularly focused on the task and inquiry at hand.

Keep your heart open, your mind calm, and count in a patient, meditative state. Shao Yong emphasizes that in order to achieve the highest kind of accuracy in predictive I Ching, the diviner's heart-mind must be tranquil and still. One reason for the rice grains counting approach to divination is to put that tranquility and stillness to the test, to ensure that you are fully emptying the mind and undertaking the ritual with the utmost patience.

Divination Methods 317

After you've counted the total number of rice grains in the second pile, divide that total by 8. Repeat the same calculation method you used with the first pile.

To illustrate, let's say for my second pile of rice, I count 189 grains. Divide that total by 8. The calculation will go as follows:

189 ÷ 8 = 23.625

Again, take the whole number 23 from 23.625 and multiply by 8:

23 × 8 = 184

Then subtract that number, 184, from the total number of rice grains, 189:

189 − 184 = 5

The remainder is 5. Thus, the assigned number for the second pile is 5. Note the trigram correspondence for the number 5.

This will reveal your upper trigram.

| 一 | 1 | 二 | 2 | 三 | 3 | 四 | 4 | 五 | 5 | 六 | 6 | 七 | 7 | 八 | 8 |
|---|---|---|---|---|---|---|---|---|---|---|---|---|---|---|---|
| ☰ | | ☱ | | ☲ | | ☳ | | ☴ | | ☵ | | ☶ | | ☷ | |
| 乾 Qián Heaven | | 兌 Duì Lake | | 離 Lí Fire | | 震 Zhèn Thunder | | 巽 Xùn Wind | | 坎 Kǎn Water | | 艮 Gěn Mountain | | 坤 Kūn Earth | |

In the case of the number 5, my upper trigram is Wind.

| | | PRIMARY HEXAGRAM |
|---|---|---|
| **SECOND** pile of rice grains: Total counted ÷ **8**. Remainder corresponds with the *upper* trigram. | Line 6 | ▬▬▬▬▬ |
| | Line 5 | ▬▬▬▬▬ |
| | Line 4 | ▬▬  ▬▬ |
| **FIRST** pile of rice grains: Total counted ÷ **8**. Remainder corresponds with the *lower* trigram. | Line 3 | ▬▬  ▬▬ |
| | Line 2 | ▬▬  ▬▬ |
| | Line 1 | ▬▬  ▬▬ |

Scoop up a third small handful of rice grains. Repeat the same process and count the total number of rice grains in the third pile.

However, this time, instead of dividing by 8, you will divide by 6 to calculate the changing line.

The resulting remainder will be a value under 5. If your total count divides evenly into 6 with no remainders, then your assigned value is 6.

That number corresponds with the line number of the hexagram. That line number is your changing line.

Let's say that the third pile yields a count of 123 grains.

123 ÷ 6 = 20.5

To determine the remainder, the whole number 20 from 20.5 is multiplied by 6:

20 × 6 = 120

That value 120 is subtracted from the total number of rice grains, 123:

123 − 120 = 3

The remainder is 3.

3 is the assigned number for the third pile.

The assigned number for the third pile corresponds with the line number in the hexagram.

|  | PRIMARY HEXAGRAM | | |
|---|---|---|---|
| **SECOND** pile of rice grains: Total counted ÷ **8**. Remainder corresponds with the *upper* trigram. | Line 6 | ▬▬▬▬▬ | **THIRD** pile of rice grains: Total counted ÷ 6. Remainder denotes the changing line. |
| | Line 5 | ▬▬▬▬▬ | |
| | Line 4 | ▬▬ ▬▬ | |
| **FIRST** pile of rice grains: Total counted ÷ **8**. Remainder corresponds with the *lower* trigram. | Line 3 | ▬▬ ▬▬  X | |
| | Line 2 | ▬▬ ▬▬ | |
| | Line 1 | ▬▬ ▬▬ | |

**Oracle message from the primary hexagram.** The Oracle (or Judgment) for your primary hexagram will read like a general summary and overall forecast in answer to your inquiry.

**Line message for the changing line.** The changing line of your primary hexagram is the Oracle's advice to you on how to proceed and what's coming up next.

**Wu Xing correspondences.** In the Plum Blossom methods of hexagram interpretation, greater importance is placed on the Wu Xing correspondences. Note the Wu Xing correspondence for the lower trigram, and then for the upper trigram. Note the alchemical reaction between those two changing phases when they interact with one another. Which is dominant and which is subservient in the interaction?

Turn to the correspondence tables for the Five Phases of Change and extract the correspondences that are relevant to the subject matter of your inquiry. You may need to take notes and create a mind map to fit the correspondences together like pieces of a puzzle. That's how you'll come to see the bigger picture and the divinatory answer to your question.

In the example we've been using so far, the resulting primary hexagram is Wind over Earth, or Hexagram 20. The Oracle section for Hexagram 20 gives insight into the matter inquired about. The changing line is line 3. Thus, turn to the text under the third line for Hexagram 20. This is the Oracle's direct advice to you.

Next, note the Wu Xing correspondences for the two trigrams. Here, it's Wood for the upper trigram Wind, and Earth for the lower trigram Earth. I like to write down notes and keywords for each of the trigrams, based on the

Wu Xing correspondences, to help facilitate insight. Write down anything and everything that you intuit might be relevant.

| | HEXAGRAM 20 | | | Wu Xing |
|---|---|---|---|---|
| Line 6 | ▬▬▬▬▬ | | | **Wind.** *Wood.* Sprouting. The dominant *qi*. A wind is blowing through that will clear the road. Spring. East. |
| Line 5 | ▬▬▬▬▬ | | | |
| Line 4 | ▬▬ ▬▬ | | | |
| Line 3 | ▬▬ ▬▬ | X | | **Earth.** *Earth.* Ripening. Overpowered by Wood. *Qilin.* Rebirth or cycle to restart. Love and marriage. |
| Line 2 | ▬▬ ▬▬ | | | |
| Line 1 | ▬▬ ▬▬ | | | |

Then you can begin crossing out what you realize is irrelevant or extraneous, and proceed with connecting the pieces to form a cohesive picture in answer to your inquiry.

In our hypothetical, a young woman asked about romantic prospects for the coming year. Wood subdues and weakens Earth. Earth has to yield to Wood. Thus, the dominant trigram here is Wind, which corresponds with Wood.

Earth, which relates to the subject matter of love and marriage, indicates that romantic prospects are strong this coming year. Since Wind (via Wood) dominates, we will place greater emphasis on the correspondences for Wood. The spring time is when the young woman will encounter strong romantic prospects, and likely someone coming from the east direction toward her. Prospects in general look good, as the *qi* of Wind will blow a clear path for her.

However, considering its alchemical reaction with Earth, there may be a romantic prospect coming in the spring; the likelihood of it being long-lasting toward marriage or long-term commitment remains to be determined.

Consider the Oracle message for Hexagram 20, Guan, meaning "reassessment; critique": "There is need for contemplation. Reevaluate your motivations." The Oracle is telling the young woman that she might not be entering into relationships for the right reasons. It's better to utilize the coming year to audit herself, to self-reflect and introspect. The Oracle even goes so far as to advise her to take some time to think over her motivations, and then when she has had some time to clear her mind, she may return for a follow-up divination.

Returning to the woman's question about romantic prospects for the coming year, the changing line marked by the X, based on the count of rice grains for the third pile divided by 6, will answer the question directly.

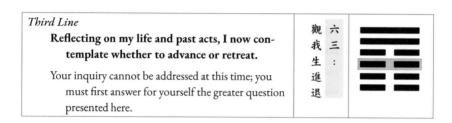

| *Third Line* | |
|---|---|
| **Reflecting on my life and past acts, I now contemplate whether to advance or retreat.** | |
| Your inquiry cannot be addressed at this time; you must first answer for yourself the greater question presented here. | |

The third line seems to repeat what has already been said, and the Oracle refuses to answer the young woman's question. The implication here is that she is asking the wrong question. Rather than asking about romantic prospects for the coming year (which the Oracle nevertheless reluctantly answers by saying there are prospects in the spring, coming from the east), she needs to focus on much deeper, probing questions relating to herself.

## Optional Additional Steps for a Follow-Up Question

Under the rice grains divination method, follow-up inquiries may be asked. However, do not repeat the same inquiry just because you didn't like or were confused by the initial answer. Instead, given what has been divined, you may ask follow-up inquiries for clarification or supplementary insight on the matter at hand.

To do so, first reflect on the divinatory response from the Book up to this point. Then formulate your follow-up question. You cannot repeat your question. It needs to be a bona fide *follow-up* that is distinct from the original question but still related to the subject matter of the original question.

Focusing on your inquiry, scoop up a fourth small handful of rice grains. Count the number of rice grains in that handful.

Divide the total by 6.

If the remainder of the division calculation for the fourth pile count is the same as the third pile result, meaning it designates the same changing line already marked, then the Oracle is insisting that all needed information has been given already, and no more follow-up inquiries may be asked. The Oracle is refusing to answer your follow-up question and is staying silent.

If, however, the remainder is different from the remainder yielded in the third pile count, then you may proceed to receive clarification from the Oracle.

|  | PRIMARY HEXAGRAM |  | TRANSFORMED HEXAGRAM |
|---|---|---|---|
| Line 6 | ▬▬▬▬▬ |  | ▬▬▬▬▬ |
| Line 5 | ▬▬▬▬▬ |  | ▬▬▬▬▬ |
| Line 4 | ▬▬  ▬▬ |  | ▬▬  ▬▬ |
| Line 3 | ▬▬  ▬▬ | X | ▬▬▬▬▬ |
| Line 2 | ▬▬  ▬▬ |  | ▬▬  ▬▬ |
| Line 1 | ▬▬  ▬▬ |  | ▬▬  ▬▬ |

To proceed, cast the transformed hexagram through the changing line. If the changing line in the primary hexagram was yin, it transforms into a yang line; if it was yang, it transforms into a yin line. The rest of the lines remain the same. Look up which hexagram this transformed hexagram is.

If the fourth pile of rice grains count yielded a different remainder from the third pile count, read both the Oracle message for the transformed hexagram and the line text designated by the fourth pile remainder.

Continuing with the hypothetical, that young woman was not satisfied with the answer. She wanted to proceed with a follow-up question and additional fourth count. She asks, "When will I get married?"

But the Book had other ideas.

The fourth pile of rice grains yielded a total of 201 grains.

$201 \div 6 = 33.5$

To determine the remainder, multiply the whole number 33 (from the result 33.5) by 6.

$33 \times 6 = 198$

Subtract 198 from the total number of rice grains, 201.

$201 - 198 = 3$

The result yields line 3, but the changing line from the third pile count was already 3, so it's a repeat. That means the Oracle is refusing to answer.

The Oracle isn't heartless, however. Note the Oracle message for the transformed hexagram, Hexagram 53: "Slow and steady to the summit."

If you read the Oracle for that hexagram, the tone has softened and is gently urging the young woman to heed the advice being given: "A tree grows at the peak of a mountain, slowly, in accordance with the natural course of growth. That is how the tree can establish firm roots deep into the soil of the mountain. Grow slow and deep . . . not fast and upward."

The closing remarks of the Oracle to the young woman: "It is an auspicious time for the maiden to marry. However, you must let the union develop in its own time. Do not rush any engagements. Take small and honorable steps."

# PRACTICUM 7.7:
# An I Ching Reading by the Rice Grains Method

Gather about one cup of uncooked rice grains from your pantry. If you don't have rice at home, beans will suffice (though if the beans are significantly larger than the size of rice grains, you may need more than one cup of the beans). Red adzuki beans are a great option in lieu of rice.

Anointing your rice or beans with a scented oil is unorthodox, but I find that it elevates my divinatory readings in such a way that I now swear by it. I craft my own anointing oil from a blend of five oils to represent the

**FIGURE 7.11** Anointing your rice grains

Wu Xing: equal parts of lemongrass, cinnamon, cedar wood, angelica seed, and myrrh, in a neutral carrier oil.

Begin by formulating a question. When you're ready, pick up a small clump of the rice grains with your fingertips, place them into a shallow dish, and count the grains. I recommend using a repurposed tool to separate the grains as you count. This is also unorthodox, but a new, unused wooden ear picker that you consecrate and repurpose as a sacred tool works really well here.

Follow the instructions for the rice grains method of divination preceding this practicum. Though tedious, the method itself is simple: the first tally of rice grains divided by 8, and the remainder yields the lower trigram. The second tally divided by 8 yields the upper trigram. A third tally divided by 6 yields the changing line. Optional: ask a follow-up clarifying question, and a fourth tally divided by 6 answers the follow-up, unless the same changing line is produced, in which case the Oracle refers you back to its initial response.

## *Horary Astrology and I Ching*

The sixty-four hexagrams follow a revealed order, which is then numbered 1 through 64, e.g., a hexagram formed from six yang lines is assigned Hexagram 1, a hexagram formed from six yin lines is assigned Hexagram 2, and so on. The synchronicity of a particular hexagram being assigned a particular number, such as the six yang lines to 1 or the six yin lines to 2, is mystically significant, or so says a key principle in the Image and Number tradition.

Likewise, the months, days, hours, and years as tracked by the movements of the sun and moon reveal a cyclical order, which is then numbered. These numbers bear significance just as the hexagram numbers do. Shao Yong emphasizes these principles in his commentaries on the I Ching. Through numbers and certain archetypes that cycle and recycle in predictable patterns, the passage of time is linked to the hexagrams.

Horary astrology is a system of divination using astrology where a querent—the person presenting a question for divination—asks a question, and an astrologer casts a chart for the precise date, time, and location when the question was presented. Certain patterns in the cast astrological chart, evaluated relative to natal astrological metrics of the querent, are believed to reveal the answer to the querent's inquiry.

In the Plum Blossom school, a form of horary astrology using the lunisolar calendar is combined with an I Ching reading. A lunisolar calendar is a calendar system that accounts for both moon phases and the degree positions of the sun. Months are based on the moon phases, and then those months are organized into seasonal terms based on the solar longitude. The seasonal terms, called solar terms, are based on agricultural cycles. From Babylonia to the east across the entirety of the continent, the calendar system used is lunisolar.

For example, table 7.8 shows the six solar terms that correspond with the first three lunar months that make up the season spring. Solar terms are subdivided based on the solar longitude degree. There are two solar terms for every lunar month. The lunar months begin on a new moon, and on about the fifteenth day of the month is the full moon, with the next month beginning on the next new moon.

Each period in the calendar cycle is numbered, and according to Shao Yong, these numbers reveal time's connection to the I Ching hexagrams.

**TABLE 7.6** Solar Terms and Lunar Months of Spring

| SOLAR TERM | SEASONAL TERM | SOLAR LONGITUDE | LUNAR MONTH |
|---|---|---|---|
| 立春 Start of spring | Early spring 寅 | 314° | Month 1 寅 Tiger |
| 雨 Spring showers | | 329° | |
| 啓蟄 Insects awaken | Mid-spring 卯 | 344° | Month 2 卯 Rabbit |
| 春分 Vernal equinox | | 0° | |
| 清明 Bright and clear | Late spring 辰 | 14° | Month 3 辰 Dragon |
| 穀雨 Gathering rain | | 29° | |

A long-division process similar to the one used for the rice grains method is used here as well. Instead of a sum total based on counted rice grains, here the sum total is based on the numerology of calendar dates under the lunisolar system.

**TABLE 7.7** Plum Blossom Calendar Numerology Formulas

| HEXAGRAM CONSTRUCTION | METHODOLOGY |
|---|---|
| Upper trigram | $\dfrac{(\text{Month} + \text{Day} + \text{Year})}{8}$ |
| Lower trigram | $\dfrac{(\text{Month} + \text{Day} + \text{Year} + \text{Hour})}{8}$ |
| Changing line | $\dfrac{(\text{Month} + \text{Day} + \text{Year} + \text{Hour})}{6}$ |

In horary astrology, the horoscopic chart cast for the month, day, year, and hour when the question is being asked is interpreted. Here, a hexagram is cast for the month, day, year, and hour for the question. The upper trigram is based on a date that the querent selects—one that is somehow significant to the matter at hand. Often the day of the divination is used. Thus, the upper trigram is simply the month, day, and year for the day when divination occurs, and the lower trigram includes the hour in the sum.

Other times, the upper trigram is the sum of two dates, especially in love and romance readings. The birthday of one lover and the birthday of the other are added together. The total sum is then divided by 8 for the upper trigram.

To ask the I Ching whether a student has passed her final exam, the upper trigram would be the date when the exam was taken, and the lower trigram would be the month, day, year, and hour of the moment when the I Ching divination commenced.

For a divination to forecast the outcome of a sustained injury, the upper trigram would be the date of injury; if for an illness, then the date when the illness was diagnosed or discovered. For general health questions—or, for that matter, any general inquiry for which you are not able to pinpoint a date—simply use the present date for the upper trigram calculation. Thus, upper and lower trigram dates would be effectively the same, but with the added difference of the hour.

If you are transitioning between careers, you might use the last date of your previous employment for the upper trigram, or if it's a more philosophical question about which direction to take from here, the date of graduation from your highest degree. If your intuition tells you that the date of graduation isn't particularly relevant to your inquiry, the go-to dates that most use are the same day for the upper and lower trigram calculations, with the addition of the hour to the sum in the lower trigram.

The rationale for using the same day, with the lower trigram accounting for the hour of the moment of divination, is that the two numbers tap in to different *qi*. The upper trigram of just month, day, and year taps in to the karma that led you to present the question for divination at that exact moment. Decisively approaching the I Ching that day is the significant event, and the *qi* of that has an impact on the outcome of the event. Whereas the lower trigram with the same month, day, and year, now adding the hour when the divination is taking place, would be the horary aspect of the procedure.

However, contemporary Plum Blossom practitioners emphasize the imperative that calendar dates must be converted to the lunisolar (農曆, *nónglì*) calendar. Thus, the number used for the month is not the Gregorian calendar month, a solar calendar that follows the mean tropical year.[12] It's going to be the lunar month. Likewise, you won't be working with the numerology for the current calendar year as you know it, but with the corresponding order number of the year per the lunisolar calendar (often referred to as "lunar calendar" for short).

Fortunately, automatic conversion calculators between Gregorian calendar dates and the lunar calendar are freely accessible.[13]

## Calculating the Lunar Month

The month number you will be using is the lunar month, not the Gregorian solar month. You'll need a calendar conversion calculator or table.

To demonstrate, I'm going to present to the Oracle this question: "What is the added advantage of integrating horary astrology under the Plum Blossom method as compared to simply asking the question by the traditional casting methods?"

My question is rather general and not date specific, so the upper trigram will be today's date, the date when the question is formulated, and the lower trigram will be the same date plus the exact hour when the divination is taking place.

The Gregorian calendar date is June 3, 2022. I used an automatic converter to convert the Gregorian calendar date to the Chinese lunar date, which is the fifth month 5, 2022 (壬寅, *ren-yin*) year of the Tiger. The lunar month number is 5, for the fifth month.

| Upper trigram: A calendar date relevant to the subject matter of the inquiry. Alternatively, use the month, day, and year of the day when the divination is taking place. | | | Month |
|---|---|---|---|
| Day | Year | 5 | |
|  |  |  | |

## Calculating the Lunar Day

The conversion calculator or table will provide the lunisolar calendar day equivalent. In the example of fifth month 5, 2022 (壬寅, *ren-yin*) year of the Tiger, the day is also 5. For another example, if the Gregorian calendar date is September 24, 1981, then per a conversion table, the lunisolar (農曆, *nónglì*) date is the eighth month 27, 1981 (辛酉, *xin-you*), year of the Rooster. The number assigned to that date would be 27. The Gregorian calendar date of December 25, 1978, would be the eleventh month 26, 1978 (戊午, *wu-wu*), year of the Horse.

| Upper trigram: A calendar date relevant to the subject matter of the inquiry. Alternatively, use the month, day, and year of the day when the divination is taking place. | | | |
|---|---|---|---|
| Month | Day | Year | 5 |
| 5 |  |  | |

## Calculating the Lunar Year

The lunar year is trickier. You're going to need to reference table 7.8. The lunar year corresponds with a combination of a celestial stem and an earthly branch. That combination then corresponds with a number 1 through 60 from the sixty-year sexagenary calendar.

**TABLE 7.8** Numerology of the Year (Stems and Branches)

| 1 | | 2 | | 3 | | 4 | | 5 | | 6 | |
|---|---|---|---|---|---|---|---|---|---|---|---|
| 甲 | 子 | 乙 | 丑 | 丙 | 寅 | 丁 | 卯 | 戊 | 辰 | 己 | 巳 |
| Jia | Zi | Yi | Chou | Bing | Yin | Ding | Mao | Wu | Chen | Ji | Si |
| Rat | | Ox | | Tiger | | Rabbit | | Dragon | | Snake | |
| 7 | | 8 | | 9 | | 10 | | 11 | | 12 | |
| 庚 | 午 | 辛 | 未 | 壬 | 申 | 癸 | 酉 | 甲 | 戌 | 乙 | 亥 |
| Geng | Wu | Xin | Wei | Ren | Shen | Gui | You | Jia | Xu | Yi | Hai |
| Horse | | Goat | | Monkey | | Rooster | | Dog | | Boar | |
| 13 | | 14 | | 15 | | 16 | | 17 | | 18 | |
| 丙 | 子 | 丁 | 丑 | 戊 | 寅 | 己 | 卯 | 庚 | 辰 | 辛 | 巳 |
| Bing | Zi | Ding | Chou | Wu | Yin | Ji | Mao | Geng | Chen | Xin | Si |
| Rat | | Ox | | Tiger | | Rabbit | | Dragon | | Snake | |
| 19 | | 20 | | 21 | | 22 | | 23 | | 24 | |
| 壬 | 午 | 癸 | 未 | 甲 | 申 | 乙 | 酉 | 丙 | 戌 | 丁 | 亥 |
| Ren | Wu | Gui | Wei | Jia | Shen | Yi | You | Bing | Xu | Ding | Hai |
| Horse | | Goat | | Monkey | | Rooster | | Dog | | Boar | |
| 25 | | 26 | | 27 | | 28 | | 29 | | 30 | |
| 戊 | 子 | 己 | 丑 | 庚 | 寅 | 辛 | 卯 | 壬 | 辰 | 癸 | 巳 |
| Wu | Zi | Ji | Chou | Geng | Yin | Xin | Mao | Ren | Chen | Gui | Si |
| Rat | | Ox | | Tiger | | Rabbit | | Dragon | | Snake | |
| 31 | | 32 | | 33 | | 34 | | 35 | | 36 | |
| 甲 | 午 | 乙 | 未 | 丙 | 申 | 丁 | 酉 | 戊 | 戌 | 己 | 亥 |
| Jia | Wu | Yi | Wei | Bing | Shen | Ding | You | Wu | Xu | Ji | Hai |
| Horse | | Goat | | Monkey | | Rooster | | Dog | | Boar | |
| 37 | | 38 | | 39 | | 40 | | 41 | | 42 | |
| 庚 | 子 | 辛 | 丑 | 壬 | 寅 | 癸 | 卯 | 甲 | 辰 | 乙 | 巳 |
| Geng | Zi | Xin | Chou | Ren | Yin | Gui | Mao | Jia | Chen | Yi | Si |
| Rat | | Ox | | Tiger | | Rabbit | | Dragon | | Snake | |
| 43 | | 44 | | 45 | | 46 | | 47 | | 48 | |
| 丙 | 午 | 丁 | 未 | 戊 | 申 | 己 | 酉 | 庚 | 戌 | 辛 | 亥 |
| Bing | Wu | Ding | Wei | Wu | Shen | Ji | You | Geng | Xu | Xin | Hai |

**TABLE 7.8** Numerology of the Year (Stems and Branches) *(continued)*

| 1 | | 2 | | 3 | | 4 | | 5 | | 6 | |
|---|---|---|---|---|---|---|---|---|---|---|---|
| Horse | | Goat | | Monkey | | Rooster | | Dog | | Boar | |
| 49 | | 50 | | 51 | | 52 | | 53 | | 54 | |
| 壬 | 子 | 癸 | 丑 | 甲 | 寅 | 乙 | 卯 | 丙 | 辰 | 丁 | 巳 |
| *Ren* | *Zi* | *Gui* | *Chou* | *Jia* | *Yin* | *Yi* | *Mao* | *Bing* | *Chen* | *Ding* | *Si* |
| Rat | | Ox | | Tiger | | Rabbit | | Dragon | | Snake | |
| 55 | | 56 | | 57 | | 58 | | 59 | | 60 | |
| 戊 | 午 | 己 | 未 | 庚 | 申 | 辛 | 酉 | 壬 | 戌 | 癸 | 亥 |
| *Wu* | *Wu* | *Ji* | *Wei* | *Geng* | *Shen* | *Xin* | *You* | *Ren* | *Xu* | *Gui* | *Hai* |
| Horse | | Goat | | Monkey | | Rooster | | Dog | | Boar | |

In the example we've been following, the year is 2022 in both the Gregorian solar and the Asian lunisolar calendars. Note that the conversion calculator lets you know that the year is *ren-yin,* year of the Tiger. In table 7.8, look for the stem-branch combination of *ren* and *yin.* A secondary point of reference is also the zodiac animal, Tiger. *Ren-yin,* year of the Tiger, corresponds with 39, 壬 *ren* and 寅 *yin,* year of the Water Tiger.

| Upper trigram: A calendar date relevant to the subject matter of the inquiry. Alternatively, use the month, day, and year of the day when the divination is taking place. | | | |
|---|---|---|---|
| Month | Day | Year | 5 |
| 5 | 39 | | |

Thus, for our example of fifth month 5, 2022 *(ren-yin),* year of the Tiger, the year 2022 is assigned the *nónglì* number 39, because 2022 is the thirty-ninth year of the current sixty-year cycle.

## Calculating the Upper Trigram

Once you've converted the Gregorian solar calendar date to the lunisolar (or lunar) month, day, and year, you're ready to calculate the upper trigram. Add the numbers together. In the Plum Blossom numerology method, always add the whole number representing each element with the whole numbers representing every other element. Thus, for the year 39, you would *not* separate it out to add 3 + 9. Instead, you add "39 +" the other whole number representations of each component of the equation.

For our example, you would add 5 + 5 + 39. Do not separate out the 3 and the 9.

| **Upper trigram:** A calendar date relevant to the subject matter of the inquiry. Alternatively, use the month, day, and year of the day when the divination is taking place. |||||||
|---|---|---|---|---|---|---|
| Month | + | Day | + | Year | | 5 |
| | 5 | | 39 | | | |

To calculate the upper trigram of our example, 5 + 5 + 39 = 49.
Once you have the sum, divide that sum by 8:
49 ÷ 8 = 6.125
Take the whole number 6 from 6.125, and multiply it by 8:
6 × 8 = 48
Then subtract that number 48 from the sum total of the calendar date, which in this example is 49:
49 − 48 = 1
The remainder is 1. Thus, the assigned number for the date of June 3, 2022, is 1. Note the trigram correspondence for your resulting remainder number. This will reveal your upper trigram. As it was with the rice grains method, if your sum divides evenly into 8, then the default number assigned is 8, corresponding with the trigram Earth.

| 1 | 2 | 3 | 4 | 5 | 6 | 7 | 8 |
|---|---|---|---|---|---|---|---|
| ☰ | ☱ | ☲ | ☳ | ☴ | ☵ | ☶ | ☷ |
| 乾 | 兌 | 離 | 震 | 巽 | 坎 | 艮 | 坤 |
| Qián | Duì | Lí | Zhèn | Xùn | Kǎn | Gèn | Kūn |
| Heaven | Lake | Fire | Thunder | Wind | Water | Mountain | Earth |

For my reading, the remainder number 1 corresponds with Heaven.

|  | **PRIMARY HEXAGRAM** |  |
|---|---|---|
| Line 6 |  |  |
| Line 5 |  |  |
| Line 4 |  |  |
| Line 3 | ▬▬▬▬▬ |  |
| Line 2 | ▬▬▬▬▬ |  |
| Line 1 | ▬▬▬▬▬ |  |

## Calculating the Lower Trigram

The lower trigram will be based on the month, day, year, and hour when the divination is taking place. If the month, day, and year to be used for your lower trigram are different from those used for the upper trigram, then follow the process again for calculating month, day, and year to get the values. You may need to do another conversion from solar calendar to lunar calendar.

In my example—and this is frequently done among the Taiwanese practitioners I've observed—I use the same month, day, and year. The lower trigram differs from the upper trigram by the addition of the hour calculation.

The hour when my divination is taking place is 7:25 a.m. The time zone isn't factored in explicitly, because it has already been factored in implicitly. The numbers are relative to your geographical location. Using the local time implicitly anchors the horary astrological reading to your location.

As it was with the number assignment for the year, you will need to consult table 7.8. One day is observed from midnight to midnight, or more precisely as noted in the table, from 11:00 p.m. of the previous calendar date through the midnight hour, and the next day begins at 11:00 p.m.

## Calculating the Hour

For the hour, like with the lunar year, do not input the actual hour numbers. Instead, you will be using the number 1 through 12 *associated with* the given hour.

**TABLE 7.9** Numerology of the Hour (Earthly Branches)

| 1 子 Zi | 2 丑 Chou | 3 寅 Yin | 4 卯 Mao | 5 辰 Chen | 6 巳 Si |
|---|---|---|---|---|---|
| Rat | Ox | Tiger | Rabbit | Dragon | Snake |
| Water | Earth | Wood | Wood | Earth | Fire |
| 11:00 p.m.–12:59 a.m. | 1:00 a.m.–2:59 a.m. | 3:00 a.m.–4:59 a.m. | 5:00 a.m.–6:59 a.m. | 7:00 a.m.–8:59 a.m. | 9:00 a.m.–10:59 a.m. |
| 7 午 Wu | 8 未 Wei | 9 申 Shen | 10 酉 You | 11 戌 Xu | 12 亥 Hai |
| Horse | Sheep | Monkey | Rooster | Dog | Boar |
| Fire | Earth | Metal | Metal | Earth | Water |
| 11:00 a.m.–12:59 p.m. | 1:00 p.m.–2:59 p.m. | 3:00 p.m.–4:59 p.m. | 5:00 p.m.–6:59 p.m. | 7:00 p.m.–8:59 p.m. | 9:00 p.m.–10:59 p.m. |

In our example, the hour of divination is taking place at 7:25 a.m. That corresponds with the period of 7:00 a.m.–8:59 a.m., or the hour of the Dragon. The earthly branch correspondence is *chen*. The hour of the Dragon corresponds with the number 5. Thus, the number assigned to this hour for the purposes of calculating the lower trigram is 5.

| Lower trigram: Use the month, day, year, and hour when the divination is taking place. | | | |
|---|---|---|---|
| Month | Day | Year | Hour |
| 5 | 5 | 39 | 5 |

Repeat the same calculation method. Here, the first step is the addition:
5 + 5 + 39 + 5 = 54
Once you have the sum, divide it by 8:
54 ÷ 8 = 6.75
Take the whole number 6 from 6.75, and multiply it by 8:
6 × 8 = 48
Then subtract that number 48 from the sum total of the calendar date, which in this example is 54:
54 − 48 = 6

The remainder is 6. Thus, the assigned number for the lower trigram is 6, or Water. The hexagram cast is Water over Heaven. Funny enough, at the exact moment of this writing, and of the casting, it's raining.

| 1 | 2 | 3 | 4 | 5 | 6 | 7 | 8 |
|---|---|---|---|---|---|---|---|
| ☰ | ☱ | ☲ | ☳ | ☴ | ☵ | ☶ | ☷ |
| 乾 | 兑 | 離 | 震 | 巽 | 坎 | 艮 | 坤 |
| Qián | Duì | Lí | Zhèn | Xùn | Kǎn | Gěn | Kūn |
| Heaven | Lake | Fire | Thunder | Wind | Water | Mountain | Earth |

## Calculating the Changing Line

To determine the changing line, return to the lower trigram calculation, which is what anchors this casting as a horary chart reading. This time, instead of dividing the total sum by 8, you will divide by 6. The remainder will correspond to your line number of your changing line.

You'll recall that my lower trigram sum was 54. To calculate the changing line, I now divide that sum by 6:

$54 \div 6 = 9$

Here, 54 divides evenly into 6 with no remainder, yielding only the quotient of 9. Since it divides evenly, the default assigned number is 6. My changing line is line 6, which I mark with an X.

|        | **PRIMARY HEXAGRAM** |   |
|--------|----------------------|---|
| Line 6 | ▬▬ ▬▬ | X |
| Line 5 | ▬▬▬▬▬ |   |
| Line 4 | ▬▬ ▬▬ |   |
| Line 3 | ▬▬▬▬▬ |   |
| Line 2 | ▬▬▬▬▬ |   |
| Line 1 | ▬▬▬▬▬ |   |

## Interpreting the Results

Look up the resulting hexagram in the Book. The Oracle message is the Oracle's answer in response to your question. The changing line denotes the line number of that hexagram entry to read. This line message imparts the Oracle's words of advice to you on how to proceed from here.

The question I had asked was: "What is the added advantage of integrating horary astrology under the Plum Blossom method as compared to simply asking the question by the traditional casting methods?"

In my example of Water over Heaven, the resulting hexagram is Hexagram 5, Xu. This is the *qi* of patience. This is the emotion of waiting for the next event to happen. Also, when numbers repeat in an unusual way that catches your attention, the sentience of the Tao is speaking to you. The whole of the universe is in your mind, is knowable by your mind, per Shao Yong's philosophies. Since numbers are the language of the universe, in an instance like this one where the number 5 repeats (the month was 5, the day was 5, the hour was 5, and the resulting hexagram is 5), ask yourself what the repeating number means. Here, I simply interpret the synchronicity as an affirmative validation of karmic or fated harmony. Everything is as it is supposed to be.

The Oracle message for Hexagram 5 suggests that there are some questions that you cannot force an answer to and know instantaneously. It requires the slow and steady nourishment of experience and dedicated study. Sometimes we just have to wait for the natural flow of the Divine. In my reading, the fact that rain was pattering on my windowsill as I received the divination of Water over Heaven revealing the watery *qi* of Hexagram 5 was a sign to me to take the reading result seriously and to contemplate its message.

The changing line, which in this case is line 6, gives the final lines of advice. Each line in a hexagram, in progression, tells one chapter of the story, designates one aspect of the matter at hand. Recall from chapter 4 that line 6 is the line of Spirit (神). This is the denouement, the closing remarks. Line 6 reveals Heaven's Will as it pertains to the *qi* of that hexagram, and expresses divine sovereignty.

*Sixth Line*
    **Entering the cave. Three uninvited guests arrive. Receive them and honor them.**
    **In the end, there is good fortune.**

Compare the innate *qi* of line 6 in hexagram constructions with the sixth line of Hexagram 8. The innate *qi* is yin, and line 6 of Hexagram 8 is also yin, forming elder yin per the yin and yang affinities. In chapter 5 we learned that the driving phase of change for elder yin is Water.

|  | INNATE *QI* |  |  | PRIMARY HEXAGRAM |  |
|---|---|---|---|---|---|
| Line 6 | ▬▬ ▬▬ | ▬▬ ▬▬ | | | ▬▬ ▬▬ |
| Line 5 | ▬▬▬▬▬ | ▬▬▬▬▬ | | Innate *qi* of line 6 | + |
| Line 4 | ▬▬ ▬▬ | ▬▬ ▬▬ | X | + | |
| Line 3 | ▬▬▬▬▬ | ▬▬▬▬▬ | | line 6 of Hexagram 8 | ▬▬ ▬▬ |
| Line 2 | ▬▬ ▬▬ | ▬▬ ▬▬ | | = | = |
| Line 1 | ▬▬▬▬▬ | ▬▬▬▬▬ | | Elder yin | ▬▬ ▬▬ |

Recall also that Heaven (Metal) nourishes Water (Water). Thus, accounting for what is happening in the skies (horary astrology) is going to nourish and support how I interpret the Tao. The metaphor of "be like water" is often used to describe how to live in alignment with the Tao.

If you read predictively, as Shao Yong was known to have done, then a close reading of the Ba Gua and Wu Xing correspondences will reveal the specifics of a prediction. Water suggests personages from overseas and an international scope. A factor in the form of a triplicity will also come in to play, per that sixth-line message. My question was framed in the form of a pair—traditional methods of I Ching divination paired with horary astrology under Plum Blossom methods—but the Oracle's answer suggests the combination of three methods, accounting for and anticipating more than what I had asked.

## PRACTICUM 7.8:
## A General Forecast for Your Year to Come

For the upper trigram, input your month, day, and year of birth, converted to the lunisolar calendar. Follow the instructions from this section for the conversion.

| **Upper Trigram** | | |
|---|---|---|
| Month | Day | Year |
| | | |

Add the month, day, and year together for the sum. (Note: If the month is 11 and the day is 24, for example, add 11 + 24. Do *not* add 1 + 1 + 2 + 4. In Plum Blossom numerology, the entire number as a whole is treated as a relevant factor. 1 + 1 under this system is an entirely different variable from 11.)

Remember that the year is not per the Western solar calendar year. You'll need to reference table 7.8 and input the two-digit year value, 1 through 60.

Divide the sum by 8. Note the remainder.

For the lower trigram, we are going to do something a bit different. Instead of doing a traditional horary chart reading, this will be more akin to a solar return reading. Use your birth month and birth day again, but for the year, put in the current year that you are running a general forecast for.

By way of example, if the date of birth used was July 15, 1985, the year 1985 corresponds with *yi-chou* (乙丑), year of the Ox. That is year 2 in the sixty-year cycle. The year number to input for the upper trigram would have been 2.

For the lower trigram, input July 15 and the current year. If the forecast is being run for the year 2028, convert that to the lunisolar calendar, which would be *wu-shen* (戊申), year of the Monkey. That is year 45 of the sixty-year cycle. The year number to input for the lower trigram is 45. Note that you will need to do another conversion for the lower trigram birthday, because the day of the month will be different.

**TABLE 7.10** Numerology of Zodiac Signs (Ascendant Hour)

| 1 | 鼠 | 2 | 牛 | 3 | 虎 | 4 | 兔 | 5 | 龍 | 6 | 蛇 |
|---|---|---|---|---|---|---|---|---|---|---|---|
|   | Rat |   | Ox |   | Tiger |   | Rabbit |   | Dragon |   | Snake |
| 7 | 馬 | 8 | 羊 | 9 | 猴 | 10 | 雞 | 11 | 狗 | 12 | 豬 |
|   | Horse |   | Sheep |   | Monkey |   | Rooster |   | Dog |   | Boar |

For the lower trigram hour, enter the number 1 through 12 that corresponds with your zodiac sign per year of birth. (See table 7.10.) For one born on July 15, 1985, the zodiac sign would be the Ox, since 1985 was the year of the Ox. Note in table 7.10 that the Ox is number 2. Thus, for the hour in the lower trigram, the number to enter would be 2.

The theoretical principle of using your own zodiac sign number for the lower trigram hour is to connect you to the year you're forecasting for.

Specifically, you want to locate the *qi* number and archetype for the forecasted year as related to your zodiac sign; then the date of birth entered for the upper trigram further pinpoints the energies that will most impact your personal *qi*.

| LOWER TRIGRAM ||||
|---|---|---|---|
| Month | Day | Year | Hour |
|  |  |  |  |

Add the four numbers together to arrive at the sum. Divide the sum by 8. Note the remainder.

Cast the hexagram with the two trigram results.

Return to the sum for the lower trigram. Take that sum and now divide by 6. Note the remainder. That will be the changing line.

| Line 6 |  |  |
|---|---|---|
| Line 5 |  |  |
| Line 4 |  |  |
| Line 3 |  |  |
| Line 2 |  |  |
| Line 1 |  |  |

The Oracle message is a general forecast for the year you divined on. The line message will be key advice the Oracle is giving you for navigating that year.

---

Are you required to convert to the lunisolar calendar, or can the horary astrology method be applied to Gregorian calendar dates? Most texts on Plum Blossom methods written in traditional Chinese insist that dates must be converted to the lunisolar calendar system. However, that's one perspective. Alternatively, consider the theories and rationales for other perspectives.

If the archetypes of the I Ching and the mathematics of numbers are indeed universal, then in theory, shouldn't any calendar system at all work here? You should be able to apply these calculation methods to the addition and long division of any calendar dates. Using the calendar system of your culture and your practice further anchors the divination in the horary aspect, because it implicitly will account for geographic location, which is often considered a critical aspect of horary readings, because ascendant hours differ depending on location.

On the other hand, an argument could be made that the I Ching and the lunisolar calendar are mathematical systems keyed to one another, and as a mathematical function, the measurement or unit system of the Western solar calendar needs to be converted to some commensurate unit of measure with the I Ching before it can be cross-referenced with the I Ching. That commensurate unit of measure under this argument is the lunisolar calendar.

Assess for yourself which rationale and therefore which perspective makes more sense to you. Experiment with both—doing horary astrology and I Ching readings with the Gregorian calendar dates as is and then after the conversions. Which have you found works the best for you?

## *Numerological Principles and Casting Hexagrams*

That such a method of divination is established canon under the Plum Blossom methods further supports the argument that you should be able to use Gregorian calendar dates in the preceding horary astrology and I Ching divination methods.

A simple method of casting hexagrams using Shao Yong's numerological principles is to sit in stillness and meditate on a question you would like an answer to. Take your time, be patient, and while meditating, attune yourself to the environment around you. Use all of the senses at your disposal to experience the world, and push the distance at which you can intuit your surroundings. That is, visualize yourself seeing beyond what you can physically see to the horizon line; hear beyond what you can actually hear. Visualize the constellations as if they are within your line of sight.

When you feel strongly attuned to the world around you, and remaining focused on the question at hand, spontaneously think up two numbers, each number consisting of three digits. For example, you could imagine the number 482, or the number 961, or 107.

The first three-digit number that spontaneously sprang into your mind is the lower trigram.

The second three-digit number that spontaneously sprang into your mind is the upper trigram.

As with the previous Plum Blossom methods, divide the number by 8. The remainder corresponds with the trigram from the Fuxi Early Heaven Ba Gua numbering of the trigrams. If the three-digit number you came up with divides evenly into 8, then the number assignment is 8, or Earth.

Now calculate the sum of the two three-digit numbers, and divide that sum by 6. The remainder is the changing line. If the sum divides evenly into 6, then the changing line is line 6.

After reading the Oracle and line messages, look up the changing phase that governs the two trigrams and the alchemical reaction between the two trigrams. Between the two, which dominates, if any? Or do they work in harmony and supportively of one another?

Look up the Wu Xing and the Ba Gua trigram correspondences for the two trigrams, and assemble the correspondences like puzzle pieces that will form a cohesive predictive picture.

# PRACTICUM 7.9:
# Plum Blossom Numerology and I Ching

Set a timer for three minutes. Close your eyes and slow your breath, arriving at a state of calm, stillness, and tranquility. Focus on a question, and take the full three minutes to refine that question, turning it over in your mind and sensing the *qi* of that question through all of your physical senses, endeavoring to see the question, hear the sounds associated with it, taste the question, smell its scent, and meditate on it. Try not to focus on the time. Remain as patient and steady in state of mind as you can.

When the timer indicates that three minutes is up, open your eyes and immediately, without thought, write down one three-digit number.

After a slight pause, again as spontaneously as you can, write down a second three-digit number. Follow the three steps in the table below, from the bottom up.

| Step 3 | [C] | Sum of [A] + [B]<br>WRITE DOWN THE SUM: | Divide sum [C] by 6<br>WRITE DOWN THE REMAINDER: | Mark the remainder line number with X |  |
|---|---|---|---|---|---|
|  |  |  |  | ▼ DRAW THE TRIGRAMS ▼ |  |
| Step 2 | [B] | SECOND three-digit number: | Divide that number by 8<br>WRITE DOWN THE REMAINDER: |  | Line 6 |
|  |  |  |  |  | Line 5 |
|  |  |  |  |  | Line 4 |
| Step 1 | [A] | FIRST three-digit number: | Divide that number by 8<br>WRITE DOWN THE REMAINDER: |  | Line 3 |
|  |  |  |  |  | Line 2 |
|  |  |  |  |  | Line 1 |

## *Channeled Method of Casting Hexagrams*

Another Plum Blossom divinatory approach involves a form of channeling. You sit in stillness after meditation and prayer, light incense, and focus on the question at hand. Then enter a natural trancelike state to "channel" six lines of a hexagram, constructed from the bottom up. Feel as if the hexagram is being channeled from beyond, and you are the medium transcribing it.

While there are no rules against using ordinary pen and paper, grinding your own ink with an inkstone and using a traditional East Asian calligraphy brush might better facilitate that transition into an altered stated of consciousness. Switching up your habits when doing sacred work versus mundane work can help your mind shift into that necessary transcendent state.

You can get as elaborate and ritualistic as you'd like with this method. The following are just a few suggestions to help inspire your own crafting of a ritualistic practice.

- If you're opting for Asian calligraphy, then for the water, use only rainwater collected at the peak of a sacred mountain, from a sacred river, or from a waterfall.
- Water collected during thunder rites harvested for the purposes of thunder magic would be great here as well.
- Have all of your calligraphy instruments consecrated before use.
- Dedicate a calligraphy set to divination and mystical workings only, never to be used for mundane purposes.
- Devote more time to preparing the sacred space than you do on the actual divination itself.
- Write out your question on joss paper (traditional Asian incense paper used for burned offerings); then burn the joss paper before an altar or a shrine to a patron deity. Mix the ashes of the burned joss paper in with the calligraphy ink.
- Integrate electional astrology (choosing a date and time per astrological methods that will be optimal for such a divination).
- Precede the divination with the Guarding of the One meditation (守一冥想, Shǒu Yī míng xiǎng), discussed in a practicum from the previous chapter.
- The practicum at the conclusion of chapter 4 walks you through one variation of the Plum Blossom channeling method by invoking the Lady of the Nine Heavens.
- For a more hyperactive approach, apply the Ascent to Heaven spirit body journeying technique from chapter 5, with your pen and paper at the ready. When your spirit body has ascended and reached the celestial court, immediately put pen to paper and, as mindlessly as you can, draw the six lines of the hexagram, as if they are being channeled by a divine being you've encountered at the celestial court.

The most crucial step when applying the Plum Blossom channeling method is to render the hexagram lines in a manner that feels involuntary and while in an extraordinary state of consciousness. The patterns of mental functioning while you are channeling the lines of the hexagram need to be distinctly different from any of your ordinary, everyday patterns of mental functioning. Remember the key principle Shao Yong repeats: the heart-mind must be in stillness and tranquility for the most accurate and powerful divinations with the I Ching to happen.

## PRACTICUM 7.10: Channeling a Hexagram from the Lady of the Nine Heavens

Attuning to the Lady of the Nine Heavens in a divination ritual isn't so much religious as it is a metaphor. It's symbolic of unveiling that latent facet of yourself empowered by those attributes we admire in her. She represents the inner self that is highly attuned to the unseen forces around you, and therefore able to foresee what is to come because your mind is accounting for more factors and variables than the average person. You're activating your subconscious to pick up on all the cues in the environment that your conscious mind is overlooking.

**FIGURE 7.12** Seal of Jiǔ Tiān Xuán Nǚ with hexagrams, stems, and branches[14]

Cut a sturdy stock of paper down to about three inches by three inches (or alternatively, seven centimeters by seven centimeters). You'll be channeling and drawing the hexagram onto this paper. Place the sheet on a reproduction of the figure 7.12 seal. You can place your paper directly atop the page in this book, or you can make a copy of the seal on a separate sheet for use.[15] By channeling the hexagram directly over this seal, you're "tracing" and drawing from the inherent powers of the seal.

For resonance with the divine yin that Jiǔ Tiān Xuán Nǚ embodies, perform this channeled divination at a late hour well after sunset. There should be no visible sunlight in the skies. An optimal time is during a full moon. For this particular ritual, face west. Light some candles, and turn off all electricity in the room you'll be divining in. Work by candlelight. Burn your favorite and most fragrant incense to consecrate the space.

With your pen close by, recite the following invocation:

| | | |
|---|---|---|
| I invoke the Lady of Mystery. | 召请玄女 | Zhào qǐng Xuán Nǚ |
| Heaven meets Earth: I enter the Temple of Mystery. | 天地玄宗 | Tiān dì xuán zōng |
| I call upon the fountain and source of *qi*. | 萬氣本根 | Wàn qì běn gēn |
| To endow me with the higher knowledge Abhijñā. | 証吾神通 | Zhèng wú shén tōng |
| To know the past, the present, and the future. To know the minds of others, to sense all influences. | | |
| Envelop me with the Golden Light. | 體有金光 | Tǐ yǒu jīn guāng |
| From within I now emanate with the light of knowledge. | 身有光明 | Shēn yǒu guāng míng |
| Jı—jı—ru | 急急如 | Jí—jı—rù |
| [Knock the table three times.] | | |

Assuming Mandarin isn't your native tongue, I recommend reciting in both English and Chinese. The invocation is excerpted and compiled from the Mantra of the Golden Astral Light 金光神咒 (Jīn Guāng Shén Zhòu) in Jiǔ Tiān Xuán Nǚ's *Book for Purifying the Heart and Eradicating Evil* 九天玄女治心消孽真經. This mantra was part of the inner alchemical and cultivation practices of Cao Xinyi 曹信義 (1908–2002), a Qing dynasty Taoist master who also went by the name Zhen Yang Zi 震陽子.[16]

The phrase for invoke "召请" *(zhào qǐng)* is used in Buddhism and Taoism as an invocation call to gods, immortals, celestials, buddhas, or bodhisattvas. Lady of Mystery is an epithet for Jiǔ Tiān Xuán Nǚ. "Jí ji rú"[17] is an utterance of sounds that connect Heaven and Earth, opening the channels of communication between gods or spirits and humans. It essentially means, "Quickly and expediently, so may it be."

Knocking the table three times is emblematic of opening the gateway to the altered state of consciousness, so that a divine consciousness can now come through. After knocking, pick up your pen and begin channeling six lines, constructed from the bottom up, to produce a hexagram. Try to keep the process as automatic as you can, without inserting your conscious thoughts.

After the sixth line has been drawn upon the paper, you feel a weight exit your hand, indicating that the spirit presence is gone. In other words, the active state of consciousness has switched back to its ordinary state. Set your pen down, clasp your hands together reverently in gratitude, and give a slight nod of a bow to say your thanks. Snuff out the candles and restore your regular lights.

The summary judgment of the hexagram's Oracle reveals the main themes of what's going on in your life right now. This is a form of taking your spiritual or psychic temperature. Read through the Oracle message text and the text for the fifth line, and try to apply that to answering the question, "What is the Oracle telling me that I do not already know?" Repeat that question to yourself a few times, then proceed to read the text.

## *I Ching and the Tarot*

Whether to use the I Ching and tarot in combination, and whether the two can or should be reconciled, is a matter of contention. A more orthodox and culturally purist approach would find such an exercise to be abominable. And yet I find that nothing is more Taoist than syncretism and looking for unity where appearances show disparity.

The tarot, as it is generally defined, is a deck of seventy-eight playing cards subdivided into a twenty-two-card set called the Major Arcana, while the fifty-six-card set called the Minor Arcana is further subdivided into four suits comprising ten pip cards numbered in sequence from ace through ten, and four court cards. It was a popular game among the aristocracy during the Italian Renaissance and gained a resurgence of interest during an occult revival of esoteric orders and mystery traditions during the Victorian era. In a noble quest for some semblance of a universal theological truth, occultists endeavored to reconcile the tarot with esoteric traditions such as the Qabalah, Hermeticism, Renaissance magic, and Hellenistic astrology. As part of this effort, ceremonial magicians such as Eliphas Levi and Aleister Crowley turned to the I Ching.

Upon an initial attempt, the seventy-eight cards of the tarot and the sixty-four hexagrams of the I Ching seem incommensurable, meaning they do not appear to share any measure in common. How do you find the common connecting point between the two systems? One is based on the cosmological principle of four fixed elements and the other on five agents of change; one is ordered in sevens and the other in eights. Nevertheless, anyone with knowledge in both systems inevitably intuits that there have to be—and that, indeed, there are—connection points between the two.

In chapter 3 we covered Crowley's approach where he assigns trigrams to the sefirot on the Qabalistic Tree of Life, renames the trigrams, and then after renaming the trigrams to fit the four alchemical elements in the Western tradition (i.e., Thunder becomes Fire, Lake becomes Water, Wind becomes Air, and Earth becomes Mountain), combines the trigrams to produce hexagram assignments for the court cards and the sun decanates from the pips.

For example, the Knight of Wands—where Knight is from the Qabalistic world corresponding with Fire, and the suit of Wands is elementally Fire, thus Fire of Fire—corresponds with the trigrams Thunder over Thunder, producing the assignment to Hexagram 51. The Princess of Swords is Earth (Qabalistic world for Princess) of Air (element for Swords), and thus the trigrams are Mountain over Wind, producing the assignment to Hexagram 18. The result of this system is that only twenty-one of the sixty-four hexagrams are assigned to the tarot.

In the 1990s, tarot artist Hermann Haindl endeavored to assign hexagrams to the cards numbered 2 through 10 of the four Minor Arcana suits, for a total of thirty-six out of sixty-four hexagrams assigned to the tarot.[18] Haindl's approach undertook to connect the hexagrams to tarot cards by core meaning. For example, the Four of Wands in tarot generally indicates the completion of a great work and feeling a sense of fulfillment; thus, Haindl connects it to Hexagram 63, per

Wilhelm's title for the hexagram, "After Completion." Citing from Wilhelm's expository text: "The transition from confusion to order is completed, and everything is in its proper place even in particulars." The Eight of Cups, which suggests a departure from a previous destination and leaving something treasured behind, is assigned Hexagram 41, "Decrease," while the Nine of Cups, the proverbial wish card, is assigned Hexagram 42, "Increase."

While there may be other attempts to reconcile the I Ching and the tarot, Crowley's and Haindl's remain the most well known.

This section will set forth my approach to reconciling the I Ching and the tarot.

**TABLE 7.11** Tarot and Trigram Correspondences

| FIRE | THUNDER | WATER | WIND | HEAVEN | LAKE | EARTH | MOUNTAIN |
|---|---|---|---|---|---|---|---|
| Fire | | Water | | Air | | Earth | |
| Younger yang | | Younger yin | | Elder yang | | Elder yin | |
| Key 4 Emperor | Key 20 Judgment | Key 12 Hanged Man | Key 13 Death | Key 0 Fool | Key 6 Lovers | Key 21 World | Key 9 Hermit |
| Key 19 Sun | Key 16 Tower | Key 2 Priestess | Key 10 Wheel of Fortune | Key 3 Empress | Key 17 Star | Key 15 Devil | Key 5 Hierophant |
| King of Wands | Queen of Wands | King of Cups | Queen of Cups | King of Swords | Queen of Swords | King of Coins | Queen of Coins |
| Knight of Wands | Page of Wands | Knight of Cups | Page of Cups | Knight of Swords | Page of Swords | Knight of Coins | Page of Coins |
| Ace of Wands | Two of Wands | Ace of Cups | Two of Cups | Ace of Swords | Two of Swords | Ace of Coins | Two of Coins |
| Three of Wands | Four of Wands | Three of Cups | Four of Cups | Three of Swords | Four of Swords | Three of Coins | Four of Coins |
| Five of Wands | Six of Wands | Five of Cups | Six of Cups | Five of Swords | Six of Swords | Five of Coins | Six of Coins |
| Seven of Wands | Eight of Wands | Seven of Cups | Eight of Cups | Seven of Swords | Eight of Swords | Seven of Coins | Eight of Coins |
| Nine of Wands | Ten of Wands | Nine of Cups | Ten of Cups | Nine of Swords | Ten of Swords | Nine of Coins | Ten of Coins |

Under the Golden Dawn system of elemental correspondences, which has become the dominant system in contemporary tarot, key 3, the Empress, corresponds with Earth; and key 10, Wheel of Fortune, corresponds with Fire.

However, here the Empress is assigned the trigram Heaven, which corresponds with Air, and the Wheel of Fortune is assigned Wind, which corresponds with Water. The connection between the Empress and the trigram Heaven is through its astrological association of Venus, which is also the planet associated with Heaven. The Wheel of Fortune corresponds astrologically with Jupiter, which is also the astrological correspondence for Wind.

In the active elemental suits for Fire and Air (Wands and Swords), the yang trigram of the two trigrams associated with each Platonic element corresponds with the king, knight, and odd pip cards. That's Fire and Heaven as noted in table 7.11. The yin trigram of the two active elemental suits corresponds with the queen, page, and even pip cards. That's Thunder and Lake.

The opposite happens in the passive elemental suits. For Water and Earth (Cups and Coins, latter of which is also known as Pentacles or Disks), the yin trigram corresponds with the king, knight, and odd pip cards—Water and Earth; and the yang trigram corresponds with the queen, page, and even pip cards—Wind and Mountain.

Doing so achieves a balance and symmetry in the yin and yang affinities.

You'll also notice in the table that only seventy-two of the seventy-eight cards in the tarot are assigned a trigram. Among the seventy-two, there's an eight-by-nine balance of trigram assignments. The seventy-two here holds resonance with the seventy-two-fold name per the Sefer Raziel and thus seventy-two angels of the Shem Hamephorash; the seventy-two languages spoken at the Tower of Babylon; the seventy-two names of God, per the Kabbalah; and the seventy-two demons from the Ars Goetia.

This leaves a remaining six cards in the Major Arcana not assigned one of the eight trigrams. These six cards correspond with six divine principles that also reveal the six lines of a "phantom" or unseen spirit hexagram, the sixty-fifth hexagram of the I Ching.

This concept of there being more than sixty-four hexagrams isn't new. Throughout the dynasties, I Ching scholars have proposed that there are more than sixty-four hexagrams,[19] though these "extra" hexagrams represent a "玄" (xuán) or dark, mysterious energy in the universe, comparable to our current concept of dark energy in the cosmos. Yes, that is the same xuán 玄 as in 九天玄女 (Jiǔ Tiān Xuán Nǚ), Lady of the Nine Heavens.

**TABLE 7.12** The Xuan Hexagram Revealed in the Tarot Major Arcana

| Key 1 | Key 2 | Key 3 | Key 4 | Key 5 | Key 6 | Key 7 |
| Key 8 | Key 9 | Key 10 | Key 11 | Key 12 | Key 13 | Key 14 |
| Key 15 | Key 16 | Key 17 | Key 18 | Key 19 | Key 20 | Key 21 |

In occult studies of the tarot, the twenty-one keys of the Major Arcana, setting aside key 0 or the unnumbered Fool card, are arranged into three sets of seven called the Three Septenaries. Six of these twenty-one keys reveal the six points of that *xuán*. Table 7.12 shows a symmetry among the six unassigned Major Arcana keys when arranged into the order of the Three Septenaries. Within tarot there are several major systems of key numbering in the Majors, with the most notable change being between key 8 and key 11. In the Tarot de Marseilles and Thoth, key 8 is Justice and key 11 is Strength; in the Rider-Waite-Smith, key 8 is Strength and key 11 is Justice. In any of the major tarot systems, both 8 and 11 are unassigned keys.

These six cards are six points of Divinity and, as the *xuán* or dark energy, express six principles of magic. The six points represent the Tria Prima in Western alchemy, or Three Primes, doubled, and echo Shao Yong's theory of the universe operating in orders of three. The doubled Tria Prima forms the Solomonic hexagram that Eliphas Levi calls the magical equilibrium.[20]

The six keys from the Major Arcana that correspond with the phantom "ninth Gua" and thus are not assigned one of the eight trigrams of the Ba Gua reveal the Six Mysteries. These Six Mysteries have correlations in science and magic, which table 7.17 summarizes.

The derivations of the six principles of magic revealed through the "ninth Gua" are based on the *Yellow Emperor's Classics of the Hidden Talisman* (AD 618–907), a Tang dynasty text alleged to have been transmitted to the Yellow Emperor by the Lady of the Nine Heavens (九天玄女, Jiǔ Tiān Xuán Nǚ). The correlations to the six scientific principles that I see as having some equivalence to the magical principle are my own musings.

Chapter 4 covered the Plum Blossom ordering of the trigrams, which accounts for a ninth sector signified by the Taiji and the Wuji, the numinous omnipresence and the numinous void. When the I Ching and tarot are merged, the presence of that ninth in its single state (not compounded with the other trigrams, creating matter and life experiences) is revealed. Table 7.13 is an expansion on the ideas first proposed by Shao Yong, illustrated earlier in table 4.10.

350   I Ching, the Oracle

**TABLE 7.13** The Ninth Trigram Revealed (the Phantom "Xuán" Gua)

| 1 | 2 | 3 | 4 | 5 | 6 | 7 | 8 | 9 |
|---|---|---|---|---|---|---|---|---|
| ☰ | ☱ | ☲ | ☳ | ☴ | ☵ | ☶ | ☷ | ☯ |
| ☰ | ☱ | ☲ | ☳ | ☴ | ☵ | ☶ | ☷ | ※ |
| 乾 | 兌 | 離 | 震 | 巽 | 坎 | 艮 | 坤 | 玄 |
| Qián Heaven | Duì Lake | Lí Fire | Zhèn Thunder | Xùn Wind | Kǎn Water | Gěn Mountain | Kūn Earth | Xuán The Void |

The six cards in the Major Arcana that do not correspond with one of the eight trigrams, but rather reveal the presence of a pure form of the ninth, the Void (Xuán), not only reveal the true presence of thaumaturgy, which is the state of nature and *qi* the Void represents; they also represent that state of innate *qi* within all of the other sixty-four hexagrams—the Tria Prima doubled.

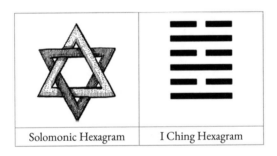

| Solomonic Hexagram | I Ching Hexagram |

Both the three sets of yin and yang lines alternating in the innate *qi* of every hexagram of the I Ching and the Solomonic hexagram of Western mystery traditions designate a cosmological holy trinity.

The Pure Ones are also known as the Three Celestial Stars 三星 (Sānxīng)—Jupiter, Ursa Major, and Canis Major—covered in the yarrow stalk divination method instructions, as part of the methodology invokes the Three Pure Ones through your gestures during the divination ritual.

**TABLE 7.14** Comparing the Cosmological Trinities in Alchemy

| The Pure Ones | 上清 Numinous Treasure | 太清 The Tao (Lao Tzu) | 玉清 Primordial Origin |
|---|---|---|---|
| Worlds | Natural (physical) | Spiritual (metaphysical) | Divine (teligious) |
| Alchemy | Earth | Man [The Mind] | Heaven |
| | Blackening | Whitening | Reddening |
| | Azoth | Incorporation | Transmutation |
| Three Jewels 三寶 | 精 *Jing* (viriditas) | 氣 *Qi* (magnetic chain) | 神 *Shen* (astral light) |
| Three Virtues 三德 | 柔克 Tenderness | 正直 Integrity | 剛克 Fortitude |

With the Tria Prima (the alchemical expression that finds equivalence in the Holy Trinity, the triple god, and the triple goddess) doubled, we have a total of six hands: a left-hand path and a right-hand path for each triple form (three yin and three yang lines in the innate *qi* of the I Ching hexagram as covered in chapter 4). And here we see a complement between Western occultism and Eastern occultism.

When one of these six cards appears in a divinatory reading, the trigram correspondence of its paired card is doubled, similar to the operations of the Spirit Helpers per the Ten Wings, covered in chapter 3. In other words, these six cards always invoke one of the eight Spirit Helpers. The eight Spirit Helpers are when the trigrams are doubled.

Note also the resonance here to the *Six Keys of Eudoxus,* an alchemical text attributed to Eudoxus of Cnidus (ca. 400–350 BC), a Greek mathematician, physician, and astronomer credited with having developed a precursor to integral calculus. However, the text itself is believed to be dated to the Renaissance by an anonymous author. Israel Regardie talks at length about the *Six Keys of Eudoxus* in *The Philosopher's Stone* (1938), noting that these Six Keys open to "the most Secret Philosophy."[21]

### TABLE 7.15 The Eight Spirit Helpers

| Heaven \| Heaven | Lake \| Lake | Fire \| Fire | Thunder \| Thunder |
|---|---|---|---|
| **1 Qián** | **58 Duì** | **30 Lí** | **51 Zhèn** |
| Summon the initiatory directive power of Heaven; contact with *yang* celestial beings. | Inner peace, happiness, and contentment; success in business deals; career or social advancement. | Casting out a fishing line to hook an objective and reel it in toward you. To tether to an object. | To absorb the powers of thunder *qi* and amplify the magus's personal power. |
| Wind \| Wind | Water \| Water | Mountain \| Mountain | Earth \| Earth |
| **57 Xùn** | **29 Kǎn** | **52 Gěn** | **2 Kūn** |
| Steady flow of profit and gains channeled toward you; financial security; prosperity. | Successful and effective shamanic journeying through the underworld or spirit realms. | To help facilitate insights, psychic visions, or spiritual awakening; improve meditation. | Fertility spells; amplifies mediumship; facilitates ghost and *yin* spirit communications. |

### TABLE 7.16 The Six Alchemical Keys of Eudoxus

| | | | |
|---|---|---|---|
| **First Key** **The Moon** | Extracting the hidden stone from the dark caverns | **Fourth Key** **The Magician** | Evaporating the liquids to reveal the pure-form, fertile solids |
| **Second Key** **Temperance** | Dissolving and separating the compounds of the stone into its elements | **Fifth Key** **Justice** | Fermentation of the stone into medicine; leavening by the same methods that bread is made |
| **Third Key** **The Chariot** | Purification in a bath of the healing tincture | **Sixth Key** **Strength** | Multiplication of the stone by dissolving and coagulating to refine the virtues of the stone—an astral fire that sympathizes with the natural fire |

**TABLE 7.17** The Science and Magic of the Six ※ Spirit Helper Cards

| KEY 1 THE MAGICIAN | | KEY 7 THE CHARIOT | |
|---|---|---|---|
|  | All manifestations of the Tao can be generated through the hand of a magus. This is knowledge of how the four seasons and four directions are the One. The Tao is contained within the mind. | Before every event, the Tao presents an opportunity to change the path of nature. Through knowledge of yin and yang and wielding it as a driver does a chariot will change that path of nature. |  |
|  | **Newton's first law.** When forces are at equilibrium, what is at rest will remain at rest, and what is in motion remains in motion. Taiji, the numinous omnipotent, and Wuji, the numinous void, express the law of inertia. | **Newton's second law.** When forces are imbalanced, they move and change. To create that change, a binary of force (a push or a pull) is driven by that imbalance, assessed through its mass and its acceleration. Imbalances create change. |  |

| KEY 8/KEY 11 STRENGTH | | KEY 11/KEY 8 JUSTICE | |
|---|---|---|---|
|  | To harness *qi* from the Tao, your mind must be awakened. This is the yang spirit and Taoist Lady in White (素女, Sù Nǚ). Interestingly, Sù Nǚ was associated with sex magic, and the Strength card in Crowley's Thoth deck is Lust. | Balance of the Ba Gua establishes order. This is the counterpart to Sù Nǚ, and that is the Mysterious Lady (玄女, Xuán Nǚ) wielding her sword, an advocate of divine justice. Both descend from the Nine Heavens. |  |
|  | **Faraday's law of induction.** An electric current (astral light) produces an electromagnetic field; a changing field creates an electric current, i.e., generates astral light. Willpower induces the current through a changing magnetized field. | **Newton's third law.** Forces are interactive and come in pairs, equal and opposite. Every interaction is a force of pairs, as expressed in the Taijitu (太極圖) yin-yang dualism of the Great Monad. |  |

**TABLE 7.17** The Science and Magic of the Six ※ Spirit Helper Cards *(continued)*

| KEY 14 TEMPERANCE | | KEY 18 THE MOON | |
|---|---|---|---|
|  | Wu Xing, or the five agents, are what trigger yin and yang to create change. This is expressed in key 14 through its numerology: 1 + 4 = 5. Temperance is the inner alchemy that cultivates a magus's *qi*. | The relationship between the outward-facing self and the shadow self will determine how weak or powerful a magus is. This is the role of a spacetime symmetry. |  |
|  | **Schrödinger's wave function.** We can predict how a quantum system (e.g., a hexagram) will behave based on a calculation of its kinetic and potential energy, and how the quantum state (state of the system) is changing with time. | **Mass-energy equivalence.** What has mass and is matter also contains intrinsic energy, or *qi*. That *qi* is a binary, and there is a relationship of equivalence between the two. All forms of energy, because of that intrinsic *qi*, interact gravitationally. | |

**FIGURE 7.13a** The ninth Gua, for marking the spirit helpers

Thus, in summary, there are six cards in the seventy-eight cards of the tarot that aren't assigned to one of the eight trigrams of the Ba Gua; rather, they correspond with a ninth trigram, marked with the symbol "※" to signify invocation of the four seasons and four directions, time and space.

If the pair of cards in a tarot reading designated for the casting of the hexagram are both from this set of six, then that indicates the presence of the Tao as Wuji (無極), numinous nothingness, and Taiji (太極), numinous omnipresence.

For example, if a two-card reading is drawn, where the first card is key 7, the Chariot, and the second card pulled is the Six of Wands, the lower trigram is formed from the first card in time while the upper trigram is formed from the second. Here, key 7, the Chariot, is one of the six spirit helpers forming the phantom Xuán hexagram, which, in lieu of a trigram, I mark with the symbol "※."

When one of these six ※ cards show up, the other trigram it comes paired with is doubled; hence, the spirit helper. Here, the Six of Wands corresponds with the trigram Thunder, so the cast hexagram in the reading is Thunder over Thunder, Hexagram 51.

**FIGURE 7.13b** *The Rider-Waite-Smith Tarot* (1911) by A. E. Waite and Pamela Colman Smith

**FIGURE 7.13C** *La Grande Tarot Belline* (1863) by Magus Edmond

Let's consider a reading where both cards correspond with the ninth Gua ※. If, for example, in a tarot reading you would like to see what Oracle message is revealed from the pairing of two selected cards in the spread, and those two are Justice (whether it is key 8 or key 11 in the system you're using) and the Moon, then we reveal the ninth Spirit Helper and phantom sixty-fifth hexagram, Xuán.

There are different layers of meaning from which you can choose to approach interpreting the double ※, or phantom sixty-fifth hexagram Xuán. I interpret it as a direct connection between my personal *qi* and the *qi* of the Xuán, which manifests to me in the form of the Lady of the Nine Heavens, Jiǔ Tiān Xuán Nǚ. The double spirit helpers ※ show up in a reading when the Lady wants her presence to be known.

Xuán, however, is a general designation for the Mystery, the darkness and that liminal space that is opaque. It's the unknown, the yet to be known. It's a space where the name and likeness of the dark goddess in a cultural form you recognize enters to commune directly with you. As the people of the Shang, that land of Yin, noted 3,600 years ago, this is the spirit of the crow.

In a mundane reading, the sentience of the Oracle has detected a concealed presence, a wild-card factor at play in the matter at hand.

TABLE 7.18 Tarot and I Ching Trigram Correspondences

### MAJOR ARCANA

| TAROT | TRIGRAM | TAROT | TRIGRAM |
|---|---|---|---|
| Key 0: The Fool | Heaven | Key 11: Justice/Strength | [Spirit Helper] |
| Key 1: The Magician | [Spirit Helper] | Key 12: The Hanged Man | Water |
| Key 2: The High Priestess | Water | Key 13: Death | Wind |
| Key 3: The Empress | Heaven | Key 14: Temperance | [Spirit Helper] |
| Key 4: The Emperor | Fire | Key 15: The Devil | Earth |
| Key 5: The Hierophant | Mountain | Key 16: The Tower | Thunder |
| Key 6: The Lovers | Lake | Key 17: The Star | Lake |
| Key 7: The Chariot | [Spirit Helper] | Key 18: The Moon | [Spirit Helper] |
| Key 8: Strength/Justice | [Spirit Helper] | Key 19: The Sun | Fire |
| Key 9: The Hermit | Mountain | Key 20: Judgment | Thunder |
| Key 10: Wheel of Fortune | Wind | Key 21: The World | Earth |

### SUIT OF WANDS

| TAROT | TRIGRAM | TAROT | TRIGRAM |
|---|---|---|---|
| Ace of Wands | Fire | Eight of Wands | Thunder |
| Two of Wands | Thunder | Nine of Wands | Fire |
| Three of Wands | Fire | Ten of Wands | Thunder |
| Four of Wands | Thunder | Page of Wands | Thunder |
| Five of Wands | Fire | Knight of Wands | Fire |
| Six of Wands | Thunder | Queen of Wands | Thunder |
| Seven of Wands | Fire | King of Wands | Fire |

### SUIT OF CUPS

| TAROT | TRIGRAM | TAROT | TRIGRAM |
|---|---|---|---|
| Ace of Cups | Water | Eight of Cups | Wind |
| Two of Cups | Wind | Nine of Cups | Water |
| Three of Cups | Water | Ten of Cups | Wind |
| Four of Cups | Wind | Page of Cups | Wind |
| Five of Cups | Water | Knight of Cups | Water |
| Six of Cups | Wind | Queen of Cups | Wind |
| Seven of Cups | Water | King of Cups | Water |

### SUIT OF SWORDS

| TAROT | TRIGRAM | TAROT | TRIGRAM |
|---|---|---|---|
| Ace of Swords | Heaven | Eight of Swords | Lake |
| Two of Swords | Lake | Nine of Swords | Heaven |
| Three of Swords | Heaven | Ten of Swords | Lake |
| Four of Swords | Lake | Page of Swords | Lake |
| Five of Swords | Heaven | Knight of Swords | Heaven |
| Six of Swords | Lake | Queen of Swords | Lake |
| Seven of Swords | Heaven | King of Swords | Heaven |

### SUIT OF COINS

| TAROT | TRIGRAM | TAROT | TRIGRAM |
|---|---|---|---|
| Ace of Coins | Earth | Eight of Coins | Mountain |
| Two of Coins | Mountain | Nine of Coins | Earth |
| Three of Coins | Earth | Ten of Coins | Mountain |
| Four of Coins | Mountain | Page of Coins | Mountain |
| Five of Coins | Earth | Knight of Coins | Earth |
| Six of Coins | Mountain | Queen of Coins | Mountain |
| Seven of Coins | Earth | King of Coins | Earth |

# Summary Outline of Hexagram Interpretation

The following checklist summarizes a general process for interpreting an I Ching reading result. It incorporates both the Image and Number Tradition and the Meaning and Principle Tradition discussed earlier in the chapter.

| | | PRIMARY HEXAGRAM | |
|---|---|---|---|
| The Oracle | ☐ | **Hexagram theme summary.** The initial box of text in the hexagram entry summarizes the divinatory message. This will give you a brief recapitulation of your reading. | |
| | ☐ | **Bold text.** These are the translations of the hexagram statements. They consist of the statements attributed to King Wen in the Zhouyi and one section of the Ten Wings. Read these statements as riddles you need to solve. | |
| | ☐ | **Annotations and commentaries.** The rest of the text in the Oracle section are my annotations and commentaries to supplement the translations. The annotations help to offer some hints on how to solve the riddles of the bold text. | |
| Changing lines | ☐ | **Bold text line statements.** The bold text line statements corresponding with each of the six lines or *yao* are translations of the statements attributed to the Duke of Zhou in the *Zhouyi*. Conceptualize these line statements as riddles you need to work on solving. How you interpret these riddles will reveal the answer. Changing lines are the Oracle's concrete advice to you, revealing what's going to happen and what actions to take going forward to ensure the best possible outcome for yourself. | |
| | ☐ | **Annotations and commentaries.** The text underneath the statements in bold are my annotations and commentaries to give some context to the line statements. These serve a supplementary purpose only. | |
| | ☐ | **TABLE 7.19** Changing Lines Position Correspondences | |
| | | Line 6 | Greater spiritual forces at play; karma or destiny. Hand of God, or acts of God. Extenuating circumstances beyond your control caused this situation, and your own actions are not to blame. Now what matters is how you respond to what has happened. A changing sixth line can also indicate that one chapter is coming to an end and a new one is beginning. Transition phase. Heading into a figurative afterlife. |
| | | Line 5 | *Hexagram ruler.* A changing fifth line can be a sign that executive leadership or decision-making is needed from you. In the situation at hand, your action will have a significant impact on others. A sign that what's to come will have long-term implications. |
| | | Line 4 | Interpersonal relationships, matters of the heart, emotional responses, or family matters are key factors. Could also be a sign that decisive action must be taken now. Time is of the essence. If you do not act quickly or implement change immediately, you might lose your window of opportunity. |

|  |  |  |  |  |
|---|---|---|---|---|
|  |  | Line 3 | Legal matters, civil affairs, or social affairs are key factors at play. This could also indicate the moment in the narrative arc when the plot thickens. Complications. Conflicts. Oppositional forces have the most impact on the situation at hand. | |
|  |  | Line 2 | Physical health, medical factors, or technological factors at play. Could also indicate the moment when a situation is beginning to gain momentum. Blooming and developmental phase. | |
|  |  | Line 1 | Short-term financial or economic factors at play. Situation is still at the onset or beginning of the narrative arc. This is still the initial setup for what's to come. Decisions made will only have short-term implications. | |
|  | ☐ | ⚏ | 太陰<br>Elder yin | Blackening, *nigredo*. Entering the dark chaos of the inner world. Catharsis. Long window of opportunity to change course. |
|  |  | ⚎ | 少陰<br>Younger yin | Whitening, *albedo*. Contemplating the "why" and coming to terms. Purification. Movement of forces is toward yin. |
|  |  | ⚍ | 少陽<br>Younger yang | Yellowing, *citrinitas*. Actualizing self-awareness. New lease on life. Motivated. Movement of forces is toward yang. |
|  |  | ⚌ | 太陽<br>Elder yang | Reddening, *rubedo*. Final achievement. Union of higher and lower. Manifestation. Short window of opportunity to change course. |
|  | ☐ | **Assess the number of changing lines.** If there is only one changing line, the solution to the matter and the action required for the best possible outcome are going to be straightforward. If, however, you have three or more changing lines, the situation right now is quite volatile. There is still a lot of uncertainty, due in large part to your own indecisiveness. | | |
| Trigrams | ☐ | **Lower trigram.** Review the metaphysical correspondences for the lower trigram from chapter 5. The lower trigram indicates people or personalities involved, the human factor, physical environmental factors and influences, or what's at the foundation. | | |
|  | ☐ | **Upper trigram.** Review the metaphysical correspondences for the upper trigram. The upper trigram indicates karmic, spiritual, or predestined influences. This is Spirit. The upper trigram reveals Heaven's Will and direct counsel coming to you from Spirit. | | |

| | | TRANSFORMED HEXAGRAM |
|---|---|---|
| The Oracle | ☐ | **Hexagram theme summary.** The initial box of text in the transformed hexagram entry gives a brief summary of the "what if." This is all prophecy and future or forward-looking projections, but they are all based on the current trajectory and are therefore fairly accurate projections of what's to come. |
| Changing lines | ☐ | **If-then statements from the primary hexagram's changing lines.** The corresponding changing lines in the transformed hexagram relate directly with the same changing line number from the primary hexagram. The primary hexagram's changing line is the "if," and the transformed hexagram's same changing line is the "then." It helps to write out the bold text riddle-like line statements from the primary hexagram side by side with the bold text riddle-like line statements from the transformed hexagram. |
| Trigrams | ☐ | **Upper trigram.** This trigram is your key when spell-crafting, praying, or petitioning for a positive outcome to your situation. The nature of actions corresponding with the Wu Xing phase of your transformed hexagram's upper trigram is the final message of what action to take in direct response to what's going on. |
| | | **IF RESULT IS A SINGLE LOCKED HEXAGRAM:** |
| The Oracle | ☐ | Follow the interpretive process as noted for the primary hexagram. A locked hexagram means all forces at play have matured, and now we're just waiting for the aftermath. The forces at play have already been simmering for far too long a time. |
| Line statements | ☐ | Read all six line statements of your single locked hexagram. Start with line 1 and progress to line 6. They will shed light on the matter at hand chronologically. Line 1 represents the past and earlier in time, the early movements of the forces at play. Line 6 represents the forecast of what's to come. |
| | ☐ | **Hexagram ruler.** Focus on line 5 of your locked hexagram. The fifth line is the crux of the Oracle's message for you. Read the statement for line 5 as the answer to the inquiry. |
| | ☐ | **Spiritual guidance.** As a supplement to the answer, I'll read line 6 as spiritual guidance for navigating the situation at hand. |
| Trigrams | ☐ | Review the lower and upper trigrams as noted for the primary hexagram. Look to the upper trigram as the key to how you might want to spell-craft, pray, or petition for the best possible outcome for the situation. |

# PRACTICUM 7.11:
## An I Ching and Tarot Card Reading

Proceed with a tarot reading using any multiple-card spread of your choosing. Alternatively, you can do a more intentional I Ching and tarot reading with a two-card spread. Either way will work here.

If you are using a multiple-card spread, once the tarot reading is complete, choose any two cards in the spread that you would like a deeper understanding of, and see how the two cards relate to one another, what forces in the universe connect them and thus make them relevant to the situation you've inquired about.

The card that was drawn into the spread earlier in time is the lower trigram. The card that came later in time when you set the cards down is the upper trigram. For a two-card draw, the first card is the lower trigram and the second is the upper trigram.

**FIGURE 7.14** Sample two-card reading. *Spirit Keeper's Tarot,* Revelation edition (2021).

Look up the cards' trigram correspondences in the preceding tables. If a card in the pair is one of the six Spirit Helper cards, then look at the trigram for the other card in the pair and double it. The two cards together form one of the eight Spirit Helpers in the I Ching.

| Heaven: 1 Qián | Lake: 58 Duì | Fire: 30 Lí | Thunder: 51 Zhèn |
|---|---|---|---|
| ☰ | ☱ | ☲ | ☳ |
| Protection of the celestial Father | Career success and inner peace | Commanding the power of attraction | Thunder magic, control of elements |
| Wind: 57 Xùn | Water: 29 Kǎn | Mountain: 52 Gěn | Earth: 2 Kūn |
| ☴ | ☵ | ☶ | ☷ |
| Prosperity and abundance | Safe journeys and the power to heal | Spiritual awakening and mastery of alchemy | Protection of the earth goddess |

For a forecast reading on the coming week, I pulled two cards using the *Spirit Keeper's Tarot*, as illustrated in figure 7.14.

The first card drawn was the Six of Chalices (or Six of Cups), corresponding with Wind (forming the lower trigram). The second card was key 6, the Lovers, corresponding with Lake (forming the upper trigram). The cast hexagram is Lake over Wind, or Hexagram 28.

Per the Oracle message for Hexagram 28, the pithy takeaway point is that the coming week will be auspicious (vs. inauspicious) for major undertakings. The card reading itself echoes similar sentiments of boding well, namely that of growth. Something I've been working on for a very long time (the "past still part of the present" theme from the Six of Cups) is coming to a head (the designation of the Lovers in the context of being paired with the Six of Cups). There may also be meetings or events (the Gemini energy of the Lovers) with family and old friends (the Six of Cups).

For those interested in delving further into the intersection of tarot and the I Ching for divinatory readings, consider the *Spirit Keeper's Tarot* deck, which blends Eastern and Western esoteric traditions. The cards were created and illustrated by me, with the trigram correspondences printed on each card.

# PRACTICUM 7.12:
## Using the I Ching to Find Lost Objects

The next time you've misplaced your wallet or keys, test-drive the I Ching to see if the Oracle can help you locate lost objects. There are a few grounding guidelines, however. First, you must have put in a sincere, good-faith effort to search for the missing item on your own, without the help of the Oracle. Demonstrate that you've already tried.

Any of the divination methods instructed in this chapter will do. However, as you perform the divination, intend that no changing lines will be observed. No matter the result, you will only be looking at a single hexagram and not at any transformed hexagrams that the changing lines yield. Instead, the changing lines in this reading will only refer to the line text for the single hexagram.

Proceed with the divination method. Once you get the hexagram result, assess the Oracle message and the line text for any changing lines. Do not cast a transformed hexagram. Let the general summary of the matter at hand sink in. Read any line text per the changing lines as specific instructions to help you narrow and pinpoint.

Then proceed with an Image and Number tradition of interpretation, where you look at the metaphysical correspondences for the pair of trigrams forming the hexagram result.

Since the subject matter is about locating a lost object, focus on the directional, materials, and land forms correspondences for the two trigrams. You'll also want to identify the ruling Wu Xing phases for the two trigrams and assess those correspondences.

What does the Oracle message tell you in terms of a general vicinity of the lost object? Now focus on the directional and land formation or building structure correspondences for the trigrams, and use the two trigrams like Cartesian coordinates $x$ and $y$ to cross-reference the precise area of where the lost object is.

Here's an example. I had misplaced my wallet, and while I was sure it was somewhere in the house, there was a chance I had lost it during my last outing. After a weekend of searching to no avail, in a moment of desperation I tried an I Ching reading.

I asked, "Where is my wallet?" The results yielded Hexagram 62, Thunder over Mountain, with line 5 as the changing line.

The Oracle message, in summary, suggested getting down low and looking up close, i.e., paying attention to details: "It is not the proper time to strive upward; instead, strive downward. Seek not from the Heavens, but seek from the Underworld." Converting that to mundane terms applicable to my inquiry, I needed to look somewhere dark, and maybe lower to the ground, not somewhere out in the open.

The line "it is not a time for expanding; it is a time for refining" and other lines in the Oracle suggested to me I'd looked where the wallet was before, but I just didn't see it. I needed to look where I'd already looked and be more vigilant about paying attention to details.

This Oracle message also reassured me somewhat that the wallet was "lost" inside my house (the reference to not needing expansion, but rather, refinement) and that I hadn't misplaced it while out. So, at the very least, I didn't need to get all my ID cards replaced.

To see just how specific an I Ching reading can get, let's apply an Image and Number tradition and look at the correspondences for the pair of trigrams.

| | |
|---|---|
| Thunder | Direction: East<br>Wu Xing: Wood<br>Materials: Wood<br>Land forms: Forest, dense woods, parched but grassy areas, dried grass |
| Mountain | Direction: Northeast<br>Wu Xing: Earth<br>Materials: Clay, stone<br>Land forms: Hills, mountains, small paths not often traveled, rocky terrain; caves or dark caverns within mountains |

Since the subject matter of my inquiry calls for pinpointing a location, I looked to the directional correspondences of the two trigrams. Thunder and Mountain correspond with east and northeast respectively. Looking at the layout of my house, I identified which rooms were in the east/northeast sector. Since I live in a three-level home, there are three possible floors and three possible rooms this could refer to. The building structures that correspond with both trigrams relate to tall buildings, so I interpreted that as the highest floor—upstairs. That would be my home office. It could also refer to a cave or dark cavern within a mountain, and interpreting "forest and dense wood" in terms of my home, perhaps somewhere cluttered with papers and "wood" like materials.

Also, the changing line yielded was the fifth line: "No rain. An image of a bird settling into a nest. The setting of the sun in the west. The duke shoots and hits one at the entrance of a cave." In addition to the land formation correspondences for Mountain, we now have a direct divinatory message relating to caves.

Next, I sat meditatively with the information provided by the Oracle. In meditation, I let the insights fine-tune themselves until a more specific and detailed revelation came through. Often people expect the divinatory result to spell out the solution for them, but my impression of the Oracle has always been that the spirit driving it will only help you help yourself.

The insight came in an instant. I got up and went straight to my home office and opened my closet door. I've looked here at least a dozen times already. Nevertheless, I got down low and stared at the monstrous pile of handbags that somewhat resembled a mountain. (Funnier yet, all of my handbags are made of vegan leather, i.e., plant-based materials; hence, the Wood reference.) "Entrance of a cave" per the fifth line message was spot-on—the mountain of handbags was at the foot of the entrance of the walk-in closet. Once I could cross-reference the directional correspondences to the northeast corner of my home, the closet was along the west wall of the room, giving meaning to "setting of the sun in the west." The "image of a bird settling into a nest" was my wallet settling inside a pocket-like location, a place for small things.

*Pay attention to details* . . . that's the core message of Hexagram 62. Within a few minutes I found my wallet in one of the zipper pockets of a handbag at the bottom of that mountain.

## PRACTICUM 7.13: 100Answering the Question "Who Am I?" with a Personality Profile

The following exercise integrates Dr. Michael McDonald's work at the intersection of personal therapy and the I Ching.[22] His Personality Profile counseling system helps begin to shed light on the question "Who am I?" utilizing the concept of archetypes and principles in transpersonal psychology.

You will be casting a set of six hexagrams, one to answer each of the questions set forth in table 7.19. Any changing lines cast from the divination method are interpreted as supplemental insights from the Oracle. The changing line corresponding with the line assignment for the question will be your main focus.

Thus, if the primary hexagram yields changing lines from the casting method, cast the transformed hexagram based on the changing lines from the casting method. If the result is a locked hexagram, interpret accordingly.

Once the hexagram results are cast, follow table 7.19 as a road map for the line text to read and focus your journaling reflections on.

The Oracle message corresponding with the cast hexagram for the question is the answer. From there, turn to the line text in that hexagram corresponding with the line number of your question, as referenced in the table.

**TABLE 7.21** Dr. Michael McDonald's Personality Profile Model[23]

| Line 6 | What is my unified self? What does you as the junzi look like? What is the personality profile of your higher self? Line 6 is also a summary that synthesizes the answers to the previous five questions. |
| --- | --- |
| | I also read this sixth hexagram as insights into the ways you best commune and connect with Divinity. What does your relationship with the Divine look like? At the end of the day, what is your philosophy of life and sense of religiosity, beyond what you are consciously aware of? What is something from your unconscious that the Oracle can reveal to you at this time? |
| Line 5 | What is my greatest gift? What is your main contribution to society? What is most likely going to be your legacy? What impact are you having on your environment? What impact are you having on the people in your life? |
| | Line 5 will give you food for thought on how you can best let your inner light shine. In what small ways do you contribute to the world? What important mission did the Divine task you with, and thus, what attributes have you been endowed with so you can complete that mission? We're not always born with the attributes necessary; perhaps the Divine has set out a path of life lessons so you can acquire those attributes along the way. If there are hardships for the learning of life lessons to cultivate the necessary attributes, those hardships are reflected in the hexagram result. |
| Line 4 | What is my vocation (or calling)? What kind of livelihood or occupation would best serve your nature, your talents and skills, and your destiny? What professional activities will yield the greatest sense of personal fulfillment? |
| | In the hexagram cast for this question, the lower trigram reveals innate archetypes you were born with, while the upper trigram reveals aspirational archetypes that will guide you toward actualizing your higher self. |
| | The lower trigram's Wu Xing correspondence will reveal skill sets to hone in the first half of your life, while the upper trigram's Wu Xing correspondence will reveal your calling. |
| | This hexagram and line 4 answer the question: "How do I interact with others most productively?" |

**TABLE 7.21** Dr. Michael McDonald's Personality Profile Model *(continued)*

| | |
|---|---|
| *Line 3* | What is my destiny? McDonald describes your destiny as "the overall shape of your life." The resulting hexagram for this question will reveal how to live your life to its fullest and how to achieve happiness.<br><br>This hexagram reveals insights into the driving force in your life path. The line 3 text in that hexagram reflects a general maxim to serve as a lifelong compass for finding your own true north. |
| *Line 2* | Why was I born this way? You were born into an environment, a family of origin, and certain personal qualities well beyond your control, some of which have become a major source of the challenges you face in life. Also, some of it has left you luckier than most in some ways.<br><br>If line 1 reveals your nature, then line 2 is a commentary on your nurture. This is a life review of the events and circumstances of your early childhood. Line 2 will also reflect past-life karma that most influences your present life path. |
| *Line 1* | What is my nature? As McDonald puts it: "The purpose of this question is to highlight the potentials, talents, abilities, and also limitations with which you were born."<br><br>What facet of fundamental human nature is most dominant in you? This is a composite profile of your inner resources. |

Consider the lower trigram formed from lines 1 through 3 and its correspondences. Dedicate time and thought to journaling your impressions on what the trigram and its Wu Xing correspondence says about the foundation of you. The lower trigram sheds light on what makes you who you are today.

The upper trigram formed from lines 4 through 6 and its correspondences will illuminate higher purpose, aspirational goals, possibilities, potential, and forecasts of what is to come in your life path. This is how karma, your most likely life choices, and disposition will most likely play out in the everyday world. The upper trigram provides a vision of the future in front of you, based on your past, and speculations on future incarnations.

For the general "auspicious to proceed" versus "inauspicious" pithy statements typically found in an Oracle message, adapt them by interpreting "auspicious" as someone born with certain privileges and dumb good luck, while "inauspicious" reveals someone born with certain setbacks or weights. Those born with such setbacks and weights have a special mission in life assigned to them from the Divine. To accomplish the great, you must be great, and greatness is not something you can be born with, because good luck does not set us up to be resilient. Setbacks are necessary to cultivate the degree of strength needed for heroism. "Inauspicious" messages in a Personality Profile reading are explanatory of the inner alchemical transformations necessary for you to undergo before you become gold, become the philosopher's stone of the gods.

Ever notice how loving parents tend to devote more attention and care to their children born with the greater obstacles in life? Whereas they tend to leave alone their independent and well-adjusted kids? I observe a similar approach from a sentient Divinity toward their human children.

This is a journaling exercise. Where you will attain the most insight is in a sincere and heartfelt rumination upon the divinatory results. Through writing, extrapolate an interpretation of the hexagram lines for yourself, based loosely on what's provided in this text. Read the text provided as merely offering core themes and general concepts, which you then need to refine and fully develop to arrive at how the Tao is answering your questions.

Consult multiple sources of I Ching hexagram interpretations, and reconcile the different perspectives. In these types of exercises, it's okay—and highly encouraged—to cherry-pick. Cherry-picking is your heart-mind's way of discernment and intuitively adjudicating what's right for you and what's not.

What you invest in this reading experience is what you will get out of it. Careless and hastily done divination tends to produce gibberish. It's also a waste of your own time. If you're going to try this exercise out and cast the set of six hexagrams for yourself to answer a question like "Who am I?", then I urge you to approach it with sincerity and earnestness, and a great deal of respect for the Oracle.

Ritualize the divinatory experience. Review preparation considerations prior to divination and how you'll invoke Divinity. If not invocation of Divinity, then think about what it takes for you, based on your personality, to take something seriously. What do you need, in terms of environmental and personal ritual considerations, for you to get into a focused, highly productive zone of concentration?

To optimize divination, you must know yourself, know the terrain. Your fundamental nature and the nurture from your environment that has molded you are the vital contextual factors for how you heed the Oracle's counsel. This set of six Personality Profile hexagrams become a lifelong handbook to help you become self-aware of your strengths and weaknesses.

**FIGURE 8.1** The six maidens of Jiu Tian Xuan Nu 六丁神女 (1493) From *The Ordination of Empress Zhang,* painted handscroll. SOURCE: San Diego Museum of Art. The Six *Ding* Jade Maidens are spirit gatekeepers at six liminal points in the cosmos who accompany the Lady of the Nine Heavens. Together with Jiu Tian Xuan Nu, the Maidens are master teachers of martial and mystical arts.[1] *Top panel, left to right:* Jade Maiden of Dinghai (丁亥玉女), protector of fortune; Jade Maiden of Dingchou (丁丑玉女), protector of the spirit; and Jade Maiden of Dingmao (丁卯玉女), protector of the body. *Bottom panel, left to right:* Jade Maiden of Dingsi (丁巳玉女), protector of destiny; Jade Maiden of Dingwei (丁未玉女), protector of the *po* soul; and Jade Maiden of Dingyou (丁酉玉女), protector of the *hún* soul.

# 8

# I Ching: The Book of Changes

子曰：「知變化之道者，其知神之所為乎。」²
*To know the methods of Change
is to know the Way of the gods.*
—CONFUCIUS

## Preliminary Notes

### The Zhouyi and King Wen's Revealed Sequence

The Zhouyi, often referred to as the Basic Classic (本經, Běn Jīng), consists of the following:

- The sixty-four six-line graphics, or hexagram figures (卦, *guà*).
- The sixty-four hexagrams, traditionally subdivided into two sequences (卷, *juǎn*), or two scrolls, where the first sequence consists of Hexagrams 1 through 30, and the second of Hexagrams 31 through 64.
- Each line of the hexagram, yin or yang, called a *yao* (爻, *yáo*).
- The hexagram names (卦名, *guà míng*).
- The hexagram statements, often referred to as the Judgment, or in this text, the Oracle (卦辭, *guàcí*).
- The statements corresponding with each *yao* (爻辭, *yáo cí*).

*I Ching, the Oracle*

The translations in this book consist of the Basic Classic and the image statements (象曰, *xiàng yuē*) from the Ten Wings. The English and the traditional Chinese are presented side by side. Text in bold is a direct translation of the received text of the Basic Classic. Where there may be ambiguities or high risk of misinterpretation, the text will be explained in the annotations and commentaries. Text in the hexagram entries that is not in bold consists of my added annotations and commentaries.

The six *yao* lines of the hexagram are titled with a demarcation of whether that line is yin or yang, noted by the numbers 6 and 9 respectively. In the Zhouyi, each line section begins with a 6 (六, *liù*) or a 9 (九, *jiǔ*), where 6s are indicative of a yin line and 9s are indicative of a yang.

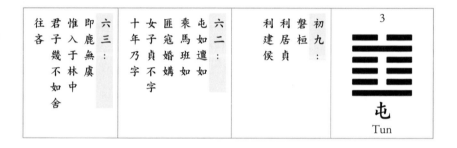

For example, in Hexagram 3, the title "初九, *chū jiǔ*" means the first 9, where 9 indicates a yang line. You'll note that line 1 of Hexagram 3 is yang. The title "六二" means the second line is a 6. Note how line 2 is a yin line. Likewise, "六三" means the third line is a 6, and line 3 is again yin.

For the line text, the boldfaced statements are the translation of the original text. The subsequent text after the boldfaced statements consists of annotations and my own explanatory additions to help supplement the translation.

Admittedly, my English translations and interpretations of the corresponding Chinese text are verbose, and I couldn't find a way around that. In Chinese, one word (one ideogram) holds multiple layers of meaning that are communicated from one person to another through shared culture. If you're both from the culture, much can be left unspoken and yet still fully expressed. More is conveyed in the subtext than what is literally stated. When translating to English, you have to translate the implied culture too; so to adequately convey those layers, I separated out the layers and tried to explain everything. Hence the verbosity.

Each entry includes the original classical Chinese text from the Zhouyi, which was originally written in an ancient form of Chinese called Gu Wen (古文, *gǔwén*). Many of the words, within the context of when they were written, meant something diametrically different from the meaning we've now ascribed to them. The syntax is different from what native speakers of Chinese would be familiar with. On innumerable occasions a single line will feature compound ideas with no discernible transitions and that are perhaps so profound that even a sophisticated reader will have difficulty finding the connections.

Among natives, this Book is coded and obscure. Many of the cultural and esoteric references are no longer part of our collective memory. And if we're being honest, a lot of it must be reconstructed . . . and fabricated, hopefully based on inductive and deductive reasoning; but it's still just a reconstruction, and ultimately, a best-effort guess. Some best-effort guesses have become authority simply by how many times those interpretations have been repeated.

There are a few different order or numbering sequences for the hexagrams. In chapter 3 we covered the latest discovery of the Mawangdui order uncovered in the 1970s, though it is believed to date back to a sequence used in 168 BC. There is also an order called the Fuxi order, though it dates to around the eleventh century AD per the writings of Shao Yong (1011–1077).

The order sequence or numbering of the hexagrams observed here—and the one that is currently considered authoritative—is the King Wen sequence (文王卦序, Wén Wáng *guà xù*). You'll often hear it referred to as the revealed sequence, the received sequence, or the classical sequence.

According to myth, this is the exact order of the hexagrams revealed to King Wen circa 1050 BC. Thus, although the reasoning for the revealed order remains vague, and it's unknown whether there is any significance to its pattern, it's commonly taken upon faith that the revealed sequence is a Heavenly determined order and thus expresses an important Mystery for the diligent I Ching philosopher-sage to discover.

## *First Sequence, Hexagrams 1–30*

The first sequence consists of Hexagrams 1 through 30, grouped into sixteen pairs. The first pair, Hexagrams 1 and 2, are yin and yang polarities of each other, i.e., Hexagram 1 consists of six yang lines, while Hexagram 2 consists of six yin lines.

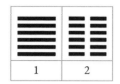

That initial pair is often referred to as the divine yang (or divine masculine in older English translations) and divine yin (or divine feminine). Following it is a train of twelve pairs that are the vertical flip of one another. For example, if you flip Hexagram 3 over vertically, it yields Hexagram 4; if you flip Hexagram 7 over vertically, it yields Hexagram 8, and so on.

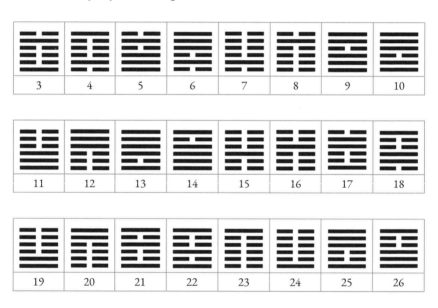

The first sequence then concludes with two pairs of yin and yang polarities. In other words, if the first of the pair has a yin line, then that same line in the latter of the pair transforms to yang, and vice versa. See how Hexagram 27 begins with a yang line for line 1 and a yin line for line 2. Its pair, Hexagram 28, thus converts line 1 to a yin line and line 2 to yang.

## Second Sequence, Hexagrams 31–64

The second sequence begins with Hexagram 31, opening with ten pairs that are the vertical flip of one another. If you flip Hexagram 31 upside down on its head, you get Hexagram 32; Hexagram 33 is the vertical flip of Hexagram 34, and so on, continuing until the pairing of Hexagrams 49 and 50.

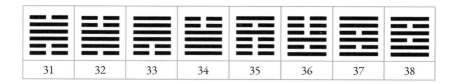

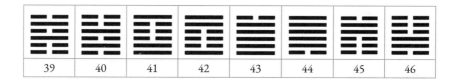

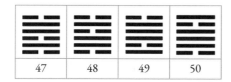

Note how Hexagrams 51 and 52 are also vertical flips of one another, but here, there is a trigram flip as well. The trigram Thunder is the vertical flip of the trigram Mountain. Hexagram 51 is Thunder over Thunder, while Hexagram 52 is Mountain over Mountain.

Next comes a single pairing consisting of hexagrams that are the vertical flips of one another, but like Hexagrams 27 through 30 in the first sequence, yin lines in Hexagram 53 transform to yang lines in Hexagram 54, and yang to yin.

| 53 | 54 |

Then three pairs of vertical flips.

| 55 | 56 | 57 | 58 | 59 | 60 |

Followed by one pair of yin-yang polarity, where yang lines in Hexagram 61 transform to yin lines in Hexagram 62, and yin to yang.

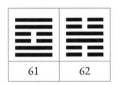

| 61 | 62 |

The second sequence concludes with one final vertical flip of two hexagrams that, like Hexagrams 1 and 2, are one another's yin-yang polarity. A yang line in Hexagram 63 transforms into a yin line in Hexagram 64, and a yin line in 63 transforms into a yang line in 64. The revealed sequence ends with the same type of pairing it begins with.

Note how Hexagrams 61 and 62 are also yin-yang polarities, but not vertical flips of one another; whereas here in Hexagrams 63 and 64, the two are both yin-yang polarities *and* the vertical flip of one another.

| 63 | 64 |

# A JOURNAL PROMPT FOR REFLECTING ON KING WEN'S REVEALED SEQUENCE

For millennia, I Ching scholars have written extensive commentaries and vehemently debated one another over the logical reasoning or explanation for King Wen's revealed sequence. What great revelation of Divine Will is illuminated by the sequence? Or are we overthinking it, and the ordering is entirely arbitrary?

Following the legacy of I Ching scholars, consider the ordering of the hexagrams in King Wen's revealed sequence, and take some time to free-write your thoughts and commentaries on whether there is any discernible pattern to the sequence.

Does it make sense to you to accept the ordering on faith alone? What does it imply about your personal spirituality if you take the ordering on faith? Do you believe there is a significance to the order? Are you skeptical and therefore will not assign any numerological or philosophical significance to the sequence? Will you simply presume that the ordering is a random matter, or a matter of convenience?

Did you catch a pattern in the ordering that I didn't cover here? Do you prefer to work with one of the alternative orders, such as Fuxi's order as espoused by eleventh-century mathematician and I Ching philosopher Shao Yong, or the Mawangdui order?

Rather than accept this as the order without any thought about why you're accepting it, take the time to reflect on the rationale for accepting (or not accepting) King Wen's revealed sequence.

## Auspicious vs. Inauspicious

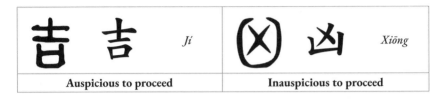

| Auspicious to proceed | Inauspicious to proceed |
|---|---|

You'll often see either of two characters in the corresponding classical Chinese text for the oracle messages: "吉" or "凶."

吉 *(jí)* indicates happiness and contentment, and therefore a good omen, prognosticating success, achievement, and a divine signal that it's auspicious to move forward as you're planning to. The ideogram here depicts a jade tablet, suggesting that Heaven's Will is aligned in your favor. The path is clear for success and advancement.

凶 *(xiōng)* indicates a bad omen, foreboding adversity and prognosticating challenges, failure, or regrets if you proceed as you're planning to. It's a word of caution from the Oracle that you don't want to move forward at this time. The situation is ominous, so tread with care. The ideogram here depicts a hole in the ground with an "X" mark as a warning not to misstep into this hole.

## To Offer Sacrifice and to Divine

| To be prosperous | To be virtuous |
|---|---|
| Sign of the sacrifice | Divination and prayer |

We addressed these two characters in chapter 3, but their significance in the context of the I Ching is worth repeating.

亨 *(hēng)* is often translated to "sign of the sacrifice."[3] You'll also see a variant on the word, 享 *(xiǎng)*, meaning to enjoy or receive good auspices. *Xiǎng* indicates that a prayer is being answered. *Hēng* is a sign from the gods that the work you have done up to this point has been accepted, and therefore you will be rewarded for your sacrifices. In the Book, it's often modified by an adjective, such as "元" *(yuán)*, meaning supreme, or "小" *(xiǎo)*, for minor, or "光" *(guāng)*, meaning illuminated by Light, shining with the Light of the gods.

貞 *(zhēn)* gets translated to "correct," "righteous," or to be "firm," in reference to firmness of integrity and conviction. The ideogram 貞 depicts a cauldron with smoke rising from its center, where the radical "卜" at the top of the character represents divination. There may be an if-then conditional statement implied here: if you prove yourself correct in your judgments, righteous in your conduct, and firm in your loyalty and virtue, then you shall be rewarded with good auspices.

These two words, *hēng* and *zhēn*, show the direct inheritances from oracle bone divination. Figure 4.8 is an etching of an oracle bone from the late Shang, circa thirteenth to eleventh century BC. It's an ox scapula and reads as follows:

辛未貞：燊禾于河，尞三牢，沉三牛，宜牢。
*Xīn wèi zhēn: Hū hé yú hé, liào sān láo, chén sān niú, yí láo.*

"辛" *(xīn)* corresponds with the Wu Xing phase Metal, the planet Venus, and the season of autumn. It can also be a reference to the western direction, the eighth year, or every eight years of the sixty-year lunisolar calendar. In this context, "辛未" *(xīn wèi)* is believed to mean day 8. Thus, "辛未貞" means

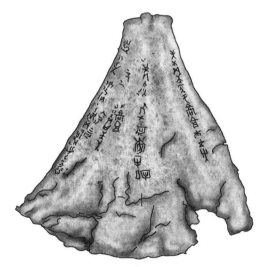

**FIGURE 8.2** Oracle bone (twelfth century BC). Oracle bone Heji 32028, Shanghai Museum.

the divination ritual taking place on the eighth day, to determine whether our prayers for an abundant harvest will be answered by the gods.

After the invocation setting the intention that this is a divination ritual praying for an abundant harvest, a note on the sacrifice offered is recorded: three oxen by "尞" *(liào)*, suggesting a sacrificial offering that involves the burning of wood or to set on fire, and three oxen by "沉" *(chén)*, suggesting that the oxen were submerged in water, perhaps drowned. Then these offerings of oxen (six in total) were placed on the sacrificial altar.

Since the Han dynasty (202 BC–AD 220), however, the two words have taken on a different patina of meaning, one rooted in Confucian values of virtue. Note how both characters are in the passage 元亨利貞 *(yuán hēng lì zhēn)*, meaning to be perfected, to be accomplished, to always advance, and to always persevere. In other words, *hēng* 亨 means you've already accomplished, and *zhēn* 貞 suggests that in order for you to achieve the success you seek, you must continue to persevere.

## The Junzi *(Sage), the Eminent One, and the Adversary*

The ideogram for *jūn* (君) depicts a person holding a scepter or rod that represents authority, lordship, and sovereignty. *Zǐ* (子) indicates a teacher, master, or the chosen son. In brief, 君子 *(jūn zǐ)* means a superior, virtuous lord. You'll see it translated as "gentleman" or "great lord." It refers generally to someone of noble, beneficent character, and in Confucian terminology, it signified the ideal man that all should aspire to be. Through a Confucian lens, 君子 *(jūn zǐ)* was intended to be gender-specific, unambiguously referring to a man.

The essential meaning of *junzi* is an aspirational version of yourself, or your higher self. Using Freudian terminology, 君子 is the superego. Thus,

I've opted to translate 君子 to "sage," though implying the full meaning of "scholar-sage."

In a literal sense, translating "君子" to scholar-sage is incorrect. Yet in the context of how I'm presenting the Oracle, "scholar-sage" or "sage" best conveys the aspirational higher self. The purpose of divination is to embody the sage within.

| 小人 xiǎo rén Xiaoren | **The adversary.** Antonym to the *junzi*. The adversary is someone in direct opposition to you, the *junzi*. This is someone with malicious intention, or more figuratively, the inner voice that tries to destroy everything your higher self wants to build. This term as used in the Oracle could also indicate someone short-sighted, self-interested, unethical, and malicious. This is an agency of social and spiritual harm. The adversary is also referred to as a common person, a commoner, the wicked, the unprincipled, or the unscrupulous, to indicate one who does not hold power but lusts after it. The designation is of low status, but one arrogant enough to be delusional. |
|---|---|
| 大人 dà rén Daren | **The eminent one.** A virtuous one who holds power and status. In the context of what your loftiest goal is, the eminent one has actualized that goal. This is someone noteworthy and of distinction. In contrast, while the *junzi* (sage) is virtuous and ethical, the sage is not one who necessarily holds power or status like an eminent one. References to an eminent one denote someone of high social rank or repute, someone prominent. Alternatively, the designation represents who you can be, and who the Oracle is pushing you to become. |

Related to the *junzi* are two epithets that repeat throughout the Book. A direct translation of "小人" might be little person or lesser, inferior person, and "大人" would be a bigger person or greater, superior person. Direct translations here do a disservice to the original meaning.

Epithets are used here by the Oracle precisely to keep the designations versatile. Depending on context, the words take on different meanings.

Confucianism focuses a great deal on social hierarchy and class rank. *Xiaoren* is used to designate a commoner, someone uneducated and unrefined. This is the one of lesser social status. *Daren* designates the eminent scholar, one who has cultivated great virtues and is educated, civilized, and cultured. This is the one of higher social status.

*Xiaoren*, from your vantage point, can indicate an opposition, an adversary, a critic, or a challenger. This is someone who is on a mission to see you fail. *Daren*, from your vantage point, is someone with more resources or more power than you, someone you can go to for advice, someone you trust and who is trustworthy.

A modern psychological interpretation would be to view them as two aspects of the inner self. They are two inner voices. *Xiaoren* is negative self-talk and the proverbial little demon on your shoulder. *Daren* is positive self-talk and your higher angel appealing to you to be a better version of yourself.

A commonly established characterization of *xiaoren* by I Ching scholars is as the antonym to *junzi*. *Xiaoren* is the personality force challenging and trying to negate the virtues of the *junzi*. In some passages, I've followed established precedent and translated *xiaoren* to the commoner. When you see the term "commoner," it refers to either you in your erred and flawed state or those around you who are flawed. The commoner or the *xiaoren* suggests one who has not yet mastered the conscious self, someone yet to master control over thoughts and emotions.

Meanwhile, *daren* is an advanced *junzi*, one with power, prestige, and authority, whereas *junzi* merely implies someone wise and ethical, but not necessarily someone holding power, prestige, or authority. A *junzi* is thus someone who idealizes about change, whereas a *daren* actually has the ability to fulfill that change.

In my translations and annotations, I've interpreted *xiaoren* as the adversary, which can be interpreted as either an actual party to the situation who is occupying that role and those characteristics, or as a figurative expression of the inner voice that's pushing you in the wrong direction. *Daren* is translated as the eminent one. If the sage is your higher self, then the eminent one is your higher self who has actualized power and prestige. The eminent one could also take on a more mundane meaning, such as a local community leader, a partner at your firm whom you can trust and who is like a mentor to you, a professor, an expert in a particular field, or someone who inspires you.

## "There Is No Blame"

| | | |
|---|---|---|
| 橆 | 無 | Negation of the subsequent word. "Not" or "no." Without. *Pictogram:* Image of two individuals holding hands in dance or movement. |
| 訡 | 咎 | Error, mistake; fault, blame. Calamity or misfortune caused by an error in judgment that could have been avoided. Failure or omission that results in harm. |

Throughout the *I Ching,* one phrase is repeated with frequency: "無咎" *(wú jiù),* "there is no blame," along with references to "no fault," "no blame," or "no errors are made." The phrase is often translated into English as "blameless."

How this line *wu jiu* or "there is no blame" is to be interpreted has been a subject of debate, with differing perspectives. Consider different perspectives and then formulate your own.

The Xici, the Great Treatise I of the Ten Wings, explains that references to "there is no blame" or "there is no error" are indications that you have been, are, or will be rectifying your own errors, and therefore all will be corrected in its own time.[4]

For me, on one level, *wu jiu* is an indication to not assign fault. What has happened was part of the natural course of events, a force majeure or "act of God" that you cannot try to peg onto any one individual or even on a group of people, so don't try.

I also interpret *wu jiu* as, essentially, "no harm, no foul." Perhaps you've erred in the past. Mistakes were made. You weren't your best self. Nevertheless, no harm was caused by the errors or omissions, and therefore no negative karma has been incurred, or no detrimental consequences will come of it.

*Jiu* also bears with it the connotation of regret, *metameleia,* a sharp form of suffering tinged by overwhelming self-condemnation, causing personal suffering and unhappiness. When "there is no blame" comes up in a reading, the Oracle is trying to coax you out of that condition. Do not wallow in that kind of suffering and self-condemnation, because in the matter at hand, it isn't warranted. There is no reason to regret your past deeds. Do not blame yourself. Do not punish yourself. As the word is often translated, the Oracle affirms that you are blameless.

Whereas *ji* 吉 is a fortuitous omen and *xiong* 凶 does not bode well for the matter at hand, *wu jiu* 無咎 in effect indicates a neutral state; the Oracle is saying, "it is what it is." Thus, when you see "blameless" or "no blame" in translations of the Zhouyi, it means that no harm will come to you despite faults made; the situation isn't ideal, but it isn't detrimental either.

## "Endeavor for Corrective Measures"

An alternate forecast of misfortune comes in the form of 吝 *(lìn)*. James Legge translates "吝" as "regret," while Richard Wilhelm (per the English translation by Cary F. Baynes) interprets it as "humiliation."

When you see references to regret, remorse, or humiliation in the Book's message, the Oracle is saying to you: "Endeavor for corrective measures."

I interpret *lìn* as a warning of a petty, suspicious, or uncharitable personality, which will result in negative consequences. This is the Oracle detecting someone who is petty, perhaps a hoarder, a pessimist, someone not being magnanimous and generous, but rather hoarding wealth selfishly. This might also indicate someone predisposed to negative thinking and therefore manifesting self-fulfilling prophecies of negative outcomes. "吝" suggests self-inflicted harm and therefore a negative outcome that is entirely within your control to prevent.

Basically, "吝" is the Oracle calling you out. There is an implication of prognosticating challenges and regret, but whereas "凶" suggests the misfortune might be beyond your control or is happening after a long chain of karmic consequences have played out, "吝" is a warning, and therefore the negative prediction is still preventable. In fact, any negative outcome when the forecast is "吝" means the cause of the outcome is your own personality. Thus, it's the Oracle counseling you to adjust your personality and correct your behavior. I've translated "吝" to "endeavor for corrective measures" as a reminder that the matter is still within your control, but an adjustment of your frame of mind is in order.

Also, whereas "無咎" *(wú jiù)*, or "there is no blame," suggests innocent errors made that won't result in detriment, "吝" *(lìn)* is a prescription for a personality adjustment. Your perspective on the matter at hand, your behavior or conduct or disposition needs to be corrected; otherwise you are causing your own grief.

## "Crossing the Great Stream"
# 利涉大川
*Lì shè dà chuān*

There are dozens of references in the I Ching to "利涉大川 lì shè dà chuān," which translates to "cross the great stream," or in the negative, "不利涉大川," meaning do *not* cross the great stream at this time. The phrase "涉大川" can also be preceded by "用," essentially indicating "action required," or employ, use, move forward in the crossing of the great stream.

When you see references to crossing the great stream, the divinatory message is to be bold and take initiative, to undertake the great challenge that is being presented to you. It's an acknowledgement that what is to come is a hazardous enterprise or a matter in which you are likely to encounter great difficulties.

Historically, "crossing the great stream" refers to the Yellow River, which King Wu of Zhou (King Wen's son) and the Zhou forces had to cross in their revolution against the tyrannical King Zhou of Shang. The crossing made by King Wu in 1122 BC was one of the great deeds in the history of China and was preceded by a long period of waiting until his success could be assured.

The image here is of one being tasked to build a boat and then to sail that boat across a great river. "To build a boat" is a metaphor for utilizing the resources you have access to, no matter how limited, and for optimizing your skills. Reflect on what your assets and talents are. Utilize those with greater effect. There's an underlying implication here that you aren't living up to your potential right now, and the Oracle is pushing you to step up and be better.

The "great stream" is a difficult and even visionary undertaking, one that will demand a great deal of labor from you. When the oracle message is "it is auspicious to cross the great stream," it means go forward. All is well. When it says "not auspicious to cross the great stream at this time," then there are still preparations that need to be made before you should go forward, so hold back for now. You still need to hone your skills and talents to a more refined level before you can utilize them to "build a boat" and cross that stream.

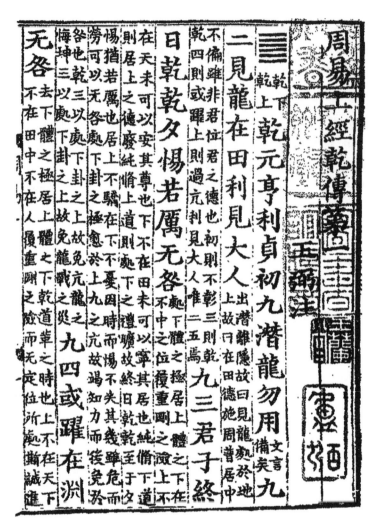

**FIGURE 8.3** Scanned page of Hexagram 1, Zhouyi in the *Siku Quanshu* (四庫全書). Sacred texts compiled by Emperor Qianlong (1711–1799).

有求必應
*Yǒu qiú bì yìng*
If there is a request, it shall be answered.

# Hexagram 1: Qián. Creative Power

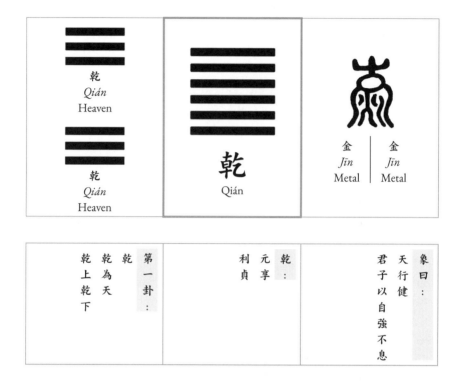

## The Oracle

Heaven's blessing: the creative power awakens a dragon. What had been hidden is now ascending. Take pause before you proceed on your endeavor. Be assured of your course of action before you proceed. Know who you are. Know where you came from. Be humble and modest. Be above reproach— then those who seek to harm will be rendered harmless. You will become the dragon that emerges from the depths, visible and rising above your peers. A pillar of beneficent astral light guides your movements. You face a moment of choice: the temporal or the spiritual. Endurance and patience will be required of you, as what is to unfold shall do so for a prolonged length of time.

**The *qi* of Heaven is full of vigor, powerful in action, and heals what is ailing. Harnessing the *qi* of Heaven, the sage strives to be strong and capable, and never ceases in that striving. Know what is weak within you and strengthen it.** The sage maintains power by using that power for the greater good, aligned with the Divine, and not to further any self-interest.

When the directive power above increases, so does the direct power below. It is now a period of expansion for you.

**Sublime success. Favors bestowed from Heaven.**

Ruling a splendorous kingdom; bestowed with the graces of Heaven and furthering the endeavor toward greatness. You are a pioneer; you wield both creativity and perseverance.

Take pause before you proceed on your endeavor. Do not act on impulse; instead, be a channel for the directive power of heaven. There is a marked difference between hearing your ego and listening to the voice of Divinity. Listen to the directive voice of Divinity.

You want to be assured of your course of action before you proceed. Once you are assured of your course of action, act swiftly, firmly, and with conviction. You will not go wrong.

You will become the dragon that emerges from the depths and becomes visible, rising above your peers.

Know who you are before you proceed. Know where you want to go.

If and when you can say for certain to yourself who you are and where you want to go, your creative power shall align with your Will, and your Will shall align with Divine Will, and Divine Will shall bring you immense success and fulfillment.

| *First Line* <br> **Hidden dragon. No movement.** | 潛龍勿用 | 初九曰： |
|---|---|---|

Great power and potential are about to burst, but at the present moment, they are still latent, hidden from view, a secret.

The lay of the land looks still, but much is going on underneath.
Power is implied.
You have not yet found the right opportunity to manifest your full capabilities. At this time, do not act on impulse. Think before you act.
"潛 Qián" suggests that the dragon is hidden submerged under water, moving beneath the surface. And yet concentrated power, force, and effort are going on. The dragon is lurking out of sight, and yet plotting, waiting to rise.

| *Second Line* <br> **A dragon seen in the field.** <br> **Favorable to meet the eminent one.** | 利見大人 | 見龍在田 | 九二曰： | ▬▬▬▬ <br> ▬▬▬▬ <br> ▬▬▬▬ <br> ▬ ▬ <br> ▬▬▬▬ <br> ▬▬▬▬ |

What had been hidden is now ascending. Great power is seen. The eminent one will show you the way. You have talent, but you need guidance.
Like will attract like, and that which is contrary will dilute you. Be cautious of who you associate with. Only associate with those who empower, amplify, and support you.
At this time it is beneficial to associate with one in a position of power who can influence others. It is now time to make your appearance. You are ready to be seen, so be seen. Make your entrance into society.
Show up, appearing as the dragon appears in the field.
You are destined to gain great influence.

| *Third Line* <br> **The sage forges and builds until the end of the day, until exhaustion. Nightfall under the light of the crescent moon, stay cautious, alert; stay sharp.** <br> **Be perseverant by day, be vigilant by night; then no harm will come.** | 無咎 | 夕惕若厲 | 君子終日乾乾 | 九三曰： | ▬▬▬▬ <br> ▬▬▬▬ <br> ▬ ▬ <br> ▬▬▬▬ <br> ▬▬▬▬ <br> ▬▬▬▬ |

When the sun shines and life-giving energy is around you, create and be productive. Persevere. Be diligent. Work.

When the day's work is done and night falls, stay alert. Be protective and guard what you've built. Power rising is seen, inviting wicked forces to tamper beneath the cloak of night.

There are risks involved, and uncertainty. Keep to the pace of the Divine, slow when it is slow, fast when it is fast. Do so and no mistakes will be made.

Be above reproach—then those who seek to harm will be rendered harmless.

---

*Fourth Line*
**Perhaps the dragon will leap into the abyss, delving upon the profound.**
**Remaining faultless; no harm shall come.**

九四曰：
或躍在淵
無咎

---

An ascending dragon comes to a crossroads. You are in a transitional period. The dragon will either remain in the profane or the dragon will take a leap of faith into the abyss, and delve into the profound.

You face a moment of choice.

One choice is a life in public service, in the sunlight where the dragon flies among the clouds.

The other choice is in solitude and privacy, where the dragon becomes king of an unknown abyss.

Both will bring you fulfillment. Both will have challenges. It is up to you which you shall choose. No choice is better than the other.

Divine Will cares not which you choose—both lead to success. Either path will yield success and fruition. No blame and no harm shall befall. You decide whether to bask in the sunlight by the shores or plunge submerged in a mysterious uncharted void.

---

*Fifth Line*
**Flying dragon in the heavens.**
**Favorable to meet the eminent one.**

九五曰：
飛龍在天
利見大人

You are destined for greatness and will attain a position of respect. Many will follow you. First, you must cultivate discipline, greater depth of knowledge, and wisdom, and gain in experience to ensure that you are worthy of the title you will be granted.

The narrative arc from the hidden dragon in the first line to the flying dragon in the fifth is symbolic of achieving prosperity and heightened status.

| *Sixth Line*<br>**The arrogant and reckless dragon will repent.** | 亢龍有悔 | 上九曰： | ▬▬▬▬▬<br>▬▬▬▬▬<br>▬▬▬▬▬<br>▬▬▬▬▬<br>▬▬▬▬▬<br>▬▬▬▬▬ |

Do not forget where you came from. Remain humble. Stay modest. Live the simple life. Be obliging and reverential.

If you misuse or misdirect your creative powers, Heaven will retract the blessings you have been endowed with.

Heed this message with care.

## THE CHANGING SIXTH LINE

If all six lines in the divination are changing lines into Hexagram 2, then the following Great Change will apply.

| *The Great Change*<br>**Encountering a flock of dragons, but no chief.**<br>　**Auspicious to proceed.**<br>**Heaven's Will is aligned in your favor.** | 吉見群龍無首 | 用九： | ▬▬▬▬▬<br>▬▬▬▬▬<br>▬▬▬▬▬<br>▬▬▬▬▬<br>▬▬▬▬▬<br>▬▬▬▬▬ |

A gathering of the powerful in need of a leader. They will look to you.

The head must be the thinker and the visionary. You have become the eminent one.

# THE JADE EMPEROR 玉帝

Heaven is an omen of the Jade Emperor 玉帝 (Yù Dì), the Heavenly Lord 天公 (Tiān Gōng). An equivalent Heavenly Lord is also found in both Vietnamese (Ông Trời) and Korean (하늘님) folk religions.

Hexagram 1 can be used in ritual magic and spell-crafting to invoke the Jade Emperor; in divination, it is a sign of a blessing from the Heavenly Lord.

The Jade Emperor is a primordial god, one of the Three Pure Ones, and ruler of Heaven. The lore around the Jade Emperor is diverse. He's a chief god in the Taoist pantheon invoked during ritual magic. Some traditions treat him as distinct from Shangdi, while others consider the Jade Emperor and Shangdi to be synonymous. Some see him as an emanation of Taiyi 太一, the divine personification of the eternal Tao and associated with the polestar, while others would say they're different gods.

The Jade Emperor is invoked and prayed to for blessings of prosperity, protection, and curing of illness.

**FIGURE 8.4** Jade Emperor and the heavenly kings (1545). SOURCE: Yonghe Temple 雍和宮, Beijing.

# Hexagram 2: Kūn. Supportive Power

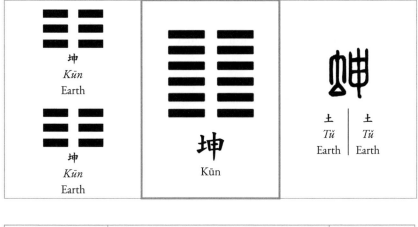

## The Oracle

To receive, be receptive. Embrace the power of yielding, and you shall receive. Clear a pathway, and what you seek shall come to you. Supportive power is the blessing of finishing to completion. In the depths of darkness, attainment awaits. Be yielding, and the powers that be will yield to you. A heart receptive to faith will never fear darkness or uncertainty. You are blessed with knowledge and intuition, twin pillars formed from the image of divine yin, and you are a vessel for healing and receiving sustenance.

**Earth yields to earth:** the way to success for you is by being receptive and yielding.

**Submit to the Divine and your journey will take you to meet a great master. Be soft, be tender, be accommodating.**

Leading yourself will lead you astray. Follow, and you will find your way.

Attainment, gains, and prosperity—**a mare gallops across the soft, fertile earth. The stallion gallops behind her.** You must be the mare.

Yielding is the true way to lead. **The aspiring sage tries to lead by charging, but takes the wrong direction and goes astray. To succeed, the aspiring sage must yield.**

**Support from the southwest proves to be allies.** Friends are found in the countryside and the small towns; among the mothers, farmers, artisans, and masses.

**Support from the northeast will bring misfortune.** Beware the caves, the dark caverns, and the dense forest.

Take instruction, and complete another's task. Then you will be closer to achieving your own.

Peace comes when you find contentment with what you possess. Your moment for achieving your greatest ambition will come. For now, receive nourishment and healing.

Harness the force and power of soft earth. Like the earth, the sage accepts the character of all, for better or for worse, and nurtures all with compassion, without exception.

*Note:* the theme of the southwest being positive and the northeast being negative appears again in Hexagram 39.

## OMEN OF THE *QILIN*

The lines "support from the southwest proves to be allies" and "support from the northeast will bring misfortune" are historical references to the rebel Zhou dynasty in the west and the Shang dynasty in the east.

The trigrams Earth and Mountain summon the *qilin* (麒麟), also known as a *kirin*. The *qilin* is a mythical beast that appears to portend a significant, transformative event relating to a sage or leader. In the I Ching, Hexagrams 2, 15, 23, and 52 are likened to the omen of seeing a *qilin* appear before you—these hexagrams are omens of a significant, transformative event to come. Here in the case of Hexagram 2, the rise to power is coming, but that moment is not here yet. Wait it out. Return for a subsequent divination to confirm when the time will be right.

| First Line<br>Treading on frost. It hardens ever so. Solid ice up ahead. | 履霜堅冰至 | 初六： |
|---|---|---|

If you know now that you are not yet ready for the hard ice, then do not proceed.

You see the frost under your feet already. It is a warning that colder weather is ahead.

Travel on designated roads only. Now is not the time to be a pioneer. Walk the path that others have paved. Follow. Be safe. What you experience now is only frost.

It will get harder before it gets easier. Thus, it is not the right time to be a pioneer.

Safety and security first. Wait until the worst is over.

| Second Line<br>Straight and forthright, generous and wide.<br>It is not yet time to take flight.<br>Not unfavorable. | 不習無不利 | 直方大 | 六二： |
|---|---|---|---|

The image here is of one fluttering your wings, endeavoring to rise. Yet the Oracle is advising that it is not the right time for you. It is more beneficial to do nothing.

What's more, your approach needs work. Instead of being efficient and taking the shortest routes to your destination, you like to wander and go on tangents. Though wandering on tangents might not be advised, broadening your base of knowledge and experiences so it is wide *is* advised.

Stay focused on the one task at hand. Stability and consistency ought to be the focus.

The second line is about being seen, but not yet heard. Be large. Occupy physical space. Be present. However, there is no need to act or speak, only be. Inaction at this time will bear advantage and gains later on.

> **Third Line**
> Contain impulses. Leave thoughts unspoken when administering the affairs of the king.
> A task left unfinished after its ending.
>
> 六三：
> 含章可貞
> 或從王事
> 無成有終

Appear to comply while quietly asserting noncompliance.

The implication of the third line is to complete the task assigned, but you won't be completing the mission, meaning your greater objective.

At this time, show restraint. In the service of a king, do not strive for accomplishment; rather, strive for completion of the task. This is not the time to exceed. Excess will be wasted effort. Hide what you are capable of for now, so as not to attract attention, especially envy or hostility.

The essence of "含章可貞" *(hán zhāng kě zhēn)* is to write what you're thinking and feeling on your chest, and nowhere else—keep your words contained within a closed mouth; harbor your emotions. Do not openly express what's really on your mind, and don't divulge your personal objectives, at least not right now and not in this particular situation.

When you have talent, do not flaunt it. The third line affirms that you are gifted and virtuous, but rein yourself in so you are being subtle and not letting all your cards show.

When you present yourself as if you don't know what you're doing, meanwhile remaining actively studious and discerning so that you know exactly what you're doing, all those around you will reveal their secrets and weaknesses to you.

Restraint is critical for future long-term success.

> **Fourth Line**
> Tie the satchel closed and knot it tight.
> There is no fault, and there is no praise.
> Neither wrong nor right.
>
> 六四：
> 括囊
> 無咎無譽

Any prominence at all will be stricken down. Do not be prominent.
What seems important to you is not essential.

Stop thinking about what you want, and you will attain it.

For now, act according to the will of others, and conceal your own intentions.
　While no praise will come to you, no blame will come either.

Success will hinge on discretion.

Tying the satchel closed and knotting it tight is a reference to keeping silent, keeping secrets. This is to contain within the mind a great deal of valuable knowledge, but concealing what you know. Here, the mouth of the satchel is being compared to your mouth—seal your lips. You won't be praised for your silence, but you won't be blamed for it either.

| *Fifth Line*<br>Wearing the golden skirt.<br>A sign of great eminence. | 黄裳元吉 | 六五： | ䷁ |

The golden skirt signifies prominence and high rank.

You are intelligent, cultured, and elegant, but to be these traits is also contingent on humility, being soft, tender, and accommodating. Harness these traits and you will achieve eminence.

It is not necessary to assert your status with words. You wear the golden skirt, meaning you embody that status with your mere presence. Approach with the disposition of conveying your status by your very presence, not by boasting, puffery, or other inferior methods. If you must tell people who or what you are, then you are not that at all.

| *Sixth Line*<br>When dragons battle in the wild,<br>their blood spills indigo and yellow. | 其血玄黄 龍戰于野 | 上六： | ䷁ |

Interpretations vary as to whether the notation means indigo, black, dark blue, or purple. In any of these instances, the indication is of a great power struggle between you and another, with injury sustained by both sides.

You leave the receptive divine yin position to emerge and overthrow the incumbent.

The sixth line is also interpreted as a cautionary tale to not become arrogant, and to not react as a result of wounded pride.

Traditionally, in the context of the sixth line, "玄" *(xuán)* is interpreted as a dark indigo color, almost black, but with tinges of deep blues and violets.

"玄" *(xuán)* is black, but not *entirely* black either, as painters might appreciate. This is the same word 玄 that appears in the name 九天玄女, Lady of the Nine Heavens. In Taoist mysticism, the Lady of the Nine Heavens is characterized as a divine, pure form of yin as expressed in Hexagram 2. There might also be a subtext here referring to the first meeting between the Mysterious Lady and the Yellow Emperor, though that reference is further obscured and presented in riddle, so that the riddle might apply to your present situation. Also, the color contrast between the dark purple tones of indigo and yellow reflects the yin–yang contrast through color theory.

If the sixth line is the changing line in the divination, then you will succeed in the overthrow. If not, then the outcome still remains uncertain at this time.

## THE CHANGING SIXTH LINE

If all six lines in the divination are changing lines into Hexagram 1, then the following Great Change will apply.

| *The Great Change* <br> **Reaping good auspices for an eon.** | 利永貞 | 用六： | ䷁ |
|---|---|---|---|

You will enjoy long-lasting prosperity. Great success that will endure. Stability, security, and good fortune will be yours.

# HOUTU, THE EARTH GODDESS 后土

Hexagram 2 brings you into the presence of Houtu, a divinity whose gender was ambiguous in early Zhou dynasty records (1050–221 BC). Early records of Houtu described a male deity, while others described Houtu as female. Hexagram 2 in ritual magic invokes Houtu, and when it comes up in divination, it is an omen that the goddess is present.

She's also known as De Mǔ 地母, or Mother Earth. Myths of Houtu often involve gender-bending, such as the goddess Houtu transforming into a man to defeat an evil ogre.[5] Only later was Houtu's gender clarified, and she was described as an earth goddess, given the title Queen of the Earth and Houtu the Sacred Mother.

Houtu has the power to grant abundant harvests and bring rain. In Taoist magic, invoke Houtu in weather magic for bringing rain, a mild winter, or a mild summer. She protects children, ensures safe childbirths, and can be invoked to bring blessings of health and longevity. Since she is the goddess of the Earth, she is also prayed to for ensuring safe travels.

The Earth Goddess is also a ruler in the underworld, similar to Emperor Dongyyue (the underworld god associated with Hexagram 52).

In addition to the myth of assisting Yu the Great, she was a patron goddess of the beneficent Emperor Wen of Han 漢文帝 (203–157 BCE) and his grandson, Emperor Wu of Han 孝武皇帝 (156–87 BCE) of the Han dynasty.[6]

# Hexagram 3: Tún. Initial Challenge

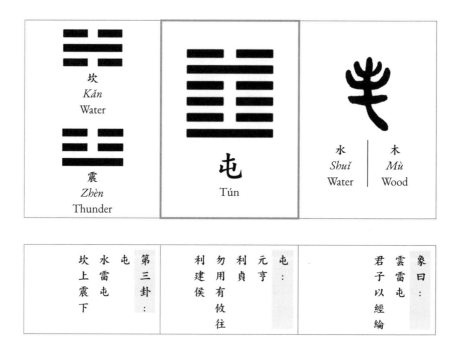

## The Oracle

Challenges at the beginning leave you feeling defeated. You have not been defeated. The matter is merely in an undeveloped stage. You have been challenged. Failures at the beginning, even repeated missteps, are blessings of strength. When you finally succeed, it will far surpass any success that came before, and you will hold on to it with longevity. Such is the blessing Heaven seeks to endow you with. Initial challenges are the mysterious ways of the Tao.

Difficulty at the beginning: a blade of grass will push against its obstacle when it sprouts out of the earth. The first meeting of heaven and earth is often beset with difficulties.

**The sage shall sort the silk threads and braid them.** By means and ability, you meet with great auspices and prosper. Your will is in alignment with Heaven's Will. Favorable gains for the marquis's undertaking.

**Rain and lightning atop the hill.** There will be a thunderstorm, then tensions will be released. Rain will fill the air, but the rain clears the chaos. You will bring order out of the confusion.

Thunder and lightning atop the hill. It is a military base.

"經綸," which is conveyed in the Oracle as the sage sorting silk threads and braiding them, is a metaphor for planning and governing a nation soon to become a rising power, or planning and organizing for a major event to come.

"勿" suggests a ritual knife used for a sacrificial offering to the gods, and "攸" is the ideogram of a purification ritual.

It is a time of personal growth. What you plant now is only a seed, dormant in the earth; but when moisture awakens it, that seed has the power to grow strong, so strong as to split rocks. Likewise, for now, you must store your energy, build momentum slowly and steadily, and prepare for the sudden breakthrough.

**You nurture within you a rising power. An auspicious omen. Favors bestowed.**

In summary, Hexagram 3 indicates environmental or social setbacks that cause initial hindrances with conception or the gestation period. However, the final prognostication is fortuitous. You'll realize that everything you went through was worth it.

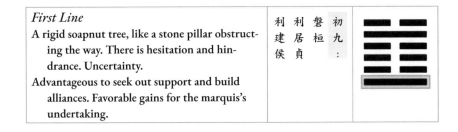

| *First Line* <br> A rigid soapnut tree, like a stone pillar obstructing the way. There is hesitation and hindrance. Uncertainty. <br> Advantageous to seek out support and build alliances. Favorable gains for the marquis's undertaking. | 利建侯 利居貞 磐桓 初九： | |

Signs point in one direction, but you contemplate walking another.

A setback leaves you hesitating and uncertain. Persevere. It is no small task for a seed to sprout and break through rock, push up against gravity, and reach up to breathe the fresh air. Yet that is the seed's destiny. You are the seed.

Pray to the Divine. Petition your gods and ancestors for support. Lean toward the sunlight. Humble acknowledgement that you don't control everything will advance you further than forcing personal control over the situation.

The historical meaning ascribed to "利建侯" is the image of constructing a clear target for your arrows, or defining your objectives before you aim and shoot. The Oracle's message in the phrase is to demonstrate clarity of mind and determination, and to persevere until the end, even if we fail in the beginning.

*Note*: In antiquity, the nuts (or berries) from the soapnut tree 桓 huán were used as medicine to treat various illnesses, such as skin diseases, eczema, epilepsy, inflammations, and stomach pains, and to ward off disease (soapnuts have antibacterial and antimicrobial properties). It was valued as a cleanser and could be fashioned into amulets to ward off evil. Here, however, the reference to a soapnut tree can also be a reference to a pillar signpost.

| | |
|---|---|
| *Second Line*<br>Ingress and egress for the hamlet are blocked: difficulty in the advance, and so you falter.<br>The cavalry is in pursuit. They attack, seizing an opportunity.<br>They are mistaken for bandits when they have come to seek marriage.<br>The maiden finds it difficult to conceive. Ten years pass before she delivers. | 十年乃字　女子貞不字　匪寇婚媾　乘馬班如　屯如邅如　六二： |

The going will get harder, and progress will be hindered. There are delays. The cavalry falls back. You now feel unsure of your own mission.

"Mistaken for bandits when they have come to seek marriage" refers to the custom of marriage abduction or kidnapping the bride before the marriage ceremony.

Ten years represents a whole cycle. You are at the beginning of a new cycle, and there is much more to endure before you attain success.

### Third Line
Chasing a deer into the forest. It is not
 a *zouyu*. Hunting unaccompanied by
 the officer of the grounds.
The sage knows when to turn back.
Going forward brings regret.

六三：
即鹿無虞
惟入于林中
君子幾不如舍
往吝

With neither guide nor direction, the hunter runs into a forest chasing after a deer. Evaluating the situation, the sage would forbear from proceeding.

Be still. In stillness, find your center. Consolidate and conserve. Endeavor for corrective measures before proceeding.

You've chased after an objective without clarity and without planning. Now you're lost in the woods. A state of confusion sets in.

When lost, do not wander. Desperation tempts you to wander, but the philosopher-sage will remain still. Stay where you are. Trace your steps backward.

The virtue to adopt is centering.

Forgo the objective. Forget the deer. It was never a *zouyu*. Priorities have shifted.

"虞" *(yú)* is an ancient officer title for one in charge of managing forests and hunting grounds. To go hunting unaccompanied by the officer of the grounds, especially when you are inexperienced, would be unwise.

The term can also be read as implying a subtext that further underscores how inexperienced the hunter is: "虞" *(yú)* can also imply through homonymy the *zouyu* (騶虞, *zōu yú*), a mythical creature likened to a *qilin*. The unspoken implication is that one is so inexperienced (to the point of being unrealistic) that a deer is mistaken for a *zouyu*, which is what compels the naïve hunter to chase the creature into the forest without a more experienced guide.

The Ten Wings commentary for Hexagram 45 draws upon the imagery of the *zouyu*, and the legend of the creature is further explained in that section of this book.

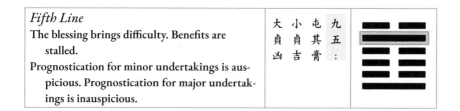

| Fourth Line |
|---|
| Horse and chariot ready, but without direction. Seek an alliance before advancing. To go forth in unity is auspicious for all. |

You think you're prepared to move forward, but you lack direction. Bring together what you have been keeping separate, and merged as one, you'll realize newfound strength.

Counsel at this stage: join an alliance. Contribute to a greater force.

| Fifth Line |
|---|
| The blessing brings difficulty. Benefits are stalled. Prognostication for minor undertakings is auspicious. Prognostication for major undertakings is inauspicious. |

External forces of opposition are substantial, and you will feel tempted to try to beat them with a greater and equal force of your own. That is unwise and will not yield positive or productive results.

Instead, acknowledge the opposition and proceed with calculated, measured, small steps. Persevere on the small scale. Small step by small step, you will wear away the opposing force and prevail.

Do not try to swing the hammer with one great force, or you will lose. Instead, chip away diligently, little by little.

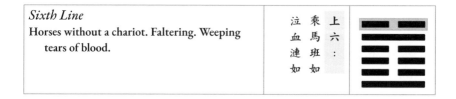

| Sixth Line |
|---|
| Horses without a chariot. Faltering. Weeping tears of blood. |

An untamed situation. You are not in control. Knowing that you are unable to control the situation is causing you to falter.

After failing to overcome initial difficulties, you falter and lose your perspective. Dangers compound when you lose your perspective.

"乘馬班如" in antiquity implies a row of four horses pulling a chariot. The four yin lines in this hexagram signify the four horses, but a single yang line breaks them up from orderly formation. Thus, here in the sixth line, there is the image of a single lost horse, out of formation and having separated from the three.

Whether you prevail or not in your endeavor hinges on whether you can handle the difficulties at the beginning. Do not lose your temper, and do not be defeated by fear or anxiety.

## Hexagram 4: Méng. Naiveté

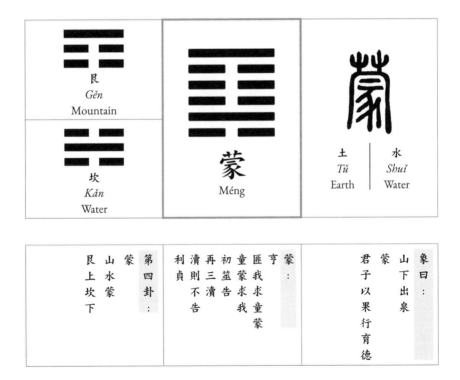

## The Oracle

> You are focused on the wrong inquiry. The Oracle shall give no further insight unless the inexperienced fool can return with proper sincerity. Seek out better teachings to learn better ways. Be aware of your inexperience. Acknowledge it. Your modesty will advance you much further than the fool feigning to be the master. This is the folly of inexperience. The solution is simple: greater nourishment and nurture.

**A favorable outcome** for the naïve but innocent. **I do not seek out the child. The child will seek me out.**
The child in the Oracle's statement is symbolic of one who is naïve, one who is still learning and in the developmental stage.
**When you encounter uncertainty, come to me. The first divination is the answer.**
**Repeated questioning shows contempt. I do not answer after the third.**
Self-correct, readjust your perspective, and you may perform a divination for the same question again. Reflect on the divination method and the state of your heart-mind before you begin. Proceed with sincerity and diligence.
I will answer the second divination.
If you are not sincere with me and you proceed with a third divination, then I will not be sincere with you.
In short, the Oracle is saying, "I will only help the self-seeker."
Yet the outcome prognosticated by Hexagram 4 is favorable. The philosophy of the Book is one of optimism—the Oracle operates on the faith that it is human nature to seek transcendence from our ignorance and naïveté. It is in our nature to want to grow.
Ignorance is pervasive. Yet to err is not evil. It is naïveté, and a result of inexperience.
Hexagram 4 comes up when one is indecisive, changing direction too often, initiating more undertakings than they can finish, and the Oracle is trying to tell you: stop, settle down, take a breath. Focus. Now try again.

# IS IT BLASPHEMOUS TO REPEATEDLY QUESTION THE ORACLE?

"瀆" *(dú)*, which appears twice in the statement "再三瀆, 瀆則不告," is translated as *contempt*. It also implies blasphemy.

Is it blasphemous to repeatedly question the Oracle? To be blasphemous is to be irreverent and impious toward that which is held as sacred, and that which concerns the Divine. If the I Ching isn't a sacred book and is just another text with historic and cultural significance, then no.

Within the context of the I Ching itself, however, the use of the word "瀆" in reference to repeating the same question to the Oracle three or more times is worth reflecting on.

At least traditionally, it was considered blasphemous to repeatedly question the Oracle, because it demonstrates that one isn't even willing to meet the Oracle halfway and try to interpret the message. It also demonstrates dissatisfaction with the answer and yet an unwillingness to take any affirmative action on our own to change the outcome.

If we are repeatedly dissatisfied with the Oracle's answer, then it proves two points to Heaven, both affirming that someone might not be the right vessel for the sacred.

First, if one does not approach divination with a methodical, orderly, and considerate process honoring the sacred so that the moment of divination is, indeed, divine, then there is too much chaos and restlessness in the heart to serve the gods.

Second, if one has approached divination in a methodical, orderly, and considerate process and received an answer but is still dissatisfied, then it's a sign of being too innately troubled and insecure to serve the gods.

| First Line |
|---|
| To enlighten the inexperienced fool, apply discipline. Fetters may be required, but in the extreme, become obstacles. Without knowledge of the terrain, a journey now will set you adrift. |

At present, you are the inexperienced fool. Law is the beginning of education. Establish an order by setting boundaries and restraints.

Stay steadfast in the moment before advancing.

Discipline ("fetters") must be applied, but take care not to become bound by regulation.

Too much binding and the mind will be constricted: injurious.

The objective of punishment is to teach, not to humiliate. Severe or prolonged punishment will do more harm than good.

| Second Line |
|---|
| Nurture the naïve: it will yield fruition. Impregnate the wife: it will yield fruition. Let the son take charge and ascend to head of the family. |

Appreciate the folly in humanity, and devote energy to develop it into wisdom.

Investments at this time will bring great returns. Now is an auspicious time for investments in the future.

It is also time for a change in leadership. Let the next generation ascend to the head. If you currently hold a position of power, it may be time to find a worthy successor.

| Third Line |
|---|
| Reject the maiden who loses possession of herself when she sees men of bronze. No grounds for harvest there. |

The maiden here is figurative, denoting a weaker character who superficially latches on to stronger characters. Weaker characters will always try to latch on to stronger characters. Reject weaker characters. They will hold you back. If someone shows you favor only when you have something material and of value to offer, decline to offer anything in return.

Likewise, if you are the one running desperately toward another to latch on to them for strength, then you are the weaker character. Audit yourself— are you showing someone favor only because that person has something material and of value to offer you? If that person had nothing to offer you, would you still show favor?

At present, it is better to stand on your own two feet and wait for others to come to you with propositions than to rush desperately toward others with yours.

Be cautious of those who only value you for what you can offer. Be cautious of the temptation to value people by their power.

| Fourth Line | | |
|---|---|---|
| The inexperienced fool is mired in confusion. Facing obstacles. Endeavor for corrective measures before proceeding. | 吝 困 蒙 | 六 四 ： |

You are not being receptive to wisdom and knowledge at this time. An adjustment of your mindset is needed.

The counsel here is to fall back. Do not proceed. You are not ready to advance yet.

| Fifth Line | | |
|---|---|---|
| Childlike naiveté is innocence. It is auspicious for the innocent to proceed. | 童 蒙 吉 | 六 五 ： |

A distinction needs to be made between inexperienced foolishness and childlike naiveté. While the former will bring you failure, the latter will bring you success.

Be humble, be open, and be receptive.

Be a child, innocent and ready to receive proper instruction. Subordinate yourself to the teachings of those wiser and more experienced.

| Sixth Line | | |
|---|---|---|
| No gains yielded from expelling the foe. No gains yielded from becoming a foe. Gains come from resisting the attack. | 利禦寇　不利為寇　上九擊蒙： | ▬▬▬<br>▬ ▬<br>▬ ▬<br>▬ ▬<br>▬▬▬<br>▬ ▬ |

Resolve darkness by shining the light in defense of your position. Do not try to resolve darkness by becoming the darkness. Defending yourself does not mean having to offend others. Prevent robbers from robbing, but do not become a robber yourself. Stand your ground against adversaries, but do not become adversarial.

# PRACTICUM 8.1:
# Reflections on the Oracle's Lesson to the Shaman-Medium

"匪我求童蒙，童蒙求我" *(Fěi wǒ qiú tóng méng, tóng méng qiú wǒ)* can bear a secondary meaning. "童" *(tóng)* is a form of shamanism found in East Asia, or *tongji* 童乩. The *tongji* is a spirit medium who channels spirits through the body and, while possessed, can then bless, heal, and prophesy.

*Tongji* is used interchangeably with *wū* 巫, a shaman (though that translation isn't precise). Note that the character for shaman 巫 is embedded into the word for divination 筮 as used in the Oracle message.

Thus, an implied secondary meaning of that passage is this:

I do not call upon the spirit medium.
The spirit medium will call upon me.

Here's how I interpret the statement: There are no chosen ones. We choose whether to take on the mantle of the medium or diviner. Like the child, we are not gifted a talent for growth; it is what we do. You do not need to be born gifted. Do not doubt whether you are a chosen one. That you doubt only means you are self-aware and humble.

Reading that line again, how would you interpret that statement?

For this practicum, free-write and journal your reflections on how you would interpret the foregoing statement and each of the progressive six lines of Hexagram 4. Apply the interpretation specifically to the framework of becoming the mystic.

Table 8.1 rephrases the six lines of Hexagram 4 to apply specifically to mystical cultivation. Read line 1 as words of advice to the mystic who is just starting out, be it as a witch, magician, psychic, medium, or occultist.

**TABLE 8.1** Interpreting Hexagram 4 as Guiding Principles for Mystical Cultivation

| | |
|---|---|
| 1 | To enlighten the inexperienced [mystic], apply discipline. Fetters may be required, but in the extreme, become obstacles. A journey [without knowledge of the terrain] will set you adrift. |
| 2 | Nurture the naïve: it will yield fruition. Impregnate the [womb of creative intuition]: it will yield fruition. Let [what you create from that womb] take charge. |
| 3 | Reject the [amateur mystic] who [prioritizes the materialistic over the spiritual]. No grounds for harvest there. |
| 4 | The [mystic] is mired in confusion. Facing obstacles. Endeavor for corrective measures before proceeding. |
| 5 | [The mystic's innocence is auspicious.] |
| 6 | No gains yielded from expelling the foe. No gains yielded from becoming a foe. Gains come from resisting the attack. |

Personally, I interpret line 2 as encouraging you to use what you learned in the stage of training in line 1 to create your own set of methods, which could very well diverge from orthodox tradition. Let your own methods take charge of your practice. You don't need to follow the old ways. Line 4 reads like the plateau, burnout stage, or midjourney crisis that advancing mystics often face. What does the "mystic's innocence" in line 5 mean to you? As for line 6, is that the Oracle advising against witch wars?

# Hexagram 5: Xū. Patience

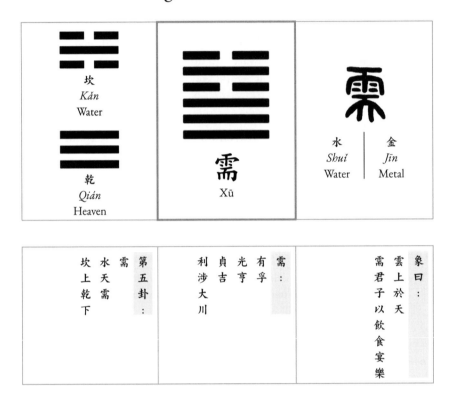

## The Oracle

You seek to advance just when dangers are at their peak. Wait it out. Cultivate patience. Let momentum build in the natural course, slow and steady. Heaven has set the course for an outcome in your favor, but patience is required. Do not force an outcome in a way that would not align with the Divine. Put your faith in the natural flow of events. Even when we pray or petition the gods and ancestors, they do not come because we've summoned them; they come because they've summoned us.

> Crows above the clouds. The sage is patient. At the banquet, match the jubilee of those at the table, and keep what is in your heart contained within the heart. Show contentment when the music plays.

# THE CROW AND THE TOTEMIC EMBLEM OF THE SHANG

"於 Yú" is a reference to a bird in the sky. As it corresponds with the trigram Water, it is implied that the bird is black, mysterious, or dark. Here, the crow is also a reference to the animal spirit associated with the Shang. The Shang had identified themselves with a bird described as a 玄鳥 *(xuán niǎo)* and adopted the bird as their totemic emblem,[7] specifically, the "天命玄鳥" (Tiān Mìng Xuán Niǎo), or Mysterious Heavenly Bird of Destiny.

Yes, that's the same "玄" as 九天玄女 (Jiǔ Tiān Xuán Nǚ), Lady of the Nine Heavens.

Over time, the Mysterious Heavenly Bird of Destiny and the Mysterious Lady of the Nine Heavens merged; thus the Lady is also associated with the Bird.

According to myth, a divine swallow-like raven, crow, or mysterious, mystical blackbird gave birth to the ancestors of the Shang.

Totemism, a word derived from the Ojibwa dialect, was first coined by French anthropologist Claude Lévi-Strauss (1908–2009) to signify that an animal serves as the emblem of a family or clan.[8] Archaeologists and scholars of ancient China then used the term *totemism* to describe the bird cult found throughout archaeological records of the Shang (1600–1046 BC).[9] Recently there has been a revival of totemistic theories to characterize the practice of identifying clans with particular animal emblems, and the religious phenomenon of a spirit animal as a tutelary deity protecting a family or clan throughout Asia since the Shang.[10]

Gaining the trust and confidence of others. Supreme auspices, illuminated by the Light of the gods.

**Auspicious to cross the great stream.** Having shown patience, aligned with Heaven's Will, the rain comes as one from Heaven descends in answer to a sage's patient prayer.

When facing a challenge, the situation will not change by a hasty force of will. One must wait and be patient. The outcome will come from the Divine. Put your faith in the natural flow of the Divine Will.

Clouds form in the sky and rise up toward heaven. The clouds must now wait for the harmony of heaven and earth to discharge its store of rain. Patience and prayers bring the rain. Do not force an outcome. Instead, have faith. All you can control is your mindset and your navigation of the situation one step and one moment at a time. Do not rush the results.

Know your purpose, and stay constant to that purpose. Crossing the great stream will be followed by meritorious achievement. Embodying perfected patience, undertake the challenge and rise to the occasion.

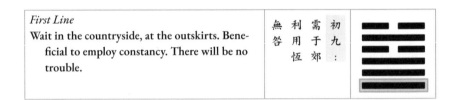

*First Line*
Wait in the countryside, at the outskirts. Beneficial to employ constancy. There will be no trouble.

In the wake of difficulties, do not react hastily. Instead, take no action. Wait.

Know your purpose and stay true. There is no need to prove anything to others right now. Stay out of visibility and there will be no trouble. Do not engage in action simply out of desperation. Wait out the storm.

To wait and confront peril with calculated inaction is the first lesson for prevailing against the turmoil of this world.

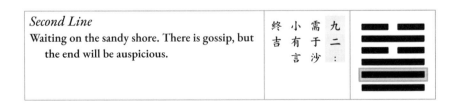

*Second Line*
Waiting on the sandy shore. There is gossip, but the end will be auspicious.

There is general unrest, and as a result, everyone is looking for someone to blame.
You must be the one who remains calm. Do not seek blame. That is not important.
Do not gratify slander with a response. Be silent. Through silence you will succeed.
Yet bear in mind the seriousness of the situation at hand. Be silent, but be alert and attentive.

| *Third Line* <br> Waiting in the mud will attract the swindler. | 致寇至 需于泥 九三： |
|---|---|

How did you end up in the mud anyway? You took action when you should have remained still. By taking premature action and leaving the sand, you end up in mud.
Where you are now exposes you to danger. Vulnerable positions attract those who seek to exploit that vulnerability.
Do not try to advance prematurely, or you will step in mud.

| *Fourth Line* <br> Lingering in blood: ominous. <br> Get out of the cave. | 出自穴 需于血 六四： |
|---|---|

You have found yourself in a perilous situation. Loss is imminent. There is risk of injury. At this point, it is not about advancing or retreating; it is about leaving the cave altogether.
Find a source of light and go in that direction. This is not the time for speaking; this is the time for listening. Run, retreat, and put as much distance between you and peril as you can.
The fourth line is also a reference to bloodletting. Drain out the toxin that is causing you illness.

| | | |
|---|---|---|
| *Fifth Line*<br>Lingering with food and wine. Perseverance brings good fortune.<br>Auspicious. | 貞 需 九<br>吉 于 五<br>　 酒 ：<br>　 食 | ▬▬▬▬▬<br>▬▬　▬▬<br>▬▬▬▬▬<br>▬▬▬▬▬<br>▬▬▬▬▬ |

There are intervals of peace between the crises. Enjoy that moment of peace, and do not lose it by worrying over the crises. Resting is not the same as procrastinating.

When the interval concludes, you will be ready to fight again and assert yourself.

Here is the underlying wisdom of the line: you must allow people their pleasure if you want them to work at their greatest capacity for you. The task will be completed faster if you give people their rest and respite. Likewise, give your body the rest and respite it needs so it can better serve your will.

| | | |
|---|---|---|
| *Sixth Line*<br>Entering the cave. Three uninvited guests arrive. Receive them and honor them.<br>In the end, there is good fortune. | 敬 有 入 上<br>之 不 于 六<br>終 速 穴 ：<br>吉 之　<br>　 客　<br>　 三　<br>　 人　<br>　 來 | ▬▬　▬▬<br>▬▬▬▬▬<br>▬▬▬▬▬<br>▬▬　▬▬<br>▬▬▬▬▬<br>▬▬　▬▬ |

Show reverence to the three uninvited guests you meet in the cave.

You will be sent three omens. Three spirits will be sent to come see you, at times when you least anticipate them—hence the "uninvited" description. They might be animal spirits, the voice of the Divine channeled through a person speaking to you, or visits in your dreams. Each arrival will bring a transcendent experience and insight.

A more mundane reading of the line is as prognostication that outside intervention will come. At first, you are reluctant to receive the help, but accept it.

It seems that after the waiting, destiny is clear: even after leaving the darkness of the cave, you are thrust right back into it. Nevertheless, yield to that fate and do not fight it. Be patient. There will be an unexpected turn of events.

There is no need to wallow alone. Accept help and honor those who help you with sincere gratitude. All will end well.

## Hexagram 6: Sòng. The Trial

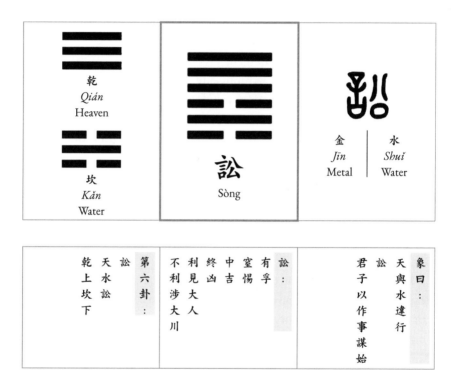

### The Oracle

Do not undertake hazardous enterprises. Conditions are ominous. Tensions beyond your control are giving rise to conflicts beyond your control, but you do possess the power to mitigate harm. This is also a time to reflect on inner conflicts and how to reconcile polarities within. Where you can reconcile, reach settlement. Do not let conflicts simmer for too long. Where you cannot make peace, move away from the conflict as expediently and quietly as you can. Heaven over Water is also an omen of entitlements clashing.

**Heaven moves upward and water moves downward.** Moving apart gives rise to tension. Tension gives rise to conflict.

**The sage will strategize a plan of action before initiating action.** Be farsighted, not nearsighted. **The sage prevails in disputes by avoiding them.**

Prisoners of war have been taken.

Stay where you are and remain alert. Let the situation come to a standstill. Challenges ahead. Foreboding adversity.

**Seek out the eminent one.** Until then, it is not auspicious to cross the great stream. Do not undertake hazardous enterprises.

Quarreling results in trials. Reflect on your own sense of entitlement to pinpoint the source of the conflict. The source of conflict is in the innate opposing tendencies. With two forces fundamentally moving away from one another, conflict is inevitable.

### AN OMEN OF CIVIL SUITS AND TENSIONS

Hexagrams 6 and 21 portend matters relating to law, governmental institutions, or politics.

Hexagram 6 can denote civil suits or tensions between two individuals head to head, or one group versus another group. In contrast, Hexagram 21 can denote criminal suits or tensions between one individual and the state, or one minority group versus the dominating majority group.

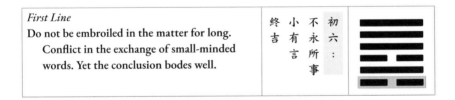

*First Line*
Do not be embroiled in the matter for long. Conflict in the exchange of small-minded words. Yet the conclusion bodes well.

You might not have been the instigator, but you had better yield, or there will be injury.

Utilize every opportunity to end conflict expediently. Break your adversary's resistance without fighting. A wise warrior avoids battle.

Words are weapons only if you let them hurt you. Resist the urge to swing back with your own words. Let the dispute dissipate by not engaging.

Do not endeavor to change your adversary. Endeavor to not let your adversary change you. Change on your own terms, and never in reaction to an opponent.

Yielding is virtuous. Asserting will exacerbate the conflict.

| |
|---|
| *Second Line* <br> It is fruitless to continue the conflict; you cannot be victorious in the contention. Retreat; return home. <br> By averting conflict, the grand master saves the three hundred families of the fiefdom. |

Your adversary has the upper hand. When you are not likely to succeed in this conflict, then it is wiser to retreat and not let the conflict start. If the conflict has started already, do your best to settle the dispute, even if it means personal sacrifice. A greater good will be served.

Be warned of trying to argue against an enemy more powerful than you. Do not let your pride, ego, or sense of honor draw you into an open conflict.

During the Zhou dynasty, a "邑 Yì" was the fiefdom of a grand master (大夫, *dàfū*), a chief administrator of a territory. The reference here is to a dispute between two grand masters, one powerful and unwise against one powerless but wise. The powerless but wise one does not engage in open conflict with the powerful, unwise one. If you are not likely to succeed in this conflict, then it is wiser to retreat and not let the conflict even start.

| |
|---|
| *Third Line* <br> Cultivate the heart-mind to be benevolent and virtuous. <br> The decision leads first into trouble, but then to prosperity. <br> If acting in service of the king, do not seek personal gain. |

Withdraw from the spotlight of the arena. Stay in the safety of the shadows. It is not yet the time to be noticed. Do not seek glory or acclaim.

Follow the prescriptions of tradition and stay strong to those traditions. In matters of public affairs or service, act for the greater good, not for your personal advancement. Think about others, and in this present matter, yield to the interest of others.

Swallow your pride. Do not start a conflict over wounded pride.

To be in service to the commoner is to be the rightful sovereign. In the way you bless the people, Heaven will bless you.

| | |
|---|---|
| *Fourth Line* <br> Do not engage in conflict that cannot be resolved. Retreat and submit to the Will of the Divine. <br> Peaceful determination and adjusting one's attitude will bring peace and prosperity. | 吉 安 復 不 九<br>貞 即 克 四<br>　 命 訟 ：<br>　 渝 |

The litigation will not be won. Your allies and your support are weak. You are in the minority position. The majority position is against you. Conflict does not end in your favor.

Therefore, it is better to do nothing so that nothing will be lost.

Accept the result peacefully and amicably. Tame your impulses. Return to an attitude of receptivity to the Divine's Will. You do not need to prove your position to others; you need to prove your position to Heaven.

| | |
|---|---|
| *Fifth Line* <br> Conflict ensues, but entering the contention can bring supreme good fortune. <br> A favorable outcome after the dispute. | 訟 九<br>元 五<br>吉 ： |

Wait for the right place and right time. When all factors are right, then you may engage in open conflict, because then you will succeed. Good omen. You may not prevail at first, but you will be the last one standing.

If the fifth line is the changing line, then you will prevail in the conflict, even against the odds. If not, then read the following counsel from the fourth line.

### THE CHANGING FIFTH LINE

**Accept the result peacefully and amicably. Tame your impulses. Return to an attitude of receptivity to the Divine's Will.**

| *Sixth Line* **Possessing the girdle of honor, and yet thrice before dawn, that honor is stripped away.** | 終朝三褫之 | 或錫之鞶帶 | 上九： |
|---|---|---|---|

Winning the conflict won't win you the respect you really want.

What you gain by force can be taken by force.

The sixth line is the image of one who has prevailed unjustly, who harms and exploits the innocent on the way to the top, who has caused disharmony in the world. The Oracle assures you that anyone engaged in such a manner will fall by the same manner. This is an assurance of karma.

If you have exploited others to enrich yourself unjustly, then beware. Before you fully ascend, all you have seized will be taken away.

If you have been the victim of one who unjustly enriched themselves at your expense, rest assured that a divine justice is in play.

# Hexagram 7: Shī. The Army

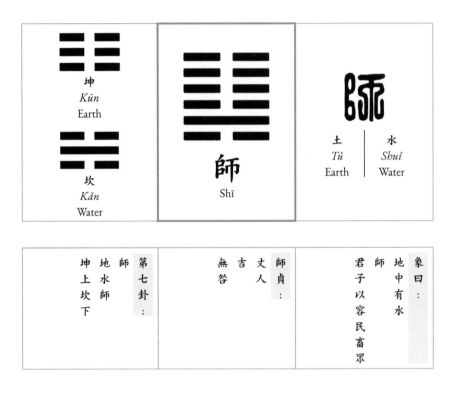

## The Oracle

Your ambitions are too scattered. The ego is a tenacious general. This general needs to enforce discipline. Your ambitions must serve as a unit, obeying the command of its general. Once you can march with a single, unified sense of purpose, nothing will stop you from accomplishing your goal. Auspicious for rallying the troops and marching forward.

**There is water deep within the center of the earth.** Be like water flowing beneath the earth; be like the hollowed pit beneath the earth. The water flowing beneath the earth is your influence and the control you are able to exert.

Conditions are auspicious when the army marches with a single, unified purpose, when the army is in proper order.

**The general works toward increasing the kingdom's people and livestock.**
Raise an army to protect their welfare, and for no other purpose than that. The general is your mind and will.

When the kingdom's people and livestock increase, your army will increase. When your army increases, your soldiers will persevere. To persevere means the army is disciplined. The army and its soldiers are the sum of your skills and capabilities. The kingdom is your world, its people your loved ones, and its livestock your assets.

To be disciplined, the army must be led by a tenacious general. May your mind and will exert such tenacity.

"容民畜眾" *(róng mín chù zhòng)* means to care for the welfare of both people and animals.

| *First Line* | | |
|---|---|---|
| The army must be ranked in the proper order; the master general will distribute according to law. To deny the proper ranking is to invite misfortune. | 否　師　初<br>臧　出　六<br>凶　以　：<br>　　律 | ▬▬　▬▬<br>▬▬　▬▬<br>▬▬　▬▬<br>▬▬▬▬▬ |

Set clearer priorities. Set clearer boundaries. Everyone should know where they stand and where you stand. If you are the one responsible for making that clear, then that should be your first order of business.

The general must know how to control the army and how to best utilize that army. Ranks must be clearly defined. Each must serve a specific purpose and must not serve any other purpose.

Take care with the power structure. Every junior must be able and willing to obey the senior. Establish a clear chain of command.

| *Second Line* | | |
|---|---|---|
| The general is positioned amid the army, centered and within. Good fortune. No harm comes despite errors made. The king bestows honors to triple the prosperity of the general. | 王　吉　在　九<br>三　無　師　二<br>錫　咎　中　：<br>命 | ▬▬　▬▬<br>▬▬▬▬▬<br>▬▬　▬▬ |

You are appointed the authority of command, but that authority comes from a higher power.

To succeed, become one with the army. When the general is aligned with the army, you, the general, will gain accolades from the king and improve your own lot in life threefold.

The outcome is safety and security. Despite missteps, all will be well.

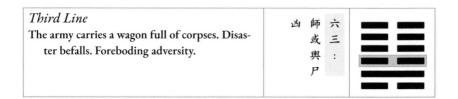

*Third Line*
**The army carries a wagon full of corpses. Disaster befalls. Foreboding adversity.**

To avoid peril, take control of your emotions. Do not let your emotions control you.

Past defeats and losses are holding you back from progress.

If you seek to advance, then there needs to be a reorganization of leadership. Install a new general, i.e., change your mind, reevaluate your intentions, consider how you have been utilizing your willpower, and shift your perspective.

You may be carrying dead weight. Reevaluate the baggage you carry. In the meantime, take a pause and do not advance any further. Correct the present before taking another step; otherwise, that step will be in the wrong direction.

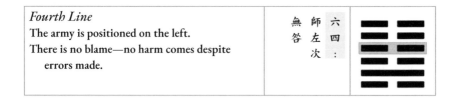

*Fourth Line*
**The army is positioned on the left.**
**There is no blame—no harm comes despite errors made.**

Assess the circumstances. If you cannot advance, then retreat. Do not engage where there is danger. Safety in the passive and receptive position.

When you are positioned incorrectly, the best strategy is to withdraw from that position and recalibrate.

"左" in this context may convey several meanings. It is a reference to the east or areas in the east, or to the left of your position; or it can indicate an unorthodox position being taken. "左" can also mean deviating from the majority, and it can imply division or divisiveness. In a political context, it's a reference to the left wing.

| *Fifth Line*<br>There is game in the field. Advantageous to hunt. There is no blame for the errors made.<br>Let the more experienced command the army. Every commoner has a role to fulfill. Collaborate in harmony. Disunity brings misfortune. |  |  |
|---|---|---|

There is bounty to be earned. There is no fault in pursuing the bounty.

However, if you pursue the bounty, let the senior in the army lead. There cannot be two heads. The junior must follow. Divisions or having both try to lead will result in injury, and an otherwise bountiful pursuit will end in failure.

To achieve your goal, you must have a clear ranking in your army, and all must be in obedient service to the general's instruction.

Unless your internal structure is in order, it is ominous to proceed. Here, the counsel is to yield to seniority, experience, tradition, and past precedent. Do not let inexperienced ambition influence the direction. Do not take unnecessary risks with what has not yet proven itself.

It is imperative to organize the internal structure now. There is bounty in the field to obtain and opportunities waiting for you to seize. Time is of the essence—unite quickly.

| *Sixth Line*<br>The Son of Heaven has a destiny to fulfill.<br>Do well with the fiefdoms inherited. Grant lordships to the meritorious. Give not power or responsibility to the wicked. |  |  |
|---|---|---|

You have been endowed with certain talents and assets for a divine purpose. Serve that purpose well. You are destined to lead the army; to do so, be wise enough to see who is meritorious and who is wicked.

A collective force does not mean that all act equally; such distribution of power will lead to failure. A collective force means all must abide by the will of the greater good and act in accordance with the will of the greater good.

The Son of Heaven is a leader and must exude confidence and authority. And yet the Son is a child who shows filial piety to Heaven.

"**大君**" in antiquity was a reference to the Son of Heaven, an emperor, or the eldest prince who is the heir apparent. There is the sense here of one who has been granted the Mandate of Heaven. "Son" is used in this context as a metaphor and not a literal reference. The literal words in classical Chinese are not gendered. However, this specific phrase has historically been translated into English as "Son of Heaven." You could alternatively translate this as "Great Sovereign Sage."

## Hexagram 8: Bǐ. Alliance

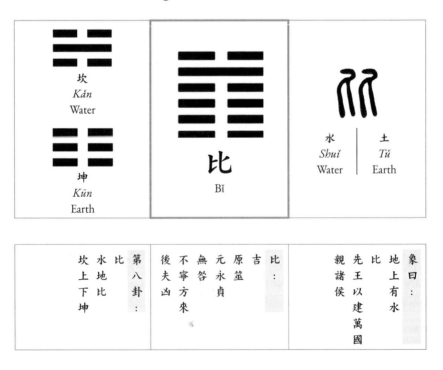

## *The Oracle*

> This is the omen of one who follows a good role model, cultivates greatness, then becomes a role model that others follow. Alliance of heart and mind. Eternal well-being is prophesied. Be a connector, one who brings people together. To bring many together, you occupy many worlds. Have your foot in many doors. Then, when tides turn, no matter in which direction, you have a safety net.

Two stand together, one linked to the other: bonding for strength; an alliance. Kinship. Seek alliances with those who share your truth.

**Kings gain innumerable territories by maintaining close relations with feudal lords.**

**Good auspices to come.**

**To conquer the great floods and enemies, hold an assembly of the gods on the mountain.**

This is an auspicious hexagram that speaks of good fortune. It bodes well-being if your intentions are in good faith. The pure of heart will be free of blame.

However, the last to arrive meets misfortune. **The last chieftain to arrive at the king's court was beheaded.**

**A budding rebellion is simmering.**

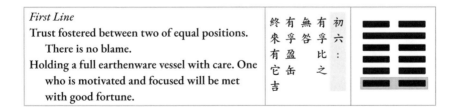

*First Line*
Trust fostered between two of equal positions. There is no blame.
Holding a full earthenware vessel with care. One who is motivated and focused will be met with good fortune.

Stay motivated. Show resilience and grit, and be perseverant. Initiate demonstrations of trust and loyalty; then colleagues will reciprocate. That is how you will rise in status.

# LEGEND OF FANGFENG ARRIVING LATE

The mention of a chieftain arriving late to the king's court and getting beheaded is a reference to the chieftain Fangfeng (防風, Fángfēng). After Yu the Great controlled the Great Floods and became emperor, he founded the Xia dynasty by annexing and subdividing the kingdom into nine regions. According to the *Bamboo Annals* (竹書紀年, *Zhú shū jìnián*), dated to sometime between 403 and 225 BC, Fangfeng refused to yield to Yu's authority, so Yu had Fangfeng executed.[11]

Yet Fangfeng was also deified, and in the Six Dynasties region, which is now Shanghai, Zhejiang, and Jiangsu, a different story is told. Fangfeng, described as a one-eyed unibrow giant with ox ears and a dragon head, was on his way to Yu the Great's court when he encountered a village trapped by one of the floods. He stopped to save the villagers, and as a result, was late to court.[12] His lateness angered the king, who interpreted the act as disrespect.

"Holding a full earthenware vessel" is a reference to a Chinese folktale: A prisoner was ordered to walk through the streets in a procession with a clay pot filled with water balancing on his head. If even a single drop of water spilled from the pot, then that would prove to the king that the prisoner was guilty of the crime. If not a single drop spilled, then it would prove his innocence. The prisoner did not spill a single drop, and when the king asked him how he did it, the prisoner said that with motivation and focus, one can achieve anything.

| | |
|---|---|
| *Second Line*<br>Bond in union all that is in you. Focus. Perseverance brings good fortune.<br>Auspicious. | 貞 比 六<br>吉 之 二<br>　 自 ：<br>　 內 |

A continuation of the folktale referenced above. Be single-minded in your decision. Before looking at others for support, be sure that all parts of yourself within are in alliance.

You are not ready to seek external support until you can act with a single mind. Know what you want before you ask anything of others.

| | |
|---|---|
| *Third Line*<br>Be wary midstream, as you hold together with the wrong people.<br>Bond in union all that is in you.<br>Do not support those with differing motivations or objectives from you. Proceed with caution. | 比 六<br>之 三<br>匪 ：<br>人 |

When you proceed with a single mind, then you will detect those who do not share your focus. Those who differ from you now will inevitably dissent against you later and bring you down. Take cautious note of those around you with ideological differences. If you ally with them, they will be the first to betray you and take you down.

Note the line "a budding rebellion is simmering" from the Oracle. Be wary of the simmering instability. Within it hides dissent that threatens your position.

| | |
|---|---|
| *Fourth Line*<br>Bond in union with those who support your motivations and focus. Hold them to that shared mission. Your perseverance will become your fortune. Auspicious to proceed. | 貞 外 六<br>吉 比 四<br>　 之 ： |

Seek alliances with those who share your mission and who can act with you as a single mind, focused on one shared objective. Seeking out those who share your single mind will motivate your own perseverance and bring about a fortuitous outcome.

| Fifth Line | | |
|---|---|---|
| The king gives chase to the birds and beasts from three sides, leaving a path for the prey to survive.<br>The fiefdom is spared. An auspicious omen. | 邑失王顯九<br>人前用比五<br>不禽三　：<br>誡　驅<br>吉 | 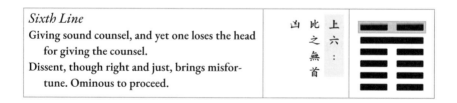 |

Let the weaker believe they've won. Be merciful to those who are lesser than you. To defeat them would be tyrannical.

When you think you have to humiliate every opponent to assert your strength, you are not strong at all. The truly strong are strong enough to appear meek.

The fifth line is a reference to benevolent and ethical hunting practices: when the king chases game, the hunt is only from three sides, always leaving the front open so a bird or beast who flees fast enough can seize the opportunity to be spared.

This is a metaphor for benevolent and merciful rulership. Always give people an out. Be humane, and show clemency.

| Sixth Line | | |
|---|---|---|
| Giving sound counsel, and yet one loses the head for giving the counsel.<br>Dissent, though right and just, brings misfortune. Ominous to proceed. | 凶比上<br>之六<br>無　：<br>首 | |

Telling the truth to one without the humility to accept that truth will bring misfortune to the truth-teller.

Giving correct counsel to one without the wisdom to accept that counsel will bring misfortune to the counselor.

There is a prognostication of injustice here—this is someone who speaks out of turn, even though the words spoken are true—and as a result is unfairly punished.

In this specific instance, in the interest of self-preservation, go with the majority and keep silent to save your own head. For your sake, now is not the time to cause disharmony. Yes, truth and integrity matter, but when and how you tell the truth also matter. What is integrity is a matter of perspective and timing.

The sixth line of Hexagram 8 is showing the fractures of the previous alliance. A rebellion is on the horizon due to quietly simmering dissent.

## Hexagram 9: Xiǎo Chù. Cultivate Gently

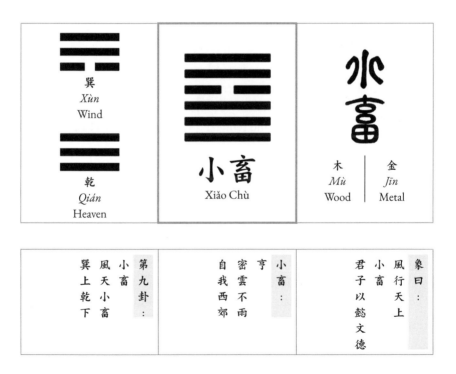

## The Oracle

> Success in minor undertakings; ominous to endeavor in major undertakings. Passivity has taming power. A storm is brewing, and it is uncertain whether the clouds bring a rain that will nourish the fields or a rain that floods the rivers. It is a period to wait and see. Secrets, confusion, clouded judgment—the only way through is to be a subtle and unseen influence. Change conditions gently.

**Winds impel the heavens above. Livestock in the sack—small gains. Auspicious to proceed. The sage cultivates refinement.**
**Dense clouds with no rain. I set upon the western threshold, passing beyond the horizon. That which has been raised now yields returns. A wind from above yields creativity below.**
You gaze at the sky and see stillness. Know that passivity has taming power. The sky is in movement. There is wind spreading out the seeds.
Wind is the least visible of all phenomena, and yet that wind spreads the seeds far and wide, yielding productivity. For now, small gains to be had as the winds continue to nurture and refine. Power is accumulated by gently withholding its expression.
Success in minor goals: you are a shepherd keeping your sheep calm with the calmness of your mind. Let the flock find their own shrubs and grass. The shepherd's only role is to see that they are safe.
And yet here is the greater wisdom of cultivating gently: do not delight in small advantages, or that is all you will ever achieve. The greatest gains are the result of benevolence and a mission to serve a greater good. The sage will always strive to achieve the impossible task of improving the world.
The line "自我西郊" appears again in the fifth line of Hexagram 62.

# PRACTICUM 8.2:
## Small Victories, Gain by Gain Mantra

The judgment lines from Hexagram 9 serve as a mantra recitation to achieve a consecutive series of small victories. Endeavoring for small victories will lead to achievement of the magnum opus you seek.

When you are feeling discouraged, invoke the higher powers of the Tao to rekindle your motivation and keep you going. This mantra helps you overcome the daily struggles of staying on task. It's divine assistance in the little steps to pave the way for something greater.

| Dense clouds, no rain— | *Mì yún bù yǔ* | 密雲不雨 |
| From my western bounds, | *Zì wǒ xī jiāo* | 自我西郊 |
| gentle wind, clear sky, gain by gain. | *fēng tiān xiǎo chù* | 風天小畜 |

The lines in Chinese are poetic. The rhythm and aesthetics of the verse add to its power, so I recommend recitation of the mantra in its classical form. The English translation is provided so you know what you're saying.

"Dense clouds, no rain" is an acknowledgement that you're feeling unmotivated and lethargic right now. As a rainmaker, this recitation sets up the forces to produce rain to come—dense clouds predict rain, which is an auspicious symbol of an abundant harvest.

Intend "from my western bounds" to mean forces of divine support from the Queen Mother of the West. West is also symbolic of the correspondence to innovation, creativity, and fertility, per the Lo Shu magic square.

"Gentle wind, clear sky, gain by gain" is an affirmative prayer—may the going be clear, may the Divine give you the gentle nudges you need to push forward, and may you achieve the progressive series of small undertakings.

Repeat the mantra daily as a prayer and petition for success. When Hexagram 9 is the divinatory result, recite the I Ching mantra to give momentum to the winds of positive change.

| First Line<br>Return to the Way. How could there be blame in such a return?<br>Auspicious. | 吉 何 復 初<br>　 其 自 九<br>　 咎 道 ： |

No fault sustained if errors are acknowledged and thus amended. Return to the righteous Path. Correct course, and nothing will be lost.

Auspicious to proceed when doing so is in the Way.

Do not follow others. Do not take the main road. Return to the path your heart most yearns to take, not because it's easy, but because it's true, and it's the path your mind in its infinite wisdom knows is right.

| Second Line<br>Pull back and return to the right path. One hand leads the other to recover lost ground. Restore your position by turning around. Good auspices. | 吉 牽 九<br>　 復 二<br>　 　 ： |

Your intuition guides you back on your own path. Do not force yourself against your own nature. The path of one hand leads the path of the other, and where you walk is the center.

| Third Line<br>The cart loses a wheel. Neither will look at the other; they avert their eyes. A quarrel. | 夫 輿 九<br>妻 說 三<br>反 輻 ：<br>目 |

Disorder within. Family relations are strained by the adversity.

Polarization of thoughts and feelings. Inner turmoil creates disunion and halts advancement.

Yet only minor impediments are frustrating your progress. Do not lose yourself to emotion simply because reason failed to solve the dilemma.

Encountering an obstacle that causes delay. Face the problem, overlook who is to blame, and work together in cooperation. Overlook self-doubt or internal conflicts. Achieve internal union and then deal with the challenge head-on.

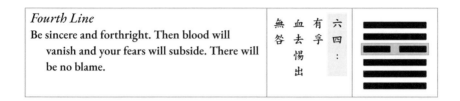

*Fourth Line*
Be sincere and forthright. Then blood will vanish and your fears will subside. There will be no blame.

Be honest with others. Take responsibility for your past acts. Do not conceal from others. By doing so, you avert the dangers of bloodshed.

The fourth line denotes the passive strength of inaction. The courage of your convictions will help you overcome a difficult situation. Sincere devotion to the Divine will help you weather the storm.

Do not choose anger. Choose to be a gentle wind. The sage's action is inaction.

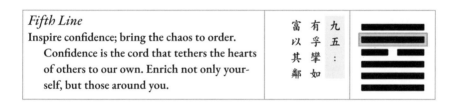

*Fifth Line*
Inspire confidence; bring the chaos to order. Confidence is the cord that tethers the hearts of others to our own. Enrich not only yourself, but those around you.

You will unite those around you behind your cause. Partnerships are reinforced with loyalty. The alchemical function is to conjoin, to negotiate opposites by finding equilibrium. Coexistence.

The image here is of bringing light to darkness, straightening what was bent, and establishing order where there was chaos. In doing so, you inspire the confidence of others. They support your objective. To receive support, you need to give support.

With such support, you succeed. On your path, make sure the success you achieve is such that all those in close proximity will also benefit from your achievements.

Reconcile the conscious mind with the unconscious mind. Search out and recognize the scattered parts of your inner psyche. Unite them. The combined force will bring small but significant victories.

| Sixth Line | 君 月 婦 尚 既 上 | ䷄ |
| :-- | :-- | :-- |
| Rains come and there is respite. Come what may, do not waver in virtue or beneficence. | 子 幾 貞 德 雨 九 征 望 厲 載 既 ： | |
| The madam confronts danger. As the moon grows full, the sage encounters misfortune. Beware of pitfalls. Take caution should you proceed. | 凶 處 | |

Rain is the union of heaven and earth. The power of passive restraint accumulates. You achieve close to your full potential. Know that after the full moon comes the waning moon, and you must embrace the waning moon. To fight against it will bring loss and disappointment. "既" is also a reference to an eclipse.

A cycle will have been completed. Seek rest thereafter. Do not persist beyond the final call. When it is over, it is over. Waning after a peak is the natural progression. To resist it is to be unwise.

A cautionary omen to proceed with care. Some baneful forces are beyond our control.

## Hexagram 10: Lǚ. Treading

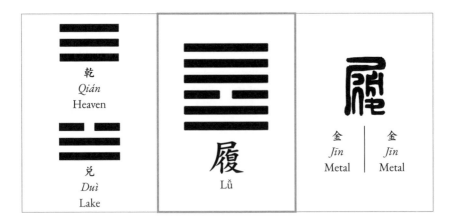

| 乾上兌下 | 天澤履 | 履 | 第十卦： | | 亨 | 不咥人 | 履虎尾： | | 定民志 | 君子以辯上下 | 履 | 上天下澤 | 象曰： |

## *The Oracle*

> Where a tiger's tail is seen, fangs and claws are not far. A risky endeavor has the potential to bring great rewards, but do not provoke the powers that be. Conditions in the environment are intense. It could all go well to the extreme, or all go badly to the extreme. Proceed with caution. Do not aggravate that which is known to bite. Remain inoffensive, and the risks you take will pay off. A generally auspicious divinatory omen, but it shows that you are the responsible party—you are the one driving the forces, which means many either rise or fall on account of the decisions you make. High pressure, high stakes. Yet the Oracle assures that you are experienced and highly competent—perfectly qualified to be the responsible party.

**Treading on the tail of the tiger. The tiger does not bite. Success.**
The sage can see how high the sky is above and how deep the water of the lake is below. Know the high from the low—pick your battles. Exercise discernment. Such differences in the ranks of people correspond with their natural endowments. The distinctions among people according to their endowments is what stabilizes society.

When the stronger is also irascible and easily irritated, do not aggravate the stronger. Do not provoke. May the weaker tread softly so as to avert danger. Then safety and security will be yours.

The sage's foot is on the tiger's tail. Proceed with caution. Keep your footsteps light, and you will be able to tread through danger without harm.

> **First Line**
> Simple conduct: tread in shoes unadorned.
> Safety. Progress without blame.
>
> 初九：素履往無咎

Right now is not the time to call attention to yourself. Maintain a humble and modest profile. Avoid boastful displays. Do not worry about what passersby think of your appearance; worry more about when you'll arrive at your destination.

Unadorned shoes suggest the rank of a commoner. The commoner is resigned to the simple conduct of a commoner. Do not pine beyond your rank. Basic values are virtuous. Your rank works to your advantage. Embrace your rank and act accordingly. By doing so, mistakes will be avoided.

One who is truly great will not be afraid of appearing little.

Do not provoke. Do not call unwanted attention to yourself.

Walk your path alone for now. Trust in your own values. Do not seek out support or aid at this time. Do not call out to others.

> **Second Line**
> Tread upon the open road, calm and content—
> walk the Path of the Tao with open heart.
> The unconventional one meets with good fortune.
>
> 九二：履道坦坦幽人貞吉

The one who diverges from the norm is the one who flourishes. Here is the image of one who leaves behind the worldly, the materialistic, and the corrupt to take a more spiritual and artistic path.

Devote time to being with yourself so you learn how to be yourself.

Know who you are so you know who to be. You do not have to be who others think you are.

The first line, "履道坦坦" *(lǚ dào tǎn tǎn),* holds double meaning. Literally, "坦坦" *(tǎn tǎn)* means a surface that is flat, level, and wide. "道" is a pathway. Thus, a pathway is flat, level, and wide. Figuratively, however, "坦坦" means to have nothing to hide, to be honest and open, and to be level-minded and thus calm. "道" is also the word for the Tao, meaning the Path of the Tao, the Way of the Sages.

The second line, "幽人貞吉" *(yōu rén zhēn jí)*, is a reference to one who lives in seclusion. The popular imagery of a "幽人" *(yōu rén)* is a hermit living in a dense forest atop a mountain.

However, the translation here for that term is "unconventional one" because "幽人" implies one who leads a musical, artistic, or spiritual vagabond lifestyle. A *yōu rén* is one who is considered unorthodox and antiestablishment and who therefore lives apart from civil society. These implications might get lost with a more direct translation to "hermit."

*Third Line*
The blind see. The lame walk. Treading on the tiger's tail: it bites. Misfortune. A warrior inherits the throne.

Those who cannot see the matter clearly feign clarity. Those who cannot walk the righteous path try to walk it anyway. Treading results in injury.

You may be exposing yourself recklessly to danger and taking on a challenge that is more than what you are capable of handling. Conditions will worsen before they turn for the better, because the path being taken is unnatural and out of course.

The warrior has great capability, but not the capability of rulership, not yet. Nevertheless, the warrior is thrust into sovereignty.

The third line is a symbol of weakness urged on by the strength behind it (the former two lines) to confront the power before it (the subsequent three lines).

The message is one of inadequate strength for dealing with a formidable opposing force. You are overexerting yourself beyond your means.

The first two oracular messages of the third line are vague as to whether the blind *can* see and the lame *can* walk, or whether the blind are *trying* to see and the lame are *trying* to walk. Thus, it can be interpreted either way, depending on the circumstances of the divinatory question.

In general, the indication here is that of the supernatural, or attempting what would otherwise be deemed beyond your means and impossible. The omen is one of misfortune and more difficulties before the path clears, but that is because you have chosen to undertake a matter that is beyond your present set of capabilities.

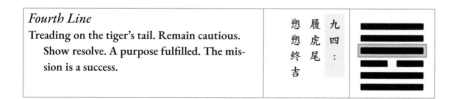

*Fourth Line*
**Treading on the tiger's tail. Remain cautious. Show resolve. A purpose fulfilled. The mission is a success.**

You succeed at a precarious and risky undertaking. You've navigated an uncertain situation with decisive and correct action. The outcome for you will be positive.

When faced with adversity, showing resolve means being firm in your virtue and reason, both of which you have in abundance.

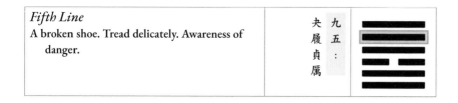

*Fifth Line*
**A broken shoe. Tread delicately. Awareness of danger.**

The path you wish to walk is dangerous, and you do not have proper footing at this time. Yet you seem aware of all this. Your awareness of the dangers ahead is what gives you strength. Note that some of the danger involves malevolence from others. Be careful of those who try to disrupt your path.

There is a fork in the path (夬 guài). One path leads to the throne, an ascent (履 lǚ), and treading upon new territory. Your divination (貞 zhēn) reveals the Will of your patron divinity; give offerings, as the Divine will protect you from danger.

*Sixth Line*
Watch your steps up to the temple of learning. Look to your conduct and weigh the favorable signs. A glorious return.

其旋元吉

上九視履考祥：

There is affinity. The endeavor will succeed. To know your future, you must review your past.

### THE CHANGING SIXTH LINE

If the sixth line is the only changing line in the hexagram, then you have passed the test, and great success will come.

## Hexagram 11: Tài. Harmony

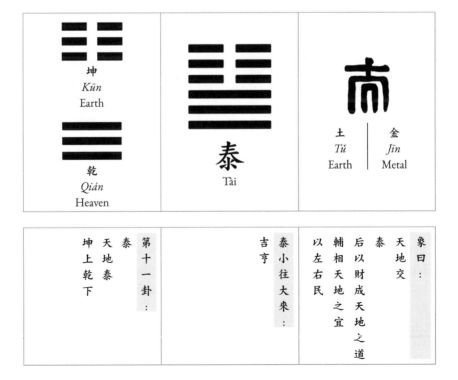

# The Oracle

Small investments yield big returns. A little risk goes a long way. And that is because conditions are in harmony to support gains and riches. Forces are aligned and conducive for well-being. The key to continued success after success is balance. Stay consistent. Strive for order and routine and yet diversity and variety for there to be harmony. Strive for a geometric congruency, and you will find that balance brings you prosperity. A symmetry produces a favorable outcome. Forecast of peace and prosperity.

**Heaven and Earth converge.** A great harmony comes forth. A holy union brings prosperity.

**The ruler gains wealth and riches, achieves success, and completes every mission with victory in accordance to the Way of Heaven and Earth.**

The inferior depart and the great arrive. **What reigns above unites in concord with what thrives below. There is peace.**

**Auspicious to proceed.**

---

*First Line*
**Pulling the reed by its root. Assembling the reeds together. The undertaking yields success.**

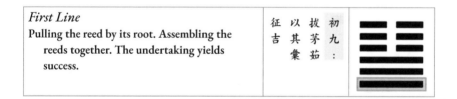

Look for the source. Find the point of origin. What at first appears disparate can be gathered together to create unity. The strength of that unity brings victory in the undertaking. Launch the campaign after you show the people their common ground—their roots are the same.

On the ninth day of the first month, pull the reeds up by their roots.

Here, the reed or "茅" *(máo)* is also an allusion to the Tao (道). Thus, the same sentences can also be read as: "Pulling the Tao by its root. Assembling the myriad facets of the Tao together."

Removal from an entrenched position advances the general welfare.

You have the grassroots support you need for victory. When you think and act for the greater good of others, your endeavor will succeed.

Auspicious to take action at this time.

| Second Line | | |
|---|---|---|
| Concealing that which is soiled and unprincipled. Wading across the river on foot. Wandering in the wilderness. Do not overlook distant or remote allies. Severing ties with friends. The right path and proper action is the middle way. | 得朋不用包九<br>尚亡遐馮荒二<br>于　遺河　：<br>中<br>行 | ▬▬ ▬▬<br>▬▬ ▬▬<br>▬▬ ▬▬<br>▬▬▬▬▬<br>▬▬ ▬▬<br>▬▬▬▬▬ |

You seek redemption to right a past wrong. You possess high intellect and great capabilities. You are willing to take risks for others, but you haven't found a worthy purpose.

Your heart is in the right place, and yet you are lost. Aimlessness.

This is how you find your way: first, build bridges to connect with distant friends; second, walk the Middle Path.

"包荒" *(bāo huāng)* or "concealing that which is soiled and unprincipled" means trying to cover up and hide one's flaws. You are wrapping what you do not want others to see in what you do want others to see.

Here, 河 *(hé)*, the river, can be a reference to the Yellow River, when King Wu of Zhou crossed the Yellow River in preparation for the attack on the Shang. Alternatively, the river can be a figurative reference to the Milky Way 銀河系 (Yín Hé Xì). In a mystical reading of this line, this is interpreted as a journey across the astral plane.

Yet another interpretation of "用馮河" (or "暴虎馮河" bào hǔ píng hé") is a reference to fighting a tiger with bare hands, an allusion to reckless heroism.

With regard to "severing ties with friends" (朋亡 péng wáng), the Han dynasty dictionary 說文解字 (Shuō Wén Jiě Zì) compiled by Xu Shen 許慎 (AD 58–148) noted that 朋 *(péng)* could be an evolved form of the Western Zhou form 鳳 *(fèng)*, meaning an imperial or mythic phoenix. Thus, the image here would be that of a fallen phoenix.

Alternatively, rather than "sever" in an intentional manner, this could be a reference to having lost friends in a manner beyond your control.

| *Third Line* | 于勿無艱無無九 | ䷊ |
| --- | --- | --- |
| No plain is without its mounds and ridges. No peace is without its discord. No departure is without return. No future is without a past.<br>There will be hardships. There is pain and suffering to come.<br>But there is no blame. Do not bemoan your goodness.<br>Having a meal to eat; fortuitous and blessed. | 食恤咎貞平三<br>有其　往不：<br>福孚　不復陂 | |

Here, the third line is the boundary between heaven and earth: change is the only constant. Both nature and human affairs will always be in a state of flux.

A prognostication of adversity to come. Those you were in conflict with left for a while to give you a moment of peace, but they return and bring trouble. Once again, you have to face difficulty. Even prosperity is not without its lower points.

That does not mean you should stop celebrating the joys of life. There is still much to be merry about. Accept pleasure and pain alike; gains and losses alike; success and defeat alike. At all times prepare yourself for the battle, and in that preparation, incur no sin and harbor no ill will toward others.

Do not bemoan your goodness—your kind heart, honesty, and integrity may not have served you, and perhaps you were taken advantage of exactly because of your goodness, but do not blame yourself and do not regret that goodness.

| *Fourth Line* | 不不翩六 | ䷊ |
| --- | --- | --- |
| Fluttering, flying—the prosperous one loses affluence on account of a neighbor.<br>Remaining unguarded, continuing to trust with open heart and sincerity.<br>Confidence without fear. | 戒富翩四<br>以以　：<br>孚其<br>　鄰 | |

A voluntary surrender of power and position, so that principles need not be compromised.

The idealism is admirable, but losses are sustained nonetheless. The willing renunciation of your assets in favor of peace, balance, and harmony puts one foot in the part of fortune and one in the part of adversity.

You gave to someone who did not deserve your kindness. Do not regret your kindness. Keep your heart free of ill will. When you build walls, you keep out the good with the bad. When you build bridges, Heaven will support the Earth.

---

*Fifth Line*
The king betrothed his daughter to the duke.
　The duke accepts.
An auspicious betrothal.

六五：帝乙歸妹以祉元吉

---

The line refers to making amends for a past wrong, though a wrong you did not yourself commit. It is a wrong perceived by others, but that perception is enough to cause possible conflict. To placate, you sacrifice a peace offering.

The king's daughter, a princess who outranks the duke, must submit to the duke for the greater good of her people. She does, and as a result, great prosperity will come to her people.

---

*Sixth Line*
The tower wall topples into the moat. Hold the army; do not use force just yet.
In a last effort at peace, the capital issues an order.
An omen of jeopardy. Endeavor for corrective measures.

上六：城復于隍勿用師自邑告命貞吝

## EMPEROR DI YI OF SHANG

This line is believed to be a reference to Emperor Di Yi of Shang, who betrothed his sister (or daughter) to King Wen of Zhou, who at the time was just a duke. Depending on dialect, "妹 Mèi" can be a reference to either a younger sister or a daughter.

Knowing the back story of Emperor Di Yi and the betrothal adds instructive layers to understanding the fifth line. To assuage tensions between Shang and Zhou, the arranged marriage between a princess of Shang and the Duke of Zhou could bring the peace that the emperor is hoping for. However, history confirms that the peace never happens. The two kingdoms go to war, and Zhou is victorious.

However, the fifth line prognosticates good fortune because what turned out to be good fortune was the betrothal. Tai Si is wise, modest, beautiful, and good, bringing great fortune and blessings to the Zhou. She gives birth to the first emperor of the Zhou dynasty, King Wu.

When the prophecy notes that "great prosperity will come to her people," at first you wonder if the Oracle means the Shang, since Tai Si, at least according to the story here, is from the Shang. And yet after the betrothal, she becomes a part of the Zhou, and her sons are all Zhou. Great prosperity *does* come to her husband and sons.

The lesson here is to be discerning, wise, and thoughtful in how we interpret the messages from the Oracle.

The legend of Emperor Di Yi and him betrothing his sister or daughter to King Wen of Zhou appears again in Hexagram 54.

An era of peacekeeping and harmony comes to its end. The tower wall toppling into the moat represents stability lapsing into chaos.

Every era of peace ends in strife. Your fortress, however strong, is still vulnerable. The higher one ascends, the farther there is to fall. That is why ambition is not wisdom.

Your beliefs may get shattered, but despite the turmoil, take no action. Do not try to prevent the toppling. Allow the transformation to complete itself. Yield to the natural course of cycles and changes.

### UNCHANGING LINE

If Hexagram 11 is your primary hexagram, and all lines but the sixth are changing lines, then the natural course of change will bring you back up to a position of prosperity shortly after the turmoil. The turmoil will be short-lived.

If the sixth line is the changing line or if Hexagram 11 is the transformed hexagram, then the prophecy of the sixth has not come to pass yet. There is still an opportunity to change course and prevent this outcome.

## Hexagram 12: Fǒu. Stalemate

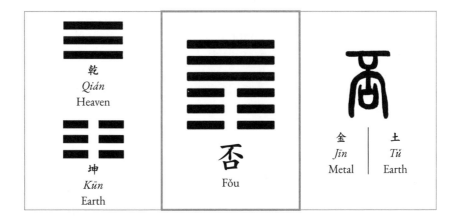

| | | | |
|---|---|---|---|
| 乾地否第<br>上天十<br>坤否二<br>下　卦<br>　　： | | 大不否<br>往利之<br>小君匪<br>來子人<br>　貞： | 不君否象<br>可子：曰<br>榮以天：<br>以儉地<br>祿德不<br>　辟交<br>　難　 |

## The Oracle

What should be flowing is going stale. The ill-intentioned are blocking the flow. Risk of loss. Practice the virtue of frugality to alleviate difficulties. Incompetence prevails. Honor the gods and ancestors for protection. And come what may, no matter how grave the inequity, you cannot falter in your own virtue. Do not let their malignity erode your integrity. If you want to know why the malevolent has come out victorious, you may ask the Oracle.

**Heaven and Earth divided. Stagnation. Cessation of movement.**
In times of poor harvest, the sage conserves. Despite difficult times, desperation does not lead to decline of virtue.
**The sage receives no blessings or gains; no favors are earned. The great depart and the inferior arrive.** The malice of others creates an impasse. There has been a halt in growth and progress. No advancing; no flow.
Boding ill for good intentions. Poor prospects if a union is contemplated. Practice the virtue of frugality to alleviate difficulties.
**Heaven and earth are estranged; as a result, big losses and small gains.**
You know it's your turn to move, but you don't know where to go. Feeling like a draw. Change the game.

| | |
|---|---|
| *First Line*<br>Pulling the reed by its root. Assembling the reeds together.<br>Prayers will be answered; good auspices to come. | 貞以拔初<br>吉其茅六<br>亨彙茹： |

The inferior gain power. A great leader who once held a high office retires from the position to preserve integrity.

Breaking a fixed position and advancing forward. Sacrifices are made.

It is auspicious to proceed at this time. Others around you have come to a stalemate, which opens up an opportunity and pathway for you to get ahead.

The lines "拔茅茹 以其彙 bá máo rú yǐ qí huì" mirror the first line of Hexagram 11. Whereas the third statement in Hexagram 11's first line was "the undertaking yields success," here, rather than conveying an expedition or campaign, the Oracle counsels that proceeding brings good auspices, and prayers will be answered.

| *Second Line* | | |
|---|---|---|
| Ceremonial meat is wrapped in palm. The adversary is faring well. The eminent one, however, is not.<br>Auspicious to proceed. | 亨　大　小　包　六<br>　　人　人　承　二<br>　　否　吉　　　： |  |

Continue to pray for guidance. The situation is bleak. Injustice prevails. There will be a time and place to act, but for now, pray, hold steady to your faith, and hold steady to your principles. Implement meditation practices.

A petition was sent up to the heavens. The people wrapped their ceremonial meats in palm as ritual offerings to the gods. These ritual offerings were then contained in a bronze vessel.

The second line denotes inexplicable injustice. The adversary is the self-interested, unethical one, and here, such a person is faring well. Meanwhile, the eminent one refers to someone who is virtuous, sophisticated in intellect, and good, and yet is not receiving blessings from the gods.

The one who sits at the head may sustain minor harms.

Nevertheless, a positive, fortuitous response to your inquiry. Injustice does not justify compromise of your principles.

| *Third Line* | | |
|---|---|---|
| Concealed by a shroud, timid. | 包　六<br>羞　三<br>　　： | |

The Oracle is expressing disapproval. Do not take the easy route.

The third line is a stalemate caused by one's own lack of self-assurance and courage.

Traditionally the third line is interpreted as forecasting disgrace or feeling shame around a situation, but the word " xiū" can simply mean timid and shy. The facet of disgrace that could come into play is if one doesn't change course.

Rather than facing a challenge head-on, you're hiding. Willful ignorance will get you nowhere; in fact, it leads to disgrace.

| *Fourth Line*<br>Heaven's Will averts a calamity. The cultivated field yields prosperity.<br>Good fortune and well-being. |  |
|---|---|

A turn for the better. Maintain Heaven's favor by remaining aligned with Heaven's Will.

Know this: you are born to fulfill a calling, but you are free to fulfill or not fulfill that calling.

Divine intervention.

| *Fifth Line*<br>After stagnation, the path is cleared for joy and good fortune. An auspicious omen for the eminent one.<br>Perishing, perishing—upon the leaning mulberry tree. |   |
|---|---|

Your fear of the current impasse motivates you to change. That change results in a favorable outcome.

Yet be careful during the time of transition. Advance cautiously; risks are high at every turn.

Realization of a divine purpose has been awakened. And with it, an old way of understanding the world perishes.

# THE TEN SUN CROWS AND THEIR MULBERRY TREE

The mulberry tree is a reference to the myth of Houyi. The god of the eastern heaven gave birth to ten golden three-legged crows who resided in a mulberry tree along the eastern horizon.[13]

The crows were ordered by their father to take turns rising in the east and setting in the west—the ten suns of earth (corresponding with the ten heavenly stems of lunisolar astrology).

But the crows rebelled and decided all ten would roam the earth at once. As a result, there were ten suns in the sky at all times. The collective heat scorched the earth and brought great suffering to humankind.

The heroic archer Houyi was called to frighten the sun birds back home, but instead, out of anger for the harm the birds had caused humans, Houyi shot and killed them one by one.

The Divine intervened at the last moment before the archer shot down the last sun, leaving only one sun crow in the sky.

In antiquity, mulberry groves were considered sacred, and shamans would go there to petition the gods for rain and abundant harvests. Mulberry trees are also the source of silkworms and thus of silk. The transformation from a silkworm chrysalis to a white silkworm butterfly was also a metaphor for Taoist immortality.

Crows and blackbirds were spiritually significant to the Yellow River civilizations of the Bronze Age. The Shang identified their clan with the totemic emblem of a blackbird, or a dark, mysterious, mythical bird described as a 玄鳥 *(xuán niǎo)*.[14]

Present-day scholars disagree as to whether "玄鳥" refers to "black bird" and thus a crow, or to "occult/esoteric/mysterious bird." Inscriptions of this black or mysterious, mystical bird have been found on oracle bones and tortoise shells dated to the Shang,[15] and the same bird design has been replicated and carved onto pottery, jade, and other precious and semiprecious stones, thus leading to the conclusion that this bird was an established emblem.[16]

Hexagram 54 is an allusion to Chang-Er, the moon goddess, Houyi's wife.

According to myth, a divine swallow-like blackbird or mysterious, mystical bird gave birth to the ancestors of the Shang. An early record of this comes from the Book of Songs (1000–600 BC)[17]:

| 天命玄鳥 | Tiān mìng xuán niǎo | The heavenly blackbird of destiny |
| 降而生商 | jiàng ér shēng Shāng | descends and gives birth to the Shang. |
| 宅殷土茫茫 | Zhái Yīn tǔ máng máng | Its descendants dwell in that vast and faraway land of Yin.[18] |

In antiquity, the kingdom that the Shang dynasty occupied was known as Yin. The passage echoes the reference to fate, as ordained by heaven (命) from the fourth line.

A champion is the savior, but at what cost? Good auspices for proceeding—intentions are pure, the purpose is virtuous. And yet perhaps the method is excessive.

The fifth line follows chronologically after the third and fourth lines. After a fall from grace, there is recovery and restoration of that grace. Reference to "否极泰来" *(pǐ jí tài lái)*, meaning once you have endured scorn and the period of embarrassment is over, good luck will come your way.

"Perishing, perishing" (其亡其亡, *qí wáng qí wáng*) suggests a spiritual death. A spiritual death is a life stage where past delusions, superficiality, and ignorance are shattered and transcendent insight is gained. Thus, one is reborn awakened into new consciousness. The fifth yang line is the light of transcendent realization.

## I Ching: The Book of Changes

| Sixth Line<br>**Overturning the opposition. First part, stagnation; final part, success. Temporary stagnation followed by jubilation.** | 上九：<br>傾否<br>先否後喜 | ䷋ |
|---|---|---|

The stalemate proves to be temporary. You seize the right opportunity to end your own stagnation.

The situation surrounding your endeavor improves, and you achieve success.

Impediments at the start, but the conclusion brings joy, celebration, and fruition—a blessing in gestation.

## Hexagram 13: Tóng Rén. Fellowship

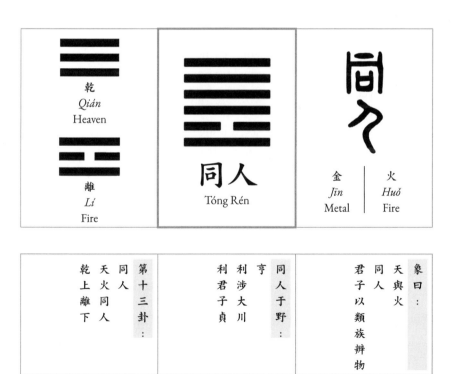

## The Oracle

> Now is a time for relationship building. Seek out a community of interest, and seek interchange. Hold in common bond. Consider the relationships you build, both social and professional. Fellowship begins with giving, and that giving becomes exchange in its own natural course. Support the happiness of others, and others will support yours. Never let a friend walk alone at night. Generosity builds bridges and networks. To be enriched by fellowship, be one who enriches others. Help others with their aspirations first, and in time you will find that you've accomplished your own.

**Heaven converges with Fire—sovereignty and sovereignty: fellowship. The sage creates order and structure for the people.** A collective is formed.

**Sign of the great sacrifice. Auspicious. Favorable for crossing the great stream.** A favorable outcome prognosticated for the sage.

**A gathering in the field. The people gather and unite.** Kindred spirits come together. Fire illuminating Heaven: radiance, innovation, and cultivation cling to the creative force; strength in the creativity; expansive creativity.

Fire ascends upward toward the sky, uniting with it. Synthesis. Heaven and Fire: together, they share universal interests and set aside private interests of the individual. Together, they pursue the goals of humanity, not the goals of one. With such unity, all difficulties and dangers can be overcome.

For such a fellowship to form, there must be one enlightened leader who inspires and guides the fellowship with the leader's inner clarity and outer strength. The leader must know that a fellowship is not a mere intermingling of different individuals; fellowship requires order and organization under the clarity, strength, and guidance of that one leader. The leader will set a specific mission, with a vision that unites the community. Inspire with a call to action. Convey the urgency and timeliness for working in unity.

| First Line | 無 同 初 |
|---|---|
| **A fellowship gathers at the entrance.** <br> **There is no blame.** | 咎 人 九 <br> 于 ： <br> 門 |

At the start of the endeavor, you open yourself up to fellowship. Proposition of a possible union.

Like minds and kindred spirits with the same goals come together. External forces assemble a strong alliance. Accord, union, and success at the beginning. Mutual honesty and candor will strengthen the start of this fellowship.

The beginning stages are crucial. Come together to reach agreements and concord, and establish shared objectives. A strategic plan is needed.

| Second Line | 吝 同 六 |
|---|---|
| **The fellowship is one clan.** <br> **Endeavor for corrective measures before** <br>    **proceeding.** | 　 人 二 <br> 　 于 ： <br> 　 宗 |

The group tends toward excluding others and elitism. That cliquish nature results in intellectual limitations. A self-serving alliance. Dogmatism.

"宗" *(zōng)* can mean those from the same ancestral temple or ancestry, those of the same family, tribe, or clan. The term can also be used to denote a lineage, tradition, sect, or school, or a group who comes together with a shared, common purpose. Can also indicate a regional or administrative district.

The second line is encouraging diversity and pluralism.

Note that if the endeavor contemplated involves family members, reconsider the alliance. Fellowship with family at this time may be regrettable, as it will result in limitations on progress.

| Third Line | 三 升 伏 九 |  |
| --- | --- | --- |
| Concealed arms in the underbrush. Ascending up a tall mound. For three years, no advancements or progress, no true coalition. | 歲 其 戎 三<br>不 高 于 ：<br>興 陵 莽 | |

You have three years to change, to undergo a full personal transformation so that when opposition and adversity really come, you'll be ready.

Securing peace by preparing for war.

Weapons were concealed in the thicket in preparation for an ambush or revolt—nurture your personal secret weapon.

Internal strife within the fellowship hinders them from uniting and launching a successful revolt. Oppositions within the fellowship and tensions among the leaders.

Victorious warriors win first before they go to war. You cannot win first if there is such strife from within. Bring peace and accord to that internal strife.

歲 (Suì) is a reference to Jupiter and the god Tai Sui, who represents Jupiter's orbital cycle. Three "歲" can also be interpreted as three cycles of crop harvests (thus, three years).

| Fourth Line |  |  |
| --- | --- | --- |
| Ascending a citadel wall. The wall is breached, but no conquest from the attack.<br>Still, it is auspicious to proceed. | | |

The citadel wall is scaled and the fortress has been breached by the rebels, but they fail to take over the fortress. A small battle won, but prospective victory in the war is still a distant matter.

Continue. You are on the right path and your mission is noble. There is much more work to be done. The fight has only just begun.

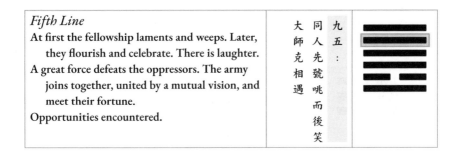

*Fifth Line*
At first the fellowship laments and weeps. Later, they flourish and celebrate. There is laughter.
A great force defeats the oppressors. The army joins together, united by a mutual vision, and meet their fortune.
Opportunities encountered.

Setting aside differences and seeking common ground, a true united fellowship is finally established. Now the fellowship must join in making a unanimous decision. In shared vision, they rise and they conquer.

Obstacles become opportunities.

There is some ambiguity as to how "大師" *(dà shī)* should be interpreted. "師" could be a reference to Hexagram 7 and could therefore be interpreted as a great army or troop. That would make sense, given the theme of fellowship here in Hexagram 13. "師" can mean a master, expert, adept, teacher, or as it was used in antiquity, a military troop of 2,500 soldiers. Depending on context, the word's meaning can range from a leader, chief, or military commander to the masses and the general public. For the sake of brevity, it's interpreted as "a great force" here, but consider the context and subject matter of the inquiry, and tailor interpretation of "大師" accordingly.

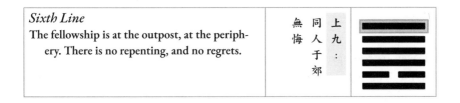

*Sixth Line*
The fellowship is at the outpost, at the periphery. There is no repenting, and no regrets.

Partial success, but that success is good enough.
It took too long for the fellowship to settle their differences and work in unison. As a result, they do not meet their lofty objectives, but what they have accomplished together is still significant and worthy of mention.
Optimal level of accomplishment is not achieved. However, there are no regrets in this fellowship. Great gains were nonetheless made.

# Hexagram 14: Dà Yǒu. Accolades

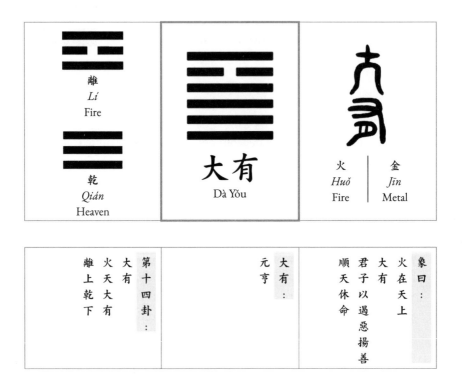

## The Oracle

**Heaven bestows great blessings when you are aligned with the Will of the Divine. This is an omen of great validation. What you have been intuiting is true and correct. What you seek to undertake is a worthy endeavor that will yield success and prosperity. Heaven supports your expansion. And yet, stay modest and heed the true lesson of this message: those blessed with abundance should not allow themselves to feel full.**

The divine flame illuminates the heavens: the bestowing of great accolades and praise. The sage neutralizes malevolence with benevolence. A great destiny awaits; align yourself with Heaven's Will.

This hexagram bodes supreme success and wealth.
**Many blessings bestowed. A great harvest.**

| | | |
|---|---|---|
| *First Line*<br>No injury sustained.<br>Bandits bring trouble.<br>Despite hardships, there is no blame. | 艱則無咎 匪咎 無交害 初九： | ▬▬▬<br>▬ ▬<br>▬▬▬<br>▬▬▬<br>▬▬▬<br>▬▬▬ |

There was a near-miss of disaster, but misfortune was averted and all begins well.

One is born positioned for success. Yet a good start does not remain good; it declines unless the advantageous position is laboriously maintained.

Those who envy what you have stir controversy. Conflicts ensue. Despite the challenges, you prevail.

Blessings from Heaven still require hard work, earning merit, and proving you are worthy. Be humble and grateful for your blessings.

| | | |
|---|---|---|
| *Second Line*<br>Loading a large wagon.<br>Go forward with the undertaking.<br>There is no blame. | 無咎 有攸往 大車以載 九二： | ▬▬▬<br>▬ ▬<br>▬▬▬<br>▬▬▬<br>▬▬▬<br>▬▬▬ |

The long journey begins. Make preparations and ensure that you have adequate resources for what is to come next.

Go forward with your endeavor. Proceed with confidence. You have support from Heaven. Be humble and grateful for your blessings, and you will continue a faultless path toward victory.

| | | |
|---|---|---|
| *Third Line*<br>Good fortune comes after the duke's service of a public good. Graces from the Son of Heaven.<br>The adversary is powerless. | 小人弗克 公用亨于天子 九三： | ▬▬▬<br>▬ ▬<br>▬▬▬<br>▬▬▬<br>▬▬▬<br>▬▬▬ |

You have a magnanimous heart and a liberal mind, so you do not regard your riches as your exclusive property. You place your assets at the disposal of the greater good. In doing so, you adopt the right attitude about possession.

Others are not capable of doing this, and as a result, they are limited by their material possessions. You, in spite of having great material possessions, can transcend those possessions and still achieve spiritual fulfillment because of your compassionate, generous view. By giving more with such a sincere heart, you will receive more from the great Divine.

One is the duke, qualified, extraordinary, and on a path to social advancement. The other is the commoner, unqualified and weak. The commoner will fail.

In a Confucian reading, "小人" *(xiǎo rén)* is translated as "commoner" and used as an antonym to *junzi,* the sage. Here it's translated to "the adversary." This is either an external opposition, someone who is trying to undermine your success, or an internal opposition, the nay-sayer voice within.

Here the Oracle is affirming that you are better than your opponent.

One interpretation is of dueling inner selves. You are both the duke and the commoner, as the terms are being used here.

If you can let the duke win out, then great gains are to be had, including social advancement and a rise in your status.

If you let your inner commoner win out, which is the person driven by self-interest, short-term gains, and being short-sighted, then you will not be able to succeed at your endeavor.

As the duke, you accept that you do not live just for yourself; you also live to serve a greater good. The beautiful paradox here is if you can sincerely live to serve that greater good, then Heaven's Will blesses you with all the merits, gains, and fortunes a selfish person would seek.

Another interpretation of the third line is that of enlisting in public service or service of a greater good; this can also be interpreted as civil service, finding a career working for the government.

| Fourth Line | |
|---|---|
| The proud can preserve what they are proud of if they are humble. The privileged can preserve their privilege if they are grateful. Let the outlaw take the divergent path. There is no blame. | 九四：匪其彭無咎 |

While pride creeps into your consciousness, the pride is well deserved.
To maintain Heaven's favor, demonstrate humility and gratitude.
To win a war, one must be adaptable and unconventional.
Focus on the morality of your own conduct, and not on the morality of others. "Let the outlaw take the divergent path," meaning do not enforce your principles onto one whose principles seem to be different from and opposite of yours.
Just as you follow your own path, let others follow theirs.
"彭 péng" evokes the rhythmic beating of ceremonial drums. The image is hearing and feeling the sound of drums (rather than seeing them). The rhythmic beating of the ceremonial drum is an omen of either a war to come or the celebration of a victory.

| *Fifth Line* <br> Foster trust to achieve ambitions. Power comes to those who can foster trust. <br> It is auspicious to proceed. | 六五：<br>厥孚交如<br>威如<br>吉 | ䷍ |

There is affinity.
To achieve your ambitious goals, you need to garner support, and to garner that support, others must find you trustworthy. Foster that trust. Trust is the one thing that the great ones cannot breach.
Should you seek to attain greater power, then you must prove yourself trustworthy. To be trustworthy, speak your truth. And yet that truth must be accessible. Not only does truth need to be accessible; it must be expressed in a dignified manner. Act sincerely and with grace, and then your path will be auspicious.

| *Sixth Line* <br> Heaven's blessing: I am your protection, and I lend my Hand in your favor. <br> Good auspices. Gains shared by all. | 上九：<br>自天祐之<br>吉<br>無不利 | ䷍ |

I see goodness in you, and it is a goodness I will protect.

There is an implication of first-person speech here. You are being assured that your work is aligned with Heaven's Will, and thus you are blessed with divine protection. Not only do you reap benefit, but a greater good shall be served as well.

## Hexagram 15: Qiān. Modesty

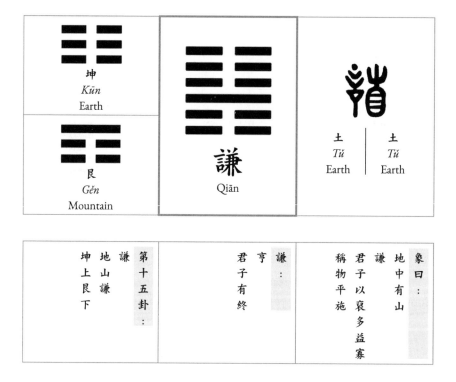

## The Oracle

If you must boast to receive honors, then no one will truly see you as honorable. Nothing is more honorable than decency. Show temperance in your conduct, temperance in your speech, and moderation in all that you do. There is no need for assuming airs of dignity or self-importance. Do not exaggerate. When you strive to be undistinguishable, you become the most distinguishable. Beyond the merits of virtue, you've unwittingly provoked the evil eye of envy and someone feels threatened by you, and this person wields power. Give no one any reason to act against you. Allow no merit to the adversary's claims.

There is a mountain within the earth. **The sage culls away where there is excess, and adds where there is shortage. Ensure temperance and fair distribution.**
Modesty will help you achieve success in your endeavor. What is most important for you is to follow through. Initiating is not the challenge; completion is the obstacle. **The sage will meet a favorable outcome.**

| | |
|---|---|
| *First Line*<br>Humble, humble is the sage.<br>Auspicious to cross the great stream. | 初六：謙謙君子<br>用涉大川<br>吉 |

### OMEN OF THE *QILIN*

The *qilin* is a mythical beast that appears to portend a significant, transformative event relating to a sage or leader. In the I Ching, Hexagrams 2, 15, 23, and 52 are likened to the omen of seeing a *qilin* appear before you. These hexagrams in general are omens of a significant, transformative event to come, one relating to the near-future rise of a sage or leader.

Here, divining Hexagram 15 relates to greatness in status, accomplishment, or knowledge yet to be revealed or manifested.

The philosopher-sage remains unaware of personal virtues. Exemplifying modesty, discretion, temperance, prudence, wisdom, and refinement grant you the powers you need to succeed in the great undertaking to come.

True greatness is unaware of its greatness.

| Second Line<br>The birds chirp of one's demonstrated modesty and charm.<br>Auspicious to persevere. | 貞 鳴 六<br>吉 謙 二<br>　　　： | 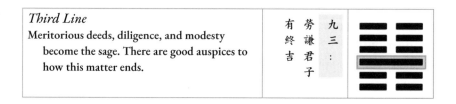 |

People are talking—you are held in high regard.

| Third Line<br>Meritorious deeds, diligence, and modesty become the sage. There are good auspices to how this matter ends. | 有 勞 九<br>終 謙 三<br>吉 君 ：<br>　 子 | |

Carry yourself with refinement.

Refinement is not in your clothes. It's in the way you think, the way you express what you think, the glint of light in your eyes, and the way you inspire others to feel better about themselves.

Carry yourself in this way and you will meet with an auspicious conclusion.

Tai Si, queen mother of the Zhou founders, carried herself with refinement but dressed modestly. When one is truly beautiful, inside and out, nothing can hide it.

Accomplishments to come for the one who exemplifies modesty and refinement.

| Fourth Line<br>There is no advantage to any endeavor that does not exercise modesty. | 無 六<br>不 四<br>利 ：<br>撝<br>謙 | |

Having achieved goals you had set out, you are now confident. Temper that confidence with humility.

Subsequent endeavors will continue to require your modesty. Though you have accomplishments under your belt, your position is still a tenuous one.

*Fifth Line*
If you are not prosperous, then your neighbor is not prosperous. If your neighbor is not prosperous, then you are not prosperous.
Gains to come from entering hostile territory.
Use force to exert influence and gain control.
Sending troops will bring advancement.

There is a difference between being modest and being weak. Be modest, not weak. When others threaten your position, assert yourself. Strike with force if necessary. Speak softly and exude a gentle demeanor, but issue justice fairly and impartially.

Be objective in your judgment of those around you. Part of being modest is to not take matters too personally and to act fairly, in accordance with laws. Even while being severe, you can maintain your modesty.

Weakness is when you are easily threatened and take matters too personally, and as a result, you strike out of pride rather than on behalf of the rule of law.

The second part of the message is about interdependent prosperity.

Your prosperity is interdependent with others' prosperity. To be independent, one must be interdependent.

In a yearning to feel safe and secure, you are tempted to fear and hoard; instead, to be safe and enjoy security, one must first have faith and foster hope.

The latter prong of the line suggests interdependent alliances with those close to you in order to gain new ground. Gaining new ground is how both you and your neighbor attain the prosperity you both seek.

| Sixth Line <br> The birds chirp of one's demonstrated modesty and charm. <br> Gains from launching the army. Send the expedition to conquer the capital; the kingdom is yours. | 上六： 鳴謙 利用行師 征邑國 |  |
|---|---|---|

It is not sufficient to merely express modesty like birds chirping, no matter how sweet the song. You are either modest or you are not; it's not found in words.

When there is enmity, do not seek to lay the blame. When there is initial failure or wounded pride, do not draw back or pity yourself. These are actions of the weak. Genuine modesty will focus on implementing order for the greater good.

In matters relating to statecraft, a challenger is favored by the people. The challenger is a scholar-teacher, of modest personal means. The birds chirping represent the people's support for the modest teacher.

The counsel being given: mobilize and advance.

"利用行師 lì yòng xíng shī" could also be interpreted to mean "call upon the masters and teachers." The meaning of the sixth line would thus change to suggest reliance on scholars and experts to help rule the kingdom.

## Hexagram 16: Yù. Enthusiasm

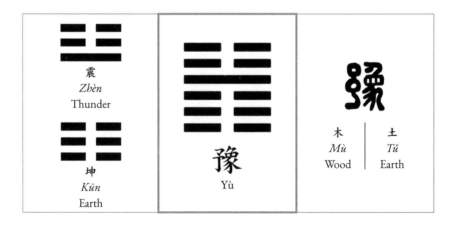

象曰：
雷出地奮
豫
先王以作樂崇德
殷薦之上帝
以配祖考

豫：
利建侯行師

第十六卦：
豫
雷地豫
震上坤下

## *The Oracle*

> Action with enthusiasm. Renounce hesitation. Do not let chronic conditions hold you back. Prepare for the advance. Demonstrate enthusiasm and you motivate not just yourself, but also the spirit realms to support you. Honor others with enthusiasm and they will reciprocate. Let the energy of life invigorate you so you can invigorate others. Know your purpose and reason for action, and you will never cease to take action. When you are relentless with your drive, nothing can or will stop you.

**Thunder shakes the earth. Prepare for an advance. Auspicious to take military action.** You will be at an advantage when you seek the counsel of a master. **Proceed with the endeavor at hand, but first seek out sage advice before initiating action.** Do not act in haste; the archer studies the target before an arrow is shot.

**The king honors the dignitaries with music and celebration. The king honors the Divine. The king honors the ancestors.**

This is a hexagram of great gusto and verve. When you can understand these honoring acts of the king, then you, too, can accomplish beyond even your highest ambitions. To be motivated to achieve, you must first be motivated by the energy of life.

An auspicious omen for taking military action.

*First Line*
**The birds chirp too indulgently.
Ominous to proceed.**

初六：
鳴豫
凶

There is a little too much devotion for one of momentary fame. Believing the rumors will result in misfortune. Unwarranted enthusiasm.

Chirping prematurely. Exhaustion; excess, leading to misfortune.

There is an upset of equilibrium, which is the source of woes. Exhaustion and excess weaken your willpower.

Perhaps you feel that you have lost your sense of direction. You feel aimless. Blocked aspirations.

Feeling sorry for yourself; lacking enthusiasm. Take some time off from the everyday.

| *Second Line* | 貞 不 介 六 |
|---|---|
| Safe within a cave. Perpetual and enduring day— good auspices to come. | 吉 終 于 二 |
| | 日 石 ： |

If the first line's advice was to take some time off from the everyday, the second line is affirming that some time as a recluse will be well rewarded.

Stabilized by rock, you will know the judgment before the end of the day. Perseverance brings good fortune.

You do not flatter those above you; you do not turn your nose up at those below you. Intuitively, you know the answer to your inquiry already.

You manifest the objectivity of a rock.

To be successful, you must be able to see the seeds, sensitive to even the most subtle and early signs of a change in conditions.

At first glimpse of the seeds, you must know whether to take action. Do not hesitate or delay.

Do not let even a day pass in hesitation. You must be able to see what is hidden. Success in your endeavor hinges on it.

"介于石 jiè yú shí" has been interpreted as one who is stabilized, wedged in securely by a rock, or being anchored securely by a rock. Yet in antiquity, "石" was also used to denote a stone cave in the side of a mountain. Consider the specific context of the inquiry to determine which interpretation applies in the matter.

Several differing interpretations of the second line are worth noting. It's been interpreted as meaning that one was trapped inside a cave or by a rock, but fortuitously, was rescued within a day's time.

Alternatively, the rock is a symbol of unwavering integrity and stability, enjoyed interminably so long as one walks the virtuous path.

Yet a third interpretation reads the line as one who is caught in the middle, but the middle position is most auspicious, and thus one remains safe and secure.

Yet a fourth reading is to see this as indicating a defensive position hiding behind a rock (or in a cave) for protection. While you are safely protected, prosperity continues to flourish.

| *Third Line* | | |
|---|---|---|
| Gazing with wide-open eyes, inciting content, discontent—regret. Hesitation and delay cause regret. |  |  |

Reflecting upon the matter with a sense of loss and sorrow. A promising opportunity incites content at the onset but later settles into discontent, and now there is a feeling of disappointment.

Anxiety causes hesitation, and the hesitation causes a delay. The delay results in missed opportunity.

There is weakness and dependency that must be eradicated. Execute the action with enthusiasm.

| *Fourth Line* | | |
|---|---|---|
| Cause for enthusiasm. Greatness is achieved. Great gains. Rallying allies to gather like a hairpin clasps the topknot in place. |  |  |

"Allies" here has also been interpreted as friends, kin, members of your clan, comrades, or fellows.

The inner source of motivation is found. You gather allies around you as a bobby pin gathers hair.

To achieve in the endeavor, renounce your hesitation.

Look inward to find what motivates you, what sparks your enthusiasm, and let that propel you forward.

When you find that inner strength and confidence, you will attract allies who believe in you, who will follow you in your cause.

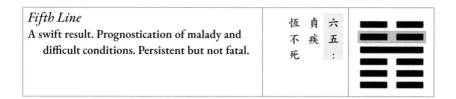

*Fifth Line*
A swift result. Prognostication of malady and difficult conditions. Persistent but not fatal.

A difficult situation; discomfort. A chronic condition in the matter at hand is holding you back; an unsolved problem persists to affect your endeavor.

Persevere through it: although the chronic condition is not likely to be curable, it does not end your pursuit, and it should not curb your enthusiasm. Injures, but does not incapacitate.

In fact, it may be that injury, the incurable chronic condition, that motivates you forward.

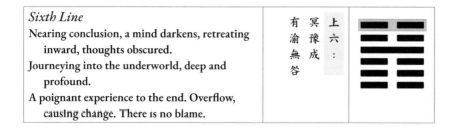

*Sixth Line*
Nearing conclusion, a mind darkens, retreating inward, thoughts obscured.
Journeying into the underworld, deep and profound.
A poignant experience to the end. Overflow, causing change. There is no blame.

As the endeavor seems to near its completion, at the denouement of the matter at hand, you see that perhaps you had been motivated by illusions, lost in a long-past memory, propelled forward by falsehoods that you wanted to see as true. A sober awakening. Just when you fear it may be too late, you arrive at a logical understanding. Yet it is not too late. So long as you are still capable of changing, of correcting, all can still end quite favorably and you will be freed of error. There is an opportunity for growth. No culpability.

A mystic might read this line as a journey into the underworld, facing one's shadow, and leaving the experience profoundly changed.

# Hexagram 17: Suí. Inspiring Followers

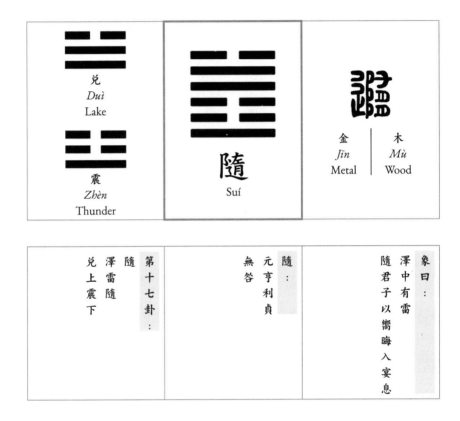

## The Oracle

To learn how to lead, you must first learn how to serve. A follower becomes the leader. To learn how to serve is to secure voluntary assent from followers. If you obtain your followers through force or cunning, by conspiracy or division, your leadership will be short-lived: there will be movements of resistance against you. Force them and they will resist. Serve them and they will serve you. Reward loyalty with generosity. Trust in your own excellence. And yet for there to be sincere trust, you must fully embody and demonstrate that excellence.

Thunder strikes at the center of fertile marshes. The sage inspires the novices to face the dark night before a new moon and guides them from uncertainty to serenity. A banquet is set for the festivity.

**Supreme good auspices are prognosticated. Advantageous to proceed. There is no blame.**

Inciting movement upward; growth and progress to come.

To lead, one must cultivate virtue (德, *dé*) and fully embody that virtue in every interaction. That is how one inspires a great myriad of followers.

Win the hearts and minds of the people. That is how you gain victory without conflict. Avoid conflict for the sake of the people.

| | | |
|---|---|---|
| *First Line* <br> **The dignitary departs from party principles. Great luck and opportunities result. Walk out the doorway and meet with allies; it will bring you productivity and success.** | 出門交有功　貞吉　官有渝　初九： | ▬▬　▬▬ <br> ▬▬▬▬▬ <br> ▬▬　▬▬ <br> ▬▬　▬▬ <br> ▬▬▬▬▬ |

You were a follower, upholding the group's principles, but now there seems to have been a change in your perspective.

You become a dissident. Before making the change known to others, be sure you are firm in your convictions, because once the change is known, you cannot vacillate.

The follower is becoming a leader through dissidence. However, keep your mind open. Be adaptable and ready to change. Remain receptive. Be actively and sincerely responsive to those who could become your followers.

Unlikely folk become the most loyal allies, so associate with people from all backgrounds. Diversity and diversifying will accomplish your objective.

| | | |
|---|---|---|
| *Second Line* <br> **Attached to the little son. Losing the husband.** | 失丈夫　係小子　六二： | ▬▬　▬▬ <br> ▬▬▬▬▬ <br> ▬▬　▬▬ <br> ▬▬▬▬▬ <br> ▬▬▬▬▬ |

You are limiting yourself to associations with the inexperienced and naïve. As a result, you may be alienating yourself from those who do have the experience, knowledge, and wisdom to help you in your endeavor.

The gendered references are used here for the purposes of metaphor. "Husband" represents one who would otherwise be an intimate partner, one of shared responsibilities, shared assets, cooperation, and mutual gains to be had. "Little son" in this context represents someone dependent on you, with potential for growth in the future; but for now, all that you give to the son is in self-sacrifice, at a loss.

Whether this line is interpreted as positive or negative is a matter of perspective. The one who inspires followers rises to the top for visibility, which is a position of solitude and isolation.

Followers are those dependent on the risen leader. Thus, they are like the little son. Tending to the son takes time away from tending to the husband, or put another way, from nurturing reciprocal and bilateral relations.

You are at a point where you must make strategic decisions about who you surround yourself with and whose interests you prioritize.

"失 shī" can mean to forfeit, fail, surrender, or neglect. Thus, depending on the context of the inquiry, it can mean failing someone or choosing to let go of someone.

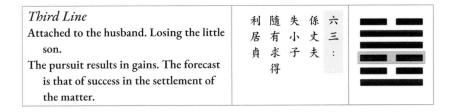

| *Third Line* | 六 | | | | |
|---|---|---|---|---|---|
| Attached to the husband. Losing the little son. | 三 | 係 | 失 | 隨 | 利 |
| The pursuit results in gains. The forecast is that of success in the settlement of the matter. | ： | 丈夫 | 小子 | 有求得 | 居貞 |

The first part of this line is the reverse of the second line. The husband is symbolic of reciprocal benefits and one with experience and knowledge, one who can yield utility right now, whereas the son is symbolic of future potential and one-way dependency.

Instead of serving the helpless, choosing the one who can help you results in achievement of your immediate objective.

| | | |
|---|---|---|
| **Fourth Line**<br>Inspiring followers yields harvest. The objective is met. But the outcome brings adversity and setbacks.<br>Have faith and trust in the Way of the Tao. Be receptive to the ways of others. That is the way to clarity of mind.<br>Is there any blame? | 何 以 有 貞 隨 九<br>咎 明 孚 凶 有 四<br>　　　在 獲 ：<br>　　　道 | ䷐ |

Follow only what can help you attain your objective. Be fierce with your conviction. Have faith in the ways of the Divine. To walk the path according to the Divine is to attain higher understanding.

There are associates in your inner circle who are not sincere toward you. They do not sincerely share the same objectives as you. In keeping these associates around you, you may inadvertently follow them to your detriment.

To achieve your endeavor, you can only keep associates in your inner circle who are sincere toward you, who share the same objectives as you. Then when you follow them, you are following them toward success.

Thus, "以明 yǐ míng" in the fourth line means to make oneself open-minded and receptive to others' way. That is the Way of the Tao.

Wisdom is attained by acquiring knowledge. That knowledge is an enduring search—the right searches for the wrong, and the wrong searches for the right. The underlying principle of the axiom: there is no right, and there is no wrong.

| | | |
|---|---|---|
| **Fifth Line**<br>Trust in your excellence.<br>Auspicious to proceed. | 吉 孚 九<br>　 于 五<br>　 嘉 ： | ䷐ |

Exude more confidence. Be self-assured. You demonstrate integrity and you work hard. Heaven's Will is aligned with yours.

Trust your position. Trust yourself. You are in the right, and the Divine is aligned in a way to support your endeavor, so it is auspicious to go forward.

What genius believes to be true, the body can surely do.

| *Sixth Line* <br> You were confined, then you were released. <br> The king makes sacrificial offerings and petitions the gods at Western Mountain. | 王用亨于西山 | 維之 | 拘係之乃從 | 上六： |
|---|---|---|---|---|

Transcendence. You've achieved more ground than those who came before you. But do not forget where you came from.

The sixth line is the main line of the Lake trigram, representing communion between gods and humans.

Generally a positive omen for long-term stability in the matter at hand. Nevertheless, the line is a reminder to continue devotionals to gods and ancestors. Hexagram 17 has been about inspiring followers; the sixth line is a reminder that the greatest leader is an inspired follower of Heaven's Will.

The popular understanding of this line is as a reference to King Wen's imprisonment by King Zhou of Shang, ultimately inciting Wen's followers to revolt and overthrow the Shang dynasty. However, scholars such as Cheng Yi (AD 1033–1107) propose that the reference is to King Tai of Zhou (周太王, Zhōu Tài Wáng).

The Western Mountain is a reference to Qishan, or Mount Qi, the birthplace of the Zhou dynasty. King Tai of Zhou was the one who moved his kingdom's capital to Qi.

# Hexagram 18: Gǔ. Decay

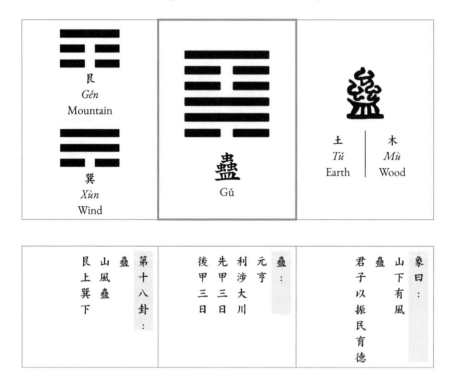

## The Oracle

**An infestation results in the decay of matter. Dogma causes degeneration. There has been spoilage and degeneration, so it is critical to take action immediately. Great obstacles to come, but take bold action to go out and confront those obstacles before they come for you. Those who can survive this stage come through the other side emanating with greatness. Sign of great power after the rebirth.**

Worms on decaying matter: pestilent. The mountain wind spreads the worms on decaying matter. There has been spoilage and the food in the bowl decays, sprouting worms, but there is still the chance to make reparations for the spoilage.

A necessary difficult part in the cycle of life.

**The sage uplifts the people by teaching them the ways of virtue.** Such teachings reverse the natural course of decay and remove the stagnation. The great sage is one who motivates the people like the wind that carries seeds up the mountain.

**Auspicious to cross the great stream.**

You have been in a state of stagnation for a while, and as a result, there is degeneration and you are headed toward a stage of decay. It is critical to take action immediately to prevent further atrophy.

"甲" *(jiǎ)* is one of the ten heavenly stems (yang in its *qi* nature) associated with the Wu Xing phase Wood, the eastern direction, the spring season, and the planet Jupiter. During the Shang dynasty, it corresponded with one of the ten days of the week.

**You will need three days before the critical point 甲, and three days after for the full endeavor to be a success.** There must be adequate preparation before that critical point, and then afterward, adequate reflection. The indication of three days prior to a critical point and three days after suggests the need for planning and a well-defined exit strategy.

For matters relating to spell-crafting and ritual work, Hexagram 18 indicates that such work is to be done between the hours of 11 p.m. and 3 a.m.

The English translation of Hexagram 18's title belies its favorable nature. This is a hexagram of great power. After all, the final message is that it's advantageous to cross the great stream.

| *First Line* <br> The father's work is decaying. There's an heir. Assured, there is no blame. <br> The whetstone comes to the end of its life— auspicious for the future to come; prosperity and great fortune. | 厲考有幹初<br>終無子父六<br>吉咎之：<br>　　蠱 |  |
|---|---|---|

Unbroken chain of succession—hand to hand, that is how decay is bypassed.

"幹父之蠱" *(gàn fù zhī gǔ)* is an allusion to a son that inherits the father's unfinished business, shares the father's vision, and completes the mission.

The whetstone, or a stone used to sharpen metal tools, axes, and daggers, symbolizes refinement and the strengthening of character through friction; it's also a symbol of cultivating a new warrior king.

The father has trained the heir well, and the heir will achieve great victories.

| | | |
|---|---|---|
| *Second Line*<br>The mother's work is decaying. This is not an appropriate time for divination. | 不可貞 幹母之蠱 九二： | ䷑ |

The first line is often referred to as "父之蠱" (Fǔ Zhī Gǔ), the Decaying Father, while the second line is the "母之蠱" (Mǔ Zhī Gǔ), the Decaying Mother.

At this time, the Oracle is maintaining silence on the matter inquired about.

| | | |
|---|---|---|
| *Third Line*<br>The father's work is decaying. The junior encounters setbacks. Feeling remorse and sorrow. No grave errors—there is no blame. | 無大咎 小有悔 幹父之蠱 九三： | ䷑ |

The heir is undertaking the challenge of finishing the father's Great Work. However, that heir, an inexperienced junior, has made errors and now feels regret. Those errors are not grave. The heir is blameless.

Crossing the great stream is met with initial failures. Nothing irreversible, so keep going.

Trust in your creativity.

Be persistent and persevere. Practicing virtues in the face of decay is how you reverse that decay.

| | | |
|---|---|---|
| *Fourth Line*<br>The father's wealth is decaying. Averting one's eyes from seeing the truth.<br>Blame. Faults may result in misfortune. An error in judgment. | 往見吝 裕父之蠱 六四： | ䷑ |

Errors result in harm. Fault lies with the one who refuses to confront the truth.

Assets are dwindling. Material resources needed to finish the father's work are scarce.

See the truth. Correct the error.

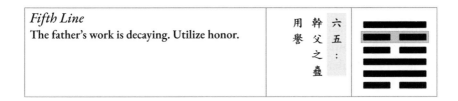

*Fifth Line*
**The father's work is decaying. Utilize honor.**

This line is generally interpreted as having to correct the errors of a predecessor. The up-and-coming generation or inheritor of a tradition must make amends on behalf of those who came before.

Foster goodwill through honesty. That is how you neutralize the decay.

The image of "譽 Yù," honor and prestige, is that of words being spoken. Use the words that are spoken to achieve what you seek.

Work toward attaining prestige. Do not yield to complacency. Have the honesty to change. Changing will avert decay.

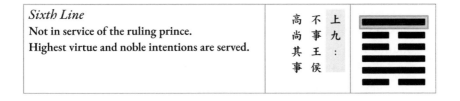

*Sixth Line*
**Not in service of the ruling prince.**
**Highest virtue and noble intentions are served.**

Serve not the person, but the purpose. Care not for the chief, but for the clan. Through legacy, that which is honest and true will live on.

## PRACTICUM 8.3:
## Poison Magic and Defenses to Ward Off Poison Magic

Gu is the most powerful poison that can be created, crafted by sealing venomous creatures into a jar and forcing them to devour one another. Specifically, the Five Poisons (五毒, Wǔ Dú) are used: snakes, scorpions, centipedes, toads, and spiders. A poison is then made from the last surviving creature.

The most powerful of Gu is crafted on the fifth day of the fifth lunar month, or "Double Five," considered the unluckiest day of the year. The venomous creatures are left sealed in that jar and placed somewhere dark and remote until only the corpse of one creature is left. The poison or baneful magic is crafted from that remaining corpse. Poison magic, curses, or hexes performed in the hour of 午 *(wǔ)*, 11 a.m. to 12:59 p.m., is also considered more potent.

Once the victim ingests the poison, it slowly infiltrates the victim's body, attacking first the abdomen and then the heart. The poison takes ten long days of pain and illness to kill the victim, causing the victim to vomit out liquified internal organs, devouring from the inside out. From Gu arose a form of baneful magic called Gu Dao. Gu Dao shares the same philosophy of curses that attack from the inside out, causing internal, psychological, or psychic damage and mental illness first before ruining the victim's livelihood, social relationships, and physical or material well-being. Culturally, Gu Dao was linked to women from minority ethnic groups in southern China and the South China Sea, who became known as masters of the craft.

As a defensive antidote against poison magic, realgar wine (雄黃酒, *xiónghuángjiǔ*) is used to counteract against curses. Sprinkling realgar wine around the perimeter of a home is a form of warding; in antiquity, this was done in the summer months not just to safeguard against evil spirits (especially during Ghost Month) but also to repel poisonous insects and snakes. Historically, realgar wine was ingested, but today we know that realgar wine itself is toxic, laced with arsenic. Thus, it should not be ingested, and if used in witchcraft, it needs to be handled with care. Red cinnabar is also used as a form of defense against poison magic.

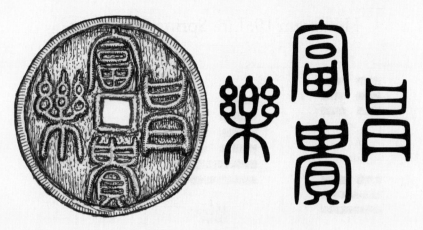

FIGURE 8.5 Protection amulet to ward against poison magic

The amulet pictured in figure 8.5 is a Fu talisman and a form of magical seal crafted into jewelry and worn. The words inscribed upon it are 富貴昌樂 *(fù guì chāng lè)*, the characters appearing in the order top, bottom, left, right forming a defensive cross. The first character means wealth and riches; the second precious and valuable or honors bestowed; the third is light that brings prosperity; and the fourth is happiness and to always be flourishing.

If a divinatory result indicates poisonous and toxic influences present in your life, craft a personal talisman for yourself using figure 8.5. Using a wood burner, inscribe the seal onto a circular wooden disk. On the other side would be an inscription of your personal seal, equivalent to a signature. Burn incense on your altar as an offering to the gods and ancestors, then place the disk on the altar for the spirits to bless. Your talisman will be ready the next day. Keep it on your person as a form of protection. If and when you lose the talisman, it's a sign that all of the poisonous magic has been neutralized and you no longer need the talisman.

# Hexagram 19: Lín. Spring Is Coming

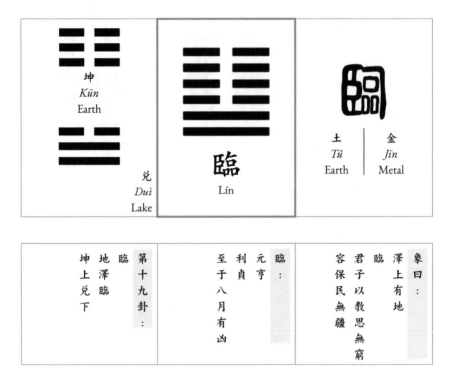

## The Oracle

Arrival of a transcendent and hallowed blessing that will bring a rebirth and renewal. That which had putrefied shall rejuvenate and be restored. A new beginning and a time to rebuild. It's a new day and a new cycle. Liberation. Opportunities are coming your way. All the work you have put in propels you toward your peak. You are about to manifest your own highest potential and destiny.

**The sign of one who prevails: ascension to greatness.** Approaching manifestation. Arrival of the light. The first light after the winter solstice. The divine light expands your power. Grace. This is the moment just before.

Prosperity and gains to come. Great benefits from completing the endeavor at hand.

**At the arrival of the eighth moon, beware of challenges.** You will enjoy an enduring period of success, but around the eighth lunar month to come, adversity, mischance, and mishaps.

Earth above lake: fertile and stable grounds for creation. Ascension to greatness. Approaching manifestation. As the great sage, in your wisdom you will look out for and protect those in your kingdom who are less fortunate.

**The divine yin above delivers an exchange and commerce to the below— a stabilizing force; your fortunes will be sustained.**

The eighth lunar month of the lunisolar calendar coincides with the autumnal equinox and represents the polarity or contrasting opposite of Hexagram 19. Thus, the Oracle's message to beware the eighth lunar month can be a metaphor for warning against trying to keep thriving what is naturally on the decline. Hexagram 19 is about rebirth and a new beginning, not about trying to prevent the inevitable.

Hexagram 19 is traditionally associated with the first light after winter, coinciding with the period from around lunar month 12 to after the new year and lunar month 1. Yet the Oracle warns of timing related to lunar month 8, which is mid-autumn, or harvest season. Thus, in terms of timing, Hexagram 19 expresses a situation that will go on for the long-term, at least one year.

After much toil and labor, and many obstacles, you are now positioned to enjoy the first light of great success. However, once you reach your pinnacle, do not look down on those below you. Do not grow arrogant or prejudiced. Do not be condescending toward the work others do that you perceive to be lesser than the work you do.

### BUDDHIST MESSIANISM

In esoteric readings of the Oracle, Hexagram 19 is resonant with messianism, such as the prophecy of Maitreya, the bodhisattva to be the successor of Sakyamuni Buddha, or the Taoist foretelling of an apocalyptic end of times and the beginning of a new world cycle.

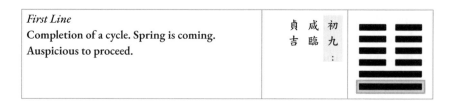

Resilience drives your ascension to greatness. You will meet with prosperity when you persevere on the virtuous and noble path.

In the ebb and flow of lucks, you are on the ascent.

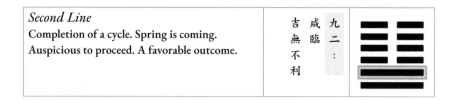

You are in control of the momentum of your present matter.

This is an omen of beneficial, growing momentum after there had been a cessation.

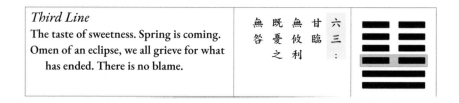

An ascension to greatness is like drinking nectar. Achievement of material success positions you comfortably in life, and life is sweet.

However, you are not advancing beyond your current point. You know this already, and it concerns you. You contemplate how you might be able to achieve more.

No misfortunes caused by errors in judgment.

"攸" *(yōu)*, the origin of "滌" *(dí)*, is the image of one pouring water over the back in a purification ritual. A ritual purification at this time may be just the right prescription.

| *Fourth Line* <br> Arriving at the crest. Spring is coming. <br> There is no blame. | 無 至 六 <br> 咎 臨 四 <br>       : | |

The arrow will hit its target. Attainment—you arrive at the destination you had set out to reach, though after great tedium and overcoming obstacles. There were miscalculations, but nothing that couldn't be corrected.

"至" *(zhi)* is the image of an arrow lodged in the ground. The arrow has reached the destination it was intended for.

| *Fifth Line* <br> Receiving knowledge; understanding. Spring is coming. <br> The great sage is coming. Favorable to proceed. | 吉 大 知 六 <br>   君 臨 五 <br>   之   : <br>   宜 | |

Prognostication of success and felicity. Sound reasoning brings success. Your prudence will be rewarded with success and good fortune. Employ your skills and intellect along with your intuition and wisdom, and you cannot go astray.

The fifth line is an omen prognosticating the rise of a great king.

The etymological root and historical form of the character "宜 yí" here is the image of two choice pieces of meat placed on a sacrificial altar as offerings. The sincerity of your devotional and ceremonial rituals will bless you with divine protection and material success.

| *Sixth Line* <br> Plentiful and enthusiastic, earnest and diligent: spring is coming. Favorable to proceed. <br> There is no blame. | 無 敦 上 <br> 咎 臨 六 <br> 吉    : | |

One achieves high esteem. Past great efforts are rewarded. Calamity averted. Errors corrected.

There is a general consensus among scholars that, although not literally in the text, the sixth line here refers to one who has achieved greatness in the world already and who has since retired or retreated from the world for solitude and inner contemplation.

Such a person is a sage or master who now returns to the world, exits retirement, or leaves solitude behind to be of use to society again, to come back and teach or help the world.

Even when expectations are not met or mistakes are made, you will go without blame, because you sacrificed time you could have enjoyed for yourself to put yourself back in service of a greater good.

## Hexagram 20: Guān. Observation

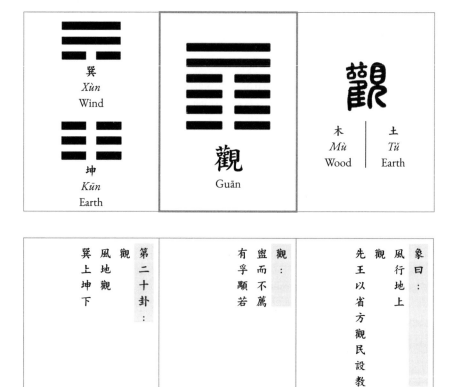

I Ching: The Book of Changes   489

## *The Oracle*

Before you proceed, give the matter a thorough reassessment. A more complete observation of the situation is called for. Do you know your own merits and your own faults? Are you sure that you are entirely in the right? Honor the gods and ancestors to receive further insight. Sometimes it is not the judgment that needs observation, but the judge. To contemplate the matter, go alone where you can observe the wind moving the earth. Nature will give you the counsel you seek.

A wind rustles the earth. **Watching, observing.**

**Kings past call upon the four guardians of the universe to aid them toward the correct guidance of their people.** You must see and also be seen. Others will then put their trust and faith in you.

In the ancient rituals of honoring the Divine, there is a moment of quiet introspection between the commencement of prayers to the Divine and the explicit appeal to the Divine for support of human endeavors (along with the ceremonial sacrifice). That in-between moment of quiet introspection is where you are now. Make the most of it. This is the time for you to cleanse yourself of inferior motivations.

Reevaluate the inquiry at hand, and restate for yourself what your motivations are.

If your true motivations do not align with the Divine, adjust your motivations. Then you are ready to ask the Oracle for the answer.

After sincere contemplation of the matter at hand, proceed with a second divination.

**There is a need for contemplation. Reevaluate your motivations behind the endeavor.** Observe. Observe the wind. Observe the earth.

---

*First Line*
A child, watching and observing.
A shaman, watching and observing.
There is no blaming the innocent.
For the sage, ominous to proceed.

初六：
童觀
小人無咎
君子吝

Reconsider the matter from a different vantage point, one oft overlooked or dismissed. The one who has no book learning teaches the one who has.

A different set of experiences is needed for the task at hand. Ominous to proceed with your current perspective; take a different approach. Going forward as you plan right now portends pain and adversity.

"童" *(tóng)* carries a dual meaning here. It can mean an innocent child, but it can also refer to a shaman. Thus, both appear in the first part of the line.

Those who are too experienced become too set in the ways of their thinking. An unconventional approach is needed. Someone inexperienced brings genius.

In a mystical reading, this line is a foretelling of either shamanic training to come or going to see a shaman. The first line is the start of a narrative arc moving toward the upper trigram Wind, which corresponds with the archetype of the shaman.

| Second Line<br>Watching and observing through a keyhole.<br>Advantageous omen of a Girl. Auspicious. | 利女貞 闚觀 六二： | ▬▬▬<br>▬▬▬<br>▬ ▬<br>▬ ▬<br>▬ ▬<br>▬ ▬ |
|---|---|---|

You do not have a clear, open view of the matter at hand, as you are looking at it through a keyhole.

Narrow view. A broader vision is needed.

In some translations, this is a crack in the door, peeping, or taking only a quick flash of a glance to see the matter. Here, the sense is that you are seeing the matter at hand through one perspective only, and other perspectives must be considered before you proceed.

The Girl is capitalized here to indicate that it can be interpreted as a proper noun (a person, place, thing, state, or quality). For example, in Chinese and Japanese twenty-eight lunar mansions astronomy, the Girl is a constellation in Aquarius consisting of four stars. The Girl can be the designation that the Oracle is using to identify a particular person in your reading.

| | |
|---|---|
| *Third Line*<br>Watching and observing my birth, my life, I advance, I retreat; step forward, then step back; rise, recede, ebb and flow; go, return. |  |

Your question cannot be answered at this time. The Oracle is being unresponsive, though the response as given answers a deeper, more profound question you've been asking.

"進 Jìn" indicates moving forward, advancing, entering, receiving, or giving, while "退 Tuì" indicates moving backward, retreating, withdrawing, leaving, receding, fading, or returning.

Is the Oracle addressing you in first person? Is this the voice of your unconscious inner self trying to communicate with your conscious mind?

| | |
|---|---|
| *Fourth Line*<br>Watching and observing the emanant light of the kingdom. Watching and observing its halo.<br>Gains to be had as a visiting guest of the king. |  |

The king honors a visiting guest. An eminent one can see the kingdom's aura, and the king invites the eminent one to share that vision.

Profound insights when you reflect upon the bigger picture, to see the forest and the trees.

| | |
|---|---|
| *Fifth Line*<br>Watching and observing my birth, my life.<br>The sage is blameless. |  |

This line is an expression of agape love. This is an emotional locution of Spirit's sublime love for and contentment with the myriad things the Three of the Tao gave birth to, and most poignantly, you—you among the myriad things that Spirit created.

While the divine sentience of the Oracle might not be answering your inquiry directly, the Oracle is speaking to you directly, expressing a sentiment that, upon further observation and reflection by you, does address the question presented.

Perhaps this is the moment to watch and observe your own life, since birth, and reflect on it. By doing so, you will arrive at the answer to your own question.

What *is* being conveyed here: You have not erred. You are perfect just the way you are.

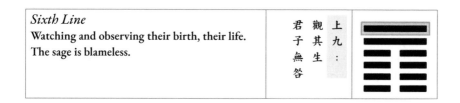

*Sixth Line*
Watching and observing their birth, their life.
The sage is blameless.

君子無咎 觀其生 上九：

What you decide, how you act, what you've done in your past—none of it matters, none of it is punishable, as long as you have been earnest and have taken every step with care. Act with care. That is all that matters.

No errors have been made. No matter what calamities seem to have befallen them, the one who is judicious and prudent is the one who has not erred.

Rather than address your inquiry directly, the Oracle has taken this opportunity to watch, observe, and reflect on this populated world. Whether the Oracle is talking about one other person or many other people, a group, a society, a civilization, or an eon's span of humanity—that is an understanding that will be reached privately between the Oracle and you.

# Hexagram 21: Shih Hé. Bite Through

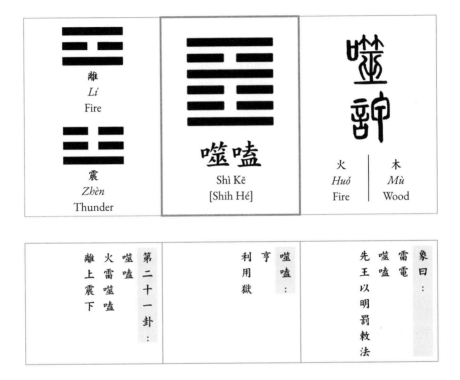

## The Oracle

A vulnerable position, outranked and overpowered. Circumstances are favorable for issuing punishment where punishment is due. Adjudicate with impartiality, and then let the punishment fit the crime. Yet in the process of penalizing another, you inflict harm onto yourself. A difficult choice. A Pyrrhic victory. If you cannot be settled until the law has been invoked, then invoke the law. Remember that there are many codes of law in this universe. Administer justice. Sign of the sacrifice.

**Cracking seeds with the front teeth.** Having the clarity to incite movement: Fire over Thunder.

There is an obstruction between the upper lip and the lower, forcing your mouth open, a vulnerable position.

**Bite down and tear through the obstruction to close the mouth again.**

This is the image of an open mouth with an obstruction between the lips. The answer is to bite through the obstruction.

**To protect from harm and to lead the way, to open the path for others, the king implements imperial orders for the law and punishment of crimes.**

**Auspicious to proceed. Favorable outcome for the trial.**

"噬" *(shì)* means to bite down, to gnaw through, though etymologically, it originates from the word "筮" *(shì)*, meaning divination with yarrow stalks, or to divine. In Chinese folk beliefs, homonyms hold power. Moreover, the word "巫" *(wū)* for shaman, witch, or medium is embedded into *shì*. Thus, to the mystic, Hexagram 21 can have the implication of seeking retributive justice through witchcraft.

"嗑" *(kē)*, in addition to the image of cracking seeds between the teeth, also means to be talkative, or to reproach, to be contentious and litigious, inclined to bicker, dispute, and be disagreeable.

Hexagram 21 pertains to legal and governmental matters.

The circumstances are favorable for you right now, and it is to your advantage to inflict punishment where punishment is due.

Bite down. Remove obstacles with force.

### AN OMEN OF CRIMINAL SUITS AND TENSIONS

Hexagrams 6 and 21 portend litigation, disputes, or legal and governmental matters, and the involvement of law, politics, or governmental institutions.

Here, Hexagram 21 can denote criminal suits or tensions between one individual and the state, or one minority group versus the dominating majority group. In contrast, Hexagram 6 can denote civil suits or tensions between two individuals head to head, or one group versus another group.

The difference between the two hexagrams is balance of power. Hexagram 6 seems to imply a more balanced distribution of power between the two adversaries, whereas Hexagram 21 implies an imbalance of power.

| First Line<br>The confining shoe maims the toe.<br>There is no blame. | 初九：<br>屨校滅趾<br>無咎 | ䷔ |

You've been walking a path without the proper footwear—inadequate preparation prior to undertaking the journey. Thus, injuries now sustained.

And yet there is also a subtext that the inadequate preparation wasn't entirely your fault or within your control.

From the start there was a lack of resources or an imbalance of power. Nevertheless, before the arc of this hexagram narrative is through, you will achieve balance. Note the balance of yin and yang lines in the hexagram composition.

A few other layers of implications from 校 *(xiào):* to resist, to oppose, to contest, to proofread, to examine, and to calculate. The original ideogram was the image of a person sitting cross-legged under a tree, perhaps contemplating a strategic plan for getting out of a precarious situation.

The original implications of 滅 *(miè)* were to destroy or extinguish by water; to flood the situation and cause destruction. Note also that the word suggests the use of water to put out a fire, suggesting the likelihood of rehabilitation, so measures to rehabilitate should be taken. Before you endeavor to punish, first try reconciliation.

Here, the translation is "maim" to indicate harm, impairment, deprivation, and a wounding. This is causing an injurious loss of use. Also, the shoe reference bears a tone of expressing repression, being bound, either by being compelled or involuntary constraint.

Nevertheless, come what may, in accordance with the Tao, this was a no-fault situation, each party foreseeably serving their own interests.

| Second Line<br>Biting through the skin maims the nose.<br>There is no blame. | 六二：<br>噬膚滅鼻<br>無咎 | ䷔ |

Offending your roots only hurts yourself—self-sabotage of your own power, assets, and social status.

In traditional physiognomy, the nose is the center of life, representing our wealth and prestige. A famous quote credited to Confucius explains filial piety as honoring one's hair, skin, and body, because it comes from our parents, and these parts of our body should not be harmed.

Be careful that you are not undermining your own success.

The second line is the first action taken in reaction to what was experienced in the first line. "Biting through the skin" implies a superficial or shallow wound. This was not intended to be a deep injury. However, it "maims the nose," suggesting harm caused to the initial stages, the beginning and the founding of the matter at hand.

Perhaps intentions were not to injure, but the end result caused an impairment. Such an impairment caused the course of events to come to an imbalance of power.

*Third Line*
Biting through preserved meat. Encountering poison. Treating the poison.
Slight regrets. A trifling sense of loss. There is no blame.

六三：噬腊肉遇毒小吝无咎

Harms inflicted seem to be intentional and premeditated.

Suggestions of meat preserved through a drying method, in contrast to the suggestions of water in the maiming process for the first and second lines.

Since 遇 *(yù)* generally suggests "encountering" or coming across the poison, it can also mean to treat, to handle, and having to deal with. The translation here endeavors to account for both possibilities.

毒 *(dú)* is accompanied by layers of implications in its subtext. Not only is it poison, as in a form of toxin (or even baneful magic); in this context, it connotes harm caused, pain and suffering, disasters or trouble, a matter that is criminal, malicious, or evil. Another layer implies that the emotions driving the event are those of hatred, resentment, malice, or the intent to harm.

The Oracle prognosticates success at overcoming the evildoing, but harms have been sustained nonetheless. You will recover.

| | | |
|---|---|---|
| *Fourth Line*<br>Biting through dried meat and bones. Attaining an arrowhead.<br>Favorable to face the hardships. Dangers ahead, yet auspicious to proceed. | 九四：<br>噬乾胏<br>得金矢<br>利艱貞吉 | |

There are advantages to be gained from persevering through the hardship. An auspicious ending if you are willing to face the difficulties. "艱 Jiān" not only means pain and suffering, serious hardships, and precarious situations, but also includes a layer that suggests a parent's death or the death of a close loved one.

Attaining an arrowhead can sometimes bear a subtext of vowing or swearing a particular oath or resolution. It's dedicating yourself in an intentional, devotional way to a specific mission.

When interpreted for metaphysical insights, "金 Jīn" suggests metal. Thus, while "矢 Shǐ" indicates an arrow, the description of it being metal is construed as pointing to a particular part of the arrow—the arrowhead. During the Shang and Zhou dynasties, 1200–901 BC, arrowheads were typically made of bronze.

The arrowhead also represents realization of the solution, the ability to gain incisive clarity.

Nevertheless, the Oracle cautions that as you tackle the heart of the matter at hand, you will encounter great difficulties that put yourself at serious risk. Still, where there is a will, there is a way, and if no matter which way you find, Heaven's Will is aligned with yours.

| | | |
|---|---|---|
| *Fifth Line*<br>Biting through dried meat. Attaining yellow gold.<br>The Oracle prognosticates no blame for the stern force exerted. | 六五：<br>噬乾肉<br>得黃金<br>貞厲無咎 | |

To rectify an excessive wrong, excessive force was used in the transmutation of the forces at play. Narratively, this is now the heart and the hollow of the matter at hand. Forceful action has already been taken, and a change in circumstance has resulted from that forceful action.

Note how the fifth line is a synthesis of the third and fourth.

The third line makes reference to just fleshy meat. The fourth line makes reference to both meat and bones, or meat that is still on the bone and then dried. Here in the fifth line, the fleshy meat referenced in the third line is dried in the manner of the fourth line.

The arrowhead (made of metal, most likely bronze) in the fourth line has now changed into yellow gold. Specifically, 黃金 huángjīn implies money, either gold coins or gold ingots. By forces put into motion, a bronze arrowhead has transformed into gold ingots.

| Sixth Line<br>Carrying the cangue maims the ear.<br>Misfortune. | 凶 何 校 滅 耳 | 上九： | ▬▬▬▬<br>▬ ▬<br>▬ ▬<br>▬▬▬▬ |

Unintended consequences. Setbacks encountered. Mistreatment of a matter at hand.

One is confined by a cangue[19] around the neck, either as a form of corporal punishment or as a self-inflicted ritual of penance. The cangue restricts the person's movements and prevents the person from being able to eat. It was intended to be a form of absolution.

Generally speaking, people were sentenced to wear a cangue for the purpose of humiliating them, not necessarily hurting them. However, unintended consequences have ensued over the course of the matter at hand; thus, the reference to the cangue maiming the ear.

Another form of carrying the cangue was self-inflicted in a form of penance ritual. To absolve one of past transgressions, a person subscribing to such folk religious beliefs would voluntarily wear a cangue to release spiritual or karmic consequences of the past transgression.

# Hexagram 22: Bì. Luminosity

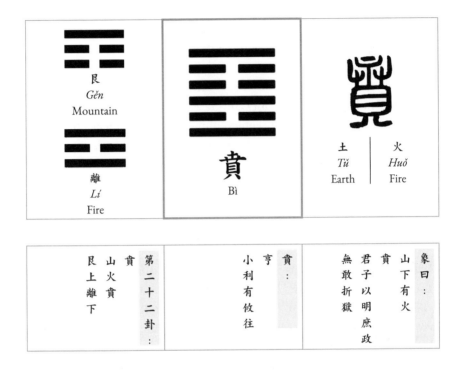

## The Oracle

Your public image now suffices for the small undertakings, but the large undertakings will exceed your beauty and grace. A personal journey will strengthen your luminosity. Strive to burn brighter, but through little steps day by day, and not by reckless compromises of yourself. To amplify your luminosity, seek advanced development of your talent and skills. It is a time for acquiring knowledge and experience. Knowledge is your beauty; experience is your grace. Be luminous.

**There is fire at the base of the mountain—luminosity.** The sage possesses clarity of insight into myriad matters of law and policy.

You possess the grace, poise, elegance, and presence to show yourself favorably to the public. The mountain fire is luminous—you are adored.

**Undertaking the endeavor can reap small gains. The adornments bring favor.** But who is the sage without the adornments?

**A pilgrimage lies ahead. Small gains made upon undertaking the pilgrimage.**

The fire illuminates a majestic mountain—there is beauty and grace in the form. Exuding luminous beauty and grace.

Gains are small when luminosity comes from wearing adornments. Beauty is not in form. Grace cannot be limited to appearances. There is no need to be proud of your adornments.

Forecast of a short-term or minor expedition.

## ON ADORNMENTS

References to "adornments" as a complete thought indicate "adornments that make you beautiful and luminous." In the interest of brevity, each time I meant "adornments that make you beautiful and luminous," I simply wrote "adornments." The concept here is an attribute that you can acquire (like jewelry, beautifying yourself, or a learned skill), one that is not necessarily inherent to you but that you have earned. Such an attribute helps you to attract attention, status, and good will.

---

*First Line*
Beautiful adornments on the feet, yet abandoning the carriage to walk as a humble apprentice. Going forth plainly on foot.

舍車而徒　賁其趾　初九：

---

The beautiful adornments on the feet suggest that you were born into some privilege and that you have enjoyed an easier life because of that privilege, for example, having a carriage to transport you about.

> **CHANGING LINES IN HEXAGRAM 22**
>
> If the primary hexagram included changing lines, then continue to the transformed hexagram for further insight into the prognosticated pilgrimage or minor expedition.
>
> If the hexagram cast is locked and you find yourself desiring more out of life than small gains, then at this time you may cast a second divination and ask the Oracle for guidance on how to attain what is needed for you to achieve your greater ambitions.

- However, you are no longer satisfied with the small gains in life. To date, you have relied heavily on your grace and beauty of form, on those assets you were born with; and while it has helped you so far, it has not been enough for your more ambitious endeavors.
- You now wish to manifest the full potential of what you are capable of, and you know you are going to need more than the superficial assets you have relied upon to date.
- To start your new journey, you must begin as a humble apprentice, at the lowest level . . . and walk onward by foot, abandoning your carriage, i.e., abandoning your reliance on those past privileges.
- Your first order of business is learning to stand on your own two feet and be independent, even if it means stumbling while you learn. Detach from the easy luxuries and privileges you used to rely so heavily on. Learn how to be helpless and weak so you can learn how to be truly powerful and strong.
- The first line indicates a form of renunciation.

| *Second Line* <br> **Beautiful adornments in the hair.** | 賁其須 | 六二： | ䷕ |
|---|---|---|---|

Traditional interpretation of this line concerns adornments in the beard, though here I've generalized it to hair. In both instances, the metaphor refers to judicious grooming.

There is a deeper spiritual meaning to the hair. In antiquity, one's hair was a symbol of one's parents and ancestors. Men wore their long, uncut hair in the form of a topknot or could wear certain headpieces, whereas women's hairstyles for managing long, uncut hair were more varied.

Whether for beards or hair, adornments and grooming were expressions of personal temperament. Leaving the beard or hair unruly and unadorned shows a wild, unsophisticated temperament, while careful grooming and adornments convey decorum and piety.

"Beautiful adornments in the hair" also conveys a sense of preparation for what's to come.

The implication here is of a calm setting and forces in cooperation with one another. The matter inquired about is in a state of lull, though in preparation for expansive, progressive action to come (implications of the Fire trigram).

A mystical reading of this line may suggest turning to your ancestors. Go to them with offerings, and reflect on what you've inherited from them. What powers lie dormant within you? Which remembrance of your ancestry will awaken?

---

*Third Line*
Beautiful adornments immersed and now in a condition of dampness.
Purified—auspicious to proceed.

永貞吉　賁如濡如　九三．

---

There is a water element to the immersion here. Perhaps one is so immersed in the beauty of the adornments that it is not unlike being intoxicated by a fine wine.

The third line signifies a potential turning point, at the cusp, and which direction you'll go from here hinges on a choice: do you wish to be a work of art, or do you wish to be the artist who creates a work of art?

The third line is that crossroads.

A purification ritual will clear the way for an auspicious outcome.

For the third line, I considered the reputation of "如," which will happen again in the subsequent fourth line. Etymologically the character depicts a woman obeying a mandate. It thus signifies compliance.

| *Fourth Line* <br> To wear the adornments that purify, purge, and refine— <br> A white horse gallops so gallantly it appears to have wings. <br> Bandits trespass, arriving like thieves, but they do not come to plunder; they come to escort the bride. | 匪寇婚媾 白馬翰如 賁如皤如 六四： |  |
|---|---|---|

Announcement of a momentous event to come. Excitement is in the air. An initial mix-up is quickly cleared, and celebration ensues.

Social advancement to come after you demonstrate who you are and what your purpose is.

Essentially, the Oracle is urging you to work on becoming more notable and noteworthy.

The white horse can symbolize literary endeavors or letters of correspondence headed your way, ones of official importance. The "white horse" can also bear a double meaning of a calligraphy brush.

The fourth line bodes well for literary and artistic endeavors.

Thus, the white horse galloping in such a way that it gives the appearance of flying can indicate creativity flowing unblocked.

The reference to "婚媾 hūn gòu" is commonly translated to bride or marriage, but historically the term can refer generally to family relatives. Thus, the bandits (who are not bandits) arrive announcing that they are distant relatives here to see family. This is cause for great joy and festivities.

The fourth line, given so much text, indicating its importance. It forecasts the announcement of a significant event.

The white horse galloping toward you in such a way as to evoke flying on wings is an omen: an incredible opportunity will present itself to you in the near future, but it is one that can vanish as suddenly as it appears, so seize the moment when you can.

# INTERMARRIAGE BETWEEN DIFFERENT CLANS

Whether "婚媾 hūn gòu" is interpreted as bride or family relatives, in either case, the fact that such an event is occurring—foreigners having to send messengers galloping on white horses to announce their arrival and state their intentions—suggests an intermarriage between different clans or dual affiliations between two kingdoms.

During the Zhou dynasty, intermarriage of different clans wasn't common, because it required one of the spouses to take a long, often treacherous journey. The story arc of the fourth line begins with an intermarriage between two different kingdoms. (Or, alternatively, relatives living in a faraway foreign kingdom arriving for a visit.)

Distinguished messengers riding white horses, to symbolize their purity of intentions, arrive in a country that isn't their own, loudly declaring that they are not bandits and clearly stating their good intentions. The gatekeepers are satisfied with the messengers' announcements and let them in. Foreigners from a faraway clan would have been an uncommon sight, so the villagers are curious.

Nevertheless, the tone of the lines is that of excitement. Finally, the messengers on white horses are welcomed. Truly, cause for celebration. Such a meeting is surely going to create new opportunities for both kingdoms.

| | |
|---|---|
| *Fifth Line*<br>A garden of beauty and bliss, adorned elegantly. Music from a lute.<br>Less and less of that precious silk. To preserve, be more prudent. A knotted cord—limits. Show restraint.<br>An auspicious outcome. | 終吝束賁六<br>吉　帛于五<br>　　戔丘：<br>　　戔園 |

Although things are going well, a general economic downturn might be up ahead, so be prepared. Start saving and conserving now for that rainy day to come.

A beautiful scene is being set here—a garden of beauty and bliss. Music is playing, the sounds from a lute. However, the storehouse of precious silk is significantly reduced. The silk is symbolic of wealth and prosperity. The advice being given here is to be more frugal and measured with expenditures.

To tie a knot at the end of the cord—this is to set limits, to count, and to keep track.

Nevertheless, the final outcome will be fortuitous.

The fifth line expands beyond luminosity in personal appearance to luminosity in the personal environment.

Per feng shui principles, Mountain corresponds with the northeast sector of the home and is where the *qi* for cultivating knowledge and education is generated.

Beautify and harmonize the northeast area of your home, and the effect will be advancement of social status and expansion of your social influence—elevating the Fire trigram below the Mountain. This would be a metaphysical measure to take to help navigate the downturn in economic times to come.

| | |
|---|---|
| *Sixth Line*<br>White adornments—graceful and beautiful, simple and pure.<br>No blame. Calamity averted. | 無白上<br>咎賁九<br>　　： |

Return to a state of grace. Transcending ornamentation. Inner beauty radiates outward.

There is no need to yearn for any more than what you have now.

Propriety and etiquette save the day. Cultivate the skill of etiquette to advance both your social and your spiritual position. Expressions of etiquette are expressions of consideration for others. By considering the interests of others, you are cultivating magnanimity and beneficence, which earns you karmic merits.

Even if at first etiquette does not feel sincere, the objective is to cultivate it in such a manner that it becomes sincere. Etiquette should, in its ideal form, reflect your sincerity of magnanimity and beneficence.

White is the color of purity. A mystic might interpret the Oracle as advising a purification ritual.

## Hexagram 23: Bō. Partition

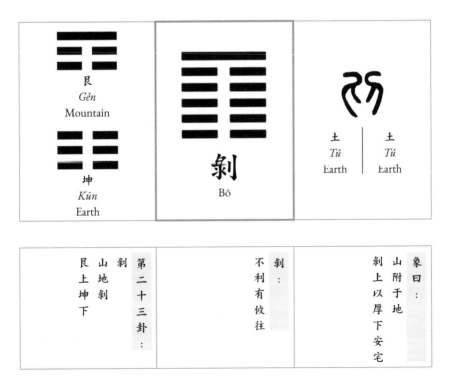

## *The Oracle*

Stay low to the ground and disturb not that which is in turbulence. Forces at large are disintegrating and splitting. Dark undermines the Light. The inferior outnumber the superior; cons outweigh the pros. Move slowly; this is the combat crawl—opposite limbs move together. Through acceptance and stillness, and an unflappable faith in your greatness, your time will come.

**The mountain rests on the earth, one tall, steep, and lacking a broad foundation; thus, with an unstable earth, the mountain is on the verge of toppling over. The dark earth is splitting apart the mountain.**
Here is a vision of the iconoclast, a challenger of orthodoxy, a destroyer of falsities that have become canonical and conventional.
**There are disadvantages to proceeding in your endeavor.**
Inferior forces with strength in numbers overtake superior forces who are in the minority. Do not act. Respond to the circumstances with stillness and tranquility.
Wisdom versus cowardice is often an issue of timing. Being the mountain for now is wisdom, not cowardice. It is not the right time to act.
When you are the mountain, positioned above those who are the earth stationed below you, a volatile condition is the result. Under such volatile conditions, your aim is to preserve your position. Give and yield generously to those below you to appease them and prevent further unrest.
Dark yin lines ascend upward to overthrow the final line of yang. Darkness defeats the Light. The force is disintegration, one of splitting.
This is not a direct means of overthrowing. In the late autumn season, the last few moments before winter arrives, dark creeps slowly, from the ground up, to consume that which was the light.
Your past conduct has developed you into a tall mountain, steep and lacking a broad foundation.
You have become too proud of yourself and too arrogant to include those lesser than you in your base. As a result, you now find yourself on the verge of toppling over.

For greater strength, the mountain must have a broad foundation as it rises out of the earth. You must always include the lesser in your base and be generous to those in the lower positions of support for you. You always want to rule a broad foundation as you ascend upward to become the mountain. For a broad base, you must be generous and benevolent; that is the way to ensure the mountain's tranquility and longevity.

Hexagram 23 expresses the decline of prosperity and influence. Discord and splits from within will give rise to a powerful opposition. Political strife is imminent.

## OMEN OF THE *QILIN*

The *qilin* is a mythical beast that appears to portend a significant, transformative event relating to a sage or leader. In the I Ching, Hexagrams 2, 15, 23, and 52 are likened to the omen of seeing a *qilin* appear before you. These hexagrams in general are omens of a significant, transformative event to come, one relating to the near-future rise of a sage or leader.

Here, divining Hexagram 23 relates to the fall, decline, weakening, recession, failure, or descent of a sage or leader. The *qilin* manifesting in Hexagram 23 prophesies the fall of an incumbent. A decline in prosperity and social order inspires the rise of a challenger. The challenger is prophesied to restore order and eradicate the chaos that the incumbent had brought on.

| | |
|---|---|
| *First Line* <br> The foot of the bed has splintered apart. <br> Attempts to further your endeavor will be futile: ominous to proceed. | 初六：剝床以足，蔑貞凶 |

A plot to overthrow the mountain. Yet the mountain still retains quiet supporters in the shadows. Seek out those quiet supporters.

Stay calm and resilient. You are positioned as the mountain, and those who wish to undermine you are the volatile earth: do not engage with them and do not incite them.

At this time, be alert, but remain silent and immovable. Plot an escape route. Prepare contingencies.

Heed this first omen of danger, and all can still end well.

"蔑 miè" is the image of a dagger striking at the lower part of the leg. Do not engage, and do not react to those who have come for your head but only struck the leg.

The theme of both the first and second lines of the hexagram, which is picked up again in the fourth, is from the legend of Wang Hai, or Prince Hai.

| Second Line | | |
|---|---|---|
| One side of the bed has splintered apart. Attempts to further your endeavor will be futile: ominous to proceed. | 凶 蔑 剝<br>　 貞 床<br>　 　 以<br>　 　 辨 | 六<br>二<br>： |

You are tempted to react and exert authority over the situation, but do not engage. Adjust to the conditions you face and stay on the defensive, adjusting yourself to avoid danger.

Do not be stubborn. Under such conditions, do not use a show of force; instead, yield and be soft. A yang disposition is ominous; a yin disposition will help you survive.

The theme of both the first and the second lines of the hexagram, which is picked up again in the fourth line, is from the legend of Wang Hai. The breakages in the bed are warning cries for you to get out of your situation and escape.

Boundary lines continue to disintegrate. The splintering is a warning of danger.

| Third Line | | |
|---|---|---|
| Cut apart and partition in the matter at hand. Erode and strip. Deprive. There is no blame. | 剝<br>之<br>無<br>咎 | 六<br>三<br>： |

Although the prognostication here is that of being blameless, this line is generally regarded as foreboding of decline, or at best inertia.

An individual is outnumbered, overpowered by extenuating circumstances, and as a result, is pressured to join the inferior position of the masses, though that single individual is aware of the inferiority of the position and seeks alliance with the mountain.

Though the individual seeks alliance with the mountain, such support must remain secret. The one who opposes the inferior masses must keep that opposition discreet for now. Give the appearance of concord with the inferior. There is no blame in the yielding position, because at this time, it is the only way to preserve the individual's position.

The passage "剝之 bō zhī" comes with a subtext of dividing to conquer or peeling and stripping away the outer layers so the people can see the truth for what it is.

The third line can often indicate slander or crisis that is causing degeneracy and chaos. Instead of letting the negativity amplify itself, partition it so that the underlying principle of the matter can be revealed.

| Fourth Line | | |
|---|---|---|
| The bed has splintered apart up to your skin. Attempts to further your endeavor will be futile: ominous to proceed. | 凶 剝 六<br>　床 四<br>　以 ：<br>　膚 | ▬▬ ▬▬<br>▬▬ ▬▬<br>▬▬▬▬▬<br>▬▬ ▬▬<br>▬▬ ▬▬<br>▬▬ ▬▬ |

Disintegrating boundaries. Splintering of the framework. Structural damage. However, the injury is only superficial or shallow. Actual harm results, but not fatal harm. Nevertheless, threats to the incumbent's position are growing near and imminent.

Calamity, but there is still an opportunity to correct course. Averting the calamity may not be possible at this time as it is beyond the point of no return, but averting permanent loss is still manageable.

The theme of the fourth line is a continuation of the first and second lines, from the legend of Wang Hai. The breakages in the bed are warning cries for you to get out of your situation and escape.

At this point you have yet to take action to save yourself, despite past warnings. Here in the fourth line, the final warning is issued. This is the last moment before it is truly too late. The key to survival is a yin disposition; a yang disposition brings adversity.

| | |
|---|---|
| *Fifth Line*<br>A string of caught fish: use the ladies-in-waiting at the palace to gain favors.<br>There is no blame for the act. |  |

An opportunity to change the direction of the tides has opened up. Appeal to those who do not appear to hold positions of power. They hold far more influence than they appear. Convince intermediary powers to mediate on your behalf.

The string of caught fish and implications of 貫 *(guàn)* can also suggest a string of coins. This is possession of currency, monies, that which holds value in trade or commerce.

The string of caught fish can also suggest the strategy to employ. Like fishing, begin by swaying one over to your position with the use of bait and a hook. One by one, with bait and hook, catch the fish and string them together one after the other to form a row of supporters in your favor.

The fish symbolize yin energy—stealth action rather than overt, visible action. Use soft power, going around and around rather than straight ahead. Using the blunt edge instead of the sharp.

The fish is also a symbol of romantic love. Here, the fifth line is expressive of the chase. One seeks to gain the favor of a romantic prospect. If you want to succeed, appeal to the friends. Ensure that they'll put in a good word on your behalf.

| | |
|---|---|
| *Sixth Line*<br>An uneaten fruit. Unmanifested fruition.<br>The sage receives a carriage. The sage has swayed public opinion.<br>Adversarial forces splinter the house. |  |

A division among the people. Differences of opinion. Prognostication of an excellent and influential orator or rhetorician.

"果" *(guǒ)* is a general descriptor for fruit and also has the double meaning of "the final result" or "conclusion of the matter." Thus, both meanings are set forth in the sixth line—its indication as a fruit and its indication as fruition.

Likewise, "輿" *(yú)* also holds dual meaning. There is a literal reference to a carriage or sedan chair, and a figurative reference to the populace and court of public opinion.

In this context, "小人" has the negative implication of villains or, more neutrally, adversarial forces. The term takes on a tone of describing miscreants in direct comparison to the honorable and beneficent sage, "君子."

The sixth line seems to imply that degeneracy and riot have won out, causing a breakdown of structure. The good sage or *junzi* is either saved by having been transported out of the precarious situation by carriage; or, even if the sage has been defeated by the adversarial forces, when all is said and done, the people realize that the sage was right all along.

## THE LEGEND OF PRINCE HAI

The bed and house references in Hexagram 23 are believed to be based on a legend dating back to China's Bronze Age. As the legend goes, Wang Hai (Prince Hai) left his home and journeyed to the kingdom of Yi.

Wang Hai rose to prestige in Yi for herding sheep. His prosperity aroused envy from many in Yi, and there were conspiracies to eliminate him and take his sheep.

An attempt to burn him alive in his own house was somehow thwarted when Wang Hai was said to have been awakened from his sleep by a mysterious rapping on his bed.

As a result, he escaped the house before it burned to the ground.

The sixth line is interpreted as Wang Hai having been saved, though he lost all his sheep, as referenced later in Hexagram 34. However, Wang Hai reinvented himself and went on to raise cattle, as will be referenced in Hexagram 56.

Wang Hai rebuilt his fortune and again aroused envy from the locals, this time as far up as the local king of Yi, King Mianshen. Ultimately, Wang Hai loses his life. His cattle are taken from him by the king of Yi himself.

# Hexagram 24: Fù. Repose

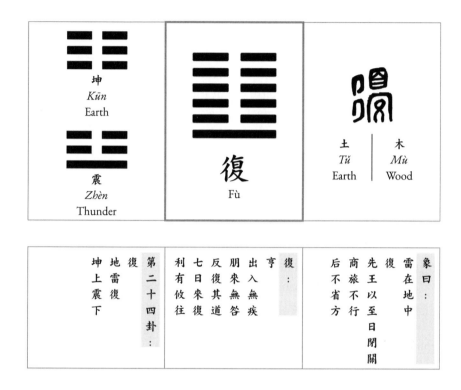

## The Oracle

A winter in the season of life, when life itself looks like death. It is a time for repose. Conserve your strength. And yet Thunder at the base means the way to conserve your strength is through movement. Auspicious to undertake action. When you move the body, the mind will move with it, and when you return to a state of rest, the mind dismounts upon inspiration. Lend powers from the Earth—immerse yourself in solitude in the world of nature. The action to undertake is to recharge the body, mind, and spirit. Focus not on the grim world around you, but on the brilliant charge within.

**A state of recovery—it is a period of repose. At the end of the winter solstice will come the warmth and the light.**
Auspicious to proceed.
You are at a turning point. The light is just beginning to emanate out of the darkness. The light does not return by force; it comes as part of a natural cycle.
Thunder is breaking upward from within the earth.
**The first offspring begins to push out of the mother's womb.** A rebirth of yang after accumulation of much yin.
**At the time of the solstice, the ancient kings would close off the gates to their kingdoms, sealing the mountain passes.** At this time, you must preserve your own energy and your own resources. Travel and commerce would remain within the realm. Take care of your own for now; do not worry about the world at large. At the moment you are not in a position to help more than your own people.
**The queen would abstain from excursions around the provinces.** It is a time for preservation of one's own culture, customs, and ways. It is a time of hibernation. Movement and innovation are at the beginning stages, so it is critical for you to get proper rest and preserve your strength. Do not waste any of your energy right now. Preserve, recharge, and rest.
You're headed toward success. Entering or leaving, there will be a full recovery from the winter. **Friends arrive—affinity. Coming and going, that is the way of the Divine.**
**In seven days, there will come the return, the turning point: seven is the number of the young light.** Seven also refers to the period of a complete cycle, such as the new first line after six lines of a hexagram have changed.
After a state of repose, it will be time for movement to stir again. It is advantageous for you to proceed on your endeavor.
**Opportunities come from travel and journeys after the winter ends.** Traditionally Hexagram 24 marks the winter season, lunar month 11 of the lunisolar calendar.

| *First Line* <br> Imminent return. No serious grief from the wrongdoing. <br> Great prosperity and gains to come. | 元 無 不 初 <br> 吉 祗 遠 九 <br> 　 悔 　 復 <br> 　 　 　 ： |
|---|---|

You may have made a minor detour diverging from the right path, but you realize your error quickly and are now turning back to find your way again.

When you are first starting out, at the immediate moment of realizing an error, correct it without delay. Do not continue doing something you know is wrong just because you are afraid of or resistant to change.

This is divine assurance of a rectified outcome.

"祇" *(qí)* holds alternate meanings of an earth spirit 地祇 *(de qí),* a divine personification of the earth and all earthly natural cycles occurring close to the ground.

After experiencing a personal winter and realizing the errors you have made, you resolve to circle back to the beginning.

Returning to the point of departure takes immense self-mastery, and you have done just that. You will be making an extraordinary comeback.

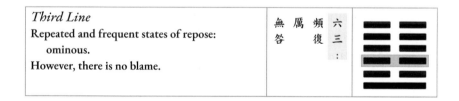

You keep changing your mind and faltering. You are being indecisive. You start on one path, feel unsure of yourself, and desert an otherwise good path. However, your intentions are good and you do not act in bad faith. You are constantly vacillating between decisions, but you are innocent in the ways you change your mind.

Note that a past unresolved issue is going to reemerge. You will now have to address that issue head-on. You cannot avoid it again or leave it pending.

The key success here is decisive action.

"厲" (lì) suggests adversity, friction, and conflict, but like a whetstone, it sharpens whatever the adversity and friction are being inflicted upon. You will come out stronger.

The word 厲 is also a reference to the powers of destruction that the Queen Mother of the West 西王母 rules over. In antiquity, 厲 was a reference to a Demon Star or constellation in the sky associated with calamities, and was considered malefic.

| *Fourth Line*<br>In the midst of many sojourners, one alone returns. | 中行獨復 | 六四： |  |
|---|---|---|---|

When the whole flock proceeds forward, you stop and return alone. Resist influence from contrary or opposing forces.

Do not compare yourself to others. Your path is going to be very different from most, so you cannot look to the sojourners to gain a true sense of your own direction.

"獨 Dú" can also mean one who is old and childless. There's a subtext of separatism or declarations of independence as well. Figuratively, the word itself asks a question, and so the Oracle is perhaps contemplating: "Is it possible that amid many sojourners going in one direction, a solitary soul turns around and dares to go the opposite way?"

| *Fifth Line*<br>The esteemed one returns.<br>There is no blame. | 無悔 | 敦復 | 六五： | |
|---|---|---|---|---|

The Oracle is urging self-reflection. Return to the point of origin, and there will be no tears shed for past errors. Knowing what is wrong is not enough; the esteemed one must take action to correct the wrong.

You'll find a range of differing interpretations for the fifth line, hinging on the word "敦" *(dūn)*. It can mean anger, but it can also mean benevolent and noble, which would seem to take the interpretation in a very different direction. The word can be used to mean diligent and earnest, honest and sincere, or thick and large. Extrapolating on "thick and large," it can mean something held in high esteem or of great importance, something to be revered. The indication is in the singular, as one, or as one who is solitary. In antiquity, "敦" was descriptive of a vessel holding grains.

"敦" is symbolic of the knowledge of the importance of knowledge, and of the strength to be strong. Thus, this line is about self-awareness.

| Sixth Line | | |
|---|---|---|
| Lost in the return. Bewitchment. Foreboding adversity. A calamity hits. Deploying the army. The army is defeated. Foreboding adversity for their kingdom's ruler. There will not be another favorable chance of attack for ten years. | 至于十年不克征 以其國君凶 終有大師敗 用行師 有災眚 凶 迷復 | 上六： |

One has lost the way. To be aimless and without purpose at this juncture is to meet with calamity. An army must have a sense of purpose and a spirit for the fight. A sovereign who cannot motivate the people will fail. You must strategize on how you can inspire.

"迷" *(mí)* not only means to become lost or confused; it also means to have been bewitched or enchanted. The trigram Earth corresponds with the mystical archetype of the Enchanter.

Thus, the sixth line doesn't just mean getting lost in the return. It perhaps suggests that in an effort to return, one gets enchanted and bewitched.

"災" *(zāi)* means a calamity or being struck by natural disaster.

The sixth line can portend an economic recession or the trough between two peaks. This is an omen of decline, one that lasts for about a decade. Flawed government policies (decision-making at the head) result in people losing confidence and therefore losing confidence in the leadership.

At the personal level, the kingdom's ruler represents your mind, willpower, and decision-making. The army is the set of skills and resources you deploy to execute your will.

# Hexagram 25: Wú Wàng. Without Folly

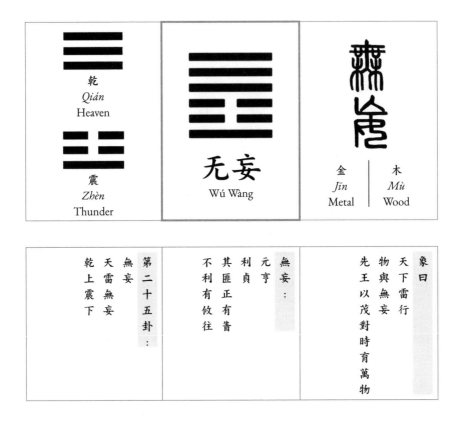

## The Oracle

*Wu wang* means do not be foolish, and do not lack common sense. Do not be bold when the time calls for meekness. Do not be arrogant when the time calls for humility. Do not be reckless when the time calls for caution. *Wu wang* is to be without folly—take care not to undertake a costly or foolish expenditure.

Choosing to strive against falsity—and yet the miscreants are truly culpable. Do not go in their direction.

All things and creatures begin without falsity—innocent. **In their times, the ancient kings flourished by providing for the ten thousand things and creatures. Rulers maintain their power only when they use that power to sustain the goodness and propriety of the kingdom.**

Your endeavor should not be one undertaken out of ambition or the need for personal validation. Undertake your endeavor with the innocence of the sky's thunder: formidable, yet with neither good nor evil intentions; the thunder is innocent, rolling and striking without falsity.

**Gains and prosperity to come: great advantage in going forward on your endeavor if you proceed without falsity.** Do not be reckless. Do not be foolish. Do not be stubborn. Do not be excessively willful. Do not be presumptuous. Be sincere and truthful, and do not be hypocritical.

Heed this counsel and all will be well—an auspicious omen for the one without folly.

**Travel or long journeys are unfavorable.**

"妄" *(wàng)* is recklessness, improper behavior; being foolish, stubborn, and excessively willful; being presumptuous; and being incorrect, untruthful, and hypocritical. "无" *(wú)* negates it. The phrase in effect means "to not be improper," so it's often translated as "propriety."

The name of Hexagram 25 is giving you wise counsel: 无妄 is a complete statement of advice in itself—do not be foolish, do not indulge fantasy thinking. You have to be realistic, not just in your awareness of the situation, but also in self-awareness. Wisdom means knowing when tinkering with the matter at hand will bring more hardships to your door than simply letting it be. You may think the situation isn't great now, but meddling with it could make it worse.

| *First Line* <br> **A pure intent in the undertaking of the endeavor yields prosperity.** | 初九：<br>無妄<br>往吉 | ▬▬▬▬▬<br>▬▬▬▬▬<br>▬▬  ▬▬<br>▬▬  ▬▬<br>▬▬▬▬▬<br>▬▬▬▬▬ |

Common sense brings success. Do not undertake foolish heroism. Do not try to force the impossible to happen. If your intentions are pure and your actions virtuous, you need not engage in pseudo-extraordinary measures—let it be to achieve prosperity.

| | |
|---|---|
| *Second Line* <br> Do not sow and reap at the same time: plow first, and then wait for the time to harvest. <br> Do not cultivate the trampled field. <br> It is auspicious to undertake your endeavor. | 六二：<br>不耕穫<br>不菑畬<br>則利有攸往 |

Part of the message here might be comparable to "don't count your chickens before they hatch." Do not rely on a presumed outcome. Circumstances could and probably will change. When you are sowing, concentrate all of your intentions on sowing the seeds, and do not immediately assume there will be a harvest.

"Do not cultivate the trampled field" is a reference to crop rotation, a practice for ensuring that the proper nutrients are retained in the soil to keep it fertile year after year. To preserve the fertility of the fields, do not grow the same crops over the waste of old crops previously harvested. Likewise, find another way to achieve your endeavor. Try a different approach, one you have not tried before.

When you proceed with the foregoing advice from the Oracle, you will find great success.

| | |
|---|---|
| *Third Line* <br> Without folly, and yet still met with calamity. <br> Perhaps like being the yoked oxen. <br> The foreign minister will succeed. <br> The villager will face calamity. | 六三：<br>無妄之災<br>或繫之牛<br>行人之得<br>邑人之災 |

Like a yoked ox, what befalls one in the pair will be sustained by the other, even if the other is innocent. Here, even though one is without folly, always proper, prudent, and judicious, because of who you're tied to, you are hit with hardships anyway.

A difficult truism underscores this third line: in life, misfortune and loss can come to the innocent—collateral damage.

In antiquity, a "行人" *(xíng rén)* was a court official position appointed to oversee international relations, likened to a minister of foreign affairs. The term could also indicate a wandering pilgrim, someone who has seen and experienced many different cultures and city-states.

As for "邑人" *(yì rén),* this could either be a reference to a citizen of the kingdom of Yi, a general descriptive for villagers, or villagers of your own locale, implying natives.

Promising potential for career advancement, but a somewhat challenging position for love and relationships.

| *Fourth Line*<br>**If you can endure and persevere, then there will be no blame.** | 九四：可貞無咎 | 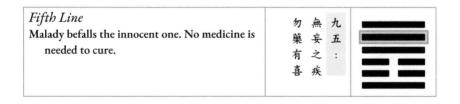 |
|---|---|---|

Circumstances will come that test your commitment to integrity. Do not waver from your values.

Do not be reckless. Do not engage in improper behavior. Do not be foolish. Do not be stubborn. Do not be excessively willful. Do not be presumptuous.

Stay true. Stay truthful. Do not act in a way that compromises your ethics. Come what may, follow your tenets.

| *Fifth Line*<br>**Malady befalls the innocent one. No medicine is needed to cure.** | 九五：無妄之疾勿藥有喜 | |
|---|---|---|

Undeserved pain and suffering shall cease on its own, in accordance with natural laws. There will be a restoration to the healthier state.

The phrase "勿藥有喜" *(wù yào yǒu xǐ)* is interpreted to mean that you may think you are ill, but you're not. Medicine isn't what's needed to "cure" the problem. More esoteric spiritual or psychic factors may be at play. This particular four-word phrase can also be used as an affirmative blessing—may your malady be cured in such a way that you don't even need to take medicine, and may you find joy and happiness, and be restored to good health swiftly. "有喜" *(yǒu xǐ)* means to be satisfied with the outcome or to be healed.

A Buddhist reading of the line construes it as the tenet of karma. Have faith that one who has accrued positive karmic merits will always be saved by the bodhisattvas.

In certain cases, this line can be interpreted as predicting the birth of a son. "Malady befalls" suggests one who feels sick and seeks medicine to cure that sickness. However, there is "喜," which doesn't just mean joy and cheer, but also includes a subtext of being pregnant. A traditionalist interpretation reads the yang line as the birth of a baby boy.

| | |
|---|---|
| **Sixth Line**<br>Without falsity: an innocent. The one who wanders meets with misfortune.<br>No advantages gained from the undertaking. | 上九：<br>無妄行<br>有眚無<br>攸利 |

The sixth line echoes the final message in the Oracle—now is not a good time to be traveling.

The time is not right for advancing, so do not advance. Either you missed an earlier opportunity for advancement and thus it is now too late, or the time has not yet come. There is nothing to be gained by forcing your way when conditions are not favorable.

You may consult the oracle again to determine the more favorable time for proceeding.

# Hexagram 26: Dà Chù. Cultivate the Supreme

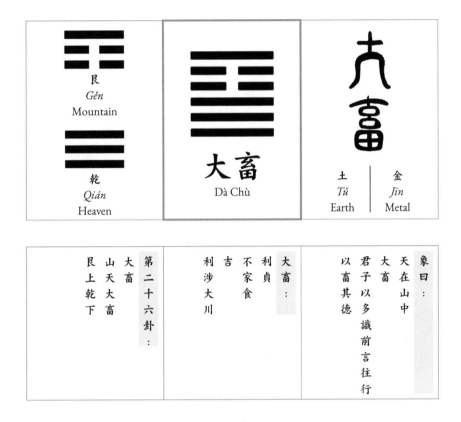

## The Oracle

You hold great power and potential, but restraint is necessary to temper that power and keep it under control. The mountain visible above the heavens is emblematic of your great power. Invest that power in a way that advances humankind. A mountain need not move or speak to awe. Nothing is more awe-inspiring than self-control. At hand is how you can tame that great power and potential. When you are accomplished, you bear the burden of using those accomplishments to give back. Power must be controlled by yielding that power to the most underprivileged. Limitations must be imposed on you to keep you on the noble path.

Study the words and deeds of the great and the wise before you; that way you can build and develop your virtue.

**Do not eat meals from home.** Officers of the nation should not accept offers of benefit from their nation; do not take from your own people; decline enrichment from those you are serving.

**It is auspicious to cross the great stream.** A promising omen for the undertaking. Advantageous for you to proceed on the endeavor.

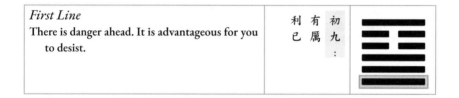

| *First Line* <br> There is danger ahead. It is advantageous for you to desist. | 利 有 初<br>己 厲 九<br>　　　： | |

Do not force the situation. The timing is not right. If you advance now, you will face adversity. Wait it out. There is a better time for you to proceed. Be patient.

There is a conflict, and you are tempted to react in a sharp, hostile manner. Forebear from doing so. Do not take any action in retaliation. If you can be beneficent no matter how hard it is to be so, the situation will turn in your favor after completion of the matter in its own natural time.

| *Second Line* <br> An axle from the carriage is broken. | 輿 九<br>說 二<br>輹 ： | |

The linchpin that holds the many parts of the whole together is fragmented. The parts of the whole are changing and moving too abruptly in conflicting directions.

Repair the axle to repair the carriage. Then there will be progress once again.

| Third Line | 九利日利良九 |
|---|---|
| A majestic horse gives chase. | 有閑艱馬三 |
| Despite difficult times, Heaven protects you. | 攸輿貞逐： |
| Train the cavalry well. Then there will be gains to be earned from undertaking the expedition. | 往衛 |

Auspicious to proceed only after adequate training and preparation. A promising omen of high achievement. The cavalry's horses are strong, healthy, and magnificent. The horses here are symbolic of natural talent. All there is left to do is to train the cavalry well. Thus, honing the innate talent is in order.

"衛" *(wèi)* could also be a reference to the state of Wei (1046–209 BC) founded during the Western Zhou dynasty, ruled by Gao, duke of Bi (畢公高), one of King Wen's sons.

In fortune-telling, this line can indicate the armed services, police, or public service for the state.

| Fourth Line | 元童六 |
|---|---|
| **Placing guards on the growing horns of the young bull.** | 吉牛四 |
| **Great auspices.** | 之： |
| | 牿 |

The theme of both the fourth and fifth lines of the hexagram is that of taming the wild instinct, the fearsome power of nature.

Here in the fourth line, a young bull is the symbol of great power and force to come. By placing horn guards on the bull as it grows, the bull's power can be controlled and tamed. Controlled and tamed power is more productive and thus will yield prosperity and good fortune. Feral, uncontrolled power is reckless and cannot guarantee prosperity and good fortune.

| Fifth Line | 吉豶六 |
|---|---|
| **The ivory tusk of a castrated young boar—** | 豕五 |
| **Auspicious.** | 之： |
| | 牙 |

Castrating a boar reduces its tendency toward aggression, thus taming it. A tamed, gentle boar's ivory tusk will contain the *qi* life force that is tamed and gentle, thus a symbol of controlled and tamed power.

Remove your arrogance, and all that you produce will be auspicious. Tame your power with the gentleness, softness, and receptivity of yin. Curb propensities for violence, hostility, or animosity. Curb the desire to be cut-throat competitive.

In certain contexts, the fifth line can be instructive on how to train mentees, employees, students, initiates, or those you are in charge of nurturing. The work product (or "ivory tusk") of those who have learned to tame their animal instincts will be of greater value and capacity.

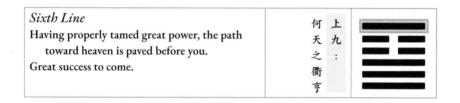

*Sixth Line*
Having properly tamed great power, the path toward heaven is paved before you.
Great success to come.

You have tamed your own great powers and potential. By maintaining proper restraint, you have stayed true to a noble path. Destined for prosperity.

## Hexagram 27: Yí. Receive Nourishment

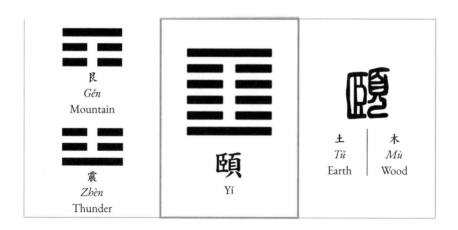

象曰：
山下有雷
頤
君子以慎言語
節飲食

頤：
貞吉
觀頤
自求口實

第二十七卦：
頤
山雷頤
艮上震下

## *The Oracle*

> Be open to receiving; receive to nourish. Good fortune can be had if you take affirmative action toward your own well-being. The true measure of who you are is in how you nourish your body, what you put into it, balanced with your speech and the words you let out of your mouth. Right now is the time to feed yourself to provide yourself with sustenance. Cherish. Enrich yourself with that which is necessary for health and growth. Nourish the Divine within.

Atop the mountain there is thunder—that which necessarily advances and grows will necessarily be weakened by the exertion. There must be nourishment.

**Nourish to sustain. The sage is prudent in speech so that only nourishing words are spoken. An open mouth is where nourishment begins.** The sage is also conscientious with food and drink.

**Pointing at the self—to know the self is to know what goes into and what comes out of the mouth.**

**Seek to feed yourself with that which is substantial, truthful, and only that which enriches.**

Strive to guard the gateway wisely. May only that which fulfills be granted entrance.

At this time, direct your energy toward cultivating character. How you nourish your body with your intake of food and how you nourish your loved ones with your words must together further tranquility. These should be your most important concerns at this time.

**Auspicious to proceed with the endeavor after one has received nourishment.**

| First Line<br>Holding your Sacred Tortoise.<br>I see bulging cheeks.<br>Maligned. | 凶 觀 舍 初<br>　 我 爾 九<br>　 朵 靈 ：<br>　 頤 龜 |  |

What you've inquired about does not necessitate a divinatory response. You are perfectly capable of addressing the matter on your own. Stop seeking validation.

The Oracle is addressing you directly. The tortoise is a symbol of wisdom. You thirst and hunger for that wisdom, for esoteric knowledge. And yet the tone here isn't one of admiration, but rather one of reprimanding.

Good intentions, but a flawed approach. Recalibrate the approach.

"Bulging cheeks" is symbolic of hoarding or going beyond what is regarded as proper.

"朵頤" *(duǒ yí)* is the image of bulging cheeks, symbolic of stuffing oneself gluttonously, at the loss of self-respect, dignity, and propriety.

This is excess of what should have otherwise been a good thing—the quest for knowledge and wisdom, the quest for spiritual nourishment.

The Sacred Tortoise is a reference to oracle bone (and tortoise shell) divination. "靈龜" *(líng guī)*, the literal translation of which might be "spirit tortoise," is a reference to the Sacred Tortoise, the tortoise shell divination method of the Shang dynasty. The tortoise shell was burned until it cracked, and the cracks were interpreted as divine omens.

| Second Line<br>The contrary of nourishment. Defiance.<br>It is a violation of canon to seek nourishment from those less fortunate than you.<br>Ominous to endeavor a conquest. | 頤 經 拂 顛 六<br>征 于 　 頤 二<br>凶 丘 　 　 ： |  |

Seek nourishment only in the ways that do not take advantage of others. Be self-reliant, but do not be selfish. This is not the time to ask others for assistance. Be mindful that the actions you take do not cause harm to those less fortunate than you.

One claims to seek nourishment, but all actions and intentions are contrary to sincere nourishment.

The line "經于丘" *(jīng yú qiū)* is a bit obscure and thus open for liberal interpretation. "經" can mean canon, a sacred text, to experience, or to engage with. It means to regulate. "丘" is to be positioned atop a mound or even a grave. There is an undertone of ruin. Thus, if construed to mean "grave," the line in effect conveys dancing on another's grave.

Thus, the image is of someone standing in a higher and more advantageous position (atop the mound) reaching down and demanding that the lower nourish the upper. Canon or propriety would call for it be the other way around—the upper should be the one nourishing the lower.

Wilhelm translates the line as follows:

Deviating from the path
To seek nourishment from the hill.
Continuing to do this brings misfortune.[20]

The final segment of the line suggests a particular type of undertaking—an expedition with the intent to attack, invade, or conquer. Should you embark upon such an ambitious endeavor under the present circumstances, the results will be ominous. The Oracle advises against proceeding.

Another implication arising from this line is of one purporting to be an expert, teaching others, when in truth one is still an amateur, in need of better teachers.

You think you are taking measures to nourish yourself, but instead, what you are doing is feeding your temptations: not the same.

Heading toward the hill represents the path toward wisdom and understanding; but here, you have deviated from that righteous path and are rejecting the proper teachings of the figurative classical canons.

In one sense, the line can be read as indicating one who is too self-righteous, a warning to not hold yourself out as a spiritual leader or beacon for others to follow when you yourself have strayed from the path of wisdom. Do not try to guide others at this time when you need guidance yourself.

There may also be a sense of improper taking from others to nourish yourself. Continuing with this improper taking will lead to misfortune. You try to lead others so that you might be able to feed on their energies in an improper effort to nourish yourself.

The proper path at this time is to be self-reliant. A strong theme in this line is that of personal misalignment.

*Third Line*
Turning away from nourishment. Foreboding adversity.
No movement for ten years. No enterprises for ten years. No gains in the outcome.

Rejecting the proper forms of personal and spiritual nourishment leads to a standstill in growth. Be mindful of the words you're speaking and putting out into this world; likewise, be mindful of the knowledge you are consuming. Be discerning of what is truth and what is illusion.

Nourishing yourself also means doing the work and holding an occupation that nourishes your spirit. Work that kills the spirit is not work worth undertaking. Formulate a plan to ensure that your labors not only nourish others, but nourish yourself.

Ten years, a decade, suggests the completion of one cycle or phase. The commitment to self-nourishment stated in the third line is that of a long-term dedicated mission.

The Oracle is being particularly stern with you because there is still an opportunity to self-correct and restore your life path to long-lasting prosperity. The stern warning at this stage is to ensure that you take the necessary measures of self-correction.

*Fourth Line*
The contrary to nourishment—auspicious.
The tiger is alert, prowling, staring, marking its prey, waiting for the choice opportunity to pounce. It desires the chase, one by one triumphing in the pursuit.
There is no blame.

The Oracle passes no judgment on this particular form of feeding, but nevertheless clarifies that it is the inverse of true nourishment.

It is auspicious to be the tiger marking its prey, readying for the ambush and chase. There is no fault in the tiger acting in the tiger's nature.

| 虎視眈眈 | Hǔ shì dān dān |
| 其欲逐逐 | Qí yù zhú zhú |

The first line in the excerpt above, *Hǔ shì dān dān*, is an adage depicting a focused, formidable tiger (虎) carefully and alertly monitoring a situation, eyes on the target, waiting for the perfect moment to strike.

The next line mirrors that structure, *Qí yù zhú zhú*, speaking to desire and a love for the hunt. Together, the two sentences can imply greed, but they acknowledge the subject's great capacity for accruing wealth and possessions.

The tiger is also a symbol of bravery. Here is one courageous, daring, and strong enough to be the hunter. A personality trait of one born to be the tiger is a love for the hunt and chase, and not just for the final result.

No divinatory forecast needs to be given. It only stands to reason that someone like the tiger will prevail in the conquest.

| *Fifth Line*<br>In defiance of the canons.<br>Follow the right path.<br>Fortunes gained, but not auspicious to cross the great stream. | 六五：<br>拂經<br>居貞<br>吉<br>不可涉大川 |

One is taking an unorthodox path. The Oracle doesn't appear to mind the rejection of canon but does offer the one reminder: "居貞" (*jū zhēn*), a maxim meaning to follow the right path.

The ideogram "貞" is the image of a cauldron with incense smoke rising from its center, with the implication of devotionals to Divinity, and divination. The "right" path isn't about aligning yourself with canon; it's about aligning yourself with the Divine. Stay in close communion with Divinity, and self-nourish through spiritual cultivation—that's what it means to follow the "right" path.

*Sixth Line*
One whom many rely upon for receiving nourishment must overcome the hardship and provide for those dependents.
Auspicious to cross the great stream.

The auspices of a destined hero. The uppermost line is yang, whom all below look up to and rely upon for support. You are the pillar of strength for many.

A positive omen. Success in the undertaking, no matter the setbacks and adversity you'll encounter before the success. Prosperity, longevity, and good fortune will be yours after you have undertaken the challenging trial of crossing that proverbial great stream.

# Hexagram 28: Dà Guò. Undertake the Great

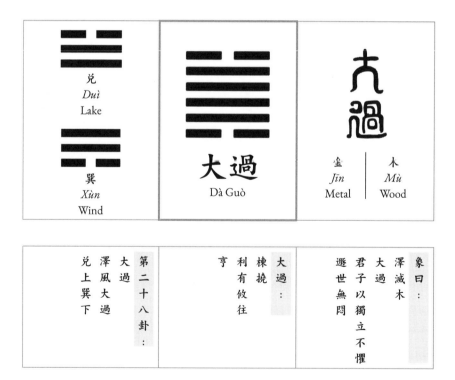

## *The Oracle*

The many steps you've taken and the changes at every step have converged. You are at a critical juncture on the cusp of undertaking the great. Wind that lifts the Lake begets excessive force, and release of that force will spread it until it becomes omnipresent. That is what you seek: to undertake the great. Relentless hard work day by day will spread your influence far and wide. A fundamental change is about to take place, and you are at its center.

The lake rises over the trees; marsh submerging wood. **Embarking on a great endeavor.**
**The sage is independent and fearless, ever concerned for the world. Let the heart be stable and calm, no matter what conditions endeavor to challenge it.**
**A fragile, unstable roof beam—a critical situation.**
Renouncing the world you knew. Expelling melancholy. It is a tipping point. You are reaching critical mass.
Yet fortune favors the inquirer—利有攸往 *(lì yǒu yōu wǎng)*. Undertaking a great challenge is likely to yield success, so proceed with confidence.
**Take the transformative path. It is a turning point in your life.**

### THE KUNDALINI SERPENT IN HEXAGRAM 28

Hexagram 28 expresses physical, ideological, and emotional injuries of long-lasting impact, experiences that remain imprinted for a lifetime and beyond. Yet it is the expression of kundalini awakening. The fourth line references a snake, reminiscent of the coiled snake Shakti divinity dwelling at the base of the spine.

| *First Line* |
|---|
| **Spread out the mat woven of white sword grass.** *Wu jiu*—**You are blameless.** 初六：藉用白茅無咎 |

Difficult times have befallen. There is every reason to be laying out the ritual mat and preparing the sacrificial offerings.

"白茅" *(bái máo)*, or *Imperata cylindrica,* also known as sword grass, is a reed that blossoms white seed heads, native to Asia. Highly flammable, it's often used as the kindling for ritual and ceremonial fires. Sword grass was a symbol of purity and purification, ideal for use in rituals.

Sword grass is also symbolic of love and prosperity between romantic couples, inspired by a reference to it in the Book of Songs (詩經, Shījīng), a collection of poems from eleventh–seventh century BC. Thus, the first line is often interpreted to indicate heartbreak or moments of challenge in a romantic relationship.

"藉" *(jí)* is a reference to a particular type of straw mat used for sacrificial offerings.

A mystical interpretation of the counsel offered here is to perform a ritual purification of your home. Do so by burning some form of aromatic dried grass or stalk (corresponding with the Wu Xing phase Wood). The smoke will help to neutralize any atrophic *qi* in your living quarters.

An animistic interpretation would be that the living Oracle feels sympathy for the predicament you're in. The Oracle offers compassion and solace.

A philosophical interpretation would be counsel that if what you feel is grief, and the true, latent underlying cause of that grief is a sense of personal failure, then engaging in a ritualized process of absolution will alleviate your grief.

One method of absolution inspired by theology is a form of ritual purification. A period of daily, dedicated prayer, speaking sacred words, is another.

On an esoteric note, "無咎" *(wú jiù)*—a reminder that you are blameless—as used throughout the Book is a form of sacred utterance by the Oracle, offering you absolution.

### Second Line
**The dried poplar gives birth to saplings.**
**The aging man takes a young woman for his wife.**
**Not an adverse decision.**

九二：
枯楊生稊
老夫得其女妻
無不利

An old idea is brought back to the forefront of your mind and, looking at it with a fresh perspective, is given new life.

Stay true to your idea, but give it a fresh, new design.

| *Third Line* <br> Tampering with the roof beam. <br> Ominous. | 凶 棟 九 <br> 橈 三 <br> ： | 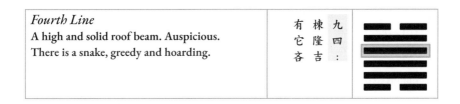 |

The pillars that hold up the frame and foundation are now breaking under the pressure from too much erratic movement. Do not change for the sake of change; change with purpose.

"棟橈" *(dòng ráo)* can mean improperly handling the roof beam, causing it to weaken, or bending it in a way that now makes it susceptible to breakage. In short, the third line is saying, "don't mess with a good thing."

The third line is advocating preservation of tradition. Maintain the current pillars as is. Now is not the time to go tampering with precedent. Keep to the tried and true.

| *Fourth Line* <br> A high and solid roof beam. Auspicious. <br> There is a snake, greedy and hoarding. | 有 棟 九 <br> 它 隆 四 <br> 吝 吉 ： | |

The fourth line can also be interpreted as the image of a curved, raised roof. This is a testament to a solid foundation and sturdy pillars. There is stability and security.

And yet there are those who are not feeling secure and are therefore hoarding and being greedy. Despite stable conditions, a threat still lurks. While also a pictorial reference to a snake, "它" is also a generic, nonspecific pronoun, indicating he, she, they, it—it's not specified.

The snake could also be interpreted as the coiled serpent or kundalini, an energy body at the base of the spine that, when awakened, induces a profound mystical experience. Positioned here, the sign of the snake is a divine call toward such an awakening. The snake in the state of "吝" suggests a closed state.

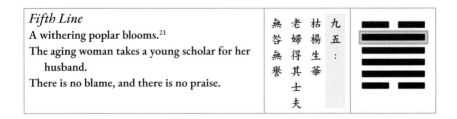

*Fifth Line*
A withering poplar blooms.[21]
The aging woman takes a young scholar for her husband.
There is no blame, and there is no praise.

Although the aging woman's marriage seems fortuitous, there is a sense of barrenness in the fifth line. The reference to the younger spouse being a scholar denotes social class. Under the Confucian system, scholars were the highest rank. Thus, the implication is she's marrying him to retain her power and prestige.

In a desperate circumstance, one who is losing power seeks an easy solution for retaining that power.

The fifth line is a parable warning against pursuing quick-fix solutions.

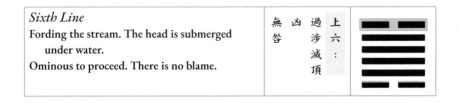

*Sixth Line*
Fording the stream. The head is submerged under water.
Ominous to proceed. There is no blame.

A bad omen for the leader or head. An overly ambitious heroic leader has overestimated what it would take to complete the mission. Do not follow the leader's doomed path.

Business trade is not advised at this time. The project being contemplated will require more resources and more time than currently estimated.

Someone incompetent and arrogant has taken on a leadership position. Listen to your instincts, which may call for disobedience.

# Hexagram 29: Kǎn. The Abyss

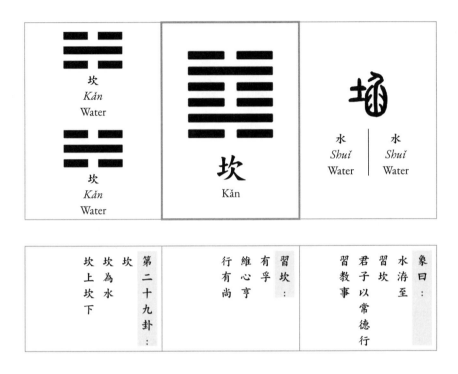

## The Oracle

A primal chaos before creation, a dark night with no glimmer of moonlight, sinking into the depths of an abyss—such is the nature of the womb that births the eminent ones. A journey at this time is favorable for avoiding the pitfalls. Move to sidestep the path of the storm. Seek refuge and be refuge. Honor the gods and ancestors to receive further insight.

**Great depths—the abyss.** Exercise caution: in such darkness and obscurity, there is potential for danger. Be wary of pitfalls, entrapment, and perils.
**However, there is a clear path to safety.** Where there is trust and sincerity, and when a heart serves an important mission, there can be prosperity in spite of the pitfalls.

**One entering the Abyss is one whose endeavor is a worthy cause.** Only in the Abyss can the worthiness of humanity shine. Who but the worthy would even dare face the Abyss.

**Water flows without impediment toward the goal.** Water flows around impediments, so there are no impediments.

When you face a pitfall, you fill the abyss of the pit with the force of Water until the abyss overflows, and in that way, you prevail in the abyss.

Study the ways of Water.

**The sage is one who remains steadfast in the path of virtue and benevolence in all undertakings.** You need ongoing study in matters of faith and philosophy. That is how you will understand Water over Water and how you can overcome all pitfalls and peril.

Sign of the Wounded Healer.

**An auspicious omen for travel. A journey can bring great rewards.**

## PRACTICUM 8.4:
## A Mantra to Reverse Misfortune

When Hexagram 29 is the divinatory result, you're probably in a state of inner chaos and confusion. You're feeling uncertain about the future, and there is a sinking feeling that the worst is still to come. Now is a good time to reverse the flow of that *qi* and revitalize it toward success and good fortune.

Use the lines of Hexagram 29 to reverse any negative flow and redirect it toward positive, productive flow. The following lines are taken word for word from the Oracle itself. Utilized as a mantra, it will control the flow of Water *qi* so that it brings clarity to your heart-mind and blessings of prosperity to your life.

Recite the subsequent lines three times in classical Chinese, then recite the translation three times. The Chinese recitation is to invoke the established pillar of power harnessed by the rhythm of the words, and the translated recitation is to amplify the mantra with your personal power—you have to understand the words to give them efficacy.

| | | |
|---|---|---|
| Water flowing, reaching Feathered wings, fluttering. A heart sincere seeks clarity and blessings of prosperity. | *Shuǐ jiàn zhì* *Xí jiāo shì* *Wéi xīn hēng* *Xíng yǒu shàng* | 水洊至 習教事 維心亨 行有尚 |

The first line of the mantra taps into and connects with the flow of the *qi* that's affecting your emotional health and your fortunes. The second line acknowledges your vulnerability, confusion, and difficulties encountered. The remaining lines are the prayer that will realign the flow of the *qi*.

| | |
|---|---|
| *First Line* Complacent to the abyss. Entering an abyss to come upon another abyss. Ominous to proceed. | 初六： 習坎 入于坎窞 凶 |

In the midst of many obstacles, you encounter more obstacles. Pitfall after pitfall.

One error is made, and known, but instead of correcting the error, you continue with the error. Doing so leads to more errors.

Losing your way at the start is innocent. Refusing to change is foolish. Ominous if you don't change course even after knowing you've erred; better to acknowledge faults. Delayed success is better than failure.

| | |
|---|---|
| *Second Line* The abyss is perilous. Seek out small gains. | 九二： 坎有險 求小得 |

The first step toward change is awareness. Here is the first light. One step at a time will lead you out of the pitfall. Journey through the abyss one step at a time.

The second line is the light that illuminates the darkness.

You are awakening.

| |
|---|
| *Third Line* |
| Coming and going from pit to pit, leaving one abyss to enter another abyss. |
| There is danger in proceeding: hold. |
| The pit becomes another pit, the abyss another abyss. |
| Stillness. |

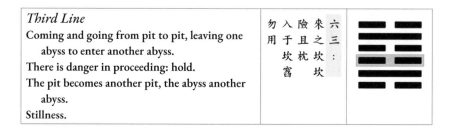

When the situation overwhelms, it is human to be frantic. The wise one knows to stay calm.

The counsel at this juncture is to do nothing. Be in stillness. Flow where the rushing waters flow. There will come the time to act, but not now.

Break the cycle.

| |
|---|
| *Fourth Line* |
| A jug of wine. Set out food for two. |
| Use an earthenware jug. Play the ritual music. |
| Leave these simple offerings for me upon a window. |
| At the end, there will be no blame. |

Mundane interpretations of this line range from a prospective business partnership to predicting romantic courtship.

Or, take it literally. Leave the offerings as instructed and in return, you will get your answer.

Pour wine into a clay, terracotta, porcelain, bone china, stone, or ceramic vessel. Place a table or altar setting of food for two by an open window along with the vessel of wine. These are the offerings your patron divinity requests. After the offerings are accepted, an omen will be sent.

"牖" *(yǒu)* also invokes the meaning of "誘" *(yòu)*. Thus, in the context of the fourth line, this conveys both the image of a window and the meanings "to enlighten" and "to guide."

"缶" *(fǒu)* is also an ancient Chinese percussive instrument made of either earthenware or bronzeware, resembling a pot. Thus, where the oracular message states "play the ritual music," you could reinterpret it as "play the ritual drum."

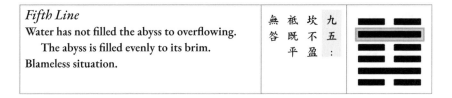

*Fifth Line*
Water has not filled the abyss to overflowing.
　The abyss is filled evenly to its brim.
Blameless situation.

You are on the brink of leaving the abyss and gaining solid ground.

The third, fourth, and fifth lines of Hexagram 29 form Mountain, a phantom trigram embedded within the hexagram, while the upper trigram is Water. This is the implied image of a mountain slowly emerging out of the waters, though its peak is not yet emerging from the abyss.

The fifth line is thus interpreted as an omen that one is no longer in imminent peril and is close to leaving the pitfalls.

"平" *(píng)*, meaning that the water is level at the brim, also means peace and calm. It's an omen that the precarious situation has been pacified or will be pacified. This can also be an omen of leveling the playing field or putting all on equal footing.

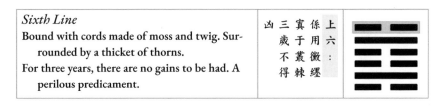

*Sixth Line*
Bound with cords made of moss and twig. Surrounded by a thicket of thorns.
For three years, there are no gains to be had. A perilous predicament.

Feeling trapped by a precarious situation, almost as if you are being punished. Unlucky circumstances and stagnation.

Difficult times to come, but this, too, shall pass. A balance will be restored, and the flow of good fortunes will return to you.

"叢棘" *(cóng jí)*, in addition to the image of thorn bushes or "thicket of thorns," was also where prisoners were kept in antiquity. The blockade of thorns prevented the prisoners from escaping.

This is the parable of one imprisoned for three years in penance for a past act, or phrased another way, one accused of three strikes of wrongdoing. It isn't entirely clear from the lines whether the prisoner is guilty or innocent.

Yet another interpretation, since this is the sixth line, is that of one who has lost their way for six years and is now paying penance for three.

In Hexagram 29, water is flowing upward, which is considered unnatural or supernatural. The sixth line conveys an impression that one has gone against nature. For going against nature, consequences will be meted out.

## Hexagram 30: Lí. The Spark

## The Oracle

> One who seeks enlightenment and then in turn enlightens others. Your luminosity comes from a fire within. Be the spark that animates the world around you. Nurture your gift of charisma. Hold tight to your community, and burn bright. Clinging is the key to cultivating charisma. When you can relate to and empathize with others, you appeal to their affections. Cling to show vulnerability; when you show vulnerability, you in turn attract empathy. The spark induces euphoria to become the prophet. Cultivation of charisma.

**One light after another—succession of sovereigns. The sun and moon coalescing.**
**The eminent one illuminates far and wide in the four directions, lighting up the four corners of the world. The luminous fire burns twice bright, in twin flames. Clarity and virtue.**
Prayers are answered.
**Raising heifers to be cows.**
**An auspicious omen.**
Fire over Fire: a yin line clings to two yang lines, one above and one below, a darkness at the center hollow of two pairs of light. What is in darkness clings to the light.
A flame has no solid form, but rather it clings to the object it burns.

---

*First Line*
**Footprints show a trail faltering between right and wrong, a confused path.**
**Honor with offerings. There will be no blame.**

初九：履錯然　敬之　無咎

---

Changing directions many times over.
Walking without thought, just to be in movement. Excitable and temperamental, but merely naïve.

"敬" *(jìng)* means to honor, but can also mean to present offerings.[22]
Common offerings implied by 敬 are tea, alcohol, food, or tobacco. The full implication of "honor with offerings" is to show reverence to gods and ancestors.

Thus, when the divinatory message is the first line, find solace in this: when you are faltering in your Path, show reverence and you will find your Way again. Endeavor with rites and rituals to rekindle a feeling of awe, spiritual transcendence, and harmony with the Tao.

The Oracle's counsel: be more orderly and methodical.

| *Second Line* <br> A curious imperial creature. <br> Sublime good fortune. |  |
|---|---|

Follow the signs that the spirit world is leaving you, and you shall achieve great success.

"離" *(lí)* can mean light, brightness, or luminosity, associations with the Fire trigram; but in this context, it can also be a reference to a rare, mythical beast. The ideogram consists of the radical "隹" *(zhuī)* meaning a short-tailed bird, likened to a sparrow, and "离" (modern: *lí*, archaic: *chī*), the image of an animal standing upright with the top "亠" indicating its head. In its modern usage, the word means to leave, depart, separate, or put distance between. I've opted to interpret it as a mythical creature, and envision it as a magical sparrow.

While "黃" *(huáng)* is more literally translated as the color yellow, as in Huang Di (黃帝), the Yellow Emperor, in antiquity the color was reserved for emperors only and was a symbol of ascension to the throne. Here, to better convey the meaning, I've interpreted "yellow" as symbolic of "imperial."

In the matter inquired about, the second line bodes positively. A strong omen of great auspices. The appearance of the animal spirit, if one envisions a mythic sparrow, symbolizes happiness and fertility. That it's an imperial color signifies an event of great importance.

Sparrows are also an omen of ancestors. The souls of ancestors can occupy a sparrow and return to earth to visit us.

| Third Line | | |
|---|---|---|
| 1. In the last light of a setting sun, beat the pot like a drum, sing the songs of lament, expressing the advancing age.<br>2. As the final light of the sun clings to the western sky, if you do not drum and sing, the great elders will lament.<br>A waning period. | 凶 則 不 日 九<br>　大 鼓 昃 三<br>　耋 缶 之 ：<br>　之 而 離<br>　嗟 歌 | ▬▬▬▬▬<br>▬▬　▬▬<br>▬▬▬▬▬<br>▬▬▬▬▬ |

This line foretells the ending of one chapter and the promise of a new chapter ascending. But at this time, one is stuck in a waning period.

You intuit an imminent ending, and that is causing you anxiety. A fear of change is causing unforced errors. Your own emotions are creating the detriment.

Release your fears. Instead of clinging, let go, and be at peace with letting go.

A shamanic reading of the line would call for a drum-and-song ritual of soul retrieval to ensure the health, longevity, and well-being of the clan's elders.

The third line consists of two variations of interpretation. The original text for the third yang line is vague and is therefore left open to either approach.

In both variations, the third line is expressing the dichotomy of song and lament, youth and old age, life and death, rising and setting, happiness and sorrow.

The setting sun in the west brings a decline. The lament signifies fear and anxiety regarding what is to come.

The third line is about legacies and remembrance. The observer sees the sun setting in the west and perceives the light lingering along the horizon as the sun's rays clinging, unwilling to set. That perception is a projection of the observer's own feelings about life and aging. This is about life review, and in that life review, settling upon a deepened sense of meaning and purpose.

Asking the youth to drum and sing, a ritual of veneration, the great elders are sharing the stories of their lives with the younger generations, passing on their wisdom, affirming their unbroken connection.

The concluding prognostication is ominous because of the observer's projections. The fear and anxiety around the setting sun, of waning life, rather than embracing the cycle of life, death, and rebirth, is why the ambiance is ominous.

| | | |
|---|---|---|
| *Fourth Line*<br>Sudden and swift, bursting forth unexpectedly—<br>As it burns,<br>As it dies,<br>Forsaken and left behind. | 棄死焚突九<br>如如如如四<br>　　　其：<br>　　　來<br>　　　如 | ▬▬　▬▬<br>▬▬▬▬▬<br>▬▬▬▬▬<br>▬▬　▬▬ |

Unexpected, unavoidable events.

Although traditionally, this line is often interpreted as prognosticating a natural disaster, the text itself is vague on that front.

The structure and tone convey a lament. The vision conjured is that of fires burning villages, villagers dying, villagers abandoning it all and fleeing.

However, note that the Oracle does not explicitly state that the matter is ominous, nor are there mentions of misfortune.

At the fourth line, the lower Fire trigram has been consumed entirely by the upper Fire, resulting in a formidable blaze at this juncture.

The line points to a moment of escalation. It is intense, rapidly expanding power, but this is both a power of destruction and a power of creation.

This stage of life is one of trial by fire, where Divinity is testing the limits and heights of your abilities. A trial by fire is a trial of character refinement.

When you have passed this stage of your life, you will be purified. And as it burns, as it dies, as it is forsaken, at every turn the gods and your ancestors are watching over you. No one will let you fall.

| | | |
|---|---|---|
| *Fifth Line*<br>Tearing, wailing such—tears streaming like rivers.<br>Sorrow and grief, alas! Take a breath. Exhale.<br>All will end favorably. | 吉戚出六<br>　嗟涕五<br>　若沱：<br>　　若 | ▬▬▬▬▬<br>▬▬　▬▬<br>▬▬▬▬▬<br>▬▬▬▬▬<br>▬▬　▬▬<br>▬▬▬▬▬ |

# THE LEGEND OF GOUJIAN, KING OF YUE

The historical account of Goujian, king of Yue (reigning 496–465 BC), is used as a parable for explaining the fifth line. Tensions were mounting between the two neighboring kingdoms of Yue and Wu. King Goujian's sister, a princess of Yue, was married to a prince of Wu in an effort to broker peace, but she left her husband and fled back home to Yue. When the prince of Wu demanded the return of his wife, Yue refused. Thus, war broke out between the two kingdoms.

The king of Wu defeated Yue in battle. Forced into servitude, Goujian and his wife ingratiate themselves to the enemy king, and with charm and cunning, Goujian eventually convinces the king of Wu to pardon and release them.

The image in the fifth line of grieving and eating bitterness is exemplified by Goujian's initial defeat, capture by his enemy, and enslavement.

Goujian returns to his kingdom and plots his revenge for ten years. After ten years of stealthy preparation, he finally launches an attack and overwhelmingly dominates the enemy kingdom.[23] Goujian shows no mercy to the enemy kingdom, executing everyone, even those who had been kind to him. This retribution is reflected in the subsequent sixth line.

History meets myth in an account of Jiǔ Tiān Xuán Nǚ, the Lady of the Nine Heavens incarnating in the form of Yuenü, a formidable swordswoman. Goujian has heard stories and high praise of this mysterious Yuenü's skills. He calls her to his court and questions

FIGURE 8.6 Script for "Yue" in bird script 鳥書 as inscribed on the sword of Goujian[24]

her: Who trained you? Who is your master? From what lineage of martial arts do you descend?[25]

Yuenü has no satisfactory answers. She tells the king that she lives in the forest alone and trained herself. She is of no lineage and has no master. Nevertheless, Goujian invites her to train his army. She teaches him thaumaturgical skills to use against the enemy and teaches his army the art of war. After Goujian's victory, Yuenü's body turns into six black stones, and Jiǔ Tiān Xuán Nǚ ascends back to Heaven.

After his enslavement, Goujian never forgets the trials and humiliation he endured. Even as king, he continued to live humbly, dress simply, and eat simply, and he was extremely frugal, making it a point to eat bitter foods every day as a reminder of what he went through, of having to eat bitterness (吃苦, *chīkǔ*) when he was a captive ingratiating himself to his enemy. (The trigram Fire corresponds with the taste of bitterness.)

After enduring great difficulties and adversity, you have truly grown from your experiences, gaining wisdom and inner strength. Crying brings a needed sense of release. You shed your ego. You shed your pride. You have nothing to lose now.

The wisdom of knowing that sends you on the path toward good fortune and success.

"若" *(ruò)*, appearing twice, could also be interpreted as an implied reference to "海若" (Hǎi Ruò), god of the northern sea, most likely in reference to the Yellow Sea, which flows into the Yellow River.

There's also a narrative flow here from the second line, with the earlier reference of the "curious imperial creature," a yellow mythic beast, to the omen of the Yellow Sea here in the fifth line.

The fifth line, the sovereign line of Hexagram 30, can be summed up with the following popular idiom: 吃得苦中苦、方為人上人 *(Chī dé kǔ zhōng kǔ, fāng wéi rén shàng rén)*. It means if you can eat the most bitter of all bitterness, then you can become the greatest above all others, peerless.

| | |
|---|---|
| *Sixth Line*<br>**The king levies his army forward for the attack, and the chieftains of the opposition are struck down.**<br>**Take the rebels as prisoners.**<br>**There is no blame.** | 上九：<br>王用出征<br>有嘉折首<br>獲匪其醜<br>無咎 |

You are the great sage whose brightness can illuminate the four corners of the world—you are the rightful king. Thus, you are in the right for quashing your opposition.

To prevail across the four corners of your endeavor, start at the head and strike down the leaders of the revolt.

There is a time to be merciful, and there is a time to show strength. The sixth line of Hexagram 30 indicates a time to show strength. Set an example.

Execute a harsh punishment to fit the transgression. You will not be faulted for showing your strength and standing your ground.

It is the sage's strong inner fire, clarity of vision, strategy for expansion, and wisdom that validate a sage as the rightful king. Thus, what action the rightful king takes is blameless in the matter at hand.

The sixth line forecasts penultimate victory over the opposition, validating one sage as the rightful, most meritorious sovereign.

# Hexagram 31: Xián. Mutual Accord

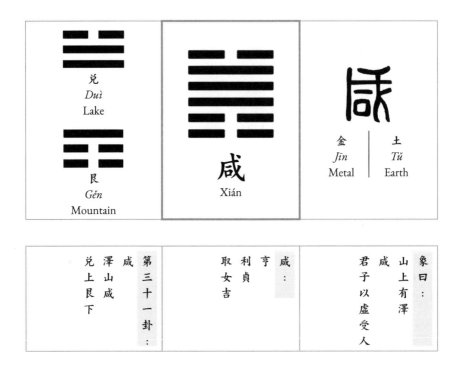

## The Oracle

**Now is the time to cultivate influence. Attract what you seek without pursuing. Receive others with humility and nonjudgment. On their own accord they'll come. Endeavor to give more than you receive, and the paradox of life is that this will grant you more than you give. To attract love, emanate with love. Be loving. Show your feelings, and people will have feelings for you. Let the people move you, and you will move the people: reciprocal attraction; mutual influence. Lovers are joyous and prosperous.**

Atop the mountain there is a lake: enduring joy and prosperity. Mutual accord and completion. The sage is selfless and open-minded toward all people.

A good omen—auspicious to proceed.

**Taking the maiden as a wife brings good fortune.** Auspicious for unions between heaven and earth, yin and yang: there is prosperity to be had in the mutual influence.

The parable of taking a maiden as a wife is a metaphor for taking a developing concept to the next level by committing to it. The Oracle affirms that what you contemplate is worthy of manifestation. Commit to the endeavor and it will yield great fruition. What you put into that endeavor is exactly what you will get out of it.

If the inquiry is about love or marriage, then this hexagram is a very auspicious omen. In business, auspicious for mergers and acquisitions.

The character 咸 (Xián) with the addition of the character for heart 心 (xīn) becomes the word for emotion and sentimentality 感 (gǎn). Thus, Xián is about sensation, feelings, and influencing another through touch, be that physical touch or touching another's heart.

Note also that implied in the subtext of mutual accord is tension. For feelings to be aroused between the lower (in this case Mountain) and the upper (Lake), there must also be an intense strain or suspense.

### THE LOVE AND ROMANCE HEXAGRAMS

There are four hexagrams that address romantic love and civil unions or marriage: Hexagrams 31, 32, 53, and 54. Here, Hexagram 31 refers to the mutual attraction and sexual chemistry experienced by the young couple in love.

| *First Line* **Sensation at the thumb.** | 初六： 咸其拇 |
|---|---|

Change is coming, though no one seems to sense it. The beginnings of movement; an idea begins to surface.

This is an idea beginning to form itself at the base of the mountain.

Whether the influence will have an impact remains to be seen; it is still too early to tell.

No clear prognostication of success or failure can be ascertained at this time. The outcome of your endeavor remains unclear, though some energy is bubbling already below the surface.

"拇" *(mǔ)* is more popularly interpreted as big toe, though the reference could also be to the thumb. This text has opted for "thumb" because the trigram Mountain is governed by the Wu Xing phase Earth, which corresponds with the thumb.

As early as the Shang dynasty (1600–1046 BC), kings and warriors alike wore archer thumb rings on their dominant hand. A slot was carved into the precious stone or bronze ring to guide and aid release of the bowstring. One such archer thumb ring was found in the tomb of Fu Hao (circa 1200 BC),[26] the female warrior general, and they were often worn linked to the archer's wrist. Moreover, the thumb ring protected the finger during hunting, battle, and sport.

*Second Line*
Sensation at the calves.
Foreboding adversity.
Holding back yields good fortune.

You feel the impulse to move, but moving now will not bode well. You are not yet strong or well-equipped enough to advance. Remain in your current position. Maintain the status quo.

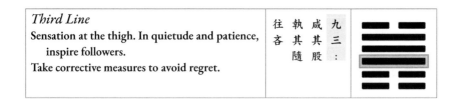

*Third Line*
Sensation at the thigh. In quietude and patience, inspire followers.
Take corrective measures to avoid regret.

This line tells the story of one who is inspired to follow those walking ahead but who is too weak to keep up. The Oracle advises not to follow, but rather, to lead. Inspire followers instead.

This is the final line of the trigram Mountain, with the two yang lines from the upper trigram Lake blocking it from ascent. The two yang lines of Lake represent obstacles in your way.

Instead of following others to become who you're not, stay who you are and lead those behind and below you.

"隨" *(suí)* is the name of Hexagram 17, Inspiring Followers.

| | | |
|---|---|---|
| *Fourth Line*<br>**Prognostication of good auspices and fortune. Regret not.**<br>**Indecisive—foolish—coming, arriving, happening—**<br>**Friends join in kinship with your hopes and wishes.** | 朋從爾思 憧憧往來 貞吉悔亡 九四： |  |

What you contemplate is auspicious and fortuitous. It will assuage all of your past regrets.

Yet you remain indecisive. You lack conviction. Wavering, tottering, and staggering the way you move—unsteady.

Your peers and colleagues believe in you. You already have the support you need.

To ascend, you must display strength in your convictions. You are on the right path. Do not doubt yourself.

| | | |
|---|---|---|
| *Fifth Line*<br>**Sensation behind the shoulders.**<br>**There is no blame.** | 無悔 咸其脢 九五： | |

Your intentions are sincere, but your actions do not advance your endeavor.

The more commonly translated reference here is the back or upper back. To clarify in meaning, here it's expressed as "behind the shoulders." This offers a more symbolic visual of the line's meaning. This is also the spine.

If your spine cannot be influenced by others, then others cannot be influenced by you. To allow room in yourself for a change of heart is virtuous, and there will be no remorse in it.

Continuing the theme of followers and influencers in Hexagram 31, the fifth
line warns of how the influencer might be the follower.

What force do you not see that is moving you from behind? The fifth line suggests an unseen influence that is moving you just as you are moving it.

"咸其脢" *(xián qí méi)* is a metaphor for deliberately avoiding reality, and yet
in this particular instance, there is no fault and no detriment caused by it.

| *Sixth Line*<br>**Sensations at the cheek and tongue.** | 咸其輔頰舌 上六： | ䷞ |
|---|---|---|

A superficial, skin-deep accord only. Charming one to follow you is not true
influence.

You may be eloquent and moving with your words, but the influence is superficial. The sense of this line is empty rhetoric.

The message: you cannot argue your way to success. To attain success in your
endeavor will require action and true influence.

Verse 81 from Lao Tzu's Dào Dé Jīng (道德經) is instructive here:

> Truthful words do not taste sweet. Sweet words are not truthful.
> The beneficent do not argue. Those who argue are not beneficent.

The Oracle is guiding you to listen closely and discern what people are
saying—and also, what you're saying to people.

The word for *cheek* (輔 Fǔ) also refers to the part of a carriage or cart that
stabilizes the vehicle. There's a subtext of support. The word for *tongue*
(舌 Shé) is also a double reference to the tongue of a bell, the hammer part
that rings the instrument.

Mutual accord between your cheeks and tongue represent their interdependence for the functions of eating, breathing, and communicating.

This is the image of people-pleasing through rhetoric, but not following up
that rhetoric with action. And yet like the first line, the sixth line of the
Oracle offers no final prognostication of a positive or negative outcome. It
merely offers its pithy statement.

# Hexagram 32: Héng. The Eternal

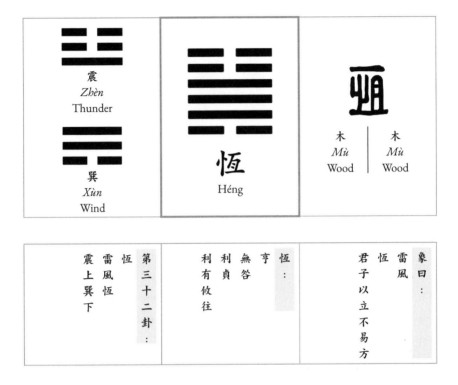

## The Oracle

You are being tasked to handle more than you should be responsible for. The action to take is to endure, and the way to endure is to change. Within you—the sage—you must pursue a constant state of transformation and change, though your outward demeanor should be one of conviction, firmness, and resolve. Be mindful—as you change, you may be tempted to call others to change. You cannot force another's transformation; that is oppressive. You can only compel your own transformation. That is how you will endure. Seek alliance with those most different from you, and find harmony. That is how you ensure your longevity and endurance. Favorable for a journey.

## THE LOVE AND ROMANCE HEXAGRAMS

Hexagram 32 can refer to the institution of marriage and continues the narrative from Hexagram 31. By yin and yang lines, the two hexagrams are reversals of one another. Hexagram 31 is the story of courtship, of yang wooing yin to copulate with yang.

Here in Hexagram 32, two have already entered a union. Wind, in the lower submissive position, exerts a gentle influence, whereas Thunder, in the upper dominant position, incites and activates. Yet both trigrams are equal in their correspondence to Wood. There is mutuality.

Now also how the Oracle's message seems to offer guidance on how a union might succeed: to be equal but interdependent, committed and loyal to one another for better and for worse, no matter how situations change. When circumstances are difficult, be dignified to one another. In the enjoyment of prosperity, be humble and modest.

The sage stands firm and resolute, steadfast, and not wavering in the Way. Not wavering in the Way means yielding to a constant state of change. That is endurance.

An auspicious omen. **There is no blame. It is advantageous to proceed. Journeys and undertakings will yield fortuitous gains.**

Endurance is the power to bear hardship with dignity, and prosperity with humility.

Hexagram 32 expresses hard work. To endure, you have to persist. Persistence is exhausting. What you seek to maintain can be accomplished, but only with highly demanding energy.

The hexagram can also refer to an ascent to leadership, governance, and the role of the leader in relation to subjects.

## THE ETERNAL

In both the received order of the hexagrams (King Wen's, which is the present order) and the Mawangdui order, Héng 恆 is the midpoint, numbered 32. While the general theme for Hexagram 32 is that of endurance, the name of the hexagram is "the Eternal" to underscore the shamanic origins of the Book of Changes.

The doctrine of the Eternal is a principal concept in the I Ching and in the shamanic cultures of both the Shang and the Zhou.[27] Lao Tzu expressed the void and emptiness of the Tao as the Eternal 恒道 Héng Dào, and to be the eternal is to attain eternal virtue, 恒德 *(héng dé)*. The Tao is the eternal name 恒名 *(héng míng)* and yet eternally without name, 道恒無名 (*Dào héng wúmíng*).

The doctrine of the Eternal as the Tao is to express enduring change, the continuance of change. The Eternal is the process of transformation, and the core message is this: to achieve immortality, to transcend and be Divine, is to never cease with one's cultivation 工夫 *(gōng fū)*.[28]

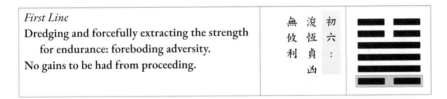

*First Line*
Dredging and forcefully extracting the strength for endurance: foreboding adversity.
No gains to be had from proceeding.

Fortitude cannot be forced. Forcing oneself to endure is not endurance.
Endurance is a refined and cultivated virtue. Reconsider your perspective of what it means to endure, to be enduring.
You want too much too soon.
Allow the matter to take its natural course, even if that means feeling like you are not in control. If you are too attached to control, you will lose that control even faster.
This is the sign of one who is trying too hard. Endeavor for inner balance and calm before proceeding.

*Second Line*
Disappointment vanishes.
Sign of repentance.

The second line expresses regret and contrition for past acts. Here the Oracle offers absolution—you are free of blame and guilt. Going forward, you will be released from consequences and penance. Divine forgiveness has been granted.

You wield immense power within. When that power is not contained and tempered, you inadvertently hurt those you care about the most.

Temperance is the solution. Exert only enough measured, tempered force necessary to advance your position. Be ever mindful and careful not to overexert. Never demonstrate the full extent of your power. Forbear, hold back, show restraint.

| Third Line | | |
|---|---|---|
| One is not being consistent and not being steadfast. Endeavor for corrective measures before proceeding. Otherwise, there will be a regrettable outcome. | 貞或不九<br>吝承恆三<br>　之其：<br>　羞德 | |

External forces cause your internal convictions to vacillate. You are inconsistent. Others are becoming aware of your inconsistency, and your reputation is at risk.

"德" *(dé)* means virtue, descriptive of a character who exemplifies integrity and one who abides by the highest code of ethics. Though a direct, literal translation of this term doesn't appear above, it's implied.

The corrective measures to take:

- Show more firmness in your sense of purpose.
- Be unwavering in your resolve.
- Do not be self-contradictory.
- Keep to your own stated principles.
- Live by those same principles that you seem to impose upon others.

Live up to these corrective measures and all will be well. Otherwise, the Oracle predicts a regrettable outcome.

| Fourth Line | | |
|---|---|---|
| Neither birds nor beasts in the field. | 田九<br>無四<br>禽： | |

You cannot hunt for what is not there. You pursue goals that are unrealistic.

No matter how much effort you exert or how intelligently you pursue the hunt, you cannot catch any game if there is none in the field. You are currently searching for what does not exist.

The field (the environment) within which you seek to undertake the endeavor is inadequate for the purpose contemplated.

| *Fifth Line*<br>They are consistent and steadfast, sincere in their divination.<br>Auspicious for the madame.<br>Ominous for the master. | 夫子凶　婦人吉　恆其德貞　六五： | ䷟ |

In a heart-mind dichotomy, follow your heart, and question the mind.

"夫子" *(fū zǐ)* is a Confucian honorific used to address someone elderly, reputed to be wise or of notable scholarship, or a master teacher.

"婦人" *(fù rén)*, or madam, is the Confucian honorific used to address a married woman.

A modernized interpretation of the fifth line is to view it as the relationship between logic and intuition. Follow your intuition ("the madame") and be wary of where your logic ("the master") is leading you.

The traditional interpretation would have been more direct, patriarchal, and literal—a wife has been living up to her duties, but a husband has not been living up to his, though acknowledging that both are devoted and sincere.

The fifth line can also be interpreted through the lens of the other Confucian relations. Thus, beyond the literal reference to husband and wife, the Oracle is siding with the subjects and against a sovereign ruler. The madame can also be interpreted as the younger generation and a more progressive movement, with the master as an older generation and a conservative movement. The madame would be interpreted as left wing and the master as right wing.

This can also relate to a parent-child relation, boding well for the child and not boding well for the parent.

| *Sixth Line*<br>Swaying, wavering endurance.<br>Setbacks and hardship. | 凶　振恆　上六： | ䷟ |

Formulate a long-term path and then commit to it. Cultivate your endurance. The ability to bear pain and hardships determines likelihood of success.

Your restlessness and state of anxiety are what prevent you from succeeding. You exhaust yourself through unproductive movement.

Perseverance must have a direction. Expending energy without a direction is mere waste.

Setbacks are causing you to waver in your personal resolve, and that will lead to an adverse outcome. Endure the setbacks with strength and stamina. Be indefatigable.

In statecraft, the sixth line is a reference to wavering, inconsistent, and excessively changing laws and policies that are causing instability in the society. A leader must give the people consistency and stability.

## Hexagram 33: Dùn. Withdraw

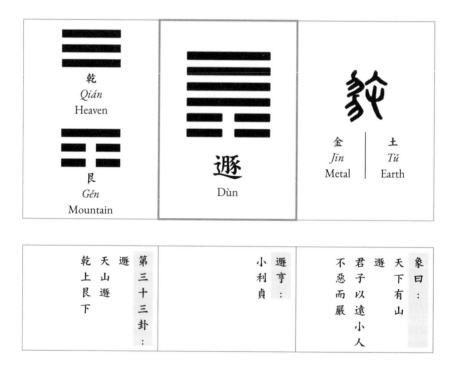

# The Oracle

> Retreat does not mean surrender. This is a strategic withdrawal into safety and seclusion while you plan your next move. When the opponent is on the offensive and you have neither the power nor support to prevail, recede and move away. Eventually the opponent will come to a rest, and that is when you strike. Return to the Oracle to affirm when the timing is right. Now is a time for self-reflection, prayer to Heaven, and personal growth.

**Beneath Heaven, there is Mountain: absconding into the darkness.**
**The sage maintains distance from those who are inferior. There is no need for enmity, but you must remain solemn and stern.**
**Better to retreat for now: there is a small gain to be had if you withdraw from the endeavor.**
Hostile forces are advancing. Confrontation will not serve your interest.
It is better to retreat for now, but do not mistake the act of retreat for fleeing. Do not flee; do not abandon the endeavor, and do not try to escape your opponent.
Giving the opponent a false impression of victory is not the same as giving the opponent a victory. Withdraw temporarily and plan a counterattack. When the opponent has come to a position of rest and complacency, that is when you strike.
The most profound degree of wisdom comes from knowing when to retreat. It is always the most difficult decision to make, and only the wisest are capable of making it.

*First Line*
**A tail in retreat: dangers lurk ahead.**
**Do not sprint in any direction.**

初六：
遯尾厲
勿用有攸往

There is an illusory, misleading escape route, and you are tempted to flee in that direction. Do not yield to that temptation, because that escape route leads to danger.

"尾 Wěi" is also a reference to the end of a matter. The first line suggests one hastily and impatiently trying to bring a matter to its conclusion, as if to escape it.

Stay in stillness. Like the trigram Mountain, stop, halt, do not move. Be in stillness, at a standstill, to preserve. In the lull you will achieve a stabilizing, balancing force. Stay quiet, but every aspect within is active and alert. Not moving doesn't mean not acting.

An alternative interpretation of the first line is in *how* to retreat. When a tiger presents itself, the deer who seeks to survive needs to be at the head of the retreat, not at the tail, so there is a buffer between you and the tiger. If you know you can gallop to the front and be at the head, then retreat.

If you know you cannot make it up to the front, then step to the side and hold still. Take no action for now. Let the stampede pass you by. Stay calm, seek shelter, and you will survive. The tone of the Oracle might imply that the chances of making it up to the front are slim, whereas the chances of survival by stepping aside are better.

**Second Line**
Use the yellow ox leather.
No one can loosen the grip.

You are in a position of hardship that is difficult to get out of.

When you cannot outmaneuver your adversary and when your adversary's physical strength overpowers yours, then craft leather rope to bind your foe.

The philosophical reading of this line is to exert greater personal resolve and willpower. Do not let hardships shake your faith.

Instead, plot the crafting of leather rope, or plot a resistance and, when the leather rope has been crafted and is capable of binding the adversary, gather the forces for a revolution.

There's a sense here of "where there is a will, there is a way." And the vision the Oracle provides is that of the yellow ox leather and what it symbolizes.

The image of the second line is of crafting leather cord. Leather cord is strong, durable, and flexible, and it can be used to bind something, likened to a binding spell or magical binding.

Leather or cowhide is a symbolic reference to liberation or revolution, as used in Hexagram 49. The ox leather represents firm willpower, resolve, and perseverance.

Another reading is a continuation of the first line—that tail in retreat is of a fleeing piglet that you can catch by using the ox leather—craft it into cord.

A mystical reading is the binding spell.

### A BINDING SPELL TO IMMOBILIZE AN ADVERSARY

A simple binding spell to immobilize an adversary and take away some of their power over you, inspired by the second line, is to mold a clay[29] poppet of the person whom you are not physically strong enough to defeat. Carve the person's name and date of birth into the poppet, or if the full date of birth is not known, the person's animal zodiac sign per their year of birth.

At a late evening hour when powerful yin spirits are active, take a spool of yellow leather cord and wind it tightly around the poppet as you recite words declaring that the named person's power is being bound and restricted.

Now you have a hold over this person, rather than the other way around. When no part of the poppet is visible anymore and the cord is tightly confining it, push pins to affix the cord firmly to the clay poppet.

Bury the poppet a safe and far distance from your home, somewhere remote.

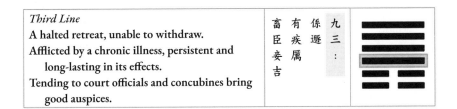

Third Line
A halted retreat, unable to withdraw.
Afflicted by a chronic illness, persistent and long-lasting in its effects.
Tending to court officials and concubines bring good auspices.

Times are difficult. There is no easy solution for getting out of the current conditions. Instead of focusing so much attention and investment on the external sphere, focus it on the internal sphere.

The state suffers from a chronic illness. It is one that cannot be instantly cured. In the effort to recover, do not forget to tend to your own house—the court officials and concubines within the palace walls.

The reference to a chronic illness is also a figurative metaphor. A hardship is plaguing present circumstances in the same way a chronic illness is persistent and never seems to withdraw, and doesn't allow the invalid to withdraw.

A subtle shift in how this line might be interpreted: 臣 *(chén)* and 妾 *(qiè)* are self-addressing pronouns used to show reverence to the one being addressed, understood to be the sovereign or the head of the royal court. In other words, instead of saying "I" or "me," when a court official addresses the king, the court official would say "臣" in place of "I." Likewise, concubines address the king with "妾" instead of "me."

That context gives this third line a more nuanced tone. In effect, "tending to court officials" becomes analogous to "tending to me." The subtle shift gives the impression of a first-person appeal, rather than the Oracle dictating to you what to do. It's the difference between "please focus your attention on me" and "go focus your attention on them." The Oracle is channeling and speaking in the voice of the figurative court officials and concubines imploring you to direct your investments to them.

Furthermore, "tending" bears a connotation of giving livestock to someone, or feeding, nourishing, and dedicating material resources to them. "Tending" also implies listening to them, appeasing them, and abiding by their wishes.

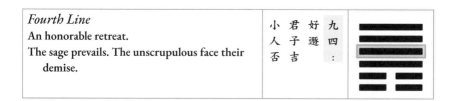

| *Fourth Line* <br> **An honorable retreat.** <br> The sage prevails. The unscrupulous face their demise. | 小 君 好 九 <br> 人 子 遯 四 <br> 否 吉 ： | |

The sage who retreats in wisdom and honor will be the one who prevails in the end.

If you retreat for now and attack another day, you will be the victor, and your adversary faces a demise.

In Confucian texts, "小人" is used as an antonym to "君子" (*junzi*).

In statecraft divination, the fourth line prognosticates the appeals of a great and virtuous leader—the sage. However, the masses are too foolish and ignorant to follow the sage.

Instead of insisting, the sage abdicates the position of power for an honorable treat. You cannot force people into wisdom.

The fourth line warns that the false prophet that the people have chosen, along with the people, are unscrupulous and therefore will face their demise.

| *Fifth Line* <br> A commendable retreat. <br> Prediction of good fortune and a favorable outcome. | 嘉 九 <br> 遯 五 <br> 貞 ： <br> 吉 | ▬▬▬▬▬ <br> ▬▬▬▬▬ <br> ▬▬▬▬▬ <br> ▬▬ ▬▬ <br> ▬▬ ▬▬ <br> ▬▬ ▬▬ |

When you have done all you can do in good faith, perhaps it's time to withdraw. The fifth line can be interpreted as properly timed retirement or wisely knowing when to bow out and take your exit.

### THE WISE DUKE OF ZHOU

The parable of the fifth line is of the Duke of Zhou, uncle to the heir apparent after the death of King Wu of Zhou.

When a rebellion led by Shang loyalists erupted in the eastern region of the kingdom, the duke successfully quashed the rebellion. He strengthened Zhou rule and became a much-beloved popular hero among the people. The duke was known for establishing more humane laws and ending human sacrifice.

The duke could have taken the title of king had he wanted to, but he didn't. Instead, after his great successes in the name of the heir apparent, King Wu's son, the Duke of Zhou, retires. When the time comes, he dutifully gives up his powers.

Alternatively, a "commendable retreat" can be applied in the art of war: when fighting means that the innocent will be hurt, retreating for the sake of the innocent is praiseworthy. In times of conflict and adversity, do not prioritize pride or vanity above the well-being of those you owe a responsibility to.

| *Sixth Line* **Portly with abundance, retreating. No adverse effects.** | 肥遯無不利 | 上九： | ䷠ |
|---|---|---|---|

Past fruits of labor are abandoned in favor of soul-searching. This is the withdrawal from the material world, feeling indifferent toward superficial riches. The sixth line is the position of seeking higher meaning from life.

There is an image here of one who is rotund from having enjoyed the good life. We're getting a vision of the torso of that tail from the first line. There is the hint of a piglet or fat little kitten.

With Heaven over Mountain, this might be in the form of spiritual retreat or becoming a recluse. The sixth line prognosticates a dramatic change in lifestyle, from a more mundane purpose to serving a higher purpose.

# Hexagram 34: Dà Zhuàng. Great Power

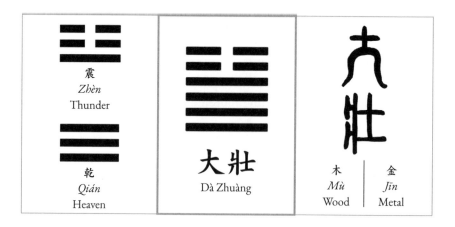

| 第三十四卦：<br>大壯<br>雷天大壯<br>震上乾下 | 大壯：<br>利貞 | 象曰：<br>雷在天上<br>大壯<br>君子以非禮弗履 |

## *The Oracle*

> Never strike until you can strike at full strength. Be alert. Be vigilant. Great power attracts great danger. Align yourself with Heaven to strike with the force of Heaven, and never with the force of arrogance or vanity. Do not use excessive force. Be tempered, measured, and fair. Only one who is weak would be merciless. Great power subjects one to great injury. A favorable omen for fulfillment of destiny, but be wise, or else your blessing can become your downfall.

**Thunder and lightning in the sky. Exalted strength. The making of greatness.**

**The sage observes the ways of ritual, ceremony, courtesy, and propriety. Every gesture of action in rites and in the details of etiquette reflect the whole of one's character.**

Favors and gains to come.

**Great power puts a flock in danger. Be alert and vigilant.**

An auspicious omen.

Hexagram 34 corresponds with the vernal equinox and thus symbolizes progress, growth, and fertile times.

### THE LEGEND OF PRINCE HAI

The narrative of Hexagram 34—about Wang Hai, the legendary wanderer who traversed into the kingdom of Yi herding sheep—picks up where

Hexagram 23 left off. He attained great prosperity and became renowned throughout the land. His prosperity as an outsider in the kingdom of Yi aroused envy, and there was a conspiracy to burn him alive in his own house.

In Hexagram 23, Wang Hai was able to escape with his life. However, he is not free of danger just yet. Here in Hexagram 34, it seems his herd of sheep is still in danger, and those who are jealous of his success still seek to inflict harm.

## THE INTERPLAY BETWEEN HEXAGRAMS 33 AND 34

Hexagram 34 denotes great personal power and accumulating an abundance of resources to further your endeavor.

If Hexagram 33 was about retreating and laying low until you're ready, then Hexagram 34 is the Oracle telling you you're ready. Strike at full strength.

However, there is a foreboding undertone, one warning of conspirators who envy your power and strength.

| First Line |
|---|
| Power in the foot. |
| To levy the troops now would be ominous. Have faith. |

征凶有孚　壯于趾　初九：

Tracking the movements of your adversary, you see that your limited strength at this time is insufficient. Your forces are not strong enough to defeat the foe.

Do not seek advancement by excessive use of a weak force. Seek advancement by measured, calculated use of a strong force.

It is not enough to be as good as your adversary or competition; you must be three times better.

|  |  |
|---|---|
| *Second Line*<br>Auspicious to proceed. | 貞 九<br>吉 二<br>　　：  |

Sign of great power. You have what it takes to succeed in your endeavor. Positive omen of success. Attainment. The best possible outcome will manifest.

|  |  |
|---|---|
| *Third Line*<br>The unprincipled uses excessive force.<br>The sage uses effortless action.<br>Forecast is that of a risky undertaking. Dangers.<br>A ram charges head-first for the fence. Its horns get entangled. | 羸 羝 貞 君 小 九<br>其 羊 厲 子 人 三<br>角 觸 　 用 用 ：<br>　 藩 　 罔 壯  |

The unprincipled and unwise wield power openly for show.
The better way is to conceal your power and give the impression of powerlessness. To display force now is risky and could bode ill for your endeavor.
Keep away from the fence and avoid further entanglement in the situation.
"罔" *(wǎng)* technically translates to nothing, not doing, not having, or staying stealthy. It is also the image of a net that catches what it needs to catch without having to take any action. I've extrapolated that meaning to *wu wei,* Taoist nonaction, or effortless action.

|  |  |
|---|---|
| *Fourth Line*<br>Auspicious omen. Disappointments vanish.<br>The fence opens. There is no entanglement.<br>Great power in the axle of a carriage. | 壯 藩 悔 貞 九<br>于 決 亡 吉 四<br>大 不 　 　 ：<br>輿 羸<br>之<br>輹  |

Forecast of success in the matter inquired about. Favorable outcome when you let natural forces flow in their own due course. Do not force the situation.

In the third line, a ram tries to break open a closed fence by charging headfirst into it, only to get its horns stuck in the fencing. Here in the fourth line, no action needs to be taken, because the fence door opens on its own, clearing a way.

Recall from the previous line that the "sage uses effortless action." The sage embodies the axle of a carriage.

An axle is what moves the wheels of a carriage forward. Without the axle, the carriage is immobile, and yet onlookers will often overlook the axles and see only the carriage.

You do not want to be the carriage. You want to be the axle hidden underneath the carriage.

| *Fifth Line*<br>Losing sheep in the kingdom of Yi.<br>There is no blame. | 無悔 喪羊于易 六五： |
|---|---|

Those who are envious of your successes and gifts take advantage of you, out of spite. Losses sustained. However, what you lose, you will gain back. Going forward, be more on guard. Protect yourself and that which is yours.

The fifth line is a continuation of the narrative from Hexagram 23, which references the legend of Wang Hai. Per folklore, Wang Hai is one of the great nomadic ancestors of the Shang people. A remarkably successful herder, he attracts the envy of his neighbors in the kingdom of Yi (all the way up to the lord of the territory), who plot many times over to have Wang Hai killed and to seize his bountiful herd.

Likewise, you have attracted the envy of others. Minor harm befalls, a loss brought on by maliciously intended neighbors.

Even someone in charge, in a position of power, envies what you have or who you are.

It will all work out in the end. Keep doing what you're doing.

| Sixth Line<br>A ram charges head-first for the fence.<br>Unable to retreat. Unable to advance.<br>No advantages gained.<br>Hardships followed by success and<br>　　blessings. | 艱無不不羝上<br>則攸能能羊六<br>吉利遂退觸：<br>　　　　藩 |   |

Caught in a precarious position. Feeling trapped by circumstances, though they were circumstances of your own doing when you acted rashly out of emotion, rather than wisely, principled and reasoned.

No good comes of the rash action that has put you in this trapped position of being unable to change course and yet also unable to complete the endeavor.

Hardships to come, but the hardships are short-lived. Blessings and good tidings will soon follow.

## Hexagram 35: Jìn. Advancement

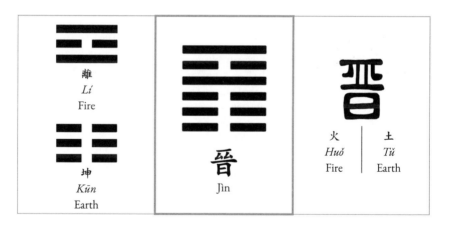

## The Oracle

> You have stood where you are for long enough. Now is a time for advancement. May the pawn become a queen. Flames must burn, and in the wake of ashes you are the phoenix that rises. Support those above you with loyalty. Support those below you with generosity. That is how you expand your influence. Advance like a mouse. Surmount the throne like a lion. All hail the Queen Mother.

A ray of light rises above the ground. Progress.

**The sage's nature is inherently good, and so as pure light shines on the sage, that nature is illuminated brighter and brighter, ever more illustrious and virtuous.**

| | |
|---|---|
| The marquis of Kang casts many extravagant horses of tin. 甲<br>And so he is beloved and treated with great courtesy. 乙<br><br>After King Wu established the Zhou dynasty, Shang loyalists in the east launched a rebellion. King Wu sends great political statemen like the Duke of Zhou to quash the rebellion, but then also sends his more romantic, charismatic brother, the marquis of Kang, to win the hearts of the people, which he does. Once united, the Zhou kingdom advances, ushering in one of China's golden ages.<br><br>You are like the marquis of Kang. You bring progress and advancement through your charisma and demonstrated virtues. You are well loved, and through your likability, you gain influence. | 甲 The reference to tin (錫) comprises metal (金) and change (易), as in the Book of Changes. There's an implied meaning from use of the word *tin:* to be wise is to know that you must be willing to change before you can create change. Hexagram 35 is first about personal advancement through cultivation, then about social advancement by nurturing the hearts of people.<br><br>乙 "晝日三接" *(zhòu rì sān jiē)*, while literally translates to "meeting three times a day," is an idiom that means to be so well loved and attended to that your presence is wanted at least three times a day. Here it's translated as "beloved and treated with great courtesy." |

# THE MARQUIS OF KANG

The marquis of Kang (衛康叔, *wèi Kāng shū*) is King Wu of Zhou's brother (and the ninth son of King Wen), who ruled one of the fiefs in the state of Wei. The territory of Wei was referenced in the third line of Hexagram 26, which described a majestic horse giving chase. Wei was ruled by the marquis's other brother, Gao, duke of Bi, also referenced in Hexagram 26.

| *First Line*<br>There is progress, though there is havoc. Pushing from behind, causing tension in the front.<br>You will still find your fortune. Favors granted.<br>To enrich and be plentiful, slow and steady.<br>There is no blame. | 裕 罔 貞 晉 初<br>無 孚 吉 如 六<br>咎　　 摧 ：<br>　　　 如 | ▬▬▬▬▬<br>▬▬ ▬▬<br>▬▬▬▬▬<br>▬▬▬▬▬<br>▬▬ ▬▬<br>▬▬ ▬▬ |

Pushing to break free from an ensnarement. Struggling causes more chaos, and chaos brings uncertainty. Take the longer route, slow and steady. That's how you'll arrive at your destination.

At the start of an undertaking for progress, there are obstacles, and now you encounter such hardships. There is devastation and damage caused, confusion and disorder.

Stay true to your path and you will be met with favor.

If you have not yet won the trust of others, be generous and kind. You will win them over.

| *Second Line*<br>There is progress, though there is sorrow; you will still find your fortune.<br>Receive now a great blessing.<br>All hail the Queen Mother. | 于 受 貞 晉 六<br>其 茲 吉 如 二<br>王 介　 愁 ：<br>母 福　 如 | ▬▬ ▬▬<br>▬▬ ▬▬<br>▬▬▬▬▬<br>▬▬▬▬▬<br>▬▬ ▬▬<br>▬▬▬▬▬ |

At the start of an undertaking for progress, there are obstacles, and now you encounter such hardships. There is loss, distress, disappointment, and affliction; grief and sadness.

# THE QUEEN MOTHER GODDESS

In the *Erya* 爾雅 *(Ěr yǎ)*, a Chinese encyclopedia and dictionary dated to the third century BC, "王母" (Wáng Mǔ) was defined as the deceased mother of the father.[30] Thus, in the context of the second line, this would be interpreted as a reference to your ancestors.

Under such a reading, the second line bestows blessings from one's ancestors, and perhaps more specifically, the paternal lineage.

"王母" (Wáng Mǔ) could also be a reference to a Queen Mother goddess whose name was found on Shang dynasty oracle bones.[31] The Queen Mother goddess's name would be invoked for divinations, prayers, and magical petitions. I connect this Queen Mother with the Queen Mother of the West (西王母, Xī Wáng Mǔ). Incidentally, Queen Mother was also venerated as a guardian goddess of ancestors.

Looking at the ideograms, "于" *(tú)* calls to mind the image of an altar, and "其" *(qí)* is a basket set upon a table, such as a basket of sacrificial offerings. A loose translation, more for the spirit of the meaning than to be literal, was "all hail," to represent veneration.

Kerson Huang translates this latter part of the second line as "Largess from the Queen Mother,"[32] affirming that from this divination at hand, the Queen Mother will generously bestow gifts upon you.

In the ideograms, we also see the image of armor, symbolic of protection. Thus, one of the great blessings bestows patronage from the Queen Mother, in the form of material prosperity, and security, in the form of safekeeping.

Stay true to your path, and you will be met with favor from the Queen Mother.

The second line is also a reference to your paternal grandmother coming through and blessing you.

Whereas the first line of Hexagram 35 gives counsel on what to do to help your own situation, here in the second line there is divine intervention.

| | | |
|---|---|---|
| *Third Line*<br>Everything, everyone is as it all should be.<br>Disappointments vanish. | 悔 眾 六<br>亡 允 三<br>　　　： | ▅▅▅ ▅▅▅<br>▅▅▅ ▅▅▅<br>▅▅▅▅▅▅▅<br>▅▅▅ ▅▅▅<br>▅▅▅ ▅▅▅<br>▅▅▅ ▅▅▅ |

All is well. The matter unfolds as it was intended. Expectations are met. Wishes fulfilled. Stay hopeful, and stay true to yourself.

| | | |
|---|---|---|
| *Fourth Line*<br>There is progress though there is a marmot, a Rat.<br>Prognostication of difficulties to come. | 貞 晉 九<br>厲 如 四<br>　 鼫 ：<br>　 鼠 | ▅▅▅ ▅▅▅<br>▅▅▅▅▅▅▅<br>▅▅▅ ▅▅▅<br>▅▅▅ ▅▅▅<br>▅▅▅ ▅▅▅<br>▅▅▅ ▅▅▅ |

At the start of an undertaking for progress, the omen of a rat appears. "鼫 Shí" can be a marmot or squirrel. "鼠 Shǔ" is the zodiac animal of the Rat. The marmot symbolizes timidity, hesitation, fears, inhibitions, and not taking action when action should be taken.

Likewise, you have the capability to advance, but timidity and inhibitions hold you back.

Rats are associated with hard work and attaining riches due to their industrious nature and their ability to acquire and hoard food. Rats are thought to be highly intelligent.

Since rats were known as carriers of parasites, which throughout the history of northern China had caused much devastation, both the marmot and the rat are associated with plagues and disease.

Thus, the Rat here represents industry, intelligence, and prosperity as driving the progress achieved up to this point, but it is also by the Rat's nature that a parasite has set in—one taking advantage of you, exploiting what you have for its own gain—and that is the cause of the difficulties forthcoming. Be wary of others' intentions toward you.

| | | |
|---|---|---|
| *Fifth Line*<br>Disappointments vanish.<br>Gains, losses—no misgivings, no sympathy.<br>Auspicious. Favorable, with potential for gains. | 往失悔六<br>吉得亡五<br>無勿：<br>不恤<br>利 | |

Opportunities will be presented if you go forth on your endeavor. The fifth line bears a connotation of financial gains and losses.

Progress toward advancement is in a steady cycle of up and down, gains and losses, though in the long run, the end result is promising.

Do not focus on the short-term yield. It may be a loss today but a gain tomorrow, or a gain today then a loss tomorrow. Consider the bigger picture at hand.

To advance, free yourself of anxieties about the future. Take the matter one step at a time, and all will be well. Progress will be made, one step at a time.

| | | |
|---|---|---|
| *Sixth Line*<br>There is progress in an advance with horns lowered.<br>Proceed with conquest of the city. A perilous undertaking, yet prospects are good.<br>There is no blame. | 貞厲維晉上<br>吝吉用其九<br>無伐角：<br>咎邑 | |

The image of the sixth line is either that of a ram with horns lowered, marching forward, or that of soldiers, advancing with spears pointed.

Rebels are causing unrest in the city. To restore peace to the kingdom, the king must go on the offensive and quash the rebellion before it spreads.

When faced with opposition, advance and use force. Go on the offensive if you have to, but be aware of the risks.

Be careful with how much force you apply. If you use excessive force, there could be a humiliating and shameful outcome. You could lose the support of the people.

Proceed in a manner that maintains the support of the people. Use just enough force to stabilize the situation. Do not implement martial law at this time.

In the matter divined upon, advance with measured yet deliberate use of force. You will nevertheless encounter backlash and challenges, but the end result will be a better position than the position you are in now.

# Hexagram 36: Míng Yí. Darkening of the Light

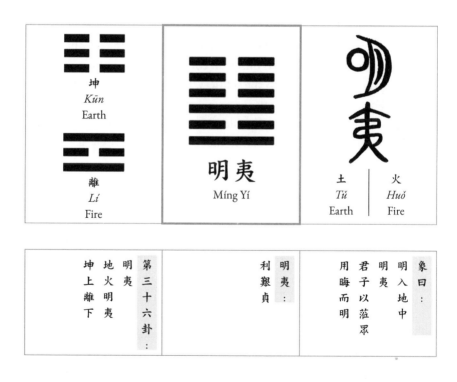

## The Oracle

It is a time of transitions, a changing of the guard. One will come to an end while another is ascending. Use the darkness to your advantage. Wait until the darkness has set in completely before you start the uprising. Use darkness to veil your light. Begin the resistance of light under the veil of darkness. Do not compel the change. Let the time of transition take place in due course. Do not draw attention to your light, but do not let that inner light go out. A push for change is in the air, but the time for change has not yet come. For the one in hardship, take heart. Divine forces are in play. Soon your light will shine in the open day.

- **Tending toward darkness. Dusk: the transitional period as night descends upon day. A darkening of the light. The sun has gone below, down to the center of the earth.**
- **The bright is wounded by darker forces; brightness being tarnished.**
- **The sage serves the many, with unselfish concern for the multitude and the myriad things. Tend to the soldiers, the farmers, the tradesmen, the scholars, and the officials.**
- Use the dark to veil your light, and under that veil, secretly begin to sway the soldiers, the farmers, the tradesmen, the scholars, and the officials to support your position.
- Build a resistance of light against the dark. This is the light of Fire concealed in stealth beneath the darkness of Earth. Use the cloak of night and the adversary's chaos to manifest your vision.
- **One is coming to an end. Another is ascending. A time of transitions.**
- **There are both advantages to be gained and great hardships to surmount.**
- Do not cause the change to take place too quickly. Do not force a change. Do not compel a transition. The sage must seek out strength in numbers and accumulate support.
- The transition time, the darkening of the light, will bring adversity—adversity is inevitable in such circumstances. When faced with adversity, you have no choice but to persevere.
- Maintain your inner light and keep it guarded. If you must, conceal it in the darkness until it is safe again. Do not draw attention to your light, but do

not let that inner light extinguish. A push for change is in the air, but the time for change has not yet come.

**An auspicious omen for one who is currently experiencing great hardships.**

## THE MANY MEANINGS OF LIGHT

明 *(míng)* is the pictograph of the rising sun and the setting moon, the image of dawn. In short, the word means light, brilliance, and brightness. There is a clarity and transparent nature to this light.

*Míng* also means vision or sight, to see with acuity and clarity. It's a figurative reference to intellect, sense, and wisdom. *Míng* means to understand, to know, and to be self-evident.

The Darkening of the Light can portend entering into a dark night of the soul. It's about undeserved challenges, but how you confront injustice will determine how bright your light shines when the sun finally rises.

Every time you see the word "light," or "darkening of the light," consider the many facets of what *light* means in the context of Hexagram 36.

## GRAND DUKE JIANG AND THE FALL OF THE SHANG

Hexagram 36 is a didactic narrative of a tyrant who is consumed by darkness and evil, a tyrant suppressing his people. In a sense, virtue goes underground, and any who are virtuous must conceal that virtue to stay alive.

Grand Duke Jiang (twelfth–eleventh centuries BC) was the military strategist who advised King Wen and his son, King Wu, on how to defeat the corrupt and tyrannical king of Shang. According to legend, King Wen prayed to Heaven to receive counsel on how he could defeat the corrupt tyrant of Shang. He then fasted, forbearing from eating meats to spiritually purify himself. In three days, King Wen chanced upon an old fisherman. Wen then appointed the old fisherman his prime minister. That prime minister, Grand Duke Jiang, would then go on to lead Wen's son to victory.

Before the Battle of Muye, Grand Duke Jiang advised the son, King Wu, to delay his revolt and allow the darkness of the Shang to descend further into chaos before attacking. The delay resulted in large numbers of the Shang army defecting, turning on the tyrannical king, and supporting King Wu of Zhou's campaign. The large numbers of defectors crippled Shang morale, leading to the Zhou's victory.

The *Six Secret Teachings* (六韜, *Liù tāo*) memorializes the military strategies credited to Grand Duke Jiang.

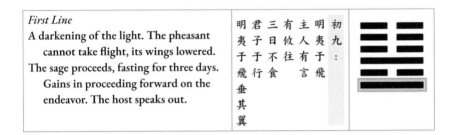

*First Line*
A darkening of the light. The pheasant cannot take flight, its wings lowered. The sage proceeds, fasting for three days. Gains in proceeding forward on the endeavor. The host speaks out.

A pheasant's wings are injured. The golden pheasant, associated with Fire, is a symbol of beauty, power, refinement, and authority, mythologized as the ancestor of the phoenix.

One's ordinary abilities have been wounded.

Those close to you, those who have hosted you, criticize or speak ill of you. Let them. So long as you understand yourself and you emanate from within with the divine light, do not be concerned with gossip or misunderstandings. Unenlightened people will talk.

Perhaps a fast, be that figuratively or a religious fasting for three days, will clear your mind and heart, and then you'll see the situation clearer.

Mind and heart cleared, proceed with the endeavor.

## **CONFUCIUS ADVISES THE PUPIL TO FAST**

The third-century Taoist text *Zhuangzi* recounts a conversation between Confucius and a brilliant pupil.[33]

The pupil conveyed his plans to the master teacher of traveling to the kingdom of Wei to teach his knowledge and wisdom. Confucius admonished the pupil, noting who would want to hear an outsider telling them how to live their lives. The pupil asked for advice. Confucius advised the pupil to fast.

> By fasting, you will learn how to hear not with your ears, but with the mind, and then not with the mind, but with your soul. After a spiritual fast, the pupil would know how to proceed and would not need to seek the master teacher for advice.
>
> Fasting, per Taoist tradition, represents discipline and modesty and is also a spiritual practice. *Bigu* (辟谷), a form of fasting where Taoist practitioners avoid grains, surviving on minimal raw foods and medicinal herbs, was believed to be a form of spiritual cultivation and rebalancing of the body's *qi*.

| | |
|---|---|
| *Second Line*<br>A darkening of the light. One from the eastern tribes has injured the left leg.<br>Rescued by a strong horse. Auspicious. | 六二：明夷于左股用拯馬壯吉 |

One has been injured in such a way as to be rendered immobilized. The injury prevents full capacity for forward movement.

The left side of the body corresponds with the right hemisphere of the brain, where intuition and emotional expression reside. The right side of the brain governs understanding, ascension, and transcendent experiences. Thus, your intuition and emotional expression are momentarily incapacitated due to an offensive attack by another, and such a wound is inhibiting the advance in your endeavor.

Here, the references to the left and to the east are also symbolic of the unorthodox path, left-wing politics, and metaphysical correspondences to the left or east.

"夷" *(Yi)* was the name of a tribe to the east of the Shang dynasty. Thus, Yi also came to describe foreigners or those outside one's clan. Therefore, the reference here is to an outsider. This further underscores the notion of one who is unorthodox or out of the ordinary. There could be references to ethnic minorities or the marginalized.

In a fortune-telling reading of the line, you'd note that it is unfavorable in near-future events to be positioned on the left.

A horse's strength represents great power, endurance, and perseverance. Do not let an injury to your emotions immobilize you. You may also be feeling that your intuitions are compromised. Persevere like a horse and you will get through.

Transcend your wound and become the wounded healer.

| *Third Line* A darkening of the light—an imperial expedition in the south. Capturing their chieftain. Proceeding when there is disease and malady is ill-advised. | 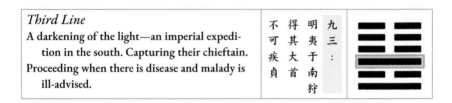 |
|---|---|

Be mindful of your own health and well-being at this time. If you are not in full operational order, do not proceed with the endeavor you're contemplating. Focus on self-recovery and healing first.

Pursuing your ambition will be productive, but long-term costs are great if you proceed right now when you are not yet at your best. Being patient and waiting to strike at another time, when you are finally at your best, will yield the same success, but without the long-term cost.

Do not be hasty.

"大首 dà shǒu" literally means "big head," though it generally refers to a chieftain, the one who leads. "大首" can also be a reference to an *okubi* per Japanese folklore, which means the sighting of a sky spirit in the form of a giant head, male or female. *Okubi* are interpreted as omens of a natural disaster to come.

The trigram Fire corresponds with the south direction. Here the third line is at the tip of the Fire right below the Earth trigram. The "imperial expedition" also implies that it's a hunt. The objective of the hunt in the south is to preserve the light of the Fire and capture the last rays of the sun before it sets.

Likewise, your objective now is to reclaim the light, and you know that to do so may require confrontation, conflict, even deception.

The third line of Hexagram 36 references a ruse that was conceived to lure the imperial court of the Shang dynasty south. The Shang king was deceived into believing that the expedition south was a hunting trip. There, at the Battle of Muye, the Shang were ambushed and defeated by the son of King Wen, thus clearing a path for the Zhou ascent to power.

Here, dusk symbolizes a transitioning period, or the transition from the Shang rule to the Zhou, a time of upheavals and transformation. That is where you are now.

| | |
|---|---|
| **Fourth Line**<br>Pierce through the left side of the belly.<br>Reach the heart of obscured understanding.<br>Exit the front courtyard gates. | 六四：入于左腹獲明夷之心于出門庭 |

The left side of the body corresponds with the right hemisphere of the brain, where intuition and emotional expression reside. Piercing through the left side of the belly suggests striking at the core of the problem at hand.

The sense here is of unveiling the darkness and exposing secrets, revealing what was hidden.

The left side is a reference to that which is unorthodox, unconventional, and unpredictable. Utilize such methods to achieve your objective.

The belly represents getting inside and to what is most vulnerable within your target. Reaching the heart of obscured understanding means to attain full and clear understanding of the matter at hand.

To exit the front courtyard gates suggests having all the information you need now to advance on your endeavor and execute it.

For the mystic, the fourth line can also be interpreted as coded instructions for how to proceed with a magical working being contemplated. It reads like step-by-step directions for where to go during an astral or shamanic journey.

When the fourth line comes up in a divinatory reading, it's because you are presently in quite a predicament. This line is the Oracle's instructions on how to get yourself out of that predicament.

| | |
|---|---|
| **Fifth Line**<br>Jizi conceals light within the dark.<br>An auspicious omen for future prosperity. | 六五：箕子之明夷利貞 |

# THE LEGEND OF JIZI (GIJA)

Hexagram 36 tells the story of Jizi (Gija in Korean), the virtuous and wise brother of the corrupt last king of Shang.[34] In some accounts, he's described as the uncle to the king. The last king of Shang falls under the evil spell of Daji, a fox spirit taking the form of a concubine. The king pulls his kingdom into poverty and turmoil as the concubine Daji exhausts the kingdom's wealth for her extravagances.

At first Gija tries to neutralize Daji's evil influence by endeavoring to teach virtue to the king. Soon Daji puts a target on Gija's back. Daji tries to convince the king to issue an order for Gija's death. To avoid the death sentence, and to avoid having to indulge the Shang court's corrupt ways, Gija feigns insanity. In lieu of a death sentence, he is imprisoned.

After King Wu of Zhou defeats the corrupt king and takes over the Shang capital, King Wu hears of the wise man Gija's many virtues. He immediately frees Gija and seeks his counsel on how to unite the territories and win over the Shang people. Gija gives his advice freely. Though King Wu offers Gija a fiefdom and an esteemed position in his court, Gija refuses, not wanting to ingratiate himself to any more kings.

Gija decides to leave his homeland and migrate eastward with a procession of five thousand followers. According to legend, he arrives at the Korean peninsula and is the mythical founder of the Gija Joseon kingdom (1120–194 BC).[35]

Gija's descendants then become the Chosŏn rulers for forty generations. Several Korean royal clans claim descent from Gija.[36] In other texts, Gija is deified and venerated by the people of Goguryeo (37 BC–AD 668), historical Korea.

However, these Chinese historical accounts of Jizi/Gija are controversial and have been challenged as apocryphal. Traditional Korean scholars tend to accept the accounts of Gija as a part of their national and cultural history, whereas modern Korean scholars are skeptical.[37] More likely, Jizi/Gija established a small kingdom in what is now Liaoning, China, adjacent to modern-day North Korea.[38]

You want to openly and vocally state your stance. You want to object. At this time, feign conformity. It is safer. A time will come for you to rise and stand up, and when you do, you will be a formidable force to contend with. Right now you are weak.

It is wiser to conceal your light within the dark, quietly rally the support you need, and speak out when your words will have the most impact. Timing matters. And right now, the timing isn't right.

Jizi, one of the wisest ministers in the court of Shang, witnesses the corruption and debauchery of the last king of Shang. As the Shang dynasty descends into darkness, the good and wise Jizi endeavors to be the light that overcomes the darkness, but to no avail. Threatened by the Shang king if he does not comply, Jizi feigns insanity rather than give in to the corruption and debauchery of the Shang. By feigning insanity, he conceals his light within the dark. Jizi goes on to be the mythical founder of a prosperous kingdom in the east.

Like Jizi, you find yourself in a perilous situation where the mainstream majority around you and the leadership are headed down a dark path. They have been led astray by malevolent forces.

If you openly refuse to comply, you will face serious repercussions and threats. If you comply, your principles will be compromised.

Like Jizi, find a clever way to not participate that will not offend those in power and also will not compel you into compliance.

The long-term result of the matter you've inquired about is great prosperity.

*Sixth Line*
**No light within the darkness.**
**First ascent to Heaven.**
**Then diffuse across the Earth.**

上六：
不明晦
初登于天
後入于地

The darkness referenced in the sixth line is a metaphor for what is in obscurity, in the unknown. It is also a reference to the dark moon—the last day of the lunar month before the new moon.

Like the sky on the eve of the dark moon, there is no visible light, and yet light is promised once the next lunar phase begins.

Thus, the omen is one of new beginnings, the end of a darkening reign and the start of a new cycle.

This is the observance of a setting sun and the promise of rising light tomorrow.

Here, the Oracle does not provide any prognostication of good fortune or bad; rather, the sentiment of the line is of neutral observation.

However, with regard to inquiries about academic achievement or an examination, since 登 *(dēng)* in antiquity signified success on the imperial civil service examination, the presence of that word here is an omen of scholarly success.

## Hexagram 37: Jiā Rén. The Family

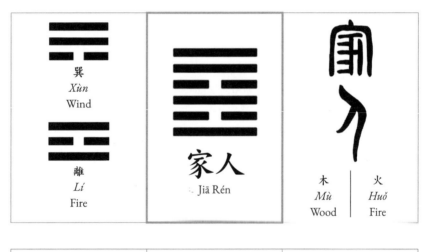

## The Oracle

Do not resist dependence on others, but be so independent that others depend on you. When there is interdependence, then there will be great success. Nurture your familial bonds. First, loyalty to the clan. Leave no housekeeping unattended. With them, you are strengthened and supported. With you, they are anchored and united.

Wind from within; fire emanates outward: synergy for movement forward.
**This is the clan, the family: interdependence.**
**The sage's words hold enduring power.**
**Prosperity pivots upon the woman.**
Traditionalists interpret Hexagram 37 as a particularly auspicious divinatory result for women. Thus, in readings for a man, the Oracle counsels the man to follow the woman in the matter at hand. Her direction is auspicious and bodes well for your own endeavors. Confucianists interpret the hexagram as moral instruction on a woman's place and influence in the family—women hold the clan together.

There is an analogy and connection made between the role of women in the clan and words in society. Both are powerful, influential forces in the shaping of a civilization's humaneness.

At the heart of Hexagram 37 is the political philosophy that the strength and power of a nation pivots upon the social and economic status of its society's women.

| *First Line* <br> **The dwelling is occupied by the family.** <br> **Disappointments vanish.** | 悔 閑 初<br>亡 有 九<br>　 家 ： |
|---|---|

Focus on the domestic front and your familial relations. Focus on housekeeping. That way unforeseen disasters can be averted.

Maintain discipline. Establish a strict code of conduct. Make sure all is organized on the home front. Make sure the logistics and administrative aspects of the matter are in order.

With implications of rules, order, discipline, and restrictions in "閑 xián" in order to maintain stability, and the need for railings or fences, the first line is interpreted as the need to regulate the matter at hand.

The first line corresponds with the familial relationship between a parent and a young child. The parent must instill discipline and restraint in a young child. The parent is also responsible for the education and development of that child.

Likewise, the theme of a relationship between a parent and a young child applies to the matter at hand. Think of the situation within that framework, and you will arrive at your answer.

| Second Line<br>Undeveloped. No fulfillment of functions.<br>Stay within the center to reap blessings.<br>An auspicious omen. | 貞 在 無 六<br>吉 中 攸 二<br>　 饋 遂 ： | 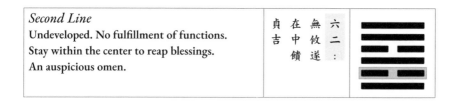 |
|---|---|---|

An auspicious omen—you get your wish granted. What you strive to make happen shall happen.

The narrative image is of one spouse burdened by defeats and misadventures out in the world, and returning home to a delicious meal cooked by the other, and the penultimate blessing of prosperity such a simple act represents.

The second line is often interpreted as gratitude for the blessings of food and abundance within the home. "Stay within the center" can mean to look for prosperity and blessings within the home rather than in career or social ambitions.

Another reading of "stay within the center" is as words of comfort from the Oracle to stay grounded, despite the challenges and hardships you've been facing.

The second line is a reminder to reflect on what blessings you do have in your life, and that you are, in fact, luckier than most, even if you did not achieve what you had set out to achieve.

Keep emotional impulses under control. Duties that ensure the welfare of the family must be attended to. Likewise, in affairs of state, the success of the nation rests on how well civil servants carry out their duties. Focus on duty, not on emotion. Stay neutral. Keep what is personal within, and keep what is social beyond yourself.

Sacrifices will be in order for the greater good of the clan. Think objectively and rationally for the sake of that greater good.

| *Third Line* | 九 |
| --- | --- |
| **The family arguing, arguing.** After remorse and adversity, the final outcome is fruition and prosperity. Wife and children laughing, laughing. There is no blame. | 家人嗃嗃 悔厲 婦子嘻嘻 終吝 |

The family argues and tempers rise because the rules implemented are too strict. Members of the clan neglect the rules altogether and overindulge. The correct path here is moderation.

The first line references a parent-and-child interaction; the second line one between spouses; and here in the third, we have a narrative image of the family, from the head of the household's vantage point.

The clan is at first in disagreement as to how best to resolve the matter at hand. Tensions rise, and heated words are exchanged. However, the tension leads to creative resolution, and conflict is at times necessary. The end result is success in the undertaking. No hard feelings after the conflict. Family will always be family.

Traditional interpretations of the third line view it as indicative of a household in disorder, and calling upon the head of the household to restore it to order.

| *Fourth Line* | 六四 |
| --- | --- |
| **Prosperous family.** Great fortune to come. | 富家 大吉 |

All who are interdependent rise together and flourish. An auspicious omen for your inquiry.

"Family" here is interchangeable with "clan." In the fourth line, the family prospers, and the clan prospers.

Historical commentaries on the fourth line commonly emphasize the yin nature of the fourth line—it is the woman who brings balance and who is the key to prosperity. The woman balances the family's accounts. Thus, a family's prosperity is credited to her prudence. Such feminine energy is representative of your emotional plane. A balanced and controlled emotional plane will be the driving force toward your success.

| Fifth Line | | |
|---|---|---|
| The principal king visits the home. Fear not the uncertainty, for there will be blessings of prosperity. | 勿恤吉 王假有家 九五： | |

Affluence comes despite the uncertainties inherent in the situation.

The principal king isn't necessarily the heir apparent to the throne, but the one who currently holds the power and status of an acting king. The reference to a principal king implies someone who holds authority, but who doesn't hold the same clan name.

The familial relationship narrated in the fifth line is that between king and subjects, but there's a twist here—the principal king is, in some respects, an outsider. Yet the prognostication is one of harmony and good tidings.

Govern the clan with love, not with fear. The king must be like a loving father. Virtuous and proper influence must be affectionate, not tyrannical.

| Sixth Line | | |
|---|---|---|
| There is trust and sincerity, discipline and order. Gains in power and prestige. A fortuitous outcome. | 終吉 威如 有孚 上九： | |

Positioned for success. All members in an interdependent family or clan have honored their duties. The team is disciplined, orderly, and there are bonds of trust between them.

You demonstrate virtue, so all around you mirror the example you set and demonstrate virtue as well.

## Hexagram 38: Kuí. Opposition

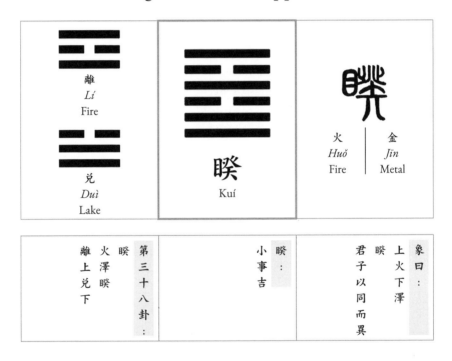

### The Oracle

Sharply opposing factions. One pushes for progressive movement and one holds back. Opposition and estrangement. Two seek the same objective, but they go in separate directions and grow apart. You feel misunderstood. Beset by alienation, hostility, and lacking affinity. And yet your individuality is critical to the matter at hand. The estrangement is necessary. Do not chase after what will return on its own. You will be making the journey in the rain. You face inclement weather throughout your endeavor.

**A flame set upon a lagoon—the two repel. A polarizing effect. The sage is not like the others. Auspicious for small matters.**

While the greater endeavor at hand is being met with opposition, take the time to settle minor tangential issues. Promising opportunities in the small.

**Two sisters live in the same dwelling, but there is estrangement between them. A wall that divides.** Where two should be in harmony, there is mutual alienation.

In statecraft, Hexagram 38 is interpreted as prognosticating the brink of civil war or threats of secession.

Minor victories, and perhaps at this time, better to focus on the minor victories anyway. Look for opportunities to gain small ground. Who will win or lose the war is still a very distant matter.

Reach for what is within your grasp. Direct your attention to what you can control.

Hexagram 38 can also be the sign of an iconoclast, one who is a perpetual skeptic.

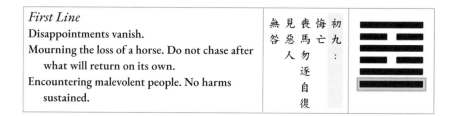

*First Line*
Disappointments vanish.
Mourning the loss of a horse. Do not chase after what will return on its own.
Encountering malevolent people. No harms sustained.

Estrangement between kin. However, do not chase down others or force unity. That will come in time. What was lost will return on its own.

Emotions are out of control at this time. There is a general loss of control all around.

Be careful. Many of prominence right now harbor malicious intentions. Tread with care and no harms will be sustained.

The horse symbolizes freedom, power, and thriving arts and culture. Forces of opposition and strife have brought about the loss of freedom, power, and what had been a thriving state of art and culture. Nevertheless, the prognostication here is that these will all return in due time. Do not force change.

The horse corresponds with the trigram Fire, so here in the first line, there is the forecast of Fire to come, represented by the yang line of the horse.

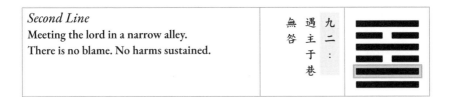

*Second Line*
Meeting the lord in a narrow alley.
There is no blame. No harms sustained.

九二：
遇主于巷
無咎

Misunderstandings in the group at large cause estrangement and opposition. At this time, consider more stealthy and covert ways to exert your influence. Formal meetings will not advance the situation. Informal and private back-alley meetings achieve the results. No one will blame you for doing so.
These informal, private meetings are needed if you are to move forward on your endeavor.

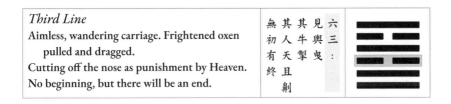

*Third Line*
Aimless, wandering carriage. Frightened oxen pulled and dragged.
Cutting off the nose as punishment by Heaven.
No beginning, but there will be an end.

六三：
見輿曳
其牛掣
其人天且劓
無初有終

Social disorder and mayhem. The one who causes the mayhem will be punished by Heaven.
No one will know how the mayhem began, its origins a matter of much speculation, but rest assured there will be an end.
You don't feel in control of the situation.
"曳 yè" suggests a listless and aimless movement, dragging or not moving in a controlled manner. Furthermore, it's pulling with it whatever has the misfortune of being attached to it. The indication here is that no one is driving the carriage and yet it is in movement. Thus, it signifies mayhem.
"劓 yì" is one of the Five Punishments from the imperial criminal code, which was to amputate the nose without anesthetics. The punishment of cutting the nose off dates back to Shang dynasty oracle bone inscriptions. Treason, causing social disorder, conspiracy, mayhem, or inciting revolt were crimes

punishable by nose amputation. In Chinese physiognomy, or face reading, the nose represents someone's social status, self-esteem, rank, and wealth. To cut off the nose was akin to a lifelong curse.

In this context, cutting off the nose is figurative, signifying that Heaven will take care of the capital punishment that the perpetrator deserves.

One need not dwell on cause, origins, or fault.

| Fourth Line<br>Isolated and lonely.<br>Fated meeting with a kindred spirit. It is a trusting friendship.<br>Despite a severe situation, no harm comes. | 厲 交 遇 睽 九<br>無 孚 元 孤 四<br>咎 　 夫 　 ： | 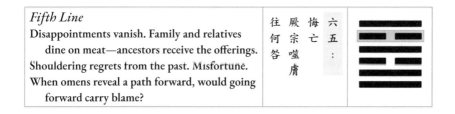 |

In the hour when you face your greatest adversity, you find a true friend. As a result, no permanent injury from the adversity is sustained.

When the fourth line comes up in a divinatory reading, you are in a state of feeling isolated or helpless. Your perspective is the minority, and you feel the opposition of the majority view.

The solution is to find one of like mind. There will be mutual benefit from the concord. Go in search of that kindred spirit.

| Fifth Line<br>Disappointments vanish. Family and relatives dine on meat—ancestors receive the offerings.<br>Shouldering regrets from the past. Misfortune.<br>When omens reveal a path forward, would going forward carry blame? | 往 厥 悔 六<br>何 宗 亡 五<br>咎 噬 　 ：<br>　 膚 | |

A very auspicious line: celebration. Bygones are bygones, and past hardships are now in the past. Ancestors assist in overcoming the opposition. Celebration and good tidings.

You have the support you need to go forward on your endeavor. A positive omen for your inquiry. There will be cause for celebration at the end. Who could blame you for moving forward, in spite of feeling the estrangement from opposition?

| | | |
|---|---|---|
| *Sixth Line*<br>Isolated and lonely.<br>Seeing the pig smeared with mud.<br>Transporting the ghosts in a chariot.<br>First draw your bow,<br>then lay aside your bow.<br>They are not bandits;<br>only here to take a bride.<br>The forward journey is met with rainfall.<br>Fortune and prosperity come after all. | 往匪先見睽<br>遇寇張孤九<br>雨婚之負：<br>則媾弧塗<br>吉　後載<br>　　說鬼<br>　　之一<br>　　弧車 | ▬▬▬▬▬<br>▬▬　▬▬<br>▬▬▬▬▬<br>▬▬▬▬▬<br>▬▬　▬▬<br>▬▬▬▬▬ |

What you feared to be a threat is just a proposal.

The sentiment of being isolated and lonely expresses one whose point of view and identity diverge from the mainstream. There's also a subtext of judgment—you are virtuous, and they are the ones who are dysfunctional. The Oracle is on your side.

The observer is seeing a corrupted or polluted environment, hence the idiom "seeing the pig smeared with mud." The observer further comments on how absurd, irrational, and dystopian the scene is—it's as strange and aberrant as "transporting ghosts in a chariot." The two thoughts taken together imply oppression, disease, misery, or squalid conditions.

The reference to marriage by bride abduction is a metaphor for an opportunity arriving in disguise. What was perceived initially as a threat (hence, drawing the bow) turns out to be a fortuitous alliance (hence, laying down the bow). The advice here is to ask questions and discern the situation reasonably before acting in haste.

Here in the sixth line, the rain brings a form of purification, washing away past transgressions, thus allowing the forward journey to be washed of the contamination that scourged the previous corrupted, polluted environment.

Yet the rainfall is also symbolic of challenges to come. It is expressive of the emotions at play, those of grieving, sorrow, and tears shed for what was lost. Moreover, making the journey through inclement weather is dangerous. It's going to be a hard road to walk, but it's the necessary road for achieving your goal.

In the end, an auspicious omen. Your actions will help many to flourish.

# TRADITIONS OF MARRIAGE BY ABDUCTION

"They are not bandits; only here to take a bride" refers to the tradition of marriage by abduction. A would-be groom whose beloved cannot afford a dowry comes to abduct and marry her, so that her family can be saved from having to pay a dowry.[39]

Among the poorest peasant classes in ancient China, marriage by bride abduction was a practical solution for avoiding the obligatory dowry that a groom's family would otherwise have to pay to the bride's family for the marriage. For most of imperial China's history, marriage by bride abduction was outlawed and vehemently condemned by the upper classes, but it was an accepted practice among the rural poor.[40]

Typically, a bride's family would have to pay a dowry to the groom's family for marrying their daughter. One way around this was for the groom to abduct the bride, which would help the bride's family "save face" from having not paid a dowry.

Marriage by abduction as an institution for socially acceptable marriages when families are too poor to pay dowries should be distinguished from instances of criminal kidnappings of girls. In the case of marriage abduction, it's a way for two lovers born into poor conditions to be together anyway.

That the line notes laying aside your bow once you realize who has entered the home indicates that there is no real threat here, no true opposition, and the one who has entered is friendly.

The final line of Hexagram 38 expresses a temporary misunderstanding that at first blush appeared to be an opposition; but once the matter was clarified, the opposition is immediately resolved and is in fact found to be a relation conducted in good faith.

# Hexagram 39: Jiǎn. An Impasse

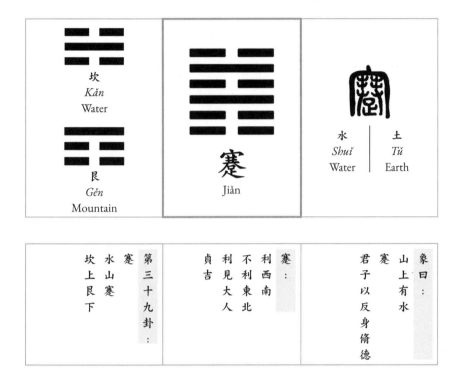

## The Oracle

Progress comes to a standstill. Every movement forward is blocked by an opposing force. Personal difficulties. When extenuating circumstances physically obstruct your path, yield to the standstill and take pause. Channel a power far beyond the reach of that obstruction, and grow it outward from within. This can only be achieved in stillness, beneficence, and calm. A favorable outcome when water carves its path through the depth of its obstruction.

Water seeks movement and momentum. The Mountain seeks to remain still. An impasse.

**The sage cultivates virtue through self-reflection.**
**The southwest is advantageous; the northeast is not.**
Good auspices to the queen, the mother, the farmer, the artisan, and the masses. Challenges faced by the politicians, the builders, the architects, and the scholars. Small towns and the countryside bring good fortune; hills, mountains, forests, and dark caverns bring misfortune.
**It serves your endeavor to seek out the eminent one. When wise counsel has been sought out, it will be auspicious to proceed with your endeavor.**
**Peril above; peril below. Adversity and troubles: take caution. Stay true to the Way of the Sages and the ending will be well.**
The theme of the southwest being advantageous and the northeast being ill-advised first appeared in the oracle message for Hexagram 2.

| | |
|---|---|
| *First Line*<br>Going forward, you encounter an impasse.<br>Returning, you gain prestige. | 往 初<br>蹇 六<br>來 ：<br>譽 |

The difficulties you face at the present time require you to wait it out. Do not be bullish and try to plow ahead.
Return to the point of origin and reevaluate your course of action.
After deliberate reevaluation, you will be back on the right track and will have a much greater chance of success.
Facing adversity, the first line is counsel to retreat. Put as much distance between you and the threat as possible. Do not confront, and do not attack.

| | |
|---|---|
| *Second Line*<br>The king's official encounters obstruction after obstruction, difficulty upon difficulty.<br>Personal interests are abandoned. | 匪 王 六<br>躬 臣 二<br>之 蹇 ：<br>故 蹇 |

You face great difficulties at the present time, but you must plow ahead and persevere.

The title of "king's official" or a minister who is a direct advisor to the king refers to one in a position of great importance, and one who cannot serve self-interest.

There is a greater good at stake, and your duty requires you to go forward, no matter how many obstructions you encounter or how difficult it gets. Despite facing an impasse, you must do everything within your power to eradicate that impasse. You have a responsibility to do so.

It is a time of personal sacrifices. Duty calls for your struggle. Meet your obstacles head-on.

Do what must be done.

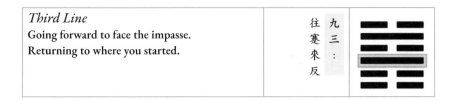

*Third Line*
**Going forward to face the impasse.**
**Returning to where you started.**

The third line is about answering a call of duty, facing danger and hardships so that the more vulnerable will not have to.

Here, "impasse" also means enduring suffering so others do not have to, putting yourself in the line of danger to protect another, or taking the hit of misfortune on behalf of the less fortunate.

One is about to embark on an odyssey that will lead you back to your point of origin, albeit changed.

If you move forward now, you will be thrust back to where you started. Fruitless labor. If you remain at a standstill, the adversity will pass you by. Then you'll be able to move forward, step by step.

*Fourth Line*
**Going forward, you encounter an impasse.**
**Returning, you enter an alliance.**

Seek out the alliance, someone in a figurative sedan carriage.

You cannot undertake your endeavor alone. You need support. Return to the point of origin and seek out partnerships, seek out counsel, seek out helpers and assistants. Once you have forged supportive alliances, go forward on your endeavor with trustworthy companions.

The journey you are on is not one you can succeed at single-handedly.

The ideogram for an alliance is that of a human-drawn sedan carriage. The image of a sedan carriage implies someone of wealth and social importance. Thus, the fourth line suggests an alliance with someone who has the means to support your endeavor.

Going forth on your undertaking alone will take you to an impasse. Seeking out someone of status who can advocate for your cause will bring the success you're looking for.

The term "alliance" in the context of the fourth line also indicates forging a connection with someone such that there will be mutual benefit. Seek unity. The term can also mean an affinity or relationship by marriage.

| *Fifth Line* <br> A major impasse. <br> Friends come. | 九五： 大蹇朋來 |
| --- | --- |

Hard times reveal who your true friends are. When you hit the worst point, kindred spirits and loved ones come to your aid. You are called to task, but friends are right there at your back, ready and willing to face the worst with you.

Great challenges ahead, and the outcome is uncertain at this time, but you persevere through those challenges with friends at your side.

The ideogram "朋" *(péng)* as it first appeared on Shang oracle bones was the image of two strings of five cowrie shells. It's the concept of a merger between two of equivalent means, yielding mutual gains.

The difference between the references in the fourth and fifth lines is that of sentiment. The fourth implies strictly business, whereas here in the fifth, your ally cares sincerely for your well-being.

The Han dynasty text *Shuowen jiezi* (說文解字, *Shuō wén jiě zì*) contended that "朋" as it appeared on oracle bones was the ancient form of "鳳," for an imperial phoenix sent to earth as a messenger from the gods.

If the *Shuowen* claim is to be believed, then the fifth line bears the omen of an imperial phoenix in the final line of the Water trigram. (In the Wu Xing, Water and Fire are in conflict.) Thus, the phoenix spirit sent by the gods is an omen that it's about to get a lot harder before it gets easier, but rest assured that your gods and ancestors will be with you every step of the way.

The omen of the phoenix and the message "friends come" is the Oracle assuring you that gods and ancestors are here to help, at your darkest moment of need.

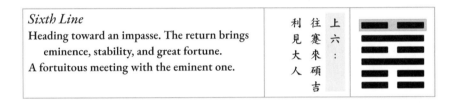

**Sixth Line**
Heading toward an impasse. The return brings eminence, stability, and great fortune.
A fortuitous meeting with the eminent one.

上六：
往蹇來碩
吉
利見大人

The preliminary Oracle section gave the advice of seeking out the eminent one. In the final prong of the narrative arc, the sixth line prognosticates a successful meeting with that eminent one.

The impasses of Hexagram 39 are in the conflicting flow of *qi* of the paired hexagrams. Mountain wants to be still and is solid; Water wants to flow and is fluid. In the rules of Wu Xing alchemy, Earth (corresponding with Mountain) weakens Water, and Water must yield to Earth.

In health and medical readings, the sixth line is interpreted as having to see a specialist (Water corresponding with healing and illness and Mountain with knowledge), with the final forecast of a full recovery.

# Hexagram 40: Jiě. Release of Tension

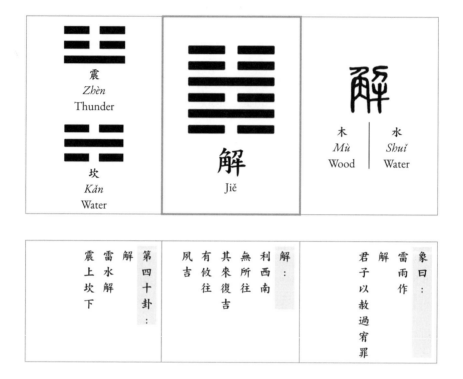

## The Oracle

When your endeavor has not been completed, do not procrastinate: bring it to completion. When your endeavor has been completed, a prompt return to stability will bring you good fortune. Do not bask in the afterglow of glory—go straight back to work. What you contemplate doing, proceed with. You will outsmart even the smart; you hunt rather than run. Sever ties with those who bring you sorrow. In your endeavor, you encounter naysayers. Cut yourself loose from their hold over you. The untying of a knot. The unraveling of a complication. Redemption is recovery.

**A thunderstorm. Release of tension.** Liberation.
**The sage will pardon their faults.** Themes prevailing: forgiveness, kindness, amnesty.
**Gains arising from the southwest.** The field is fertile. Sign of the bull.
**Without a destination, do not go.** Return to the point of origin.
**With a destination, go forth with swift motion and speed.** There is urgency.
**Early mornings are auspicious. Old ways are favorable.** What you are going through—one who came before you went through it too. They are the old ways, and they will guide you until you are set free.

The old oracle bone script for "夙" *(sù)* is that of a man holding or venerating the moon, hands lifted in prayer toward the crescent. Another interpretation of the script image is that of a person working judiciously under the light of the moon, suggesting tenacity, perseverance, and dedication to one's work.

More commonly, Oracle messages offer a little more insight before they state a judgment of no blame, blameless, no faults, or no errors. Here, this recurring phrase throughout the Zhouyi—無咎 *(wú jiù)*—is the whole of the first line. What is not said is just as important as what is said.

*Wu jiu* means that no fault is being assigned. Errors are inconsequential. What you're experiencing now isn't the consequence of mistakes made in the past; it just is what it is. One sense of the term is denoting an act of God and therefore assuring you that you are absolved of any culpability for what has transpired.

In revelations of *wu jiu*, the Oracle is also reassuring you not to condemn yourself and not to be the cause of any unnecessary further suffering or unhappiness. Do not punish yourself. You are blameless.

That no other context is offered as the Oracle gets straight to the point is
poignant. You've been blaming yourself. You think what happened was
within your control, and some misstep of yours caused it all to go in the
direction that it did. All untrue. There is no blame to go around in the
mortal world. What happened was an act of God.

| | |
|---|---|
| *Second Line*<br>Catching three foxes in the field.<br>Attaining a yellow arrow.<br>Good fortunes and success forthcoming. | 九二：<br>田獲三狐<br>得黃矢<br>貞吉 |

Foxes represent the afterlife, magic and witchcraft, cunning, and sophistication, and they embody the trickster. They are both uncommonly benevolent and uncommonly evil. Offend them, and surely you will perceive them as demonic; respect them, and they are fiercely loyal allies. Under Confucianism, foxes serve an important role in ancestor veneration, as guardians and protectors of our departed.

"Attaining a yellow arrow" is a metaphor for walking the straight, center path of 義 (yì). The path of *yi* is righteousness, upholding justice, sincere concern for the public good, and putting public good above self-interest.

Moreover, hunting is a metaphor for military expeditions. Altogether, the second line prognosticates success in exerting and maintaining your political or social power. "Catching three foxes in the field" means to prevent malfeasance before it becomes a problem. The omen of the fox spirit also means that your ancestors are close by and watching—where there are many foxes, there is also much spirit activity.

Having "獲 huò" (fox) in one line and "得 dé" (earn, receive) in the next suggests that the foxes are received by you, perhaps implying that they allowed you to get close.

| | |
|---|---|
| *Third Line*<br>Burdened with carrying the sack, steering a<br>    wagon. Attracting thieves.<br>Remorse. A sense of loss. | 六三：<br>負且乘<br>致寇至<br>貞吝 |

To prevent a regrettable outcome, endeavor for corrective measures before proceeding. Adjust your perspective. Otherwise there will be remorse.

The narrative told by the third line is that of a porter. While most porters travel by foot, here is one who has become quite well-to-do and thus reaches just a little beyond his means to travel by wagon, as one of the wealthier merchants would do. Here is one displaying wealth in a manner that will attract envy and thievery.

Also, the line suggests one whose head is in the clouds and is shirking responsibility.

In the matter at hand, do not take shortcuts. Under no circumstances should you take the easy way out, or else you will lose all you have gained up to this point.

An adjustment of perspective is in order. Be more frugal and appear more modest.

"且 Qiě" here also carries a connotation of your male ancestors or a stone altar for offerings to your ancestors. Thus, the subtext reminds you to venerate your male ancestors. This evening, burn incense and place out choice dried meats as an offering for them. In the morning, burn another stick of incense as an offering, pray for a message from them, and then perform another I Ching divination. That subsequent divination will be a direct message from your ancestors.

| *Fourth Line* <br> Untangle your toe (from the hemlock). <br> Friends come—they are trustworthy. | 朋解九<br>至而四<br>斯拇：<br>孚 | 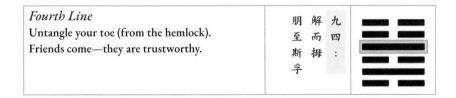 |
|---|---|---|

Sever ties from toxic associates. Then trustworthy friends will come. The implication of hemlock in the fourth line is to represent poisonous influences. Since the hemlock has not been ingested and is merely tangled with the toe, no harms sustained, but free yourself of the influence quickly before the risk becomes an actual threat.

The fourth line can suggest interpersonal challenges with colleagues.

| Fifth Line | | |
|---|---|---|
| The sage releases the tension. Auspicious omen. The sage wins the trust of the commoners. | 六五：君子維有解有孚于小人吉 | ䷧ |

Your endeavor serves many. Success and gains prognosticated for the matter at hand.

The fifth line narrates a story of a village in distress. The sage comes and solves the problem. The villagers are grateful and pledge their faith and loyalty in the sage. Winning the villagers' support will bring the sage a great advantage in a future matter.

An alternative perspective on the fifth line is to interpret "小人" as the unprincipled, the antihero, or your adversary. From this perspective, you are being called to help someone you dislike. Win the trust and loyalty of one you dislike. By doing so, you pave your own path to success and gains in the future.

| Sixth Line | | |
|---|---|---|
| The duke aims and shoots a falcon from atop a high tower. Catching the falcon. Harvest. A win. A favorable outcome. | 上六：公用射隼于高墉之上獲之無不利 | ䷧ |

Eliminating a potential threat before it becomes a threat. Quashing internal strife. The sixth line is the release of tension within.

In antiquity, the sixth line was interpreted as swiftly penalizing civil disobedience.

In a contemporary reading, this is dealing with the inner naysayer.

The falcon is a bird of prey, symbolizing raptors that are trying to intimidate you from action.

The importance of quick timing is also implied in the sixth line. You must act quickly. Do not procrastinate, delay, or hesitate. Deal with the problem as soon as it is detected. Do not let it fester, and do not let it breach the fortress wall.

## Hexagram 41: Sǔn. Debilitation

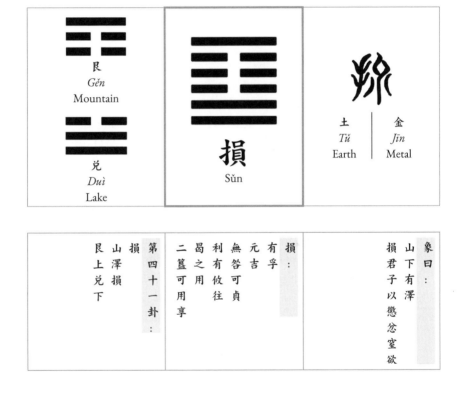

## The Oracle

What goes stale will enter a state of rot. Growth and well-being require dedication. Eradicate what is decaying immediately before it spreads. Never let mold fester. When movement takes a natural course toward decline, it becomes more advantageous to take up movement toward advancement. The question to ask is how one might achieve advancement in spite of the ongoing state of debilitation. A great upheaval is coming, but Heaven will protect you. Walk the path of light. Honor the gods and ancestors with prayer, incense, offerings, and song. You will remain protected by the Divine. Do not linger or dwell on matters that have come to their conclusion. Do not fault yourself for outcomes you couldn't control. Taking time for yourself in the mountains, at a lake, or by the seas will cleanse your heart-mind and replenish what had been lost due to the woes of the everyday.

At the base of the mountain, a lake.
**When there is distress, the sage will tame anger and desire.**
The Book of Rites 禮記 Lǐjì outlines five emotions that are powerful driving forces: joy, anger, sorrow, love, and hatred. Like the Wu Xing, they are agents of change. Love and hatred can both become desire. The uncultivated let the five emotions control them. The sage controls the five emotions.
Where there is tamed anger and desire, there will be gains and prosperity to harvest.
**In spite of the distress, a sacrifice made sincerely from the heart will bring good fortune. Two baskets may be used for the sacrifice. Use great earnestness when imploring the Divine for an intervention.**
When there is faith and trust, there will be enduring wealth and prosperity.
You remain protected by the Divine. Hexagram 41 can be a sign of one with an external aspect of the self that is visibly debilitated but internally is strong and resilient in spirit. Thus, you are one of Heaven's beloved ones.

| *First Line* | | |
|---|---|---|
| Complete the current matter expediently. Carry onward to the next matter expediently. Then there will be no remorse. Assess how time weakens matter. | 酌損之 無咎 已事遄往 | 初九: |

The first line is in effect the Oracle telling you to quicken your pace. You're going too slow.

Be more expedient in finishing what you're currently working on, and get to the next endeavor that you've been contemplating as soon as possible.
One reason for this, notes the Oracle, is that a critical window of opportunity is quickly closing.

| *Second Line* <br> Gains and prosperity achieved from the current matter. <br> Difficulties in proceeding on the next matter. <br> No long-lasting harm sustained. Affluence and flow of gains to come. | 益 弗 征 九 <br> 之 損 凶 二 <br> 　　　貞 ： |  |

The current matter concludes with gains. A difficult start to the future matter you will undertake. Such is the cycle of life. In the end, net gain.
Note the parallel structure to the first line. The current matter you're working on will yield success. However, a window of opportunity has been missed, so challenges are forecasted for the next matter you're embarking upon.
Overall, no long-term consequences. Everything will work out well for you.
The last message in the second line is a reference to Hexagram 42, Burgeoning, where the flow of affluence is on the increase.

| *Third Line* <br> There are three sojourners. <br> One sojourner will leave. One sojourner walks on alone. That sojourner will meet another. Affinity. |  |  |

A gathering of three brings one too many ideas, leaving one feeling excluded. It becomes inevitable that the excluded one departs. Thus, the group disbands. A gathering of one is lonely, and because one is lonely, the one only stands to gain—there is no one to lose.
Two ways this third line gets interpreted.
The first is as a total of three together at the start. One leaves. Now you have two. Among the two, one walks "alone" even though physically there is still that other companion. One meets a friend. Now there's three again.

The second interpretation of this otherwise vague and ambiguous line is that there are only two people together at the start of this narrative. One leaves, so only one is left and is alone. Then this one meets another, so there is a pair again. Thus, at all points of the story, there are just two together, but in total, three characters.

Which way do you interpret the line?

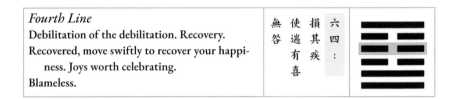

*Fourth Line*
Debilitation of the debilitation. Recovery.
Recovered, move swiftly to recover your happiness. Joys worth celebrating.
Blameless.

As a predictive oracular message, the fourth line prognosticates healing and full recovery after having sustained an illness or loss.

As philosophy, the line is about self-correcting a character flaw, one that has been weakening us and preventing us from truly ascending to higher achievement. Thus, now is the time to self-correct. That way we can more expediently achieve what we've undertaken.

Implied herein is that one of the five driving forces of emotion has become imbalanced in our personality—joy, anger, sorrow, love, or hatred—noting that either love or hatred can become desire. Thus, the sage is being called to cultivate greater control over these emotions, especially the one of these five that is most debilitating at this time.

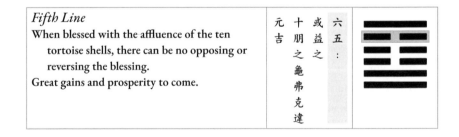

*Fifth Line*
When blessed with the affluence of the ten tortoise shells, there can be no opposing or reversing the blessing.
Great gains and prosperity to come.

One of the most beautiful lines received in the I Ching. The supreme good fortune and prosperity prognosticated in the fifth line of "Debilitation" is akin to the aphorism that failure is the mother of success (失敗乃成功之母, *Shī bài nǎi chéng gōng zhī mǔ*).

This is a sentient Divinity assuring you, in no uncertain terms, that you are protected.

The Zhou dynasty monetary system consisted of five materials: gold, silver, copper, tortoise shells, and cowrie shells.[41] Tortoise shells held both mundane value as currency (thus as a symbol of wealth) and spiritual value as divination tools. Moreover, the northern skies are guarded by a sacred Black Tortoise.

The *Yiwen leiju* 藝文類聚 (AD 624) is instructive in understanding the meaning of "十[朋之]龜,"[42] which translates to "ten [unknown units] of tortoise shells."

| The ten [units] of tortoise shells are as follows: | | 十朋之龜者，[43] | |
|---|---|---|---|
| 1. Divine Tortoise, | 一曰神龜， | 6. Tortoise of Divination, | 六曰筮龜， |
| 2. Spirit Tortoise, | 二曰靈龜， | 7. Tortoise of the Mountains, | 七曰山龜， |
| 3. Tortoise of the Stars, | 三曰攝龜， | 8. Tortoise of the Lakes, | 八曰澤龜， |
| 4. Precious Tortoise, | 四曰寶龜， | 9. Tortoise of the Waters, | 九曰水龜， |
| 5. Tortoise of Arts and Culture, | 五曰文龜， | 10. Tortoise of the Flames. | 十曰火龜。 |

The "Tortoise of the Stars" is an astrological consideration, significant in fate and destiny calculations, often assessed alongside Tai Sui (the orbit of Jupiter).

It's also a reference to the Buddhist principle of *prajñapti*. The concept is difficult to translate. Essentially, it's a form of corresponding virtual truth to every truth in reality. It's like a photograph of the truth, or a string of code to produce a simulated version of physical forms.

The blessing "Tortoise of the Stars" implies having the power to think something into existence by creating a photographic mental image of it, and then materializing the physical reality of it. Essentially, it's the power to design your own fate and destiny.

"Precious Tortoise" implies financial prosperity, wealth, and being blessed with always having all that you hold precious.

The fifth line is fatalist, in the best possible way. When you are meant to achieve a mission because it was ordained so by the gods, then there is no stopping the manifestation of it. Nothing, not this Oracle, not any force in this universe can prevent that achievement because it has been ordained by the most powerful force in the universe.

In short, although you face challenges, the final outcome will be auspicious—great success to come.

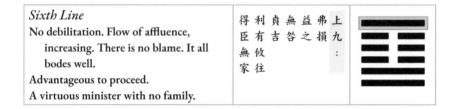

**Sixth Line**
No debilitation. Flow of affluence, increasing. There is no blame. It all bodes well.
Advantageous to proceed.
A virtuous minister with no family.

上九：損之益之弗
　　　益之无咎
　　　貞吉利有攸往
　　　得臣無家

The sixth line is the image of a good minister who acts selflessly, with nothing personal to gain from their endeavors.

In a mundane interpretation of the sixth line, the message might be to hire more assistants or employ additional personnel. Find those who are aimless or lacking direction, and give them your direction. Find those without a mission, and give them your mission. Find those who do not feel a sense of solidarity, and give them a newfound sense of solidarity.

Generally, this line is auspicious in matters of career, business, health, and luck.

## Hexagram 42: Yì. Burgeoning

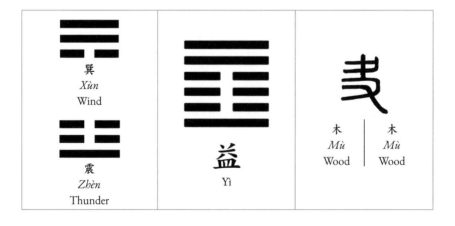

| | | |
|---|---|---|
| 第四十二卦：<br>益<br>風雷益<br>巽上震下 | 益：<br>利有攸往<br>利涉大川 | 象曰：<br>風雷<br>益<br>君子以見善則遷<br>有過則改 |

## The Oracle

A state of increase and expansion. Opportunities come knocking. As you gain, ensure that others gain. What you receive, you must give. That is the only way to ensure further increase and ascent. Time is of the essence in the matter. Your window of opportunity will not remain open for long. The time for increase and ascent is now. Accept the challenge; rise to the occasion. Never lose your kindness. You know you are aligned with Heaven's Will when what you seek for yourself will in turn benefit the collective and achieve a greater good.

Thunder incites a new development and wind disperses it, giving it momentum. A state of increase and expansion. The image of burgeoning is a vessel with water overflowing.

A sage learns honor from the honorable, and honor from the corrupt. Learn beneficence from the beneficent, and beneficence from the malicious.

"君子以見善則遷，有過則改" *(Jūnzǐ yǐ jiàn shàn zé qiān, yǒu guò zé gǎi)*. Here is the translation of this oft-quoted proverb:

**When sages see the good of others, they are inspired to be better; and when they see the fault of others, they correct that fault in themselves.**

**Auspicious to cross the great stream.**

Heed those words, and the gods will bless you with ever-increasing and overflowing prosperity.

Yi is a symbol for the prosperous and ever-continuing flow of growth, gains, benefits, profit, and affluence.

### First Line
It is a time of accomplishing the great deed.
Good tidings and fortune.
There is no blame.

初九：
利用為大作
元吉
無咎

As the Oracle section of the hexagram noted, it is auspicious to cross the great stream.

You are worth your greatest ambition. That most lofty goal you aspire to can be achieved. Pursue it.

### Second Line
Perhaps there is a burgeoning.
When blessed with the affluence of the ten tortoise shells, there can be no opposing or reversing the blessing.
Eternal and prolonged divine blessings.
Even the king humbly serves the Great Lord.

六二：
或益之
十朋之龜弗克違
永貞吉
王用享于帝吉

Gains and increases are promised on the condition that you stay humble and modest. Even the king serves the Great Lord in Heaven. There is always someone better than the best, higher than the highest.

The tortoise shells reference invites you to continually commune with the Divine through divination, so that you stay true to the Path set out for you by the Divine.

The second line includes the same ten tortoise shells reference from the fifth line of Hexagram 41, and both are yin. Refer to Hexagram 41's fifth-line commentary on the interpretation of ten tortoise shells, which in summary is an affirmation that you are blessed by Heaven.

The reference to the Great Lord in Heaven here means Shangdi, the supreme being in Heaven referenced in Shang oracle bones.

### Third Line
Burgeoning. Calamity. There is no blame.
There is a sincere, centered heart, speaking only truths.
For petitions to the duke, use a jade tablet.

六三：
益之用凶事
無咎
有孚中行
告公用圭

Aspirations inspire a beautiful beginning. Then trouble hits. There will be no irreparable harm.

Stay honest. Stay faithful. From the adversity comes an opportunity for advancement. The third line can prognosticate career successes after grueling hard work and demands. The counsel given here would be to keep at it; your grit will get you through.

Jade tablets were inscribed with prayers to the gods.[44] They're symbolic of important messages. The third line recounts a promising start that was then met with major challenges.

The rest of the line can be interpreted either as advice to petition or pray to "the duke" with your request, or as an allusion to a forecast that you will be receiving an important message soon. The duke can be a reference to a minor deity or spirit. Lei Gong, for example, the thunder god in Thunder Rites, is a duke.

Considering that this is the final line of the trigram Thunder, it isn't entirely absurd to identify the reference with Lei Gong (雷公) and proceed with a petition to him. The jade tablet becomes a metaphor for a form of Fu sigil talisman crafting.

| *Fourth Line* <br> Take the Middle Path. <br> Proceed with petitioning the duke. <br> Counsel to move the capital: advantageous. | 利用為依遷國 告公從 中行 六四： | ䷩ |

This is the position of an intermediary, go-between, mediator, or ambassador. Moreover, be balanced, objective, and try to see both sides. Walk along the center.

The same reference to petitioning the Duke from the third line (in the lower Thunder trigram) is repeated here in the fourth (beginning formation of the Wind trigram).

If the Duke is interpreted as a spirit entity, then the fourth line's counsel is that of prayers and offerings to gain the favor of the gods. This might refer to particular minor deities, divinities relating to weather or natural phenomena, or a genius loci (the protective spirit of a place).

A secular interpretation of petitioning the duke is appealing to someone in a position of power and gaining that person's favor.

The moving of the capital is a reference to the capital city of the Zhou dynasty being relocated eastward. Western Zhou fell to invasions from the far west, invaders that the Zhou referred to as "barbarians" and a "wild tribe" who had their hair unbound and bodies tattooed, and who wore animal skins. They ate a more meat-centric diet, noted the Zhou, rather than a grain-based diet like theirs (with the implication that the grain-based diet was more civilized). The constant invasions from these outsider groups prompted the Zhou court to move the capital to the east, with the subsequent period in history referred to as the Eastern Zhou.[45]

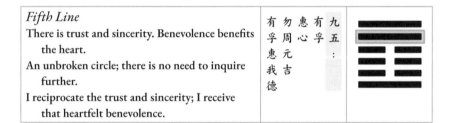

*Fifth Line*
There is trust and sincerity. Benevolence benefits the heart.
An unbroken circle; there is no need to inquire further.
I reciprocate the trust and sincerity; I receive that heartfelt benevolence.

Here's the Oracle's answer to you in plainspeak: In your heart, you already know the answer. You don't have to be asking this question.

The fifth line is one of the rare instances when the message is received in first person and the Oracle self-addresses with "I."

And with that "I," the Oracle assures you that all you've spoken to the gods in your heart is heard by the gods. If a specific divinity or ancestor was invoked for the divination, that voice is speaking through the text and self-addressing with "I."

Everything that you think and feel about Spirit is reciprocated back at you.

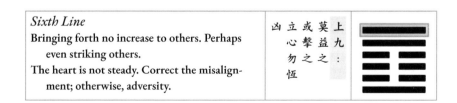

*Sixth Line*
Bringing forth no increase to others. Perhaps even striking others.
The heart is not steady. Correct the misalignment; otherwise, adversity.

When you enjoy burgeoning prosperity, the only way to keep it enduring is to give it away. If you do not pay your good fortune forward, you will lose it.

Corrective measures to behavior, conduct, way of life, and mindset are in order. If one does not make the self-corrections soon, fortunes will dissipate.

Think about how you are in service of others. How are you contributing? To align personal will with Heaven's Will means that what you pursue is not just for your own gains, but will result in collective gains and achievement of a greater good.

# Hexagram 43: Guài. Decisive Action

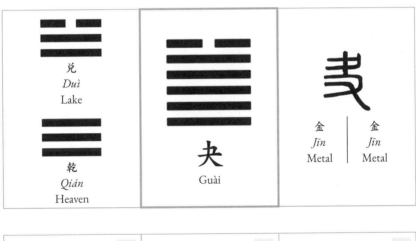

## The Oracle

After a long period of tension, there will be a breakthrough. Be careful, as there may be risks ahead. Your interests are not the only ones at stake in the endeavor; be sure to warn others about the risks involved, but do not yet reveal your intentions. No gains from reactive combat. You intuit that you must take decisive action, but how? In which direction will you go? Send a prayer upward to Heaven. Place full faith in the Divine that blesses your path, and your prayer shall be answered. The solution will be a different path from the one initially conceived.

---

The image of Hexagram 43 is that of an impending flood, and having to plan, execute the plan, and undertake the building of levees (embankments to stop the flooding of rivers) swiftly, decisively. The image calls to mind how Yu the Great saved ancient China from the great floods.

**The sage will share the kingdom's abundance and prosperity downward to all people.**

**In all laws, embody virtue and benevolence; the sage must be seen to embody virtue and benevolence.**

**Make known throughout the king's court: a sincere and stern warning cry declared throughout the capital.** "戎" *(róng)* is a reference to a tribe or clan in the west.

**Unfavorable to respond with arms.** This is not a martial incident.

**Favorable to embark on the journey.**

Take decisive action.

---

| *First Line* |
|---|
| Arm and protect your toe before advancing. Advancing at a disadvantage. Errors that could have been avoided are made. |

初九：壯于前趾，往不勝為咎

An imbalance of power and strength. You are not prepared for a fight. Susceptible to injury, one that would prevent you from moving forward.

Do not walk a blistering journey without the proper footwear. Defense is better than offense at this time.

Unexpected setbacks at the beginning.

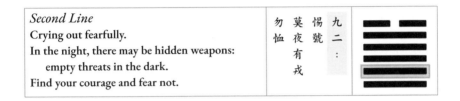

*Second Line*
Crying out fearfully.
In the night, there may be hidden weapons: empty threats in the dark.
Find your courage and fear not.

A state of stress and distress, but the situation is not as dire as you think it is. Here, the word for "weapons" is the image of one holding a polearm in one hand and a shield in the other. Thus, it's often translated to "soldiers." The symbol represents military or martial action. In other words, there is fear of an attack or hostile conflict, but the Oracle forecasts that it won't happen, or at least it will be successfully thwarted.

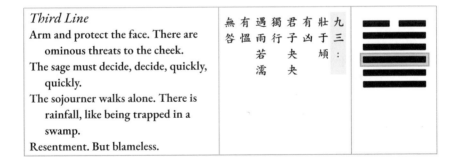

*Third Line*
Arm and protect the face. There are ominous threats to the cheek.
The sage must decide, decide, quickly, quickly.
The sojourner walks alone. There is rainfall, like being trapped in a swamp.
Resentment. But blameless.

The Oracle is insisting that you decide and act quickly, almost conveying a sense of urgency.

This is a warning of a threat to the face. The reference can also be to your cheek. Like a slap in the face, there could be an unexpected or sudden affront. The threat could involve humiliation.

The next scene in the narrative is of one walking in the rain alone, and the torrential downpour is so heavy that it's almost like wading through a swamp.

Feeling resentment for what you have to endure. If it turns out you weren't
able to act quickly in time to thwart the affront, the Oracle wants you to
know that this was not your fault. You did nothing wrong.

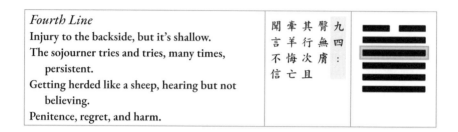

*Fourth Line*
Injury to the backside, but it's shallow.
The sojourner tries and tries, many times, persistent.
Getting herded like a sheep, hearing but not believing.
Penitence, regret, and harm.

Injury sustained, causing difficulties with advancing, but the injury is minor.
Nevertheless, you're feeling restless, anxious, and a little aimless, too.
You're given sound advice. You hear but you're not listening. You still think
you know better. You refuse to acknowledge that in this situation, you are
the sheep, and it might serve your own interests to be herded.
Take the advice. Otherwise there will be remorse, and greater injury to come.

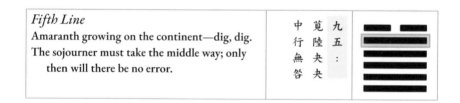

*Fifth Line*
Amaranth growing on the continent—dig, dig.
The sojourner must take the middle way; only then will there be no error.

You are letting others who are inferior overrun you. However, the reason you
have let them overrun you is because you do not seem to be fully aware
that they are weeds.
They have a superficial appearance of brilliance, which is why you let them
persist. Note that amaranth growing on the continent could also indicate
rampant corruption among the highest offices in the state. Such corruption must be uprooted or it will only spread.

You have to act decisively and be resolute. You have to lead with a firmer hand. You cannot let the inferior control the decisions you make.

In acting, take the middle way, meaning avoid the extremes.

The phrase "dig, dig" is an indication to arrive at a resolute decision quickly, and then act quickly. Do not procrastinate and do not hesitate.

In many translations, instead of amaranth, the reference is to weeds. The implication of this line is the rapid spread of inferiority that you must uproot if you are to succeed at your endeavor. Thus, translations using the term *weeds* clearly convey that point.

Amaranth, however, displays brilliant red, pink, and purple perennial flowers that bloom in clusters, and to use the word *weeds* may risk oversimplifying the matter.

| *Sixth Line*<br>Sounding a bark but no command.<br>At the end, there is misfortune. | 終有凶 無號 上六： | ▬▬ ▬▬<br>▬▬▬▬▬<br>▬▬▬▬▬<br>▬▬▬▬▬<br>▬▬▬▬▬<br>▬▬▬▬▬ |

Warning of dangers to come, complaints, wailing, and lament, but no constructive counsel on how exactly to proceed; no orders issued, no plan of action.

When faced with an imminent threat, instead of expending your voice to complain about the situation or warn people of impending doom, use your voice to give an actionable plan.

If you can conceive of an actionable plan, then the prognostication of misfortune may be diverted. Otherwise, if it's just the sound of barks without method or action, the end result will be dire.

## Hexagram 44: Gòu. Improper Meeting

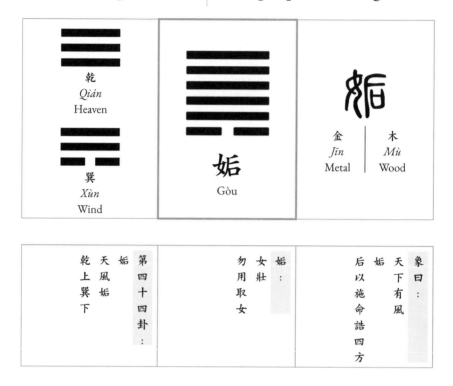

## The Oracle

Unions and partnerships are not auspicious at this time. Resist encounters that will undermine your sincerity. Honor and nurture personal independence. Keep temptations in check. If error is left uncorrected, faults and infractions unaddressed, then corruption sets in. Complacency turns a minor defect into a grave danger. Abuse of opportunities.

A meeting that is not proper. The result is betrayed trust.
The sage's rule, in accordance with the Mandate of Heaven, commands the four corners of the world. One in bad faith is inserted into a position of power and begins to gain influence.

**Inferior forces begin to gain power. That power must be subdued.**
If the situation worsens, then the sage is counseled to go forth with resistance and civil disobedience. Eradicate the evil influence.
**A maiden is placed where she should not be.**
**Marrying the maiden would be an improper meeting.**
If the inquiry is about romance, love, or marriage, then there are adversity and troubles: take caution. Unions and partnerships are not auspicious at this time.
Traditionally Hexagram 44 corresponds with the summer solstice, around the fifth lunar month of the lunisolar calendar.

## KING ZHOU OF SHANG AND HIS CONCUBINE DAJI

Hexagram 44 is an account of the favored and corrupt consort Daji (妲己) of the last Shang king. According to legend, a demonic fox spirit possessed a beautiful maiden's body, and when the lustful Shang king heard of a maiden who resembled the goddess Nǚwā, he arranged for the maiden to be brought to his court.

Daji corrupts the king, and together they empty the kingdom's treasury with their extravagances, inflicting much torture, suffering, and pain upon all; thus the king loses the Mandate of Heaven. A revolt led by the Zhou ensues and brings about the fall of the Shang.

| | |
|---|---|
| *First Line*<br>Halt the endeavor with a metal brake.<br>Virtue brings prosperity.<br>There is a matter to undertake. Ominous if matters take their own course.<br>A weak, emaciated pig flounders and falters, mistrustful. | 羸見有貞繫初<br>豕凶攸吉于六<br>孚　往　金：<br>蹢　　　柅<br>躅 |

The path you're headed on is not the right one. Do not continue. Instead, there's another path for you to walk. Change course and begin the new journey

The pig is a symbol of good fortune, generosity, trust, trustworthiness, and peace. When the pig is weak and emaciated, good fortune and trust are running thin. The pig's floundering and faltering suggest compromise of a good work ethic, of truthfulness and sincerity.

*Second Line*
A bag of fish. There is no blame.
There are no gains to be had from inviting guests.

What you've attained is enough for you, but not yet enough for two or three.
The bag containing fish is symbolic of catching a spouse or romantic partner, but the implication is that the timing isn't right. This can also mean having attained small gains in business or work, but it's not yet the right time to share in the spoils.
Traditionally, the second line was interpreted as third parties going after your lover or what you have because you invited them into your life and trusted them. Thus, it's about being wary of someone you invited into your life who has ulterior motives and wants what you have.

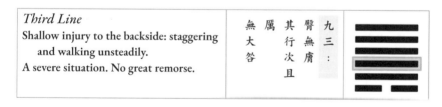

*Third Line*
Shallow injury to the backside: staggering and walking unsteadily.
A severe situation. No great remorse.

You perceive the complication to be worse than it really is. Regain perspective.
This is the image of one attempting to scale great heights, but slipping and falling. An alternate image is of one with a minor wound, and letting what should just be a minor wound negatively affect your confidence.
The third line prognosticates a severe situation to come, but the actual harm sustained by you is minimal.
Omen of a crisis, but if you steady your walk and stop staggering, you'll make it out of it relatively unscathed.
The third line has also been historically interpreted to indicate that inferior elements or toxic influences were threatening your situation. You made

poor choices with regard to alliances and partnerships. Either circumstances or the gods pushed you off that path in the hopes you'd stop walking in the wrong direction.

However, instead of changing course, you dust off your backside and walk unsteadily down the same wrong road—even worse.

| *Fourth Line*<br>No fish in the bag.<br>Going forth brings misfortune. | 起 包 九<br>凶 無 四<br>　 魚 ： | |
|---|---|---|

The timing is not yet right. Hold back. Forbear. Show restraint.

Fishing with a net and unable to catch any fish. In statecraft, this is interpreted as a monarch who has lost the support of the people. It can predict a downturn in the economy, a rise in unemployment, and scarcity.

In matters of love and romance, the fourth line's forecast is not promising.

"起" in this context presents a few other meanings to consider:

| | | |
|---|---|---|
| • to rise | • to instigate | • to initiate |
| • to move forward | • to trigger | • to attempt to move up |
| • to stand up | • to extract | • to prepare or draw up a |
| • to break out | • to remove | plan |

If you're thinking of acting in any of the ways listed above, perhaps think twice. Going forth in the manner currently being contemplated invites adversity and mishaps.

| *Fifth Line*<br>A melon wrapped in willow leaves.<br>A concealed emblem.<br>Wrath from the Heavens. The Mandate brings a downfall. | 有 含 以 九<br>隕 章 杞 五<br>自 　 包 ：<br>天 　 瓜 | |
|---|---|---|

A power that had been hidden now rises. Heaven revokes the Mandate from a previous ruler and grants it to a new one.

Your endeavor has borne fruit already, but the results remain hidden from view. The answer is in plain sight, though presently covered by willow leaves.

The reference to a concealed emblem is based on the Taoist principle of latent knowledge deep within that you are not conscious of at the moment. But you will soon stumble upon the answer to your question. At first you will not recognize it as the solution.

Your purpose will soon become clear, and it will be a purpose in service of the Divine. When the answer and your purpose finally come to you, keep it to yourself for the time being; do not share your plans with others, as the time is not yet ripe.

At the point in time marked by the fifth line, keep intentions concealed for the time being, and continue to cultivate the foolproof plan.

You will soon realize your full potential, and what had been granted to another will soon be granted to you. To ensure your rise to success, embody benevolence, act with wisdom, be loyal and faithful, speak only true words, and serve a greater good. Follow these principles, and Heaven will bless you. Violate these principles, and the downfall will be yours.

The fifth line narrates the final hour of the Shang dynasty and the ascendant hour of the Zhou.

"杞 Qǐ" can be interpreted to be wolfberry (goji berries), a willow tree, or any small tree. Wolfberry and willow trees both symbolize healing, and both have been known for their medicinal properties since antiquity.

The white muskmelon, or snow melon, is a symbol of moral righteousness, virtue, and being endowed with blessings from the Divine to fulfill a special purpose.

| Sixth Line |
| --- |
| To meet with their horns locked. |
| Regrets, but not an irredeemable disaster. |

Like locked horns, you have to face a conflict, and it proves to be quite the challenge, bringing troubles but no disaster.

The only way forward is to confront the opposition head-on, like locked horns.

Either you are stronger or you are more cunning—that is the only way to get out of the deadlock.

## JIANG ZIYA, THE WHITE MUSKMELON

In the *Records of the Grand Historian* 史記 (91 BC) compiled by Sima Qian, the state of Qi, a feudal territory during the Shang dynasty, was written as "杞." The state of Qi became somewhat of an independent kingdom after the overthrow of Shang, and during the Zhou, it was governed by Jiang Ziya 姜子牙, the duke of Qi, one of King Wen's legendary ministers and a Chinese cultural hero. He was referenced earlier in Hexagram 36 as Grand Duke Jiang.

Jiang served in the court of the corrupt last king of Shang. As the king descended into corruption along with his concubine Daji, Jiang resigned from court life, retiring to the Zhou countryside.

According to legend, he'd go fishing without hooks, deep in his faith that fish meant for him to be eaten would come by their own free will. King Wen encountered Jiang while he was fishing, found him to be wise and virtuous, and entreated the elderly Jiang, then seventy-two, to advise him on how to defeat Shang. After King Wen's death, Jiang continued to advise Wen's son, King Wu.

If "杞" as referenced in the fifth line of Hexagram 44 was intended as a reference to the duke of Qi, the line would read, in effect, "a melon," symbolizing virtue and one tasked to fulfill a divine purpose, concealed within (the state of) Qi, the place "wrapped in willow leaves."

Thus, Jiang Ziya is represented by the white muskmelon. The concealed emblem is a reference to Jiang Ziya's high status as a former court minister, but as the elderly man in plain clothes fishing by a river in the foreign state of Zhou, his true identity was not known to King Wen.

Moreover, this interpretation would give the fish and fishing references in the second and fourth lines another layer of meaning.

# Hexagram 45: Cuì. Assembly

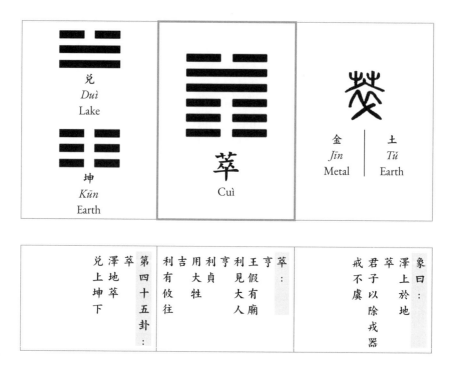

## The Oracle

A leader rises among them. You are destined to gather the people in congregation and unite them under your purpose, but take care that when you do, you are also prepared to handle the strife that is bound to arise when people congregate. This is your forewarning. Have a contingency plan in place. It's not about personal sacrifice; it's about aligning personal will with Heaven's Will. Choose progress. Start now.

The lake collects water, which seeps into the earth and enriches it. A fish and a dragon gather in assembly.
The sage is called to refine another, a warrior of great talent and ability.
Stop not the *zouyu*.

The king enters the ancestral temple. Favorable to go meet the eminent one.
An auspicious omen. An honorable leader or messiah arrives.
The sage must sharpen the weapons. The weapons will be needed to battle dangers ahead.
Regarding the warrior, 戎 could also be a reference to the Quanrong (犬戎), an ethnic group that often invaded the Zhou. The Quanrong claimed ancestry from two sacred white dogs and venerated the white dog spirits as the emblem of their clan.
The king entering the ancestral temple is a reminder to be humble and honor your roots.
Great fortunes to come from proceeding.

## THE *ZOUYU*

The *zouyu* (騶虞) was a mythical creature of Chinese lore that symbolized benevolence, virtue, loyalty, and righteousness. Like the *qilin*, the *zouyu* appears as an omen of a coming great leader. The *zouyu* appears to forecast the rise of a spiritual leader or a kindhearted sovereign, one who is a paragon of goodness and who is religiously devout. The *zouyu* was said to be a creature that resembles a white tiger with black spots.

According to the *Book of Mountain and Seas* 山海經 (Shānhǎi Jīng), a pre-Qin dynasty text (221 BC), the *zouyu* is a sacred animal resembling a white tiger with black markings. There are also five magical attendant grasshoppers (or scorpions) in service of the zouyu.

Figure 1.2 at the end of chapter 1 is a Qing dynasty (AD 1644–1911) painting of a *zouyu*.

| | | |
|---|---|---|
| *First Line*<br>There is trust, but it will not last to the end.<br>Disorder, confusion. An assembly, a gathering.<br>If you cry out, there will be laughter.<br>Show concern and pay mind—<br>Go forth. There is no blame. | 無往勿若乃有初<br>咎 恤號亂孚六<br>　 一乃不：<br>　 握萃終<br>　 為<br>　 笑 | ▬▬ ▬▬<br>▬▬▬▬▬<br>▬▬ ▬▬<br>▬▬ ▬▬<br>▬▬▬▬▬<br>▬▬ ▬▬ |

A productive start to an undertaking loses its momentum and incurs trouble. You lose faith, and this is the source of the problem. Rekindle your faith in the gods to course-correct the situation. Another way to phrase this is to rekindle your faith in yourself.

Forecast of a matter incurring some chaos and disorder. Regain order, and disaster will be averted.

One in the assembly must stand up as a leader, inspire confidence, restore the faith of the assembly, and teach the assembly to act as one again. Right now they are disintegrating and feeling aimless.

| Second Line |
|---|
| Drawing the bow brings good auspices. |
| Have faith. Blameless. |
| It benefits you to offer a small sacrifice at the ancestral temple. |

六二：引吉無咎 孚乃利用禴

It is time to act. Aim. Lead. Induce, trigger, instigate. Attract. Arouse. Stir up.

"引 Yǐn" is the image of a bow being drawn, so the action evoked is aiming, guiding, leading, to induce, to arouse, or to attract, to trigger and instigate.

The second line is also interpreted as an acknowledgement that a great talent is present, and now you are being called to utilize that talent in a more active and productive way.

In antiquity the "禴 Yuè" was a ritual offering kings made to the gods. A mystical reading of the second line would be to burn incense and leave out offerings to your ancestors. Reach out to their spirits, as they have a message for you.

| Third Line |
|---|
| Such is the assembly; such is it lamenting. Unfavorable to proceed. Yet no blame in moving forward. |
| Regret over a small error. |

六三：萃如嗟如 無攸利 往無咎 小吝

This is a forecast of personality issues causing a standstill in progress.

Endeavor for minor corrective measures before proceeding. Adjustments to the details are needed.

Another theme from the third line is to let it go. What happened has happened, and you have to move on. Do not dwell on past resentment. Choose progress.

The image of the third line is of one endeavoring to bring the assembly together, to no avail. Sighing at the fallibility of human nature—people are behaving selfishly and arrogantly.

The third line also carries with it an implication of a self-professed leader, but one who is incompetent, self-centered, and not up for the task. Changes must be made to resolve that situation.

| *Fourth Line*<br>Great fortune.<br>There is no blame. | 九<br>四<br>： | 大<br>吉 | 無<br>咎 |  |

Auspicious to advance.

A favorable outcome for your endeavor: passive virtue attracts the devotion and admiration of others. You become a focal point for the assembly. You were not seeking fame or validation intentionally, but you receive both.

| *Fifth Line*<br>A gathering into position. There is no blame—outlaws prove to be trustworthy.<br>Supreme and enduring good fortune when virtue is maintained. Disappointments vanish. | 九<br>五<br>： | 萃<br>有<br>位 | 無<br>咎<br>匪<br>孚 | 元<br>永<br>貞 | 悔<br>亡 | |

A gathering into position represents a group unified by a singular mission or purpose. One whom the group has judged as lacking virtue is the most virtuous of them all. Those you might not ordinarily ally with prove to be effective allies.

If unity can be achieved, the prognosis is success, with gains to come. Circumstances have brought a group together. Now they must learn to trust and rely on each other.

"匪" *(fěi),* often translated as "outlaw," can also mean a political opponent, or it can be a figurative indication of political opposition.

*Sixth Line*
With both hands, I weep tearfully.
There is no blame.

You proposition another, and you are rejected. You are misunderstood.

The rejection stings, and you lament. The other sees you lament, and through that, finds you sincere. Your intentions are made clear. The other will have a change of heart and accept your proposition.

In the end, after the weeping of tears, the union you seek will come to fruition.

The sixth line implies a first-person perspective, and an expression of anxiety that you are at risk of erring or that any successes are short-lived due to a great deal of uncertainty.

This is someone at the top whose position is threatened.

That there is no blame is a reference to one's innocence as difficult circumstances arise. This is not a matter of cause and effect that you put into motion, and it's not a matter of karmic retribution. There is a great sense of injustice to the matter at hand.

Final prognostication here suggests that no irreparable harm will come to pass, however.

# Hexagram 46: Shēng. Hoist

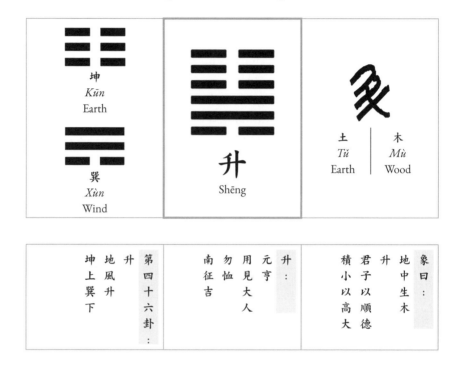

## The Oracle

Step up and push up. It is time to rise up the ranks. Reach above and beyond. Expand. Small victories accumulate to become greatness: one victory hoists up another until you attain supreme success. The winds of change are blowing in your favor, and the resources of the earth present themselves to you. How a tree grows, resilient and adaptable, yet solid and stable, inspires the path you will take to glory. Honor your roots, for your roots determine your staying power.

Within the earth, a tree grows. The tree grows atop a high mountain. The sage adheres to virtuous practice and grows upward like the tree.
    Favorable to meet with the eminent one.

Small victories accumulate to become greatness: one victory hoists up another until you attain supreme success.

Oppositional forces attempt to bury you, but they did not know that you are a seed.

**A seed deep within the earth begins its push upward as it grows into a tree.**

Give the seed time to push through the resistance of the earth. In time, the seed will flourish. New opportunities will open for you. Do not overlook the small gains. They will accumulate and push you upward closer to the greater gain you are after.

Wind hoists up the Earth: great gains and prosperity to come.

**A southbound journey yields fruition.**

| First Line<br>Pushing upward with conviction: great gains and fortune. | 允升大吉 | 初六： | ䷭ |

If you push upward toward your goal, you will succeed. The winds of change are blowing in your favor, and the resources of the earth make themselves available to you. Wealth and honor come to you when you assert yourself and reach for what you want.

| Second Line<br>Faith and sincerity advance the endeavor.<br>Offer a small sacrifice at the ancestral temple. There is no blame. | 無咎 孚乃利用禴 | 九二： | ䷭ |

A sense of not belonging, questioning where your place is in this world and what purpose you serve. Here is one who has less than the others but is expected to be equal to if not surpass the others.

The Divine will guide you every step of the way. Stay close, remain faithful and sincere in your inquiries. The path will clear.

In spite of modest resources, pay heed to the counsel of this line and you can still achieve your goal.

You feel like you are wrong, but you are not. You need only pray, and you will be hoisted. Consider daily devotionals or a routine meditation practice. Overall, a promising omen.

| *Third Line*<br>1. Ascending a city of nothingness.<br>2. Scaling a defenseless city. | 升虛邑 | 九三: | |
|---|---|---|---|

A groundbreaking expedition. New discoveries to come. The omen of a pioneer.

There are two versions of interpretation to consider here. The third line could be translated as "ascending a city of nothingness" or as "scaling a defenseless city." The city is symbolic of a subject, a topic, a field of study, a professional field, or a division of a territory of some kind.

In both versions of the translation, the third line is a push for you to act decisively, refrain from hesitating, and advance now. There are no obstacles to hinder you. However, it is uncultivated, untrodden land. You may be breaking new ground. Move forward boldly.

Note also a possible interpretation of a reference to the constellation 虛宿 Xū sù, an equivalent to Aquarius and Equuleus, ruled by the Black Tortoise in the north. 虛 is one of the twenty-eight lunar mansions in Chinese astrology, associated with the Rat, and generally considered an unlucky omen. Thus, it can prognosticate family conflicts, illness, and losses.

Other associated meanings include unpreparedness, lacking adequate resources, lack of organization, or events not going as expected.

Taken altogether, you feel inadequately prepared for the task at hand, but the yang line at the third-line position (in terms of ranking, this position is associated with legal matters, external or social affairs, and matters of social standing) portends good auspices if you tread with care at every step.

| *Fourth Line*<br>The king makes offerings at Mount Qi.<br>Auspicious. There is no blame. | 吉無咎 | 王用亨于岐山 | 六四: | |
|---|---|---|---|---|

Honor your roots, optimize the gifts and talents you've inherited, and you will succeed.

## MOUNT QI

The fourth line is a reference to King Wen of Zhou establishing a prosperous settlement near Mount Qi, the birthplace of the Zhou dynasty and origin point of his ancestry.[46] Mount Qi was the first home and the site of the founding of the Zhou clan by King Wen's ancestors. The settlement near Mount Qi also helped the Zhou to establish control over an important trade route.[47]

| Fifth Line<br>Auspicious to rise up the ranks. | 貞吉升階 | 六五: | ䷭ |

Your perseverance yields prosperity. The fifth line portends a promotion, rise in status, and one on the ascent to the top. This is also an advance from a lower stage to a higher stage.

Yet do not become overly eager in your ascent. Calm, steady progress and remaining humble are the keys to retaining a healthy momentum hoisting you up to the top.

| Sixth Line<br>In darkness deep, hoisting.<br>Steady breaths, resting to rest, staying calm, and control of your breath will hoist you to attain that which you seek. | 利于不息之貞 | 冥升 | 上六: | ䷭ |

The sixth line begins with a bit of a paradox—declining or descending to hoist and ascend. "冥" is also the underworld. It's a reference to that which is obscured, deep, profound, or esoteric.

A mystical reading of the sixth line is a call to journey into the underworld in order to advance a matter or to cause a matter to ascend. A parable of that is the monk who journeys into hell to find his mother's soul so he can save her and restore her soul to the earthly realm for rebirth. A contemporary mystical reading might be a call for shadow work.

The latter part of the sixth line is practical advice on how to proceed with the descent into the darkness deep so that there can be a future ascent.

A more mundane reading of the sixth is as a promising forecast that despite being mired in confusion, chaos, or a declining state right now, steady and perseverant movement upward will result in transcendence of that declining state. Great potential for regrowth and recovery.

The sixth line can also be interpreted as someone already at the peak of success, who now risks a decline. The latter part then offers instruction on how to stay at that peak and put off the decline for as long as possible—right now is not the time to attempt to go up even higher, because that approach will lead to decline. Instead, if you truly seek to go higher, then the actual approach to take to achieve that goal is to maintain the status quo, and maintain equilibrium.

## Hexagram 47: Kùn. Blockade

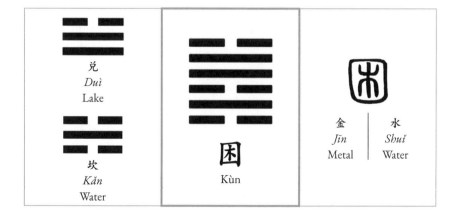

| | | | | |
|---|---|---|---|---|
| 兌上坎下 | 澤水困 | 第四十七卦： | 有言不信 | 無咎 | 貞大人吉 | 亨 | 困： | 君子以致命遂志 | 困 | 澤無水 | 象曰： |

## The Oracle

Ambitions hit a wall. Feeling exhausted and worn down, you are overwhelmed, unable to cope with your feelings of entanglement. Barriers of entry to the next level of advancement. Forces cause you to become isolated, closed off, and surrounded. Obstruction of passage and progress. A state of inner oppression. In the darkness, you do not yet see how the restraining bonds can be broken. First, do not let external forces restrain you. Restrain yourself. Control what you can control. Cultivate an inner strength that becomes an outer strength, and you can shatter the iron hand that is otherwise holding you back.

Exhausted and entangled. Feelings of hardship bring on a depression.

The sage subscribes to the conviction that destiny is leavened by free will and determination. Yet the sage also knows that destiny is written into the annals, and to know destiny so that one might navigate it is to consult the annals.

Forecast of triumph over the hardships. Auspicious for the eminent one.

Truth presents itself, but there is no truth. Trust presents itself, but there is no trust.

There is a message, but it is not a message. Words spoken, but there is no meaning.

**Sign of the Sacrifice:** losses sustained for a greater good or greater subsequent success. Hexagram 47 describes one with great ambitions, but with that comes great demands. Pursuit of big rewards comes with big risks. At this particular point in time, challenges and barriers hold you back from movement forward.

**Perseverance will bring you good fortune.**

The etymology of the ideogram for Kun 困, Hexagram 47, is Wood 木, symbolic of growth and prosperity, boxed in and surrounded 囗. This is the *qi* force that besieges with difficulties.

When Hexagram 47 comes up, increase Wood *qi* in your surroundings.[48] The trigram Thunder is also utilized in metaphysical measures to counteract the blockade. When the fifth line of Hexagram 47 is changed from yang to yin, the hexagram becomes 40, Jie, meaning to release the tension and untie the knots. That upper trigram transformation is from Lake to Thunder.

Likewise, Hexagram 47 was traditionally used in baneful magic to blockade someone and prevent that person from achieving prosperity or advancement.

---

*First Line*
Caned on the backside. Surrounded and besieged. Difficulties. Sitting beneath a barren tree.
You enter the darkness, a river valley between the two mountains.
Nothing is seen and unseen for three years.

三歲不覿　入于幽谷　臀困于株木　初六：

---

Oppressed by self-doubt, you are unable to see the situation with clarity.

Feelings of ennui. One is weary and discontent. Restlessness. That which used to fulfill you no longer fulfills you. Discontent with the status quo and entering a personal dark night of the soul.

You are now reflecting on what your options are, looking for a solution, but you don't see one. You feel confined to the status quo.

"幽 yōu" can mean concealed, imprisoned, trapped somewhere deep and remote, or the netherworld. "谷" is a valley between two mountains, a gorge, a ravine, or a river between two mountains. It's a term used figuratively to indicate being trapped in a difficult predicament.

"歲 Suì" refers to Jupiter, and the god Tai Sui associated with Jupiter, symbolic of years. It's also a reference to the annual harvest. Each "歲" is one harvest, so a figurative reading of the line can be "three harvests." Tai Sui/Jupiter is also associated with Wood, which is the symbol 木 being blockaded 囗 to form Kun 困.

| *Second Line*<br>Satiated by food and wine. Excess.<br>A vermillion sash wearer arrives. A sacrificial offering brings good fortune. Advancing brings adversity. |  |  |
|---|---|---|

A state of inner strife and self-imposed oppression. Satiating excessively through food and wine, or immediate gratification to numb the pain and dull the senses. You try to give the superficial impression that all is well with you. But there is oppression within. You have imprisoned a part of yourself inside of yourself.

The vermilion sash wearer is a harbinger of change. You are tempted to make rash, hasty, dramatic changes to your life, changing just for the sake of changing. Doing so would be ill-advised. Thus "advancing brings adversity."

Official seals worn by ministers were often hung from a vermilion sash.

Thus, an alternate interpretation of the vermilion sash would be as government action, law and policy, systemic or institutional influences on the situation at hand. This can be a foreshadowing that some form of punishment is imminent.

A "sacrificial offering" can mean self-reflection and deeper contemplation of the matter at hand before taking any action, or it can mean consulting your ancestors for counsel.

| *Third Line*<br>Trapped among the high rocks; a rugged, rocky terrain, surrounded by thorns and thistles.<br>Returning, man enters his palace, but cannot find his wife. It is foreboding. |  |  |
|---|---|---|

You are overwhelmed, unable to cope with your feelings of entanglement. There is indecisiveness in the face of what you see as your adversity. Yet you are being oppressed by that which is not oppressive.

The man symbolizes logic, reason, and rationality. The wife symbolizes emotional expression, intuition, and spiritual understanding. You are not trusting your intuitions, or you are not in control of your emotions.

The third line narrates the story of a man who is trapped atop a steep crag or cliff, and then finds himself surrounded by thorns, making it even more difficult to extricate himself from the predicament.

Finally, he manages to free himself, so he returns home to his estate, but he cannot find his wife. The implication is of further misfortune.

The meaning of the story is one experiencing adversity after adversity, each one different yet possibly related to the previous, unable to catch a break.

The wife not being home has led to two different interpretations. It can be interpreted as you having to help yourself, because there is no one you can depend on for support.

Another interpretation is that the wife has been kidnapped, her whereabouts unknown, and now you have to undertake an investigative adventure. This might represent the loss of something valuable to you that now you need to retrieve.

Not an auspicious forecast. Outlook in the matter at hand isn't great. Challenges ahead if one undertakes the endeavor contemplated. Perhaps it's better to stay home and keep safe. Travel and risky journeys are ill-advised at this time.

If your divinatory result is the third line, it could be an indication that extenuating forces beyond your control, or that have been maliciously cast onto you, are causing stagnation in your progress. To remove the blockage, counteract that baneful force.

| *Fourth Line* | | |
|---|---|---|
| Slow passage homeward. Trapped in a golden carriage. Adversity, yet there will be an ending to that adversity. | 九四：來徐徐，困於金車，吝，有終 | 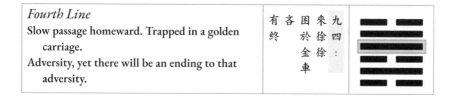 |

Difficulties with understanding who you really are. In a way, this is a questioning of personal identity, or challenges with the "Who am I?" philosophical inquiry.

Journeying forward will be difficult, and while it may feel like there is no end in sight to the adversity experienced, it will come to its cessation. A good outcome prognosticated, not so much in the sense of good fortune, but more in the sense that you will be able to overcome the adversity and return to neutral.

In a lighter mundane reading of being trapped in a golden carriage, it can indicate obstacles encountered when traveling, such as flight delays, traffic jams, getting stranded somewhere, and so on.

| | |
|---|---|
| *Fifth Line*<br>Cutting off the nose. Cutting off the feet.<br>Bound by the vermilion sash.<br>Speak with poise, calm and steady, a quiet tone, and thus shall there be progress.<br>Favors granted after the ceremonial offering. | 九五：劓刖，困於赤紱，乃徐有說，利用祭祀。 |

You have been wronged, and you feel alone. No one will hear your appeal. A divine intervention is needed.

The Five Punishments (五刑) of imperial China were: 墨 (tattooing the face), 劓 (cutting off the nose), 刖 (cutting off the feet), 宮 (castration), and 大辟 (execution).

Two of the five—cutting off the nose and cutting off the feet—are stated here. Cutting off the nose was symbolic of loss in social status and condemning one to lifelong bad fortune (the nose represented one's luck). Cutting off the feet was punishment for stealing, trespassing, treason, or sedition.

The vermilion sash was worn by officials of the king or government, upon which they'd hang their seals. To be bound by the vermilion sash could mean feeling the restrictive consequences of law and policy, institutional or systemic influences. Or it could mean you are the one who is carrying such a seal, and now you are feeling bound by your status and position.

Recall the foreshadowing in the second line, where the vermilion sash reference first appeared. There it was suggested that punishment might be imminent. The narrative progresses to this point of the fifth line, the climax, where indeed there has been a sentencing—two of the Five Punishments, no less.

Guilty or innocent, justified or unjustified, you've been punished, or you feel like you're being punished. You're feeling confined by the situation at hand.

Appeal your case and save yourself through discussion, negotiation, and keeping your tone quiet and calm. Stay composed and have poise.

Additionally, "祭 jì" means to go before the altar with offerings and a ceremony to petition the spirits for help. Your petition will be answered. Divine intervention may be the only way out of the situation. "祭" is the image of an altar, and a hand with a piece of meat as an offering coming before the altar in ceremony.

"祀 sì" means both to sacrifice and to venerate.

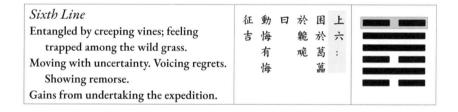

| Sixth Line | | |
|---|---|---|
| Entangled by creeping vines; feeling trapped among the wild grass. Moving with uncertainty. Voicing regrets. Showing remorse. Gains from undertaking the expedition. | 征動曰於困上<br>吉悔　　六<br>　有臲葛：<br>　悔卼藟 | ䷮ |

The expedition includes implications of an attack or strike, with the objective to conquer. Thus, it is symbolic of an ambitious undertaking.

An auspicious outcome is prognosticated.

## Hexagram 48: Jǐng. Fountainhead

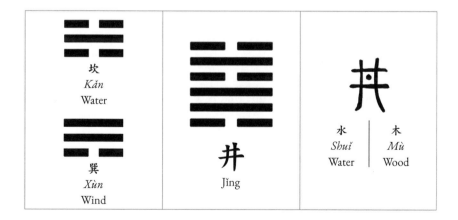

| | | | |
|---|---|---|---|
| 坎水井<br>上風井<br>巽<br>下 | 第<br>四<br>十<br>八<br>卦<br>： | 凶贏亦井往無改井<br>其未汔來喪邑：<br>瓶繘至井無不<br>井　得改<br>　　　井 | 君木象<br>子上曰<br>以有：<br>勞水井<br>民井<br>勸<br>相 |

## The Oracle

Society may change, but people's primitive needs never do. Nourish the people's primitive needs. Failing to reach the depths of people's inner essentials will cause your undertaking to fall short. To succeed, reach deep into the people's hearts and deeper into the tempest. The situation at hand is much deeper, much more meaningful than you initially perceive it to be. Tensions arise from an ideological struggle. Adversity and troubles: take caution. Keep the name of the Divine close by and at the ready, and invoke Heaven in your times of need.

**Dispensing nourishment, the wood draws up the water through the well, like the stems of plants draw up water to the blossoms.**
**The village has changed. Its well has not. Coming and going, the well is in frequent use.**
Although politics can change society, the people's primitive needs will always remain the same. No matter how people develop or society advances, there will always be a return to the fountainhead.
**Well water near depletion. A rope that is too short and a cracked water jug bring misfortune.**
A "rope that is too short" symbolizes efforts that fall short of reaching the fountainhead or source of all life. Failing to reach the depths of the fountainhead means failing to truly understand life. A "cracked water jug" symbolizes human negligence, not instilling enough care into the study of philosophy and divinity.

For your endeavor to succeed, you must extend a rope long enough to reach the fountainhead. You must understand the source of the situation at hand.

**The sage motivates the people to work and appeals to them to help one another.**

The primary message of this hexagram is that of rejuvenation and plenitude for the masses, nourishment for the people. Your endeavor is one that must be expanded to include nourishment for a greater good.

At this time you are still being shortsighted. The situation at hand is much deeper, much more meaningful than you initially perceive it to be.

**Adversity and troubles: take caution.**

| *First Line* <br> Do not drink the muddy well water. <br> Neither bird nor beast come to this dilapidated well. | 舊井無禽 | 井泥不食 | 初六： | |
|---|---|---|---|---|

You are exhausted, and the exhaustion has inhibited you from being productive. What once had worked for its intended purpose is no longer serviceable.

That not even birds and beasts find the water fit to drink conveys a sense of deep despair, lacking any source of inspiration, and feeling uninspired by life.

Rediscover your fountainhead, or find a new one. What is the source of your motivation for life?

In the later Hexagram 50, the Cauldron, the vessel you are using to produce your objective needs to be reworked. Here in the first line of Hexagram 48, Fountainhead, the source of the problems is with the system of beliefs or philosophies that are driving your objective.

| *Second Line* <br> Shooting arrows down the well at the koi. <br> The leaky water jug is cracked. | 甕敝漏 | 井谷射鮒 | 九二： | |
|---|---|---|---|---|

A well's water jug being cracked and leaking indicates an operation that no longer works as it should; something is out of service. The reason you haven't been successful in the endeavor is because you have the equivalent of a leaky water jug, and it's leaking because it's cracked.

You're also not supposed to be fishing at a well of drinking water. There's a sense of being unfit for the purpose. What you're doing to achieve your objective has no bearing or connection to the objective. There's an inherent absurdity here.

"谷 gǔ" also has a double meaning implying a difficult position. You're forced to act the way you do out of circumstances.

"射 shè" is the image of one shooting with a bow and arrow. It means to shoot, to fire or launch, and bears a reference to archery.

"鮒 fù" indicates carp, though in this context, that can mean goldfish or koi. Koi symbolize prosperity, love, affinity, and peace. Here they represent personal happiness.

Happiness and contentment are elusive; your desperate approach to be happy is ineffective.

| *Third Line* <br> **The well water is drinkable, but no one drinks. This brings great sadness to my heart.** <br> **Drink from the well. If only the king would understand—then good fortune would come to them all.** | 並受其福 | 王明 | 可用汲 | 為我心惻 | 井渫不食 | 九三： |
|---|---|---|---|---|---|---|

An unused asset is a wasted asset. The line references a well with clear drinking water, but no one is using it. Here the Oracle speaks in first person, i.e., "my heart."

In the cultural context, the heart 心 represents not just emotions, but thoughts as well. A better way to conceptualize "心" is as heart-mind. One way to read that line is: "This brings great sadness to my state of mind." This is the motif of a weeping god, Heaven shedding tears because the god's creation has turned out in a way unintended.

Divinity has endowed you with certain powers and talents. It was predestined that you would utilize these blessings, but such blessings have gone neglected, unused. "The king," symbolic of personal willpower, doesn't realize the blessing. If only you would come to the understanding of your greater purpose, then destiny can finally be fulfilled.

| *Fourth Line*<br>**Repairing the bricks of the well.**<br>**No errors are made.** | 井甃无咎 | 六四： | ䷯ |

It is a time for personal transformation. A reconstruction of what had gone into disrepair.
Adjusting to a new or current situation.
Reorganize the priorities in your life. All will be well.

| *Fifth Line*<br>**The well is clear and pure. Cleansing and cooling. Springwater flowing.**<br>**Drink.** | 食洌寒泉 | 井 | 九五： | ䷯ |

One has connected to a source of inspiration and creativity again. Life-giving rejuvenation.
The fifth line is said to prognosticate a great leader who brings prosperity to all, one who will cleanse and purify the land of its own past wrongs.
A time of purification.
"泉" as a reference to "黄泉 Huángquán" (yellow spring) also means the land of the dead. In Shinto, this is *yomi*, the World of Darkness, where the souls of the deceased go in their afterlife. After drinking and eating at the heart of *yomi*, there is no returning to the mortal world. This was a region believed to be located underground, below the earth.

The word preceding it "寒 hán" is the image of a house and someone dwelling within.

Rereading the line with "泉" meaning the land of the dead, the line would be: "The well is clear and pure; I am home, here in the afterlife." This is interpreted as an answer from one who has died and is reaching out to let you know that all is well in the afterlife.

### Sixth Line
Collecting water from the open well: no hindrances; dependable.
The well yields supreme good fortune.

Great prosperity and accomplishment.

Whereas the fifth line of Hexagram 48 is about an inner world and great inner potential, here the sixth line is a prognostication of manifested potential.

You become a fountainhead providing knowledge, service, and great good to others. You nourish the people like an open well, and for that, you will enjoy great prosperity.

The sixth line is, in effect, Divinity saying, "I am so proud of you."

## THE CHANGING SIXTH LINE

If the sixth line is the only changing line in a divination, then you are about to embark upon a grand accomplishment.

# Hexagram 49: Gé. Revolution

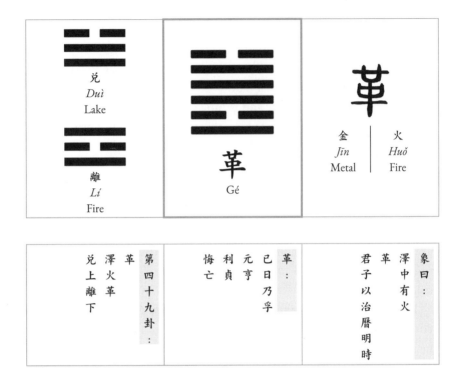

## The Oracle

Revolution to rectify injustice begins with revolution of the heart. First change inner misalignments before seeking a transformation of others. It is your responsibility to affirm that a call for change is for the better, and not for a different form of the same. Thus, true change comes when you are aligned with Heaven's Will. What you seek requires momentum, and to drum up that momentum, live and abide by higher principles. Those who see you embody the higher principles will be attracted to you, and you will gain momentum. Having that majority support is the authority you need for a just revolution.

A leather hide born of a magnificent fire. A change. To remove, to expel. Reform.
The talons of the bird cling to its offspring.
Prosperity and material gains. **A great position of advantage. Disappointments vanish. An auspicious omen.**
At the heart and center is a magnificent fire. The methods to be employed are like the art of tanning a leather hide.
**The sage must set the calendar and timing of events to come.**
Inspire confidence. When the people see that you have a vision, a plan, and the talent to carry forth that plan, they will be joyful and loyal.

### SOCIAL CHANGE

The leather hide is a metaphor for social change. It signifies removing or expelling an old and installing a new. Thus, Hexagram 49 is often interpreted as prognostication of reform or revolution. There are political or social implications.

Hexagram 49 expresses the passing of the Mandate of Heaven. The current ruler has violated the moral obligation to care for the people. Thus, the right to revolt is granted to the people, and through it, the new Son of Heaven will be revealed.

| First Line |
| --- |
| Using cord of yellow cowhide to bind them. |

鞏用黃牛之革 初九：

Omen alerting to the condition of oppression. Reform is needed. This is also the initial stage of revolution—the beginnings of an awakening.

| | |
|---|---|
| *Second Line*<br>The day of change has come. Call upon the troops—forward march.<br>Auspicious to advance; no blame for taking casualties. | 六二：<br>已日乃革之<br>征吉<br>無咎 |

If mediation and peaceful negotiation did not bear positive results for your position, then you have no choice but to assert that position.

This is the second stage of revolution. You've already tried the easy way. Now it's time to go with the hard way.

| | |
|---|---|
| *Third Line*<br>Call upon the troops—forward march.<br>Advancement then meets with danger. Foreboding adversity.<br>It is said that revolution requires the three axioms.<br>Stay virtuous. | 九三：<br>征凶貞厲<br>革言三就<br>有孚 |

The third line warns that the initial battles are unsuccessful, and yet advancing to meet those battles head-on is necessary. To mitigate harm, be patient, and take care not to act rashly.

The three axioms of a successful revolution are the following:

First, before you speak words of change, you must have studied change.

Second, to study change means knowing how to win the people's hearts.

Third, winning the people's hearts is the only way to successfully change.

Stay true to the three axioms and you will succeed in the endeavor.

| | |
|---|---|
| *Fourth Line*<br>Disappointments vanish.<br>Virtue, trust, and sincerity change the Mandate.<br>A favorable outcome. | 九四：<br>悔亡<br>有孚改命<br>吉 |

"命" *(mìng)* is both a reference to the Mandate of Heaven (the Mandate) and to fate or destiny.

The Oracle message is a conditional: if you have "孚 *fú*," then you can change destiny. Or as it is used here, when Heaven sees another to be virtuous, trustworthy, and sincere, Heaven will change the Mandate.

孚 means to have gained the trust of, to convince. Thus, you need to gain the trust of the Divine, and in more practical considerations, you need to gain the trust of the people you are hoping to serve.

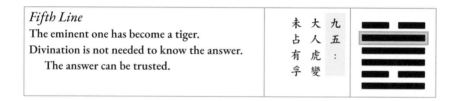

*Fifth Line*
The eminent one has become a tiger.
Divination is not needed to know the answer.
　The answer can be trusted.

"Become" as used here carries a tone of magical or miraculous transformation, and it is a sudden change, one that is unexpected. It becomes a game changer.

The eminent one is a sage who has attained power, prestige, and status.

The outcome is like the distinct, bold markings of a tiger. You already know what you're seeing, so there is no need to inquire about it.

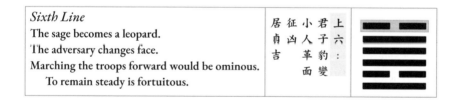

*Sixth Line*
The sage becomes a leopard.
The adversary changes face.
Marching the troops forward would be ominous.
　To remain steady is fortuitous.

The leopard (豹, *bào*) is a symbol of courage, military prowess, and martial arts. The sage was virtuous and sincere, but without power. Having transformed into a leopard means having succeeded in military campaigns when one did not have a military background.

"Become" as used here carries a tone of magical or miraculous transformation, and it is a sudden change, one that is unexpected. It becomes a game changer.

The adversary changing face is a reference to one who changes rhetoric, but the ulterior motives and selfishness remain the same.

While the sage has truly changed for the better, growing stronger and more fearless, the adversary's deceit proves to be more vicious.

Do not attack. Right now is not the time for bold action. Lay low in stealth. Remain steady and keep the physical position unchanged, even if you yourself have undergone a transformation.

The right time will come.

## Hexagram 50: Dǐng. The Cauldron

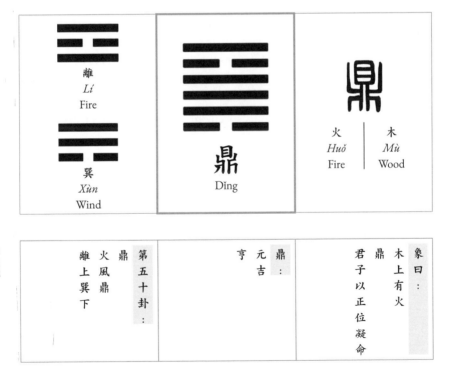

## *The Oracle*

You are in the developmental phase. Nourish the inner temple. At issue is the alchemy for nurturing talent and virtue so that there may be progress, innovation, and success. That alchemy, however, is reserved exclusively for the worthy. What is needed right now for you to prevail in your endeavor is a personal catharsis. Greater nourishment is needed. Bring forth offerings of sustenance to both the inner temple and to the outer temple of the gods. Be sure to cleanse and purge the cauldron thoroughly of its grime before you cook with it. Good fortune and favors bestowed upon the one who first purifies, then alchemizes.

**Supreme good fortune and favors from Heaven.**
You embark upon a direct and straight path to higher rank. Go forth, focused and steady, in alignment with the divine command, and find your destiny.

In Wu Xing alchemical principles, Wood creates and empowers Fire. Fire corresponds with the alchemical processes of synthesis, integration, assimilation, and illumination.

Kindling from the challenges you've overcome now light the fire empowering you to shine.

**The sage will inspire the people to serve in accordance with their capacity, as ordained by fate.** Or so goes the Confucian commentary appended to Hexagram 50.

Moreover, **the sage must now complete the mission.** The sage's mission: Heaven's Will is the sage's will; bringing peace and prosperity to the people is the sage's destiny; to unceasingly cultivate knowledge and wisdom is in the sage's nature.

This is the developmental phase. The fire is burning upon the gathered wood, and the cauldron is ready.

Offerings of sustenance are given to both the inner temple for personal nourishment and the outer temple of the gods, to carry forth the will of the gods.

Nurture your talent and virtue to initiate great progress, innovation, and success.

## CULTURAL SIGNIFICANCE OF THE CAULDRON

The cauldron is an alchemical vessel of great cultural and spiritual significance. The myths begin with the Yellow Emperor (2697–2597 BC) forging three precious tripod cauldrons, representing Heaven, Earth, and Humanity forged from copper.[49]

Yu the Great casts nine tripod copper cauldrons that the Xia dynasty (2100–1600 BC) passes on to the Shang, and when the Zhou defeat the Shang, the nine cauldrons pass on to the Zhou.[50] The nine cauldrons represented the Mandate of Heaven and were an insignia of imperial authority. By the time of the Qin (221–206 BC), the nine cauldrons were lost. According to legend, they were washed away and consumed by a river during a flood.

Cauldrons were used to cook the food that would be given as offerings to ancestral spirits. Incense burners for shrines and altars are commonly in the shape of a cauldron.

## HEXAGRAMS 49 AND 50

Whereas the theme of Hexagram 49 was dissent and a reform to or revolution of a systematic social order, Hexagram 50 expresses the events after the regime change.

Hexagram 50 is restoration and reconstruction of what the dissent had destroyed. This is a developmental phase and the building of new foundations. Establishing a new order after dismantling an old one is much harder than the dismantling process of revolution itself. Thus, after revolution, the hard part begins—having to design and build a new structure that will be better than what preexisted.

> **First Line**
> The upturned cauldron will be easier to clean.
>   There is grime and grit to be dredged.
> Taking a concubine to bear a son. Blameless.

初六：鼎顛趾利出否得妾以其子無咎

Overturn the cauldron. Clear out the filthy matter. Reconsider what you've been developing. Do not continue cooking in a cauldron filled with grime. Clean it first, then try again.

Personal catharsis to come. A purge.

Correct course and no irreparable harm will come from the past errors made.

"Taking a concubine to bear a son" calls on a traditional notion of marrying a second wife if the first wife is unable to produce a male heir. If and when the second wife gives birth to a son, her son becomes the heir, and her position, although she is a concubine, is now elevated higher than that of the first wife.

Likewise, in the matter at hand, you may need to "take a concubine to bear a son." The endeavor you are trying to develop into fruition is not going to take hold as is, so consider a different vessel for your concept.

> **Second Line**
> The cauldron is bountiful. Fruition.
> My counterpart is feeling malaise, and thus cannot approach the cauldron to dine with me.
> A favorable outcome.

九二：鼎有實我仇有疾不我能即吉

An undertaking of ambitious proportions and a lofty mission was prepared with great care.

The first part of the Oracle's advice here is to handle such a cauldron with great care.

Since everything about its inception and purpose is aligned with Heaven, there is fruition—a great start as the foundations are being built. However, now the plot thickens.

"仇 chóu" could be translated as a companion, spouse, peer, or mate, but it can also be translated to indicate an enemy or the opposition.[51]

The support for interpreting it as opposition (an adversary) comes from the image of the six-line hexagram. The three yang lines at lines 2, 3, and 4 represent the belly of the cauldron, full. The yin line 5 represents your opponent, someone who is occupying the position of opposition against you.

The two yang of lines 3 and 4 represent the obstruction between you, a yang line, and the one occupying a polar opposite position from you, the yin line of line 5. Hence, this "other," be that a companion, spouse, or enemy, cannot approach to dine with you, because the yang of lines 3 and 4 keep the two of you apart.

Here, the translation for "仇" is "counterpart," a neutral way to account for both interpretative approaches. Essentially this "other" who is feeling unwell and thus unable to come dine by the cauldron occupies whatever position and perspective are the opposite of yours.

This "counterpart" is the yin to your yang, which could be complementary, but is also by nature adversarial, because you two represent polar opposites. When you want to go right, this counterpart wants to go left. This is one who always has an objection to your proposal. There is innate rivalry between you and the counterpart.

Nevertheless, the position is at the base of a full belly, so the final prognostication is favorable.

The oracle bone script for "即 jí" is the image of a person sitting and facing a food vessel, with its original meaning "approaching to eat" or "getting ready to eat."

The second part of the Oracle's advice to you is this: there is a tension between two sides, one occupied by you and one occupied by the other. This could very well be a division within yourself, where logic and pragmatism (the yang) are dominant and seek to go in one direction, but your intuition and irrational feelings (the yin) won't support this direction. Be it one against another or one against the self, the two sides are unable to meet and arrive at an agreement. There's an unsteadying imbalance, and it needs to be resolved as your next course of action.

A traditional parable for the second line is of a court official from the old regime who does not support the newly ordained king, so when the king holds a great feast, that court official refuses to attend the banquet and thus refuses to dine with the king. Counsel to the king is this: the court official doesn't have enough power or support from the opposition to do harm, but it's a tension you'll need to eventually address, so bear that in mind.

The situation is favorable, so continue to advance on your endeavor, but remain on guard for the opposition, one who will surely become more vocal and combative in the times to come.

| Third Line<br>Broken handles on the cauldron.<br>Their endeavor comes to a stop.<br>Cannot dine on the pheasant soup.<br>Liberating rains bring catharsis.<br>Ending will be favorable. | 終方雉其鼎九<br>吉雨膏行耳三<br>　　虧不塞革：<br>　　悔食 | |

Dramatic events leading up to this point have caused one to be purged of emotions.

A sudden, profound realization comes to light. What had been blocked and suppressed deep within is finally let out.

Thus, a good omen.

Notice how the word for "broken" here is "革 gé," the name for Hexagram 49, Revolution. Thus, in a metaphorical way, one could say that the handles of the cauldron are in revolt.

The word used for "their" by the Oracle is "其" *(qí)*, a gender-neutral pronoun that could indicate his, her, its, their, or one.

The image here is of one seeking to undertake an activity or journey somewhere, but that intention is being blocked, suppressed, or stalled.

Copper ritual cauldrons were enormous and heavy, so the only way to move one would be to affix chains to them by their handles (which resemble ears) and have several persons lift them for transport. If the handles have broken off, then the cauldrons cannot be moved. Thus, the endeavor has come to a stop. Likewise, the Oracle's counsel here is to listen to what others have to say. You'll hear the solution to the problem you face if you'll only listen.

The pheasant in the Oracle text is described as greasy, fat, and oily. Traditionally this was a descriptive for a creamy pheasant soup.

The "方" from the passage "方雨虧悔 fāng yǔ kuī huǐ" as used on Shang oracle bone inscriptions meant to exile, to cut off the shackles from, to send far away, to banish. The meaning of this passage can be translated as: "The falling rain cleanses away the contrite."

The passage is a metaphor, where rain "雨" bears the figurative meaning of teachings and instruction, lessons learned. Another meaning for "方" is rule, law, and reason. Thus, like tanning the cow leather is a figure of speech for a revolution in Hexagram 49, falling rain cleansing away the contrite is a figure of speech for the idea that if you bring teachings and moral instruction on the rule of law and reason, then grief will subside.

The meaning is that of catharsis, a purging and purification that the rain brings, whether it's literal rain falling from the sky or as teachings and life lessons.

| *Fourth Line*<br>**A broken cauldron. Tripod capsized, the rice porridge spilling.**<br>**The duke's robes have been stained. Foreboding adversity.** | 凶 其 覆 鼎 九<br>　形 公 折 四<br>　渥 餗 足 ： |  |

A promising event has turned out quite badly. You failed at discharging your duties competently because of inadequacies that you could have avoided had you been more careful with who you relied on.

At this time, halt any advance, and instead of seeking progress, seek correction. Rectify all wrongs before proceeding.

In the fourth line of the Hexagram 50 narrative arc, the feet on the cauldron have broken off, so the cauldron capsizes. Since it contained a carefully prepared meal (the triple yang of lines 2, 3, and 4 resembling the full belly of a cauldron), the contents spill everywhere, and the duke's robes are stained.

The duke's robes getting stained represents one feeling embarrassed or humiliated by the incident. One's image and appearance have been stained.

When the fourth line comes up in a reading, pay attention to who you trust as a member of your inner circle, or be more mindful of how you select employees.

The reference to a cauldron's broken legs is also symbolic of censure or failing to overcome obstacles and thus receiving backlash.

| *Fifth Line*<br>Yellow handles on the cauldron, gold chains attached.<br>Auspicious omen. | 利貞 鼎黃耳金鉉 六五：  |
|---|---|

The fifth line represents a golden age. The times ahead are those of peace and stability. There are thriving arts and culture, and a flourishing civilization. This can be credited to a wise and beneficent ruler occupying this fifth line.

The yellow color calls to mind the Yellow Emperor, the Yellow Dragon, and the Yellow River valley civilizations. Yellow corresponds with Earth in the Wu Xing cycle, where the *qi* of yin and yang are balanced and symbolic of the center.

Thus, as an omen, seeing yellow here is an affirmation that you are in the right and that you have Heaven's blessing.

Yellow is also the color of neutrality, so to hold on to Heaven's blessing, cultivate neutrality and objectivity. Never be prejudiced toward any one side. Have the beneficence and virtue to feel compassion for all.

The fifth line portends success in work or career matters, professional advancements, glory, and promotions, and it affirms one whose competency inspires trust from others.

The final message of the fifth line is to remain humble. Every figure of authority will answer to a higher power of authority.

As applicable, when the fifth line comes up and you have to make a judgment, follow past precedent. The narrative here is of a humble king who has the wisdom to consider how past great kings ruled, and to emulate their ways. Thus, as applied here, rather than diverging from precedent, honor it.

"鉉 xuàn" referenced in both the fifth and sixth lines has been translated as "chains," though it can also be rings or a rod. The reference is to the device used for carrying cauldrons. In both instances, that the "鉉" is present means the cauldron is being prepared for transport.

| *Sixth Line*<br>Jade chains on the cauldron.<br>Great fortune and favors. No losses sustained. | 無不利 大吉 鼎玉鉉  上九：  |
|---|---|

Jade represents spiritual cultivation. You are virtuous, sincere, wise, and one that the leader trusts, though you yourself are not the head.

If the fifth line with the references to yellow and gold were about the sovereign or career success, the sixth line is more internal. This is about spiritual advancement. Jade was believed to improve health, bring longevity, and protect souls from evil. Taoist alchemists associated jade with immortality. An auspicious omen. The inner self has reached a highly developed stage. The endeavor ends well for you.

## Hexagram 51: Zhèn. Jolt

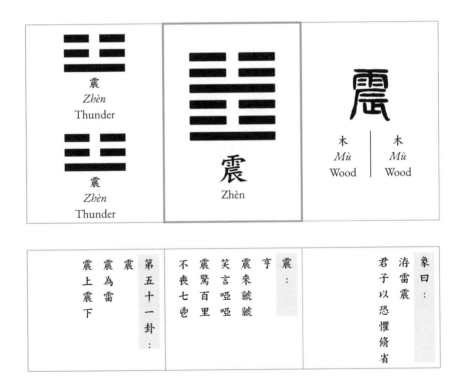

## The Oracle

> The shock of fate has hit you. Circumstances seem beyond your control. This is the hexagram of force majeure—unforeseeable situations that prevent you from fulfilling what you seek to fulfill. Do not allow cataclysm to weaken your will to survive. While you cannot control the circumstances, you can control your response. In time, you will fully recover what you have lost. It is still auspicious to go forth on your endeavor. Find the eye of the storm. That is the calm at the center of a cyclone. New beginnings brought on by sudden sharp turns.

Flowing water: here comes a downpour, a great thunderstorm. There is a sudden change of course. Auspicious to petition the gods. Pressing upward, valiantly.

A sage is humbled by the Will of the Divine. It serves one's purpose to fear the gods. Thunder strikes, trembling, trembling. Exchanging smiles, laughing, laughing.

The boom and crack strikes fear far and wide. Do not let spill the chalice of sacrificial wine. Keep your heart-mind aligned.

Seizing control and power. Thunderclap. A sudden change. There will be an upheaval.

"鬯" *(chàng)* is a reference to sacrificial or ceremonial wine. The oracle bone script for it is the image of a chalice containing the symbol "※" for blessings and divine protection through the four seasons and covering the four directions.

The image of "不喪匕鬯" *(bù sàng qī chàng)* evokes a sacrament, a rite in which one has come before the ancestral temple with offerings to appease the gods and bless our ancestors. We hope that by blessing our ancestors, they will bless us in return.

The rite includes goblets filled with ceremonial wine, copper and bronze daggers, and scorpions. In Thunder Rites, a branch of Taoist magic, such daggers are used in exorcisms and in ritual dances honoring the gods. The reference to the daggers in the context of Hexagram 51 is to evoke martial prowess.

The scorpion is another symbol thematic in Thunder Rites and in the previously referenced poison magic from Hexagram 18. The scorpion is both toxic, used for crafting poisons, and also an antidote, used to craft medicines that dispel toxins. Since antiquity, scorpion has been used as a cure for convulsions, spasms, and epilepsy.[52] Interestingly, one of the adverse effects cited from overuse of scorpions as a treatment for nervous system diseases is liver failure. Liver corresponds with Wood from the Wu Xing cycle, and Wood corresponds with Thunder.

Hexagram 51 expresses military discipline for the establishment of peace and stability within a kingdom. There's a sense here that the best defense is a good offense. Here, we also see advancement and progress, accruing of great powers and resources, so long as one keeps the sacrificial wine flowing.

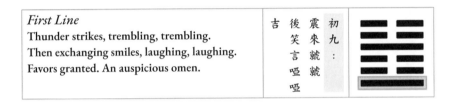

*First Line*
**Thunder strikes, trembling, trembling.**
**Then exchanging smiles, laughing, laughing.**
**Favors granted. An auspicious omen.**

You dreaded what would happen. Fear took hold of you. However, the outcome is not as bad as you dreaded. Initial apprehension becomes relief.

The first experience of the Divine was intimidating, but once we realize that Divinity comes to bring us blessings, our tensions ease and we laugh in cheer. The exchanging of smiles is also a reference to realization, and coming to an understanding of the laws of nature.

There will be good fortune.

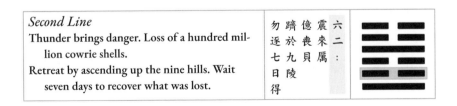

*Second Line*
**Thunder brings danger. Loss of a hundred million cowrie shells.**
**Retreat by ascending up the nine hills. Wait seven days to recover what was lost.**

The second line portends financial loss, but also a full recovery.

Do not rush to restore that loss. View the situation from a higher perspective—hence ascending up nine hills—before you act. In time, you will fully recover what you have lost.

When we face dismaying losses of fortune, rather than resisting the experience, accept the loss with grace and calmly formulate a plan for achieving greater gains. Meaning, when you have incurred loss, don't focus on the loss or on how to recover that loss. Instead, your mind should be focused on how to gain. By focusing on how to gain, you in turn recover the loss.

Take time to strategize and prepare a plan for how to gain. The adversity will be short-lived.

| *Third Line*  Thunder—*su, su,* **trembling, trembling.**  Thunder passes. The eclipse subsides. No harms come. Diseases cured. | 震 震 六<br>行 蘇 三<br>無 蘇 ：<br>眚 | ▬▬ ▬▬<br>▬▬▬▬▬<br>▬▬ ▬▬<br>▬▬ ▬▬<br>▬▬▬▬▬<br>▬▬ ▬▬ |

Adversity comes and there is distress, but just as it had arrived, it departs. "眚 hěng" is also evocative of an eclipse and represents recovery from disease.

You feel powerless in the face of cataclysm, and while you cannot control the circumstances right now, you can control your mental response. Persist and be resilient. Advance onward. All that you lose you will recover again.

When you can remain calm in the face of the storm, your mind will be able to see the opportunities for action. If you stay distraught, you will miss those opportunities.

| *Fourth Line*  **Lightning strikes mud.** | 震 九<br>遂 四<br>泥 ： | ▬▬ ▬▬<br>▬▬ ▬▬<br>▬▬▬▬▬<br>▬▬ ▬▬<br>▬▬ ▬▬<br>▬▬▬▬▬ |

Movements restrained. Progress inhibited. An unyielding situation.

Ambitions cannot be carried forward. The shock of unexpected and disappointing circumstances has reduced you to inertia.

Do not let your inhibitions hinder your progress. Push movement forward against the odds.

The fourth line can also indicate unlikely alchemy.

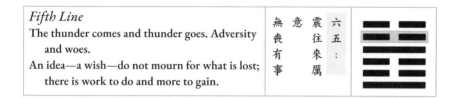

*Fifth Line*
The thunder comes and thunder goes. Adversity and woes.
An idea—a wish—do not mourn for what is lost; there is work to do and more to gain.

An unfavorable situation, but you need to persist forward. This is the Oracle saying to you: chin up, take the hits like a champ, then come back swinging.

Find the eye of the storm. That's the small region that remains calm at the center of a cyclone. Weather through the dangers from that center.

By maintaining a central position, you will stay safe through these shocks of fate. In the end, your losses will be mitigated.

Your work is not done. Your mission remains incomplete. After the storm, there are matters for you to attend to. Remain steady.

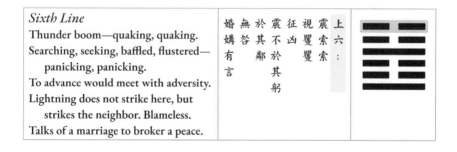

*Sixth Line*
Thunder boom—quaking, quaking.
Searching, seeking, baffled, flustered—panicking, panicking.
To advance would meet with adversity.
Lightning does not strike here, but strikes the neighbor. Blameless.
Talks of a marriage to broker a peace.

The first part of the sixth line conveys panic and anxiety. In such a state of instability, there is no point in attempting to move forward. Thus, before you can find your center and restore calm, stay put. Do not undertake any ambitious or heroic acts.

The forecast in the sixth line is that you are not the one who sustains the hit; rather, a neighbor, someone close to you, is the unfortunate one in the line of sight of the storm. Thus, you do not sustain irreparable harm from the adversity.

In statecraft, the sixth line offers counsel that the conflict between two states can be assuaged through the brokering of a marriage or accord. This is symbolic of a merger—when an adversary threatens your security, instead of attacking, propose an alliance.

The sixth line can be interpreted as an impending natural disaster, one brought on by angry gods. As long as you stay virtuous, god-fearing, and humble, the gods will spare you.

# Hexagram 52: Gěn. Listen to the Wind

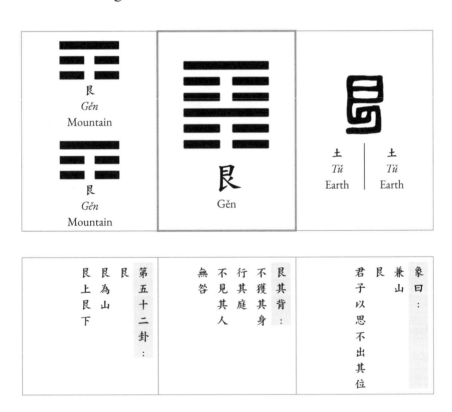

## *The Oracle*

Quiet your heart and be calm. Remember that even stillness can be a form of movement. The sage contemplates the situation in stillness. It is natural for the heart to fluctuate and a mind to flutter, but exercise restraint. Listen to the wind. That is how you will hear the answer to your inquiry—the wind will carry an important omen to you. Silence is the way to self-mastery. You show your strength to others when you sit tall like a mountain, walk with the formidable presence of a mountain, all the while calm and serene. Think before you speak. Silence is the way to prevailing in your endeavor. Present inaction paves the way for future gains.

---

**Be still like a mountain. The sage moves without moving. The sage advances and evolves, is changing by standing still.**
**Lying on the back—the body cannot move. Wandering into the courtyard—there is no movement.**
**No irreparable harm comes. There is no blame.**
Matters have come to a standstill. No movement or action. That's because you're in movement and trying to take action.
It is natural for the heart to fluctuate and a mind to flutter from thought to thought, especially in the aftermath of adversity, but exercise restraint and keep still.
You will hear the answer to your inquiry by listening to the wind.
Be still, with your back straight, in repose.
When you are lost, do not wander. Remain still and a path will be cleared.
In rest there is movement.
Hexagrams 51 and 52 are related. After the quake of Hexagram 51, Thunder over Thunder, *qi* changes into its inverse, Hexagram 52, Mountain over Mountain. Flip 51 upside down and you get 52, and vice versa. Hexagram 52 expresses the sentiment of seeking return to normalcy after a shock of circumstances.
"身" can evoke pregnancy or rise in social status. The preceding "其" is a neutral pronoun, which could mean his, her, its, their, that, or one. Thus, "不獲其身" *(bù huò qí shēn)* is a prognostication that there will be no

harvest, no manifestation or receiving of one's "身," be that a figurative reference to pregnancy or social status, or to a certain corpus, a person's body or body of work.

Finally, listening, as used in this context, is not about hearing, but about paying close attention and being attentive.

### OMEN OF THE *QILIN*

The *qilin* is a mythical beast that appears to portend a significant, transformative event relating to a sage or leader. In the I Ching, Hexagrams 2, 15, 23, and 52 are likened to the omen of seeing a *qilin* appear—these hexagrams are omens of a significant, transformative event to come, one relating to the near-future rise of a sage or leader.

Here, divining Hexagram 52 can portend a great awakening or epiphany, but one that is contingent upon the seeker heeding the counsel of Hexagram 52's lines.

### ASTRAL PROJECTION

In both Taoism and Buddhism, the mountain is often used as a metaphor for proper form in meditation. Thus, I interpret the lines "Lying on the back—the body cannot move. Wandering into the courtyard—there is no movement" as the Oracle offering instruction on astral projection. The lines are describing a mystical out-of-body experience. What's more, the progressing lines of the hexagram read like traditional step-by-step instructions for how to astrally project.

When Hexagram 52 comes up in divination by or for a Taoist mystic, bring the physical energy body to stillness to awaken the psychic or astral energy body. The Oracle becomes the voice of a spirit messenger, announcing that an astral journey will take you to an ascended master or divinity, who awaits with an important spiritual directive for you.

| *First Line*<br>The feet at rest, calm and tranquil.<br>No harm comes. Gains to come in steadfast passage forward. | 初六：<br>艮其趾<br>無咎<br>利永貞 |  |

The feet are symbolic of initial movement. Keeping the feet at rest is the Oracle's counsel to be patient and not engage. This is the omen of undertaking a journey without taking a single step.

In the matter at hand, stay steady without the intention of advancing. Instead of indulging ambition or desiring progress, seek to maintain the status quo. The paradox of intention and result will be that by intending to maintain the status quo, you shall advance and attain what you seek.

It is not yet time for you to engage. Rather than saying "a journey of a thousand miles begins with a single step," here the first line is telling you that your journey of a thousand miles begins with quiet contemplation of the journey.

| *Second Line*<br>The calves at rest, calm and tranquil.<br>No relief to their followers. The heart is not content. | 六二：<br>艮其腓<br>不拯其隨<br>其心不快 |  |

What's in the heart is not truthfully spoken. The secrecy and concealment are burdening. When you can't save yourself, how can you save those who depend on you?

Calf muscles support you when you stand. They are what enable movement. "腓 féi," while an anatomical reference to the calves, is also a reference to being ill or in a state of declining; so here, there is a halt to illness, and a state of decline has been put to a stop.

While one's own state of decline has come to a stop, unfortunately the predicament of those in a lesser position, and those who look to you as a leader, is growing dire. The circumstances are such that you do not have the ability to save them.

Feeling powerless to save them, your heart is discontented. You cannot be happy when others are in such a state of suffering, with no salvation in sight. "拯 zhěng" bears an undertone of salvation or being lifted up, raised.

The second line implies the Cassandra metaphor—one knows of an impending threat and tries to warn the people, but the people will not listen or don't believe the wise one. This is the unfulfilling position of knowing what will happen, desiring to prevent it, but not having the power of persuasion to keep it from happening.

| Third Line | | | | | |
|---|---|---|---|---|---|
| The midsection at rest, calm and tranquil. <br> Wounded back, cauterize the aching heart. | 厲薰心 | 列其夤 | 艮其限 | 九三： | |

The image of the third line is of sundered flesh along the backside, where your waist and loins are. Adversity and difficult circumstances have also damaged the heart, bearing the implication of a sharp object having been thrust there.

"限 xiàn" is a reference to a boundary, a threshold, a liminal space forming a veil. Anatomically, this is the waist, loins, back, and spine, or midsection of the physical body.

The third line is a quiet struggle, expressing a tragedy so big yet so small that there are no words, no means of comfort to lessen the pain.

If interpreting the lines through the lens of a mystic, then the third line reads like the critical transition point, shifting you from one realm or state of consciousness into the next. This is the entrance point. This is entering the courtyard by way of the astral body.

Your emotions resent the instruction to keep still. You are feeling a disquiet and distress that provoke you to move, as if movement can help you escape your feelings. Yet the Oracle is counseling you to hold still, calm and tranquil, perhaps the very words you do not want to hear right now.

| *Fourth Line*<br>The torso at rest, calm and tranquil.<br>No irreparable harm done. | 無 艮 六<br>咎 其 四<br>　 身 ： |
|---|---|

This is the image of one seated in meditation. Maintain repose to mitigate the harm. If you remain still, calamity will pass you by.

The torso is a reference to our anatomical center and site of our organs. This is what holds us upright.

Show restraint. Even when you are well within your rights to act, hold yourself back. Keep your composure.

The fourth line is a preemptive admonishment from the Oracle to not judge other people. Like the image of one in sitting meditation, focus on yourself, judge yourself. Do not give unsolicited advice, and do not concern yourself with whether another is contributing their part. Just make sure you contribute yours.

As a narrative progression of astral journeying, the fourth is a moment of personal achievement—you've successfully arrived at your intended destination.

| *Fifth Line*<br>The face at rest, calm and tranquil.<br>Keep your words in their proper order. Disappointments vanish. | 悔 言 艮 六<br>亡 有 其 五<br>　 序 輔 ： |
|---|---|

"輔 fǔ" is a reference to the cheeks and the surrounding skin of the mouth. The fifth line is counsel to keep your mouth at rest. Show restraint with your words. In fact, perhaps not speaking at all would be wisest.

The Oracle is reminding you to be judicious with your choice of words. Think before you speak, not the other way around.

There are few things more difficult than keeping silent about matters that are significant to you. Silence is therefore the most difficult abstinence.

Yet silence is the way to self-mastery. What's more, silence is the way to prevailing in your endeavor.

| Sixth Line<br>Desires and emotions at rest.<br>Attainment of great fortunes and the favor of the gods. | 上九：敦艮吉 |
|---|---|

At the sixth line, the epiphany is realized. Staying in a state of repose is the demonstration of a benevolent heart. When the one with a benevolent heart can stay at rest, great fortune and reward will come. Present inaction paves the way for future gains.

This is an affirmation of one who has tamed one's state of mind.

Desires and emotions at rest yield fruition and success.

## GOD OF THE UNDERWORLD, DONGYUE 东岳大帝

Hexagram 52 invokes Emperor Dongyue 东岳大帝 (Dōng Yuè Dà Dì), god of the underworld, and is also an omen of his presence. Emperor Dongyue is the god of Mount Tai, the sovereign ruler of all mountain gods and Taoist god of the underworld. The trigram Mountain is also associated with the deep caves in the mountainside that lead to the underworld.

In antiquity, the souls of the dead return to Mount Tai, so Emperor Dongyue was designated as a ruler of the underworld. Although he isn't one of the Eight Immortals, he's the first of all humans to have become immortal. In Mahayana Buddhism, he is a dharma protector, or a Guardian of the Law.

If Hexagram 52 becomes a recurring presence, the Taoist mystic might understand it as a call from the god of the underworld to appear before his court. Astrally journey to the underworld court of Dongyue, a journey that takes you on an ascent up a steep mountain to a cave, then into the cave and on a descent deep below the earth. The underworld is dark, cold, but dry.

Dongyue can also be invoked in mediumship readings to send and retrieve souls of the dead between the realms. Perhaps Hexagram 52 is an omen that the god of the underworld is calling to you, beckoning you to his court, for he has an important mission he'd like you to fulfill.

# Hexagram 53: Jiàn. Steadfast

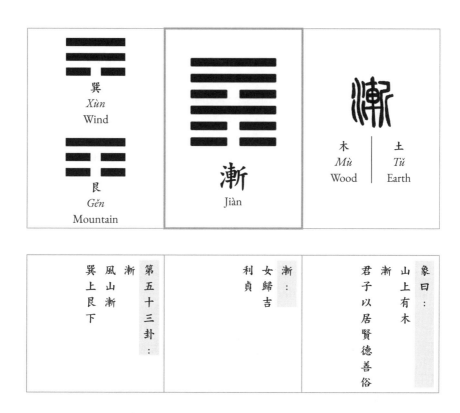

## The Oracle

Do not seek overnight success. Forgo instant gratification. A tree can grow at the peak of a mountain if it grows slowly and steadily, with deep roots. Building a strong foundation is more important than endeavoring for high branches. Do not try to change your nature; instead, embrace your nature. Play to your own strengths. You are at the beginning of a long journey. You find yourself in the midst of unfamiliar circumstances, and you will have to adapt quickly. Before you know for sure what you are up against, retreat to a position of safety. Slow and steady to the summit.

**A tree grows at the peak of a mountain, slowly, in accordance with the natural course of growth.** That is how the tree can establish firm roots deep in the soil of the mountain.

Grow slow and deep into the mountain, not fast and upward toward the sky. Stable roots and a strong foundation are more important to your endeavor than high branches.

**When faced with vulgarities, the sage responds with dignity, virtue, and benevolence.**

Slow, steady, and gradual development: progress one step at a time. Do not seek overnight success; forgo instant gratification. Do not be anxious when you see others appear to advance more quickly than you. Your success will come in time, and gradual success will be more enduring and powerful than their instant success.

**It is an auspicious time for the maiden to marry.** Matrimony brings prosperity. However, you must let the union develop in its own due time. Do not rush any engagements. Take small and honorable steps.

**Gains and favors bestowed.**

### THE LOVE AND ROMANCE HEXAGRAMS

There are four hexagrams that address romantic love and civil unions or marriage. Hexagram 31 refers to the mutual attraction and sexual chemistry experienced by the young couple in love. Hexagram 32 refers to long-term commitment and a civil union between two people.

Here, Hexagram 53 refers to the engagement and building the foundation of a relationship. Finally, Hexagram 54 refers to the propriety that must be maintained and the social conduct necessary for two in a civil union if that union is to endure.

# TOTEMIC ANIMAL SPIRIT OF THE WILD GOOSE/SWAN

The six lines of Hexagram 53 follow the narrative of a wild goose. The goose symbolizes loyalty and devotion in conjugal relations, and more broadly, represents teamwork, cooperation, and integrity.

Geese are said to mate for life and are protective of their mates and offspring. If a goose's loved one is injured, the goose will stay by the loved one's side, risking its own life, even when winter is coming, and will not join the flock in migration.

Geese also form communities, and when one member of the community is injured, there will be members who trail behind to care for the injured. When geese fly in the *V* shape, it is to reduce air resistance for the geese flying in the back so the group collectively can fly faster, farther, and more efficiently.

"鴻" is also the word for swan.

Thus, rather than being a narrative of a wild goose, Hexagram 53 can be interpreted as narrating the chronicle of a swan.

In both Chinese and Japanese myths, swans are spirit messengers between the celestial and human worlds. Used interchangeably, both the swan and the goose hold religious and spiritual significance in Zhou dynasty marriage rites.[53] Likewise, in traditional Korean marriage ceremonies, the groom's procession to the bride's house included a servant carrying a life-size statue or likeness of a goose, and once the procession arrived at the bride's home, the goose was symbolically placed atop a bowl of rice.[54]

The Khitan, a seminomadic people of the Korean peninsula who established an independent state along the northern borders of what is now Manchuria,[55] would sacrifice a white goose before the winter solstice as an offering to the gods.[56] The goose as a totemic animal spirit was a part of initiation rituals in Siberian shamanism.[57]

> *First Line*
> The wild swan dawdles toward the shore.
> Foreboding adversity for the young offspring.
> There is talk, but there is no blame.

You are at the beginning of a long journey.

You are lacking the support needed to assist you in your endeavor. You feel alone, like you are embarking on your journey alone. Not only do you feel alone, but others criticize your approach.

Although you lack experience, keep your pace slow and steady, focusing more on growing roots than growing branches, and in the end, you will prevail.

Though others criticize you, you make no errors. There are discussions, but no fault. You are in the right. Ignore what others say. Focus on growing those roots. It is not an unfortunate incident.

> *Second Line*
> The wild swan dawdles toward the boulder.
> A celebration with food and drink.
> Prosperity.

The boulder is a symbol of seeking shelter and safety. It's an omen of stability to come.

The Oracle affirms that you have built a proper, solid foundation. You now begin to enjoy the first signs of success after those initial difficulties.

Share your prosperity. Celebrate with others and display generosity, even to those who may have criticized you or declined support. Doing so will build their trust and devotion toward you. As you continue onward, such trust and devotion from those behind you will be highly advantageous.

You want to court loyalty and cooperation right now.

> **Third Line**
> The wild swan dawdles toward the highlands.
> A husband going on an expedition does not return. A wife becoming pregnant does not deliver.
> Hardships. Safeguard against those who invade and plunder.
>
> 九三：鴻漸于陸　夫征不復　婦孕不育　凶　利禦寇

The highlands represent infertile prospects. It is wiser for the swan to remain close to bodies of water. To dawdle toward the highlands, on plateaus that are dry and barren, is ominous for the wild swan.

The wild swan is foolishly ambitious.

The third line is an admonition to stay close to the herd, and do not wander alone too far from the flock, or you will get lost.

The parable of the husband setting out on a journey but not returning and a wife pregnant but not delivering represents ill-timed pursuits. The parable is an omen of good intentions that are improperly executed.

Furthermore, consider the context and why the Oracle tells the specific story of a husband and wife after the vision of the goose, a symbol of marital union. The implication is that at this particular point in time, neither the proverbial husband nor the wife are destined to be carrying forth their undertakings, and if it wasn't meant to be, then it wasn't meant to be. Instead of attempting to independently carry out separate ambitions, at this time, the two should be in harmonious union as one, a team.

Likewise, at this time the group needs to stay together as a group. Individuals ought not set out on their independent ambitions just yet. If instead of staying together as a group individuals wander off on their own, you'll leave the collective assets vulnerable to plunder. An outsider or interfering party will come in and exploit the situation, causing harm to all.

Right now it is better to be on the defensive than to be on the offensive.

The time is not right for trying to conquer something new (parable of the husband) or trying to create and develop something new (parable of the wife).

> *Fourth Line*
> The wild swan dawdles toward the woods.
> Perhaps it will find a log to perch on.
> No irreparable harm will come.

Rather than woods and a log, the fourth line has also been interpreted as the swan flying to a tree and then perching upon a branch.

An ambitious undertaking where you put yourself far outside your natural element will turn out well. To be more precise, the Oracle does not portend success but notes that there will be no disaster, and no harm will come from the ambitious undertaking.

Furthermore, the advice to give here is after having started the ambitious undertaking, once you realize you're out of your element and far from home, find somewhere stable to rest. In other words, yield to the situation rather than attempting an even more ambitious escalation.

> *Fifth Line*
> The wild swan dawdles toward the summit.
> For three years the one who conceives cannot conceive.
> Yet all will be well—good auspices.

When you achieve greatness and ascend to the summit, you will find yourself isolated and lonely. The higher you go, the more you realize how alone you are.

Be wary of deceitful people around you. Due to how high you have ascended, you are now a visible target for attack.

You have surpassed expectations, but be cautious of the darker aspects associated with success and achievement. Tread carefully toward that summit you've aspired to.

"歲" refers to Jupiter, and the god Tai Sui associated with Jupiter, symbolic of years. It's also a reference to the annual harvest. Each "歲" is one harvest, so a figurative reading of the line can be "three harvests," i.e., after three consecutive successes, the fourth will not yield fruition.

> *Sixth Line*
> The wild swan dawdles toward the highlands.
> Its feathers can be used for the sacred rites.
> Good auspices.
>
> 上九：
> 鴻漸于陸
> 其羽可用為儀
> 吉

If the first line of Hexagram 53 expresses the beginning of a journey, then here the sixth line expresses its end. Even an end is not an end, but rather, a transformation.

Feathers being used for sacred rites represents legacies.

The feathers are also a reference to the feathers worn during ceremonial rites and shamanic dance.[58] The mystic reads this as a divine call to perform a sacred rite, which will then assure that what you want to happen will come true.

"陸 lù" can be interpreted as the swan dawdling toward the shores, or the swan dawdling toward the highlands. Depending on the context, either can apply.

The sixth line prognosticates a harmonious union, marriage, or ascent in rank in one's career.

Good fortune for all.

The third and sixth lines mirror each other in structure. In the third, the wild swan dawdles toward the highlands, but the timing isn't right, so those who go off on independent endeavors fail in those endeavors while leaving the collective vulnerable to exploit. Thus, hardships ensue.

Here in the sixth line, the swan dawdles toward the highlands and achieves a greater spiritual purpose. Here, the timing is right.

# Hexagram 54: Guī Mèi. The Marrying Maiden

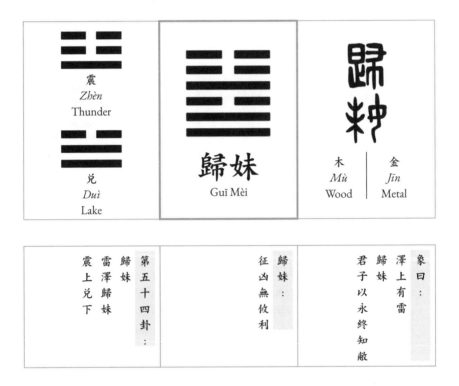

## The Oracle

Do not rush a life-altering commitment. Do not accept the first proposition that comes your way. A postponement can work to your advantage. Know your worth, and stand in that worth with modesty and sincere self-awareness. When you are strong in your sense of self-worth, you need not try to convince others of your value. Win your own approval first. In all matters, high or low, do not let them see you losing your composure. The undertaking will meet with great hardships, but the endeavor is well worth the pain endured—great advantages to be gained if you can overcome the adversity.

A change has come, beyond your control. You have been swept up by the tides of fate. What is happening at the moment is part of enduring the path to fulfilling a greater destiny.

**Thunder strikes the marshlands. The young maiden is wed.**

The marrying maiden is not the head wife; she is a concubine.

The current efforts you contemplate do not advance your endeavor. Circumstances did not turn out as you had hoped.

A disappointing situation. Feeling as if exhaustive efforts have been in vain. A sense of defeat. Lack of confidence in what is to come. Uncertainty abounds.

To break the perpetual cycle, bring it to its end. **The sage knows the only circumstance that is eternal is change.**

Embarking on a long journey in search of conquest. Prolonged efforts achieve the solution and break the cycle.

**Inauspicious—a bad harvest.** You begin powerless, but by the end, you will be the one holding the power. Use cleverness and cunning within the constructs of propriety and you shall prevail.

What you seek to achieve will call for great hardships to be endured. Are you ready for that? Think about the cost you are willing to pay for what you want to gain. **Be cautious and avoid proceeding unless you have determined that it is critical and necessary.**

At the moment you may find yourself in a position of low status. Do not be tempted to elevate your status through impropriety. Seek power through ways that are dignified and ethical. **Dispense efforts in moderation.**

## THE LOVE AND ROMANCE HEXAGRAMS

There are four hexagrams that address romantic love and civil unions or marriage. Previously in Hexagram 53, the Oracle narrates the engagement period and the foundation of a relationship.

Hexagram 54 refers to the mutual obligations that must be fulfilled for a civil union to thrive. *Guī* "歸" can mean to return or to seek patronage. The underlying *qi* is to move in the direction of convergence. The more archaic use of the word is to take a bride.

# THE LEGEND OF CHANG-ER AND HOUYI

While "知" *(zhī)* means to know, knowledge, and comprehension, the ideograph is of someone shooting an arrow straight toward a target, conveying the idea that knowledge and understanding strike like arrows shot from a bow.

Hexagram 54 is often interpreted as a reference to Chang-Er (嫦娥, Cháng'é), a folk Chinese goddess of the moon, and her husband, Houyi (后羿, Hòuyì), the archer who shoots down nine of the ten suns scorching the earth. Thus, I thought it would be apropos to highlight the etymological reference to shooting arrows behind the word that means "to know."

Note that the fifth line of Hexagram 12, 否 (Stalemate), also includes an allusion to Houyi and Chang-Er.

Chang-Er was a maidservant in the Jade Emperor's celestial palace in heaven. When she inadvertently broke a vase, she was punished by being sentenced to live out life as a mortal. As karmic punishment, she was born into a poor peasant family. However, her beauty captivated the attention of the gifted archer Houyi.

One day ten suns appeared in the skies, scorching the earth. To save humanity, Houyi shoots down nine of the ten suns, and for his heroic deed, is made king. Houyi becomes a corrupt, despotic ruler. He seeks to create the elixir of life so he can rule for eternity.

To save the people from a despotic king, Chang-Er takes the elixir of life and drinks it. In doing so, she floats up to the moon and lives there for eternity.

**FIGURE 8.7** *Chang-Er Flees to the Moon* (1868–1892) by Yoshitoshi Taiso. Woodblock print.

# THE LEGEND OF TAI SI, CONCUBINE WHO BECOMES EMPRESS

An alternative theory is that Hexagram 54 references Tai Si (太姒), King Wen's wife. In this mythical telling of the story, Tai Si was a maiden taken as one of King Wen's concubines, but he so loved her that Tai Si eventually became the empress and bore the king ten sons. She is the mother of King Wu of Zhou and the Duke of Zhou.

In all accounts, Tai Si is venerated as an ideal concubine, then queen, wife, and mother. When she first enters the Zhou royal palace as a concubine, she is humble and respectful toward the queen. She has the intelligence and wisdom to counsel her husband, King Wen, on matters of state, and to do the same later for her son King Wu. Tai Si is credited as the reason why her sons, such as King Wu and the Duke of Zhou, came to be such wise men. Tai Si was described as modest, avoiding opulence and dressing simply.

Hexagram 54's references would suggest that Tai Si is the sister (or daughter) of Emperor Di Yi, a good king of the Shang dynasty, and father to the corrupt King Zhou of Shang, who imprisons King Wen (technically his uncle-in-law or brother-in-law). Though historians have not been able to verify the accounts as narrated in Hexagram 54, according to the fifth line, Di Yi marries off his younger sister (or daughter) to King Wen of Zhou in hopes that doing so would maintain peace between the kingdoms.

Unfortunately, such hopes are not fulfilled, as the Zhou ultimately revolt and defeat the Shang.

*First Line*
Marrying the maiden as a concubine.
The crippled can walk.
Advancing is auspicious and yields fruition.

征跛歸初
吉能妹九
　履以：
　　娣

In the imperial court, a concubine ranks below the queen. If the concubine is modest and humble, and if she respects the queen's status, then the concubine will be welcomed into the family and can thrive.

Likewise, junior officials who remain modest and humble and who respect the senior officials can accomplish far more than the senior officials who try to assert their power.

A concubine who knows how to play to hierarchies can ascend the ranks in the natural course and achieve the same power as the queen.

Likewise, the junior official who plays to hierarchies can eventually assert even more power than the senior official. Seemingly severe setbacks do not deter you from achieving your objectives.

Win the confidence of a superior by being modest and humble.

Appear as if you blend into the background. Let another assert the appearance of authority.

Conceal your ambitions so as not to appear as a threat to those in power. By doing so, you can become the one with true power, orchestrating events to your will.

Influence the situation at hand by convincing those who hold superior titles that the idea was theirs all along.

Appear crippled and conceal that you can walk. Appear frail and fragile when you are strong and capable.

Sun Tzu's *Art of War* teaches cultivating and accruing power while concealing your power. Hide your skills under a cloak of feigned incapacity. Overestimate your adversaries and then be better than that overestimation, all while conducting yourself such that your adversaries underestimate you.

| Second Line<br>Blind in one eye; you can still see.<br>A solitary one advances forward. | 利 眇 九<br>幽 能 二<br>人 視 ：<br>之<br>貞 | ▬▬ ▬▬<br>▬▬ ▬▬<br>▬▬▬▬▬<br>▬▬▬▬▬<br>▬▬ ▬▬<br>▬▬▬▬▬ |
|---|---|---|

Currently you are not seeing the entire situation clearly, but you still see enough to assess the circumstances and take action.

You will still succeed at the undertaking.

Matters remain concealed, but you won't be deterred.

Appeal to the gods and petition them for assistance. Divination will reveal their answer.

| Third Line<br>The marrying maiden is cast aside.<br>She returns home and, in her place, her sister. | 反 歸 六<br>歸 妹 三<br>以 以 ：<br>娣 須 | ▬▬ ▬▬<br>▬▬ ▬▬<br>▬▬▬▬▬<br>▬▬ ▬▬<br>▬▬▬▬▬<br>▬▬ ▬▬ |
|---|---|---|

The outcome falls short of your expectations. Unfulfilled desires.

Nonetheless, accept the outcome for what it is. It may fall short of your expectations, but the matter can still end well for you. Do not be tempted to engage in improprieties or unethical behavior in an attempt to meet those expectations.

Let what happens happen. Do not try to manipulate the outcome.

| Fourth Line<br>The marrying maiden delays the marriage for a more proper time.<br>There are gains to be had in doing so. | 遲 歸 九<br>歸 妹 四<br>有 愆 ：<br>時 期 | ▬▬ ▬▬<br>▬▬ ▬▬<br>▬▬▬▬▬<br>▬▬▬▬▬<br>▬▬▬▬▬<br>▬▬ ▬▬ |
|---|---|---|

Do not rush a life-altering commitment. Hold out for better prospects to come.

Do not accept the first proposition that comes your way. A postponement can work to your advantage.

| | |
|---|---|
| *Fifth Line*<br>**Emperor Di Yi gives his sister in marriage.**<br>　　**His robes are not as well-embroidered**<br>　　**as the prince's.**<br>**The waxing moon is almost full.**<br>**A favorable outcome.** | 吉　月幾望　其君之袂不如其娣之袂良　帝乙歸妹　六五： |

Throughout imperial China, the embroidery on the robes of the aristocracy noted their rank and status. It would follow logic that the sitting emperor's robes must be better embroidered than a mere prince's. That the prince's robes are better embroidered is a prophecy that one day soon, that prince will outrank the sitting emperor.

The line is a reference to King Wen, who is then a prince, defeating the Shang dynasty, currently ruled by the elder Emperor Di Yi, the father to the corrupt last king of Shang.

The moon is currently waxing, which means the matter inquired about is in a progressive growth and development stage, moving toward final manifestation.

A waxing moon suggests the heights of success to come.

If read predictively, the fifth line is calling attention to the coming full moon. Another omen will come to you at that time.

An alternate translation of the fifth line is that rather than comparing Emperor Di Yi's robes to the unnamed prince's, the reference is to Tai Si the concubine (who later becomes queen). In the alternate translation, the robes that the concubine wears upon her person are not as beautiful as the robes that have been gifted as part of her dowry. That is to say she is worth more (her dowry) than she appears (what she's actually wearing). Such a reference would also echo the cultural depiction of Tai Si as modest and always dressing humbly.

A takeaway lesson from the parable of the fifth line would thus be that modesty and humility will pay off in the long run.

| Sixth Line<br>The maiden carries a basket, but the basket holds nothing of substance.<br>Sacrificing a sheep in ritual; there is no blood.<br>No harvest comes from the sacrifice. | 無攸利 士刲羊無血 女承筐無實 上六： | ䷥ |
|---|---|---|

When the sheep is sacrificed in ritual to petition the gods for a bountiful harvest, the sheep does not bleed, which is seen as a bad omen—the gods have not accepted the offering.

You've undertaken a fruitless endeavor.

## CONCLUDING THE LEGEND OF TAI SI

The sixth line is a continuation of the narrative in the fifth line. There were tensions between the Shang and Zhou states predating King Zhou of Shang and King Wen of Zhou. King Zhou of Shang's father, Emperor Di Yi, attempts to broker a peace between the two states by marrying off his sister (or perhaps his daughter) to King Wen of Zhou.

The efforts toward peace are fruitless. War breaks out between the states regardless, and the Shang dynasty is overthrown.

The woman carrying a basket is a reference to a traditional wedding custom of the bride presenting the groom with a basket of offerings. Here, the basket holds nothing of substance, suggesting that the groom gains nothing. During the Shang, blood sacrifices were made to the gods for a good harvest. The bloodletting during a ritual sacrifice was also believed to end disasters and to purify.

Thus the sixth line is considering the situation from the Shang's vantage point. The whole purpose of giving Tai Si in marriage to King Wen of Zhou was to broker peace. That purpose was not achieved. Emperor Di Yi's hope for peace was not fulfilled by the maiden.

## Hexagram 55: Fēng. Opulence

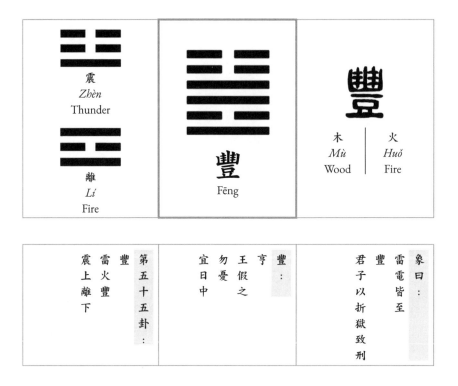

### The Oracle

Honors bestowed. There is progressive movement, and there is clarity in the mind. You are in a position of great influence. You rise like the sun at the highest point in the sky. Be mindful when abundance becomes opulence. When abundance becomes opulence, the king will fall. Every Age of Enlightenment comes to a decline. A period of tremendous power is upon you, but bear in mind that this, too, shall pass. Embrace the tides of change, come what may.

**Thunder and lightning: fullness for all.**

**The sage renders judgments and verdicts, handing down punishments that fit the crimes.** You are in a position of great influence, and you use your authority to bring justice.

**The king attains abundance and is free of worries. Prosperity and fortune at the noon hour.** You will reach great heights of success, like the sun at the highest point in the sky.

The inciting of movement brings light, clarity, and success.

However, abundance soon becomes opulence. When abundance becomes opulence, the king will fall. Thus, abundance comes in cycles; opulence comes in cycles. Every age of enlightenment will decline. Every king's reign will end.

To know when you have enough is to be immune from disgrace. To know when to stop is to be preserved from perils. Only thus can you endure for long.[59]

A period of tremendous power is upon you. A time of advancement: the height of social and civil progress. However, keep in mind that this, too, shall pass. What goes up will come down. Embrace the tides of change, come what may. Enjoy the moment of power and prestige while it lasts.

| *First Line* <br> Meeting their match. <br> For a while, no troubles. Endeavoring forth, the matter is yet to be valued. | 往有尚 雖旬無咎 遇其配主 初九： | ䷶ |

The subtext of "meeting their match" is that both are equally powerful rulers in their own rights. There is affinity. Moreover, the meeting is one of mutual benefit and opportunity.

Translated as "a while" here, "旬 xún" can indicate ten days or ten years; it's a general indication for a period of time. "尚 shàng" is translated as "valued," meaning the final accounting of lucks has yet to be assessed. There is still some uncertainty for the long-term future.

Xún 旬 is also a reference to the Shang dynasty god associated with the passage of time, corresponding with the ten-day week (the ten heavenly stems of lunisolar astrology) and the trigram Fire. Thus, the first line can be interpreted as an omen or call from a Fire god or the personification of Time.

To ensure long-term success, elevate the match to more than just a fair-weather friendship. Demonstrate loyalty, and loyalty will be reciprocated.

The matter you are consulting the Oracle for meets with tentative approval from the Oracle.

| *Second Line* | | |
|---|---|---|
| Opulence veiled. The Big Dipper and pole star are seen at noon. Casting suspicions spread like a disease. Inspire trust and faith. An auspicious outcome. | 吉 有 往 日 豐 六<br>　孚 得 中 其 二<br>　發 疑 見 蔀 ：<br>　若 疾 斗 | ▬▬　▬▬<br>▬▬　▬▬<br>▬▬▬▬▬<br>▬▬▬▬▬<br>▬▬　▬▬<br>▬▬▬▬▬ |

Interpersonal hostilities abound. The mistrust must be changed to trust for the matter to succeed. The forecast is that such will be achieved; thus, fruition.

Traditionally, the second line was interpreted to indicate a foreigner, or foreign relations. In state craft, this would be an international treaty or accord between two who are matched in wealth and resources, and who mutually harbor distrust for the other.

Alternatively, the second line might be expressing an outsider who comes in and becomes the leader of the pack. Now members of that pack are expression displeasure for the situation and do not trust an outsider to be leading them.

In the story of a king told through Hexagram 55, the second line offers some character development—this king is an outsider. To stay in power, the king will need to inspire trust.

A heavy veil cloaks the light—clarity, understanding, knowledge, and the right path are obscured. Mistrust and envy come to rule.

You can navigate the darkness by remaining sincere and truthful, no matter how the power struggle ends.

The second line is describing a solar eclipse that's occurring during the day. Thus, the sky is darkening and even stars like the Big Dipper and polestar are visible at noon.

| *Third Line* <br> Opulence swift upon them; abundance. The lesser constellations can be seen at noon. <br> Droplets of stardust glimmering in the sun. A misty veil over the light. <br> A broken right arm. No irreparable harm. | 無 折 日 豐 九 <br> 咎 其 中 其 三 <br> 　 右 見 沛 ： <br> 　 肱 沫 | ▬▬　▬▬ <br> ▬▬▬▬▬ <br> ▬▬　▬▬ <br> ▬▬　▬▬ |

The third line continues the narrative of the king. After reaching the heights of prosperity, the king's reign is now on the decline. The king is about to be overthrown. It is an unsettling time of changes.

That "lesser constellations can be seen at noon" suggests a darkened sky, significantly darker than the second line. The sky has darkened to the point where even the lesser constellations are now visible at high noon.

The solar eclipse narrative from the second line has now reached such occultation that the daytime sky is in total darkness by the third. This is a total eclipse. Day has become night.

The king calls upon a magus to reverse the eclipse and bring back the sun. The magus tries, but is unable to reverse the eclipse. The king breaks the magus's arm as punishment for the failure.

Though the final outcome has not passed yet, the story foreshadows that the eclipse will subside and the light will return, hence the yang line of the third. The magus is pardoned—thus, no irreparable harm.

The "misty veil" shrouds understanding, clarity, truthfulness, and integrity. Do not make your judgment of the situation yet, because you do not have all the facts. You do not yet know the whole truth of the matter, so refrain from taking sides.

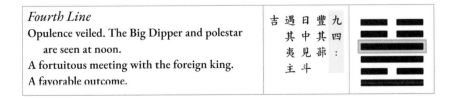

At the moment of the fourth line, the eclipse underway since the second line is still ongoing, though it is subsiding a bit—the phrasings in the second and fourth lines mirror each other, whereas the third line denoted the darkest point of the eclipse.

The worst is now over and it is the lightening of the dark, though at this point the sky is still in partial darkness, which means clarity, truthfulness, and integrity are still obstructed. However, the fourth line predicts that the darkness is finally coming to an end. Light is visibly returning.

An auspicious time for an alliance. Like the theme expressed earlier in the narrative arc, this is an opportune encounter between two equally capable kings.

In divination, "fortuitous meeting with the foreign king" is interpreted as a new opportunity coming your way. You're emerging from darker times, and soon a great offer with the promise of abundance and prosperity will present itself. The "foreign king" here is also a specific reference to an eastern tribe or clan. Thus, the king is from a land east of the inquirer.

| *Fifth Line* | | |
|---|---|---|
| Comes a new order, an enlightened period. | 吉 來章有慶譽 | 六五： |
| There is celebration and glory. | | |
| A favorable outcome. | | |

There is a new leadership. The old king of the preceding lines is overthrown. A new king ascends the throne. The new king has won the favor of the people.

The fifth line also suggests recruiting enlightened ministers to counsel the new king.

A period of prosperity for the kingdom. Full light has been restored.

| | | |
|---|---|---|
| *Sixth Line*<br>House of opulence. Installing curtains in the house. Peering out through the doorway.<br>Alone, in stillness—quiet—not another person in sight, for three years they see no one.<br>Foreboding adversity. | 凶　三　闃　闚　蔀　豐　上<br>歲　其　其　其　其　六<br>不　無　戶　家　屋　：<br>覿　人 |  |

The sixth line is a metaphor for hoarding and miserliness. One of wealth and riches puts up curtains so no one can look inside, then peers out through slats in the doorway. This person ends up alone, a recluse, isolated from the world for three years.

The image of the house is a tall fortress of a structure, and the family within it living isolated, in seclusion from the rest of society. In a reading, this could suggest elitism, snobbery, and arrogance, believing one to be so superior to others as to not even allow intermingling. As a result, there is a period ("three years") of stagnation, and no further prosperity is had.

Isolated, the miser exhausts the accrued abundance and ultimately loses everything.

The sixth line can also be interpreted as a metaphor for a gatekeeper or gatekeeping.

In Chinese astronomy, 蔀 *(bù)* is a cycle of seventy-six years. Nineteen years is one 章 *(zhāng);* four 章 is one 蔀; thus, one 蔀 is seventy-six years.[60] Therefore, an esoteric reading of "installing curtains in the house" from the sixth line might be that a 家 holds power or opulence for seventy-six years. 家 *(jiā)* can mean a family, a house (thus a clan), a school of thought, an ideology, a tradition, or a lineage.

## THE ECLIPSES OF 1088 BC AND 1070 BC

A total solar eclipse took place on June 19, 1088 BC, the longest total solar eclipse to have taken place in that century.[61] The longest annular solar eclipse of that century took place soon afterward, on December 25, 1089 BC. The eclipses would have taken place during King Di Yi's reign.

Di Yi's youngest son, King Zhou of Shang, takes the throne in 1076 BC. An eclipse that brought about darkness at noon was recorded on June 20, 1070 BC.[62]

Blending popular fiction with history, I'd like to imagine that, if King Zhou of Shang's offensive act toward the goddess Nǚwā had indeed taken place, then it fits the astronomical timeline to suppose that the 1070 eclipse was the day Nǚwā summoned the fox spirit to earth to corrupt King Zhou of Shang. The Battle of Muye happens in 1046, and the last king of Shang is defeated by King Wen's son, Wu of Zhou.

After the Zhou forces took the capital, the king of Shang hoarded his treasures all around him inside his palace, setting himself and the palace on fire. Perhaps that is alluded to by the lower Fire trigram of Hexagram 55.

Moreover, references to the Big Dipper in the second and fourth lines are significant, as the Big Dipper was considered the throne or chariot of Shangdi (上帝), the Supreme Emperor oft referenced in Shang dynasty oracle bones. The Big Dipper was considered the mark of death, as it was situated in the northern skies, the territory of the Black Tortoise. Thus, a total eclipse darkening the skies of day such that the Big Dipper in the northern skies would be visible at noon would have been interpreted as a fatal omen, especially for a king.

However, whether Hexagram 55 is in reference to either of these major eclipses is a matter for speculation.

# Hexagram 56: Lǚ. The Wanderer

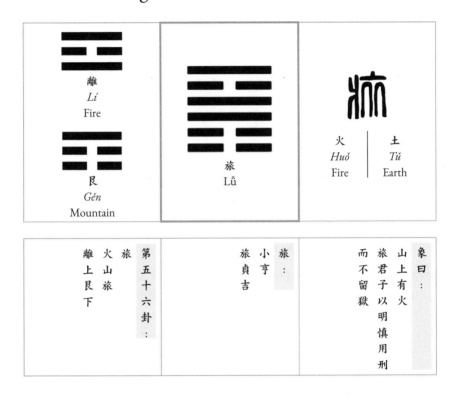

## The Oracle

The enterprising wanderer is a stranger in a new land, among unfamiliar people. Be knowledgeable and cautious. You are on a probationary period. To integrate yourself with the group, be humble, respectful of the group hierarchy, and let your humor be tactful. Be dignified. You are not yet familiar with inner politics, so do not engage in gossip and do not publicly declare loyalties just yet. Conceal your assets. Do not dismiss the oracle's warnings: stay guarded and protect yourself from those who want what you have.

Atop the Mountain, there is Fire. The wandering sage is knowledgeable and cautious.
Do not unduly punish others, and do not delay in hearing the cases.

One who was persecuted flees home and is now the wanderer, itinerant and traveling about; a peripatetic; a stranger in a new land.

**There are small gains to be had for the wanderer.** Go forth in your travels and you will find good fortune.

The theme of Hexagram 56 is a lack of home-court advantage. You are far from home. You are a stranger in these lands. Thus, many unexpected situations will arise, situations you might not be equipped to handle. Lacking cultural knowledge.

## THE LEGEND OF WANG HAI

Hexagram 56 is inspired by Wang Hai (王亥), the legendary wanderer who was clever, enterprising, wealthy, and a restless peripatetic. Wang Hai left his homeland and migrated to the kingdom of Yi.

In the kingdom of Yi, Wang Hai attains great prosperity raising sheep, and as a result, the Yi locals envy his wealth. The locals conspire to burn down Wang Hai's house and kill him to take his sheep. References to that are embedded in Hexagram 23.

Wang Hai is able to escape with his life, but he loses his flock of sheep, as referenced in the fifth line of Hexagram 34 (see "丧羊于易").

A resilient man, he rebuilds his fortune by raising cattle, and the invention of the yoke is even attributed to him. However, the locals do finally succeed at usurping Wang Hai's wealth, and here in the sixth line of Hexagram 56 (see "丧牛于易"), Wang Hai loses his cattle.

According to a chronicle of ancient China found in the *Bamboo Annals,* Wang Hai is the ancestor of the Shang dynasty, and he lived six generations after Yu the Great.[63] He's credited with developing the concept of the merchant. The Shang clan advanced in both agriculture and animal husbandry, enjoying a surplus, and Wang Hai came up with the idea of taking that surplus to neighboring clans for trade. He was, in summary, an ancient Chinese traveling businessman.

| First Line | 斯 旅 初 |
|---|---|
| The wanderer—*suo, suo!* | 其 瑣 六 |
| foolish and full of swagger, | 所 瑣 ： |
| strays upon disaster. | 取 |
|  | 災 |

You've reached beyond your means and have digressed from your own Path.
   Where you've wandered to, you've invited trouble.
A misadventure.
"瑣" *(suǒ)* translates to petty, trivial, and insignificant, though it can also be
   used as an onomatopoeia, to mimic the sound of ancient money clinking
   as a person walks. Jade or bronze replicas of cowrie shells would be strung
   together on a cord and carried on the person, with the cord acting like a
   wallet.
The sound *suo, suo* implies that the wanderer is moving with arrogance and
   swagger, causing all the money in the wallet to clink loudly for all passersby to hear. Basically, an ancient Chinese way of flexing (showing off).
   Here is someone acting upon foolish ambition. "Stray" conveys that
   the wanderer has deviated from the right path[64] and gone beyond the
   wanderer's personal limitations.
"災" *(zāi)* is the ideogrammic compound image of flooding and fires.

| Second Line | 得 懷 旅 六 |
|---|---|
| The wanderer comes upon a guest house. | 童 其 即 二 |
| Money held close to the bosom, the wanderer | 僕 資 次 ： |
|    hires a child servant. | 貞 |
| Stay on the virtuous path. |  |

There is one last clear chance to avert trouble. Stay modest, be prudent, be kind.
The second line can also prognosticate travel.
In contrast to the wanderer in the first line who is flaunting wealth, the wan-
   derer of the second line conceals it. Be humble about your capabilities.
      Being modest will gain you trust and acceptance.
In statecraft, when navigating a new environment, earn the trust and loyalty
   of assistants. Retain support from the locals, those who are young and still

naïve about interpersonal politics. Doing so can help ensure success and acceptance in the new environment.

| Third Line<br>The guest house that the wanderer stays at is burned to the ground.<br>Mourning over the misfortune of the child servant.<br>Brewing troubles. | 旅焚其次 喪其童僕 貞厲 九三： | ▬▬▬<br>▬ ▬<br>▬ ▬<br>▬▬▬<br>▬▬▬<br>▬ ▬ |
|---|---|---|

Losing support and favor, tensions between peoples, redressing a wrong with more wrong. Forgiveness is the only way to redress the wrong.

Efforts to rebuild relationships are in order. Demonstrate sincere care for and interest in others. Then they will care for and be interested in you.

One must be the first to step forward to forgive. If there is no such one, then the storm that comes will ravage all.

The translation describes the child servant's fate euphemistically as "misfortune." The original line implies death.

The guest house is symbolic of a migrant or immigrant community living within the kingdom. That it's burned to the ground suggests that they are unwanted visitors, inciting such vitriol from the locals that they are willing to burn down the village guest house. There's collateral damage—one of their own, the child servant, dies from the violence.

In the first line, an outsider's conduct came across as overbearing and boorish to the locals. The guest house represents a particular group, institution, or community. The house burning to the ground represents being unwelcome. When one is a guest, one must be respectful to the host. But a host retaliating by burning down their own house (harming their own institutions) will result in misfortune to that group's most vulnerable, represented by the child servant.

| Fourth Line<br>The wanderer builds a shelter. Gaining in fortune. Obtaining a hatchet.<br>My heart is sorrowful. | 旅于處 得其資斧 我心不快 九四： |  |
|---|---|---|

Seeking acceptance in a new environment, but hiding away and wielding a hatchet. Your actions are not helpful in achieving your goal.

Continuing the parable of the wanderer, there is now shelter, increase in material resources, and a weapon. Yet there is a tone of lament in the first-person perspective of the fourth line.

You are resourceful in your new environment, and in spite of earning little help or support from the group, you manage to stand on your own two feet anyway.

Gains in resources suggest that opportunities arise for you, and obtaining a hatchet suggests that you are becoming self-sufficient. The hatchet can also be used for self-defense, suggesting that you are not yet secure or safe in your new environment.

Threats against you still loom, and you must be careful and alert. You are a stranger to them.

There is a profound loneliness expressed in this line. Material success is not enough. You still seek something of the heart.

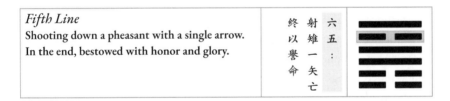

*Fifth Line*
Shooting down a pheasant with a single arrow.
In the end, bestowed with honor and glory.

A striking accomplishment wins respect. You are finally accepted by the group. An omen of glory and advancement in social status.

The wanderer in the narrative of the fifth line finally earns the respect of the locals. Shooting down a pheasant with a single arrow represents an impressive act.

The pheasant in Chinese cosmology symbolizes ambition, honor, and fame, as well as innovation and progress. It also corresponds with Fire.

*Sixth Line*
A bird burns its nest.
At first the wanderer laughs,
but then weeps loudly, lamenting.
Lamenting and mourning the loss of his cows in the kingdom of Yi.
Foreboding adversity.

At the position of the top line of the upper trigram Fire, the image is of past hard work in flames.

The bird is symbolic of a message or omen. The wanderer overlooked all of the earlier omens presented and now is in dire circumstances. Thus, the sixth line is a caution to heed the omens.

Written with syntax from a bygone time, speculations on the meaning of "鳥焚其巢 niǎo fén qí cháo" hold that it means either "the bird burns its nest" or "the bird's nest is burning." Also, it's not entirely clear whether we're talking about a bird in the singular or birds in the plural.

This question of bird or birds is worth considering because if we follow lore, the mention of a cow in the latter portion is in the plural in reference to Wang Hai's loss of his cattle. Since the possessive pronoun "其" referring to the subject "鳥" is neutral, the line could be bird/it or birds/they.

The translation here is to the bird burning its own nest as a reasonable speculation for why, in the next passage, the wanderer is laughing and then crying.

The wanderer is a passerby who observes a bird making a grave, unintentional error that, as a result of the bird's mistake in judgment, causes its own nest to go up in flames.

The wanderer laughs at the irony. The wanderer is also laughing because he, too, made the same grave error in judgment. He was too arrogant, and so his room and board went up in flames like the little bird's nest. But then the wanderer is reduced to tears, because the loss was tragic. He mourns both the bird's loss and his own loss of cattle. The account of what happened to the wanderer in the preceding five lines suggests that the story of the bird and the burning nest mirrors his own experience. That's why he both laughs and cries.

The pronoun "his" is used here in reference to the parable of Wang Hai, who lost his cattle in the kingdom of Yi.

Also, "易" here, in addition to referencing the kingdom of Yi, happens to be the same word for the Book of Changes, I Ching (Yi Jing).

# Hexagram 57: Xùn. Use Gentle Force

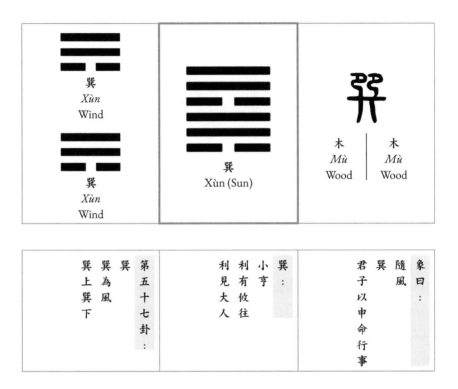

## The Oracle

The power you exert must be a gentle force. The wind is powerful because time is its power. The wind uses time to accomplish all endeavors. So you, too, like the wind, must use time to accomplish your endeavor. Be the unseen influence. The magus casts a spell that will produce an unseen influence. Whether the warrior advances or retreats, both decisions will bode well so long as the decision is made with conviction. One must delve below the surface, perhaps into the unconscious mind, to understand the situation at hand. Do not change paths time and time again. Open your heart-mind to Heaven. You'll be led to the right course of action. Take that path, step by step, the same path time and time again. The wind is favorable. Small gains to be had.

**Follow the order that has been predestined. The sage is given a decree.**
Submit to the direction of the winds.
A favorable wind—there are small gains to be had. **A journey will be auspicious. Go forth to see the eminent one.**
There is a need for self-correction. The sage's destiny is to embody the eminent one.
The sage cultivates wisdom, learning that the relationship between the eminent one and the people is like that between the wind and the grass. The grass bends to the will of the wind.
The wind is powerful because time is its power. The wind uses time to accomplish all endeavors. You, too, like the wind, must use time to accomplish your endeavor.
"申," *shēn,* is one of the earthly branches and is a timing reference. It corresponds with the zodiac sign Monkey. *Shēn* could relate to the seventh lunar month, corresponding approximately with August through September.
The ideogram "巽" *(xùn)* depicts two people sitting side by side on a table.
"共" also means to share, to be together. Considering the meaning of the hexagram, the most probable meaning for the word is that of peace talks, negotiation, conference, and accord.
Thus, Hexagram 57 and "巽" refer to soft power, shaping people's cultural and political values to shape culture and politics.

| *First Line* |
|---|
| Advancing and retreating. |
| The warrior utilizes military strategy and follows an honor code. |

The warrior raises a sword in defense only, and for just cause. One first advances along the correct path, but then chooses to retreat, turn, and walk away from the sun.
The ideogram 武 depicts a soldier raising a blade in defense. The etymological root of the ideogram 退 suggests one walking away from the sun, in retreat.

Do not let your mind vacillate like the wind. Rather, be the wind that moves and influences others. The wind uses soft force to sway, not the hard edge of the blade.

Any direction the warrior goes, whether advancing or turning back to take another path, the Divine is with you. Auspicious to go in any direction, so long as the warrior exemplifies a code of honor and utilizes military strategy.

| *Second Line* <br> A gentle force moves beneath the bed. <br> Call upon the scribe and the shaman. <br> To disturb, to obey; to dispute, to comply; in this way—auspicious to proceed. <br> There is no blame. | 無 紛 用 巽 九 <br> 咎 若 史 在 二 <br> 　 吉 巫 床 ： <br> 　 　 　 下 | ䷸ |

Commanding the power of the universe, one changes the path of nature.

Exert willpower and petition spirit forces to assist in the endeavor. Summon both the inner scribe and the inner shaman to command nature. Will the forces to change course in your favor. To create enduring change, the wind must change from the foundation.

The narrative of the warrior that began in the first line continues.

Note also that the trigram Wind is assigned the archetype of the Shaman.

More commonly, the second line is interpreted as only referencing a shaman. However, in archaic uses, "史" also represented a court historian or scribe. The original ideogram depicts a hand holding a brush pen. It then later developed the meaning of "to send for, to employ."

"史巫 shǐ wū" could also be interpreted as "magi and witches."

The second line can also be interpreted as a reference to dreamwork, lucid dreaming, or astral shamanic journeys in your dream state.

The ambiguity of juxtaposing "紛 fēn," which means to disturb, to dispute, or disorder, and "若 ruò," to obey, to be compliant, has left this line rather open for interpretation.

| *Third Line* <br> Frequent and repeating, the gentle forces. <br> Adversity. | 頻 九 <br> 巽 三 <br> 吝 ： | ䷸ |

Unsuccessful and yet unchanging. Endeavor for corrective measures.

The image of the third line is of one who tries to persuade another through repeated soft appeals but not getting through to them. Yet instead of changing strategy, the same unsuccessful strategy is tried over and over. Thus, a disappointing outcome. Difficulties ensue.

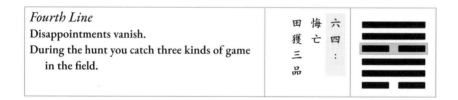

*Fourth Line*
Disappointments vanish.
During the hunt you catch three kinds of game in the field.

A forecast of a good hunt. Glory earned from the merits you've demonstrated in your field of work. Past troubles are left behind you.

All past disappointments and challenges disperse from this great success.

You attain three "品 pǐn," essentially three articles of value. Alternatively, it reads as you advancing by three ranks. Yet this could also be a reference to having caught three animals during a hunt. That could be three different kinds of game or just three in number.

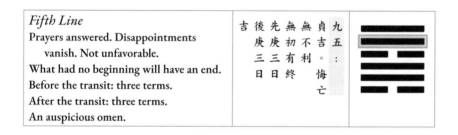

*Fifth Line*
Prayers answered. Disappointments vanish. Not unfavorable.
What had no beginning will have an end.
Before the transit: three terms.
After the transit: three terms.
An auspicious omen.

Social ills call for social reform. For change to occur peacefully and in a manner that the people can accept, there must be a trine of time in advance of the change to prepare the people, and there must be a trine of time after the change for them to acclimate.

What you did not start, you will end.

"日 rì" is more commonly translated to "days," in which case the line would read three days before the event horizon and three days after. To clarify that it's more likely to be figurative, it's translated as "terms" here. 日 is the image of the sun. Work with that symbolism to consider how it applies to the matter inquired about.

"庚" *(gēng)* is one of the ten heavenly stems. It is ruled by Metal and expresses maturation, autumn, the west wind, or twilight hours. It can also be symbolic of a battle victory or event likened to a battle victory. Here, I've opted to translate it as an astrological transit. The transit signifies a decisive moment from which there cannot be a full return—a life-changing or course-altering event that results in a directional shift.

This line can be interpreted as a regime change, passing rulership from one to another.

The Oracle is alerting you to pay attention. Shifting forces in play three days (or terms) before the event horizon and three terms after will give you a window of opportunity to create any change you want.

| Sixth Line<br>A gentle force moves beneath the bed. Mourning one's fortune and grief over a hatchet. Foreboding adversity. | 貞 喪 巽 上<br>凶 其 在 九<br>　 資 床 ：<br>　 斧 下 |  |
|---|---|---|

The image of the sixth line is of a crown prince staging a coup to assassinate his father, the king. Alternatively, it's one political faction trying to overthrow another. The theme is an attempt at a regime change, but it is unsuccessful.

Do not be impatient with change. To use gentle force means to use soft power. Create the social or political change you seek through soft power, not by force. An ominous forecast for one who seeks change by force.

The sixth line can also forecast a volatile economy or an unstable society.

Recall from the fourth line of Hexagram 56, the wanderer gains a fortune and a hatchet. In contrast, here in the sixth line, the warrior mourns over a fortune and a hatchet. "喪" bears an implication of misfortune befalling, or a misadventure.

Meanwhile, "a gentle force moves beneath the bed" mirrors the earlier second line.

### OLD WOMAN OF THE WINDS 風婆婆

Hexagram 57 invokes Fēng Pópo 風婆婆, or Madame of the Winds, a crone goddess of the winds and storms. She rides upon a tiger and carries the winds in a magical sack. Fēng Pópo is a grandmother-like figure who can be both gentle and powerful. She'll bring you blessings, lost objects, and that which you need most, and she can also wreak havoc when angered.

Perhaps the eminent one referenced in the reading is old Madame Wind inviting you to call upon her for divine assistance.

## Hexagram 58: Duì. Joyous Exchange

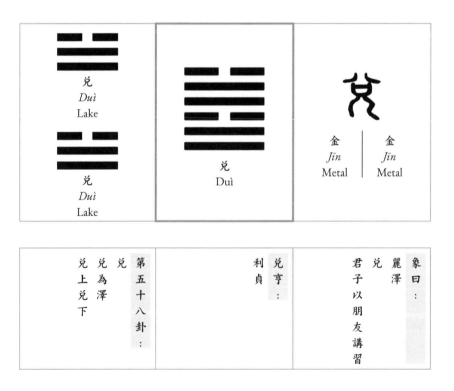

## *The Oracle*

> Inner light shines outward and attracts a kindred spirit. To seek joy is to seek discourse that will advance knowledge and deepen your compassion. To maintain joy, engage in lively intellectual discourse with your peers. Exchange and interchange are the themes du jour. A new experience brings joy. Reach out to old friends, and connect heart to heart. Engage in that which is fun. May your mind be pure so joy follows as a guardian angel.

**A serene lake. Joyous exchange. The sage engages in discourse and study with friends.**
**Prognostication of success—a favorable outcome.**
Win over the hearts of others through your friendliness, not by force.
A lake on its own evaporates sooner. Joined together, they replenish each other. Such is the way of knowledge. Learning on your own is not enough; amplify that education by studying further with others.
Sharing knowledge. Insights cross-pollinate. Sign of benevolence.
A final, gentle warning: remain guarded when you share your joy or exchange knowledge. No matter how sincere you are, there will be those who seek to exploit your knowledge.

| *First Line* <br> A harmonious exchange. <br> Auspicious. | 初九: 和兌吉 |
|---|---|

An exchange of kind, gentle words. An exchange of peace. Reconciliation.
Direct, honest conversations. Knowledge is shared and thus amplified. All parties are enriched. The path you walk is virtuous, and the joy you achieve is sincere.
The virtues of conscientiousness, gentleness, and generosity of spirit are prevalent.

| Second Line | 悔 孚 九 |
| --- | --- |
| An exchange in confidence. Auspicious. Disappointments vanish. | 亡 兌 二　吉 ： |

An exchange that fosters mutual trust; an exchange to persuade and influence.
Know who you can trust; you must be able to distinguish between those who seek you out to exploit your knowledge and those who can share knowledge with you in a mutual, rewarding exchange.

| Third Line | 來 六 |
| --- | --- |
| Arriving for an exchange. Foreboding adversity. | 兌 三　凶 ： |

Unfinished conversations. Lacking reciprocity. One-sided exchanges. Forecast of delays.
The third line is interpreted as reliance on external stimuli for joy, mirth, and merriment. Enduring, sustainable joy must come from within.
When the inner self is not stable, external stimuli for joy can quickly become temptations, which can lead you astray in your quest for knowledge and truth. Do not look to others for comfort or reassurance.

| Fourth Line | 介 商 九 |
| --- | --- |
| Trade and commerce before the full moon—a tipping point. In between melancholy there is joy. | 疾 兌 四　有 未 ： 喜 寧 |

A business deal goes well. And yet the feeling is one in between melancholy and joy.
Contemplating the exchange and feeling restless. Confronting that restlessness and the ailments in the heart is how you find peace.
You are plagued by indecision, and that feeling of indecision causes anxiety.

To dilute those feelings of anxiety, you seek festivities and pleasures, but that melancholy remains wedged within the festivities. It will fester until it becomes disease.

If you want to find inner peace, then you must confront your anxieties.

The fourth line is expressive of one in search of happiness, looking in all the wrong places, and finding instant gratification instead.

The first part, "商兑未宁 shāng duì wèi níng," includes an innuendo referring to the Shang dynasy. Knowing the legend of Wang Hai, an ancestor of the Shang dynasty, and Wang Hai's importance to the Shang adds a depth to the word "商," which means trade, business, and commerce. *Shāng* 商 means business, but it also refers to the Shang clan. Wang Hai was said to have invented trade and commerce. A summary of Wang Hai's legend was provided with Hexagram 56.

"未" is one of the twelve earthly branches in the lunisolar calendar system, corresponding with late summer and the zodiac sign of the Sheep. "未" also signifies a waxing moon phase, right before it enters the full moon. Thus, here the passage is translated to "tipping point."

In fortune-telling, the line can forecast an unexpected pregnancy that leaves the parents uncertain how to feel.

| *Fifth Line*<br>**Trusting that which should not be trusted.**<br>**There is danger ahead.** | 有孚 九<br>厉 五<br>于 ：<br>剥 |
|---|---|

Naïve exchanges. Lacking due diligence or having acted hastily, an exchange took place that should not have happened.

You are associating with destructive people. Negative influences push you off your path and toward peril.

Others are using your knowledge for ill intentions. Be careful that those closest to you are not exploiting you.

| *Sixth Line*<br>**Inducing the exchange.** | 引 上<br>兑 六<br>： |
|---|---|

An exchange gone awry; mirth and merriment go astray.

An imbalanced exchange or relationship where one enables the other to pursue self-destructive tendencies. One side is self-sacrificing in excess.

Mirth must come from within and emanate outward. You cannot seek out mirth from external sources and hope that it will penetrate inward to affect your heart.

The heart must sustain its own mirth. Otherwise, it runs the risk of exposing the spirit to temptations and evil.

The sixth line warns of deception. People pretty up their words and flatter or delude you. This is an omen of manipulation or under-the-table negotiation tactics.

Cultivate a stronger sense of self-worth. If you don't even know what you're worth, why are you bargaining for an exchange?

## Hexagram 59: Huàn. Making Waves

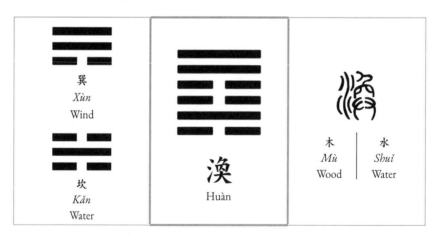

## *The Oracle*

A very important task is at hand, and to make waves, you will be the driver of the forces. Like wind breaking waves, a voice of reason, virtue, and compassion rises to reform what is broken and severe. Omen of one with a strong sense of purpose, who understands exactly what must be done to make waves and create necessary change. Set aside personal interest and pursue public interest. Heaven seeks you as a vessel to carry forth its mission. Dispel what has been oppressive. Honor the gods and ancestors to receive further insight: prayer, petitions, meditation, and music.

**The Wind pushes the Water upward:** subtle thoughts and intentions push forward. It is auspicious to cross the great stream and take risks: an auspicious omen. Thoughts beget movement.

**To commune with the gods, the first kings made offerings and built temples to honor Shangdi, the Sovereign of Heaven.**

A boat traverses across the river. Wind disperses the water, rocking the boat forward.

**Auspicious to cross the great stream.**

A cold wind chills the water to ice. A fevered wind will melt it. Likewise, when you are cold, all that you disperse is cold. When you are warm, all that you disperse is warm.

Who you are is what you create in this world. **A favorable omen.**

The hexagram name "渙" initiates the second through fifth lines, creating a dactylic pattern. In these instances, the single word is translated into a phrase: "渙" becomes "like wind breaking waves."

The story of Hexagram 59 features a protagonist horse who is introduced in the first line and then implied in the second through sixth lines. The "wind's breath on wings of water" is the image of the horse in movement and an image of the totemic horse's power.

# SHANGDI, THE SUPREME BEING IN THE I CHING

The "帝" *(dì)* in the Oracle message refers to Shangdi 上帝 (Shàng Dì), or the Heavenly Emperor. Hexagram 59 reveals the presence of Shangdi as the voice of the Oracle.

"Shangdi" means "Supreme Sovereign" or the highest god in Heaven per Shang dynasty theology. There is one other reference to Shangdi in the original Zhouyi, and that is in the second line of Hexagram 42, Burgeoning, 王用享于帝吉, noting that even earthly kings must humbly submit to the Great Lord in Heaven.[65]

For clarity, the "Shang" 上 of Shangdi is not the same as the "Shang" 商 of the Shang clan. 上 means high or above. Today, 商 has evolved to mean business, trade, and commerce. The ancestor of the Shang, Wang Hai, was the first or at least the most famous ancient Chinese merchant. 商人, which once meant "one from the Shang," now means merchant or businessperson.

According to Shang oracle bones, yearly sacrifices are made to Shangdi and had been made even before the times of the Xia (2070–1600 BC), the dynasty preceding the Shang.

Unlike other gods in the pantheon who would descend to earth to help mortals, Shangdi is considered to be beyond our capability of understanding. The god is Tao, and Tao is everything, so Shangdi is everywhere, and yet nowhere, because the god is separate and apart from this universe. The universe is but Shangdi's creation.

The Heavenly Emperor doesn't appear to us and has no human-like (or animal-like) form. Instead, the high god communes with humans through messenger gods, spirits, and our ancestors. Ancestors often transmit messages to us from Shangdi.

Shangdi is often used interchangeably with Heaven (天, *tiān*) and Heaven with Shangdi. Throughout the I Ching, references to Heaven are self-referential by the Oracle to Shangdi. The word "Shangdi" itself is descriptive, *shang* meaning high and *di* meaning god or sovereign; *shangdi* describes a deity who dwells above.

> As for powers, the high god is considered omnipotent and omniscient, ordaining all events—past, present, and future—in the cosmos. It's likened to the Tao (道). Like Shangdi, the Tao is described as the "the origin of all things. . . . It unties all tangles, it harmonizes all lights, it unites the world into one whole. Hidden in the deeps, yet it seems to exist forever. I do not know whose child it is; it is the common ancestor of all, the father of all things."⁶⁶

| | |
|---|---|
| *First Line*<br>**Rescued by a strong horse.**<br>**Auspicious.** | 初六：<br>用拯馬壯吉 |

A blessed appearance comes to save the day.

An image, statue, or effigy of a horse represents social or career advancement. Historically, such a gift would be given as a blessing for a student to pass the imperial examinations and become an official. Horses are associated with business, entrepreneurship, pragmatism, and diplomacy, as well as the hopeless romantic—one who would leave it all behind for that one true love.

The image here is of an injured person who climbs atop a horse and drives it forward in full gallop across a stream. The wind and force created by the horse splashes and disperses the water.

The first line is the same passage as the latter portion of the second line of Hexagram 36, the darkening of the light. It is thus implied that an injury has occurred, but one is rescued by the horse.

The ambiguity of the original line has given rise to two diverging interpretations: one rescues a strong horse, and that is auspicious; or one is rescued by a strong horse, which is auspicious. Here, both the second line of Hexagram 36 and this line are interpreted as using a horse to rescue oneself from a precarious situation.

| | | |
|---|---|---|
| *Second Line*<br>Like wind breaking waves, a horse escapes from the stall.<br>Disappointments vanish. | 悔 渙 九<br>亡 奔 二<br>　 其 ：<br>　 机 | 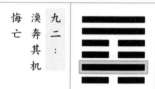 |

A horse breaks free of its stall and gallops away, its hooves dispersing the waters, splashing as it dashes toward freedom.

The second line can express someone unjustly confined who has broken free. The rider leaps atop the horse and escapes. You catch your moment and you are set free. You sever old bonds.

As horse and liberated rider hasten across a stream, they make waves.

Release from a period of confinement. Severing old bonds that were tying you down.

In mundane divinatory readings, the second line is interpreted as leaving a dead-end job and finally transitioning into a career that's more aligned with your life purpose, or finally leaving a stifling relationship; thus, while it is about the end of a situation, that situation was harming you, so the end result is beneficial.

| | | |
|---|---|---|
| *Third Line*<br>Like wind breaking waves, one's body cuts like a spear.<br>There is no blame. | 無 渙 六<br>悔 其 三<br>　 躬 ： |  |

The third image is of one diving into the waters to save those who are drowning.

A hero, one of generous spirit, gives what is received and helps wherever possible.

In the matter at hand, think beyond personal interests. Think about a greater collective's well-being.

To walk the path of virtue, one must be loyal, and to be loyal means to be brave. Bravery means sacrifice, and in sacrifice, love and trust are forged. In love and trust, one's body feels graced by Divinity.

A very important task is at hand, and you are the driver of the forces.

The third line describes a heroic act, someone putting another's interest or life before one's own; this is transcending self-interest. The overarching theme from Hexagram 59 is that of having faith in providence—when you serve a greater good, a greater power will be there to provide for you. There is never any loss in generous giving.

*Fourth Line*
Like wind breaking waves, separating from the flock. Supreme good auspices.
Brimming and overflowing upon the hill, the heretics deluge the mound with their grievances.
Such waves lead to graves. The dishonorable are none the wiser.

六四：
渙其群
元吉
渙有丘
匪夷所思

The fourth line expresses dissent, but how does one go about dissenting?

Dispersing from the flock to stand independent and free-thinking: that's good, according to the Oracle. The fourth line endorses civil disobedience, if it is aligned with Heaven's Will.

Causing a riot to overflow in numbers and dispersing a torrent of grievances such that, from afar, the gathering people resemble a hill: that's not good, according to the Oracle.

The latter form of dissent will lead to tragedy, one that doesn't hurt the dishonorable ones but only the innocent. The sage must have the wisdom and compassion to prevent tragedy from happening to the people. The people partaking in that mound are innocent; those with another agenda who have led them there are not.

The spirit behind and justification for the dissent are aligned with Heaven's Will. The method of dissent must also align with Heaven. To align with Heaven, every measure must be taken to reach an accord.

The minister of peace is one who can draw both groups to the center point between them. Set aside personal friendships and adjudicate objectively, fairly, and impartially.

Setting aside translation, even the interpretation of "匪夷所思 fěi yí suǒ sī" could go in very different directions. We could be talking about robbers, bandits, thieves, and outlaws, or the people from the kingdom of Yi, or the dishonorable. We could also be talking about rioters. And is it a mound, a hill, the village square where the people are gathering in protest, or a gravesite?

Here, two different interpretations of "匪夷所思" are provided in the second and third paragraphs. Instead of "robbers and bandits," the word choice was "heretic," to express that the dissenters are those who refuse to conform to the establishment.

| *Fifth Line* | |
|---|---|
| Like wind breaking waves, sweating—the sovereign's royal decree. Like wind breaking waves—the sovereign's dwelling place is spared. There is no blame. | 无 渙 渙 九<br>咎 王 汗 五<br>　 居 其 ：<br>　 　 大<br>　 　 號 |

The fifth image is of yielding one's own home to house others, giving of one's own wealth to enrich others.

A sovereign, one of generous spirit, gives what is received, and helps wherever possible. Note the continuity here from the third line.

In the matter at hand, think beyond personal interests. Think about a greater collective's well-being.

To walk the path of virtue, one must be charitable, and to be charitable means to be merciful. Even when one has acted against you, outright dissented against you, be merciful. Mercy means self-control, and in self-control, love and trust are forged. In love and trust, one's body feels graced by Divinity.

To disperse the dissent and restore unity, the sovereign issues a royal decree.

The perspiration symbolizes emotional catharsis and spiritual rejuvenation: the releasing of old tensions and steps taken forward, toward a healthier, united body.

A policy is proposed during a time of discord. The policy inspires a rallying cry from the people in favor of that policy.

Social reform. The sovereign is a peacemaker.

Moreover, in the royal decree, the sovereign announces renunciation of personal interests and dedicates assets to the public interest (represented by the sovereign's dwelling place). The latter portion of the fifth line expresses self-sacrifice and renunciation in the form of dispersing one's personal wealth and contributing it to the people's wealth.

When there is disagreement, disperse the discord and bring unity by conceiving of a new idea. The innovative proclamation does not include any of the old ideas. It feels like a new policy, and the people are pleased that the new policy will be a reform. No one feels favored or disfavored.

The fifth line tells the story of a severe flood dispersing across the kingdom—wind breaking waves. But because the sovereign listened to the people and agreed to social reform, the setting of better policies inspired Heaven to show mercy. The flood is stopped just before it reaches the sovereign's dwelling place.

Likewise, there is a prophecy here: A leader will face a choice of yielding to the people's demands for change or continuing with old policies. If the leader continues with old policies, natural disasters will plague the lands, provoked by Heaven's wrath. If the leader listens to the people and changes the policies, then the leader will thrive.

| *Sixth Line*<br>Like wind breaking waves, overflowing with bloodshed.<br>Leave: go far from here. To do so, no harm befalls. | 上九：渙其血去逖出無咎 |  |
|---|---|---|

It takes wisdom to know when you are the problem. A matter has gone beyond the point of no return and now, the course of action is to mitigate the harm.

Sometimes it is heroic for us to stay, and sometimes it is heroic for us to go. In the matter at hand, it is heroic for you to go.

The sixth line has been interpreted as pertaining to refugees, the theme of 逃難 *(táo nàn),* meaning to flee from calamity, be a refugee, run from authoritarian oppression.

The line "渙其血, 去逖出" *(huàn qí xuè, qù tì chū)* evokes the image of running away from bloodshed, or endeavoring to avoid bloodshed by going away and never returning.

The forecast is that one shall leave behind what one had once called home, and never look back.

## Hexagram 60: Jié. Boundaries

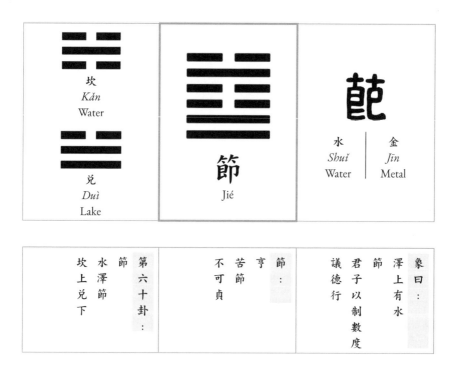

## *The Oracle*

> Right now, you are aimless. You have not set the proper limits on yourself. Without boundaries, there can be no identity. Without identity, you have no sense of yourself. Without a sense of yourself, you do not know what you really want and feel no purpose. Without feeling a purpose, you will remain aimless. Your way to success now is through self-discipline, and through self-discipline you will realize what you really want. Tame your emotions. Know who you are.

Water is beneficent when it occupies a limited space. **The Lake must contain Water, but it should never overflow with Water.** To ensure neither scarcity nor overflow, the level of the Water must be checked constantly.

**The sage will devise measures to regulate and examine virtue, and then implement regulation and examination of virtue. That is how virtue can thrive among humankind.**

**Every sage must set laws for the kingdom to flourish.**

The sage lives in accordance with systems of laws, and to live within boundaries, one must count, enumerate, reckon, and critique.

Discuss matters of morality and virtue, matters of the heart and mind. Live what you discuss, your heart guiding your morality, and mind guiding your virtue.

Venerate the gods and ancestors.

Right now, you are aimless. You have not set the proper limits on yourself. **You find such boundaries to be difficult and bitter. It is not an appropriate time for a divination.**

The main reason you have not attained the success you are looking for in your endeavor is your aimlessness: you do not know what you really want. You do not know where you are going.

Without boundaries, there can be no identity. Without identity, you have no sense of yourself. Without a sense of yourself, you do not know what you really want and feel no purpose. Without feeling a purpose, you will remain aimless.

Your way to success now is through self-discipline, and through self-discipline, you will realize what you really want. Then the path to success will open up to you. Make an offer in reverence, a pledge to strive for higher good, and I will be there when you need me.

For the group or an alliance working cooperatively toward a goal, regulations must be set, and boundary lines drawn.

Do not let the Lake overflow with Water, or there will be a flood.

| *First Line*<br>Not leaving the courtyard.<br>There is no blame. | 無 不 初<br>咎 出 九<br>　 戶 ：<br>　 庭 |
|---|---|

You have the power to move, but not the will.

You decide to stay back and remain with the familiar. You wish to advance.
  You wish to undertake the challenge, but the obstacles seem insurmountable at this time, so you fall back and restrain yourself.

You exercise judicious discretion. You are wise. Do not advance in haste. Work within your limitations for now.

Also, when there is adversity, disorder, or conflict, the impulse is to speak out.
  At the present moment, speaking out will bring disfavor and will not solve the matter at hand.

Stay silent. Be discreet. For now, holding back and not taking action proves to be the better judgment.

## THE CHANGING FIRST LINE

If the first line is the only changing line in the cast hexagram, then discretion is the better part of valor, and you should remain where you are. Do not advance. Do not proceed. Do not act and do not react. Accept the limitations of the situation at hand.

  The transformed hexagram resulting from the changing first line will reveal follow-up insight into why the Oracle cautions against proceeding.

| *Second Line* <br> **Not leaving the front doorway.** <br> **Foreboding adversity.** | 凶 不 九 <br> 出 二 <br> 門 ： <br> 庭 | ䷻ |

While the first line conveys wisdom in knowing your own limitations and not acting beyond those limitations, here the second line conveys foolish hesitation that results in failure.

If you hesitate, you will miss out on a great opportunity.

When the time for action comes, you have to seize it immediately. If you hesitate, your endeavor will not succeed because your hesitation will result in a missed opportunity for advancement.

There is a difference between waiting and hesitating.

Waiting is staying attentive for the right time and the right opportunity to come. Waiting is calculating.

Hesitating is being presented with the opportunity, but lacking the courage and determination to act. Hesitating is faltering.

Do not inhibit yourself unnecessarily. Seek out wider horizons.

Be ambitious when you consider your goals. Know your limitations, but you must be able to distinguish that knowledge from self-doubt.

Do not doubt your own capacity. If you do, you will only be holding yourself back.

| *Third Line* <br> **No boundaries to regulate one's principles.** <br> **But alas, to regulate, to be principled.** <br> **There is no blame.** | 無 則 不 六 <br> 咎 嗟 節 三 <br> 若 若 ： | ䷻ |

You are undisciplined and testing your boundaries. Unwise and ill-advised, but at least no harm will come of it.

The Oracle's tone in the third line is like that of a parent's sigh of mild lament, watching a child foolishly err; but the child is innocent, and fortunately for the child, the error is harmless.

Yet after the sigh, a serious life lesson is being imparted to the child. The parent takes the child aside and gives a lecture.

What is your limit? Where do you draw the line? If you do not set a boundary before embarking and vow never to cross that boundary, then you risk losing your way.

You are just lucky that this time, no harm has come from your naivete.

Dutifully obey decrees from the sovereign within.

If you do not set limitations for yourself, you will lack focus. Without focus, you cannot aim. If you cannot aim, you will never hit your target. Do not indulge in extravagances. Nonetheless, there is no fault to your idealism.

| *Fourth Line* <br> Peaceful and natural boundaries. <br> Success. | 六四：安節亨 | |

Understand the nature of regulations, and accommodate accordingly. By working within those limitations, you will become unlimited in your success.

You must always adapt to the fixed conditions of your situation.

Also, understand that there are limitations that are the work of nature and universal laws. These natural limitations provide balance. To work within those limitations is to live in harmony with the universe.

To be in harmony with the universe is to become limitless in power like the universe. That is the paradox that the sage will comprehend.

| *Fifth Line* <br> To enjoy boundaries. Good auspices to come. <br> Attainment of high esteem. One is truly virtuous. | 九五：甘節吉往有尚 | |

The fifth line expresses reciprocal boundaries. How you expect others to be restrained is how you must restrain yourself.

To restrain another, you cannot use force. Set an example by first restraining yourself. Your virtue inspires others to voluntarily set restraints upon themselves.

In the eyes of Heaven, one who can inspire others to enjoy boundaries without commanding or compelling it is the sovereign of highest esteem, nobility, and virtue.

When you achieve through self-restraint and setting boundaries, others will follow.

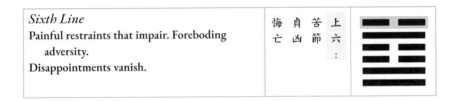

*Sixth Line*
**Painful restraints that impair. Foreboding adversity.**
**Disappointments vanish.**

Boundaries are necessary if one is to flourish, but in excess, they will debilitate and enfeeble. Your measures need to be tempered, not extreme. The intent is not to overcompensate; the intent is to balance.

A restraint should challenge you to become stronger and more refined. A restraint should not cause undue hardship.

Be wise enough to know the difference between discipline and oppression. Then expectations will be fulfilled. If you confuse oppression for discipline, then you threaten the balance, and expectations will not be fulfilled.

# Hexagram 61: Zhōng Fú. Faith Within

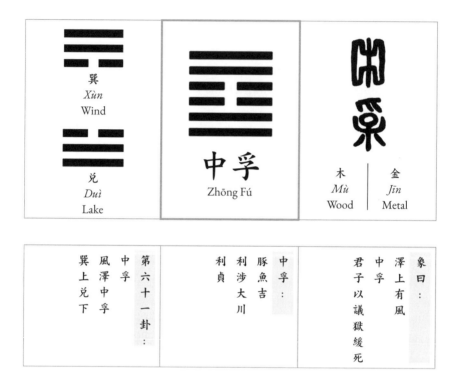

## The Oracle

Do not rush to judge others. Gain a deeper understanding of why they act the way they do. The answer to a difficult question is arrived at only when you are receptive to truth. On the brink of an awakening. The time for harvest is coming. You will soon manifest your full potential. There is a certain affinity between the Oracle and you.

**A Wind blows across the Lake: gentle thoughts nourish and bring joy.**
   The image of faith (孚) is a mother bird's foot placed protectively over her fledgling.

**The sage deliberates on the transgressions of humankind but delays executions.** Do not rush to punish others. Respond, but do not react—be responsive, not reactionary.

To unravel the truth, first you must gain a deep understanding of why the transgressor acted. Open the heart to truth. To be superior in strength is to show mildness in punishment. Let your sense of justice be guided by that principle.

The answer to a difficult question is arrived at only when you are receptive to truth.

**Persuading a piglet and fish: good fortune and prosperity arrive for you. Favors granted.**

The greatest challenge to the sage is not in the persuasion of the highest members in society to be open to truth; the greatest challenge is the persuasion of the most inferior members to accept moral obligation.

The greatest work of the sage is not in supporting the eminent ones in embracing truth; the greatest work is supporting the adversary in embracing truth.

Fellowship is not in itself noble. The unprincipled have fellowship, but such bonds can be broken without principles.

Peace and unity come not from fellowship, but from faith.

The truest bonds, ones that cannot be broken, are forged when all hearts are open to truth. When all hearts are open to truth, they are united by it.

Fellowship alone is not enough. There must be faith within. The sage must persuade the adversarial ones to open their hearts to truth. Then unite them with the eminent ones.

**Auspicious to cross the great stream.**

Hexagram 61 expresses the forces that move people to tell the truth.

A secondary implication of the revelation "persuading a piglet and fish: good fortune and prosperity" is as support for biological diversity. Hexagram 61 is the image of Wind dispersing the seeds of life across the Lake, the figure of the fertile womb.

| *First Line*<br>**Sighting of a *zouyu*. Favors bestowed.**<br>**Where there is a snake, there is no swallow.** | 初　虞　有<br>九　吉　它<br>：　　　不<br>　　　　燕 | ▬▬▬▬▬<br>▬▬　▬▬<br>▬▬　▬▬<br>▬▬▬▬▬<br>▬▬▬▬▬<br>▬▬▬▬▬ |

A perilous environment, and yet take heart—one will rise, one who shall change that environment and bring back the swallows (symbolic of beauty, grace, an empress, messenger of good news, and the ushering in of a spring period).

"虞" is emblematic of the *zouyu*, a mythical creature that appears to announce the arrival of a rising spiritual leader, one who is benevolent, virtuous, and kindhearted. The first line indirectly implies the sighting of one. The oracle bone script for the word is the image of a tiger-like creature.

A prudent swallow will not flit about a garden when a snake is present. A prudent swallow will assess the safety of an environment before flying into it.

The current state of affairs is perilous, absent of swallows.

The first line can reveal a climate that is overly dominated by masculine forces, where a balance with more feminine forces (represented by the swallow) is needed.

No major changes to the situation in the short term, but in the long term, great changes to come, changes with a spiritual implication.

*Second Line*
A crane is crooning in the shade. Its chicks answer the call.
I have a vessel of good wine; I will share it with you so we can drink to intoxication.
I am with you, diffused everywhere.

九二：鶴鳴在陰，其子和之。我有好爵，吾與爾靡之。

The second line suggests a certain affinity between the Oracle and you.

The greatest and the most noble among us lead like a nurturing mother. You are not one who seeks glory, attention, or the spotlight.

As you croon from the shade, all will answer the call because truth as spoken by a great spiritual leader has a way of resonating. You do not need to be seen to be heard.

That is how you know the Divine is present. When you are wallowing in your darkest moment, call out and the Divine will answer. You do not need to see me to hear me.

When the call of the crane is principled, then the answer from the chicks will echo the principled call.

You are to be a spiritual inspiration to others. Just as the Oracle serves as spiritual inspiration to you.

The second line echoes the sighting of the *zouyu* earlier in the first line.

When your heart is open to truth and you are not speaking for the sake of ego or attention, but speaking for the sake of truth, others will join and follow you on the virtuous path.

| *Third Line*<br>Combating a formidable foe.<br>To beat the drum or surrender—<br>To lament or to sing. | 或 成 得 六<br>泣 鼓 敵 三<br>或 或 ：<br>歌 罷 | ▬▬▬<br>▬  ▬<br>▬  ▬<br>▬▬▬ |
|---|---|---|

One is faced with an equal and opposing adversary. This is a war between equals.

At this time of divination, either side could be the victor, either side could lose. There is currently a hollow opening for either to seize upon the chance and get ahead.

In the hexagram image, notice how the third line is yin and begins to form the shape of a hollow center (the third and fourth yin lines). This hollow center resembles a narrow opening, symbolic of an opportunity for either side to advance or retreat—there is a path to success from here, but it is a precarious one.

The text itself is instructive on how to gain the advantage and make it through that narrow opening of opportunity first, before your adversary.

The one who makes it through first will be fighting on their own terms. In military strategy, the one who fights on their own terms is the one more likely to prevail.

That action to take—beat the drum and fight if you are five times stronger than the adversary; avoid battle if you are not. Feign weakness when your adversary is arrogant—feign the lament, and later you will be the one singing.

The third line of Hexagram 61 echoes the emotional value of the third line of Hexagram 30. Hexagram 30 expressed the point of decision between beating the drum or singing the song of lament. Hexagram 61 expresses two separate points of decision: the first is between beating the drum and thus advancing into battle or surrounding before the battle begins; the second is to lament over your decision or sing in contentment from it.

In fortune-telling, the third line does not bode well for the matter inquired about. There is a great deal of uncertainty and volatility.

The only true solution is to cultivate faith within and return to consult with the Oracle again, to see if the situation has shifted.

| Fourth Line<br>A waxing moon is near full. A horse's mate has gone astray.<br>No harm is caused by the fault. | 無 馬 月 六<br>咎 匹 幾 四<br>亡 望 ： |  |
|---|---|---|

An awakening is about to take place. The time for harvest is coming. You will soon manifest your full potential. In doing so, others may be left behind.

Your position right now can be likened to a waxing gibbous moon phase; you are about to enter the full moon phase of the matter.

In matters pertaining to career, you are trusted and respected by those in power; it's a good opportunity to seek advancement or promotion. Whether you'll get it is another story altogether, given that the fourth line doesn't explicitly forecast a favorable outcome; it forecasts no harm or fault sustained from the outcome.

However, in matters pertaining to love and romance, the fourth line is less encouraging. In response to such an inquiry, the fourth line simply urges you to arrive at a decision soon and act upon it. The Oracle refrains from telling you what to do, only telling you to make the decision.

There is no error in the sacrifice. At this time, seek counsel from one who is in a superior position. Through that counsel, a path to success will be illuminated. Such advice is delineated in the fourth position yin line moving toward the fifth position yang line.

"匹 pǐ" could mean a mate, someone's counterpart, an equal match, an adversary, an opponent, or a spouse. The term is also used to indicate the power or force generated by running horses.

"亡 wáng" could mean to perish, to have become deceased, to lose, or to have become lost. Here, the translation is reduced in severity to "astray." "亡"

is a reference to something you had that you now do not have, something that has fled or slipped away from your reach.

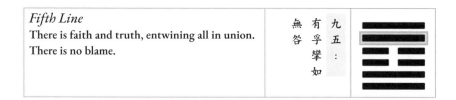

*Fifth Line*
There is faith and truth, entwining all in union.
There is no blame.

Present a gift of good faith. Foster trustworthiness.

You are the sovereign who can bring all the forces together under one virtuous rule.

Your subjects cling together in union. The ruler and the kingdom are intertwined.

Execute the decision that best serves your kingdom.

The fifth line hearkens back to the *zouyu* vision in the first line—a positive forecast for the matter inquired about.

In matters of love and romance, the one your heart has committed to is right for you; remember to treat your love with sincerity, a heart always open to truth and faithfulness.

In matters of career and ambitions, be open and honest, be yourself, be sincere, stay faithful to those you answer to, and you will find yourself unimaginably successful.

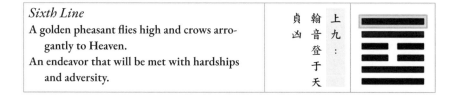

*Sixth Line*
A golden pheasant flies high and crows arrogantly to Heaven.
An endeavor that will be met with hardships and adversity.

One who boasts extravagantly of one's faith and virtues is one who lacks faith and virtue. One with prodigious talent should humble oneself before Heaven. In summary, do not be performative, and do not be pretentious.

"翰音登于天 hàn yīn dēng yú tiān" is figurative of a secondary meaning. While "翰" can be a golden pheasant in flight, it is also a writing brush or a literary work, or it is representative of one's literary talent.

"音" means sound, timbre, speech, pitch, and news. "登" as it is translated in the sixth line means to ascend upward, mount, rise, and head up, but it also means to publish a story. In antiquity, the word denoted success in passing the imperial examinations.

Thus, the secondary meaning of the golden pheasant is a work of writing that is coming across as pretentious, claiming more than the truth.

The solution is to hold back, show restraint and modesty. Revisit what you are presenting to others, and endeavor for modesty.

# Hexagram 62: Xiǎo Guò. Pay Attention to Details

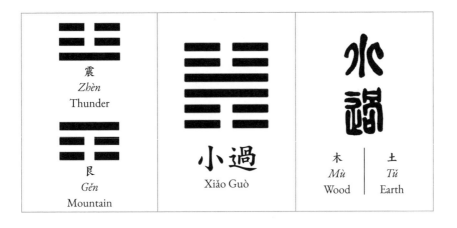

## *The Oracle*

Do everything there is to do a little bit better than everybody else. Pay attention to the details, and in that way you shall achieve success. The timing for your intentions is not right at the moment. It is still premature for you to take action. Initiate small changes toward your goal. Do not petition for a dramatic change or instant results. Advance up the ladder one rung at a time. Great prosperity if you heed the message.

- **There is thunder atop the mountain: inciting small movements but keeping the greater matter at rest.** Maintain stability in the wider foundation, but pay attention to the details and initiate small changes toward progress.
- **A bird in flight delivers a message: it is not the proper time to strive upward; instead, strive downward. Seek not from the Heavens, but seek from the Underworld.**
- Seek not to compete with Heaven, but if you strive ambitiously, then seek to understand the shadows. Strive downward, not upward. Let the downward striving hoist you up.
- **Great prosperity and fortune if you heed the message.**
- **It is not a time for expanding; it is a time for refining.**
- The sage is humbler than the humble, expressing more heartfelt sorrow than the sorrowful, and is more frugal than the frugal.
- Do everything there is to do a little bit better than everybody else. Pay attention to the details, and in that way, you shall achieve success.
- There will be fruition if you persevere through your endeavor, but undertake it one small step by one small step. Pay attention to the details.
- In the opening lines, Hexagram 62 warns not to be overly ambitious in trying to overpower Heaven's Will and nature. The short-term gains yielded from such ambition will be eclipsed by the long-term disasters that ensue.

The progression of the first to sixth lines relay that narrative and what will happen if the warning in the opening lines is not heeded—**do not ascend, but you may endeavor to descend.**

| | |
|---|---|
| **First Line**<br>Bird in flight meets with misfortune. | 飛 初<br>鳥 六<br>以 ：<br>凶 |

Year of a bad harvest. Famine and challenge.

The timing for your intentions is not right.

Stay with the tried-and-true Path. Your time will come. It is not now. Inauspicious to ascend. Remain at the base of the mountain. Seek safety.

| | |
|---|---|
| **Second Line**<br>Surpassing one's ancestors. Meeting one of mother's foremothers.<br>Not reaching one's ruler. Meeting one's subject.<br>All is well. | 無 遇 不 遇 過 六<br>答 其 及 其 其 二<br>　 臣 其 妣 祖 ：<br>　 　 君 |

You undertook the path with one intention, only to meet with a different result.

You assume the one you seek is one who can help, but it is the other, the one you overlooked, who can influence the situation.

"祖 zǔ" is one's ancestors (generally, not accounting for gender), one's grandparents (either grandfather or grandmother), or a founding ancestor.

"妣 bǐ" is also a deceased mother. In the second line, it can refer to one's matrilineal ancestors, whereas the preceding "祖" generally presumes the patrilineal ancestors.

If one's mother is deceased, a mystical reading of the second line would interpret it as a sign that your mother is connecting with you through the Oracle. Your mother is present.

The second line makes reference to one of the five Confucian relations: ruler (君) to subject (臣), which corresponds with the Wood phase of the Wu Xing cycle.

| | | |
|---|---|---|
| *Third Line* <br> Leaving the fortress unprotected to go destroy another. <br> Foreboding adversity. | 凶 從 弗 九<br>　 或 過 三<br>　 戕 防 ：<br>　 之 之 | ䷛ |

Be content with the present situation. Leaving the security of your own stronghold to potentially exploit and harm another for personal gains will result in misfortune.

The third line can also come up for a reading when you have unseen adversaries and the Oracle is warning you about the envy your accomplishments have unintentionally stirred up. Be careful of who you are letting into your home, and who you are trusting.

In a very mundane and lighter reading of the third line, do not leave your home unprotected. It may be vulnerable to intruders. "戕 qiāng" in such a context is less about going out to destroy than it is about "picking up your axe and heading out to hunt," or in present-day terms, going to work.

In all instances, tread forth with care.

| | | |
|---|---|---|
| *Fourth Line* <br> There is no blame. That which should have come to pass was missed. <br> Forward movement will surely encounter adversity. <br> Do not unduly delay. Do not engage in prolonged undertakings. | 勿 往 弗 九<br>用 厲 過 四<br>永 必 遇 ：<br>貞 戒 之 | ䷛ |

Time is of the essence. For matters in progress, get them to completion as quickly and expediently as you can. Do not delay, and do not procrastinate.

The fourth line suggests powerful human intervention that diverts the course of nature. This is an instance where human will was able to override Divine Will. As a result, an event that should have come to pass by Divine Will was diverted from its course. That thing that should have happened did not happen.

However, at the fourth line position, no harm, no foul. (This is not going to be the case at the subsequent sixth line position.)

Before engaging in long-term projects right now, think twice and take caution. Consider what you are capable of at this time and whether a long-term project is reasonable.

The first line, "There is no blame," suggests that the situation "is what it is." Various moving parts and factors have brought you to your present circumstances and the limited forward-moving options.

You head out in search of an opportunity (or person), but such an opportunity passes you right by. Do not force your way forward. It is better to stay out of the way.

The fourth line is also a forecast of the general climate of your environment at the time of divination. As it seems, the future is volatile, and you do not want to be in the direct path of the storm. Take care of yourself.

In the narrative of the fourth line, an ambitious minister seeks to surpass and overthrow the reigning sovereign. Note the "greatness" of the fourth yang line versus the "inferior" or weaker of the fifth yin line.

Thus, the minister's ambition is not unfounded—perhaps the minister would rule better than the incumbent—but seizing the reign by force will end in calamity for the minister.

It is better to wait patiently for the natural course of events to take place. Take small, unseen steps toward your ambitious goal. Do not try to force immediate change.

| *Fifth Line*<br>Dense clouds, but it doesn't rain.<br>I am the western hinterlands.<br>The duke shoots a retrievable arrow into the cavern. | 公<br>弋<br>取<br>彼<br>在<br>穴 | 自<br>我<br>西<br>郊 | 密<br>雲<br>不<br>雨 | 六<br>五<br>： |

You seek understanding of your present circumstances. There are unseen forces at play, which your intuition has picked up on; hence you aim an arrow into the darkness of the cave, knowing somehow that something lurks within.

"Dense clouds, but it doesn't rain" is essentially conveying that something is brewing, and great happenings are afoot. This is a developmental or preparation stage for a great thing to come.

An exceptional ruler born of virtue is prophesied by the Oracle to achieve greatness. (This is expressed by the auspicious yin line in the yin position of the ruling fifth of the hexagram image.)

The ruler is destined to make a profound difference, but that ruler cannot manifest full potential without wise counsel and supporters. Seek out these counselors and supporters where you might least expect them. They are ones who have bowed out of public service, who prefer not to be at the center of attention. They will help the ruler achieve full potential.

Such a path is the one determined by the Divine.

The duke will become a king someday, but you are not ready yet. Seek out wise counsel and supporters.

"I am the western hinterlands," where the Oracle addresses itself in first person, was historically interpreted as a reference to the western region of Chaoge, the capital of the Shang dynasty and site of the Battle of Muye. The Oracle's voice is channeling the voice of the Zhou dynasty forefathers and foremothers. The "I" is an ancestral voice. Also, note how this line appeared first in Hexagram 9. Also, whether to translate this line as "I am the western hinterlands" or "I am in the western hinterlands" is unclear.

Another reading of the line is: "Come to me along the western gates," with *gates* meaning a threshold or liminal space. This would be the astral bounds of Mount Kunlun, where the Queen Mother of the West resides, and the site of a paradise reserved for shamans, the *wū* 巫.

The line "密雲不雨 mì yún bù yǔ" translates to dense clouds, no rain, but it is also symbolic of keeping secrets and withholding knowledge. "密" carries an implication of that which is concealed and kept secret, left a mystery. "雨" or the symbol of rain here is quenching the thirst for knowledge, to wash away what was causing a thing to be opaque or impenetrable.

The "弋" is a very particular type of arrow. It's attached to string that is then attached to a bow. So when the archer shoots the arrow, after it hits its target, the arrow can be easily fetched. In a way, it symbolizes a safety net or measure of security.

Among those who practice traditional Chinese medicine, "公弋取彼在穴 gōng yì qǔ bǐ zài xué" can be a reference to acupressure points in the human anatomy. The "弋" represents acupuncture needles. The duke refers to the acupuncturist or healer. In summary, the fifth line is proposing the healing of an unsolved problem by treating its invisible trigger point.

| Sixth Line | | |
|---|---|---|
| That which should have come to pass was missed. | 上六：| |
| Bird in flight ensnared by a net—Foreboding adversity. | 弗遇過之 飛鳥離之 是謂災眚 凶 | |

Troubled times ahead.

The flying bird is soaring intellectualism that turned into arrogance. At first the intellect and arrogance are empowering, and human ingenuity outruns the preordained course of nature. Now nature is catching up and coming for humanity with a vengeance.

Act within the scope of your position. No matter how elevated your thoughts are, your actions cannot reflect where your thoughts are—they should reflect no more than the actual authority you command.

At the personal level, the sixth line is about ambitions gone awry.

At the global level, the sixth line is about human invention that surpassed nature for a while, but now the repercussions are being felt in the form of natural disasters and civil strife.

"弗遇過之 fú yù guò zhī" from the fourth line is repeated here in the sixth. Human will diverted the path of Divine Will, and as a result, an event that Divine Will had ordained to be did not come to pass. The skipping of that destiny point creates a new path of destiny, one that leads to calamity.

A bird in flight is caught by a net, symbolic of human-made disasters and social or geopolitical conflicts. Likewise, natural disasters come to plague the people.

All because that which should have come to pass was missed. It's not always in our best interest to divert the course of nature. We cannot be myopic. Changing the near future for ourselves could result in disaster for our fate in the long-term future.

The specific reference to a flying bird and the Fire trigram or Hexagram 30 is perplexing. "飛鳥 fēi niǎo" means a flying bird, which most translations agree with. The rest of the passage has been interpreted as the flying bird being ensnared by a net, and that has become unquestioned precedent for interpretation.

The question presented is what to do with the reference to "離," which is the designation for the Fire trigram, and also Hexagram 30.

The Fire trigram could be a foreshadowing of the lower trigram of Fire in the next hexagram (Hexagram 63). Recall further the ambiguous reference to a curious imperial creature 離 in the second line of Hexagram 30.

"飛鳥離" could perhaps be a cryptic reference to the Flaming Phoenix ruling the southern region of heaven.

The developing narrative here in Hexagram 62 begins with the flying bird in the first line, and by the plot point of the sixth, perhaps it is being revealed that the flying bird is the Flaming Phoenix of the four directional guardians.

Thus, it is not a mere bird in flight one has caught; a mortal has dared interfere with the flight of a celestial being—ominous indeed.

"眚 shěng" also denotes an eclipse, which is a foreshadowing of disaster to come. In fortune-telling, the "眚" could be interpreted to indicate cataracts or a disease of the eye.

## THE MORAL OF THE STORY THAT
## HEXAGRAM 62 TEACHES THE SPELLCASTER

The eight trigrams are assigned eight archetypal facets of the Taoist mystic. The Thunder trigram, which is the upper trigram of Hexagram 62, corresponds with the Spellcaster. What lessons on the ethics of spell-crafting and greater rules of law can be learned from Hexagram 62? When one induces magical effects, compelling the path of nature of its divinely intended course, are there long-term ramifications to our short-term successes?

## Hexagram 63: Jì Jì. After the Ending

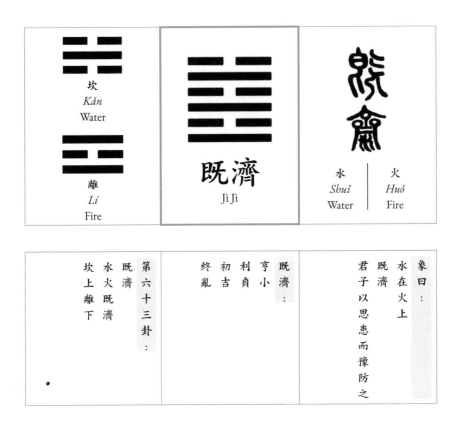

### The Oracle

Anticipates pitfalls before advancing. How might your actions affect others? A noble leader puts the people's welfare before self-interests. You have done what you have done. The matter now is what happens next. It is the time after an ending and at the start of a new beginning. Call upon the Illustrious Ancestor. When it comes to receiving favor from the Divine, the extravagance of your offerings does not matter; the sincerity of your heart and piety matter more.

**An auspicious omen for minor affairs. Gains to be had.**
**At the inception, favorable proceedings. At its cessation, chaos, disorder, and unrest.**
Water atop Fire. **A kettle is burning over the stove. The result is steam: be cautious, as tensions abound.**
Water over Fire is unstable for both. If the water in the kettle boils over, then the fire will be extinguished. If the fire burns for too long or the heat is too high, the water evaporates and vanishes. It is true that great energy is generated by Water over Fire, but it is still a hostile relationship.
Exercise caution.
**The sage anticipates possible misfortunes and pitfalls before advancing, to best protect the people.** Think about the consequences that your actions may have for others, not just yourself. The endeavor you contemplate is indeed highly attractive to you, with great prospects for glory and success.
However, it creates a volatile environment that could be adverse to those who depend on you. A noble leader puts the people's welfare before self-interests.
Ferrying relief across the river: it is the aftermath. You have crossed the great stream. The matter now is what happens next.

| *First Line* | | |
|---|---|---|
| The journey is delayed. | 無 濡 曳 初 | |
| A fox's tail gets wet. There is no blame. | 咎 其 其 九 | |
| | 尾 輪 ： | |

"曳其輪 yè qí lún" is more often translated to "the wheel drags behind." The understood meaning is that road conditions cause a carriage to decelerate and slow the pace.
Then the scene jumps to the story of a fox crossing a stream, which the fox hoped would be shallow, but the actual depths result in the fox's tail getting wet.
This translation merges the figurative meaning of the first part with the parable of the fox so as to streamline the narrative.

The key point of the first line is an analogy. The first part of the analogy is the carriage that is forced by road conditions to cross a shallow stream, and in wading through the waters and mud, the wheel drags behind. The carriage is then compared to a fox wading through a stream getting its tail wet.

No major harms result.

It is the lull after one chapter of your life has come to an end. A new one is about to begin. It is a period of transitions for you. Take it slow until you know where you want to go.

Transition periods are often difficult and riddled with minor obstacles, which is what you are currently experiencing.

| *Second Line* | 七 | 勿 | 婦 | 六 |
| The woman laments the loss of her veil. | 日 | 逐 | 喪 | 二 |
| Do not give chase. In seven days, you will have it back. | 得 | 其 | 其 茀 | ： |

The purpose of the woman's veil is to preserve her modesty. To lose that veil and thus have her full face be exposed would be construed as a disgrace, but here, the Oracle instructs not to chase after the lost veil.

What you feel you have lost is not really a loss.

An intention of yours that you had kept hidden is now exposed. Do not try to cover it up again or make excuses. Do nothing and respond gently.

The exposure was necessary for the completion of a cycle in your life path. It is a point of new beginnings.

| *Third Line* | 小 | 三 | 高 | 九 |
| Ancestor Wu Ding vanquishes the Guifang devils. It took three years to fully subdue them. | 人 | 年 | 宗 | 三 |
| The unprincipled are inept at achieving such feats. | 勿 用 | 克 之 | 伐 鬼 方 | ： |

Expand your domain. Like Ancestor Wu Ding, it is a time for conquests.

After one conquest, another begins. The power accrued is so formidable that all oppositional forces are subdued.

In the matter at hand, the key to success is to call upon the greatest military and divinatory counsel you can, and that greatest counsel will come from one you may least expect.

Whom you keep as counsel is determinative of your likelihood of success. Surround yourself with people who support your ambitions.

If you are in the midst of an ambitious undertaking, give it three years' time for it to fully manifest as the victory you're seeking.

## KING WU DING AND THE WARRIOR QUEEN FU HAO

The third line of Hexagram 63 references Emperor Wu Ding (1250–1192 BC) of the Shang dynasty, referred to as Ancestor Wu Ding. The specific name used in the statement is Gaozong 高宗, which is the temple name for King Wu Ding of the Shang.

Wu Ding led many military campaigns into foreign lands, such as the Yi, Qiang, and Ba kingdoms, to expand his dominion.

His favorite wife, Lady Fu Hao, was appointed a military general by Wu Ding, and was also a high priestess. Lady Fu Hao led the oracle bone divinations for the court, an unusual privilege for a woman at the time. It would thus be highly unusual for a woman, a concubine, to be providing military or divinatory counsel.

Likewise, when the third line comes up in a reading, call upon an unusual person for service. You will find greater success in your endeavor that way. Do not go for the usual candidates.

## CULTURAL PRACTICE OF TEMPLE NAMES

The cultural practice of temple names is traced back to the Shang. A temple name was used posthumously in place of the ancestor's given name as a title of honor, and it was used during ancestor worship. King Wu Ding's temple name begins with the prefix "高" to indicate that he was a monarch being honored for a notable achievement. The highest honorific was the prefix "太" indicating the founder of a dynasty.

## THE "GUIFANG DEVILS"

The reference to the Guifang devils in the third line and later in Hexagram 64 in the fourth is a term used by the Shang to describe a clan that they often went to war with. They called that clan the Guifang, meaning "people of the devil lands." The reference is to the historical wars fought between King Wu Ding of the Shang and the people from the region they called Guifang, the Devil Kingdom.[67] It took three years for the Shang to defeat Guifang.

Thus, "高宗伐鬼方" *(Gāozōng fá Guǐ Fāng)* translates to "Gaozong [Ancestor Wu Ding] defeats the Devil Territories." When referring to people, it might be translated to the Guifang devils.

| *Fourth Line*<br>Fine silks become rags.<br>Take caution throughout the day. | 終日戒 繻有衣袽 六四： |
|---|---|

Every golden era must come to an end, and how it ends is dependent on the ruler. Here, "day" can be symbolic of an era or a chapter in your life path. Although you are enjoying prosperity and good fortune, be cautious and stay modest. In spite of abundance, fruition, and a verdant, picturesque landscape in your current line of sight, there are elements of decay in the situation at hand.

# USING HEXAGRAM 63 IN EXORCISM RITUALS

## "ANCESTOR GAOZONG VANQUISHES THE DEMONS" 高宗伐鬼方

The word for vanquish "伐" *(fá)* used in the third line also happens to be a reference to the Three Stars, a constellation symbolic of the Three Stellar Gods that is often represented at the top of Taoist Fu talismans.[68]

Moreover, in Taoist traditions, martial arts and the military are connected to ritual magic and the mystical, such as the Lady of the Nine Heavens being a patron divinity that teaches both military strategy and occult practices.

Thus, the passage from the third line "高宗伐鬼方" can be repurposed and reinterpreted as "Ancestor Gaozong vanquishes the demon." Repurposed, it becomes an incantation used for exorcising a ghost or demon.

A Fu talisman or sigil is crafted to petition Ancestor Gaozong. The incantation is recited in an exorcism ritual to call upon that ancestral power. The demon and exorcism connection continue when Thunder Rites are implied in the next reference to the "Guifang devils," in Hexagram 64, line 4.

The Western Han dynasty (221–207 BC) text *Interpretations and Incantations of Celestials in the Zhouyi* (周易乾鑿度, *Zhōuyì qián záo dù*) from the *Yì wěi* 易緯 noted that Hexagram 63, Ji Ji, could be used to subdue ghosts and demons.[69] Thus, there is a long history and precedent for using Hexagram 63 in exorcism rituals.

### Fifth Line

The eastern neighbor slaughters oxen to the gods.
And yet they do not receive the blessings that the western neighbor receives.
The western neighbor need only make small, simple sacrificial offerings.

When it comes to receiving favor from the Divine, the extravagance of your offerings does not matter. It is the sincerity of your heart and piety that matter more.

Happiness cannot be quantified. It is the quality that counts.

Ostentatious displays of your success will not bring joy.

Success in small, humble undertakings. Disappointments in extravagant ambitions.

The fifth line is a reference to the Shang practice of sacrificing animals to their gods and ancestors. They're referred to as the eastern neighbor. Meanwhile the Zhou shifted the people away from animal sacrifice to what they deemed more civil forms of worship. The Zhou are the western neighbor.

## COMPARING SHANG AND ZHOU SACRIFICIAL OFFERINGS

Chapter 3 covered one of the major shifts of religious practice between the Shang and the Zhou dynasties. The Duke of Zhou is credited as having shifted the culture from human and animal sacrifice, which had been a norm during the Shang, to a society that focused more on rites and rituals.

The Zhou venerated their gods and ancestors through ceremonies, poetry, and songs. Per the Book of Rites, a classical treatise dated to the Zhou dynasty on the rituals and etiquette of the Zhou, offerings to gods and ancestors could include cooked meals, incense, jade and precious stone tokens, and cups filled with spirits (alcohol).

A fox is crossing a stream, which the fox hoped would be shallow, but the actual depths result in the fox getting wet. The obstacle faced is overwhelming.

Likewise, you've bitten off more than you can chew in your extravagant ambition for perfection. Perfection is the beginning of the defect.

The moral lesson of the sixth line position is to not strive to be the best, to not endeavor to outdo everyone else. Know your own limits. Ambition is encouraged, but it must be tempered with humility.

You might be in over your head.

# Hexagram 64: Wèi Jì. Toward an End

## The Oracle

> What is to be has not yet come to pass, but as you ford the river, you see the banks on the other side. You are about to peak in the situation at hand, but know that after every peak, there comes a time of stagnation and then an inevitable decline. No one is above regulation. There is an order that every one of us must follow, a higher authority that each one of us must submit to. When you forget that, then that is the start of the decline. Remember: reaching the top is only the halfway point.

**Fire above Water: one repels the other—incompatible principles.**
> Fire moves upward; Water moves downward. It is not yet time for ferrying relief across the river: reaching toward an end; at the point of climax. You are about to ford the great stream, but what is to be has not yet come to pass. There is prosperity to be had, and from where you stand, you can gauge how much farther you must go to attain that prosperity.

**The sage exercises caution in determining a proper order and must understand the power of the four cardinal directions.**
> You are about to peak in the situation at hand, but know that after every peak, there comes a time of stagnation and then an inevitable decline. Remember: reaching the top is only the halfway point.

**There will be a favorable outcome.**

**A little fox wades across a stream.**
> It is close to reaching the shore. **The fox's tail gets wet.**

> There is one last obstacle to overcome before you reach the top, and then after you reach the top, there is still the descent to be concerned about.

> Such is the cycle of changes that we are all subjected to. **No easy gains.**

## HEXAGRAM 64: THE HEXAGRAM OF CHANGE

Hexagram 64 reaffirms the overarching theme of the Book of Changes—and that is change. The final hexagram is not about completion; it is about incompletion. The end is only a beginning. There is no end. The hexagram expresses a period of transition from the peak of a situation to a time of standstill after that peak to the time right before the inevitable decline.

Considering chronology and timing, you would assume that the final hexagram in the revelation would be one of completion, but the theme of conclusions is found in Hexagram 63, not 64. Hexagram 63 was about closing and what comes after a closing. Here, Hexagram 64 is about the last mile before arriving at a finish line. In Hexagram 64, you are close to achieving the goal, but not quite there yet.

Nevertheless, it is generally considered an auspicious hexagram in divination because it indicates that only small, reasonable efforts are needed to achieve great success and final accomplishment of what you seek to attain.

| *First Line* | 吝 濡 初 |
| A fox's tail gets wet. | 其 六 |
| Remorse. Hardships. | 尾 ： |

Endeavor for corrective measures before proceeding.

The first line of the hexagram mirrors the structure of the first line in Hexagram 63. There, the fox's tail gets wet, but there is no blame. Here, the fox's tail gets wet, and hardships ensue.

An error of judgment results in injury.

Do not rush hastily into a situation. Be more methodical and discerning. Be self-aware of your personal limitations.

Hasty decisions will put you in perilous situations. At present, you may be prone to miscalculation.

You can get through the situation with success if you are careful and steady, and you take your time. If you are hasty or underestimate the matter at hand, then you will expose yourself to vulnerability.

| Second Line<br>The journey is delayed.<br>Forecast of an auspicious outcome. | 貞 曳 九<br>吉 其 二<br>　 輪 ： | |
|---|---|---|

You exercise prudence, and you know your own limitations. You delay the journey for a better time.

Such prudence is rewarded. There will be a favorable outcome.

The parable of the fox wading across the stream continues. Hexagram 64 reads like an alternative ending to the narrative that began in Hexagram 63.

If in the matter at hand you've been hesitating, thus delaying, because you are unsure which path to take, the second line counsels to take the middle path. This is the single yang line sandwiched in between two yin for the lower trigram.

Thus, at this position, the path forward for yielding a favorable outcome is right at the center. By staying centered, no matter what the conditions are on the path you take, your virtue and sincerity will attract support and success.

| Third Line<br>Crossing the stream during the time of Wei.<br>　Undertaking the expedition is unfavorable at this time.<br>[Not] Auspicious to cross the great stream. | [不] 征 未 六<br>利 凶 濟 三<br>涉 　 　 ：<br>大<br>川 | |
|---|---|---|

Here is one who is idealistic, with grandiose visions, courageous and lion-hearted, but naïve. You tend to think you're ready when you're not. You try to run before you can crawl. You say you rely on instinct, but really you are just too impatient to think it through.

Slow down. Unwind. This is currently an unfavorable time.

Do not undertaking long journeys or ambitious undertakings. Now is not the right time to launch an attack, endeavor to conquer or invade, or take retaliatory measures. This is not the right time for aggression.

The time of "未" *(wèi)* refers to one of the twelve earthly branches, the Sheep 羊, and is the seasonal term corresponding with late summer. This is the time of the Coming Heat and Great Heat in July. For ascendant hours, it corresponds with 1:00 p.m. to 3:00 p.m.

You are going through a period of transition, but at this time, you still lack the necessary resources and are ill-prepared for the transition ahead.

Delay your endeavor momentarily. Wait for a more opportune time.

In Kerson Huang's translations, there is an annotation that the original line "利涉大川," meaning "auspicious to cross the great stream," should be "[不]利涉大川," or "it is [not] auspicious to cross the great stream."[70]

Whether the line originally read "auspicious to cross" or "not auspicious to cross," considering the preceding passages, the interpretation in the short term remains the same—do not rush headfirst into the undertaking. Take your time. Formulate a strategic plan. Return to the Oracle for another divination, and do not undertake the expedition until the Oracle has deemed it favorable.

If the line originally read "auspicious to proceed," then perhaps in the long term, the undertaking you have contemplated is noble and worth pursuing, just not at this time.

If the line originally read "not auspicious to proceed," then even in the long term, the undertaking you have contemplated is ill-advised.

Since the ambiguity remains, it's safest to simply return for a subsequent divinatory reading and clarify with the Oracle later.

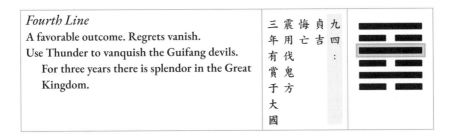

*Fourth Line*
A favorable outcome. Regrets vanish.
Use Thunder to vanquish the Guifang devils.
    For three years there is splendor in the Great Kingdom.

九四：貞吉悔亡震用伐鬼方三年有賞于大國

It is now an auspicious time to launch an attack. Proceed with the ambitious expedition. Though now is the time to start, completion of the expedition will take some time, so be patient. Stick to the same path, for it is the path of splendor, for the next three years, consistent and relentless.

# THE "GUIFANG DEVILS" AND THE SHANG

The fourth line reference to "震" *(zhèn)* is a reference to either the trigram Thunder or Hexagram 51, Zhen, meaning to jolt, creating an unexpected sharp turn.

The Oracle's reference to Zhen forecasts that there could be a change in leadership or control.

It is a time for instigating change and conquests. It is a time of movements, of taking initiative, excitation, revolution, or division. Exorcise the demons (oust those who are wreaking havoc, causing a decline in society, and oppressing the people). Methods in Thunder Rites will be indispensable.

The reference to the Guifang devils continues from Hexagram 63. Compare the two lines side by side.

| Hexagram 63 ※ Line 3 | Hexagram 64 ※ Line 4 |
| --- | --- |
| Ancestor Wu Ding vanquishes the Guifang devils. It took three years to fully subdue them. | A favorable outcome. Regrets vanish. |
| The unprincipled are inept at achieving such feats. | Use Thunder to vanquish the Guifang devils. For three years there is splendor in the Great Kingdom. |

The annotations for line 3 of Hexagram 63 covered the history of wars between the Shang and a clan that they referred to as "鬼方," a pejorative term for a distant clan that the Shang often went to war with. They called that clan the Devil Kingdom, or devil people. "鬼" *(guǐ)* also means ghost or demon, so it could have been Ghost Kingdom and ghost people.

In the present line, the Great Kingdom is a reference to the Shang (at the time, the Shang were referred to as the Yin (殷). They used "國" or kingdom to identify their domain, conveying civilization. Thus, "鬼方" wasn't even really referred to as a kingdom. "方" is a more generic term for territory, place, or region, and it does not have the same connotation of civilization that the Shang "國" does.

The fourth line prognosticates career or academic success and high achievements. Take decisive action now, and reap the rewards later.

It is your time to be seen and to be heard. Speak loudly, boldly, and do not be afraid to incite. Heaven calls you to it, to instigate much-needed change.

Seizing control will require the exertion of great power. It is now time to launch your forces in full. Do not hold back. Advance. Incite. Conditions may not seem perfect for attack right now, and there will be collateral loss, but attack is the optimal action to take.

A period of peace and prosperity will follow.

### A REPURPOSED MEANING FOR THE FOURTH LINE: "USE THUNDER TO VANQUISH THE DEMONS" 震用伐鬼方

The Taoist mystic might repurpose the meaning of the fourth line. Since military campaigns and sorcery are often linked in Taoist traditions, the passage "震用伐鬼方" *(zhèn yòng fá guǐ fāng)* can be reinterpreted as spell-crafting instructions to the Taoist mystic.

The fourth line of Hexagram 64 is a divine omen to engage in Thunder Rites as the method for undertaking the matter at hand. Repurposed, the line reads: "Use the quake of thunder to exorcise the ghosts and demons."

In other words, thunder magic. The trigram Fire corresponds with the immortal Lü Dong Bin 呂洞賓 of the Taoist Eight Immortals. Lü Dong Bin was a renowned master of thunder magic (雷法, Léi Fǎ).

| *Fifth Line* | 六五：貞吉無悔君子之光有孚吉 |
|---|---|
| A favorable outcome. There is no blame. A radiant aura—the sage has Awakened. Patience is rewarded. An auspicious sign. | |

An awakening. This is the sign of one who is wise beyond their years, wise with the knowledge and experience of myriad lifetimes. This is one who has advanced to a heightened level of their craft.

"有孚" *(yǒu fú)* is often directly translated to "there is sincerity," "there is trust," or "there is good fortune," all of which are correct and apply in this context.

Additionally, the term here expresses a more complex narrative statement: you have worked hard, you have been honest and sincere at every point in your journey, and you have persevered; and now your patience is going to be rewarded. Not only is this an omen of success to come, and the greatest degree of it, but you deserve it. You worked for this. Your heart never wavered. You've always been faithful and true.

A new leadership has ascended to power, and a time of prosperity is upon us. The fifth line depicts clouds receding and sunlight shining through.

Always seek out the light above you and take the path that leads to the light.

| Sixth Line |  |
|---|---|
| Patience is rewarded and we feast, we drink. There is no blame. A fox's head gets wet. Patience is rewarded and wrongdoing is made right. | 上九：有孚于飲酒無咎濡其首有孚失是 |

You have overcome the worst of the struggles. A time of calm and well-being has arrived. It is a time of inspired confidence and contentment. It is also a time to consolidate your gains.

Enjoy tempered celebration: be modest, and continue to prepare for tomorrow. Do not be overly indulgent. Be content with what you have gained, and enjoy the blessings in your life. Do not become tethered to the desire to acquire more and more. Avoid excess.

Temperance and maintaining equilibrium is in order. Exercise restraint and know the limits of your power. There must be moderation in all things that you do.

No one, no leader, is above regulation. There is an order that every one of us must follow, a higher authority that each one of us must submit to. When you forget that, then that is the start of the decline.

Note how "有孚" *(yǒu fú)* from the fifth line is repeated twice in the sixth, symmetrically at the top of the first statement and at the top of the last statement.

The reference to the fox's head getting wet is a restatement of the sixth line of Hexagram 63. Here, we may be seeing a subtext emerging. "首," or head, can also mean a chieftain or leader. Most poignantly for the final line of the final hexagram, "首" can also imply a return to the beginning.

An ending is never just an ending; it's always the fodder for a new beginning.

# WU YI OF SHANG, THUNDER, AND GOD

King Wu Yi 武乙 of Shang (reigning 1147–1112 BC) was a formidable ruler, leading the Shang to some of the dynasty's greatest military conquests, but he was also known as a cruel, brutal, and arrogant monarch.

According to the *Bamboo Annals,* in 1117–1118 BC, King Wen's father, Ji of Zhou, captured twenty chieftains of the Guifang devils from the Devil Kingdom referenced in the hexagrams, and brought them to King Wu Yi of Shang. Ji of Zhou pledged submission to the Shang. For his loyalty, Wu Yi rewarded Ji of Zhou with jade and horses.

Despite Ji of Zhou having pledged his loyalty, later Wu Yi's son would betray him, luring him to a specified location on false pretenses and having Shang forces assassinate him. Ji of Zhou was King Wen's father, and needless to say, King Wen vowed vengeance.

An account of Wu Yi's arrogance is documented in the *Records of the Grand Historian* 太史公書, a chronicle of ancient China begun by Sima Tan 司馬談 (165–110 BC), an imperial court astrologer, and completed by his son Sima Qian 司馬遷 (145/35–86 BC).

Wu Yi carved a wooden idol or effigy (偶, *ǒu*) of Shangdi, the Supreme Sovereign of Heaven. The king then challenged the effigy of Shangdi to *liubo* (六博), an ancient form of gambling and board game between two players. *Liubo,* meaning six sticks, is played on a square chess board. Each player is given six chess pieces.

The idol of Shangdi lost, according to Wu Yi, and the king humiliated the god for losing. According to Sima Qian's *Records,* after that incident, "when he was out hunting, [King Wu Yi of Shang] was struck down by a violent thunderclap, and killed."[71]

History gives the fourth line statement "use Thunder to vanquish the demon" another layer of meaning. Especially when you consider it as spoken by the voice of the Oracle—Shangdi. Moreover, in the Shuo Gua or Eighth Wing of the Ten Wings, it's noted that Di [Shangdi] comes forth in the sign of Thunder—帝出乎震, *dì chū hū zhèn*.[72]

FIGURE 9.1 Nine-headed phoenix 九鳳 SOURCE: From the *Book of Mountain and Seas* 山海經. Originally written pre-Qin, before 221 BC; illustration is from a Qing dynasty (1644–1911) edition. Animal totem of the kingdom of Chu 楚 during the Zhou dynasty.

# 9

# Ancestral Veneration and the I Ching

IN THE WAY that a shaman, medium, or mystic can become possessed by a spirit entity and speak the words of that spirit, the Oracle can become possessed by a spirit, too. The Book of Changes is a ritual tool that amplifies and strengthens the psychic connection between the living and the dead. Thus, through the Book, the two worlds can communicate with each other. This chapter will discuss how you can utilize that feature of the Book to contact the spirit of an ancestor.

We won't be able to provide the specificities of ancestor veneration traditional to your ethnic group or heritage. However, this chapter celebrates in a general way what is shared in common by Asians from north of the mainland, through the central plains, and into the peninsulas, encompassing the Pacific islands. And I say with relative confidence that no matter the ethnic group, if you hail from this part of the world, it's in your blood to honor your ancestors.

Our observances, our holidays, what we eat, what we use as offerings, when and where we venerate the dead, how and why, and the specific rituals around how we mourn are certainly different. Funeral rites can vary from fists beating chests and performative wailing to total silence, from dancing and music[1] to definitely no dancing or music.

Among the Confucian-influenced traditions (China, Vietnam, Korea, Japan), we might disagree on exactly how many sticks of incense to burn, but we agree there will be incense. There's going to be food, lots of it. Some cultures eat the food after it's been offered to ancestors; others will not. What we wear to ancestral rites will vary from region to region, but we all concur that you had better be respectably dressed. Also, somehow tea is always involved.

To be Vietnamese is to feel connected to your ancestors; it's part of the cultural identity.[2] In Shinto, an Indigenous religion of Japan, there are three tiers of ancestor veneration to observe: imperial ancestors, local tutelary gods or the ancestors of place, and the ancestors of the family.[3] To this day, ancestor veneration is the foundation of Japanese social life and political life. The word for government, *matsuri-goto,* means "government administration," and it also means "affairs of worship," with the most minute details of ancestral rites codified by law, enduring even into the twentieth century.[4] Korean death rites represent a complex interplay of Confucian and Christian values, often resulting in profound struggles with balancing filial duty or *hyo* to ancestors and religious piety to God.[5]

At minimum, we remember our departed parents and grandparents on the anniversaries of their deaths and the Lunar New Year, inviting them into our homes, leaving out offerings, and burning incense as we pray for their blessings. Koreans celebrate *jesa* 제사, a memorial ceremony held on the anniversary of an ancestor's death. Ritual greetings call the spirits home, and male descendants lead the offering rites.[6]

Anniversaries of deaths are traditionally calculated per the lunar calendar. When my mother-in-law passed on March 1, 2021, the anniversary of her death was honored on February 18, 2022. That's because March 1, 2021, converts to the eighteenth day of the first lunar month in the year of the Ox. In the subsequent year of the Tiger, the eighteenth day of the first lunar month converts to February 18, 2022.

Ancestors are those you share a bloodline with—your parents when they pass on, your grandparents, great-grandparents, great-great-grandparents, and so on. In your blood and bones is the psychic link that connects you to everyone since the dawn of time who shares your mitochondrial DNA.

Those psychic links can also be established through adoption rituals. I have an aunt who was adopted into the family. Since she is now a part of our family name, we believe that with the adoption ritual, she is as connected to the clan's blood as I might be. Moreover, she continues to retain connection to her biological family through blood, so she can connect to both the lineage she became a part of spiritually and the biological lineage she was initially born into.

Ancestral Veneration and the I Ching 757

**FIGURE 9.2** *A Child Worshipping the Sage* SOURCE: From *Chinese Thought* (1907) by Paul Carus.[7]

Let's define "worship." When we say ancestor worship, we mean continuing to respect them in death just as we did in life. We continue to feel their presence and influence in all that we do. On special occasions, we remember to cook them a special meal and burn joss sticks or joss paper as offerings for them—the equivalent of gifts. We go to them in our times of need. We go before the ancestor altar and open the doors of communication, dial in, and ask great-grandma for her advice. Ancestor veneration is filial piety. It's to "drink water to remember the source."[8]

We don't deify them, and they do not replace the gods or God of our religious faith. However, within folk beliefs, the oldest generations of our lines have been venerated for so long, remembered for centuries, that the collective remembrance has the effect of empowering them in a way that is *like* deity. Our oldest of ancestors become very powerful spirits who have the ability to influence natural forces and assist us when we ask for help. As a collective, the spirits of all your ancestors combined become a very effectual force in helping to create change, should they wish to act in unison for you. Thus, we invoke them to help us pass final exams, bless a marriage, or bless a new home we've just moved into. From their vantage point, they can see more of the past, present, and future than we can as mortals, so they can answer questions when we call upon them in divination.

A belief called soul dualism explains how ancestral spirits can return to visit us and also reincarnate. Like yin and yang, the soul consists of a binary—the *hún* 魂 and the *pò* 魄. The *hún* aspect of your soul is yang, where karma is accounted for, and this is the part that reincarnates. The *pò* aspect of your soul is yin, and it remains part of the unseen energy present in our cosmos.

The memories of the life one has lived remain with the *pò*. When you call upon your ancestors, it's their *pò* that answers. Their *hún* is reborn and reincarnated into a new body, with that rebirth formulated per their soul's karmic accounting. According to Taoist beliefs, the *hún* is the part of you that travels astrally, though that belief isn't unanimously shared. Still other traditions further subdivide the soul into three aspects of *hún* and seven of *pò;* divisions of three and five or five and eight are also common. Regional beliefs will vary.

In addition to the lunar calendar death anniversary dates of parents and grandparents, there are three key holidays when ancestral veneration is significant: Lunar New Year, Tomb-Sweeping Day, and the Mid-Autumn Moon Festival.

The Lunar New Year occurs on the first new moon of the year, or first lunar month, and the first solar term, the Start of Spring (立春, Lìchūn). This is a time for cheer and festivities. Around 11 p.m. on the eve before Lunar New Year, a delicious meal is prepared for ancestral spirits and placed on the altar. This is construed as a family reunion dinner. Joss sticks are burned as offerings.

Tomb-Sweeping Day (or Qingming Festival) coincides with the fifth solar term, Bright and Clear (清明, Qīngmíng) and the third lunar month of the Dragon (辰, Chén). While the corresponding Western calendar dates vary, it's when the solar longitude is 14° or on the fifteenth day after the spring equinox, when solar longitude is 0°. Most Asian ethnic groups celebrate a version of Tomb-Sweeping Day where we visit our family's burial grounds to clean the gravesites, pray, and leave ritual offerings.

So far, you've got lunar month 1 solar term 1, then lunar month 3 solar term 5, and the third key holiday for ancestral veneration occurs on lunar month 7 solar terms 13 and 14—the Start of Autumn (立秋, Lìqiū) and Dissipating Heat (處暑, Chùshǔ).

Ghost Month 鬼月 corresponds with the earthly branch *shen* 申, a different word from *shen* 神 meaning spirits; but yes, they are homonyms, and the Chinese place a great deal of importance on synchronicities such as homonyms.[9] The historical form for "申" from Shang oracle bone scripts and Zhou dynasty bronze inscriptions was the image of a lightning bolt, traced back to the same pictogram for thunder (雷, *léi*) and lightning (電, *diàn*). It's meaningful to me that the final Gua in the Zhouyi is Hexagram 64, Fire over Water, where we have this line: "Use Thunder to vanquish the demons."

The Ghost Festival is the day of the full moon during Ghost Month. We say this is the day when the gates between realms are left open, allowing spirits, hungry ghosts, and demons to wander the earth. For the whole month, the veil is thin, so spirit activity purportedly heightens, most notably reaching us through water and reflective surfaces. Then on the day of the full moon, the Ghost Festival, all hell literally breaks loose. What the Ghost Festival means to you is dependent on how sensitive you are. I grew up edified with enough rules and admonishments to fill their own handbook.

Ghost Month coincides with typhoon season all across the Pacific, which might be why so many different Asian cultures observe a version of the Ghost Festival during this time. Although we may differ on the finer points, I'm a bit amused that all of us unanimously warn: "Stay out of the water." The closer to the ocean an ethnic group gets, the more superstitious dos and don'ts they seem to have for Ghost Month.

With a collective mind and intention set on family reunions, any of these three holidays will be more conducive for an I Ching mediumship reading to communicate with ancestors. Thoughts are powerful, and when a lot of people everywhere think the same thoughts at the same time, physical realities are created. Thus, if you're not exactly a trained psychic medium, then it might be easier to try establishing contact on one of these three holidays.

Set up an ancestral altar for the evening. Approach the divination ritual with sincerity. I sympathize with the skepticism people have toward psychics who claim that your doubts will impair the accuracy of their readings. That can feel like a cop-out when their psychic readings are wrong. However, in this case, doubt and rejection of the unknown will cloud your mind and block you from receiving messages from beyond. You don't have to believe hook, line, and sinker, but come with an earnest wish to connect. And that earnestness is demonstrated by how much thought you're willing to give to the ritual process.

The thoughts and emotions generated by doubt create interference and will affect the frequency that the spirits are using to communicate with us. A *shi fu*, or master teacher, once explained to me that there is an electromagnetic wave frequency of sound and light associated with the spirit realms. Much of what goes into rituals and ceremonial rites is intended to access those frequencies of sound and light. True or not, it's an instructive analogy.

# PRACTICUM 9.1:
## Setting Up a Basic Ancestor Shrine or Altar

A shrine is a sacred space that has been thoughtfully arranged and is dedicated to your gods or ancestors, and you keep it as a permanent fixture in your home. From time to time or per the seasons and holidays, you might change up what's on your shrine, but it's always there. You might go before the shrine for your daily prayers or meditation.

An altar is a sacred space set up for a specific type of work, which could include all of the same features of your shrine, but it's temporary. You might convert a desktop in the den to an altar space for a divination ritual to contact your ancestors, but then you'll clear that table once the divination ritual is over. The altar table is where you do ritual magic or divination.

However, I'm constantly confusing myself and will use shrine and altar interchangeably. It's okay if you do, too.

Figure 9.3 is a shrine and altar setup, called a Gòngfèng 供奉, from my father's childhood home. The main table is the shrine for honoring both

FIGURE 9.3 Shrine and altar

gods and ancestors. There is a pull-out table in front for an altar. When not in use, it's tucked underneath the larger table for the shrine. When in use, a tablecloth is spread over it, and the offerings are placed on the altar.

Ideally your shrine or altar will be set up in a way that reflects the cultural heritage you share with your ancestors. For those who are a blend of different cultures, your sacred space will reflect that blend. For those who don't have access to an established family or cultural tradition for how to honor your ancestors but would like to start, here are some thoughts.

It's common to see a special type of furniture that's a shrine with a pull-out table that can be used as an altar in front of the shrine. The altar of offerings to ancestors is only displayed in front of the shrine on holidays. Ordinarily, only the shrine is visible.

Personally, I don't have an ancestor shrine in my home because, as I like to irreverently joke, I don't have to—I'm a girl, and I don't have any sons. One of the enduring residuals of Confucian thought is that women really aren't integral to ancestor veneration. For funerals, only the men lead the important parts of the ritual, with disproportionate honors bestowed upon the eldest male. So, if that's how it's going to be, why should I set aside precious limited space in my home for a shrine? Irreverence aside, I do, however, work with altars, and will set one up to honor my ancestors on holidays or when I'd like to contact them for divination or blessings.

In terms of directionality and placement of the altar, I've heard it all:

It must be placed in the east because the Wood phase corresponds with ancestors, and Wood corresponds with spring, and spring corresponds with east.

It must be placed in the west because the dearly departed have set like the setting sun in the west. Buddhists would also say that the west corresponds with the Pure Land western paradise, which obviously is where your ancestors ended up, right?

I've heard that it better be placed in the north because that is the realm of the Black Tortoise, who is the guardian of the underworld and is the psychopomp who guides ancestral souls.

Per feng shui principles, it had better be placed in the south, because that is the most auspicious placement.

Which set of instructions do you heed?

Whenever possible, follow the principles of your specific heritage. Otherwise, lean into your intuition, listen from the heart, and you'll know exactly where your altar needs to go.

Flower arrangements on the altar express the importance of the occasion—and guests—to you. Candles help with ambiance. Also, at least in Mahayana Buddhism, I was taught that the light from the candles is symbolic of enlightening knowledge and wisdom. In Taoist magic, two candles on the altar represent the light of the sun and the light of the moon.

You'll also want to place delectable offerings on the altar. If around the holidays you see boxes of assorted preserved and candied fruits out on the front display of Asian grocery stores, one reason they're so popular is because it's a no-fuss one-stop-shop for your ancestor offerings. The folks on my paternal side tend to love nuts, so for them I need to get nuts. The folks on my maternal side really like black and red melon seeds. My husband's side of the family prefers sunflower seeds. My maternal grandmother has a thing for McDonald's french fries. No credible source is going to tell you that fries are a traditional ancestor offering, but if I want her to show up, I'm going to have fries.

A common centerpiece on an ancestral shrine or altar will be photographs of the dearly departed. However, personal sensitivities will vary, and it's more important for you to honor your own sensitivity. After my mother-in-law's passing, my husband put up an ancestral shrine in the family room so she could still be with us and stay updated on our daily activities. However, having to confront the framed photographs of her daily was inhibiting my father-in-law from living his life fully. Either he actively avoided seeing the shrine, or when he did, he'd break into tears. So we took down the shrine, and an altar to honor her only goes up on special occasions. Ancestor veneration should be beneficial in your life and support your well-being. If it's doing the opposite, then you need to prioritize your well-being.

For the specific purposes of an altar set up to communicate with your ancestors through the I Ching, the key features will be the incense, candles, and offerings. If you're calling on someone specific, then framed photographs of them are helpful. Offerings are typically selected and arranged to represent a sacred trinity, the Wu Xing, and for the extravagant, the Ba Gua,[10] but it's unlikely that your ancestors will be that picky.

If I had to name the most important principle for altar setup, I'd say it's purification. Make sure you've thoroughly cleaned the space where you plan on setting up a shrine or altar. Clean and dust as you normally would, though perhaps a little more thoroughly than normal. Burn incense smoke to clear the air. Read and chant sutras aloud. I consider purification the most important because atrophic *qi* accumulates in collecting dust, increasing in potency over time, which can interfere with the nature of ritual work you're trying to do. Considering the medical research on microbial communities and bacteria in house dust[11] and how they can cause resistance to antibiotics,[12] regular cleaning and dusting just makes sense.

Can non-Asians use the I Ching to communicate with the spirits of their non-Asian ancestors? I believe anything's possible. I also think there are probably better mediums for that than the I Ching.

Culture is one of the strongest anchoring bonds in genetic memory. Our cultural experience while living is so strong that it remains a psychic attachment. Optimizing that psychic attachment improves your chances of a successful spirit contact. If you're trying to connect with an ancestor who has that psychic attachment of culture that can be traced to the Yellow River and Yangtze civilizations, then using the language of the I Ching can be a highly effective way to communicate. If the ancestor you are trying to connect with would view the I Ching as entirely foreign and unfamiliar, then the Book isn't the best option for establishing connection.

## PRACTICUM 9.2:
## Cowrie Shell Divination and Invoking a Twelfth-Generation Ancestor

Applying Shao Yong's nine categories of time, twelve generations (12 × 30 years) ago will refer to an ancestor of yours who lived around 360 years ago, which is also one revolution (運, *yùn*). This practicum will use six cowrie shells to cast a single locked hexagram, on the premise that you're invoking an ancestor and the Oracle is channeling your ancestor's message. This is a modified method of cowrie shell divination from the approach in chapter 7, which had mirrored the coin toss method.

Thoughtfully and with great sincerity, prepare a dish of fresh fruits and vegetables as offerings for the Black Tortoise. In Vietnamese folk religion, the sacred Black Tortoise spirit is Huyền Vũ (Korean 현무 *[hyeonmu]*; Japanese げんぶ *[genbu]*), envisioned as a black turtle-snake.

**FIGURE 9.4** Cowrie shell divination

The Black Tortoise is a messenger to the underworld and guardian over the souls of ancestors. You'll find several references to the Tortoise in the lines of the I Ching. In this practicum, the Tortoise will help escort your ancestor to and from realms.

Is calling a psychopomp or other spirit to accompany the soul of a loved one necessary? No, not at all. Typically, someone you've had a close relationship with in the living is not going to need a spirit attendant to guide them to you. You can call upon that person directly. However, if calling upon an unnamed or unknown ancestor, as we are doing here, I'd call the Black Tortoise, or for the more Buddhist-leaning, one of the Buddhas or bodhisattvas.[13]

There are no absolute rules for what to prepare as offerings for the spirit Tortoise, but I like to go with five, in the Wu Xing colors:

1. **Green:** leafy greens for Wood.
2. **Red:** red apple or tomato slices for Fire.
3. **Yellow:** corn or banana for Earth.
4. **White:** radish or a hardboiled egg for Metal.
5. **Black:** currants, purple grapes, purple cabbage, blueberries, raisins, or elderberries. (Dark blue or purple will suffice.)

The night hours between 11:00 p.m. and 3:00 a.m. are best for spirit summoning and spirit communication. These ascendant hours correspond with Wood, which is also associated with our connection to ancestors. An I Ching mediumship reading to speak with your twelfth-generation ancestor would be optimized at those hours. If this is your first attempt at spirit contact, then perhaps waiting until midnight can help you optimize your chances of success.

Have three candles prepared. The three represent the celestial, earthly, and underworld realms. Light the center candle and place it upon your altar. Then turn off the electricity in the room so the only illumination is that single candle. With that center candle, light the other two. Dip a stick of incense into the center flame and restore it to its incense holder, which should be positioned in front of the three candles. Arranged in front of the incense are the offerings to the sacred Black Tortoise. Place this book to the right side of the offerings. This is your altar, which ideally should be on a raised platform.

Have sacred religious relics on the altar and also worn upon your person. Examples are sacred books placed on the altar in addition to this text you're holding, which has been preemptively fortified with sigils within these pages to ward off unwanted spirit guests. Upon your person, wear religious jewelry or mala prayer beads. Measures such as these, along with having thoroughly cleaned and purified the altar area ahead of time, will help prevent the ritual from going awry.

I then like to kneel next to the altar and perform this divination ritual by tossing the six cowrie shells to the floor, but I wouldn't consider that necessary. If you prefer to be seated in a chair at a table, that's fine, too.

Place the six cowrie shells between cupped palms, emulating the sound of a rattle. Shake the cowries rhythmically, hearing the sound of the rattle. That light and pleasant clacking attracts beneficent spirits.

I start by permitting myself to be mesmerized by the curling wafts of incense smoke. Continue shaking the cowries like a rattle. Feel yourself getting drowsy, entering a dreamlike state. Your eyelids are heavier, so you close your eyes. The rattling sound continues at an even, steady, hypnotic tempo.

Speak aloud, slowly, and let the beats of the rattling sound punctuate your words:

> "Black Tortoise, my family name is [announce your surname]. I seek to speak with a twelfth-generation ancestor of mine. Please guide the spirit of my ancestor to me. As a humble token of my gratitude, please accept these offerings."

Repeat the petition as many times as you intuit is necessary. Lean into the sensations you feel. Observe the patterns of the candle flames and incense smoke. Together, they will let you know when the ancestor has arrived.

Once you feel a shift within you, pause the rattling of the cowries. Feel the presence of the spirit. How does the air feel? How does your skin feel? Your body?

Promptly introduce yourself. This is just good manners. Thank the ancestral spirit for taking the time to see you. Then state your request: "Please reveal to me something about my family. Please share with me an insight into who I descend from and where I come from that will help me better understand who I am."

Resume shaking the rattle formed by your closed, cupped palms and the cowries. Continue to repeat your request as many times as you intuit is necessary. Through trial and error, you'll learn how your physiology reacts to spirit contacts. For me, it's a gentle nudge behind my elbows that didn't come from my own force. That's when I let the nudge guide my forearms and release the cowries onto the ground.

In the same way most East Asians will consider it more polite to wait until the giver of a gift has left before opening the present, at this time, do not focus on the cowries or think about what the reading result might be. Try in earnest to focus on the spirit presence and caring about that spirit's presence.

Turning your attention to the ancestor presence, convey your heartfelt thanks and bid the spirit farewell. For the farewell, sit meditatively in silence and communicate through your emotions. Not a word need be exchanged; only the emotions you're emanating. When you've "said" (through feelings) all that you've wanted to say, recite only once: "Ancestor of my blood and bone, thank you for all that you have done. May your return be safe and sound."

The Black Tortoise will know to come and guide the ancestral spirit's return. Clasp your hands together in prayer and bow. Stay bowing until you feel a shift in the air and know that the spirits have left. The exact etiquette of your bowing will depend on your cultural heritage. The way you've been taught to bow to elders and eminent ones is how you should be bowing here. If you're uncertain, then nod your head forward slightly, chin down, and keep your eyes to the ground, with hands clasped in prayer until you feel the shift and intuit that the spirit presence is gone.

Restore the lights, and now you can assess the divination result.

The shell landing closest to you indicates line 1 of the cast hexagram. Each shell indicates successive lines of the hexagram from the bottom up, according to its distance from you, so that the shell that's farthest away is line 6. The smooth, convex side of the cowrie is yang, and the hollow, concave side is yin.

Some of the shells might land very close to one another. Look carefully to discern distance. If two or more are truly *exactly* the same distance from you, the lines are constructed in order from the rightmost shell to the left, as the Asian languages are classically written. For example, if the second and third shells are at the exact same distance from you, the one to the right is line 2, and the one to the left is line 3.

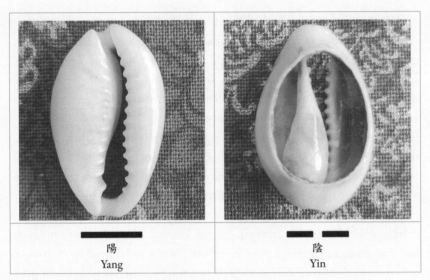

**FIGURE 9.5** Cowrie shell correspondences

For the divination result pictured in figure 9.4, the following hexagram is constructed:

Read the entire hexagram entry. The Oracle section will give you the ancestral spirit's response to your inquiry. You will also be reading all six of the line statements of the hexagram as a narrative.

Line 1 reveals what life was like at the time for the family—the life your twelfth-generation ancestral spirit was born into. Line 2 is that ancestral spirit's childhood. Line 3 conveys the ancestral spirit's adulthood and own family life. Line 4 conveys what it was like toward the ancestor's end of life. Line 5 is the legacy that has endured over the centuries, that you've inherited. Line 6 is a final revelatory and prophetic message the spirit would like to leave you with.

**TABLE 9.1** Ancestral Spirit Communications through Hexagrams

| Line 6: | Final revelatory message for you | **Upper trigram:** Livelihood, personality, life's work, own family, what you've inherited |
|---|---|---|
| Line 5: | Legacy that endured over the centuries | |
| Line 4: | Matters relating to end of life and death | |
| Line 3: | Adulthood and own family life | **Lower trigram:** Foundations of the ancestor's life, place, family economics, identity |
| Line 2: | What childhood was like | |
| Line 1: | What life was like for the family | |
| **The Oracle message:** General summary of the life your ancestor lived and what the ancestor most wants to convey to you about your heritage | | |

References to "auspicious," "favorable," or "gains" relate to socioeconomic privilege; "ominous" connotes socioeconomic hardship; and "blameless" or "there is no blame" means fairly middle-class or middle of the hierarchy for their time. "Auspicious to cross the great stream" means the ancestor wants you to know about a notable achievement.

If the hexagram number is odd, then the ancestor that came to visit took on a more historically masculine role in the family. If the hexagram number is even, then the ancestor that came to visit took on a more historically feminine role.

In the example of casting Hexagram 31, a male ancestor came through per the odd number value. In the subsequent photograph of the reading result where all six shells turned up yin, Hexagram 2 denotes a female ancestor coming through.

**FIGURE 9.6** Cowrie shell casting for Hexagram 2

The Oracle message will need to be deciphered. Think of it as a riddle to solve. Moreover, your ancestor can and will use trigram correspondences to communicate specific details. Trust your intuition. A good I Ching reading is an interplay between the themes the hexagram lines convey to you and your gift for identifying how those themes play out in concrete human language. The questions you most want to know in terms of specificities are answered by those trigram correspondences. It's a matter of whether you can decode the message.

For the lower trigram, look to correspondences from chapter 5 that indicate which region they lived in or the landscape of their hometown (mountainous, close to a large body of water, north, south, etc.), and look to the weather correspondence for that region's climate. The lower trigram will shed light on the family circumstances that supported them and social class that the ancestor was born into.

For the upper trigram, the correspondences will indicate the ancestor's livelihood and the family they created and supported. Also look at the traits corresponding to the upper trigram. This sheds some light on the ancestor's personality and disposition. The Wu Xing phase correspondence for the upper trigram will also reveal the ancestor's key character traits. Consult chapter 6.

Afterward, the fruit and vegetable offering that had been given to the Black Tortoise spirit can be eaten. The Black Tortoise is a celestial spirit, so consuming the earthly *qi* of the fruits and vegetables is what the spirit enjoys. By consuming the earthly *qi* for itself, the spirit leaves behind its celestial *shen*, meaning those fruits and vegetables are now blessed. You eating those fruits and vegetables now brings blessings to you.

This practicum is one I would recommend to anyone who is interested in learning a little more about their Asian heritage.

To adoptees, while meeting biological relatives just one or two generations from yourself can be a roll of the dice, one thing I can say with fair certainty is that your ancestors from twelve generations ago, no matter what they might have been like while living, are more than eager to embrace you. They'll enthusiastically share with you what their lives were like and who they were, and you'll find those insights in the correspondences to the trigrams and the Wu Xing.

To those leading nontraditional lives who are worried whether their ultratraditional family would accept them, this of course is on a case-by-case basis, and no universally true statement can be made. That said, a twelfth-generation ancestor is not going to be as judgmental as you might fear. Being in spirit and having that transcendent view of this world that being mortal couldn't have provided them with means they're much more open-minded and compassionate than they were while living.

They're curious about you. They're intrigued by your world. They're accepting and tolerant because the superficialities and social norms they would have been restricted to as humans are no longer there. Having existed for 360 years as a spirit compared to the number of years they lived as human means they've evolved. Just as you wouldn't want to be judged right now by how you behaved as a toddler, it wouldn't be fair to judge the spirit of a twelfth-generation ancestor by how they were as humans.

# 10

# The *Yì*, the *Wū*, and Shamanism

## Shamanic Origins of the I Ching

The origins of the I Ching are shamanic.

The rhythmic and ritualistic yarrow stalk method of divination pulls you into a different state of mind, trancelike and meditative. The rattling sound of metal coins and cowrie shells produces music. The voice that responds to your inquiry is a channeled spirit.

The I Ching was first and foremost intended for prayers to gods and ancestors, through which the spirits answer.[1] The Book is a mediator between worlds. More importantly, the Oracle reveals Heaven's Will to you.[2]

According to the Ten Wings, we can communicate with spirits (神 shén) through dancing and drumming, in the form of rites and rituals (變 biàn).[3] The Book of Rites 樂記 (Lè Jì) emphasizes that rites—including rituals involving dancing and drumming—unite Heaven with Earth and placate the spirits.[4] The music that holds such power comes from instruments made of metal and instruments made of stone.[5] Music pleases the gods, leads you to Heaven, and leads the demons back to the underworld.[6] Ritual is to music as Heaven is to Earth, as interconnected as yin and yang, linked to the realms of demons and gods.[7]

Chinese philosopher Li Zehou 李泽厚 (1930–2021)[8] said the two most important characteristics of the Chinese civilization are (1) the clan system of relationships bound by kinship, and (2) shamanism within the shamanistic-historical traditions.[9] Li contends that King Wen, who received the hexagrams, and the Duke of Zhou, who received the line statements, were shamans.[10] Writes Li:

> The research of archaeologists from Chen Mengjia[11] to Zhang Guang-zhi[12] has shown that kings were the head shaman. The work of many scholars has shown the ancient sage-kings of Chinese tradition to have been shaman leaders, including those celebrated in Confucianism—Yao,[13] Shun,[14] Yu,[15] Tang,[16] King Wen, King Wu, and the Duke of Zhou. . . . The shaman was able to communicate between heaven and human, imploring and exhorting heaven to rain. Scholars have shown King Wen to also have been a shaman, and the Duke of Zhou's legendary offering of himself to the spirits to relieve King Wu's illness likewise involved shamanism,[17] as recorded in the Book of Documents.[18]

Thus, the Book of Changes descends from the *wū* 巫, China's shamanistic-historical traditions.[19] According to lore, King Wen and the Duke of Zhou *received* the Yì 易. As shamans, they were representing, conveying, and carrying out Heaven's Will. The Oracle teaches us this: divination reveals how to be in alignment with Heaven's Will, and when you are in alignment, you are divine. To be divine means to be protected and to thrive in a transcendent state.

Shamanism 巫術 *(wū shù)* is a religious culture premised on the belief that selected members of society possess the ability to communicate with or be vessels to gods, spirits, and ancestors.[20] A shaman can also traverse between worlds. There is a cosmological belief in a tiered cosmos, with a heavenly level, the middle realm of Earth, and an underworld.[21] Shamans traverse to the underworld to rectify imbalances in the cosmos that were causing plagues and disease.[22] A *wushi* shaman 巫師 *(wū shī)* is a healer, exorcist, medium, diviner, prophet, and magus. The shaman is one who is able to commune with spirit entities from other realms.

The *Guo yu* 國語 (453 BC), or *Discourses of the States*, is a compendium of eight books transcribing the speeches of kings and other prominent court officials of the Zhou. The text differentiates between a male shaman, called a *xi'* 覡, and a female shaman, called a *wū* 巫.[23] However, in modernity *wū* 巫 is applied as a general term for a shaman, irrespective of gender identity.

**FIGURE 10.1** Oracle bone script for *wū* 巫

The word for I Ching divination, *shì* 筮, is the character for shaman 巫 paired with bamboo or yarrow stalks, *zhú* ⺮ (竹).[24] Consider the opening operations in yarrow stalk divination. The formations of the stalks resemble the upper and lower horizontal stalks plus the connecting vertical stalk, as you see in the character for shaman 巫.

As for the etymological origins of the word *wū* 巫, one theory for the ideogram's original meaning is the depiction of a ritual dance or two people praying and dancing for rain.[25] I lean toward an alternative theory. The arrangement that resembles the formation of stalks during divination is a symbol of what the shaman does—bridge different realms so exchanges and interchange can happen between the two realms. The two figures on either side can represent ritual dance, yes, but it also represents astrally journeying and soul dualism. It's the binate of the shaman's consciousness when channeling spirits from other realms. Thus, to me, the ideogram depicts communication between worlds.

In oracle bone inscriptions, the word 巫 was used in both the context of referencing a shaman and in the context of referencing dance.[26] The interchangeability of the word for the two meanings might suggest that to the Shang, shamanism was dance, and dance was shamanism. Dance was not merely an artistic performance; rather, it held sacred significance. Dance was prayer. Shamanistic dance was the earliest spiritual and cultural practice unique to humanity.[27] In the later *Shuowen jiezi* 說文解字, compiled AD 25–220, the *wū* 巫 was defined as a supplicant, a female who is able to serve the formless 無形 *wú xíng* and through dance bring the spirits downward.[28]

## PRACTICUM 10.1: I Ching Divination by Dance

Take pause to reflect on what you are unhappy about. What induces worry? What negative thought or concern has been plaguing you? What are you insecure about? As your focus concentrates around this unhappiness, that negative feeling begins to aggregate, and you can feel it clump up in your throat.

With a strong, sharp exhale, make an audible guttural sound as you blow that clump out of your throat. It is now a hanging orb, suspended in the air. This negativity is an imbalance in the universe. Through sacred movements in rites, you'll be transmuting that negativity to restore balance.

Play a traditional folk instrumental song, and let the music enchant you. Alternatively, play music with a strong, pulsating vibration that you can hear through your skin, that you can feel moving your heart-mind. Dance to the music, every movement inspired by the divine. There is a numinous wind that you are able to sense when in dance, and your every movement is shifting, stimulating, and influencing that numinous wind, a *qi* life force.

As you progress, move in such a way that you know intuitively is taming that numinous wind. There's a sentience to that wind that's coming alive and is now listening to your movements. You've convinced that numinous wind to follow you and support you.

Now move that wind around the negative orb you ejected and expelled out of your body. The numinous wind is stronger and is now overpowering the negative orb, which in turn restores balance as the wind consumes and neutralizes the orb.

Slow down your movements so you can steady your heart rate. This can be walking in circles until you've calmed back down, or if you've remained seated and are not pacing, temper and relax the movements of your body.

As you slow down, the wind your dance movements generated converts into a psychic or unseen energetic power. The way you know to eat and drink, you know to absorb that energetic power to nourish your body, mind, and spirit.

Close your eyes. Sit in stillness, now fully relaxed. Feel a divine presence, that numinous wind. That presence is beneficent and fulfilling, and it feels like contentment. Now that the wind has consumed and neutralized the negative orb, it will reveal to you what more to do going forward to ensure security and prosperity, and to maintain contentment.

Before you start the I Ching divination, feel yourself open and receptive to a flickering light source in the universe, but that light source is also a sound wave, and you can hear it through clairaudience—your astral ears, not your physical ones. This is the voice of that numinous wind.

Put pen to paper and channel the impulses you feel vibrating and palpitating through your body like wavelengths, which you are now converting into words. There won't be more than a few key phrases.

Then proceed with the I Ching divination. I recommend the coin toss method. Let the metal coins jangle rhythmically in your cupped hands. The rattling sounds they make form language. If you prefer the traditional yarrow stalk method, that's perfect as well.

When you have concluded the divination, integrate what you channeled from listening to the voice of the wind with the message from the Oracle. There will be resonance between the two. The divinatory message you receive is counsel on how to maintain the balance that your dance has begun to restore. By maintaining balance as counseled by the Oracle, you can ensure prosperity, a more enduring sense of security, and happiness.

## The Loanword "Shaman" and the *Wū*

This text adopts a descriptive meaning for "shaman" to be applied in an overbroad manner that covers a diverse range of folk traditions. I'll be using it as a loanword to cover folk practices inclusive of and extending beyond the shamanistic practices of northeast China, central Asia, and Siberia.[29] Let's start with where this loanword might have come from. Several theories circulate about the etymological origins of the word *shaman*.

One theory is that it comes from the Tungusic word *šaman* (шаман or саман).[30] The Tungusic are a collective of ethnic groups native to Siberia, north central Asia, and northeast Asia. *Šaman*, in short, means "priest of the Uralic-Altaic peoples (those who speak Uralic-Altaic languages)," originating from the Turkish-Mongol languages.[31] Per this theory, Russian explorers migrated the word westward into Europe during the seventeenth century.[32] Personally, I think it might have been earlier than that, during the thirteenth-century Mongol expansion and conquests. When the word *šaman* appeared in a twelfth-century Chinese dictionary, the term was defined as "sorceress."[33]

A second theory for the origins of the word "shaman" is from *shraman* श्रमण, derived from Pali (and *çramana* in Sanskrit),[34] meaning an ascetic spiritual seeker, or more specifically, a Buddhist ascetic.[35] One of the earliest mentions of the word *shramana* dates back to around 700 BC, in the Brihadaranyaka Upanishad बृहदारण्यक उपनिषद्.[36] The term denoted a mystic cultivating transcendence of humanity's worldly nature, striving for a heightened state of consciousness. Then, just as Buddhism migrated from the Indian peninsula to north Asia, *shraman* was introduced to the Turkic-Mongol lexicon.[37]

Beginning in the Jin dynasty (1115–1234), the Manchus of northeast China differentiated themselves from the ethnic Han people through their religious identity of shamanism (*saman* or *sama* in Manchu).[38] A Manchu *saman* was one who had experienced a spiritual death and rebirth, and as a consequence, could travel to and from the world of spirits.[39] By the Ming dynasty (1368–1644), *wū* 巫 shamanism as practiced by the ethnic Han had waned in favor of Confucianism, Taoism, and Buddhism. When the Manchus ruled China during the Qing (1636–1912), they instituted state shamanism, and in 1747 the Qianlong emperor (a Manchu) standardized Manchu shamanism in a commissioned Shamanic Code.[40] The ethnic tensions between the Manchus and Hans has also meant that among the Chinese, there's controversy over whose system of magico-religious practices can be called *wū* 巫 shamanism. Thus, the moniker of 巫 can become a matter of sensitive identity politics.

While the shamanic traditions of Asia are vibrantly diverse, what seems to unite the shamans of the Manchus and the Hans with Tengrism in Mongolia, the Buryat and Tungus in Siberia, the Indigenous practice of Bön བོན in Tibet, the *tangki* 乩童 of Taiwan, the *jhakri* झाक्री of Nepal,[41] and the *mudang* 巫堂 of Korea is this word "shaman"—or, more specifically, their nonuse of the word.

Today, the word "shaman" has become a marketing tactic to attract outsiders. Among themselves, these mystics do not self-identify as shamans. In Mongolia, use of the word "shamanism" has become a product of the Euro-Western gaze. Native practitioners would simply call it Tengrism. The "shaman" is a priest of Tengrism, one who divines the future, communes with spirits, and heals the sick.

The more commonly used equivalent terms for "shaman" in Mongol are *böö* (Buryat) and *bügä* or *bögä* (Mongolian), which gets translated to "sorcery."[42] *Bü/böö* is then translated to *wū* 巫 in Chinese, bearing some relation to *bo/bǔ* 卜, meaning to divine, which is connected to the term *ki/ji* 乩, used in various parts of China and Mandarin-speaking Asia to indicate a spirit medium. The Tibetan term for sorcerer is *aba/ba*.[43]

Even use of the word *wū* 巫 by the Chinese and *mu* 巫 by Koreans to denote a shaman is a postmodern reclaiming of the term. Native practitioners of *wū* in Asia, especially from the rural regions less affected by globalization, don't identify as shamans or witches. As I've often heard from my own mother and relatives in Taiwan, *wupo* 巫婆 (a female shaman or witch) is a term used by people they'd call outsiders—those who do not practice the mystical arts—to describe those who do. Someone who is actually a *"wupo* 巫婆" would not self-identify with that term unless they're an educated urban millennial or younger who fancies a reconstruction of the distant past. At best, an equivalent term might be "spirit medium."

On the mainland in Wenzhou, China, male shamans are called *shén hàn* 神漢 and female shamans *shén pó* 神婆. Spirit mediums who drum, dance in a trancelike state, and speak or sing in tongues are called *shén tóng* 神僮, meaning a child of Spirit. Colloquially, they're still known as *wū* 巫, and the women are described as *wupo* 巫婆 (female shamans or witches), but the term *wupo* bears a pejorative connotation, as it does to most native practitioners of it in Taiwan. The shamans themselves prefer *not* to use the designation *wū*.[44]

Similar to the Chinese shamans of Wenzhou, many of the older shamans in Seoul consider the term *mudang* 巫堂 disrespectful, and they prefer the title *mansin* 萬神.[45] The centuries of persecution and social backlash that the *wū* and *mudang* were subjected to have effectively tainted the connotations of these titles.[46] It's only in recent decades that the sentiment has changed, with an active reclaiming of the term *mu* 巫, just as there is an active reclaiming of the term *wū* 巫.

The commonality in sentiments across Asian ethnic groups and cultures is striking. Notice how the preferred title in Korean, *mansin* 萬神, is not too different from the preferred titles in Chinese, *shén hàn* 神漢 for male shamans and *shén pó* 神婆 for female shamans, or the alternative, *shén tóng* 神僮. The titles share the term "神" to replace "巫."

## Shamanistic-Historical Traditions

Shamanism was practiced in ancient China as far back as 5000 BC. The Yangshao 仰韶 were a Yellow River civilization that existed between 5000 BC and 3000 BC. Neolithic art and gravesites confirm that Yangshao shamanism is one of the earliest examples of a system of rites and rituals in China.[47] Chieftains who led the Yangshao were shamans or *wū* 巫 who would use effigies of animals such as dragons, tigers, and deer as their spirit helpers, where the animals represented particular spirits assisting the shaman in communicating with the other realms.[48] It's speculated that the drums crafted by the Yangshao served the purpose of empowering a shaman's spirit contacts and journeys to other realms. The invention of the drum is even attributed to the *wū*.[49]

Excavation of a Jiahu burial site in China dated to the early or middle Neolithic Age unearthed pairs of turtle shells with pebbles placed between the paired shells, as if forming rattles, and proto-characters inscribed on the shells.[50] One burial of a shaman-chieftain had eight such relics made of turtle shells and pebbles placed on different parts of the body of the deceased. Archaeologists believe that these turtle shell rattles were either a divination tool or a healing talisman.

Among the Hongshan 紅山, a Neolithic culture in northeast China between 4700 and 2900 BC, religious and military power was consolidated in a shaman king.[51] It was not uncommon at all for military leaders and great

**FIGURE 10.2** Illustration of Jiahu turtle shells

warriors to be shamans, and vice versa. Hence, one of the archetypes of the mystic covered by the eight trigrams is the Warrior (corresponding with Lake). Even into the Shang, historic figures such as Fu Hao 婦好 served as both military general and high priestess or shaman.

Oracle bones further affirm the existence of a thriving shamanistic culture that was the religious backbone of ancient China, reaching its peak during the Shang and Zhou of the Bronze Age.[52] Shang dynasty shamans (商巫, *Shāng wū*) held political authority because their connection to the gods and ancestors could validate the sovereign rights of a king or state.[53] During the Shang, the king was the kingdom's chief shaman.[54] Thus, since the Neolithic era, shamanism has played a central role in China's foundational political history.[55]

Beyond their political authority, the *wū* occupied a specialized class in society for one key reason: generally, humans and spirits should not and do not intermingle, with one exception—the *wū*. Thus, shamans were the only designated class of humans excepted from that rule. They were the ones with illuminated or specialized knowledge of the other worlds above and below ours. They possessed a prescience that empowered them to divine the future. They could hear messages from gods, spirits, and ancestors. What's more, they could understand and thus decipher the cryptic signs and omens of the spirits. During the Shang and Zhou, shamans were also mathematicians and geometers.[56]

A principal tenet of Shang shamanism was belief in the power of animal spirits. Animal spirits, mythical and real, such as dragons, scorpions, and toads, were venerated as manifestations or messengers of the gods. The Shang venerated the black crow as the ancestral animal spirit they descended from,[57] referenced in Hexagrams 5 and 12. Of particular note was a mythical beast called the Hànbá 旱魃, a scorpion-like flying creature with martial skills who could take the form of a goddess.[58] She wore blue robes and wielded the power to emit light and heat. However, the creature-goddess was also the cause of droughts and was therefore both feared and shunned.

It's unclear whether Hànbá is a mythical animal, goddess, demon, or all of the above. The Hànbá also came to be associated with death. She was the goddess who transformed into a raven to look after the corpses of the recently departed, guiding their souls to the afterlife. Female shamans 女巫 *(nǚ wū)* during the Shang would channel Hànbá,[59] who in turn empowered the shamans with supernatural and magical abilities.

Perhaps what most defines the work of a shaman is astral journeying for the purpose of exchange with the spirit world or to rectify imbalances in the spirit world causing harm in the physical world. Asian shamanic traditions will vary in this regard. Some traditions conceptualize the journey as ascent versus descent along an axis mundi, which is what you'll often hear from north Asian shamanism. In the south, journeying is conceptualized as lateral, "crossing over." A shaman becomes a vessel for gods or spirits to "cross over" laterally and mount. Mirrors become emblems of portals or keys to cross over liminal gateways between worlds.[60]

Another aspect of astral journeying is dreamwork, which can also serve as a form of divination, or oneiromancy. Dreamwork is the shamanistic practice of going to an underworld or netherworld while in a sleep state or as a lucid dream. A part of your soul (recall the belief in soul dualism or multiple facets of soul covered in chapter 9) journeys to the realm of the dead, a realm of demons, hungry ghosts, dragon kings, and dragon spirits under water, or a realm of fox spirits, among other spirit planes, to mediate an adverse situation that is happening on earth in the physical plane.

By the late Zhou, however, the shaman's role changed to be more ceremonial than political. They presided over state-sponsored rites, prepared the sacrificial offerings, and looked after the temples. Well into the Han dynasty (202 BC–AD 9; AD 25–220), *wū* were appointed to the imperial court.[61] They would oversee rituals, perform divinations, and serve as healers alongside court physicians.

Both Confucianism and Taoism are birthed from *wū* shamanistic-historical traditions, and to that end, the whole of Chinese culture is built on the foundations of those traditions.[62] China's clan society heavily emphasized the importance of ritual and music, a value sourced back to the Duke of Zhou. Ritual governs the body, and music governs psychology.[63] Ritual dance was also intended to be magical. A shaman's ceremonial shooting of an ox effigy during a dance was intended as a blessing to ensure a successful hunt of oxen the next day.[64] It is also through leading ritual that the shaman is a historian—ritual is cultural history.

Shamanism is central to the cultural identity of Korea as well, as documented in the compilations in state history of shamanistic rituals, dating back to AD 375 under King Kunchogo of Paekche.[65] The *kut* rituals of Korean shamanism are the most instructive for understanding the importance of rites. During a *kut* ritual, the *mansin* 萬神 shaman invokes a spirit entity, and the spirit displaces the *mansin*'s personality and takes over. In the shaman's body, the spirit can drive away misfortune, increase prosperity, and give divinatory readings. Each movement in the ritual dance is deeply symbolic and is a way of modifying metaphysical energy that is creating changes in the earthly plane, in real time as the dance progresses.

The *kut* are typically performed in the shaman's altar room or god hall (神堂 *sindang*), with the altar positioned along the north side of the hall, because guardian spirits descend from the north.[66] This reminds me of the *Yili* 儀禮 (475–221 BC) noting that an I Ching diviner faces north,[67] and the general belief that the north corresponds with ancestors, the afterlife, and the underworld. Likewise, when the Duke of Zhou petitioned the Zhou ancestors and divined for blessings, he built his altars facing north.[68]

To guide the dead through a safe transition to the afterlife, the *mansin* performs a ritual called the *ogu* 誤鬼 *kut*. The *pyong* 病 *kut* heals the sick. There are also rites for venerating particular gods and spirits, such as the *yongsin* 龍神 *kut* for honoring the dragon spirit.

Implicit within the responsibility of conducting rites and rituals is knowledge of astrology so the shaman can pick auspicious calendar dates for state events and, most importantly, military activities.[69] You may have noticed that even in the I Ching, many of the lines are structured to prognosticate whether to advance a military campaign or launch an attack.[70]

It was during the Han (202 BC–AD 220) that the tension between the institution of Confucian scholars and the institution of the *wū* culminated.[71] Starting in the first century BC, the status of shamans in a Confucian-dominant society declined.[72] Specifically, Confucianism was a humanist and rationalist tradition of philosophy. The ecstatic dance and spirit mediumship of the *wū* stood in stark contrast to rationalist Confucian thought. Confucians emphasized the I Ching's literary, aesthetic, and philosophical value, and they cast a sharply skeptical eye at using the Oracle for spirit mediumship.

During the Song (960–1279), the *wū* were differentiated from Taoist ceremonial magicians, and the ceremonial magicians denounced the *wū*.[73] The tension might be comparable to the present-day tensions between ceremonial magic and folk witchcraft—aren't they the same thing? And yet dare assert that in a room full of ceremonial magicians and witches. Likewise, shamans and Taoist priests both engage in divination, faith healing, astral journeying, sorcery or spellcasting, soul retrieval, and rituals while emphatically demanding that each faction be seen as unrelated to the other.

Thus, while Confucianism and Taoism both scorned *wū* shamanism, they both arose from *wū* shamanism.[74] Despite the aversion Taoist ceremonial magicians might have historically felt toward the *wū* shamans, *wū* shamanism indisputably cemented the foundation of Taoist magic.[75] The ceremonial magician's pacing rituals, astral projection techniques, and methods of petitioning gods and spirits through modes of magical writing come from the shamans they denounce.

Most importantly, the fundamental cosmological basis of both the *fashi* 法師 Taoist methods master and the *wushi* 巫師 shaman is the I Ching, from the metaphysical theory of yin and yang to the eight trigrams. Today, both the Taoist ceremonial magician and the folk shaman craft magical talismans called *fu* 符, perform soul retrievals, channel spirits, and tell fortunes. They use magical mirrors and wield similar ritual tools. They face the same condemnation and censure from mainstream society.

Whether the *tâng ki* 乩童 of Taiwan are shamans is a matter of contention. In southern Taiwan, the *tâng ki* are spirit mediums who dance into an ecstatic frenzy, enter a trancelike state, and proceed to speak in tongues that mimic the speech of infants. The spirit mediums engage in religious self-flagellation with weapons until rivulets of blood stream down their heads and bodies. The self-flagellation purifies the body so a god can enter and possess that body, and it demonstrates the spirit medium's devotion to the god.

Channeling spirit entities is a prominent feature among the *tâng ki* 乩童. The spirit medium allows a god to take possession of the physical body and mind in a process called 上身 *shàng shēn*, meaning "mounting the body." The god then speaks through the possessed medium, sending its powers through the medium to heal the sick or give prophecies.

A similar question is raised as to whether the Hmong *txiv neeb* are considered shamans. I would say yes, absolutely. To heal an illness, the *txiv neeb* of the Hmong enter a trancelike state to journey into the spirit realm and converse with the person's spirit body or other knowledgeable spirits on that astral plane to determine what is wrong.

Often to achieve good, the *txiv neeb* has to broker a deal, a *puaj dab*,[76] with evil. In general, concepts of "good" versus "evil" aren't clear-cut in the Hmong belief system and don't have any equivalent concept in the Western Christianized lexicon. A spirit entity attaches to the afflicted—or, if not attached, then has stolen a fragment of soul from the afflicted—out of retaliation for some wrong that the spirit entity believes was perpetrated by the afflicted. Whether the spirit's actions are justified or not, now the *txiv neeb* must mediate, talk it out with the spirit, talk it out with the person, and figure out how to reach a settlement. In one sense, you could say a *txiv neeb* is practicing both law and medicine. The *puaj dab*, or settlement, might call for the exchange of spirit money *(ntawv nyiaj)* or the sacrifice of an animal in exchange for return or restoration of the afflicted person's soul fragment.

Today, Taoist priests from the many ethnic groups across southern China and mainland Southeast Asia syncretize Taoism, Buddhism, and folk practices of magic, rites, divination, and faith healing. Each tradition has specialized names for their priests, be that a *hmxphī* หมอผี, a master of spirits in Thailand, or a *thầy cúng* in Vietnam, which translates to shaman, and yet is often used interchangeably with *Đạo sĩ*, meaning a Taoist priest. Are they unambiguously distinct in cultural practice from each other and from the Tenger *böö* in Mongolia or the *mansin* 萬神 *(mudang* 巫堂*)* of Korean shamanism? Yes, absolutely.

Historically in Japanese shamanism, distinctions were made between the *echiko* 市子 blind woman[77] who engaged in spirit possession and the *miko* 巫女 priestess in Japanese Shinto, though both are still described as shamans. The *miko* performed a ritual dance called the *kagura* 神楽, intended as an offering to the *kami* 神,[78] similar to the dances performed by the *wū* 巫 shamans of China, with their foremost role as spell-crafters, casting talismans.[79] The *echiko* or *itako* イタコ were typically blind women who were spirit mediums channeling the voices of *kami* and the dead.[80]

Whether these diverse and disparate traditions should all fall under the umbrella of shamanism, and how fine a point to make in distinguishing the Taoist priest from the shaman, comes down to a matter of perspective. Do you want the label of *wū* 巫 to draw boundaries or to unify?

Shamanism is not a primitive, archaic magico-religious practice that remains frozen in time, unchanged for millennia.[81] It is a dynamic, living tradition.

I define a shaman as one who navigates liminal spaces, treading where most people don't go and can't go. Their purpose for navigating such spaces is to acquire knowledge that is otherwise inaccessible. Their functions of healing and divination are byproducts of acquiring that knowledge. Just as humans evolve and nature changes, gods and spirits change too. The relationship between spirits and the shaman evolves.

All of these traditions we've skimmed across in this chapter are modalities of shamanism. Their practitioners are shamans. The *wū* of 1046 BC may look very different from the Manchu *wū* of the seventeenth century, and certainly different from the present-day *tâng ki* 乩童 spirit mediums of Taiwan, but that doesn't mean they're mutually exclusive from each other; it means there has been change. The Taoist priest is not mutually exclusive and separate from the shaman, and we see this in the immortal He Xian Gu 何仙姑, both a Taoist priestess (道姑, *Dào gū*) and a shamaness (女巫, *nǚ wū*).

The *miko* 巫女 performing the *kagura* 神楽, who approaches spirit work with a very different aesthetic from the *thầy cúng* or *txiv neeb* performing a soul retrieval, share the same sensitivity to the unseen. A *mansin/mudang* from Korea has more in common with the *txiv neeb* from Laos than she does with the uninitiated profane of her own culture, because the *mansin* shares a spiritual heritage with the *txiv neeb*. The *jhakri* of Nepal and the *shén pó* 神婆 are both communicating with spirits through dancing and drumming, which the I Ching instructs as the way we communicate with spirits.[82]

Thus, what remains as the common axis that defines the shaman is one who navigates the thresholds between life and death.[83] The Korean *mansin* performs the *ogu* 誤鬼 *kut* to guide the recently departed, ensuring safe transition into the afterlife. The *tâng ki* 乩童 of Taiwan and *echiko* 市子 of Japan channel the dead so that the living might find closure. Even the shaman's role as healer is about decay, about knowing what has separated and disintegrated in the spirit realm, causing harm in the earthly counterpart.

Moreover, the shared nonuse of the word "shaman" uniting the previous generation of Asian mystics is the same as the shared reclaiming of that word today by the up-and-coming generation of shamans now navigating the liminal spaces between globalization and the digital revolution.

# PRACTICUM 10.2:
# An Ancestral Shaman Spirit's Blessing

Wuxian 巫賢 was a chief shaman 大巫 or grand high priest who served the Shang dynasty court. He lived some time during the fifteenth century BC. According to the Book of Documents 尚書 (Shàngshū), dated to the Shang and Zhou: "During the reign of King Zu Yi of Shang, the devoted and faithful Wuxian was the chief shaman 大巫 who served as the mediator between Shangdi 上帝 and the King of Shang."[84]

A powerful diviner, astrologer, rainmaker, and healer, Wuxian is considered the great ancestor of the 商巫 *Shāng wū*, or Shang dynasty shamans. He is credited as having invented the drum 鼓 *gǔ* that *wū* shamans use in their rites, and a form of divination 筮 *shì* using stalks of grass. The *Liezi* 列子 (fifth century BC) traces Wuxian's lineage back to the Yellow Emperor, and from Wuxian came a long lineage of great *wū* 巫, shamans and healers.

The chief shaman was then deified 神化 *(shén huà)* and venerated as an ancestor spirit who can gift shamans with blessings.

An ancestor or deified shaman spirit who can bless present-day shamans is a recurring and unifying motif found across Asian cultures. The *txiv neeb* shamans of the Hmong spiritually descend from Siv Yis, the first shaman, a divine being with the knowledge of healing and defeating evil.[85] The *jhākri* of Nepal hold a similar belief: the first and primordial shaman was Mahādev, who created shamans and taught them the magical arts, *tantra-mantra*.[86] Mahādev gifted the descendant shamans with magical drums and knowledge of how to heal the sick and exorcise evil. Likewise, the *tâng ki* of the cultures by the Pacific Ocean venerate Matsu, who was a shaman in her mortal life and was then deified as Wuxian was. Matsu is now a patron goddess whom shamans pray to for blessings.

This practicum will call upon the ancestral spirit of Wuxian in prayer to receive a divine omen on how you might advance in your metaphysical and spiritual studies from where you are now. Using the yarrow stalk method instructed in chapter 7, you'll be constructing a trigram of the Ba Gua, rather than the six-line hexagram.

For this divination ritual, opt for all-blue ceremonial wear. You do not need special articles of clothing; rather, from what you already have, go with an outfit that is predominantly a medium to dark blue. One common association I found among north Asian and southeast Asian shamanistic practices was the color blue in traditional ceremonial wear.

You'll also want to prepare three small dishes of offerings, such as uncooked grains, nuts, seeds, candies, fresh fruits, or pastries, and three cups (a small teacup size will suffice) of drinks, such as a good liquor, tea, and juice/nectar.

After the spirit has accepted the *qi* of these offerings, the spirit will replace that consumed *qi* with *shen* 神, meaning the offerings become blessed. When you consume those offerings after the divination ritual, they will bless you with good health and prosperity.

Begin by washing your hands and rinsing your mouth thoroughly. This is symbolic of personal purification. Light one stick of incense. Next, tap a wood block instrument three times. Alternatively, in lieu of a wood block, you can beat a ritual drum or ring *tingsha* cymbals three times. You'll want to beat at about forty beats per minute.

Recite the following:

| I call upon Ancestor Wuxian and pray for your Great Blessing | *Bài qǐng Wū Xián Zǔ qí shòu zī jiè fú* | 拜請巫賢祖<br>祈受茲介福 |
|---|---|---|

Then rap the instrument three more times to conclude, again at forty beats per minute.

Proceed with the yarrow stalk divination where three operations of counting will yield a single *yao* line. However, you'll be stopping at three rounds of the counting operations, to produce a three-line trigram rather than a six-line hexagram.

| Counting Operations | | | | Sum of Three Counts | | |
|---|---|---|---|---|---|---|
| First count → | 5 stalks | = | 3 | 6 | X | Changing yin |
| | 9 stalks | = | 2 | 7 | | Unchanging yang |
| Second count → | 4 stalks | = | 3 | 8 | | Unchanging yin |
| | 8 stalks | = | 2 | 9 | X | Changing yang |
| Third count → | 4 stalks | = | 3 | | | |
| | 8 stalks | = | 2 | | | |
| | Sum of Three Counts | | | | | |

If the resulting trigram had changing lines, cast a second transformed trigram using the same method for casting a transformed hexagram. If the result of your trigram was all unchanging lines, producing a locked trigram, then you will double the trigram, similar to receiving the "※" result.

The primary trigram you received in the divination invoking Ancestor Wuxian will reveal to you what your greatest gift is as a metaphysician and what area of study or spiritual cultivation to advance. This is Ancestor Wuxian revealing to you what facet of the mystic you are growing into right now.

If, for example, the received primary trigram is Thunder, turn to the corresponding entry in chapter 5. The trigram is interpreted as an omen from Ancestor Wuxian. Read through the entry for your primary trigram. What is the ancestral shaman spirit pointing you toward? Bridge the gap with your intuition.

The archetype of the mystic corresponding with your primary hexagram reveals your strongest talent or ability as a mystic. In the example of Thunder, the corresponding archetype is the Spellcaster. This is someone with an innate above-average aptitude for spell-crafting. Ancestor Wuxian is advising you to further hone that skill.

| RECEIVED PRIMARY TRIGRAM | | | TRANSFORMED HEXAGRAM |
|---|---|---|---|
| Third operation | 6 | ▬▬ ▬▬  X | ▬▬▬▬▬ |
| Second operation | 8 | ▬▬ ▬▬ | ▬▬ ▬▬ |
| First operation | 7 | ▬▬▬▬▬ | ▬▬▬▬▬ |

If, for example, the primary trigram is Fire, then the corresponding archetype is the Philosopher. You probably apply academic rigor to metaphysics. You care deeply for the theoretical because you want to answer how and why. You also have the potential to become a leading luminary. These next few months, lean in more to book study of the occult arts.

The Warrior archetype in this context refers to activism in your community. Consider the metaphor of the military strategist, which was a key role of the Shang dynasty shaman. What social change or movement are you being called to contribute to?

The trigram Heaven, corresponding with the Virtuoso, is an omen to embrace music and dance as forms of personal ritual and expressions of spirituality. Bring more music and dance into your life. You are probably one with a natural talent for choreography rites and ceremonies. Optimize that.

If the archetype of your received trigram is the Shaman, this is perhaps a most affirming sign. If your received archetype is The Healer, you probably would have made a great medical doctor, no matter what professional field you've ended up in. Consider serious dedication to study of the healing arts. Learn arts such as reiki, aromatherapy, or herbalism, for example.

The sign of the Alchemist appearing in such a divination ritual right now is the ancestral shaman spirit letting you know that you are on a defined, specialized path toward achieving a personal Great Work. Now, your focus should be entirely on completing that Great Work, an undertaking that is your magnus opus.

The Enchanter is one who understands the deeper and more profound value of aesthetics. This is one with innate charisma, which you can cultivate into gains of social influence. When you consume the blessed offerings, your charisma is going to be augmented, and the next chapter of your life path is about achieving heightened social influence.

Next, note the Wu Xing cycle correspondence for your primary trigram. In the example of Thunder, the governing Wu Xing phase of change is Wood.

Wood corresponds with spiritual cultivation, from the Five Mystical Arts of Taoist metaphysics. Thus, to advance in embodying the facet of the mystic that is the Spellcaster, dedicate the next three moon cycles (i.e., lunar months) to the mystical art corresponding with Wood, which is spiritual cultivation.

This is how you best solidify your own foundations so you can be a more powerful, effective mystic.

**TABLE 10.1** Eight Trigrams and Five Mystical Arts Correspondences

| TRIGRAMS | | | | WU XING | | FIVE MYSTICAL ARTS |
|---|---|---|---|---|---|---|
| ☳ | Thunder | ☴ | Wind | 木 | Wood | Spiritual Cultivation |
| ☲ | Fire | | | 火 | Fire | Divinatory Arts |
| ☶ | Mountain | ☷ | Earth | 土 | Earth | Study of Appearances |
| ☰ | Heaven | ☱ | Lake | 金 | Metal | Study of Fate |
| ☵ | Water | | | 水 | Water | Study of Healing Arts |

Assign the transformed hexagram as the upper trigram, and the received primary trigram as the lower trigram. If there were no changing lines in your divination, then double the trigram. For example, if none of the lines were changing in the primary trigram of Thunder, then the resulting hexagram would be Thunder over Thunder.

In the example of the top changing line in the trigram Thunder, the transformed hexagram is Fire. Thus, the hexagram result is Fire (the assigned upper trigram) over Thunder (the assigned lower trigram). This is Hexagram 21.

Read the Oracle message for your resulting hexagram. This is the ancestral shaman spirit guiding you on what you most need to do next to advance in the most self-empowering way. To achieve that, the *qi* to cultivate and master now relates to the correspondences of your primary trigram.

After the divination ritual, bow your head to give thanks for the blessed food and drink. You may then consume the offerings you had given to the ancestral shaman spirit.

Anyone from any walk of life can call upon Ancestor Wuxian. If you feel a closer connection to the goddess Matsu, then invoke her by replacing the preceding invocation with the following:

| I call upon Shamaness Matsu and pray for your Great Blessing | *Bài qǐng Wū Mā Zǔ qí shòu zī jiè fú* | 拜請巫媽祖 祈受茲介福 |

Of course, this divination ritual for receiving blessings from an ancestral shaman spirit can be modified to reflect your culture, heritage, or spiritual path. You're invited to invoke either Ancestor Wuxian or the goddess Matsu, but feel free to adjust any part of the instructions for invocation of your own tradition's ancestral shaman spirit. If you're of Hmong ancestry, for instance, that might be Siv Yis.

When approached with sincerity and earnest heart, you may find that any physical or emotional ailments you had been afflicted with will have improved. The ancestral shaman spirit has empowered you with what you need to advance faster in your metaphysical studies; what's more, no ancestor shaman is going to leave without a little bit of healing magic applied to what's been ailing you. It's just the nature of the shaman.

## The Eight Gods of Shang Shamanism

The *wū* 巫 shamans of the Shang invoked eight emanations of divinity: (1) Tiāndì 天帝, a heavenly emperor synonymous with invocations to a high god Shangdi 上帝; (2) Shè 社, a god of the soil; (3) Fēng 風, a deity of the wind; (4) Xún 旬, a divine personification of time, characterized as the ten-day week; (5) Hé 河, a divine personification of the rivers; (6) Yuè 岳, a divine personification of the mountains; (7) Dōng Mǔ 東母, the Eastern Mother; and (8) Xī Mǔ 西母, the Western Mother.[87]

**TABLE 10.2** Eight Gods of the *Wū* Shamans and the Ba Gua[88]

| Tiāndì 天帝 | Shè 社 | Fēng 風 | Xún 旬 |
|---|---|---|---|
| Heaven | Earth | Wind | Fire |
| Hé 河 | Yuè 岳 | Dōng Mǔ 東母 | Xī Mǔ 西母 |
| Water | Mountain | Thunder | Lake |

Aside from the highest god in heaven, Shangdi, major rivers were thought of as the source of rain, and thus Hé 河 was invoked alongside Shè 社, the god of soil, for abundant harvests. Sacrificial offerings to Hé and Shè were made by sinking or drowning the sacrifices into the rivers and by burial. These offerings ranged from jade objects and precious silk to sheep, pigs, cows, horses, and even human sacrifice.[89]

**TABLE 10.3** Eight Trigrams and Corresponding Gods

| TRIGRAM AND EIGHT INNER ARCHETYPES OF THE MYSTIC | | EIGHT IMMORTALS AND THEIR MAGICAL WEAPONS | SHANG GODS OF THE WŪ AND CORRESPONDING DIVINITIES |
|---|---|---|---|
| ☰ 乾 | Heaven 乾<br>The Virtuoso | Han Xiangzi 韓湘子<br>Flute 笛子 | Tiāndì 天帝<br>God of the skies<br>*Also*: Shangdi 上帝 |
| ☱ 兌 | Lake 兌<br>The Warrior | Zhong Li Quan 鍾離權<br>Fan 葵扇<br>*Also*: Iron war fan | Xī Mǔ 西母<br>Western Mother<br>*Also*: Xiwangmu 西王母 |
| ☲ 離 | Fire 離<br>The Philosopher | Lü Dong Bin 呂洞賓<br>Peach wood sword 寶劍 | Xún 旬<br>Personification of time<br>God or goddess of the sun<br>*Also*: Zhurong 祝融 |

**TABLE 10.3** Eight Trigrams and Corresponding Gods *(continued)*

| | | | | |
|---|---|---|---|---|
| ☳ | 霊 | **Thunder** 震<br>The Spellcaster | Cao Guo Jiu 曹國舅<br>Clappers 雲陽板 | **Dōng Mǔ** 東母<br>Eastern Mother<br>*Also*: Dong Wang Gong 東王公<br>or the god of thunder 雷神 |
| ☴ | 巽 | **Wind** 巽<br>The Shaman | He Xian Gu 何仙姑<br>Lotus 莲 | **Fēng** 風 God of the wind<br>*Also*: Fengbo 風伯 or Feng Po Po 風婆婆 |
| ☵ | 峪 | **Water** 坎<br>The Healer | Li Tie Guai 李鐵拐<br>Longevity gourd 葫芦 | **Hé** 河 God or goddess of the moon<br>*Also*: Xuanwu 玄武 or Beidi 北帝; Matsu 媽祖 |
| ☶ | 艮 | **Mountain** 艮<br>The Alchemist | Zhang Guo Lao 張果老<br>Drum 鱼鼓 | **Yuè** 岳<br>Dongyue 东岳 or the mountain god Sanshin 山神/산신 |
| ☷ | 堉 | **Earth** 坤<br>The Enchanter | Lan Cai He 藍采和<br>Flowers 花籃 | **Shè** 社<br>*Also*: Houtu 后土; Tudigong 土地公 (tutelary god of the soil) |

References to the *shen* 神 or spirit of the eight trigrams are woven through the subtext of the I Ching. Dongyue 东岳 is referenced in Hexagram 52. Houtu 后土 is referenced in Hexagram 2. This is also the Mother Goddess of Vietnamese folk beliefs.[90] Xún 旬 is referenced in the first line of Hexagram 55, Thunder over Fire. These are just to name a few of the many shamanistic undercurrents of the Oracle.

Whether you conceptualize the eight trigrams in the abstract, as awareness of concepts, or you personify the eight trigrams as spirits and give those spirits names, the destination remains the same: self-awareness and utilizing that self-awareness to achieve personal balance. One type of person might prefer to focus on programming code, which are the trigrams, while another type prefers the humanized visual.

The eight inner archetypes of the mystic, the Eight Immortals, and the Shang gods all represent *shen* 神, spirit.

*Shén* 神 refers to gods and ancestors, deities, and that which is magical, mystical, or considered supernatural. This is the 神 of *mansin* 萬神 and *shén tóng* 神僮 of *kami* 神.

*Shén* 神 is also your spiritual center, your mind (心神, *xīn shén*), psyche (精神, *jīng shén*), and consciousness (神志, *shén zhì*). It is your higher self, that which inspires you toward wisdom, compassion, and beneficence. It is the divinity within. A healthy spiritual center will heal what is afflicted in the body or the mind; likewise, afflictions of the body or mind will affect the spiritual center, your inner 神 (*shén*).

Shamanism isn't that far removed from psychology. Both, at their core, address mental health. *Shén* 神, be that gods, ancestors, spirit, or inner psyche, is in, is every part of, and manifests as the myriad mysterious things.[91]

## Soul Retrieval: Theory and Practice

The practice of soul retrieval is a form of healing. It's premised on the belief that physical and mental illness is caused by imbalances or fragmentation of the soul. Chronic physical conditions, incurable diseases, anxiety disorders, ADHD, and every assortment of afflictions were attributed to aspects of the soul leaving the body, wandering off and getting lost, or getting stolen by demons. A ritual to call the soul back home, or soul retrieval, was seen as the cure.

In Hmong shamanism, the *ua neeb khu* is the healing ritual in which the shaman, the *txiv neeb*, who is the master of spirits, a title given to shamans, enters a trancelike state. The *txiv neeb* shaman crosses over beyond the thresholds of earth and sky to investigate the cosmological imbalance causing one to be sick.[92]

Communicating with the spirits in that realm, the *txiv neeb* is then able to restore balance and thus heal the illness or retrieve lost souls.[93] In Hmong cosmology, the human body hosts many souls, each serving a different function. Physical and mental illnesses are attributed to one or more of these souls leaving the body. When a person's soul fragments or pieces of it leave the body, the body becomes imbalanced, and that imbalance is the cause of ill health or peculiar behavior. Soul retrieval is a ritual that calls that lost fragment of soul back to its body, restoring that body to whole. A similar belief is found among the traditions of Mongolian shamanism, a belief in achieving a state of *tegsh*, or balance in the world, between Father Heaven and Mother Earth.[94] Each person's body is like a micro-universe that can become imbalanced when there has been disaster (causing part of the soul to flee from the body) or spirit interference (causing part of the soul to have been abducted).

*Ua neeb khu* rituals are not a relic of the past but still very much a vibrant practice in the present within the Hmong American community.[95] Peer into any Asian enclave or any rural community in Asia and you will still find practices of shamanic soul retrieval.[96]

The Hakka 客家 are an ancestral group considered part of the Han, though they're often segregated or marginalized from the majority Han. My father is Hakka, while my mother is Minnan 閩南, also called Hoklo and Hokkien (the name of the ancestral group varies depending on region). Beliefs in soul retrieval are found in the traditions of both groups.

Among the Minnan, soul retrieval practices are not as common as *shou jing* 收驚, a form of faith healing found in Taiwan, Hong Kong, and Macao, among other regions of the south. For various reasons, from trauma or grief to demons or another witch's curse, a part of the soul can be shocked, frightened, or terrorized into leaving the body. Since part of the soul is now missing, the person will experience physical or mental illness. *Shou jing* retrieves that lost fragment of soul and thus cures the illness. Two different practices are both considered *shou jing*.

The first is to call a soul back home, similar to the soul retrieval discussed earlier. Rituals vary from region to region, but essentially, there is a ritualistic calling out or shouting of the person's name, telling that fragment of soul to return to its body. A bundle of incense sticks is burned all at once and often waved around in the air as you shout or call, so the soul can follow the scent and smoke of the incense back to the body.

The second form of *shou jing* typically involves a Fu talisman and incantations of spells and invocation of powerful deities. In southern Taiwan, Kuan Yin and Matsu 媽祖, the goddess of the Pacific Ocean and a patron ancestor deity of shamans,[97] are commonly petitioned. However, different lineages, traditions, and even individual spirit mediums will venerate different patron deities. Another frequently invoked deity is the Queen Mother of the West. Those who identify as *shén tóng* 神僮 might venerate Nezha 哪吒, a deity who takes on the form of a child; thus, when Nezha possesses a spirit medium, the medium will speak and behave in a childlike manner, chewing on pacifiers and baby bottles.

The *wū* shaman or a Taoist priest (both practice *shou jing*) will then place the talisman on the afflicted, with a laying on of hands, and will continue the incantations to draw out a demon believed to be attached to the soul. Once the demon is drawn out of the soul and into the paper talisman, the talisman is burned and the affliction is cured.

Table 10.4 is an example of a popular *shou jing* incantation among the Minnan and Fujianese. If we're applying a critical analysis of the incantation, it seems to be both a soul retrieval and an exorcism, conflating the two. This particular *shou jing* incantation exemplifies real-life shamanic practices that don't fit neatly into academic categories.

The first part calls upon divine forces to retrieve or harvest the fragment of soul that has been frightened away from the body. It can also be translated to "stop and put an end to this fright." The second part is in effect an affirmation. The third is exorcising the demon causing the affliction. In short, the incantation retrieves what was lost and then banishes the demon that caused the soul fragmentation.

**TABLE 10.4** *Shou Jing* Incantation for an Exorcism and Soul Retrieval[98]

| I call upon Kuan Yin and Matsu to retrieve the lost soul, to put an end to this fright. | Bài qǐng Guān Yīn Fó Zǔ, Mā Zǔ lái shōu jīng. | 拜請觀音佛祖、媽祖來收驚。 |
|---|---|---|
| [Name of the afflicted], fear not, hold your courage, resolute and unflinching, your heart-mind is steady and restored. | [Name of the afflicted], wú jīng wú dǎn xià, xīn gān tóu àn dìng dìng. | [Name of the afflicted] 無驚無膽嚇，心肝頭按定定。 |
| Shou qi qi shou li li<br>Evil spirits be ousted—<br>You are banished away, a thousand miles from here. | Shōu qǐ qǐ shōu lí lí<br>Xiōng shén 'è shà chū qù, zǒu qiān lǐ. | 收起起收離離，凶神惡煞出去，走千里。 |

For the line, "*Shōu qǐ qǐ shōu lí lí*" from the English translation, I've left the line as a direct transliteration, since the sounds and rhythm of the line are more important than stating its meaning. In essence it means "the soul fragment has been restored; the demon is gone," but it's the sound of the words that hold power. Note also the repetition of the word "離" *(lí)*, which is the trigram for

Fire. The word "起" *(qǐ)* appears in the fourth line of Hexagram 44, which uses an account of the corrupt last king of Shang and his concubine Daji as a parable. (Later mythologized accounts of Daji would characterize her as a demon fox spirit.)

The Darkhad shamans of northern Mongolia have a belief and practice similar to *shou jing*.[99] They believe that there are multiple facets to the soul, and the portion of it that is the vital soul can leave the body due to fright, shock, or trauma (not unlike the psychological concept of dissociation).[100] The shaman would then need to engage in a ritual of soul retrieval to call that fragment of vital soul back to the body.

The Khalkha use metal mirrors to reintegrate a soul fragment.[101] The mirror is placed over the chest or the spiritual spine of the afflicted so that that the soul fragment can safely return. Alternatively, a mirror can be used to draw out a demon from a body, and that demon spirit trapped within the mirror.

Ethnic groups such as the Yao or người Dao of Vietnam and Mien 瑶族 in southern China have practices similar to *shou jing* that involve drawing the demon out of the body and into either a Fu talisman or an egg. In the syncretizing of Buddhism and Taoism, Buddhist sacred texts such as the Heart Sutra, the Diamond Sutra, or the Great Compassion Mantra are recited for exorcising the demons. In Yao/Mien *shou jing* rituals, you'll also find invocations of the Three Pure Ones or the Jade Emperor. Other ethnic groups, such as the Hakka, also place the Three Pure Ones as central in their theology. The ink scroll painting featured on my family's shrine shared in figure 9.3 in chapter 9 features the Three Pure Ones.

## PRACTICUM 10.3:
## Soul Retrieval Ritual Invoking Kuan Yin

This is not a practicum for everyone to perform and is not to be used irresponsibly. It's provided here as a "break glass in case of emergency" last resort for self-healing.[102] The following is a Hakka soul retrieval, integrating elements of Hmong shamanic traditions.

How do you know when would be an appropriate time to perform a soul retrieval ritual on yourself? If a fragment of your soul is lost, you'll know. It's a feeling of emptiness, a hollow within, and you just *know* a part of you has gone missing. No matter what you do, you feel off balance. You feel listless, melancholic. Physically you might be experiencing chronic illness, aches, or pains, as if the rest of your body is trying to overcompensate for what is lost.

Most important of all, you've exhausted all avenues of resources accessible to you. You have sought every means of expert medical and qualified health care available to you. Traditionally, the soul retrieval ritual was performed on children or young women suffering from illness, be that physical or mental. In the present day, the shaman is sought alongside a medical doctor, and both modern medical or psychological treatment and soul retrieval work in tandem with each other.

A fair question to ask might be: how can you successfully perform a soul retrieval ritual when you are not an initiated or even trained shaman? This soul retrieval ritual isn't exclusive to shamans. The matriarch of a family was

**FIGURE 10.3** Kuan Yin from the Heart Sutra by Zhao Mengfu 趙孟頫 (AD 1254–1322)

considered more than authorized to perform such a ritual for the young ones. Also, in this specific practicum, you're doing it on yourself, so the ritual is innately more powerful because of your intention-setting and strong bond to the lost fragment of soul.

The traditional Hakka soul retrieval ritual consisted of burning gold and silver joss paper as offerings to gods (the gold) and ancestors (the silver). Burn a total of fifty sheets to represent yin and yang in balance, and gods and demons in balance. (The number fifty is used for the same reason that fifty yarrow stalks are used.)

Traditionally, an article of clothing belonging to the sick child would be passed through the smoke of the burning joss. The one performing the ritual would repeatedly call out the sick child's name, along with the command to return home. The child would be seated close by. You won't need an article of clothing if you're performing the soul retrieval ritual on yourself.

As you burn the sheets of joss paper one by one, repeatedly recite the invocation below. It's one often used by shamans and spirit mediums in Taiwan. The invocation calls upon Kuan Yin, the bodhisattva of mercy and compassion. I've adjusted the pinyin romanization for nonnative speakers, to help with pronunciation. I would strongly urge recitation first in Mandarin, and then follow up with a recitation in English. The Mandarin recitation is for summoning the power from beyond and to tap in to a preexisting old channel of established ancestral shamanic power. The English is to summon the power from within, because you need to know what you're saying for the words to have force.

| | |
|---|---|
| *Bài qǐng Guān Yīng lái shōu jīng.* | 拜請觀音來收驚。 |
| *Wú jīng wú dǎn xià,* <br> *xīng gān tóu àn dìng dìng.* | 無驚無膽嚇， <br> 心肝頭按定定。 |
| *Shōu qǐ qǐ shōu lí lí,* <br> *Xiōng shén 'è* <br> *shà chū qù, zǒu qiān lǐ* | 收起起收離離， <br> 凶神惡 <br> 煞出去，走千里。 |
| I call upon Kuan Yin to retrieve what has been lost. | |
| I banish all fears. I am not threatened, I am not scared. <br> My heart, my mind, steady and restored. | |
| Give me strength to rise, to be made whole. <br> I take back what is mine; Kuan Yin, retrieve my soul. <br> I vanquish you, demon—I banish you far from here. | |

The recitation has two objectives. The first is to restore your strength so that when the soul fragment returns, your body can repair itself. The second is put as much physical and psychic distance between you and the perpetrator as possible. In the recitation, the perpetrator is characterized as a demon.

Note that the "離" in the line *"Shōu qǐ qǐ shōu lí lí"* is the Fire trigram. For emphasis, the English has a second recitation of Kuan Yin's name that isn't in the Mandarin.

Continue doing this until all fifty sheets of joss paper have been burned. Put out the fire and collect the ashes into a pouch. Seal the pouch shut. Keep this pouch on you at all times and on your nightstand while you sleep.

Additionally, a knotted red string bracelet is put on the wrist of the child's weaker hand. The string bracelet is inspired by the Hmong string-tying ritual, though it is a common folk practice found across the south of Asia. Here, you'll tie the bracelet onto yourself.

There would typically be a final affirming statement to close, such as 急急如律令 *(jí jí rú lǜ lìng)*, or "So may it be." A Buddhist-leaning family would recite 南無阿彌陀佛 *(Námó Amítuófó)* as a mantra to the Amitabha Buddha.

Since you're invoking Kuan Yin, recite:

*Námó Guānshìyīn púsà* 南無觀世音菩薩

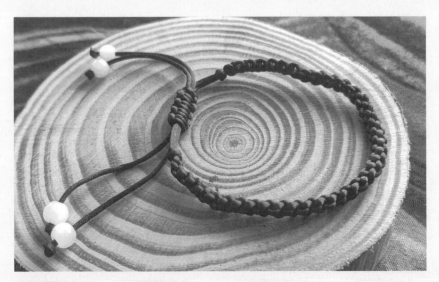

**FIGURE 10.4** Knotted red string bracelet of protection

It essentially means: "With reverence, I hereby invoke the bodhisattva Kuan Yin."

Keep the talisman pouch on you at all times, and continue wearing the knotted red string bracelet until you feel restored to wholeness. The sealed pouch of ash is in effect a medicine bag. It performs the function of a spiritual homing beacon to guide all that you've lost back to you. It also strengthens your system so that, once all of you has returned, your body, mind, and spirit will heal itself. The red string bracelet represents sutures, to tie everything in place while you heal.

If the red string bracelet falls off on its own, take a moment to self-assess. Intuitively scan and feel your body. How do you feel? Did the bracelet fall off because the spirits are confirming to you that you no longer need it? Or did the demon who took the fragment of soul overpower the ritual working and cause the bracelet to fall so you will be more vulnerable?

An I Ching divination will also answer that question promptly. A response of "auspicious" means all is well. A response of "ominous" means you'll want to repeat the entire ritual again and replace the lost red string bracelet. You need to fortify yourself more; sadly, your first attempt wasn't enough.

When all is well and restored, put the talisman pouch away in storage. It is now transformed into a blessed object that's lucky to keep around. As for the red string bracelet, continue wearing it until it falls off on its own.

If you have been severely wronged, violated, and hurt while the perpetrator seems to go unpunished and unscathed, that feeling of injustice tinged with resentment festers and can cause the soul to fragment. Also, the perpetrator who inflicted a serious moral transgression has, whether knowingly or not, served a demon, and in that sense, possessed by a demon, has taken away a piece of your soul. When any part of you feels broken, even if it is your heart, a soul retrieval ritual can help to patch you back up.

If nothing else, a soul retrieval psychologically helps to bring solace. It is a way to reclaim your power and restore yourself to whole when no one else will do it for you. You can also perform it on a close friend who has experienced such a violation. While the impulse may be to go with a more aggressive magical approach, such as a curse, bear in mind that in such a situation, your first priority should be to heal. If you really seek to punish, wait until you're back to full strength.

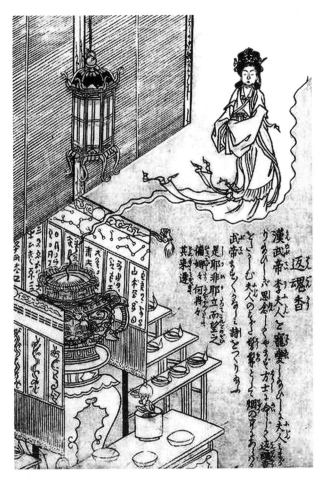

**FIGURE 10.5** Hangonkō 返魂香 (1780) by Toriyama Sekien. According to a legend from the Han dynasty, Fǎn Hún Xiāng 返魂香 (Japanese はんこんこう, Hankonkō) is a magical incense the size of a swallow's egg and black as a mulberry. When this incense burns, the sick will recover and the dead will rise within three days. Emperor Wu of Han 漢武帝 (156–87 BC) used this magical incense to bring his beloved dead concubine back to life. An early record of this magical incense is sourced from *Shizhouji* 十洲记, a collection of fantastical fiction from the Han. Later, Taoist alchemists and mystics took inspiration from the stories, such as using black styrax/storax resin incense in soul retrieval rituals.

## Xī Wáng Mǔ, Goddess of the *Wū*

In Taoist mysticism, the Queen Mother of the West, Xī Wáng Mǔ 西王母, is one of the most important goddess figures in the pantheon. Taoist *fangshi* 方士 invoke the Queen Mother to help them cultivate the Tao. *Fangshi,* translated as "methods master," can refer to occultists, ceremonial magicians, alchemists, diviners, exorcists, astrologers, holistic healers, and every variety of mystic. First and foremost, Xī Wáng Mǔ was the goddess shamans called upon, and she chooses shamans and *fangshi* as her medium for communicating with humanity.

The earliest records we have of a Western Mother date back to the Bronze Age,[103] when a Western Mother (西母, Xī Mǔ) and her counterpart, the

**FIGURE 10.6** Queen Mother of the West 西王母 (Qing dynasty) by 金廷標. SOURCE: National Palace Museum, Taipei.

Eastern Mother (東母, Dōng Mǔ) were invoked together for divination. These records were first found on oracle bone inscriptions (殷墟卜辞, yīn xū bǔcí) from the matriarchal societies of the early Shang (1600–1046 BC).[104] According to these inscriptions, offerings were being made to the Western Mother and Eastern Mother in hopes that prayers would be answered. One of the earliest mentions of Xī Mǔ was an invocation inscribed upon oracle bone: "We divined: if we make offerings to the Eastern Mother and Western Mother, there will be approval."[105]

Over the next several millennia, oral tradition would maintain that the Western Mother, a Queen Mother (王母, Wáng Mǔ) as found in the I Ching, and the Queen Mother of the West 西王母 (Xī Wáng Mǔ) were one and the same goddess. Twenty-first-century historians have their doubts, though I'll honor tradition and continue to view them as an unbroken lineage of veneration. In the southern regions of Taiwan, the Queen Mother and the Golden Mother 金母娘娘 (Jīn Mǔ Niáng Niáng), through their astrological connection to Venus, are venerated as one and the same goddess.

She is also known as Lady Queen Mother 王母娘娘 (Wáng Mǔ Niáng Niáng), though this is a later evolution of the goddess, and Lady Queen Mother 王母娘娘 is nearly always depicted as younger, beautiful, and elegant. Meanwhile, Xī Wáng Mǔ's depictions have greater range, from a crone with wild, untamed hair and a tail to a fuller-bodied stern woman wearing an ornate *feng guan* 鳳冠 or phoenix headdress.

Within the time period of her early veneration, the western region that she ruled would have been west of China's central plains.[106] The west was where the sun set and thus became associated with the unknown, with mysteries, death, and the afterlife. Due to her connection with death and the underworld, she works closely with the Black Tortoise of the north, a guardian spirit over our ancestors.

Popular myth today has her residing on celestial Kunlun Mountain, though earlier accounts had her residing on Jade Mountain. Kunlun is the pillar that connects heaven, earth, and the underworld, the axis mundi of Taoist mythology. Xī Wáng Mǔ is sovereign over the axis mundi. At the peak of the axis in heaven is a tree that grows the peaches of immortality, an ambrosia. The peaches on the world tree only bloom once every three thousand years.[107] Ritual swords and the magical tools of Taoist *fangshi* 方士 are crafted from peach wood to connect their craft to the goddess. The Queen Mother's palace is the most opulent and lavish imperial palace a mortal has ever seen, where the Queen is attended to by beautiful Jade Maidens 玉女 *(yùnǚ)*.[108]

On the peak of Mount Kunlun adjoining the Queen Mother's residence is a paradise reserved for shamans, the *wū* 巫.[109] Go there and you'll meet Wuxian 巫賢, the great ancestor of the shamans and the many notable *wū* and witches through the ages. There they tend to their gardens of numerous medicines. Through these canons, Xī Wáng Mǔ is associated as a patron goddess of the *wū* 巫. She is invoked for every form of sorcery, from love spells to curses. Taoist *fangshi* study the scriptures of the Queen Mother to cultivate stronger *qi* specific to spiritual cultivation.

The earliest depictions of Xī Wáng Mǔ showed her as a demon of plagues and a dark goddess of destruction. The West Mountain Sutra 西山經 from the *Classic of Mountains and Seas* 山海經 (circa 300 BC) describes the Queen Mother as a human with a leopard's tail and tiger's teeth. Her hair is long and wild, and upon her head she wears an ornate *sheng* 笙, a regal crown with detailing that resembles the plumage of a rare bird.[110] The *Classic of Mountains and Seas* also describes the nine-tailed fox 狐狸精 *(hú lí jīng)* as one of the Queen Mother's close companions, along with a winged wolf-like beast 獸焉 *(shòu yān)* with the horns of an ox, and a mythical crimson-feathered pheasant 鳥焉 *(niǎo yān)*.

Of particular note, pottery unearthed in the Qinghai province at the Lajia archaeological site, where archaeologists have excavated artifacts from the early Bronze Age (2300–1500 BC), bears illustrations depicting dancing figures that are part human and part animal. These figures had human faces and torsos, a leopard tail, and sharpened tiger's teeth.[111] Whether there are any connections between Xī Wáng Mǔ and these Bronze Age depictions of ritual are unclear, but the specificity of the details might suggest that there are.

The white tiger is the totemic animal spirit associated with the west, and thus is also associated with the Queen Mother. Other animal spirits associated with her range from wildcats and foxes to three-legged crows and scorpions. The scorpion association is what connects her as a key divinity in *wū* shamanism.

In Taoist and Chinese shamanic lore, Heaven is subdivided into nine regions, just as Yu the Great subdivided his kingdom into nine regions, with nine tripod cauldrons as the emblem of an emperor's divine right to rule. While the Queen Mother resides in the western region of Heaven, it's nevertheless understood that she rules over all nine of them. Thus, her most well-known protégé, 九天玄女 (Jiǔ Tiān Xuán Nǚ), is referred to as the Lady of the Nine Heavens. Jiǔ Tiān 九天 is a reference to the zenith point in the sky. In Taoist cosmology, Jiǔ Tiān 九天 is also a reference to the nine tiers of Heaven, 九重天 (jiǔ chóng tiān).[112]

In the I Ching, the second line of Hexagram 35 references a Queen Mother: 于其王母 (tú qí Wáng Mǔ), meaning in honor of Grandmother or to be blessed by the Queen Mother. In antiquity "Queen Mother" was the title for a deceased paternal grandmother and thus signifies one's ancestor. Likewise, the Wáng Mǔ (王母) in Xī Wáng Mǔ is a reference to our ancestral grandmother spirits.

Recall the creation myth of Nǚwā we covered in chapter 2. Nǚwā had to remake humans from clay after an apocalyptic flood wiped out the first humans that populated earth. Those first humans were created by Xī Wáng Mǔ, one of the first divinities to arise from the Taiji 太極 (numinous omnipresence) and Wuji 無極 (numinous nothingness).

The "Inner Chapters" 內篇 ("Nèi Piān") from the Zhuangzi 莊子 (350–250 BC) describes Xī Wáng Mǔ as an immortal spirit dwelling in the far west, one of the first and primordial gods birthed from the Tao.[113] "Nobody knows her beginning, and nobody will know her end."[114]

She is considered a dark goddess because she was created from a pure form of divine yin. "Queen Mother" isn't just a reference to a powerful goddess; she is a creator goddess whom we honor as an ancestor spirit.

Xī Wáng Mǔ is the ruler of Heaven's wrath (天之厲, tiān zhī lì), the bringer of calamities, and the Wu Can (五殘, wǔ cán), meaning Five Destructions, a star (or multiple star system) observed in ancient times believed to be malefic, similar to the Demon Star (Algol) of ancient Egyptian astronomy. The star's name translates to the Five Destructions. "厲" appears in the I Ching several dozen times.[115]

Whether the malefic star referenced as the Five Destructions is the same as or even related to Algol, a multiple-star system in the constellation Perseus, is unclear. However, we do know that in Eastern astrology, Perseus is 大陵 (dà líng) and Algol is counted as the fifth star of the constellation, or 大陵五 (dà líng wǔ). Algol is in the western mansion (a similar concept to a horoscopic house) of the White Tiger 白虎 báihǔ. Thus, the Demon Star is still under the purview of Xī Wáng Mǔ.

In Songs of the Eminent Ones 大人賦 (Dà Rén Fù) by Sima Xiangru 司馬相如 (179–117 BC), an Eminent One journeys through astral worlds of dragons, spirits, and other mythical beings. The world is subdivided into four directions. In the west is Xī Wáng Mǔ's imperial palace on Kunlun Mountain, where an Eminent One can only enter guided by a Jade Maiden, one of the Queen Mother's celestial attendants. Xī Wáng Mǔ is described as having white or silver hair, wearing an ornate crown, with three-legged blackbirds as her companions.

**FIGURE 10.7** The Banquet of Seowangmo (Joseon, 1392–1910). SOURCE: Los Angeles County Museum of Art.

The Living Sutra of the Queen Mother of the West 洞眞西王母寶神起居經 (Dòng Zhēn Xīwángmǔ Bǎo Shén Qǐjū Jīng), of unknown authorship dated to the Eastern Jin (AD 266–420), is a collection of Taoist alchemical practices utilizing qigong and acupressure. The text is also used in exorcisms.[116] According to the Living Sutra, the Queen Mother grants immortality to those who are worthy and will share secret formulas of mystical practices with those who are devoted to her.

By AD 400 to 500, she is revered in many schools of Taoism.[117] The White Lotus, a Taoist secret society and mystery tradition in China founded in the twelfth century, venerated the Queen Mother of the West 西王母 (Xī Wáng Mǔ). She is a frequently invoked patron goddess among the *wushi* 巫師, holistic healers, spirit mediums, and diviners. The Yaochidao 瑤池道 in Taiwan is a Taoist lineage that venerates the Queen Mother as the principal divinity and path to salvation.[118]

You'll have noticed that the Qing dynasty silk paintings of 西王母 featured in this chapter depict a significantly tamed version of Xī Wáng Mǔ. Most of what has survived are imperial palace paintings, which tend to avoid the version of the Queen Mother who is a feral dark goddess with wild hair, sharp teeth,

The Yì, the Wū, and Shamanism 809

**FIGURE 10.8** Seiōbo, Queen of the West. SOURCE: By Keishu Takeuchi (1868–1912). Woodblock print.

and a leopard's tail. By the *Bamboo Annals* 竹書紀年 (299 BC), descriptions of the goddess took a notable turn for the gentler, regal, refined queen. Through the dynasties, she became a venerated patron goddess of women and was prayed to for blessings of love, marriage, and safe childbirth.

The Queen Mother of the West embodies divine yin. What that means to humans will vary and even change over time. Within China, presentations of her are diverse. Similar to how Fuxi and Nǚwā are depicted as a pair, the Queen Mother is commonly paired with either the Jade Emperor or the Grand Duke of the East. The *fangshi* traditions of the south, however, will often depict her as an independent all-powerful goddess, without a partner. Unlike Fuxi and Nǚwā, the Queen Mother has her own temples and orthodox sutras or devotionals that invoke her alone, with no Jade Emperor or Grand Duke in sight.

The Queen Mother is divine yin, but she transcends the locked interdependent binary of yin and yang. She is the feminine personification of Wuji 無極, the numinous void, and was self-birthed from the Wuji. Another name she goes by is Wujimu 無極母, divine mother of the numinous void. Self-birthed from that darkness, she began life as a powerful demon. According to Taoist lore, she was a demon who taught herself the Tao and ascended to Heaven, now eternally ruling as a celestial from her palace in the west. It is her demon origins that keep her connected to the underworld, even though she's now part of the heavenly court.

Today, there has been a reclaiming of her fearsome dark goddess aspect. The new up-and-coming generation of Asian witches and Taoist mystics is hearing her call. In Korea, she is known as Seowangmo 수왕모. In Japan, she is Seiōbo せいおうぼ; in Vietnam, *Tây Vương Mẫu*.

As a self-birthed dark goddess from the numinous void and one of the first gods to be birthed, her powers are formidable and far-ranging. She has a gentle side to help in matters of the heart and in matters relating to family planning. Yet she also has a fearsome side you can appeal to when you've been unjustly wronged. Among witches and occultists, she's a go-to divinity to invoke for exorcisms, penal spell-crafting, baneful magic, and curses.[119]

When you work with the Lady of the Nine Heavens, the Queen Mother is never far. Fox spirits are only ever a few degrees of separation from Xī Wáng Mǔ. In the various sutras and canons associated with her, she is a celestial teacher to the *fangshi* 方士 and *wū* 巫. Within the Taoist pantheon, she's considered one of the more earnestly interactive of gods, willing to mentor, to guide, and to offer divine intervention.

This book is crafted to help mediate a connection between you and Xī Wáng Mǔ, the Queen Mother. The I Ching becomes the communication tool. You'll discover for yourself the path to reaching Mount Kunlun, however you might conceptualize the axis mundi. We start building our way to that connection by first working with your spiritual mentor, should you seek to receive her—the Lady of the Nine Heavens.

# PRACTICUM 10.4:
## Invoking the Queen Mother of the West

In this practicum you will be calling out to Xī Wáng Mǔ. The Oracle will be the medium through which the goddess delivers her message to you. An optimal time for this practicum will be between a waning crescent moon and the dark moon, just before the new moon. The darkness is symbolic of the numinous void Wuji 無極 that she came from and of her role as Wujimu 無極母, divine mother of the numinous void.

I recommend utilizing either the yarrow stalk method or the cowrie shell toss method. This practicum will also introduce an alternative short-form yarrow stalk divination method. One of these three would be ideal, though lean into your own intuition and go with what works for you.

Work by candlelight. Select an evening hour after sunset. I would recommend as close to your bedtime as possible, as you will be continuing the divinatory process in your dream state.

Switch off the electricity in the room and illuminate with candles. Candle color is not significant. Go with what you have on hand. Light incense. Sit in stillness for a moment to ground and center yourself. Take deep, slow breaths. Wait until you are fully relaxed, feeling empowered and psychically receptive.

We'll be using the second line from Hexagram 35, Jìn, as the invocation prayer. Note that we're omitting the two-word divinatory statement "貞吉." That leaves us with the following recitation:

| There is progress, and there is sorrow. | jìn rú chóu rú | 晉如愁如 |
| May I now I receive Her blessings. | shòu zī jiè fú | 受茲介福 |
| All hail the Queen Mother. | yú qí Wáng Mǔ | 于其王母 |

The beauty of reciting it in Mandarin is the rhythm and the perfect tercet of the poetic verse. The poetic form adds power to the recitation. However, reciting in English will work just fine. Likewise, you can translate the lines and recite in your native tongue.

Essentially, the meaning of your recitation is first an acknowledgement that you've had your ups and you've had your downs, followed by your petition to the goddess. You are calling out to the Queen Mother and asking that she hear your call.

Bow your head slightly and recite the invocation prayer.

**FIGURE 10.9** Short-form method for yarrow stalk divination

Then begin the divination. The subsequent paragraphs will instruct on an alternate short-form method with yarrow stalks, but feel free to skip and instead work with one of the divinatory methods you've already learned.

**FIGURE 10.10** Bridging the worlds

Similar to the traditional long-form yarrow stalk method presented in chapter 7, you'll need a bundle of fifty stalks. Begin by setting down a single vertical stalk. Divide the bundle (forty-nine stalks remaining) in your hand into two bundles. One goes atop the single stalk, signifying Heaven. The other bundle goes below the single stalk to signify Earth. The single stalk now connects Heaven and Earth. Pick up one stalk from the bottom Earth bundle and place it between your ring and pinky fingers.

Start with the bottom Earth bundle, pick it up, and sort the stalks into groups of 4 until you have a remainder of 4 or fewer stalks in hand. Move on to the Heaven bundle and sort them into groups of 4 until you have a remainder of 4 or fewer. This is invocation of the four guardian spirits of the four directions and four seasons (space and time).

The total count of remainder stalks from the Heaven and Earth bundles combined will be *either* a total count of 5 stalks *or* a total count of 9 stalks. If you don't get exactly 5 or exactly 9, then there was a miscalculation, and you'll need to review your count.

| First Count | | Resulting Line |
|---|---|---|
| 5 stalks | Yin | ▬▬ ▬▬ |
| 9 stalks | Yang | ▬▬▬▬▬ |

If the total of stalks for the first count was 5, then draw a yin line for line 1 of your hexagram. If the total of stalks for the first count was 9, then draw a yang line.

| | | | |
|---|---|---|---|
| Second round with 50 stalks | | Third count (4 or 8) | Line 6 |
| | | Second count (4 or 8) | Line 5 |
| | ↑ | First count (5 or 9) | Line 4 |
| First round with 50 stalks | | Third count (4 or 8) | Line 3 |
| | | Second count (4 or 8) | Line 2 |
| | | First count (5 or 9) | Line 1 |

Set aside the 5 or 9 stalks from that remainder pile. They will not be counted in the next operation.

With what's left, either forty-five or forty-one stalks, repeat the process once again to yield the second count.

Set down a single vertical stalk to anchor. Here, I like to repeat the invocation prayer again. Then divide the bundle in two—one bundle calls forth the spirits of Heaven, and one calls forth the spirits of Earth. The vertical stick in the center connects them.

The visual of the stalk formation resembles the frame of the word for shaman, 巫. The two figures of 人 dancing around the frame represent the dance of the shaman, and here, the shaman occupying two minds—your own and the mind of a god.

Start with the Earth bundle. Sort into groups of 4 as you did with the traditional yarrow stalk method. You'll have a remainder of 4 or fewer stalks.

Then move on to Heaven. The total second count of the Earth remainder and Heaven remainder will yield either 4 stalks or 8 stalks.

This produces line 2 of your hexagram.

| Second Count | Resulting Line | |
|---|---|---|
| 4 stalks | Yin | ▬▬  ▬▬ |
| 8 stalks | Yang | ▬▬▬▬▬ |

Set aside the remainder stalks from the second count above the remainder stalks from the first count.

Then gather up all stalks not set aside and proceed with the operation again. Repeat the invocation prayer. You will now have recited it three times over the course of casting the lower hexagram.

Like the second count, the third count will yield either 4 stalks or 8 stalks. The resulting number of stalks will instruct whether a yin line or yang line has been produced.

| Third Count | Resulting Line | |
|---|---|---|
| 4 stalks | Yin | ▬▬  ▬▬ |
| 8 stalks | Yang | ▬▬▬▬▬ |

The three counts have now yielded a trigram. Note the trigram. This will be the lower trigram of the final divined hexagram. Gather up all fifty stalks again and start the operation over once more. Recite the invocation prayer as you set down that first anchoring vertical stalk. Connect Heaven and Earth, and in total you'll repeat the invocation prayer six times as you cast the six lines of the hexagram.

Your final result will be a single hexagram. We won't be observing changing lines. Start by reading the summary section in the Oracle. Continue on to read the full text for the Oracle, which corresponds with the received text attributed to King Wen in the Zhouyi and one part of the Ten Wings. This section reveals overarching themes, a summary of your marching orders, and how to solve the problem. This is giving you the pulse and temperature of the situation. Envision this as the Queen Mother face to face with you, speaking to you.

| Second round with 50 stalks | Third count (**4** or 8) | Line 6 | ━━  ━━ |
| --- | --- | --- | --- |
|  | Second count (**4** or 8) | Line 5 | ━━  ━━ |
|  | First count (5 or **9**) | Line 4 | ━━━━━ |
| First round with 50 stalks | Third count (**4** or 8) | Line 3 | ━━  ━━ |
|  | Second count (**4** or 8) | Line 2 | ━━  ━━ |
|  | First count (**5** or 9) | Line 1 | ━━  ━━ |
|  |  | Hexagram Result: | **Hexagram 16. Yù** |

The example of a resulting Hexagram 16 is my own reading done during a dark moon, just before the new moon phase. In the table, I've bolded the stalk remainder count for each operation. For example, in the first round, the first count yielded 5 stalks in my reading, which corresponds with a yin line. In the second count, I counted 4 stalks, so another yin line. The only received yang line is in the second round first count, when I counted 9.

For the next part of the practicum, you'll need pen and paper to copy and write out the text for the six lines of your cast hexagram. The text is just the sentences in bold, which are the translations of line statements attributed to the Duke of Zhou. (Everything other than the bolded line statements are my commentaries, which can be ignored.)

In the example of Hexagram 16, for line 1, only copy down "The birds chirp too indulgently. Ominous to proceed." Then skip the rest of the text and copy down line 2, "Safe within a cave. Perpetual and enduring day— good auspices to come," and so on to line 6.

Write out the Duke of Zhou line statements for all six lines, in succession like a narrative. However, there's a slight catch. As you write each word from the Oracle, feel as if your hand is being guided by a force that is not your own—the Queen Mother's hand over yours.

This is a form of training. Feel the goddess's presence as if she is the driver within your body and you've shifted over to the passenger seat. You are still conscious and aware of all that is going on, but what is happening in terms of motor functions is not you—it's her. This training is a form of attunement to get your personal frequency aligned with hers, so that in the future, channeling her and being her vessel will come more naturally.

Before you close the session, review what you've just written. What visions are being triggered by the text? Do not force any thoughts or analysis into your mind. Instead, do the opposite. Try not to think at all. Try to *receive*. Endeavor to be *told* what the meaning of the oracle message is, by way of divine insight, and don't critically process the message.

What comes through might be nonsensical or illogical. It might not even flow from the I Ching text in any rational or discernible way. This is training yourself to let synchronicity happen, rather than compelling the divinatory experience to follow a logical flow.

At the end of the handwritten text, write out the invocation prayer.

Place this written sheet on your nightstand when you go to sleep.

Before you fall asleep, read the divinatory message you received. The six lines all together will imply a particular setting, like a story. Fill in the details with your imagination and intuition. What is the backdrop and landscape of the oracle message?

Recite the invocation prayer one final time.

As you fall asleep, visualize the world that the lines of the Oracle message built. Like focused meditation, keep your thoughts tethered to that visualization.

When you wake in the morning, try to recall your dream. Write down anything that comes to you immediately upon waking. Where did you go? What did you experience? If no recollections come to mind, instead of assuming that you didn't dream or can't remember, assume that your mind must have blocked the dream. Resolve to yourself that going forward, at least for the next few months, you will be unblocking your dreams. Then try again the next evening, and again, being persistent and patient with yourself, until a dream triggers deeper insight into the goddess's message for you.

Next, let's focus on the two trigrams that your hexagram consists of.

If you are at a juncture point in your life where you would like to maintain the status quo, or fortify to build a stronger foundation, then focus on the lower trigram. Turn to chapter 5 and select a practicum to work with associated with your lower trigram.

If you are seeking to manifest a major change in your life, or you want significant advancement or improvement in your status quo, then focus on the upper trigram. Turn to chapter 5 and select a practicum associated with the upper trigram.

When you feel confident that you've understood the message received, repeat this divinatory practice invoking the Queen Mother. Do not seek external validation to affirm what you understand or don't—learn to find that confidence from within, to be self-aware enough to simply know.

This practicum uses the established and reliable medium that is the I Ching Oracle as a tool for strengthening your attunement to Xī Wáng Mǔ. Repeated, albeit methodical, applications of it exercise your psychic muscles.

## Healing the Inner *Shén*

In "The Eightfold Gods Discourse" 八正神明論 from the *Yellow Emperor's Classic of Internal Medicine* 黃帝內經 *(Huángdì nèi jīng)*,[120] a book formulated from the I Ching, a young Yellow Emperor asks his teacher, the mythical healer Qibo 岐伯, "What is 神 *(shén)*?"[121]

On its face, the dialectical exchange is about acupuncture, but implied within the subtext is another conversation altogether, as every word in the discourse holds double meaning. I bring up the "The Eightfold Gods" from *Huángdì nèi jīng* because it emphasizes diagnosis of the *shén* in internal medicine, and yet the text reads like a treatise on *wū* shamanism, overlapping with concepts of soul retrieval.

The question refers to the *shén* from Jīng Qì Shén 精氣神, which signifies the trinity of essences in our bodies that govern physical, mental, and spiritual health. They're referred to as the Three Jewels 三寶 (Sān Bǎo), triplicities that are composed of yin and yang. There are eight characters of such triplicities, fashioned after the theory of the eight trigrams of the Ba Gua.

The young emperor's question itself holds several inquiries in one. On the face of the discourse, this is an inquiry about how a physician can access a patient's *shén* 神 to heal the spiritual center and thus heal body and mind.

The undercurrent to that inquiry is a philosophical questioning of god— how do you call upon god as Spirit 神? What is the meaning of Spirit 神? What is god? How do you invoke god? To heal the inner *shén* 神 is to achieve attunement with a higher sense of Spirit 神 beyond yourself.

Thus, to his pupil's question "What is 神?", Qibo responds:

Invoke the name of Spirit,
for here is what Spirit is:
that which ears cannot hear,
the Eye that sees All,
a heart-mind aligned with its Purpose,
a solitary wisdom, awakened and self-aware,
the voice that speaks all words,
the eyes that see what cannot be seen,
realized at the dusk and twilight of your senses,
that which only you can know,
a wind that moves the clouds—
the dead, afflictions, catastrophe are also called Spirit.
Three parts, originating from the nine governances,
these are the nine principles, the Nine Needles.[122]

In traditional acupuncture, the Nine Needles were the nine types of medical instruments of the healer. The theoretical principle underlying the Nine Needles of the healer is the principle of nine heavens.

That there is a connection here to the Lady of the Nine Heavens, Jiǔ Tiān Xuán Nǚ, just feels intuitive. She is a divine messenger for the Queen Mother of the West and a powerful divinity in her own right associated with healing magic.

The esoteric teaching that Qibo is conveying to the Yellow Emperor is that the Nine Needles, or the nine tools of the healer, are purposed to connect one to the Nine Heavens. When you can connect yourself to every tier of Heaven, you can heal every nature of affliction.

Shamanism, and by extension work with the I Ching, is purposed for healing.

# PRACTICUM 10.5:
## Healing Your Spiritual Center

You can divine with the I Ching to heal your inner *shén* 神, your spiritual center. This will be a combination method between yarrow stalk and rice grain. To cast a single hexagram, follow the short-form yarrow stalk method presented in the previous practicum. Then to reveal the changing line, you'll count rice grains and divide by 6. The remainder of the division calculation will note the changing line to read.

I had been experiencing an emotional and creative slump in my life and going through a bout of depression. It was spilling over into my physical health as well, resulting in lethargy and unusual weight gain. I could intuit that something was wrong, but I could not logically identify what that was. So I consulted the I Ching. I lit a stick of incense at the hour of sunrise and proceeded with the short-form yarrow stalk method. The following were my results:

| | | | |
|---|---|---|---|
| Second operation | Count 3. Result = 8 | ▬▬▬▬▬ | ▬▬▬▬▬ |
| | Count 2. Result = 4 | ▬▬  ▬▬ | ▬▬  ▬▬ |
| | Count 1. Result = 5 | ▬▬  ▬▬ | ▬▬  ▬▬ |
| | | | Mountain |
| First operation | Count 3. Result = 8 | ▬▬▬▬▬ | ▬▬▬▬▬ |
| | Count 2. Result = 4 | ▬▬  ▬▬ | ▬▬  ▬▬ |
| | Count 1. Result = 5 | ▬▬  ▬▬ | ▬▬  ▬▬ |
| | | | Mountain |

Mountain over Mountain yields Hexagram 52. Listen to the Wind. The abstract summary judgment of the Oracle message ("No irreparable harm comes. There is no blame.") assured me that whatever was going on inside, this was manageable. If, for example, your reading result yields a more severe message (e.g., "Ominous to proceed."), the situation might require greater work to cure. If the result is "Auspicious" or words to that effect, perhaps you're overthinking the situation.

No matter what the result is, your divinatory message will yield practical advice on how to balance your spiritual center. You may need to dive deeper into the words to understand what the Oracle is saying. The purpose of the riddles is to make you work for the answer, because the journey is part of the solution. If you don't work for the answer, you won't fully "know" the answer.

**FIGURE 10.11** Combining yarrow stalk and rice grain methods

In the specific case of my reading, the hexagram result is one of the eight Spirit Helpers (since it's a trigram doubled). As a Spirit Helper, Hexagram 52 helps facilitate psychic visions and spiritual awakening, and it improves meditation. Mountain corresponds with the bodhisattva Samantabhadra, or Puxian, as noted in appendix D. Thus, for the next few months, I'll implement routine mantra recitations of Puxian.

Rice grains symbolize good health and longevity, so utilizing them infuses your ritual with the *qi* of the rice grains, an incidental blessing while you divine. Since the short-form yarrow stalk method only yields a single hexagram, scoop up about a teaspoon of grains to count, while focusing on the health of your mind, body, and spirit.

Count the total grains and divide the total by 6. The remainder from the division calculation will be the corresponding changing line. If the total number of grains divides evenly into 6, then your changing line is line 6.

In my reading, I counted a total of 88 grains. (I also noted the synchronicity of the 8, since the trigram Mountain corresponds with the number 8 when superimposed over the Lo Shu magic square.) Dividing 88 by 6, you get a quotient of 14 and a remainder of 4. My changing line is line 4 of Hexagram 52. In short, to help restore balance to my spiritual center, the Oracle advised meditation and to remove myself from situations where I would be temped to be judgmental of others. Hexagram 52 also happens to correspond with astral projection. An astral journey to Mount Kunlun, envisioning myself accepting healing herbs from an ancestral shaman spirit, really helped to rejuvenate me.

Likewise, extract the practical advice that the Oracle is trying to give you about how to restore your spiritual center. What is it about your inner *shén* 神 that needs healing, and *how* can you heal it? The trigram that your changing line is in can also reveal corresponding spiritual healing practices.

Needless to say, these types of practicums should never replace qualified health care or psychological counseling. They should be used in tandem with science, not in opposition against it.

# 11

# Returning Full Circle

THE I CHING FORMS the pattern of a circle,[1] a never-ending book that returns to Hexagram 1 after Heaxagram 64, and with every revolution, it evolves—in the eye of the beholder, the Book changes. As a mandala, it is a map of the labyrinthine mind of the Tao. As a sacred text, every copy of the Book is imbued with divine power, in the view of animists. The totality of words becomes a spell, and the printed text a sigil.

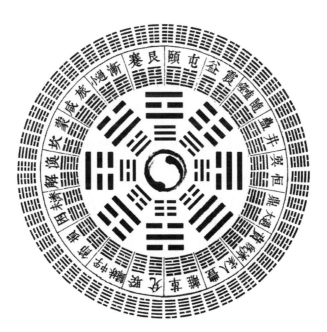

**FIGURE 11.1** A cyclical Book of Changes

I took that premise a step further, inspired by the Yao *người Dao* shaman priests of Vietnam. Upon every Yao shaman's altar are devotional paintings of patron deities. For the shaman, the artist who creates a painting matters. The artist must observe strict religious practices while painting the deity. Once complete, the painting must undergo a ritual to enliven it, to consecrate it so it can be a residence for a god.[2] Taoist and Buddhist traditions observe similar rituals, called *kai guang* 開光, the opening of the Light.

Thus, every featured work of art was thoughtfully curated, its metaphysical properties considered. For the entire duration of my writing of this book, I invoked the Lady of the Nine Heavens and lit incense offerings before I sat down to write. For guidance I would recite mantras.

In our time together, we've covered a lot of ground. The cultural heroes of Chinese lore have personalized the I Ching as a storybook. If you revisit the myths and legends of the I Ching, perhaps you'll now see the influences of the Queen Mother. Both the Queen Mother of the West and the Lady of the Nine Heavens are connected to Nǚwā, the mother goddess. Fox spirits answer to the Queen Mother.

Having gone through three thousand years of Yì Xué scholarship and interpretive traditions, you've seen how the Book has evolved. Early in its history, the Oracle's primary use was political, wherein shaman priests would consult the Yì to advise kings on matters of statecraft.

We went into a granular study of the Ba Gua and Wu Xing, empowering you with a core set of technical knowledge that you'll take into every other branch of East Asian metaphysics. You learned the traditional methods of divination, but also, I hope you feel encouraged to devise your own.

Most important of all, you now have a portfolio of meaningful practicums you can turn to. I strived to ensure that the practicums in this book are self-empowering. They'll offer just enough guidance to keep you feeling safe within guardrails, but give you ample space to do as you will. The practicums are intended to teach techniques that you can then mix and match at will. Keep a notebook to document your I Ching readings and the practicums you've tried. Start assembling your own Taoist grimoire, a Book of Methods or *fāng shū* 方書.

In my experiences with the Book, every time my life has gone through a revolution and I return to the Oracle, I find myself reading a changed text. I project onto the Book the changes that have happened within me, and in doing

**FIGURE 11.2** Summary of divination methods

so I see myself with newfound clarity. Life experiences deepen my understanding of the lines, and each revisit to the Oracle deepens my understanding of life.

Like reading scripture, study of the I Ching inspires us to be more benevolent, to cultivate patience, and to embody the three virtues—integrity, fortitude, and tenderness.[3] The I Ching is a book of moral philosophy, and it is also a book of occult secrets. The Oracle is a master teacher to both the rationalist scholar and the spiritualist mystic.

Yet reaching for the Book of Changes does not always need to be a deep endeavor. To settle a lighthearted dispute over whose sports team will win or where to go for vacation, I've turned to the Oracle. Have I asked irreverent questions? Yes. Has the Oracle returned with Hexagram 4, Naiveté, or 44, Improper Meeting, as the answer? Yes.

I turn to the Book when I'm at my worst, at my best, and everything in between.

We write the books we want to read. This book is mentorship in the esoteric arts. Contained within a primer on the I Ching and Yì Xué scholarship is a Taoist grimoire. Sure, the theoretical matters, but *how* do I apply the knowledge in practice? That's the book I endeavored to write.

As the Yellow Emperor received esoteric teachings from the Lady of the Nine Heavens, as Yu the Great received the Lo Shu Book of the River Maps, which squares the circle of hexagrams as received by King Wen, and as the Duke of Zhou received transmissions of the line statements, the Book of Changes has come into your hands because you are ready to receive. Receiving the Oracle is itself an omen that you are ready for Change.

**FIGURE 11.3** The Queen Mother's Shòu Yān 獸焉

## PRACTICUM 11.1: Where Do I Go from Here?

This is one of my favorite go-to inquiries. The phrasing is broad, and yet the divinatory results are astoundingly specific. I recommend either the coin toss method or using three cowrie shells.

Start by meditatively contemplating the question, "Where do I go from here?" Ruminate freely, in a stream-of-consciousness style in your mind, letting your thoughts wander. After a few minutes, round up and gather your thoughts to contain them in an imaginary pen. Put a visual to it: picture yourself on horseback wrangling a herd into an enclosure and closing the gates. You are herding your thoughts. After you've closed the gates, take a few deep breaths and begin.

Shake the three coins or cowrie shells for the first toss and recite the question, "Where do I go from here?" three times, then toss. Record the line result. For each of the six tosses, recite the inquiry three times before tossing.

Consider what actionable advice the Oracle is presenting you with. Perhaps the lower or the upper trigram in the primary and transformed hexagrams are the same, and the recurrence is an omen of a correspondence to that trigram that contains the answer. Look to the Wu Xing correspondence of the transformed hexagram's upper trigram—it will reveal the dominant nature of changing forces or *qi* at play. Revisit the "Summary Outline of Hexagram Interpretation" section at the end of chapter 7.

There is also a secret implied hexagram in your divinatory result. Lines 2, 3, and 4 from the primary hexagram form the lower trigram. Lines 3, 4, and 5 of your transformed hexagram form the upper trigram. If the reading result was locked, yielding a single hexagram, combine lines 2, 3, and 4 to reveal the lower, and lines 3, 4, and 5 to reveal the upper.

To demonstrate, table 11.1 features an actual reading result during a full moon in Capricorn. Three cowrie shells were used for the divinatory method. The cast hexagram yielded one changing line (elder yin) in the sixth. Note how lines 2, 3, and 4 of the primary hexagram form the lower trigram (Thunder) of the secret hexagram. Lines 3, 4, and 5 of the transformed hexagram form the upper trigram (Mountain).

**TABLE 11.1** Revealing the Secret Hexagram

| | PRIMARY HEXAGRAM | | TRANSFORMED HEXAGRAM | SECRET HEXAGRAM |
|---|---|---|---|---|
| Line 6 | ▬▬ ▬▬ | | ▬▬▬▬▬ | ▬▬▬▬▬ |
| Line 5 | ▬▬▬▬▬ | | ▬▬▬▬▬ | ▬▬ ▬▬ |
| Line 4 | ▬▬ ▬▬ | ※ | ▬▬ ▬▬ | ▬▬ ▬▬ |
| Line 3 | ▬▬ ▬▬ | | ▬▬ ▬▬ | ▬▬ ▬▬ |
| Line 2 | ▬▬▬▬▬ | | ▬▬▬▬▬ | ▬▬ ▬▬ |
| Line 1 | ▬▬▬▬▬ | | ▬▬▬▬▬ | ▬▬▬▬▬ |
| | Hexagram 60 | | Hexagram 61 | Hexagram 62 |

Every divinatory result contains an implied secret hexagram. Even if you don't acknowledge it in the reading, it's still there. It is the occult, unseen side of nature. It is the sustaining counterpart to your reading result. The judgment summary of the Oracle message for this secret hexagram reveals arcane, mystical, and psychic forces that you can harness.

# 12

# Appendices

**FIGURE 12.1** Leaf 2 from the *Landscapes* 山水 by Jiao Bingzhen (1689–1726).
SOURCE: National Palace Museum, Taipei.

# APPENDIX A: Twenty-Four Solar Terms

TABLE 12.1 Solar Terms to Solar Longitude and Lunar Months

| SOLAR TERM | SEASONAL TERM | SOLAR LONGITUDE | LUNAR MONTH |
|---|---|---|---|
| Start of Spring 立春 Lìchūn | Early Spring 寅 Yín Wood | 314° Feb. 3–5 | Month 1 虎 Tiger |
| Spring Showers 雨水 Yǔshuǐ | | 329° Feb. 18–20 | |
| Insects Awaken 驚蟄 Jīngzhé | Mid-Spring 卯 Mǎo Water | 344° Mar. 5–7 | Month 2 兔 Rabbit |
| Vernal Equinox 春分 Chūnfēn | | 0° Mar. 20–22 | |
| Bright and Clear 清明 Qīngmíng | Late Spring 辰 Chén Earth | 14° Apr. 4–6 | Month 3 龍 Dragon |
| Gathering Rain 穀雨 Gǔyǔ | | 29° Apr. 19–21 | |
| Start of Summer 立夏 Lìxià | Early Summer 巳 Sì Fire | 44° May 5–7 | Month 4 蛇 Snake |
| Green Buds Form 小滿 Xiǎomǎn | | 59° May 20–22 | |
| Blossoms Form 芒種 Mángzhòng | Midsummer 午 Wǔ Fire | 74° June 5–7 | Month 5 馬 Horse |
| Summer Solstice 夏至 Xiàzhì | | 89° June 21–22 | |
| Coming Heat 小暑 Xiǎoshǔ | Late Summer 未 Wèi Earth | 104° July 6–8 | Month 6 羊 Sheep |
| Great Heat 大暑 Dàshǔ | | 119° July 22–24 | |

**TABLE 12.1** Solar Terms to Solar Longitude and Lunar Months *(continued)*

| SOLAR TERM | SEASONAL TERM | SOLAR LONGITUDE | LUNAR MONTH |
|---|---|---|---|
| Start of Autumn 立秋 Lìqiū | Early Autumn 申 Shēn Metal | 134° Aug. 7–9 | Month 7 猴 Monkey |
| Dissipating Heat 處暑 Chùshǔ | | 149° Aug. 22–24 | |
| White Dew 白露 Báilù | Mid-Autumn 酉 Yǒu Metal | 164° Sept. 7–9 | Month 8 雞 Rooster |
| Autumnal Equinox 秋分 Qiūfēn | | 181° Sept. 22–24 | |
| Cold Dew 寒露 Hánlù | Late Autumn 戌 Xū Earth | 194° Oct. 8–9 | Month 9 狗 Dog |
| The First Frost 霜降 Shuāngjiàng | | 211° Oct. 23–24 | |
| Start of Winter 立冬 Lìdōng | Early Winter 亥 Hài Water | 224° Nov. 7–8 | Month 10 豬 Boar |
| Light Snow 小雪 Xiǎoxuě | | 244° Nov. 22–23 | |
| Heavy Snow 大雪 Dàxuě | Mid-Winter 子 Zǐ Water | 251° Dec. 6–8 | Month 11 鼠 Rat |
| Winter Solstice 冬至 Dōngzhì | | 271° Dec. 21–23 | |
| Coming Cold 小寒 Xiǎohán | Late Winter 丑 Chǒu Earth | 284° Jan. 5–7 | Month 12 牛 Ox |
| Great Cold 大寒 Dàhán | | 301° Jan. 20–21 | |

The twenty-four solar terms mark approximately every 15° of the sun's position on the celestial sphere along its ecliptic. (Recall the numerological importance of 15, and the Lo Shu magic square's connection to 15.) Though the first solar term is designated the "Start of Spring," that first week of February for most of the Asia mainland would still feel like winter; however, early February begins to show the first signs of life, and whether the summer will yield a good or bad harvest can often be determined by this time.

At 0° solar longitude, the vernal equinox is when the lengths of day and night are equal. "Gathering Rain" is when rains begin to nourish the fields of grain and millet, and the rice paddies. Around July 22–24 commences the hottest period of the year, until the first week of August. While temperature-wise the "Start of Autumn" solar term is still considered summer (commences after the first week of August), at this time the productivity of the final autumn harvest (the mid-Autumn harvest festival) can be predicted; hence, experienced farmers know to look for the first signs of autumn during this week of August. At around 271° is the time of the winter solstice, when the hours of day are the shortest and the hours of night are the longest.

The Start of Spring, Start of Summer, Start of Autumn, and Start of Winter mark four cardinal points. On the Lo Shu, they correspond with the southeast, northeast, northwest, and southwest respectively. The equinoxes and solstices correspond with due east, north, west, and south respectively. Note the Later Heaven arrangement of King Wen's Ba Gua, the Lo Shu, and the seasonal cycle in table 5.13 from chapter 5.

**TABLE 12.2** Solar Terms, Eight Trigrams, and the Lo Shu

| 4 — Xùn Wind Southeast | 9 — Lí Fire South | 2 — Kūn Earth Southwest |
|---|---|---|
| NATURAL CYCLE OF THE TAIJI: Start of Summer | NATURAL CYCLE OF THE TAIJI: Summer Solstice | NATURAL CYCLE OF THE TAIJI: Start of Autumn |
| THAUMATURGE'S TAIJI: Start of Spring | THAUMATURGE'S TAIJI: Winter Solstice | THAUMATURGE'S TAIJI: Start of Winter |
| 3 — Zhèn Thunder East | 5 King Wen's Ba Gua (Later Heaven), the Lo Shu Square, and Solar Terms | 7 — Duì Lake West |
| NATURAL CYCLE OF THE TAIJI: Vernal Equinox | | NATURAL CYCLE OF THE TAIJI: Autumn Equinox |
| THAUMATURGE'S TAIJI: Vernal Equinox | | THAUMATURGE'S TAIJI: Autumn Equinox |
| 8 — Gěn Mountain Northeast | 1 — Kǎn Water North | 6 — Qián Heaven Northwest |
| NATURAL CYCLE OF THE TAIJI: Start of Spring | NATURAL CYCLE OF THE TAIJI: Winter Solstice | NATURAL CYCLE OF THE TAIJI: Start of Winter |
| THAUMATURGE'S TAIJI: Start of Summer | THAUMATURGE'S TAIJI: Summer Solstice | THAUMATURGE'S TAIJI: Start of Autumn |

In the subsequent tables, note the two differing systems of correspondences between the trigrams and the solar terms. The Thunder correspondence to the vernal equinox and the Lake correspondence to the autumnal equinox are the points of similarity between the two systems.

The rows for the Natural Cycle of the Taiji reflect the yin and yang trigram characterizations of the solar terms. This is the frequently cited majority view of correspondences between the solar terms and King Wen's Ba Gua.

The rows for the Thaumaturge's Taiji reflect the nature of yin and yang, the forces of *qi* that a metaphysician would want to harness corresponding to the seasonal cycle, to ensure productivity, good harvests, and personal success. This is the system of correspondences I use, and the one I recommend the alchemist, shaman, and mystic to adopt. The Thaumaturge's Taiji represents the correspondences of metaphysical measures to take during each season, to balance out the natural cycle of the Taiji.

During cardinal spring or the Start of Spring, for example, Wind represents gentle influences and cultivation of growth, whereas Mountain reflects the innate stillness of the natural cycle. At the Start of Summer, however, continued success is often contingent on knowledge and experience. The natural cycle corresponds with Wind because this is when forces are in constant flow; the Mountain lets us know to tame that natural flow of Wind.

**TABLE 12.3** Solar Terms and Taiji Trigram Systems, Part 1

| SOLAR TERM | | NATURAL CYCLE OF THE TAIJI | THAUMATURGE'S TAIJI |
|---|---|---|---|
| Start of Spring | 立春 Lìchūn | | |
| Spring Showers | 雨水 Yǔshuǐ | 艮 Gèn Mountain | 巽 Xùn Wind |
| Insects Awaken | 驚蟄 Jīngzhé | | |
| Vernal Equinox | 春分 Chūnfēn | | |
| Bright and Clear | 清明 Qīngmíng | 震 Zhèn Thunder | 震 Zhèn Thunder |
| Gathering Rain | 穀雨 Gǔyǔ | | |

**TABLE 12.3** Solar Terms and Taiji Trigram Systems, Part 1 *(continued)*

| Start of Summer | 立夏 Lìxià | | |
| --- | --- | --- | --- |
| Green Buds Form | 小滿 Xiǎomǎn | | |
| Blossoms Form | 芒種 Mángzhòng | 巽 Xùn — Wind | 艮 Gěn — Mountain |
| Summer Solstice | 夏至 Xiàzhì | | |
| Coming Heat | 小暑 Xiǎoshǔ | | |
| Great Heat | 大暑 Dàshǔ | 離 Lí — Fire | 坎 Kǎn — Water |

By the summer solstice, the natural world is represented by Fire at its hottest, but the metaphysical measure to take should be that of Water, to balance the innate Fire and keep it from going to excess in a way that would harm. Water is essential during the seasonal period of Great Heat. Thus, throughout the hottest of the summer months, Fire represents the natural cycle, but Water represents the active measures to engage in, to balance out that Fire and prevent overheating or dehydration.

**TABLE 12.4** Solar Terms and Taiji Trigram Systems, Part 2

| SOLAR TERM | | NATURAL CYCLE OF THE TAIJI | THAUMATURGE'S TAIJI |
| --- | --- | --- | --- |
| Start of Autumn | 立秋 Lìqiū | | |
| Dissipating Heat | 處暑 Chùshǔ | | |
| White Dew | 白露 Báilù | 坤 Kūn — Earth | 乾 Qián — Heaven |
| Autumnal Equinox | 秋分 Qiūfēn | | |
| Cold Dew | 寒露 Hánlù | | |
| The First Frost | 霜降 Shuāngjiàng | 兌 Duì — Lake | 兌 Duì — Lake |

**TABLE 12.4** Solar Terms and Taiji Trigram Systems, Part 2 *(continued)*

| Start of Winter | 立冬 Lìdōng | ☰ 乾 Qián Heaven | ☷ 坤 Kūn Earth |
|---|---|---|---|
| Light Snow | 小雪 Xiǎoxuě | | |
| Heavy Snow | 大雪 Dàxuě | | |
| Winter Solstice | 冬至 Dōngzhì | ☵ 坎 Kǎn Water | ☲ Lí Fire |
| Coming Cold | 小寒 Xiǎohán | | |
| Great Cold | 大寒 Dàhán | | |

The Start of Autumn and Dissipating Heat are the solar terms coinciding with Ghost Month (lunar month 7). Earth is the natural expression of nature during this time—pure yin *qi* at play, as yin corresponds with the realm of ghosts and demons. However, the active measure to take would be represented by the opposite—Heaven, pure yang *qi* to counteract the detrimental influences of ghosts and demons during this time.

Meanwhile, during cardinal winter, beginning with the solar term Start of Winter, the whiteness of the snow is expressed in the whiteness of the trigram Heaven, but the metaphysical action to take is conservation and to be as yin as possible, which corresponds with Earth.

During the winter solstice, the natural cycle of *qi* in the season corresponds with the trigram Water, but the metaphysical measure to take during the cold winter months is Fire, because Fire ensures warmth and nourishment through the cold.

# APPENDIX B:
## Stems, Branches, and Trigrams

The trigrams correspond to the heavenly stems through the Wu Xing as the common connecting point, i.e., Wu Xing correspondences to the trigrams link to the Wu Xing correspondences of the heavenly stems.

**TABLE 12.5** Heavenly Stems, Trigrams, and Wu Xing

| HEAVENLY STEM | BINARY | WU XING | TRIGRAM | HEAVENLY STEM | BINARY | WU XING | TRIGRAM |
|---|---|---|---|---|---|---|---|
| 甲 jiǎ | yang | 木 Wood Mù | Wind Xùn | 己 jǐ | yin | 土 Earth Tǔ | Earth Kūn |
| 乙 yǐ | yin | 木 Wood Mù | Thunder Zhèn | 庚 gēng | yang | 金 Metal Jīn | Heaven Qián |
| 丙 bing | yang | 火 Fire Huǒ | Fire Lí | 辛 xīn | yin | 金 Metal Jīn | Lake Duì |
| 丁 ding | yin | 火 Fire Huǒ | Fire Lí | 壬 rén | yang | 水 Water Shuǐ | Water Kǎn |
| 戊 wù | yang | 土 Earth Tǔ | Mountain Gěn | 癸 guǐ | yin | 水 Water Shuǐ | Water Kǎn |

The trigrams correspond to the earthly branches through the twelve zodiac signs as the common connecting point, i.e., zodiac correspondences to the trigrams link to the zodiac correspondences of the earthly branches.

**TABLE 12.6** Earthly Branches, Trigrams, and Wu Xing

| EARTHLY BRANCHES | BINARY | ZODIAC SIGN | TRIGRAM | EARTHLY BRANCHES | BINARY | ZODIAC SIGN | TRIGRAM |
|---|---|---|---|---|---|---|---|
| 寅 *yín* | yang | 虎 Tiger | Mountain Gěn |  申 *shēn* | yang | 猴 Monkey | Earth Kūn |
| 卯 *mǎo* | yin | 兔 Rabbit | Thunder Zhèn | 酉 *yǒu* | yin | 雞 Rooster | Lake Duì |
| 辰 *chén* | yang | 龍 Dragon | Wind Xùn | 戌 *xū* | yang | 狗 Dog | Heaven Qián |
| 巳 *sì* | yin | 蛇 Snake | Wind Xùn | 亥 *hài* | yin | 豬 Boar | Heaven Qián |
| 午 *wǔ* | yang | 馬 Horse | Fire Lí | 子 *zǐ* | yang | 鼠 Rat | Water Kǎn |
| 未 *wèi* | yin | 羊 Sheep | Earth Kūn | 丑 *chou* | yin | 牛 Ox | Mountain Gěn |

# APPENDIX C: Trigrams and Feng Shui

**TABLE 12.7** Trigrams and Feng Shui Correspondences

| South—**Red Phoenix** | | |
|---|---|---|
| **4** Xùn / Wind<br><br>Wealth, finances, income, assets<br><br>Element: **Wood**<br>Empowered by: **Water**<br>Weakened by: **Metal**<br><br>Vibrant green plants, a prosperity bowl, prosperity tree; a water fountain or fish tank with flowing water increases wealth. | **9** Lí / Fire<br><br>Honor, status, victories, fulfillment, happiness<br><br>Element: **Fire**<br>Empowered by: **Wood**<br>Weakened by: **Water**<br><br>MARS (in July after the summer solstice, Mars is visible in the south); Mars corresponds with Fire. | **2** Kūn / Earth<br><br>Love, romance, domestic matters<br><br>Element: **Earth**<br>Empowered by: **Fire**<br>Weakened by: **Wood**<br><br>The condition and appearance of the southwest corner of the home reflects the relationship of the domestic partners who live here. |
| **3** Zhèn / Thunder<br><br>Ancestry, family, roots, past life<br><br>Element: **Wood**<br>Empowered by: **Water**<br>Weakened by: **Metal**<br><br>JUPITER (on the vernal equinox, Jupiter is seen in the east); Jupiter corresponds with Wood. | **5** ☯<br><br>Health, fate, luck, trials, challenges<br><br>Element: **Earth**<br>Empowered by: **Fire**<br>Weakened by: **Wood**<br><br>SATURN (visible in the middle of the sky in May, with Wood, Fire, Metal, and Water of the Wu Xing flowing around Earth). | **7** Duì / Lake<br><br>Creativity, progeny, fertility, innovation<br><br>Element: **Metal**<br>Empowered by: **Earth**<br>Weakened by: **Fire**<br><br>VENUS (on the autumnal equinox in September, Venus is seen in the west); Venus corresponds with Metal. |
| **8** Gěn / Mountain<br><br>Education, knowledge, arts, culture<br><br>Element: **Earth**<br>Empowered by: **Fire**<br>Weakened by: **Wood**<br><br>The northwest corner of the home reflects the collective values and philosophy of those who live here. | **1** Kǎn / Water<br><br>Career, goals, drive, willpower, motivation<br><br>Element: **Water**<br>Empowered by: **Metal**<br>Weakened by: **Earth**<br><br>MERCURY (in November before the winter solstice, Mercury is visible in the north); Mercury corresponds with Water. | **6** Qián / Heaven<br><br>Blessings; guardians, clan, community, allies<br><br>Element: **Metal**<br>Empowered by: **Earth**<br>Weakened by: **Fire**<br><br>The traditional placement for a shrine or altar. Where gods and ancestors are invited. Consecrate this corner to receive divine blessings. |
| North—**Black Tortoise** | | |

East—Azure Dragon (left side) · West—White Tiger (right side)

# APPENDIX D:
# The Eight Bodhisattvas and the Ba Gua

**TABLE 12.8** Eight Bodhisattvas and the Ba Gua

| | | |
|---|---|---|
| **Qián**<br>Heaven | 乾 | **Akashagarbha** 虛空藏菩薩 (Xū Kōng Cáng Púsà), the sky jewel, bodhisattva of the infinite sky and space itself. Personification of the *ākāśa* आकाश or Akasha. Shakyamuni Buddha described Akashagarbha's magical powers as boundless.[2] Depicted with blue, yellow, or green skin and wielding a sword of truth and spiritual knowledge. |
| **Duì**<br>Lake | 兌 | **Maitreya** 彌勒菩薩 (Mí Lè Púsà), the emanation of agape love and messianic future Buddha, successor to the Shakyamuni Buddha. Represents the promise of a brighter future. Currently resides in Tushita, the western heaven, or deva world. Prophesied to return to earth at humanity's darkest hour, reincarnated as a prophet. In Song dynasty lore, Maitreya reincarnated as the eccentric Laughing Buddha (Bùdài 布袋, Vietnamese Bố Đại), who brings blessings of abundance, fortune, and joy. |
| **Lí**<br>Fire | 離 | **Mañjushri** 文殊菩薩 (Wén Shū Púsà), the emanation of wisdom *(prajñā)* and considered the oldest of the eight bodhisattvas. According to the Lotus Sutra, Mañjushri dwells in Vimala, a Pure Land in the east. He is often depicted with a flaming sword of wisdom and riding a blue lion, symbolic of taming the beast mind. The mantra of Mañjushri is: *oṃ arapacana dhīḥ*. The five syllables *"arapacana"* invoke Mañjushri. The mantra is used to bring clarity and insight into a situation. |
| **Zhèn**<br>Thunder | 震 | **Vajrapani** 金剛手菩薩 (Jīn Gāng Shǒu Púsà), the emanation of power (in Taoist mysticism, Vajrapani is often invoked in thunder magic). A fierce protector bodhisattva. Symbolic of the Buddha's power; the hand of god. Invoked to protect against demons and ghosts, and to increase the power of spell-casting. Vajrapani's epithet is the Lord of Secrets or Master of Secrets. The mantra of Vajrapani is: *oṃ vajrapāṇi hūṃ phaṭ*. The mantra is used by Taoist ceremonial magicians to cultivate thunder *qi*. |

**TABLE 12.8** Eight Bodhisattvas and the Ba Gua *(continued)*

| | | |
|---|---|---|
| **Xùn**<br>Wind | ☴<br>巽 | **Sarvanivaranavishkambhin** 除盖障菩薩 (Chú Gài Zhàng Púsà) removes obstacles for clear focus and concentration. Bodhisattva of abandoning all shadows. He is invoked to clear afflictions, doubts, regrets, physical pain, and that which has been preventing spiritual cultivation. Depicted holding a flower, a wheel of jewels, or wish-fulfilling jewel. Mantra: *namaḥ saman ta buddhā nām—aḥ—sattva hitā bhyud gata—traṃ—traṃ—raṃ—raṃ—svāhā*. To consecrate a work space for divination, light incense, then pass a clear crystal quartz over the work space and recite the mantra. |
| **Kǎn**<br>Water | ☵<br>坎 | **Avalokiteshvara** 觀世音菩薩 (Guān Shì Yīn Púsà), or Kuan Yin, the emanation of mercy and compassion. While Avalokiteshvara is depicted as male, since the Tang dynasty, Kuan Yin has been depicted as female and wearing a white robe. Kuan Yin is a miracle worker who will assist anyone who calls to her, unconditionally. She doesn't condition her help on offerings, worship, or devotion. The Great Compassion Mantra 大悲咒 (Dà Bēi Zhòu) is recited to purify karmic merit and to help facilitate a peaceful transition to the afterlife, spiritual healing, and consecration or purification. A shorter mantra used for invoking Avalokiteshvara: *oṃ mani padme hūṃ*. Invocation of Kuan Yin in Mandarin: 南無觀世音菩薩 (*námó* Guān-shìyīn Púsà). |
| **Gěn**<br>Mountain | ☶<br>艮 | **Samantabhadra** 普賢菩薩 (Pǔ Xián Púsà), a spiritual teacher who offers guidance in how to practice the tenets of Buddhism. Teaches that wisdom only exists for the purpose of putting it into practice. Depicted mounted on a white elephant. Reciting the secret name of the Lord of Secrets 祕密主 (Vajrapani) will vanquish all demons and remove all curses. The secret name is Samantabhadra (Pǔ Xián Púsà). |
| **Kūn**<br>Earth | ☷<br>坤 | **Kshitigarbha** 地藏王菩薩 (Di Zàng Wáng Púsà), the emanation of fertility and abundance; shows mercy upon hell beings and the oppressed. Depicted as carrying a wish-fulfilling jewel and a staff that opens the gates of hell. In Japanese culture, he is Jizō, guardian of deceased children and aborted fetuses. According to lore, prior to becoming a bodhisattva, Kshitigarbha was a maiden with deep compassion for those suffering in hell. |

**FIGURE 12.2** *Immortals Gathering around the Buddha* (Qing dynasty). SOURCE: National Palace Museum, Taipei.

# APPENDIX E:
# Map of Shang and Zhou

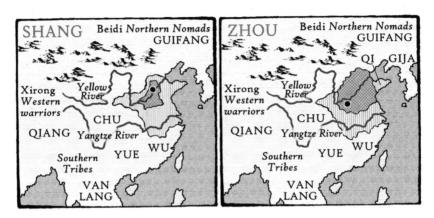

**FIGURE 12.3** Map of the Shang and Zhou dynasties. *Note: not drawn to scale.*

|  | Capital city and central court of the dynasty. Site of the central administrative government. |  | Feudal city-states and fiefdoms. These are territories controlled by the dynasty. |
|---|---|---|---|

| | |
|---|---|
| 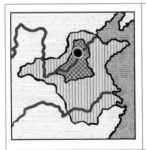 | **Shang Dynasty**商 (1600–1046 BC)<br>In antiquity, the Shang was known as the Yin 殷. The Yin claim descendancy from a mythical blackbird 玄鳥. The crow as a totemic emblem of the Shang is explained in Hexagram 5. In 1250 BC, King Wu Ding designated Yin (later known as Anyang) as his capital.[3] Wu Ding is referenced directly in the third line of Hexagram 63. Prior to that, the Shang capital was moved several times. When the Shang were overtaken by the Zhou, the capital was Chaoge 朝歌. |
| 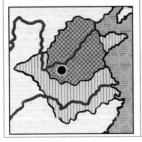 | **Zhou Dynasty** 周 (1046–256 BC)<br>One of the longest-reigning dynasties in Chinese history (789 years). The ruling family of the Zhou were the Ji 姬, who claimed descent from the cultural hero Hou Ji, conceived when his mother stepped into a footprint of the god Shangdi. Initially Zhou's capital was Haojing 鎬京 (also known as Zhongzhou 宗周),[4] but it was later moved to Luoyang during the Eastern Zhou (770–255 BC).[5] |

Shang's capital was in the northeast, while Zhou's was in the southwest. Recall how in both Hexagrams 2 and 39, there are references to the southwest being auspicious but the northeast being inauspicious.

| | |
|---|---|
| **Guifang** 鬼方 | The Guifang are the people referenced in Hexagrams 63 and 64. They were among the Beidi northern nomads that were often at war with the Shang and later the Zhou. "Guifang" could also be a reference to the Xirong western warriors. Another theory is that the Guifang were the descendants of the Xiongnu,[6] a confederation of nomadic tribes indigenous to Mongolia, Kazakhstan, Kyrgyzstan, Manchuria, Xinjiang, Gansu, and southern Siberia. They may have also been the indigenous ancestors of the Uyghurs. They were located northwest of the Shang. |
| **Qiang** 羌 | The Qiang were a people of Tibeto-Burman origin who were mainly shepherds and horse breeders. Interactions with the Qiang and their contributions were frequently referenced on Shang oracle bones. Clans of the Qiang occupied the Tibetan Plateau and claimed ancestry from the Yellow Emperor. Qiang prisoners of war captured by the Shang were the skilled artisans who crafted the oracle bones.[7] |
| | The Qiang consisted of a confederation of diverse clans. Some used the sheep as their totemic symbol. The sheep was considered a psychopomp, whose spirit could lead the deceased safely to the underworld. Thus, at the funeral ceremony, a sheep would be sacrificed so that its spirit could accompany the loved one to the afterlife. Other clans of the Qiang were known as the White Wolf people.[8] |
| **Chu** 荆楚 | Chu, also known as Jingchu, is the state ruled by leaders who claimed ancestral lineage from the Ji 姬 clan (King Wen and the subsequent rulers of the Zhou). The Chu were a prominent confederation of clans during the time of Shang. They succeeded at annexing numerous fiefdoms and expanded their kingdom, coexisting peacefully alongside the Shang and Zhou through political prowess. One of the early totemic animal emblems of the Chu ruling family was the bear.[9] Later, during the Zhou, the Chu were associated with the animal totem of the nine-headed phoenix 九鳳. (See figure 9.1 from chapter 9.) |
| **Wu** 吳國 | One of the early Yangtze River civilizations that rose concurrently with the Yellow River civilizations. The Wajin 倭人, an ethnic group in Japan who formed the kingdom of Wa, are believed to be descendants from the ruling family of the Wu.[10] During the Eastern Zhou period, Wu and Chu were rivals. The famous military strategist Sun Tzu was an advisor in the court of Wu. The Wu are renowned for metalwork, weaponry, and sharp acumen. |

| | |
|---|---|
| **Yue** 越 | King Goujian, who went to war with the kingdom of Wu, was from the kingdom of Yue. The state of Chu allied with Yue in their efforts to defeat Wu. The legend of Goujian is often used as a parable for explaining the fifth line of Hexagram 30. Current speculations connect the Yue with the Austronesians that migrated south into pre-Han Taiwan around 1500–1000 BC.[11] The Wu and Yue spoke a different language from the dominant Shang and Zhou, and they tattooed their bodies, so they were often described as barbarians. |
| **Qi** 齊 | The state of Qi, located around present-day Shandong, was founded after the Zhou overthrew the Shang and was ruled by Jiang Ziya 姜子牙, referenced in Hexagram 44. The kingdom of Yi 夷 referenced in Hexagrams 23, 25, 34, and 56 was absorbed into the state of Qi. Mount Tai, which in antiquity was believed to be an entrance or gateway to the underworld, is located in Qi. |
| **Gija** | Hexagram 36 tells the story of Jizi (Korean Gija). Pre-Qin Chinese records claim that Jizi 箕子, dissenting against Shang rule but refusing to submit to Zhou, became the founding ruler of Gija Joseon 기자 조선, the region that is presently North Korea. However, no archaeological evidence of Gija Joseon has been found. |
| **Van Lang** | Văn Lang was the legendary kingdom of Vietnam that lasted from 2800 to 258 BC.[12] Shang and Zhou dynasty references to southern tribes 南蠻 *(nán mán)* were likely in reference to the Văn Lang.<br><br>Later the kingdom of Văn Lang and a neighboring kingdom of Thuc would merge to become Âu Lạc (257–180 BC).[13] The name Âu Lạc is in reference to a goddess who took the form of a bird.[14] Note some of the overlap with the totemic emblem of the Lady of the Nine Heavens merged with the Mysterious Heavenly Bird of Destiny, referenced in Hexagram 5.<br><br>By 179 BC, Âu Lạc became part of Nam Viet.[15] |

# BIBLIOGRAPHY

Adler, Joseph A. *The Yijing: A Guide.* New York: Oxford University Press, 2022.
Asprem, Egil. "Rejected Knowledge Reconsidered: Some Methodological Notes on Esotericism and Marginality." *New Approaches to the Study of Esotericism* 17 (December 2020): 127–46.
Ball, Jacqueline, and Richard H. Levey. *Ancient China: Archaeology Unlocks the Secrets of China's Past.* Washington, DC: National Geographic, 2006.
Birdwhistell, Anne D. "The Philosophical Concept of Foreknowledge in the Thought of Shao Yong." *Philosophy East and West* 39, no. 1 (January 1989): 47–65.
Blagov, Sergei. *Caodaism: Vietnamese Traditionalism and Its Leap into Modernity.* New York: Nova Science Publishers, 2001.
Carus, Paul. *Chinese Thought: An Exposition of the Main Characteristic Features of the Chinese World-Conception.* Chicago: Open Court Publishing Co., 1907.
Castro-Chavez, Fernando. "Defragged Binary I Ching Genetic Code Chromosomes Compared to Nirenberg's and Transformed into Rotating 2D Circles and Squares and into a 3D 100% Symmetrical Tetrahedron Coupled to a Functional One to Discern Start From Non-Start Methionines through a Stella Octangula." *Journal of Proteome Science and Computational Biology* 1, no. 3 (2012). http://www.doi.org/10.7243/2050-2273-1-3.
———. "A Tetrahedral Representation of the Genetic Code Emphasizing Aspects of Symmetry." *BIO-Complexity* 2 (2012): 1–6. https://doi.org10.5048/BIO-C.2012.2.
Chang, Kwan-chih, et al., eds. *The Formation of Chinese Civilization: An Archaeological Perspective.* New Haven, CT: Yale University Press, 2002.
Chang, Wonsuk. "Reflections on Time and Related Ideas in the *Yijing*." *Philosophy East and West* 59, no. 2 (April 2009): 216–29.
Chen, Mengjia 陳夢家. "The Ancient Writings of the Shang and Zhou" 古文字中的商周祭祀. *Yenjing Journal* 19 (June 1936): 125–29.
Chen, Sanping. *Multicultural China in the Early Middle Ages.* Philadelphia: University of Pennsylvania Press, 2012.
Chen, Shih-Chuan. "How to Form a Hexagram and Consult the *I Ching*." *Journal of the American Oriental Society* 92, no. 2 (1972): 237–49.

Chen, Yong Zheng, 陳永正 and Gu Jian Qing 古健青, eds. 中國方術大辭典 [Encyclopedia (or dictionary) of Chinese alchemy and ritual magic]. Guangdong: Sun Yat-Sen University Press 中山大學出版社, 1991.

Cheng, Chung-ying. *The Primary Way: Philosophy of Yijing*. Albany: State University of New York Press, 2020.

Cheng Yi. *The Yi River Commentary on the Book of Changes* [伊川易傳]. Translated by L. Michael Harrington. New Haven, CT: Yale University Press, 2019.

Chih-Hsu Ou-I. *The Buddhist Yi Jing*. Translated by Thomas Cleary. Boulder, CO: Shambala Publications, 1987.

Childs-Johnson, Elizabeth. "Fu Zi: The Shang Woman Warrior." In *The Fourth International Conference on Chinese Paleography Proceedings*, 619–51. Hong Kong: Chinese University of Hong Kong, 2003.

Chinese Text Project 中國哲學書電子化計劃. "'Dì wáng shì jì' 帝王世紀 [The age of kings] by Huángfǔ Mì" 皇甫謐. Edited by Donald Sturgeon. Accessed May 11, 2022. https://ctext.org/wiki.pl?if=gb&chapter=838808.

Chinese Text Project 中國哲學書電子化計劃. "Huángdì nèijīng 黃帝內經" [Yellow Emperor's classic of internal medicine]. Edited by Donald Sturgeon. Accessed May 11, 2022. https://ctext.org/huangdi-neijing.

Chinese Text Project 中國哲學書電子化計劃. "Shān hǎi jīng 山海經" [Classic of mountains and seas]. Edited by Donald Sturgeon. Accessed June 11, 2022. https://ctext.org/shan-hai-jing.

Chinese Text Project 中國哲學書電子化計劃. "Shàng shū 尚書" [The book of documents, or the classic of history]. Edited by Donald Sturgeon. Accessed May 11, 2022. https://ctext.org/shang-shu.

Chinese Text Project 中國哲學書電子化計劃. "Shiji 史記" [Records of the grand historian]. Edited by Donald Sturgeon. Accessed May 11, 2022. https://ctext.org/shiji.

Chinese Text Project 中國哲學書電子化計劃. "Wǔ xing dà yì 五行大義" [The great meaning of the five changing phases]. Edited by Donald Sturgeon. Accessed May 29, 2022. https://ctext.org/wiki.pl?if=en&res=601464.

Chinese Text Project 中國哲學書電子化計劃. "Wǔyīng diàn shísān jīng zhùshū 武英殿十三經注疏" [Commentary on the thirteen classics]. Edited by Donald Sturgeon. Accessed June 18, 2022. https://ctext.org/library.pl?if=en&res=77712.

Chinese Text Project 中國哲學書電子化計劃. "Yi jing 易經" [I Ching, Book of Changes, English translation by James Legge]. Edited by Donald Sturgeon. Accessed May 11, 2022. https://ctext.org/book-of-changes/yi-jing.

Chinese Text Project 中國哲學書電子化計劃. "Yì wěi 易緯" [The occult I Ching]. Edited by Donald Sturgeon. Accessed May 17, 2022. https://ctext.org/library.pl?if=en&res=82580.

Chinese Text Project 中國哲學書電子化計劃. "Yīn běnjì 殷本紀" [Annals of yin]. Edited by Donald Sturgeon. Accessed May 9, 2022. https://ctext.org/shiji/yin-ben-ji.

Chinese Text Project 中國哲學書電子化計劃. "Zhōu lǐ 周禮" [The rites of Zhou]. Edited by Donald Sturgeon. Accessed May 11, 2022. https://ctext.org/book-of-changes/yi-jing.

Chinese Text Project 中國哲學書電子化計劃. "Zhūzi yǔ lèi 朱子語類" [A collection of conversations of Master Zhu]. Edited by Donald Sturgeon. Accessed May 17, 2022. https://ctext.org/zhuzi-yulei/zh.

Crowley, Aleister [the Master Therion]. *Magick in Theory and Practice*. Paris: Lecram Press, 1929.

Eaves, Lindon J., Katherine M. Kirk, Nicholas G. Martin, and Robert J. Russel. "Some Implications of Chaos Theory for the Genetic Analysis of Human Development and Variation." *Twin Research* 2, no. 1 (1999): 43–48.

Ebrey, Patricia B. *Cambridge Illustrated History of China*, 26–27. London: Cambridge University Press, 1997.

———, Anne Walthall, and James B. Palais. *East Asia: A Cultural, Social, and Political History*. New York: Houghton Mifflin, 2013.

Eco, Umberto. "From Marco Polo to Leibniz." In *Serendipities: Language and Lunacy*, translated by William Weaver, 53–76. San Diego: Harcourt Brace & Company, 1998.

Elman, Benjamin A. *A Cultural History of Civil Examinations in Late Imperial China*. Berkeley: University of California Press, 2000.

Feng, Shi 馮時. *Chinese Astronomy and Archaeology* 中國天文考古學. Beijing: China Social Sciences Press 中國社會科學出版社, 2010.

Fu, Peirong 傅佩榮. *Fu Peirong's Interpretation of the Book of Changes* 傅佩榮譯解易經. Taipei: Taiwan Oriental Publishing House 台灣東方出版社, 2011.

Gan Bao. *In Search of the Supernatural: The Written Record*. Translated by Kenneth J. DeWoskin and James Irving Crump. Stanford, CA: Stanford University Press, 1996.

Gao, Heng 高亨. *A General Introduction to the Ancient Classic* Zhouyi 周易古經通說 *(Zhōuyì gǔ jīng tōng shuō)*. Hong Kong: Zhonghua Shuju, 1963.

———. *The Old Classic with a New Exegesis* 周易古經今注 *(Zhōuyì gǔ jīng jīn zhù)*. Beijing: Běijīng Chóng Huà Shùjù 北京崇化數據, 1984.

Hon, Tze-ki. *The* Yijing *and Chinese Politics: Classical Commentary and Literati Activism in the Northern Song Period, AD 960–1127*. Albany: State University of New York Press, 2005.

Horthemels, Daniel. *Confucius Cinarum philosophus, sive, scientia Sinensis Latine exposita* [Confucius the philosopher of China, or, the knowledge of China translated into Latin]. Translated by Philippe Couplet, Christian Herdtrich, Prospero Intorcetta, and Francis Rougemont. Paris, 1687.

Huang, Alfred. *The Complete I Ching: The Definitive Translation by Taoist Master Alfred Huang.* 10th ed. Rochester, NY: Inner Traditions, 2010.

Huang, Kerson. *I Ching: The Oracle.* Singapore: World Scientific Publishing Co., 1984.

Jammes, Jeremy, and David A. Palmer. "Occulting the Dao: Daoist Inner Alchemy, French Spiritism, and Vietnamese Colonial Modernity in Caodai Translingual Practice." *Journal of Asian Studies* 77, no. 2 (May 2018): 405–28.

Jung, Carl Gustav. *The Collected Works of Carl Jung.* Edited and translated by Gerhard Adler and R. F. C. Hull. Princeton, NJ: Princeton University Press, 1969.

Keightley, David N., ed. *The Origins of Chinese Civilization.* Berkeley: University of California Press, 1983.

Kim, Yung Sik. *The Natural Philosophy of Chu Hsi (1130–1200).* Philadelphia: American Philosophical Society, 2000.

Ko, Young Woon. *Jung on Synchronicity and* Yijing: *A Critical Approach.* Newcastle upon Tyne, UK: Cambridge Scholars Publishing, 2011.

Lauren F. Pfister. "Clues to the Life and Academic Achievements of One of the Most Famous Nineteenth Century European Sinologists—James Legge (AD 1815–1897)." *Journal of the Hong Kong Branch of the Royal Asiatic Society* 30 (1990): 180–218.

Lee, Jung Young. "The Book of Change and Korean Thought." In *Religions in Korea: Beliefs and Cultural Values,* edited by Earl H. Phillips and Eui-young Yu, 5–24. Lanham, MD: Rowman & Littlefield, 1982.

Legge, James. *I Ching: Book of Changes.* New York: Bantam Books, 1964.

Lewis, Mark Edward. *The Flood Myths of Early China.* Albany: State University of New York Press, 2006.

———. *Writing and Authority in Early China.* Albany: State University of New York Press, 1999.

Li, Weirong. "Striving for the 'Original' Meaning: A Historical Survey of *Yijing*'s English Translations." In *Encountering China's Past: Translation and Dissemination of Classical Chinese Literature,* edited by Lintao Qi and Shani Tobias, 165–84. Singapore: Springer, 2022.

Li, Xiaobing. *China at War: An Encyclopedia.* Santa Barbara, CA: ABC-Clio, 2012.

Liao, Mingchun 廖名春. *I Ching: Classical and New Theories on the History of Yi Xue* 《周易》經傳與易學史新論. Jinan: Qilu Publishing 齊魯書社, 2001.

Liu, Da. *I Ching Numerology: Based on Shao Yong's Classic Plum Blossom Numerology.* New York: Harper & Row, 1979.

Liu, Haifeng. *The Examination Culture in Imperial China.* Translated by Weihua Yu. Reading, UK: Paths International Limited, 2018.

Liu, JeeLoo. "Reconstructing Chinese Metaphysics." *Journal of East-West Thought* 1, no. 1 (December 2011): 151–63. http://hdl.handle.net/10211.3/130846.

Liu, Peng. "'Conceal My Body So That I Can Protect the State': The Making of the Mysterious Woman in Daoism and Water Margin." *Ming Studies* 74 (November 2016): 47–71.

Liu, Yujian 劉玉建. *An Examination and Study of Han Dynasty Gua Qi Traditions* 漢易卦氣學研究 *(Hàn yì Guà Qì xué yán jiū)*. Jinan, China: 齊魯書社 *(Qí Lǔ Shū Shè)*, 2007.

Lui, Adam Yuen-Chung. "Syllabus of the Provincial Examination (Hsiang-Shih) under the Early Ch'ing (1644–1795)." *Modern Asian Studies* 8, no. 3 (May 1974): 391–96.

Ma, Zhen G., and Hua C. Zeng. *Hexagram-Allocated Table of Shao Yong's 129,600-Year Supreme World-Ordering Principles* (邵雍皇极经世 129,600 年配卦表). Montreal: Paramita Publishing Studio, 2020.

McClatchie, M. A. *A Translation of the Confucian Yi Jing or the "Classic of Change" with Notes and Appendix.* Shanghai: American Presbyterian Mission Press, 1876.

McMahon, Keith. *Women Shall Not Rule: Imperial Wives and Concubines in China from Han to Liao.* Lanham, MD: Rowman & Littlefield, 2013.

Murray, Julia K. "The *Ladies' Classic of Filial Piety* and Sung Textual Illustration: Problems of Reconstruction and Artistic Context." *Ars Orientalis* 129 (1988): 95–129.

Ng, Benjamin Wai-Ming, ed. *The Making of the Global* Yijing *in the Modern World: Cross-Cultural Interpretations and Interactions.* Singapore: Springer, 2021.

Ng, Wai-Ming. "The Assimilation of the *Yijing* in Tibetan History and Culture." *Sungkyun Journal of East Asian Studies* 19, no. 1 (April 2019): 19–36.

———. "The *I Ching* in Late-Choson [Joseon] Thought." *Korean Studies* 24 (2000): 53–68.

———. *The I Ching in Tokugawa Thought and Culture.* Honolulu: University of Hawai'i Press, 2000.

———. "Study and Uses of the *I Ching* in Tokugawa Japan." *Sino-Japanese Studies* 9, no. 2 (November 1990): 24–44.

———. "*Yijing* Scholarship in Late Nguyen Vietnam: A Study of Le Van Ngu's *Chu Dich Cuu Nguyen* (An Investigation of the Origins of the *Yijing*, 1916)." *Review of Vietnamese Studies* 3, no. 1 (2003): 1–14.

Nielsen, Bent. *A Companion to Yi Jing Numerology and Cosmology: Chinese Studies of Images and Numbers from Han (202 BC–220 CE) to Song (AD 960–1279).* New York: Routledge Curzon, 2003.

Ou-I, Chih-hsu. *The Buddhist I Ching.* Translated by Thomas Cleary. Boston: Shambhala Publications, 1987.

Palmer, David A., and Xun Liu, eds. *Daoism in the Twentieth Century: Between Eternity and Modernity*. Berkeley: University of California Press, 2012.

Peterson, Barbara Bennett. *Notable Women of China: Shang Dynasty to the Early Twentieth Century*. London: Routledge, 2015.

Pulleyblank, E. G. "The Chinese and Their Neighbors in Prehistoric and Early Historic Times." In *The Origins of Chinese Civilization*, edited by David N. Keightley, 411–66. Berkeley: University of California Press, 1983.

Rothschild, N. Harry. *Emperor Wu Zhao and Her Pantheon of Devis, Divinities, and Dynastic Mothers*. New York: Columbia University Press, 2015.

Rutt, Richard. *The Book of Changes (Zhouyi): A Bronze Age Document*. Richmond, UK: Curzon Press, 1996.

Schönberger, Martin. *I Ching and the Genetic Code: The Hidden Key to Life*. Santa Fe, NM: Aurora Press, 1992.

Sears, Richard. Chinese Etymology 字源. Accessed July 11, 2022. https://hanziyuan.net/.

Shaughnessy, Edward. *Unearthing the Changes: Recently Discovered Manuscripts of the Yi Jing (I Ching) and Related Texts*. New York: Columbia University Press, 2014.

Shchutskii, Julian. *Researches on the I Ching*. Princeton, NJ: Princeton University Press, 1979.

Sherrill, W. A., ed. *The Astrology of I Ching: Translated from the "Ho Map Lo Map Rational Number" Manuscript by W. K. Chu*. New York: Penguin Books, 1993.

Smith, Richard J. *Fathoming the Cosmos and Ordering the World: The Yijing (I Ching, or Classic of Changes) and Its Evolution in China*. Charlottesville: University of Virginia Press, 2008.

———. "How the Book of Changes Arrived in the West." *New England Review* 33, no. 1 (2012): 25–41.

———. *The I Ching: A Biography*. Princeton, NJ: Princeton University Press, 2012.

Smith Jr., Kidder, Peter K. Bol, Joseph A. Adler, and Don J. Wyatt, eds. *Sung Dynasty Uses of the I Ching*. Princeton, NJ: Princeton University Press, 1990.

Sun, Weimin. "Features of Chinese Cosmology." *Journal of East-West Thought* 1, no. 2 (March 2012): 133–44. http://hdl.handle.net/10211.3/131584.

Theobald, Ulrich. ChinaKnowledge.de: An Encyclopaedia on Chinese History, Literature and Art. Accessed June 18, 2022. http://www.chinaknowledge.de/.

Thu, Nguyen Tai, and Hoang Thi Tho, eds. *The History of Buddhism in Vietnam*. Washington, DC: Council for Research in Values and Philosophy, 2008.

Turner, Kevin. *Sky Shamans of Mongolia: Meeting with Remarkable Healers*. Berkeley, CA: North Atlantic Books, 2016.

Van Ess, Hans. "The Old Text/New Text Controversy: Has the 20th Century Got It Wrong?" *T'oung Pao* 80, no. 1/3 (1994): 146–70.

von Franz, Marie-Louise. *On Divination and Synchronicity: The Psychology of Meaningful Chance.* Toronto: Inner City Books, 1980.

Wang, Bi 王弼. *A Collection of Writings by Wang Bi* 王弼集校釋 *(Wángbì jí xiào shi).* Edited by 樓宇烈 (Lóuyǔ Liè). Beijing: Zhonghua Shuju 中華書局有限公司, 1980.

———. *The Classic of Changes: A New Translation of the I Ching.* Translated by Richard John Lynn. New York: Columbia University Press, 1994.

Wang, Fen-sen. "The Impact of the Linear Model of History on Modern Chinese Historiography." In *Transforming History: The Making of a Modern Academic Discipline in Twentieth-Century China,* edited by Peter Gue Zarrow and Brian Moloughney, 135–68. Hong Kong: Chinese University Press, 2011.

Wang, Qingshu. "The History and Current Status of Chinese Women's Participation in Politics," in *Holding Up Half the Sky: Chinese Women Past, Present, and Future,* edited by Shirley L. Mow, Jie Tao, and Zheng Bijun, 92–106. New York: Feminist Press at the City University of New York, 2004.

Wang, Rui. *The Chinese Imperial Examination System: An Annotated Bibliography.* Plymouth, MD: Scarecrow Press, 2013.

Wang, Shizhen 王世真. *The Complete Biography of the Immortals* 列仙全傳 *(Liè xiān quán chuán).* Beijing: Cultural Relics Press 文物出版社, 2018. First published 1651.

Wilhelm, Hellmut, and Richard Wilhelm. *Understanding the I Ching: The Wilhelm Lectures on the Book of Changes.* Princeton, NJ: Princeton University Press, 1979.

Wilhelm, Richard, trans. *The I Ching or Book of Changes.* Rendered into English by Cary F. Baynes. Princeton, NJ: Princeton University Press, 1977.

Yan, Johnson F. *DNA and the I Ching: The Tao of Life.* New York: Penguin Random House, 1993.

———. *DNA and the I Ching: The Tao of Life.* Berkeley, CA: North Atlantic Books, 2014.

Yan, Wenming, and Wang Youping. "Early Humans in China." In *The Formation of Chinese Civilization: An Archaeological Perspective,* edited by Kwan-chih Chang, Xu Pingfang, Lu Liancheng, Shao Wangping, Wang Youping, Yan Wenming, Zhang Zhongpei, Xu Hong, Wang Renxiang, and Sarah Allan, 11–26. New Haven, CT: Yale University Press.

Yang, Li. *Book of Changes and Traditional Chinese Medicine.* Beijing: Beijing Science and Technology Press, 1998.

Yang, Mayfair 楊美惠. "Shamanism and Spirit Possession in Chinese Modernity: Some Preliminary Reflections on Gendered Religiosity of the Body." *Review of Religion and Chinese Society* 2 (2015): 51–86.

Yang, Shengyong 楊勝勇, ed. *Military History of the Three Dynasties of China* 中國元古暨三代軍事史. Beijing: 人民出版社 People's Publishing House (Rénmín Chūbǎn Shè), 1994. Volume 3 from *The Hundred Volumes of the Complete History of China* 中國全史百卷本).

Yi, Cheng. *The Yi River Commentary on the* Book of Changes. Translated by L. Michael Harrington. New Haven, CT: Yale University Press, 2019.

Yong, Ma, Su Hongxia, Jin Qian, Feng Wei, Liu Jianuo, and Huang Wenying. *The General History of Chinese Tourism Culture*. New York: SCPG Publishing, 2016.

Zhang, Qi-cheng 張其成, ed. *Encyclopedia of the I Ching (Vol. 1)* 易經應用大百科全書(上篇). Taipei: De Jǐng 地景, 1996.

Zhang Shanwen 张善文, ed. *Zhouyi Dictionary* 周易辞典. Beijing: China Encyclopedia Publishing House 中国大百科全书出版社, 2005.

Zhang, Yuanshan 張遠山. *The Way of Fuxi* 伏羲之道. Hunan: Yuelu Publishing House 嶽麓書社, 2015.

Zheng, Jixiong 鄭吉雄 (or Cheng, Kat-hung). *A Philological Approach to the Philosophies of the* Zhouyi 周易玄義詮解 (*Zhōuyì xuán yìquán jiě*). Taipei: Institute of Chinese Literature and Philosophy, Academia Sinica, 2012.

Zhu, Bo-kun 朱伯崑, ed. *An Introduction to the Studies of the* Yijing 易學基礎教程 (*Yì xué jīchǔ jiàochéng*). Beijing: Jiuzhou Chubanshe, 2012.

Zhu, Xi 朱熹. *The Original Meanings of Changes of the Zhou Dynasty* 周易本義 (*Zhōuyì běnyì*). Edited by Liao Mingchun. Beijing: Zhonghua Shuju 中華書局有限公司, 2009.

———. *The Original Meaning of the Yijing: Commentary on the Scripture of Change*. Translated by Joseph A. Adler. New York: Columbia University Press, 2020.

Zou, Xue Xi 鄒學熹 and Zou Cheng Yong 鄒成永. *Traditional Chinese Medicine and the I Ching* 中國醫易學. Szechuan: Sichuan Science and Technology Press 四川科學技術出版社, 1989.

# NOTES

## 1. Preface

1  "A path is made by walking it" is an oft-quoted aphorism associated with fourth-century BC Taoist philosopher Zhuangzi 莊子. The original text reads: "道行之而成 物謂之而然" *(Dào héng zhī ér chéng wù wèi zhī ér rán)*. From: 內篇 ("Nèi piān") in "Qí wù lùn" 齊物論, the second chapter of Zhuangzi's "Inner Chapters" 莊子・內篇. 齊物論, Chinese Text Project, ed. Donald Sturgeon, accessed July 4, 2022, https://ctext.org/zhuangzi/adjustment-of-controversies/zh.

2  Chen Shu 陳書 (1660–1735) is credited as the first female literati painter for the Qing imperial court and is the founder of the Xiushui School painting style. During a time when educating a woman was discouraged, Chen Shu was able to study the classics and the arts. She specialized in landscape paintings, considered rare for a woman. *Reading the I Ching in a Mountain Study* 山窗讀易圖 (1735) is one of her more well-known landscape paintings and is iconic of her style. Try this thought exercise: visualize your astral self at the foot of that path in the foreground along the bottom right. One path, long and winding, leads you to the base of that mountain. The other leads you to that small cottage. Which path do you take?

3  Benjamin A. Elman, *A Cultural History of Civil Examinations in Late Imperial China* (Berkeley: University of California Press, 2000), 316; Haifeng Liu, *The Examination Culture in Imperial China*, trans. Weihua Yu (Reading, UK: Paths International Limited, 2018); Rui Wang, *The Chinese Imperial Examination System: An Annotated Bibliography* (Plymouth, UK: Scarecrow Press, 2013); Adam Yuen-Chung Lui, "Syllabus of the Provincial Examination (Hsiang-Shih) under the Early Ch'ing (1644-1795)," *Modern Asian Studies* 8, no. 3 (May 1974): 391–96.

4  The Five Classics were considered the seminal texts on Confucianism, dating back to before 300 BC. They were: (1) the Book of Documents (書經, Shūjīng), a book on Chinese political philosophy and a saga of philosopher-kings during the Xia, Shang, and Zhou dynasties; (2) the Book of Songs (詩經, Shījīng), literary poems dated between the eleventh and seventh centuries BC; (3) the Book

of Rites (禮記, Lǐjì), delineating ceremonial rites from the Zhou dynasty, social decorum, and etiquette; (4) Book of Changes, the I Ching (易經, Yìjīng); and (5) the Spring and Autumn Annals (春秋, Chūnqiū), a historical chronicle of the state of Lu, or the period of Chinese history during 722–481 BC.

5   Wai-ming Ng, "Study and Uses of the *I Ching* in Tokugawa Japan," *Sino-Japanese Studies* 9, no. 2 (November 1990): 24–44.
6   Wai-Ming Ng, "*Yijing* Scholarship in Late Nguyen Vietnam: A Study of Le Van Ngu's *Chu Dich Cuu Nguyen* (An Investigation of the Origins of the *Yijing*, 1916)," *Journal of Vietnamese Studies* 3, no. 1 (2003): 2.
7   Ng, "Study and Uses," 27.
8   Benjamin Wai-ming Ng, "Forward: Globalizing and Localizing the Yijing," in *The Making of the Global* Yijing *in the Modern World: Cross-Cultural Interpretations and Interactions*, ed. Benjamin Wai-ming Ng (Singapore: Springer, 2021), x.
9   Lê Quý Đôn (Lí Guì Dūn, 1726–1784) was a polymath, poet, government official, and member of the Nguyễn dynasty literati, and was documented as having an eidetic memory. In his life he served in both the courts of the Trịnh clan in the Lê dynasty (north Vietnam) and the Nguyễn dynasty (central and southern Vietnam). He wrote several volumes of encyclopedias on the sciences and treatises on history and philosophy, in addition to writing about the I Ching. One notable feature of Vietnamese scholarship on the I Ching is its treatment of the text as classical literature rather than as having metaphysical or spiritual implications. On the other hand, among the people, the I Ching's eight trigrams were frequently used in Vietnamese talismans and were prevalent in Vietnamese folk magic. Ng, "*Yijing* Scholarship," 5.
10  Ng, "*Yijing* Scholarship," 3.
11  Wai-ming Ng, "The *I Ching* in Late-Choson [Joseon] Thought," *Korean Studies* 24 (2000): 53–68.
12  Wai-ming Ng, "The Assimilation of the *Yijing* in Tibetan History and Culture," *Sungkyun Journal of East Asian Studies* 19, no. 1 (April 2019): 19–36.
13  The *Zuo zhuan* (左傳, *Zuǒ chuán*) is a narrative history covering 722–468 BC. The Qiang (羌) people are believed to be the early predecessors of the Tibeto-Burmans, who migrated south to these regions from Gansu and Mongolia. E. G. Pulleyblank, "The Chinese and Their Neighbors in Prehistoric and Early Historic Times," in *The Origins of Chinese Civilization*, ed. David N. Keightley (Berkeley: University of California Press, 1983), 418.
14  Richard J. Smith, *The I Ching: A Biography* (Princeton, NJ: Princeton University Press, 2012).
15  This might be a good place to talk about the inconsistency of romanization throughout this book. From grade school through part of my university years, I

Notes to Chapter 2. Myths, Legends, and Cultural Heroes of the I Ching  857

learned the Wade-Giles system of romanizing Mandarin Chinese and the Bopomofo Zhuyin approach to transliteration. Thus, I still use the spelling "Taoism" and the "Tao" and have not been able to switch my brain over to "Daoism" or the "Dao." Likewise, it's "I Ching" for me, not "Yijing." By the twenty-first century, however, Hanyu Pinyin replaced the Wade-Giles system, so from college onward I had to learn Hanyu Pinyin and stopped using Wade-Giles. Most Generation X and Millennial Taiwanese Americans share this inconsistency. I've preserved that trait in the romanization to express my particular intersectional identity. The Wade-Giles and Pinyin inconsistency is a very Gen X/Millennial Taiwanese American thing to do.

## 2. Myths, Legends, and Cultural Heroes of the I Ching

1  The spelling "I Ching" is from the Wade-Giles romanization system primarily used in Taiwan. The spelling "Yijing" is per the Hanyu Pinyin system used in mainland China. Also, some diacritic notation has been included to refer to differentiating pronunciation as it appears in the standard pinyin pronunciation. However, diacritics have not been included in all instances in order to honor the diversity of pronunciations found among the Chinese and diasporic Chinese communities.
2  In 1059 BC, a rare planetary stellium of Mercury, Venus, Mars, Jupiter, and Saturn is interpreted by the Zhou people as foretelling that the Mandate of Heaven would pass. King Wen believes that Heaven has granted that mandate to him and declares himself the rightful destined king. That's likely why the Shang imprison him. However, that destiny wouldn't be fulfilled by Wen, but rather, by his son, King Wu of Zhou, in 1046 BC. This also raises the question: did King Wen sincerely predict the fall of Shang and rise of Zhou with I Ching yarrow stalks? Or was that merely confirmation bias? A decade earlier he was already interpreting astronomical phenomena as prophetic of his clan's rise to power.
3  Kanō Sansetsu (1589–1651) was an Edo-period Japanese painter renowned for his historical and Buddhist paintings.
4  The oldest Chinese creation myth, predating the myth of Pangu (盤古), who was the primordial man born from an egg and who separates Heaven from Earth, is that of Fuxi and Nǚwā. Archaeological relics of their depictions show Fuxi holding up the sun and Nǚwā holding up the moon; one holds a compass while the other holds a ruler.

The earliest written source of the Nǚwā myth comes from a Taoist text called Lièzǐ (列子), dated to around 475 BC, consisting of eight chapters on the Tao In the text, Nǚwā repairs Heaven after a Great Flood—a flood caused by a battle between the God of Fire and the God of Water. The flood killed off the first humans, so Nǚwā molds new people out of clay.

After creating these new humans, envious demons try to destroy the world by breaking the pillars holding up Heaven so that it might collapse onto Earth. Nǚwā creates five colored stones and uses those stones to mend the pillars. As a child listening to these stories, I remember wondering, *Where was Fuxi during all this? Why didn't he help?* One speculation that has emerged among contemporary scholars is that the story of Nǚwā is a testament to China's early matriarchal society, symbolic of how women, with the capability of childbirth, are the better creators.

5 Throughout prehistoric China, with records dating to the Warring States period (approximately 2221 BC–475 BC), dragons, serpents, and snakes were linked to the *wū* (巫), spirit mediums and shamans. The serpents of the *wū* were also associated with childbirth and fertility.

6 Mark Edward Lewis, *Writing and Authority in Early China* (Albany: State University of New York Press, 1999), 204–5.

7 In goddess-worshipping Taoist lineages that venerate the Queen Mother of the West 西王母 (Xīwángmǔ) as Wujimu 無極母, mother of the infinite and numinous void, the Queen Mother is the creator goddess of the first people from a previous eon. After the first people were wiped out in an apocalyptic Great Flood, Nǚwā remakes humans from clay, commencing a new eon. We are the descendants of the people created by Nǚwā, but we still venerate the Queen Mother as a grandmother or crone figure, while Nǚwā becomes the primary mother figure.

8 Lewis, *Writing and Authority*, 197.

9 Guo Xu (1456–1526/32) was a Ming dynasty court minister turned painter. Fatigued by the corruption of the Ming, he abandoned his government post to pursue art. After making a name for himself as an artist and poet, the imperial family invited him back to the palace as a court painter, but he declined, preferring the life of a commoner.

10 Yu the Great (大禹, Dà Yǔ) is a well-documented figure in Chinese history, though scholars now speculate that he might have been mythical. He is often characterized as one of the great philosopher-kings of the ancient Xia dynasty, though he was more likely an engineer for the imperial court who was awarded grand titles posthumously in honor of his achievements. In Chinese historical paintings, the myth of Yu the Great and the floods was a common theme and was even given a name: "Great Yu Who Controlled the Waters" (大禹治水, Dà Yǔ Zhì Shuǐ). Figure 2.9 is an example of this genre of historical painting. In southern regions of China, Yu the Great is deified as a water god. That Yu the Great might have simply been an engineer even though he is revered now is an interesting

implication of cultural values, in light of how Nǚwā and Fuxi are commonly depicted holding the tools of trade for an engineer or architect.

11  Lihui Yang and Deming An, with Jessica Anderson Turner, *Handbook of Chinese Mythology* (New York: Oxford University Press, 2005), 135–37.

12  A Han dynasty text dated to 206 BC–AD 8, *Dai the Greater's Book of Rites* (大戴禮記, *Dà dài lǐ jì*), explains that the Lo Shu magic square is assigned the numbers one through nine, with each of the nine sectors envisioned as a chamber, and all together the nine chambers are the Hall of Light (or Temple of Light).

13  It is uncertain whether the Nine Tripod Cauldrons were real or mythical. They were lost during the reign of Qin Shi Huang, the first emperor of the Qin dynasty, around 200 BC. References to the Nine Tripod Cauldrons are found in the Confucian text *Gongyang zhuan* (公羊傳): "天子九鼎，諸侯七卿大夫五，元士三/天子九鼎，諸侯七，卿大夫五，元士三。" The text is written in the form of a Socratic dialogue between Confucius and a pupil, in reference to the nine tripod cauldrons of the emperor, seven princes, five court ministers, and three emperors. The text authored by Sima Qian, *Records of the Grand Historian* (太史公書, *Tài shǐ gōng shū*), written around 94 BC, also references the nine tripod cauldrons, describing them as having been cast by Yu the Great and as being made from gold, along with precious metals from Heaven and Earth.

14  Paul Carus, *Chinese Thought: An Exposition of the Main Characteristic Features of the Chinese World-Conception* (Chicago: Open Court Publishing Co., 1907), 48. The Mystic Tablet illustrates the eight trigrams as they were revealed to Fuxi (spelled Fuh-Hi in the text) on the back of a tortoise. The Carus text notes that the illustration of the Mystic Tablet was reproduced from Waddell's *Buddhism of Tibet*. The center nine-sector Lo Shu magic square is written in Tibetan characters. Encircling the Lo Shu magic square are the twelve animals of the zodiac.

15  Mark Edward Lewis, *The Flood Myths of Early China* (Albany: State University of New York Press, 2006).

16  One of the most repeated lines from the Taoist classic (or scripture) Tao Te Ching reads: 道生一，一生二，二生三，三生万物 (*Dào shēng yī, yī shēng èr, èr shēng sān, sān shēng wàn wù*), or "The Tao produces one; one produces two; two produces three; three produces all manifestations of nature in this universe." The last two words "万物" (*wàn wù*) mean, essentially, the myriad things of this cosmos, anything and everything that manifests in physical nature, all that exists. Multiplication begets creation in the natural world, but division brings order to the humans who live in that natural world.

17  Taoist cosmogony proposes that the Tao as a unity is subdivided into the binary of yin and yang so that the unity might be understood. Yin and yang can each in turn be subdivided into inherent yin and yang within each. In other words, yin

is not pure yin, but rather is innately a combination of yin *and* yang; likewise with yang, which contains within it a particle of yin. Since a singular yin, despite possessing an innate binary of yin and yang, is dominant yin, yin + yin + yang expresses a subdivision into a trinity; singular yang, being dominant yang, is subdivided into yang + yang + yin. Eight trigram subdivisions of the Tao result from this division process. Yet the paradox and wisdom of the Tao is that the division process is also equivalent to an addition and combination process. This is likened to the Western alchemical principle of *solve et coagula,* or dissolution and coagulation.

18 *Annals of Yin,* Chinese Text Project, ed. Donald Sturgeon, accessed May 9, 2022, https://ctext.org/text.pl?node=649067&if=en. The *Annals of Yin* is a chronicle of ancient Chinese history attributed to Sima Qian, a Han dynasty historian and scholar.

19 Edward L. Shaughnessy, *Unearthing the Changes: Recently Discovered Manuscripts of the Yijing and Related Texts* (New York: Columbia University Press, 2014), 12.

20 N. Harry Rothschild, *Emperor Wu Zhao and Her Pantheon of Devis, Divinities, and Dynastic Mothers* (New York: Columbia University Press, 2015), 109.

21 Jiao Bingzhen 焦秉貞 was a seventeenth- and eighteenth-century painter and astronomer who converted to Roman Catholicism. His art style is heavily influenced by Western artistic techniques, such as two- and three-point perspective.

22 Rothschild, *Emperor Wu Zhao,* 109–23.

23 This well-known legend part of popular lore is inconsistent with the references made in the I Ching, however; for example, the fifth line of Hexagram 11 and the underlying narrative of Hexagram 54.

24 In the *Shiji* (史記), or *Records of the Grand Historian*—a historical chronicle attributed to Sima Tian, a chief astrologer in the imperial court of the Han dynasty, and his son Sima Qian—Tai Si (太姒, Tàisì) was also described as having been beloved and admired by the women of the court. If true, then Tai Si possessed a particularly exceptional set of skills and personality traits.

25 Rothschild, *Emperor Wu Zhao,* 109.

26 The novel 封神演義 *(Fēng shén yǎn yì),* written during the Ming dynasty (AD 1368–1644), has also been translated as *Investiture of the Gods, Romance of the Gods,* and *The Complete Biography of Shang and Zhou.* From prison, King Wen uses the eight trigrams of the I Ching to accurately predict what will happen to his kingdom, the Zhou, including their rebellion against the Shang. Throughout the novel, the cultural heroes are aided by gods, goddesses, and celestials. Nǔwā is a mother goddess featured in the novel.

27 Nüwā's birthday is noted as the fifteenth day of the third moon, meaning the third full moon of the lunar calendar year. The mythology of Nüwā begins with her and her brother-spouse Fuxi as the survivors after a great flood, who then create the humans we descend from. She is later deified as a mother goddess.

28 Xiaobing Li, *China at War: An Encyclopedia* (Santa Barbara, CA: ABC-Clio, 2012), 293–94.

29 The most popular and oldest known Chinese text on dream interpretation, *The Duke of Zhou's Interpretation of Dreams* (周公解夢, *Zhōu Gōng jiě mèng*), and the idiom "梦见周公" *(mèng jiàn Zhōu Gōng),* translated as "dreaming of the Duke of Zhou" (meaning to have a prophetic dream), are modern-day hallmarks of the Zhou period's influence on the development of Chinese culture.

30 Yong Ma et al., *The General History of Chinese Tourism Culture* (New York: SCPG Publishing, 2016).

31 Wang Qingshu, "The History and Current Status of Chinese Women's Participation in Politics," in *Holding Up Half the Sky: Chinese Women Past, Present, and Future*, eds. Shirley L. Mow et al. (New York: Feminist Press at the City University of New York, 2004), 92–93.

32 Jacqueline Ball and Richard H. Levey, *Ancient China: Archaeology Unlocks the Secrets of China's Past* (Washington, DC: National Geographic, 2006), 22–23.

33 Barbara Bennett Peterson, *Notable Women of China: Shang Dynasty to the Early Twentieth Century* (London: Routledge, 2015); Elizabeth Childs-Johnson, "Fu Zi: The Shang Woman Warrior," in *The Fourth International Conference on Chinese Paleography Proceedings* (Hong Kong: Chinese University of Hong Kong, 2003), 619–51. Note: Fu Hao is often referred to in the oracle bones as Bigui (Chinese: 妣癸).

34 Yan Wenming and Wang Youping, "Early Humans in China," in *The Formation of Chinese Civilization: An Archaeological Perspective*, eds. Kwan-chih Chang et al. (New Haven, CT: Yale University Press), 3.

35 Wang Fen-sen, "The Impact of the Linear Model of History on Modern Chinese Historiography," in *Transforming History: The Making of a Modern Academic Discipline in Twentieth-century China*, eds. Peter Gue Zarrow and Brian Moloughney (Hong Kong: Chinese University Press, 2011), 150, noting that "at some point during the Xia or Shang dynasty, the matriarchal tradition transformed into a patriarchal one."

36 Zhang Zhongpei, "The Yangshao Period: Prosperity and the Transformation of Prehistoric Society," in *The Formation of Chinese Civilization: An Archaeological Perspective*, eds. Kwan-chih Chang et al. (New Haven, CT: Yale University Press, 2002), 68, 72, and 83 (noting that social organization transitioned from a

matriarchal to a patriarchal society during the Yangshao period, or 5000–3000 BC). The complete evolution from matriarchal to patriarchal ends in the Longshan period, or 3000–1900 BC. Kwan-chih Chang et al., eds., *The Formation of Chinese Civilization: An Archaeological Perspective* (New Haven, CT: Yale University Press, 2002), 286.

37 Keith McMahon, *Women Shall Not Rule: Imperial Wives and Concubines in China from Han to Liao* (Lanham, MD: Rowman & Littlefield, 2013), 17.

38 For a rather gory example, during the Shang, as a sacrificial offering to the gods for rain, a female witch/shaman 女巫 *(nǔ wū)* would be stripped naked and violently burned under the scorching sun so she would be rendered as red as possible, a form of offering called the Chì 赤. The hope was that the level of cruelty would cause the gods to mourn, cry a torrent of tears, and thus bring rain. From *Myths and Witchcraft of the Shang Dynasty* 商代的神話與巫術 by Chen Mengjia 陳夢家 (Beijing: Yenching University 燕京學報, 1936), 563–66.

39 "Shang Tomb of Fu Hao," in *A Visual Sourcebook of Chinese Civilization,* edited by Patricia Buckley Ebrey, University of Washington, accessed May 14, 2022, https://depts.washington.edu/chinaciv/archae/2fuhmain.htm. Ball and Levey, *Ancient China*, 22–23.

40 *The Literature and History Series* 文史版系列节目, season 1, episode 1, "The Battle of Muye" 牧野之战, directed by 陳鶩 (Chén Zhuó), aired January 8, 2021, on CCTV.

41 By the time of the Western Zhou dynasty, or 1045–771 BC, oracle bone divination becomes obsolete and is replaced by yarrow stalk divination using the I Ching (or Zhouyi). In addition to I Ching divination, moon block divination (珓杯, *jiào bēi*) and sacred lots (籤, *qiān*), known as *omikuji* in Japan, were also popular. Joseph A. Adler, "Zhu Xi's Conception of *Yijing* Divination as Spiritual Practice," in *The Making of the Global* Yijing *in the Modern World: Cross-Cultural Interpretations and Interactions*, ed. Benjamin Wai-ming Ng (Singapore: Springer, 2021), 12.

42 In the sexagenary (sixty-year) lunisolar calendar system, the earth's orbit around the sun is called the Yellow Path, which is subdivided into twenty-four segments, called twenty-four solar terms. Each term corresponds with a set position of the earth along the Yellow Path, rendering that period of time auspicious or inauspicious for certain human activities. Marked by ten heavenly stems and twelve earthly branches cycling through the five changing phases of the Wu Xing, the calendar system is based on sixty-year cycles. For a discussion on the lunisolar calendar, see my book *The Tao of Craft* (Berkeley, CA: North Atlantic Books, 2016), 179–82, 482, 495–98, 511.

43  Kerson Huang, *I Ching: The Oracle* (Singapore: World Scientific Publishing Co., 1984), 13.

44  Bokun Zhu (朱伯崑), ed., 易學基礎教程 *(Yì xué jīchǔ jiàochéng) An Introduction to the Studies of the* Yijing (Beijing: Jiuzhou Chubanshe, 2012): 54–103.

45  Daniel Horthemels, *Confucius sinarum philosophus, sive, Scientia sinensis latine exposita* [Confucius the philosopher of China, or, the knowledge of China translated into Latin], trans. Philippe Couplet et al. (Paris, 1687). This is the first major translated work of Confucius in Latin, printed by Daniel Horthemels, which was to be dedicated to King Louis XIV. The four named translators were Jesuit priests on mission in China: Philippe Couplet (1623–1693), Christian Herdtrich (1625–1684), Prospero Intorcetta (1625–1696), and Francis Rougemont (1624–1676). See: "Confucius Sinarum," *Beyond Ricci: Rare Books from the Jesuitica Collection at Boston College,* accessed May 10, 2022, http://ricci.bc.edu/books/confucius-sinarum.html. I opted to showcase the Latinized perspective of Confucius rather than one of the traditional or iconic Chinese paintings of him.

46  Given the general audience for a text like this, the term "Confucianism" and even "neo-Confucianism" will be used, somewhat reluctantly, throughout the book. The better term is Ruism, a classical philosophy of humanism and rationalism that dominated—but also evolved—over time. In Chinese, the term for the philosophy is 儒家 (Rújiā) to mean the school of Ru thought, or 儒學 (Rúxué), meaning Ru studies. An intellectual movement toward Ru thought began well before Confucius, though he is one of the most famous philosophers of Ru. What Western scholars call neo-Confucianism is simply a progression of Ruism during the Song dynasty, spearheaded by philosophers such as Zhu Xi 朱熹 (AD 1130–1200), whom we cover in chapter 3. Interestingly, in antiquity the term "儒" *(rú)* was used to denote shamanic rites and rituals. This and the changing of the meaning of "貞" *(zhēn)* from "divination" to "virtue and morality" and "亨" *(hēng)* from "sacrificial rites" to "Confucian (Ru) virtues" further inspires the premise that the I Ching was shamanic in origin, which will be one of the key suppositions of this book.

47  An oft-quoted line from the Xici, one of the Ten Wings (the appendices to the I Ching), is: "Master Confucius said, 'The Yi is perhaps the most illustrious book. It was by the I Ching that the saints/ascended masters refined their virtue" (子曰：「易其至矣乎」夫易，聖人所以崇德). The text goes on to describe the Book of Changes as the gate of all good paths and righteousness. "繫辭上 - Xi Ci I, Also Known as: The Great Treatise I," Chinese Text Project, ed. Donald Sturgeon, accessed June 25, 2022, https://ctext.org/book-of-changes/xi-ci-shang.

48  Qingshu, "History and Current Status," 92–93.

49 However, there is now general consensus that the attribution of the Ten Wings as being authored personally by Confucius is apocryphal. And while authorship credit for King Wen and the Duke of Zhou has endured for millennia, there is no indisputable proof of that either.

50 The *Ladies' Book of Filial Piety* was written by Madame Zheng during the Tang dynasty, addressing the rules of behavior for women and consisting of a series of texts and images painted on silk scroll. This copy of the *Ladies' Book* was created during the Song dynasty. Although the paintings in the *Ladies' Book of Filial Piety* are credited to the famous painter Ma Hezhi (馬和之), the style is more in line with the painter Ma Yuan (馬遠) or Ma Lin (馬麟), dated to the twelfth and thirteenth centuries. Julia K. Murray, "The *Ladies' Classic of Filial Piety* and Song Textual Illustration: Problems of Reconstruction and Artistic Context," *Ars Orientalis* 129 (1988): 95–129.

51 Recall figure 1.1, the landscape painting by the female literati painter Chen Shu 陳書 (AD 1600–1735), titled *Reading the I Ching in a Mountain Study*. This is a close-up view of the cottage house. In the endnote corresponding with that figure, you were invited to choose either the path to the cottage house or the path up toward the mountain. If you had chosen the cottage, your tendency is toward a Rationalist approach, emphasizing the practical use of the I Ching to solve immediate worldly affairs. However, at this juncture, the sage within is calling you toward deeper self-knowledge. Study the I Ching to understand who you are, your purpose, and how you can achieve the transcendental experience of inner peace. Perhaps what you most need at this moment is balance. Your first objective, with this book as your companion, is a transcendental spiritual experience. Broaden your horizons and challenge everything you thought you knew so you might endeavor to know more.

52 Zhu Xi, *The Original Meaning of the Yijing: Commentary on the Scripture of Change*, trans. Joseph A. Adler (New York: Columbia University Press, 2020), 8.

## 3. Yì Xué: An Overview of I Ching Discourse

1 Dennis Kat-hung Cheng, "Reexamining the English Translation of the *Yijing*," in *The Making of the Global* Yijing *in the Modern World: Cross-Cultural Interpretations and Interactions*, ed. Benjamin Wai-ming Ng (Singapore: Springer, 2021), 26.

2 The Book of Rites is a collection of essays on rites and rituals. The date of origin is uncertain, though archaeological findings from a tomb in Hubei where fragments of the Book of Rites were found date at least parts of it to the Warring States period, 475–221 BC.

3   Yun Shouping 惲壽平 (1633–1690) was one of the most acclaimed calligraphers and painters from the Qing dynasty, regarded as one of the Six Masters 清六家 *(Qīng liù jiā)* whose style and techniques have become canonical. Yun was born into an impoverished family from the Jiangsu province and could not afford to sit for the imperial civil service examinations. He thus dedicated himself to art and gained prominence through his calligraphy.
4   From "The Deeper Implications of the Book of Changes," chapter 4 of the Xici, or the Fifth Wing of the Ten Wings.
5   Edward L. Shaughnessy, *Unearthing the* Changes: *Recently Discovered Manuscripts of the* Yijing *and Related Texts* (New York: Columbia University Press, 2014), 14.
6   Martin Kern, "*Fénshū kēng rú* 焚書坑儒" [Burning the books and executing the *ru* scholars], in *The Encyclopedia of Confucianism*, ed. Xinzhong Yao (New York: Routledge, 2003), 213.
7   Kerson Huang, *I Ching: The Oracle* (Singapore: World Scientific Publishing Co., 1984), 21.
8   Tze-ki Hon, "The *Yijing* in Twentieth-Century China," in *The Making of the Global* Yijing *in the Modern World: Cross-Cultural Interpretations and Interactions*, ed. Benjamin Wai-ming Ng (Singapore: Springer, 2021), 139.
9   Benjamin Wai-ming Ng, "Forward: Globalizing and Localizing the Yijing," in *The Making of the Global* Yijing *in the Modern World: Cross-cultural Interpretations and Interactions*, ed. Benjamin Wai-ming Ng (Singapore: Springer, 2021), x.
10  Historian, philosopher, and scholar Li Zehou contends that Confucianism, or the development of rationalist philosophy in China, caused a gradual evolution in the understanding of "the divine" from a *magic force* to *magic morals,* wherein internalizing virtue bestowed personal mystical power. Li Zehou, *The Origins of Chinese Thought: From Shamanism to Ritual Regulations and Humaneness*, trans. Robert A. Carleo III (Leiden: Brill, 2018), 33–34.
11  Kern, "*Fénshū kēng rú* 焚書坑儒."
12  Hans Van Ess, "The Old Text/New Text Controversy: Has the 20th Century Got It Wrong?" *T'oung Pao* 80, no. 1/3 (1994): 162.
13  Ess, "Old Text/New Text," 148.
14  Ess, 148.
15  Ess, 146–170.
16  Wang Bi (王弼) (AD 226–249) grew up during the turmoil and political instability of the Three Kingdoms period. He's best known for his interpretations and commentaries on the Zhouyi, or *Zhouyi zhu* (Commentary on the *Zhouyi*), which is credited as the first philosophical commentary on the I Ching. He synthesized Confucianism, Legalism, and Taoism in his I Ching discourse. Wang Bi was

known to be a precocious child, recorded as having understood the Tao Te Ching by the age of ten. As predominantly a Confucianist, Wang Bi held some ideas that might not be palatable to modern sensitivities. He advocated for a patriarchal state and a patriarchal family order; in his view, human society could only function if it was strictly hierarchical. Wang Bi died at the young age of 23.

17 王弼 (Wang Bi), 王弼集校釋 *(Wángbì jí xiào shì)* [A collection of writings by Wang Bi], ed. 樓宇烈 (Lóuyǔ Liè) (Beijing: 中華書局有限公司 [Zhonghua Shuju]), 1980.

18 Richard John Lynn, trans., *The Classic of Changes: A New Translation of the I Ching as Interpreted by Wang Bi* (New York: Columbia University Press, 1994), 28.

19 Lynn, *Classic of Changes, Wang Bi* 120.

20 Zhu Xi (朱熹) (AD 1130–1200), was a Song dynasty Confucian polymath who passed the imperial examinations at the age of nineteen, when the average age of passing students was closer to thirty. Though he was appointed to prestigious official positions, he was demoted each time he received an appointment because he openly attacked more powerful officials and accused them of corruption. In terms of spirituality, Zhu Xi advocated for a form of neo-Confucian meditation (靜坐, *jìngzuò*) for the purpose of self-cultivation. He believed that in order to achieve enlightenment, one had to actively seek knowledge, investigate ideas, and adopt a meditation practice to reflect upon that knowledge and those ideas. Zhu Xi faced much opposition for his radical ideas, though he continued to garner a cult following. The emperor posthumously recognized him with the title "Venerable Lord of Culture." He is now recognized as one of the Twelve Philosophers of Confucianism.

21 "Zhu Xi's fundamental hermeneutic principle regarding the Yijing was that 'the Yi was originally created for divination' (*Yi benwei bushi'er zuo* 易本為卜筮而作)." Zhu Xi, *The Original Meaning of the Yijing: Commentary on the Scripture of Change,* trans. Joseph A. Adler (New York: Columbia University Press, 2020), 11. See also: Kidder Smith, Jr., Peter K. Bol, Joseph A. Adler, and Don J. Wyatt, "Chu Shi and Divination," in *Sung Dynasty Uses of the* I Ching (Princeton, NJ: Princeton University Press, 1990), 169–205.

22 朱熹 (Zhu Xi), 周易本義 *(Zhōuyì běnyì)* [The original meanings of changes of the Zhou dynasty], ed. Liao Mingchun (Beijing: 中華書局有限公司 [Zhonghua Shuju]), 2009.

23 張其成 (Zhāng Qí-chéng), ed., 易經應用大百科全書(上篇) [Encyclopedia of the I Ching (vol. 1)] (Taipei: 地景 [De Jǐng], 1996.

24 易緯 *(Yì wěi),* Chinese Text Project, ed. Donald Sturgeon, accessed May 17, 2022, https://ctext.org/library.pl?if=en&res=82580. Source: Zhejiang University Library.

25  *Yì wěi* (易緯), *Encyclopedia of Chinese History, Literature, and Art*, ed. Ulrich Theobald, accessed May 17, 2022, http://www.chinaknowledge.de/Literature/Classics/yiwei.html.
26  The full moon, when the sun, earth, and moon are in alignment, falls on the fifteenth day of the lunar month. Each trigram combines with the other trigrams fifteen times in the sixty-four hexagrams. The factor of five for the Wu Xing five agents of change multiply with the trinity of Heaven, Earth, and Humanity, and with the trinity of the trigrams, to produce fifteen hexagrams (5 phases x 3 factors of yin and yang = 15). Thus, fifteen is considered the numerological resonance of the Tao.
27  "Interpretations and Incantations of Celestials in the Zhouyi" (周易乾鑿度, *Zhōuyì qián záo dù*), Chinese Text Project, ed. Donald Sturgeon, accessed May 23, 2022, https://ctext.org/datawiki.pl?if=gb&res=659075.
28  Gao Riguang 高日光, "Han Kangbo 韓康伯," in 諸子百家大辭典 [Dictionary of the hundred schools of masters], eds. Feng Kezheng 馮克正 and Fu Qingsheng 傅慶升 (Shenyang: 遼寧人民出版社 [Liaoning People's Publishing House], 1996), 91.
29  Li Binghai 李炳海, "Xuanxue 玄學" in 諸子百家大辭典 [Dictionary of the hundred schools of masters], eds. Feng Kezheng 馮克正 and Fu Qingsheng 傅慶升 (Shenyang: 遼寧人民出版社 [Liaoning People's Publishing House], 1996), 735.
30  劉玉建 (Liu Yujian), 漢易卦氣學研究 *(Hàn yì Guà Qì xué yán jiū)* [An examination and study of Han dynasty Gua Qi traditions] (Jinan, China: 齊魯書社 [Qí Lǔ Shū Shè], 2007).
31  "易緯" *(Yì wěi)*, Chinese Text Project, ed. Donald Sturgeon, accessed May 17, 2022, https://ctext.org/library.pl?if=en&res=82580. Source: Zhejiang University Library.
32  馮友蘭 (Féng Yǒulán), 中國哲學史 [History of Chinese philosophy] (Taipei: 臺灣商務印書館, 1994).
33  Zhu Xi, *Original Meaning*, 26.
34  龐樸 Páng Pǔ, ed., 中國儒學 *(Zhōng guó Rú xué)* [Confucian studies of China], vol. 2 (Shanghai: 東方出版中心 Dōngfāng Chūbǎn Zhōngxīn [Oriental Publishing Center], 1997), 51–52.
35  張善文 (Zhāng Shànwén), ed. 周易辞典 [Zhouyi dictionary] (Beijing: 中國大百科全書出版社 [China Encyclopedia Publishing House], 2005), 213.
36  Shànwén, Zhouyi dictionary, 213.
37  Son Kizen, "Early Gua Qi Thoughts: Seeking the Roots of Early Gua Qi Thoughts," *Journal of the Institute of Chinese Culture* 69 (July 2019): 35.
38  "說卦 – Shuo Gua [the Eighth Wing]," Chinese Text Project, ed. Donald Sturgeon, accessed June 25, 2022, https://ctext.org/book-of-changes/shuo-gua.

39 Liao Mingchun 廖名春, *I Ching: Classical and New Theories on the History of Yi Xue* 《周易》經傳與易學史新論 (Jinan: Qilu Publishing 齊魯書社, 2001), 37–38.
40 Vu Hong Van, "Restoration of Confucianism and the Phenomenon of Three Religions of the Homeland under the Nguyen Dynasty," *Turkish Online Journal of Qualitative Inquiry* 12, no. 3 (July 221): 1520–33.
41 Pham Thi Lan, "The Role of Confucianism in Sociopolitics of the Nguyen Dynasty in the First Half of the 19th Century," *Linguistics and Culture Review* 5, no. 4 (2021): 2403–12.
42 Neo-Confucianism reaches its height during the Song and Ming dynasties. It is a revivalist movement of Confucianism, but it rejects the more mystical and supernatural elements of Confucianism influenced by Taoism and esoteric Buddhism. Under neo-Confucianist thought, emotions (or sentimentality) needed to be carefully controlled and cultivated. Emotions were seen as self-centered; therefore, to cultivate sagelike consciousness, one had to evolve beyond being ruled by emotions and sentimentality. Also, emotions got in the way of rationalism and caused imbalances in a person's *qi* life force. However, while that perspective was characteristic of neo-Confucianism, it was not determinative. Equally compelling was a defense of sentimentality, most notably propositioned in the *Three Wives Commentary* by three female scholars from the late Ming and early Qing dynasty literati. The *Three Wives Commentary* was significant for its positive reception by male scholars at the time, who saw the discourse as a testament that women could be capable of the same intellectual rigor as men. Neo-Confucianist thought had an even greater impact beyond China. In Joseon Korea, the ideology was adopted by the state. When Japan invaded Korea between 1592 and 1598, Korean neo-Confucian scholars were taken to Japan as hostages. Once there, these scholars heavily influenced Japanese scholars, thereby advancing the development of Japanese neo-Confucianist thought.
43 Sergei Blagov, *Caodaism: Vietnamese Traditionalism and Its Leap into Modernity* (New York: Nova Science Publishers, 2001), 1.
44 Caodaism is an Indigenous folk religion of Vietnam with a strong emphasis on the esoteric and mystical. It syncretizes Buddhism, Confucianism, and Taoism with mediumship and shamanic practices. The literal translation of the term Cao Dai means "celestial palace." The cosmological beliefs of Caodaism are similar to those of Taoism. Yin and yang principles are personified as deities; the universe began as a dark void of chaos; yin and yang crystallized to form Light; and from that Light emerged Cao Dai, or God. Some adherents of the religion focus on Cao Dai as a Heavenly Father, while others recognize the main divine force as a Mother Goddess. In a world where political leadership often turns corrupt, the spirit worlds communicate divine truths directly to the people (through divination and

mystical practices). There are four categories of spirits (Phat, Tien, Thanh, and Than), with each category subdivided into three ranks *(thien, nhan,* and *dia)*, creating a twelvefold pantheon of spirits. After death, humans also become part of the spirit world, and those who are still alive can communicate with them for insight. Victor L. Oliver, *Caodai Spiritualism: A Study of Religion in Vietnamese Society* (Leiden: Brill Publishing, 1976).

45  Blagov, *Caodaism,* 1–15.

46  Daehwan Noh, "The Eclectic Development of Neo-Confucianism and Statecraft from the 18th to the 19th Century," *Korea Journal* 43, no. 4 (Winter 2003): 87–112.

47  According to the entry on Huang Tsung-hsi (Huang Zongxi) in the biographical dictionary *Eminent Chinese of the Ch'ing Period,* Huang and I share the same birthday, September 24. Tu Lien-Che, "Huang Tsung-his," in *Eminent Chinese of the Ch'ing Period,* ed. Arthur W. Hummel Sr. (Washington, DC: United States Government Printing Office, 1943), 351–54.

48  經部 and 易類, eds., 四庫全書總目提要編委會 (Shanghai: 上海古籍出版社 [Shanghai Ancient Books Publishing House], 2015), 35.

49  Benjamin Wai-ming Ng, "Nemoto Michiaki's Use of the *Yijing* in Meiji State Ideology," in *The Making of the Global* Yijing *in the Modern World: Cross-Cultural Interpretations and Interactions* (Singapore: Springer, 2021), 124–25.

50  Ng, "Nemoto Michiaki," 126–27.

51  Wai-ming Ng, "Study and Uses of the *I Ching* in Tokugawa Japan," *Sino-Japanese Studies* 9, no. 2 (November 1990): 39.

52  Ng, "Nemoto Michiaki," 126.

53  Gan Bao, *In Search of the Supernatural: The Written Record,* trans. Kenneth J. DeWoskin and James Irving Crump (Stanford, CA: Stanford University Press, 1996).

54  Ng, "Nemoto Michiaki," 129.

55  Ng, "Study and Uses," 38.

56  Ng, 40.

57  Ng, 40.

58  Tze-ki Hon, "The *Yijing* in Twentieth-Century China," in *The Making of the Global* Yijing *in the Modern World: Cross-Cultural Interpretations and Interactions,* ed. Benjamin Wai-ming Ng (Singapore: Springer, 2021), 139–40.

59  Xing Lu, *The Rhetoric of Mao Zedong: Transforming China and Its People* (Columbia: University of South Carolina Press, 2017).

60  Hon, "The *Yijing* in Twentieth-Century China," 148.

61  Miki Shima, *The Medical I Ching: Oracle of the Healer Within* (Boulder: Blue Poppy Press, 1992), 195.

62 Shaughnessy, *Unearthing the* Changes; Edward L. Shaughnessy, *I Ching: The Classic of Changes, the First English Translation of the Newly Discovered Mawangdui Texts of I Ching* (New York: Ballantine Books, 1997).
63 Hon, "The *Yijing* in Twentieth-Century China," 149.
64 Shaughnessy, *Unearthing the* Changes, 5–7.
65 For a complete table comparing all sixty-four hexagrams in the King Wen order (also referred to as the "received text") to the recently discovered Mawangdui manuscript, see Shaughnessy, *Unearthing the* Changes, 7–8.
66 Geoffrey Redmond and Tze-Ki Hon, *Teaching the I Ching (Book of Changes)* (New York: Oxford University Press, 2014).
67 Richard J. Smith, "How the Book of Changes Arrived in the West," *New England Review* 33, no. 1 (2012): 25. The I Ching is first translated into a European language around 1736 by a French Jesuit missionary, Jean-Baptiste Regis (1663–1738). Weirong Li, "Striving for the 'Original' Meaning: A Historical Survey of *Yijing*'s English Translations," in *Encountering China's Past: Translation and Dissemination of Classical Chinese Literature*, Lintao Qi and Shani Tobias, eds. (Singapore: Springer, 2022), 167.
68 Ming-che Lee, "The Early Transmission of the *Yijing* and the Figurists' Renditions," in *The Making of the Global* Yijing *in the Modern World: Cross-Cultural Interpretations and Interactions*, ed. Benjamin Wai-ming Ng (Singapore: Springer, 2021), 87.
69 In Mandarin Chinese, Shangdi (上帝) was co-opted by Protestant missionaries to mean the Christian God. Thus, in most people's minds today Shangdi no longer refers to the Heavenly Father of our Bronze Age ancestors. Catholics use the term Tianzhu (天主) to mean the Christian God.
70 This is a well-known, oft-repeated reference from chapter 42 of the Tao Te Ching.
71 Lee, "Early Transmission," 91.
72 Charles Porterfield Krauth, *A Vocabulary of the Philosophical Sciences* (New York: Sheldon & Company, 1879), 933.
73 Hellmut Wilhelm and Richard Wilhelm, *Understanding the I Ching: The Wilhelm Lectures on the Book of Changes* (Princeton, NJ: Princeton University Press, 1979), 8.
74 Smith, "Book of Changes," 25–26.
75 Li-jing Wu, "Historicizing the *Yijing* in the Anglophone World," in *The Making of the Global* Yijing *in the Modern World: Cross-Cultural Interpretations and Interactions*, ed. Benjamin Wai-Ming Ng (Singapore: Springer, 2021), 44.
76 M. A. Canon McClatchie, *A Translation of the Confucian Yi Jing or the "Classic of Change" with Notes and Appendix* (Shanghai: American Presbyterian Mission Press, 1876), ii.

77 McClatchie, *Translation*, 2. The Stoic hero-sage or *sapiens* is described as the "Model Man," or one who is courageous and who bravely endures adversity, passionless and calm.
78 John Tsz-pang Lai, "Thomas McClatchie's Mythological Interpretation of the Yijing," in *The Making of the Global Yijing in the Modern World: Cross-Cultural Interpretations and Interactions*, ed. Benjamin Wai-Ming Ng (Singapore: Springer, 2021), 112.
79 Vincent Hale and Nicholas Croce, eds., "Marduk," In *Mesopotamian Gods & Goddesses* (New York: Rosen Publishing Group, 2013).
80 McClatchie, *Translation*, 443–53. In the preface to McClatchie's 1876 translations, he affirms that the I Ching shouldn't be read through a Christian sensibility; rather, it should be investigated as the pagan system that it is, and readers should "take especial care to ascertain the ideas attached to important terms and phrases by heathen writers themselves." McClatchie, *Translation*, iv.
81 McClatchie, 451.
82 McClatchie, 452.
83 McClatchie, 443.
84 McClatchie, 452–53.
85 McClatchie, 452–53.
86 Smith, "Book of Changes," 28.
87 Smith, 29–30.
88 A. H. Sayce, "Babylonian Augury by means of Geometrical Figures," in *Transactions of the Society of Biblical Archaeology*, vol. 4 (London: Longmans, Green, Reader, & Dyer, 1876), 302. Sayce writes, "To this day this pseudoscience flourishes among the Chinese, and the eight trigrams of Fohi [Fuxi] are not only supposed to be the bases and principles of all things, but to act as efficacious charms as well."
89 Sayce, "Babylonian Augury," 303–4.
90 Sayce, 306.
91 Smith, "Book of Changes," 29.
92 In Legge's own letters and writings, he refers to the Chinese as peddlers, servants, or his disciples who obediently convert to Christianity. To be fair, he did count selected Chinese Christians as friends, such as saying "my old friend Hung Jin" or holding "in loving remembrance the old Chinaman, Ch'ea Kin Kwang. Who can say, knowing the story of Ch'ea, that Chinamen are incapable of enthusiasm and heroism?" Helen Edith Legge, *James Legge, Missionary and Scholar* (London: Religious Tract Society, 1905), 102. From Legge's tone, he tended to view himself as a savior to the Chinese people. Furthermore, he seemed to have only surrounded himself with the Chinese who were already Christian or interested in accepting Christianity. Boasting of his own abilities, he recounts a conversation he had with a

Chinese boatman ferrying him across Canton: "You Chinese despise us foreigners because we cannot speak your language, but here, you see [referring to himself], is an Englishman who does speak Chinese." Legge claims the boatman replied, "He speakee Chinese more better I." Legge, *James Legge*, 80. Legge also recounts a time when he succeeded at converting a Taoist priest. In another recounting, Legge instructs a "Chinaman" to burn all of his idols to receive baptism. Legge, *James Legge*, 84–85, 89. A Chinese wedding is described as having frustrated the Westerners and keeping them up all night by being a "continual uproar." He emphasizes the "rudeness of the ceremony" led by "mock priests" who were "filthy": "One would imagine the arrangements had been the product of some infantile brain, rather than the product of a fully developed capacity." Legge, *James Legge*, 124–25. Local streets were described as crawling with "outcast wretches." All that said, if his daughter's biography of him can be believed, then Dr. Legge bestowed generous charity upon the poverty-stricken Chinese, often at great risk to his own life and limb, as it seems that everywhere Legge went, Chinese mobs were surrounding him, striking to chase him off their lands, even attempting to stone him. At one point, a Buddhist priest tries to save Legge, saying to him, "You had better be off. The people talk of stoning you; they are enraged owing to Canton being taken by foreigners." Legge, *James Legge*, 89. In contrast to Legge, Wilhelm was more open to befriending non-Christian Chinese. "In his autobiography, Wilhelm describes the diverse people at his banquet table, ranking from former high officials to Daoist practitioners and diviners." Lu Zhao, "Richard Wilhelm's *Book of Changes* and the Science of the Mind in the Early Twentieth Century," in *The Making of the Global Yijing in the Modern World: Cross-Cultural Interpretations and Interactions*, ed. Benjamin Wai-Ming Ng (Singapore: Springer, 2021), 157.

93 Wu, "Historicizing the *Yijing*," 47.
94 Shiyin Liu, "Deciphering James Legge's 'Confucianism'" (PhD thesis, University of Glasgow, 2020), https://doi.org/10.5525/gla.thesis.79032.
95 N. J. Girardot, *The Victorian Translation of China: James Legge's Oriental Pilgrimage* (Berkeley: University of California Press, 2002), xv. Note: Slur in original quote redacted.
96 Lai, "Thomas McClatchie," 116.
97 Lai, 116.
98 Legge, *James Legge*.
99 Not only did Wilhelm translate texts from Chinese to German; he also translated texts from German to Chinese, as he had done with Immanuel Kant's *On the Power of the Mind to Master Its Morbid Feelings* (1798). Wilhelm believed that bridging European psychology with Asian philosophy could reveal universal truths on the science of the mind. Zhao, "Richard Wilhelm," 156.

100  Bettina Wilhelm, "My Grandfather Richard Wilhelm" (presentation to the Taiwan Institute of Psychotherapy, Taipei, Taiwan, October 5, 2013).
101  Zhao, "Richard Wilhelm," 161.
102  Richard Wilhelm, trans., *The I Ching or Book of Changes,* rendered into English by Cary F. Baynes (Princeton, NJ: Princeton University Press, 1977), 84–85.
103  There isn't concrete proof that the White Lotus were behind the Boxer Rebellion, but per oral tradition, that remains the understanding of the people.
104  Yingong Dai, *The White Lotus War: Rebellion & Suppression in Late Imperial China* (Seattle: University of Washington Press, 2019).
105  Carl G. Jung, foreword to Richard Wilhelm, trans., *I Ching or Book of Changes: The Richard Wilhelm Translation,* rendered into English by Cary F. Baynes, 3rd ed. (London: Penguin Books, 1967), xxii. For additional context regarding Jung's thoughts on the East, in his foreword for Wilhelm's translation of *The Secret of the Golden Flower,* a Taoist alchemical text, Jung says that he finds in it what he "had sought for in vain among the Gnostics." Carl G. Jung, foreword to Richard Wilhelm, trans., *The Secret of the Golden Flower: A Chinese Book of Life,* rendered into English by Cary F. Baynes (San Diego: Harcourt Brace Jovanovich, 1962), xiv. Jung cautions Western readers not to dismiss *Secret* as mystical, and he asserts that it is "based on the practical insights of highly evolved Chinese minds, which we have not the slightest justification for undervaluing." And yet a few paragraphs down from that, he stresses that as much as he appreciates Eastern thought, it should not "depreciate the tremendous differentiation of the Western intellect; compared with it the Eastern intellect must be described as childish. (Naturally this has nothing to do with intelligence.)" R. F. C. Hull, trans., *C. G. Jung: Psychology and the East* (Princeton, NJ: Princeton University Press, 1978), 8. Like the other European writers commenting on Eastern thought cited for this chapter, Jung was a product of his time and culture.
106  Jung, foreword to *I Ching,* xxii.
107  Jung, xxii.
108  Jung published his own commentary on *The Secret of the Golden Flower,* which Wilhelm translated. It was only after his study of Taoist alchemy that his interest in Western alchemy grew. C. G. Jung, *Memories, Dreams, Reflections,* ed. Aniela Jaffe, trans. Clara Winston and Richard Winston, rev. ed. (New York: Vintage Books, 1989).
109  Jung, *Memories,* xxiv.
110  Young Woon Ko, *Jung on Synchronicity and* Yijing: *A Critical Approach* (Newcastle upon Tyne, UK: Cambridge Scholars Publishing, 2011), 101.
111  Explaining the connection between the I Ching and modern physics, as well as his theory of synchronicity, Jung writes: "The ancient Chinese mind contemplates

the cosmos in a way comparable to that of the modern physicist, who cannot deny that his model of the world is a decidedly psychophysical structure. The microphysical event includes the observer just as much as the reality underlying the I Ching comprises subjective, i.e., psychic conditions in the totality of the momentary situation. Just as causality describes the sequence of events, so synchronicity to the Chinese mind deals with the coincidence of events. The causal point of view tells us a dramatic story about how D came into existence: it took its origin from C, which existed before D, and C in its turn had a father, B, etc. The synchronistic view on the other hand tries to produce an equally meaningful picture of coincidence. How does it happen that A', B', C', D', etc., appear all in the same moment and in the same place?" Carl G. Jung, foreword to *I Ching*, xxiv.

112 Zhao, "Richard Wilhelm," 165.
113 Jung, foreword to *I Ching*, xxiii.
114 Jung, xxvii.
115 Ko, *Jung on Synchronicity*, 142.
116 "For more than thirty years I have interested myself in this oracle technique, or method of exploring the unconscious, for it has seemed to me of uncommon significance." Jung, foreword to *I Ching*, xxii. Jung also says: "The method of the I Ching does indeed take into account the hidden individual quality in things and men, and in one's own unconscious self as well." Jung, xxviii.
117 Ginette Paris, *Wisdom of the Psyche: Depth Psychology after Neuroscience* (New York: Routledge, 2007).
118 Ko, *Jung on Synchronicity*, 100, 102.
119 Jung, foreword to *I Ching*, xxiv.
120 Jung, xxv.
121 "But needless to say, nothing 'occult' is to be inferred. My position in these matters is pragmatic." Jung, xxxiv.
122 "Jung came to believe that the key to decoding the conditions of neurosis lay within the history of civilization and mythology.... With his eye on history, he developed the concepts—archetypes, New Age, collective unconscious, synchronicity, anima, the two dimensions of personality (extroverted, introverted), man's four basic functions (thinking, feeling, sensation and intuition)—that made him famous." Robert S. Boynton, "In the Jung Archives," *New York Times Book Review,* January 11, 2004, 8. https://www.nytimes.com/2004/01/11/books/in-the-jung-archives.html.
123 Antoine Faivre, *Theosophy, Imagination, Tradition: Studies in Western Esotericism* (Albany: State University of New York Press, 2000); David Allen Hulse, *The Eastern Mysteries: An Encyclopedic Guide to the Sacred Languages and Magickal Systems of the World* (Woodbury, MN: Llewellyn Publications, 2000).

124 Éliphas Lévi, *Dogme et rituel de la haute magie* (Paris: Germer Bailliére, Libraire-Éditeur), 1861.
125 Reuben Swinburne Clymer, *Alchemy and Alchemists: Giving the Secret of the Philosopher's Stone, the Elixir of Youth, and the Universal Solvent*, vol. 3. (Allentown, PA: Philosophical Publishing Co., 1907), 209.
126 Clymer, 209–10.
127 Smith, "Book of Changes," 32.
128 Redmond and Hon, *Teaching the I Ching*, 234.
129 Richard Kaczynski, *Perdurabo: The Life of Aleister Crowley*, rev. ed. (Berkeley, CA: North Atlantic Books, 2010), 724–25, 524, 528, 533, 545, 584, 602. The I Ching predicted that a proposal of marriage was imprudent. Kaczynski, 644. He divined on the prospects of friendship with Bobby Barefoot. Kaczynski, 725. A synchronicity occurs when he casts Hexagram 14, Great Happenings, and that same day a letter arrives for him with the words "great happenings" written upon it. Kaczynski, 746. He consulted the I Ching to track the progress of a libel lawsuit and, essentially, took legal advice from his I Ching divinatory results. Kaczynski, 688.
130 Aleister Crowley [the Master Therion], *Magick in Theory and Practice* (Paris: Lecram Press, 1929), 160.
131 Crowley, 160.
132 Crowley, 161.
133 Crowley, 161.
134 Nevertheless, despite how temperamental gnomes and Mercury might be, a magician whose research is fully adapted to his Neshama (הנשמ), i.e., the magus's soul or spirit, will still find geomancy and tarot lucid and reliable. Ibid.
135 The Master Therion [Aleister Crowley], *The I Ching: A New Translation of the Book of Changes*, Internet Sacred Text Archive, accessed August 5, 2022, https://www.sacred-texts.com/oto/lib216.htm.
136 Crowley said "the existence of two such superficially different systems is transcendent testimony to the truth of both." Smith, "Book of Changes," 32. Crowley equated the Tao with *ain* (Nothingness in the Kabbalah/Qabalah), yin and yang with the Lingam and Yoni, *jing* in Taoist metaphysics as *nephesh* ("animal soul"), *qi* as *ruach* ("spirit; breath") and *shen* with *neschamah* (the "intuitive mind"). Smith, 32. Likewise, the Confucian virtues espoused in the I Ching had parallels in the Kabbalistic principles of the *sephirot*.
137 Redrawing of Aleister Crowley's *The Chinese Cosmos* diagram in "The Book of Thoth: A Short Essay on the Tarot of the Egyptians," from *The Equinox* 3, no. 5; from The Master Therion [Aleister Crowley], *The Book of Thoth (Egyptian Tarot)*, 1st ed. (1944; repr., Newburyport, MA: Samuel Weiser, 1974), 270.

138 References herein will be to the Christianized Qabalah influenced by Hermeticism as found in Western occultism, to be distinguished from the Kosher Kabbalah, or authentic Jewish Kabbalah.

139 The Master Therion [Aleister Crowley], *The Book of Thoth (Egyptian Tarot)*, 1st ed. (1944; repr., Newburyport, MA: Samuel Weiser, 1974). Citations refer to the Samuel Weiser edition.

140 "Liber LVIII (Number 58) - The Qabalah from The Temple of Solomon the King," Hermetic Library, accessed June 25, 2022, https://hermetic.com/crowley/libers/lib58.

141 Redmond and Hon, *Teaching the I Ching*, 234.

142 Geoffrey Redmond, "The *Yijing* in Early Postwar Counterculture in the West," in *The Making of the Global* Yijing *in the Modern World: Cross-Cultural Interpretations and Interactions*, ed. Benjamin Wai-Ming Ng (Singapore: Springer, 2021), 197–221.

143 Robert S. Ellwood and Harry B. Partin, *Religious and Spiritual Groups in Modern America* (New York: Routledge, 1973), 81.

144 Lindon J. Eaves et al., "Some Implications of Chaos Theory for the Genetic Analysis of Human Development and Variation," *Twin Research* 2, no. 1 (1999): 43–48. https://doi.org/10.1375/twin.2.1.43.

145 Umberto Eco, *Serendipities: Language and Lunacy*, trans. William Weaver (San Diego: Harcourt Brace & Company, 1998), 69.

146 David E. Mungello, *Leibniz and Confucianism: The Search for Accord* (Honolulu: University Press of Hawai'i, 1977), 46.

147 Mungello, 46. However, Bouvet still insists that assertions that the I Ching was a form of divination were "pure superstition."

148 Mungello, 49.

149 Mungello, 46.

150 Mungello, 46–47.

151 Wai-ming Ng, *The I Ching in Tokugawa Thought and Culture* (Honolulu: University of Hawai'i Press, 2000), 143–45.

152 Mungello, *Leibniz and Confucianism*, 53.

153 Mungello, 54. Interestingly, this is also my approach to reconciling Eastern and Western occult correspondences: finding the energetic common denominator of the eight trigrams from Taoist alchemy and the Aristotelian four elements from Hermetic alchemy.

154 Mungello, 60.

155 David J. D'Onofrio and Gary An, "A Comparative Approach for the Investigation of Biological Information Processing: An Examination of the Structure and Function of Computer Hard Drives and DNA," *Theoretical Biology and*

*Medical Modeling* 7, no. 3 (January 21, 2010). https://doi.org/10.1186/1742-4682-7-3.

156 "Deoxyribonucleic Acid (DNA)," National Human Genome Research Institute, accessed May 20, 2022, https://www.genome.gov/genetics-glossary/Deoxyribonucleic-Acid.

157 "Deoxyribonucleic Acid (DNA)."

158 "Ribonucleic Acid (RNA)," National Human Genome Research Institute, accessed May 20, 2022, https://www.genome.gov/genetics-glossary/RNA-Ribonucleic-Acid.

159 Johnson F. Yan, *DNA and the I Ching: The Tao of Life* (Berkeley, CA: North Atlantic Books, 1991), 106.

160 Yang Li, "*Book of Changes* and Genetics," in *Book of Changes and Traditional Chinese Medicine* (Beijing: Beijing Science and Technology Press, 1998), 485.

161 Yan, *DNA and the I Ching*, x.

162 Fernando Castro-Chavez, "A Tetrahedral Representation of the Genetic Code Emphasizing Aspects of Symmetry," *BIO-Complexity* 2 (2012): 1–6. https://doi.org10.5048/BIO-C.2012.2.

163 "Genetic Code Chart, Nirenberg," Smithsonian National Museum of American History, Behring Center, accessed May 22, 2022, https://americanhistory.si.edu/collections/search/object/nmah_688714.

164 Castro-Chavez, "Tetrahedral Representation," 7.

165 Castro-Chavez, 9.

166 Yan, *DNA and the I Ching*, xiii.

167 Joseph A. Adler, "Zhu Xi's Conception of *Yijing* Divination as Spiritual Practice," in *The Making of the Global Yijing in the Modern World: Cross-Cultural Interpretations and Interactions*, ed. Benjamin Wai-ming Ng (Singapore: Springer, 2021), 15.

168 Exorcism is the expelling of an atrophic or adverse energy form. Thus, it can mean the purification of water, wine, liquor, or a ritual tool. It also refers to the more common understanding of an exorcism, which is the expelling of a demon that is possessing a body or occupying a place. In Taoist mysticism, thunder magic or thunder rites are perhaps the most well-known methods of demon banishment and vanquishing.

169 "史記 – Shiji, Records of the Grand Historian," Chinese Text Project, ed. Donald Sturgeon, accessed May 11, 2022, https://ctext.org/shiji.

170 Yang Li, *Book of Changes and Traditional Chinese Medicine* (Beijing: Beijing Science and Technology Press, 1998), 21.

171 Li, *Book of Changes*, 21.

172 The *Yellow Emperor's Classic of Internal Medicine* 黃帝內經 *(Huángdì nèi jīng)* is a treatise on ancient Chinese internal medicine, but it is also a treatise on

Taoist cosmology. Oral tradition attributes the text as being compiled during the early Han (202 BCE–9 AD), with book I of the *Inner Canons* dated to 400 BC, though historians today dispute that claim. The text (or collection of texts) is structured as a dialectic, a conversation between a young Yellow Emperor presenting inquiries to Qibo 岐伯, a mythical healer who himself learned the healing arts from an ascended celestial master.

173 Li, *Book of Changes*, 21.
174 Jung, foreword to *I Ching*, xxv–xxvi.
175 Jung, xxvi.
176 "I have questioned the I Ching as one questions a person whom one is about to introduce to friends: one asks whether or not it will be agreeable to him. In answer the I Ching tells me of its religious significance, of the fact that at present it is unknown and misjudged, of its hope of being restored to a place of honor." Jung, xxviii.
177 The seal featured in figure 3.16 comprises Chinese oracle bone script for the eight trigrams and animal spirits governing the four directions. The center four characters constitute the seal for the Mysterious Lady of the Nine Heavens. "※" is a symbol for protection and is used in craft to manifest abundance or prosperity. It is also found in Fu sigils for exorcisms to ensure divine protection from the four directions. Your intention is what powers the "※" glyph. The background features superimposed layers of Fuxi's Early Heaven Ba Gua of trigrams, sixty-four hexagrams, and the Lo Shu magic square (representing King Wen's Later Heaven Ba Gua). The characters along the four corners are: 富貴昌樂 *(fù guì chāng lè)*, which we'll cover in Hexagram 18. In short, they signify wealth and riches; precious honors bestowed; prosperity; and happiness, to always be flourishing. When you invoke divine blessings, they emanate out of the circle, enliven the scripts along the four corners, and incidentally increase these four blessings in your life.
178 These myths are sourced to the Dragon and Fish River Map (龍魚河圖, *Lóng yú hé tú*) from the Han dynasty (202 BC–220 AD).
179 There are also popular myths of this celestial coming as a pair: the Mysterious Lady of the Nine Heavens (九天玄女, Jiǔ Tiān Xuán Nǚ) and the White Lady of the Nine Heavens (九天素女, Jiǔt Tān Sù Nǚ). The White Lady is more often referenced as Sù nǚ (素女), or Lady in White. She's often conceptualized as the yang, and the Lady of the Nine Heavens as the yin.
180 Another text on the myths about the Mysterious Lady of the Nine Heavens is *The Mysterious Lady's Art of War* 玄女兵法 *(Xuán nǚ bīngfǎ)*, ca. AD 557–641 AD during the Tang dynasty.

181 In chapter 3 of my book *The Tao of Craft*, the 黃帝陰符經 *(Huáng dì yīn fú jīng)*, translated as the *Yellow Emperor's Classics of the Esoteric Talisman*, is distilled into thirteen guiding principles. To name a few of the principles, the book proposes that within your mind you can contain the whole of the Universe, which is the Tao. To do so, you align yourself with the Tao, and then you will be aligned with the Universe. All manifestations of the Universe can be generated through your own hand, and from your hand can flow Heaven's Will. No one holds special favor in the court of Heaven, but anyone can gain favors from the court of Heaven. To harness the energy of higher spirits, use yang; to harness the energy of lower spirits, use yin. Benebell Wen, *The Tao of Craft: Fu Talismans and Casting Sigils in the Eastern Esoteric Tradition* (Berkeley, CA: North Atlantic Books, 2016), 61–70.

182 Recall figure 1.1, the landscape painting titled *Studying the I Ching by a Window*. This is a close-up view of the mountains along the horizon line. In the endnote corresponding with that figure, you were invited to choose either the path to the cottage house or the path up toward the mountain. If you had chosen the path up toward the mountains, you tend toward an Originalist approach to the I Ching, meaning you emphasize the experience of divination as an experience of the Divine itself, and perhaps you've picked up this book in an endeavor of spiritual journeying. You're striving for self-cultivation. Yet at this time, your higher self is calling you toward knowledge of the universe and the world around you. Study for the purpose of partaking in important social change. You are what the world needs most right now. After your spiritual journeying, consider how you can be a part of the change that your world needs.

## 4. Interpreting the Hexagrams

1 Cai Yuanding (蔡元定), son of the famous physicist Cai Fa, was an independent scholar, a disciple and close friend of Zhu Xi, a feng shui master, and a polymath from the Song dynasty. He tried actively to avoid political life, unlike most I Ching scholars of fame, who were invariably always involved in politics. Nevertheless, he was charged with heresy and exiled for his teachings, despite his attempts not to be political. Cai also wrote many influential treatises on the I Ching and feng shui, such as his writing on the Lo Shu magic square and how the five changing phases of the Wu Xing flow through the Lo Shu. 庹永 (Tuǒ Yǒng), "蔡元定父子易學思想闡釋" [Cai Yuanding's commentaries on I Ching studies] (Fujian: 人文學院－學位論文 [Xiamen University Institutional Repository]), 2016.

2. Bent Nielsen, *A Companion to Yi Jing Numerology and Cosmology* (Abingdon-on-Thames, UK: Taylor & Francis, 2013), 25.
3. In my 2016 book *The Tao of Craft,* figure 1.16 in chapter 1 labels Elder Yin and Yang as "Plenary" to indicate completed or matured formation, and it labels Younger Yin and Yang as "Adjusting" to indicate that it is still in transition.
4. "說卦 – Shuo Gua [the Eighth Wing]," Chinese Text Project, ed. Donald Sturgeon, accessed June 25, 2022, https://ctext.org/book-of-changes/shuo-gua.
5. "說卦 – Shuo Gua [the Eighth Wing]."
6. Bent Nielsen, *A Companion to Yi Jing Numerology and Cosmology: Chinese Studies of Images and Numbers from Han (202 BC–AD 220) to Song (AD 960–1279)* (New York: Routledge Curzon, 2003).
7. Xuezhi Zhang, *History of Chinese Philosophy in the Ming Dynasty* (Singapore: Higher Education Press, 2021), 521.
8. Nielsen, *Companion*, 2.
9. Daniel Tong, *A Biblical Approach to Feng Shui and Divination* (Millcreek, UT: Genesis Books, 2006), 84.
10. Chung-ying Cheng, "*Yi li zhi xue* (Learning of meaning and principle)," in *The Encyclopedia of Confucianism*, ed. Xinzhong Yao (New York: Routledge, 2003).
11. Joseph A. Adler, *The Yijing: A Guide* (Oxford, UK: Oxford University Press, 2022), 90.
12. Cheng Yi, *The Yi River Commentary on the* Book of Changes, ed. L. Michael Harrington (New Haven, CT: Yale University Press, 2019), 2.
13. Yi, 11.
14. L. Michael Harrington and Robin R. Wang, "Introduction," in *The Yi River Commentary on the* Book of Changes, ed. L. Michael Harrington (New Haven, CT: Yale University Press, 2019), 12.
15. M. A. Canon McClatchie, *A Translation of the Confucian Yi Jing or the "Classic of Change" with Notes and Appendix* (Shanghai: American Presbyterian Mission Press, 1876), 282.
16. James Legge, trans., *I Ching: Book of Changes* (New York: Bantam Books, 1969), 201.
17. Richard Wilhelm, trans., *The I Ching, or Book of Changes,* rendered into English by Cary F. Baynes, 3rd ed. (Princeton, NJ: Princeton University Press, 1977), 503–4.
18. The Master Therion [Aleister Crowley], *The I Ching: A New Translation of the Book of Changes,* Internet Sacred Text Archive, accessed August 5, 2022, https://www.sacred-texts.com/oto/lib216.htm.
19. Kerson Huang, trans., *I Ching: The Oracle* (Taipei: World Scientific Publishing Co., 1991), 163.
20. Yi, *Yi River Commentary,* 486.

21 Zhu Xi, *The Original Meaning of the Yijing: Commentary on the Scripture of Change,* trans. Joseph A. Adler (New York: Columbia University Press, 2020), 250.
22 Alfred Huang, *The Complete I Ching: The Definitive Translation by Taoist Master Alfred Huang,* 10th ed. (Toronto: Inner Traditions, 2010), 639–48.
23 Thomas Cleary, trans., *I Ching: The Book of Change* (Boston: Shambala, 2011), 98–99.
24 The five great Confucian scholars of the Northern Song period (AD 960–1126) are: Shao Yong 邵雍 (1011–1077), Zhou Dunyi 周敦頤 (1017–1073), Zhang Zai 張載 (1020–1077), Cheng Hao 程顥 (1032–1085), and Cheng Yi 程頤 (1033–1107).
25 For those who would like to make a deep dive into Shao Yong's work, read the *Book of Supreme World Ordering Principles* (皇極經世, Huáng jí jīng zhì), which presents his philosophical investigations into the origins of the cosmos and his Map of the Earliest Heaven (先天圖, Xiān Tiān Tú), a diagram accompanied by a theory so esoteric that few of his peers—and few people today—could follow it, which could be the reason why his works eventually fell into obscurity.
26 One of Shao's contemporaries, Cheng Hao 程顥 (1032–1085), remarked about Shao Yong: "[He] has the learning of the inner sage and outer king. When something is about to happen, Yong is able to know beforehand." Said Hsieh Liang-tso (1050–1103), another prominent Confucian thinker of Shao Yong's time: "Shao is skilled in the numerical matters of the I Ching. When he calculates the success and failure, the beginning and the end of things, of disasters and good fortune, and the long or short lives of people, he is never mistaken by the slightest hair." Anne D. Birdwhistell, "The Philosophical Concept of Foreknowledge in the Thought of Shao Yong," *Philosophy East and West* 39, no. 1 (January 1989): 47–48.
27 Johannes Kepler, *Harmonice mundi* (The harmony of the world), 1619.
28 Yiu-ming Fung, *Dao Companion to Chinese Philosophy of Logic* (New York: Springer International Publishing, 2020), 357–62.
29 Chih-hsu Ou-I, *The Buddhist I Ching,* trans. Thomas Cleary (Boston: Shambhala Publications, 1987); Beverly Foulks McGuire, *Living Karma: The Religious Practices of Ouyi Zhixu* (New York: Columbia University Press, 2014).
30 Inscription from the mural tomb of Du Jiyuan (AD 940), Nanjing. Source: Cultural Relic Series (文物資料丛刊, Wenwu ziliao congkan), vol. 10, 160. Beijing: Cultural Relics Publishing House (文物出版社, Wénwù chūbǎn shè), 1987.

## 5. The Eight Trigrams (Bā Guà)

1 The word "red" 赤 here has some interesting subtext. It not only refers to the color; it can also mean "loyalty" and "sincerity." Red also represents revolutions,

which echoes the earlier correspondence of cycles. The word for "cycle" 圜 *(huán)* cited from the Ten Wings is another word for revolution.
2 From Shuo Gua 說卦 in the Ten Wings.
3 Per the Shuo Gua 說卦 in the Ten Wings, "帝出乎震" (Dì *chū hū zhèn*). The reference to "帝" (Dì) is Shangdi 上帝.
4 In the Fifth Wing of the Ten Wings, it's noted that "the way of the Creative brings about the male. The wing of the Receptive brings about the female." While that has been interpreted as referring to yin and yang at that binary-code level, it has also been interpreted to indicate Hexagram 1 and Hexagram 2 respectively.
5 Li Zehou 李泽厚, *The Origins of Chinese Thought: From Shamanism to Ritual Regulations and Humaneness,* trans. Robert A. Carleo III (Leiden: Brill, 2018), 50.
6 Zhu Xi (朱熹, Zhu Xi) was a philosopher, politician, and poet (AD 1130–1200). He was formative in the development of Chinese philosophy, in particular Neo-Confucianism. Zhu espoused a philosophical theory that although there is evil in this world, humans are fundamentally good. How we manifest or nurture that original nature of goodness determines whether we preserve that fundamental goodness. The level of effort it takes one to manifest goodness will depend on that person's innate talents and skills, family upbringing, and social environment. Different personalities, characters, aptitudes, and intelligences are a result of variations in talents and environment. He was considered unorthodox during his time, applying Confucianism to Taoism and Buddhism, though he was highly critical of Buddhism. Earlier in Chinese history Zhu Xi wasn't well known for his work in I Ching studies, but in the West he's best known for annotating and writing commentaries on the Changes. In terms of Zhu Xi's approach to the I Ching, his writings emphasized combining principles in the Book of Changes with the Wu Xing, or five phases (Wood, Fire, Earth, Metal, and Water). These five changing phases are values of *qi* that affect cosmic and human creativity. Yung Sik Kim, *The Natural Philosophy of Chu Hsi (1130–1200)* (Philadelphia: American Philosophical Society, 2000). Kidder Smith Jr. et al., eds., *Sung Dynasty Uses of the* I Ching (Princeton, NJ: Princeton University Press, 1990).
7 杜永明 Du Yongming, ed., 來注易經圖解 [Lai Zhide's annotated Book of Changes] (Beijing: 中央編譯出版社 Central Compilation Press, 2010).
8 Zhang Yuanshan 張遠山, 伏羲之道 [The Way of Fuxi] (Hunan: 嶽麓書社 Yuelu Publishing House, 2015); Feng Shi 馮時, 中國天文考古學 [Chinese astronomy and archaeology] (Beijing: 中國社會科學出版社 [China Social Sciences Press], 2010).
9 "河出圖，洛出書，聖人則之," from "繫辭上 - Xi Ci I, also known as The Great Treatise I," Chinese Text Project, ed. Donald Sturgeon, accessed July 6, 2022, https://ctext.org/book-of-changes/xi-ci-shang.

Notes to Chapter 5. The Eight Trigrams (Bā Guà)    883

10  Feng Shi [Chinese astronomy].
11  Per Chinese tradition, the number 15 represents the harmony of life and the order of the universe. The number 15 is a product of the factor of 3, for the trinity of Heaven, Earth, and Man, multiplied by the factor of 5, for the Wu Xing five phases and the five directions per Chinese geomancy, north, south, east, west, and center. It is the number of the Tao, the Way. Also, there are a total of 384 lines in the I Ching (64 hexagrams × 6 lines or *yao* each), whereby 3 + 8 + 4 = 15. The three digits also represent the holy trinity, the eight trigrams, the four directions, and the four seasons of space and time. Finally, within the 64 hexagrams, 8 are the spirit helpers, where the trigrams are doubled. Each grouping of hexagrams ordered by their trigram arrangements yields a total of 8 groups of 15 hexagrams in each group. The 8 groupings of 15 hexagrams by spirit helpers is covered in chapter 5.
12  Biographical profiles of the Eight Immortals from: （明）王世真 (Ming) Wang Shizhen, 列仙全傳 *(Liè xiān quán chuán)* [The complete biography of the Immortals] (Beijing: 文物出版社 [Cultural Relics Press], 2018) (first published in 1651).
13  邹学熹 (Zōu Xué Xī) and 邹成永 (Zōu Chéng Yǒng), 中國醫易學 *(Zhōng guó yī Yì Xué)* (Szechuan: 四川科學技術出版社 [Sichuan Science and Technology Press], 1989), 108.
14  Plus, if we're really going to go with the gender identity rationale for correspondences, then the trigram Earth corresponds with the Wu Xing changing phase of Earth, and the agent of change that is Earth happens only when yin and yang are in balance. Yin dominance, for example, corresponds with the phases Metal and Water. Under the gender identity rationale, then, Lan Cai He, who is either nonbinary or gender fluid, makes more sense for Earth, where yin and yang are in balance, than does He Xian Gu, who is decidedly feminine presenting and, using the traditionalist's logic, pure yin.
15  Baolin Wu, Michael McBride, and Vincent Wu, *The Eight Immortals' Revolving Sword of Pure Yang* (Dunedin, FL: Three Pines Press, 2011), 33.
16  Mantak Chia and Johnathon Dao, *The Eight Immortal Healers: Taoist Wisdom for Radiant Health* (Rochester, VT: Destiny Books, 2017), 16.
17  安陽源易緣, ""入選道教 "八仙"：一個重要條件，與《易經》八卦有關" [The Eight Immortals of Taoism as related to the Ba Gua of the I Ching], 安陽市作家協會, September 20, 2017.
18  Xī and Yǒng, *Zhōng guó yī Yì Xué,* 108.
19  The totemic animal correspondences to the eight trigrams are sourced from the Ten Wings, chapter 3 of the Eighth Wing, "說卦 – Shuo Gua [the Eighth Wing]," Chinese Text Project, ed. Donald Sturgeon, accessed June 25, 2022, https://ctext.

org/book-of-changes/shuo-gua. This should be differentiated from the zodiac animal correspondences.
20. W. Perceval Yetts, "The Eight Immortals," *Journal of the Royal Asiatic Society of Great Britain and Ireland for 1916*, 773–807.
21. Suzanne E. Cahill, *Transcendence & Divine Passion: The Queen Mother of the West in Medieval China* (Stanford, CA: Stanford University Press, 1993), 13–15.
22. The reference to the Lake (Dui) trigram corresponding with the Sorceress comes from the Ten Wings itself, in the Shuo Gua, or Eighth Wing: 兌為澤，為少女，為巫 *(Duì wèi zé, wèi shàonǚ, wèi wū)*. "為" essentially means to become, turns into, is or to be, to beget, governs, or gives power to. Thus, the line reads: "Lake (Dui) gives power to the marshes, gives power to the maiden [or youngest daughter], gives power to the *wu* shaman." "說卦 – Shuo Gua [the Eighth Wing]," Chinese Text Project, ed. Donald Sturgeon, accessed June 25, 2022, https://ctext.org/book-of-changes/shuo-gua.
23. Yetts, "The Eight Immortals."
24. Yetts.
25. Homayun Sidky, "On the Antiquity of Shamanism and Its Role in Human Religiosity," *Method and Theory in the Study of Religion* 22 (2010): 72.
26. Homayun Sidky, *Haunted by the Archaic Shaman: Himalayan Jhakris and the Discourse on Shamanism* (Lanham, MD: Lexington Books, 2008), 69.
27. Yetts, "The Eight Immortals."
28. Yetts.
29. Chuang Tzu, *Wandering on the Way: Early Taoist Tales and Parables of Chuang Tzu*, trans. Victor H. Mair (New York: Bantam Books, 1994), 38.
30. Yetts, "The Eight Immortals."
31. The dog is an important totemic animal spirit for several Chinese ethnic groups, including the Mien, the Yao 瑤族, who are also an ethnic minority in Vietnam, and the She 畲, tracing back to the myth of Panhu 盤瓠. Panhu is a dragon-dog with five-colored fur. Emperor Ping of the Kingdom of Chu 楚 (1030–223 BC) promised his daughter's hand in marriage to anyone who could bring him the head of his enemy, King Gao 高王. Panhu successfully met that challenge, and true to his word, the king married his daughter to the dragon-dog. Their children became the ancestors of the Mien/Yao. In honor of Panhu, their traditional clothing features the five colors of Panhu's fur.
32. Yetts, "The Eight Immortals."
33. *Fāngshì* 方士 is a term that surfaced around the Han dynasty (206 BC–AD 220) to describe those who specialize in occult or mystical arts. You'll find several mentions of *fāngshì* in Sima Qian's *Shiji* 史記 [Records of the Grand Historian], such as a reference to *fāngshì* dedicated to bringing peace and harmony to the world

and who are working on formulating a panacea, or *qí yào* 奇藥, miracle medicine, along with passages depicting *fāngshì* speaking in tongues, giving sage counsel to the Son of Heaven (the emperor), and communing with gods, immortals, and mythical beasts to learn the secrets of healing herbs. The term *fāngshì* covers alchemists, astrologers, diviners, ceremonial magicians, exorcists, sorcerers, necromancers, and shamans. *Fāng* 方 means "methods," and *shì* 士 means "scholar or master who specializes in a particular study." Thus, *fāngshì* translates to "methods master." They were typically Taoist priests, but not necessarily, as there was already a term for that—the *Dàoshi* 道士, or Taoist master, which included alchemists, astrologers, diviners, ceremonial magicians, and others who practiced the occult arts and who self-identified as Taoist. In contrast, a *fāngshì* isn't necessarily a Taoist. Any specialist in a divination method would have been a *fāngshì*. Likewise, one who practiced shamanic healing, *wū yī* 巫醫, would have also been called a *fāngshì*.

34 Yetts, "The Eight Immortals."
35 Yetts.
36 Li, *Origins of Chinese Thought*, 25–26.
37 Wang Mingming, "All under Heaven *(Tianxia):* Cosmological Perspectives and Political Ontologies in Premodern China," *Hau: Journal of Ethnographic Theory* 2, no. 1 (Spring 2012): 340–41.
38 The four stages are also referred to as the "fourfold fireball," wherein each stage cumulatively involves greater struggles. Heraclitus referenced four stages of the alchemical opus: *melanosis, leukosis, xanthosis,* and *iosis.* Much later, in the fifteenth or sixteenth century AD, the four were reduced to three: *nigredo, albedo,* and *rubedo.* Mary Ann Mattoon, ed., *Personal and Archetypal Dynamics in the Analytical Relationship: Proceedings of the Eleventh International Congress for Analytic Psychology, Paris, 1989* (Switzerland: Daimon Verlag, 1991), 77. Henrik Bogdan, *Western Esotericism and Rituals of Initiation* (Albany: State University of New York Press, 2012): 113, 197 (explaining *nigredo, albedo,* and *rubedo*). *Nigredo (melanosis)* is separation from your previous decaying state, a purging and catharsis. This is entering the dark chaos of your inner world, the unconscious mind. This is the watery element. *Albedo (leukosis)* is a liminal state, the stage of the moon. Here the psyche is purified. The soul becomes conscious and aware of itself. This is a period of contemplation and coming to terms with your soul purpose. *Citrinitas (xanthosis)* is the stage of the sun, of directing that self-awareness from *albedo* outward and externalized. Awakening to a rebirth and new life. The final alchemical stage of *rubedo (iosis)* is the aggregation and integration phase. This is purification by fire and the culmination of the previous three stages, thus the most arduous and difficult to get through. *Rubedo,* the reddening,

is likened to the reddening color of the trigram Heaven in Taoist symbolism. This is materialization of the spiritual.

39  Vajrabhairava is believed to be an incarnation of the bodhisattva Mañjushri 文殊菩薩 *(wén shū púsà)*, one of the Eight Great Bodhisattvas. He is also associated with the Amitabha Buddha 阿彌陀佛. Vajrabhairava, alternatively known as Yamāntaka, is a god of death, or one who conquers death. Vajrabhairava is often invoked in exorcisms for his powers to subdue and control demons. Recitations of the Vajrabhairava mantra—*om Yamantaka hum phat*—prolong life and protect one from demons. The mantra itself has the power to vanquish and ward.

## 6. The Five Phases of Change (Wu Xing)

1  尚書洪範 [Book of Documents], Chinese Text Project, ed. Donald Sturgeon, accessed May 31, 2022, https://ctext.org/shang-shu/great-plan/zh.
2  Ang Tian Se, "Five Phases (Wuxing)," In *Encyclopedia of the History of Science, Technology, and Medicine in Non-Western Cultures,* ed. Helaine Selin (New York: Springer Science & Business Media, 2008), 939.
3  Se, 939–40.
4  Se, 940.
5  For those interested in learning more about the Wu Xing and curating a diet per the Wu Xing, I recommend Paul Pitchford's *Healing with Whole Foods: Asian Traditions and Modern Nutrition* (Berkeley, CA: North Atlantic Books, 1993).
6  "Xi Ci I or The Great Treatise I 繫辭上" from the Ten Wings: 易與天地準，故能彌綸天地之道。仰以觀於天文，俯以察於地理，是故知幽明之故。
7  Mozi 墨子 (470–391 BC) was the founder of Mohism, a school of ethics that espoused altruism and universal love, in contrast to what had become entrenched in Chinese culture by then—limited family love and clan love, or tribalism. Mozi tried to break through China's long system of tribalism to apply a more Buddhist concept of altruistic love for all people, beyond family and clan. Central to Mohism are the Ten Doctrines, subdivided into five pairs corresponding with the Wu Xing: (1) Wood: Promote the educated, and promote everyone to become educated. (2) Fire: Universal love for all humanity beyond one's tribe, and universal rejection of military aggression and conflicts, no matter who it favors or who it's against. (3) Earth: Moderation in use of resources for the living, and moderation in use of resources for the dead (more modest and less wasteful funeral rites). (4) Metal: Respect Heaven, and respect the underworld of ghosts.(5) Water: Condemn waste and extravagance, and condemn fatalism (to inspire a strong sense of individual agency).

8 The eight trigrams featured in the pentagon connecting the Wu Xing represent the cycles of nature. Beginning at the ascendant point, or bottom-left corner just above Metal, is the trigram Heaven. Heaven then creates the precipitation that is Water. Water has to transmute between aether and earth. On earth the rain becomes Thunder. Thunder becomes Fire. Fire transmutes between aether and earth. Fire forms Earth. Earth forms Mountain. Mountain forms Lake. Lake, symbolic of a womb, begets Heaven, and the cycle starts over again.
9 Yang Li, *Book of Changes and Traditional Chinese Medicine* (Beijing: Beijing Science and Technology Press, 1998), 143.
10 Li, *Book of Changes,* 145.
11 Li, 143.
12 Li, 153.
13 Li, 143.
14 Li, 145.
15 Li, 143.
16 Li, 145.
17 Li, 143.
18 Li, 145.
19 "太平經 *(Tàipíng jīng),* or Scriptures of the Great Peace (37–32 BC)," 古典文學網 (Classical Literature Network), accessed May 31, 2022, http://www.cngdwx.com/xianqinlianghan/taipingjing/.

## 7. Divination Methods

1 In calligraphy and ink brush painting, a thick cloth mat is placed under the rice paper to protect the tabletop. The cloth also keeps the paper from sliding around. Since hexagram lines were drawn with ink on rice paper, the cloth mat concept transferred to divination methods. Having a dedicated and consecrated mat for drawing the hexagram lines or tossing coins isn't a requirement, but it will help keep your coins in pristine condition (and also protect your table). Since I divine with Qing dynasty coins I inherited from my maternal grandmother, using a cloth divination mat helps slow down the wear and tear on the coins. A benefit of the divination mat, especially one consecrated for divination purposes, is that it helps to create a nexus or connection point between Heaven and Earth, much like the process of setting down the first vertical stick in the yarrow stalk method, then dividing the bundles in two and casting them in an "as above, so below" ritualistic manner, in effect connecting Heaven and Earth through ritual. Likewise, a consecrated divination mat creates a liminal space for Heaven and Earth to converge.

Placing crystals or stones charged with thunder *qi* in a thunder rites ritual around the mat effectively creates such a liminal space. Fu talismans crafted for the purposes of consecration, protection, and *qi* empowerment placed underneath the mat or inscribed onto it also work. Or, just spread out a sturdy piece of cloth, simple and clean, and that's it. The extent to which you want to get ceremonial with a divination mat is dependent on what works for you. Figure 5.1 from chapter 5 is a historical example of a talismanic magic square design that can be referenced as inspiration for crafting your own divination mat.

2  Several texts are used by devotees of the Lady of the Nine Heavens, including: *Jiǔ Tiān Xuán Nǚ's Book of Salvation* (九天玄女救世真經, *Jiǔ Tiān Xuán Nǚ jiùshì zhēn jīng*); *The Book of Exorcisms* (消孽真經, *Xiāo niè zhēn jīng*), which covers the Lady's mythology and lists her powers, such as exorcising demons from Earth and sending them back to hell, curing the world of disease, and teaching the worthy how to wield such powers; and the Earth Mother Sutra (地母經, *de mǔ jīng*), which blends Buddhism and Taoism, covering the accounts of Kuan Yin and Jiǔ Tiān Xuán Nǚ, and how the Lady of the Nine Heavens contributed to the revelation of the I Ching to the people.

3  Zhu Xi, *The Original Meaning of the Yijing: Commentary on the Scripture of Change,* trans. Joseph A. Adler (New York: Columbia University Press, 2020), 261.

4  Xici (繫辭傳, *Xìcí chuán*), Fifth Wing, first section, chapter 9 on the Oracle.

5  Xi, *Original Meaning,* 319, citing Zhu Xi's 易學啟蒙 [Introduction to the study of the *Yi*] (AD 1186).

6  Wang Bi , *The Classic of Changes: A New Translation of the I Ching,* trans. Richard John Lynn (New York: Columbia University Press, 1994), 18.

7  Xi, *Original Meaning,* 317.

8  Bin Yang, "The Rise and Fall of Cowrie Shells: The Asian Story," *Journal of World History* 22, no. 1 (March 2011): 1–25.

9  Yang, "Rise and Fall," 6.

10  Yang, 4.

11  Anne D. Birdwhistell, "The Philosophical Concept of Foreknowledge in the Thought of Shao Yong," *Philosophy East and West* 39, no. 1 (January 1989): 52.

12  A tropical year is the length of time it takes the Earth to complete an orbit around the sun, which varies from year to year and is approximately 365 days, varying plus or minus five to six hours, with leap years at approximately 366 days. In Western astrology, tropical zodiac wheels are based on the tropical year, whereas sidereal charts are cast per the sidereal year, or sidereal orbital period, which is the time that the Earth takes to orbit the sun with respect to the fixed stars. The exact

length of time of the sidereal year will differ from the exact length of time of the tropical (or solar) year.

13  Google.com has a free calendar conversion calculator built into the search engine. Run a keyword search for "convert [Gregorian calendar date] to lunar calendar." The search engine will provide an automatic output at the top of the page with the equivalent date in the Chinese Lunar calendar (though this same lunisolar calendar is also used by other parts of Asia, notably Vietnam, Korea, and Japan). For example, when running the search "convert June 3, 2022 to lunar calendar," the result given is "Fifth Month 5, 2022 (ren-yin), year of the Tiger." You'll need to then cross-reference that data with the stems and branches tables provided in the chapter. You can also download Gregorian–lunar calendar conversion tables free of charge from the Hong Kong Observatory at https://www.hko.gov.hk/en/gts/time/conversion.htm.

14  The background center of the seal featured in figure 7.12 is an invocation seal for the Lady of the Nine Heavens (*Jiǔ Tiān Xuán Nǚ yìn shì*, 九天玄女印式) sourced from the *Língbǎo liù dīng mì fǎ* 靈寶六丁秘法. Authorship and date of the text are unknown, but are likely sourced to the Northern Song (AD 960–1127). The center focal point is "九天玄女" in stylized oracle bone script. The rings around the seal feature the heavenly stems and earthly branches, along with thirty-six hexagrams in the inner circle and sixty-four along the outer circle. Both the Early Heaven and Later Heaven Ba Guas are layered behind the center seal. The *Língbǎo* text instructs that invocations of the Lady or crafting her seal should happen on the day of 甲 (Jiǎ), which corresponds with the Wu Xing phase Wood, or Thursday per the modern calendar. In the calendar of antiquity, however, 甲 (Jiǎ) would have been the first day of the ten-day week. The text also instructs that seals for the Lady of the Nine Heavens should be crafted from jujube wood 龍棗木 *(lóng zǎo mù)*. In Taoist mysticism, bracelets and mala prayer beads were commonly made from jujube wood. Wearing a bracelet of jujube wood beads was thought to bring health, longevity, and physical protection.

15  If you're decent at arts and crafts, you can draw, use a wood burner, paint, or inscribe the circular medallion seal from figure 3.16 to use in lieu of figure 7.12. Both are seals for invoking the Lady of the Nine Heavens. The *Língbǎo* text (see note 14, this chapter) instructs that the Seal of the Lady of the Nine Heavens should be carved on a plaque of jujube wood. Traditionally the seal would be painted onto the wood using red vermilion ink from an inkstone.

16  I wasn't able to locate an original source for this mantra, though it is unlikely to have been authored by Cáo Xìnyì. It is more probable that Cáo sourced it from Taoist scriptures he would have had access to as a temple master, and that he cited it in his own writings.

17  This is a shortened form of what you've also seen within the pages of this text as the closing affirmation of a Taoist spell: 急急如律令 *(jí jí rú lǜ lìng)*. The full five-syllable version is more commonly found in exorcisms and ceremonial spell-crafting. "急急" means urgently or expediently. Thus, in full, it would be: "Expediently carry forth this decree of the gods." The shortened three-syllable version found here, 急急如 *(jí jí rú)*, is an affirmation to the effect of: "Expediently may my will and intentions come to manifest." The shortened version is used to summon from within your own latent powers.
18  Hermann Haindl, *The Haindl Tarot Deck* (Stamford, CT: U.S. Games Systems, 1990).
19  For example, *Jiao's Book of Yi* 焦氏易林 *(Jiāo shì Yì lín)* by Jiao Gan 焦贛 proposed that there were a total of 4,096 hexagrams. *Yì lín* means a forest of changes. The sixty-four hexagrams are combined with one another sixty-four times to produce 4,096 prophetic divinatory verses.
20  Eliphas Levi, *Transcendental Magic: Its Doctrine* (*Dogme et rituel de la haute magie)*, trans. Arthur Edward Waite (London: George Redway, 1896). See chapter 6, "The Magical Equilibrium."
21  Israel Regardie, *The Philosopher's Stone: Spiritual Alchemy, Psychology, and Ritual Magic*, eds. Chic Cicero and Sandra Tabatha Cicero (Woodbury, MN: Llewellyn Publications, 2013), 129–78.
22  Michael McDonald, *I Ching Self-Change: Ancient Oracle, Modern World* (self-pub., 2019).
23  McDonald, *I Ching*, 261.

## 8. I Ching: The Book of Changes

1  Peng Liu, "Conceal My Body So That I Can Protect the State: The Making of the Mysterious Woman in Daoism and Water Margin," *Ming Studies* 74 (November 2016): 51.
2  "繫辭上 - Xi Ci I, Also Known as: The Great Treatise I," Chinese Text Project, ed. Donald Sturgeon, accessed June 25, 2022, https://ctext.org/book-of-changes/xi-ci-shang.
3  Kerson Huang's translation of the I Ching translates "亨" to "sign of the sacrifice." For instance, in the Judgment for Hexagrams 1 and 2, "元亨" is translated to "Sign of the Great Sacrifice." Kerson Huang, *I Ching: The Oracle* (Taipei: Bookman Books, 1991), 40–43.
4  "繫辭上 - Xi Ci I."
5  Lihui Yang and Deming An with Jessica Anderson Turner, *Handbook of Chinese Mythology* (New York: Oxford University Press, 2008), 137.

6. Emperor Wen of the Western Han dynasty acceded to the throne at the age of twenty-three. He was by all accounts a beneficent and kind ruler, ushering China into one of its golden ages. Emperor Wen implemented one of the earliest social welfare programs by giving tax exemptions to the poor, widowed, and elders without surviving children, and sending monthly stipends of grain, wine, and meat to seniors over the age of eighty, in addition to stipends of clothing to seniors over ninety. He brokered peace treaties with neighboring kingdoms and permitted government officials to give him honest criticism. Hing Ming Hung, *The Magnificent Emperor Wu: China's Han Dynasty* (New York: Algora Publishing, 2020), 85–108.
7. Chen Zhi, "A Study of the Bird Cult of the Shang People," *Monumental Serica* 47 (January 1999): 142.
8. Zhi, "A Study," 128.
9. Zhi, 127–47. Totemism as applied to Bronze Age Chinese civilizations was first proposed by Guo Muoro 郭沫若 (1892–1978), who proposed that the animal pictographs found on Shang oracle bones and bronze vessels were clan signs, or 族徽 *zú huī*.
10. Zhi, 147.
11. Wang Zhongfu [王仲孚], *A Special Study on Chinese Ancient History* [中國上古史專題研究] (Taipei: Wunan Book Publishing [五南圖書出版股份有限公司], 1996).
12. Yang and An with Turner, *Handbook of Chinese Mythology*.
13. Yang and An with Turner, 95–96.
14. Zhi, "A Study," 142.
15. Zhi, 129.
16. Zhi, 142–43.
17. Zhi, 129.
18. The Shang were historically known as the Yin (殷代, *Yīn dài*). References to the Shang as the Yin are also found in the Zhouyi.
19. A cangue (枷, *jiā*) is a wooden yoke placed around a person's neck as a form of corporal punishment and public humiliation. Its use was popular for most of East and Southeast Asia's history. The cangue was constructed as a large, heavy tablet with descriptions of the person's crimes painted on the wooden boards. One sentenced to wear the cangue would then be placed in the public square, exposed to both the elements and condemnation from the community.
20. Richard Wilhelm, trans., *The I Ching or Book of Changes,* rendered into English by Cary F. Baynes. (Princeton, NJ: Princeton University Press, 1977), 109.
21. "枯楊生華" *(kū yáng shēng huá),* or "a withering poplar blooms," has become an idiom meaning a much older woman marrying a much younger man.

892   *I Ching, the Oracle*

22   The character 敬 *(jìng),* meaning reverence and implying a transcendent experience, appeared often in Zhou dynasty texts. The original meaning of the word 敬 was "shamanistic ritual ceremony." Li Zehou, *The Origins of Chinese Thought: From Shamanism to Ritual Regulations and Humaneness,* trans. Robert A. Carleo III (Leiden: Brill, 2018), 33.

23   The legend of one of the Four Beauties of ancient China intersects with the legend of Goujian. In his plot for revenge against the king of Wu, his ministers find one of the most beautiful women of Yue, Xi Shi 西施, and send her as a tribute to the king of Wu. The legend went that Xi Shi was so beautiful that when she gazed into a pond, the fish would be so enchanted by her beauty that they'd forget how to swim. Xi Shi was in fact acting as a spy for Yue. As the king of Wu's concubine, she succeeded at distracting him to such an extent that he neglected the affairs of state. Xi Shi also managed to convince the king of Wu to execute his best and most loyal military generals. Having weakened the state of Wu, King Goujian of Yue was able to invade and defeat the Wu.

24   Bird script 鳥書 *(niǎo shū)* was an ornamental calligraphic script used in the southern regions of mainland Asia, as would be found in the kingdom of Yue. Bird script is found primarily among the Chu, the Wu, and the Yue south of the Shang and Zhou dynasties.

25   A full recounting of both history and legend can be found in Paul A. Cohen, *Speaking to History: The Story of King Goujian in Twentieth-Century China* (Berkeley: University of California Press, 2009), 1–35.

26   Eric J. Hoffman, "Chinese Thumb Rings: From Battlefield to Jewelry Box," Asian Art, https://www.asianart.com/articles/rings/index.html, accessed June 14, 2022.

27   Li, *Origins of Chinese Thought,* 86.

28   Li, 87.

29   If clay cannot be sourced, mix one cup flour, a quarter cup salt, one tablespoon oil, and one cup water into a pot and stir vigorously while heating the pot. In about three to five minutes, the dough will form a ball and will no longer stick to the sides of the pot. Let the dough cool, and knead until smooth.

30   "爾雅 - Er Ya," Chinese Text Project, ed. Donald Sturgeon, accessed June 14, 2022, https://ctext.org/er-ya.

31   Guohui Huang 黄国辉, 從親屬稱謂看殷墟甲骨的分期問題 [Study of the oracle bones] (Beijing: 北京師範大學歷史學院 [Department of History, Beijing Normal University]), 52.

32   Huang, *I Ching,* 109.

33   This endnote has only a tangential relation to the text, but I've been looking for somewhere to put this Zhuangzi quote, which feels unfortunately timeless, and

in its own way, relates to Hexagram 36: "Steal a dagger, get executed. But steal a country, and get appointed the feudal lord" 彼竊鈎者誅, 竊國者為諸侯 *(Bǐ qiè gōu zhě zhū, qiè guó zhě wéi zhū hóu)*. Zhuangzi 莊子 (350–250 BC), from Qū Qiè 胠篋 (300 BC). "胠篋," Chinese Text Project, accessed August 28, 2022, https://ctext.org/zhuangzi/cutting-open-satchels/zh.

34  Huang, *I Ching*, 11.
35  Jae-Hoon Shim, "A New Understanding of Kija Choson as a Historical Anachronism," *Harvard Journal of Asiatic Studies* 62, no. 2 (December 2002): 271–305.
36  Three major Korean royal clans are said to be descendants of Jizi: the Cheongju Han 청주 한씨, the Haengju Gi행주 기씨, and Taewon Seonu 태원 선우씨.
37  Shim, "A New Understanding," 273.
38  Shim, 292.
39  Anne E. McLaren, "Marriage by Abduction in Twentieth Century China," *Modern Asian Studies* 36, no. 4 (October 2001): 952–84.
40  McLaren, "Marriage by Abduction," 956.
41  Bin Yang, "The Rise and Fall of Cowrie Shells: The Asian Story," *Journal of World History* 22, no. 1 (March 2011): 9.
42  "*Yiwen Leiju* (藝文類聚)," Chinese Text Project, ed. Donald Sturgeon, accessed June 16, 2022, https://ctext.org/yiwen-leiju/zh.
43  "Tortoise 龜" from volume 96 卷九十六 of *Yiwen leiju* (藝文類聚), accessed August 28, 2022, https://ctext.org/yiwen-leiju/zh.
44  Feng Shi, "A Study on Wang Mang's Jade Tablet for the Feng-Shan Ceremony of the Xin Dynasty," *Chinese Jiu Tang Shu Archaeology* 7 (2007): 165.
45  Chonglan Fu and Wenming Cao, *Introduction to the Urban History of China* (Singapore: Springer Publishing, 2019), 83. See also Frank M. Flanagan, *Confucius: The Analects and Western Education* (New York: Bloomsbury Publishing, 2011), 14.
46  Maria Khayutina, "King Wen, a Settler of Disputes or Judge? The 'Yu-Rui Case' in the *Historical Records* and Its Historical Background," *Das Bochumer Jahrbuch zur Ostasienforschung* [Bochum Yearbook of East Asian Studies] 38 (2015): 267.
47  Khayutina, "King Wen," 271.
48  Here are a few recommended measures for amplifying Wood and Thunder to counteract the blockading effects of Hexagram 47. Petition a dragon spirit as a guardian protector, or invoke a deity associated with the east, Jupiter, or Thunder. On a plaque of wood, inscribe the four ideograms as shown in figure 8.5. Draw a circle around the four ideograms and a square in the center as depicted in the illustration. Place this along the easternmost wall of your home. Keep a potted green or bamboo plant next to the plaque, and maintain that plant daily. This is a measure to strengthen the Wood energy for progress and gains in income to such

a point that it will break the barriers that had kept it enclosed. You can also combine the talisman with the bamboo plant by painting the talismanic design onto the pot that holds the plant.

49 Tao Wang, *Mirroring China's Past: Emperors, Scholars, and Their Bronzes* (New Haven, CT: Yale University Press, 2018), 26.
50 Imperial Japanese Government Railways, *An Official Guide to Eastern Asia, Vol. IV, China* (Tokyo: Imperial Japanese Government Railways, 1915), cxx–cxxi.
51 In the English translations I've consulted, "仇" is translated as "wife" (Kerson Huang), "mate" (Alfred Huang), or "comrades" (Richard Wilhelm/Cary Baynes). In contrast, most Chinese interpretations of the Zhouyi interpret this word as "enemy," "opponent," or "opposition." 傅佩榮 Fu Peirong, 傅佩榮譯解易經 *Fu Peirong's Interpretation of the Book of Changes* (Taipei: 台灣東方出版社 [Taiwan Oriental Publishing House], 2011), 466.
52 Ping Rong et al., "Chinese Herbal Compounds Containing Scorpion in the Treatment of Epilepsy: A Protocol for Systematic Review and Meta-analysis," *Medicine* 100, no. 10 (March 12, 2021): e25134, https://www.doi.org/10.1097/MD.0000000000025134.
53 Edward A. Armstrong, "The Symbolism of the Swan and the Goose," *Folklore* 55, no. 2 (June 1944): 56.
54 Armstrong, "Symbolism," 56.
55 Michael J. Seth, *A Concise History of Korea: From the Neolithic Period through the Nineteenth Century* (Lanham, MD: Rowman and Littlefield, 2006), 83–85.
56 Armstrong, "Symbolism," 57.
57 Armstrong.
58 Li, *Origins of Chinese Thought*, 61.
59 Lao Tzu, *Tao Teh Ching,* trans. John C. H. Wu (Boulder, CO: Shambhala, 2006), 103.
60 周髀算經 *Zhoubi suanjing* (1046–256 BC), a mathematical text dating back to the Zhou dynasty.
61 "Five Millennium Catalog of Solar Eclipses: 1100 BCE to 1001 BCE," National Aeronautics and Space Administration, accessed June 18, 2022, https://eclipse.gsfc.nasa.gov/SEcat5/SE-1099--1000.html.
62 S. J. Marshall, *The Mandate of Heaven: Hidden History in the* Book of Changes (Abingdon, UK: Routledge, 2015), 50–66.
63 The *Bamboo Annals* (竹書紀年, *Zhú shū jìnián*) is a chronicle of events from the time of the Yellow Emperor (ca. twenty-sixth century BC) to around 300 BC. The date of authorship is unknown, but the earliest version discovered dates to around 296 BC from the tombs of King Xiang of Wei, where copies of the I Ching were

also found. The *Annals* offers more insights into the account of Wang Hai, one of the early ancestors of the Shang dynasty. Wang Hai lived sometime during the Xia dynasty (2070–1600 BC), six generations after Yu the Great stops the floods. Wang Hai is the leader of the Shang clan. They develop advanced techniques in agriculture and animal husbandry, leading to overabundance. Through Wang Hai's business acumen, they develop profitable trade with nearby kingdoms and clans, including the Kingdom of Yi. Wang Hai travels to the Kingdom of Yi to establish these trade connections. King Mianchen of Yi initially welcomes Wang Hai with open arms, but Wang Hai falls in love with Mianchen's wife. Mianchen plots to murder Wang Hai, sending a guard to assassinate Wang Hai in his sleep. Wang Hai's body was found the next morning chopped into eight pieces by a hatchet. Mianchen then takes all of Wang Hai's cattle and sheep.

64  The first line of Hexagram 56 can be used as an effective curse to knock down someone wealthy, privileged, and arrogant, especially one who has in effect intruded on others' land to gain riches from or exploit that land. This method of baneful magic works on one in power who has gravely wronged you, and where any other form of recourse is not possible, because that person is too powerful and you're otherwise powerless. "旅瑣瑣,斯其所.取災。" is pronounced: *Lǚ suǒ suǒ, sī qí suǒ. Qǔ zāi!* " If you're reciting the line to lay down a curse, you'll want to be emphatic with those last two words. If Mandarin isn't your first language and English is, alternate between recitation of it in Mandarin and in English. The point of reciting in a language you're more familiar with is to drum up your own power and combine it with the intention. "[Recite the name of the target]—*suo, suo!*—foolish and full of swagger, shall stray upon disaster." Since that last word *zai* means by fire or water, burn or drown an effigy of the target while reciting the words. Write the target's name and a few identification numbers or data points on an unlucky number of toilet paper sheets and flush the written-on sheets down the toilet one by one, reciting the curse words emphatically. Alternatively, burn something with the target's personal *qi* or energy on it, and as you set it on fire and watch the flames consume it, recite the words. Finally, every prudent spell-crafter will warn of unintended consequences and the ethics of spell-crafting. While I could hop on a soapbox and give a full-day lecture on morality and the repercussions of cursing, I'll summarize it all with this: only curse when you are at such a low point that you really have nothing left to lose, and the target is truly a malicious bad actor, not just someone you disagreed with or who called you a bad name.

65  Shangdi (上帝) is mentioned a third time in the "象曰" from the Ten Wings discussing Hexagram 11, in the line "殷薦之上帝," meaning the many offerings and blessings to Shangdi.

66 Tzu, *Tao Teh Ching*, 9.
67 Yáng Shèngyǒng 楊勝勇, ed., *Military History of the Three Dynasties of China* 中國元古暨三代軍事史 (Beijing: 人民出版社 [People's Publishing House] Rénmín Chūbǎn Shè, 1994), vol. 3 of *The Hundred Volumes of the Complete History of China* 中國全史百卷本, 53.
68 benebell wen, *The Tao of Craft: Fu Talismans and Casting Sigils in the Eastern Esoteric Tradition* (Berkeley, CA: North Atlantic Books, 2016), 90–91.
69 "Interpretations and Incantations of Celestials in the Zhouyi (周易乾鑿度, Zhōuyì Qián Záo Dù)," Chinese Text Project, ed. Donald Sturgeon, accessed May 23, 2022, https://ctext.org/datawiki.pl?if=gb&res=659075.
70 Huang, *I Ching*, 166–67.
71 Herbert A. Giles, *Religions of Ancient China* (Chapel Hill, NC: Project Gutenberg, 2006), https://www.gutenberg.org/files/2330/2330-h/2330-h.htm.
72 "說卦 – Shuo Gua [the Eighth Wing]," Chinese Text Project, ed. Donald Sturgeon, accessed June 25, 2022, https://ctext.org/book-of-changes/shuo-gua.

## 9. Ancestral Veneration and the I Ching

1 The Tujia, an ethnic minority in China, perform a funeral dance called *sayerhe* around the coffin, drumming, singing, and dancing while wearing festive colors. The celebratory funeral dance is premised on the belief that souls are immortal and that the deceased have only changed from their physical bodies to a spirit form. The celebration is for the living to accompany the dead in their transition. Zhenhua Guo, Jun Yang, and Meirong Tang, "Research on Tujia *Sayerhe* Dance" (paper presented at the Sixth International Conference on Social Network, Communication and Education, September 15, 2016).
2 Vu Hong Van and Nguyen Trong Long, "Identify the Values of Ancestor Worship Belief in the Spiritual Life of Vietnamese People," *International Journal of Philosophy* 7, no. 4 (2019): 160–66. doi: 10.11648/j.ijp.20190704.14.
3 Nobushige Hozumi, *Ancestor Worship and Japanese Law* (Tokyo: Maruzen Kabushiki-Kaisha, 1912), 30–31.
4 Hozumi, *Ancestor Worship*, 73–76.
5 Chang-Won Park, *Cultural Blending in Korean Death Rites: New Interpretive Approaches* (New York: Continuum International Publishing, 2010), 2.
6 Charles Courtney and Jung Young Lee, eds., *East Wind: Taoist and Cosmological Implications of Christian Theology* (Lanham, MD: University Press of America, 1997).

7   Paul Carus, *Chinese Thought: An Exposition of the Main Characteristic Features of the Chinese World-Conception* (Chicago: Open Court Publishing Co., 1907), 121.
8   Van and Long, "Identify the Values," 165.
9   The belief that homonyms hold metaphysical importance began early in the history of Chinese thought. The Ten Wings commentaries for Hexagram 1, Qian, address the concept this way: "同聲相應,同氣相求" (Things with the same sound resonate together; things with the same vital energy seek out one another) *(Tóng shēng xiāng yìng; tóng qì xiāng qiú).* From the Seventh Wing, commentary on the Words of the Text: 易經・乾卦・文言. In the Huainanzi 淮南子 of the early Han: "The mutual resonance between the various things is deeply mysterious and profound. It cannot be evaluated through knowing, nor understood through explanation. This is perhaps the emotional resonance between things. This is perhaps the dynamic movement among things." *"Lan ming xun"* 覽冥訓, in He Ning 何寧, ed., *Huainanzi jishi* 淮南子集釋 (Beijing: Zhonghua Shuju, 1998), 6.450. Sounds a bit like Jungian synchronicity . . . written in 139 BC.
10  My book *The Tao of Craft* has a section on setting up an altar (see citation at the end of this note). However, discussions on how an altar or shrine "should" be set up are a touchy subject. There's no unanimous consensus, and every Taoist lineage has its own set of beliefs around the altar or shrine. Moreover, traditions will vary by region. Traditions even vary by family; if your family has consistently set up ancestor shrines in a particular way for generations, then nothing is more powerful to follow than that, no matter what authoritative canon says. benebell wen, *The Tao of Craft: Fu Talismans and Casting Sigils in the Eastern Esoteric Tradition* (Berkeley, CA: North Atlantic Books, 2016), 121–25.
11  Helena Rintala, Miia Pitkäranta, and Martin Täubel, "Microbial Communities Associated with House Dust," *Advances in Applied Microbiology* 78 (December 2012), 75–120. doi: 10.1016/B978-0-12-394805-2.00004-X.
12  Sarah Ben Maamar et al., "Mobilizable Antibiotic Resistance Genes Are Present in Dust Microbial Communities," *Plos Pathogens* (January 23, 2020), https://doi.org/10.1371/journal.ppat.1008211.
13  As a general rule of thumb, if you're calling upon a nature spirit or Taoist divinity, you'll want to prepare thoughtful offerings. In Buddhist traditions, offerings are not necessary. Thus, if you're praying to Kuan Yin, a commonly invoked bodhisattva for accompanying our ancestors to and from worlds, no offerings are necessary. However, it's considered good practice to offer merit in honor of her instead, meaning that in gratitude for Kuan Yin's assistance, after the ritual you will do good in this world, such as giving to charity, being generous, being kind, going vegan for a set period of time so you aren't harming animals, and so on.

## 10. The *Yi*, the *Wū*, and Shamanism

1. I Ching divination was aimed at foretelling the future by way of an inquiry presented to ancestral spirits, and through the Book of Changes, ancestral spirits would respond. Thus, divination practices such as the I Ching were interconnected with ancient shamanism. Li Zehou, *The Origins of Chinese Thought: From Shamanism to Ritual Regulations and Humaneness*, trans. Robert A. Carleo III (Leiden: Brill, 2018), 24.
2. Liao Mingchun, *Mawangdui boshu Zhouyi jingzhuan shiwe*, "Xi Ci" 繫辭, 24.
3. "Xi Ci I or The Great Treatise I 繫辭上," from the Ten Wings: 精氣為物，遊魂為變，是故知鬼神之情狀。
4. Interpreting "大樂與天地同和，大禮與天地同節。和故百物不失，節故祀天祭地，明則有禮樂，幽則有鬼神," from "樂記, verse 12," Chinese Text Project, ed. Donald Sturgeon, accessed June 29, 2022, https://ctext.org/liji/yue-ji/zh.
5. "樂記, verse 12," Chinese Text Project, ed. Donald Sturgeon.
6. Interpreting "樂者敦和，率神而從天，禮者別宜，居鬼而從地," from the 樂記, verse 17.
7. Interpreting "及夫禮樂之極乎天而蟠乎地，行乎陰陽而通乎鬼神," from the 樂記, verse 20.
8. Li Zehou 李泽厚 is considered one of the most important modern scholars of Chinese history and culture, and a central figure in the Chinese Enlightenment 啟蒙 (Qǐméng) of the late twentieth century. He was a scholar exiled from his home country of China, but well loved and admired by the Chinese and globally. His works have been characterized as neotraditional, neo-Kantian, post-Marxist, Marxist-Confucianist, and romantic. Greater insight into the man and his works can be found in Jana S. Rošker's *Following His Own Path: Li Zehou and Contemporary Chinese Philosophy* (Albany: State University of New York Press, 2019).
9. Li, *Origins of Chinese Thought*, 13.
10. Li, 16.
11. Chen Mengjia 陳夢家 (1911–1966) is considered a leading authority on Shang oracle bones and is the author of the seminal work *The Myths and Wū Shamanism of the Shang* 商代的神話與巫術 (1936). He was a law student who then turned his interest toward studying classical Chinese literature, religion, and archaeology. Due to his scholarly writings opposing China's simplification of Chinese characters, he was persecuted as being antigovernment from 1957 to 1966. He died of either suicide or persecution on September 3, 1966.
12. Also transliterated into English as Kwang-chih Chang 張光直 (1931–2001) and often attributed as K. C. Chang. Chang was a Taiwanese-Chinese archaeologist

and scholar of premodern China, the Bronze Age, and shamanism. Some of his most notable contributions are on Shang dynasty societies and the prehistory of Taiwan.

13  Yao refers to Emperor Yao 堯 (2356–2255 BC), a mythic king during a golden age of China, before the Shang. He was extolled by Confucius as being a virtuous, selfless, and devoted king. He was also known for the extraordinary lengths he went to in an effort to subdue the Great Flood of Gun-Yu 鯀禹治水, which lasted for two generations beginning with Yao's reign.

14  Shun refers to Emperor Shun 舜 (2294–2184 BC), whom Emperor Yao abdicated his throne to. Likewise, Shun would voluntarily abdicate his throne to Yu the Great, who founded the Xia dynasty, believing his own son to be unworthy of kingship. Shun was known for his reverence toward the god Shangdi 上帝, veneration of nature spirits, and filial piety.

15  Yu refers to Yu the Great 大禹, who finally succeeded at taming the Great Flood that had started two generations previously during Emperor Yao's reign.

16  Tang refers to King Tang of Shang 成湯, who overthrew the Xia and founded the Shang dynasty. Tang is considered a well-respected leader who succeeded at uniting many tribes or clans. When his kingdom suffered from a drought, Tang had gold coins minted and distributed to the poor.

17  In *Records of the Grand Historian* (94 BC), early Han historian Sima Qian (145–86 BC) recorded that after defeating the Shang, King Wu (King Wen's son) fell gravely ill. The Duke of Zhou built three earthen altars that faced north, capped them with ceremonial jade, and called upon the spirits of their great-grandfather King Tai, his grandfather King Ji, and King Wen for divine assistance. The duke then proceeded with a divination, and the result was auspicious. The slip of paper bearing the prayer petition and oracle message was sealed in a coffer bound with metal bands, and the duke instructed everyone not to speak of the divination until the king recovered. The following day, King Wu recovered. Taking inspiration from the Duke of Zhou's divination/spell, pray for a certain objective to manifest, then consult the I Ching for the response. If the response is auspicious, write out both the prayer and the Oracle message noting good auspices. Place the slips of paper into a sealed box or pouch, and put it away. Do not speak a word about the spell until after your objective has come true.

18  Li, *Origins of Chinese Thought*, 99–100.

19  One significant point to mention, though I don't want to belabor it, is Li Zehou's emphatic distinction between what he referred to as the shaman of shamanistic-historical tradition, which he somewhat romanticizes as noble and exalted, and the later phenomenon of the shaman of "lesser traditions." He refers to the forms of spirit mediumship, spellcasting, and talisman sigil-crafting of the lower classes

as the "lesser tradition" of shamanism. He notes that during the Shang, the *wū* 巫 was a leader, a supplicant whom the gods would listen to, a diviner, and a historian, but over the passage of time and through the changing of collective consciousness, the *wū* 巫 became thought of as one engaging in "elaborate folk rituals of warding off spirits." According to Li, these latter "marginal traditions of shamanism are of little consequence." Li, *Origins of Chinese Thought*, 18–19. Personally, I do not make that distinction, and I consider the two to be one and the same. There is an evolution and transformation of the practice of shamanism that occurs over the millennia, but they are not two separate and distinct threads.

20 Mayfair Yang 楊美惠, "Shamanism and Spirit Possession in Chinese Modernity: Some Preliminary Reflections on Gendered Religiosity of the Body," *Review of Religion and Chinese Society* 2 (2015): 52.

21 Robert E. Murowchick, *Cradles of Civilization: China* (Norman: University of Oklahoma Press, 1994), 55.

22 Arthur Waley, *The Nine Songs: A Study of Shamanism in Ancient China* (London: Allen & Unwin, 1955), 9.

23 Section 10 of the 楚語下 *(Chǔ yǔ xià)* from the *Discourses of the States* reads: "如是則明神降之，在男曰覡，在女曰巫," meaning when gods or spirits descend into particularly blessed, illuminated, and enlightened individuals and possess them, when they are men, they are called *xi*, and when they are women, they are called *wū*. 《楚語下》, Chinese Text Project, ed. Donald Sturgeon, accessed June 27, 2022, https://ctext.org/guo-yu/chu-yu-xia/zh.

24 Li, *Origins of Chinese Thought*, 23.

25 Li, 19.

26 Li, 101.

27 Li, 102.

28 Wuxian was a diviner and high priest who led the sacrificial rites, as well as a rainmaker and healer, although he was best known for being a gifted astronomer/astrologer. He's considered the great ancestor of *wū* shamans and was later deified. From the *Shuowen jiezi*: "巫,祝也:女能事無形 以舞降神者也" *(Wū, zhù yě: nǚ néng shì wúxíng yǐ wǔ jiàng shén zhě yě)*. In the entry for *wū* 巫, the text references Wuxian 巫咸 from the Shang dynasty, a renowned shaman who lived between 1600 and 1046 BC, serving under King Tai Wu 太戊 of Shang. (Note, however, that in the *Records of the Grand Historian* by Sima Qian, Wuxian was recorded as serving King Zu Yi 祖乙, who reigned 1428–1409 BC, so there may be conflicts in the historical records.)

29 In some academic circles, "shamanism" and *wū* are used to denote a limited segment of Chinese folk traditions. On this model, only those from northeast China, central Asia, or Siberia can call themselves a shaman, and in China, only those of

northeast Asian descent are *wū*. The rationale given for limiting these terms is the contention that applying a unifying term of solidarity to cover all marginalized folk practitioners would be "a strenuous and worthless project." Liu Guiteng, "Shamanism and the Musical Instruments Used in the Manchurian Shamanistic Sacrificial Rituals," *Journal of the Association for Chinese Music Research* 9, no. 2 (fall 1996): 2. I disagree with that perspective and tend to agree with academics such as Li Zehou, Homayun Sidky, and Mayfair Yang on a broader applicability of the terms "shamanism" and *wū*.

30 Michael Winkelman, *Shamanism: A Biopsychosocial Paradigm of Consciousness and Healing* (Santa Barbara, CA: Greenwood Publsihing, 2010), 65.
31 Berthold Laufer, "Origin of the Word Shaman," *American Anthropologist* 19 (1917): 367.
32 Laufer, "Origin," 361–71.
33 Laufer, 369.
34 Laufer, 362.
35 N. D. Mironov and Sergeĭ Mikhaĭlovich Shirokogorov, *Śramana-Shaman: Etymology of the Word "Shaman"* (Cambridge, UK: Royal Asiatic Society, 1924).
36 Brihadaranyaka Upanishad, verse 4.3.22.
37 Buddhism was introduced to Nepal and then inner Asia and Mongolia from about 200 BC to AD 300. Shamanism and Buddhism were pitted against each other and yet also integrated into one another. Kevin Turner, *Sky Shamans of Mongolia: Meetings with Remarkable Healers* (Berkeley, CA: North Atlantic Books, 2016), 68–69.
38 Pamela Kyle Crossley, *Orphan Warriors: Three Manchu Generations and the End of the Qing World* (Princeton, NJ: Princeton University Press, 1990), 28–29; Mark C. Elliott, *The Manchu Way: The Eight Banners and Ethnic Identity in Late Imperial China* (Stanford, CA: Stanford University Press, 2001).
39 Patricia B. Ebrey, Anne Walthall, and James B. Palais, *East Asia: A Cultural, Social, and Political History* (New York: Houghton Mifflin, 2013), 314–15.
40 Nicola di Cosmo, "Manchu Shamanic Ceremonies at the Qing Court," in *State and Court Ritual in China*, ed. Joseph P. McDermott, ed. Cambridge: Cambridge University Press, 1999, 359.
41 Homayun Sidky, *Haunted by the Archaic Shaman: Himalayan Jhakris and the Discourse on Shamanism* (Lanham, MD: Lexington Books, 2008).
42 Laufer, "Origin," 370.
43 Laufer.
44 Yang, "Shamanism and Spirit Possession," 59.
45 John A. Grim, "*Chaesu Kut*: A Korean Shamanistic Performance," *Asian Folklore Studies* 43 (1984): 235.

46  During the Qing dynasty and through the Cultural Revolution on mainland China and Korea's colonial period of Japanese occupation, the *wū* and the *mudang* were persecuted and subjected to intense social criticism. As a result, many of the *wū/mudang* from that period want to distance themselves from the negative connotations of that word. Two phenomenal works to read are Yang, "Shamanism and Spirit Possession," and Merose Hwang, "The Mudang: Gendered Discourses on Shamanism in Colonial Korea" (PhD thesis, University of Toronto, 2009).
47  Murowchick, *Cradles of Civilization*, 63.
48  Li Liu, *The Chinese Neolithic Trajectories to Early States* (Cambridge, UK: Cambridge University Press, 2005), 155.
49  Liu, *Chinese Neolithic*, 123.
50  Anne P. Underhill, ed., "Chapter 10: the Jiahu Site in the Huai River Area," in *A Companion to Chinese Archaeology* (Hoboken, NJ: Wiley-Blackwell, 2013), 194–212.
51  Li, *Origins of Chinese Thought*, 30.
52  Murowchick, *Cradles of Civilization*, 55.
53  Yang, "Shamanism and Spirit Possession," 53.
54  Li, *Origins of Chinese Thought*, 15.
55  Li, 101.
56  Li, 26.
57  Chen Zhi, "A Study of the Bird Cult of the Shang People," *Monumental Serica* 47 (January 1999): 127–47. doi: 10.1080/02549948.1999.11731325.
58  One of the early descriptions of the Hànbá 旱魃 comes from the Classic of Poetry 詩經, or Book of Songs, circa eleventh–seventh century BC, describing the creature as cruel and burning. *The Classic of Mountains and Seas* 山海經 (475–220 BC) describes the Hànbá as a scorpion. In volume 4 of *The Children's Book of Qionglin* 幼學瓊林, an ancient educational text for children, in the chapter on Taoist ghosts and demons 釋道鬼神類, the Hànbá is described as a demoness.
59  陳夢家 [Chen Mengjia], 商代的神話與巫術 ["Myths and wū shamanism of the Shang dynasty"], *Yenjing Journal* 20 (December 1936): 525–26.
60  However, mirrors are also an essential shaman's tool in north Asian traditions, such as the *toli* mirror of Buryat shamanic sorcerers. A *toli* mirror can be used for healing and protection but is itself enlivened with a spirit. Turner, *Sky Shamans*, 133. Among the Khalkha, a subgroup in Mongolia, *toli* mirrors are a shaman's or sorcerer's defensive weapon for protection, often decorated with the twelve animals of the lunisolar zodiac or the eight trigrams of the Ba Gua. Turner, 115; photographic essay insert between 178 and 179.
61  Yang, "Shamanism and Spirit Possession," 55.

62 Li, *Origins of Chinese Thought,* 49.
63 Li, 45.
64 Li, 103.
65 R. Guisso and Chai-Shin Yu, eds., *Shamanism: The Spirit World of Korea* (Singapore: Asian Humanities Press, 1988), 14–15.
66 Grim, *"Chaesu Kut,"* 236.
67 Zhu Xi, *The Original Meaning of the Yijing: Commentary on the Scripture of Change,* trans. Joseph A. Adler (New York: Columbia University Press, 2020), 319.
68 Sima Qian 司馬遷 (145–86 BC), in *Records of the Grand Historian* (94 BC), also referred to as the *Shiji* 史記, noted that the Duke of Zhou petitioned the Zhou ancestors for blessings to cure his nephew King Wu's illness, then performed a divination for the ancestor spirits' response. In doing so, he constructed three altars and performed the sacrificial rites facing north.
69 Zehou, *Origins of Chinese Thought,* 30.
70 Line statements in the Zhouyi including the word "征" *(zhēng)* refer to omens on whether to go on a military expedition, whether to invade, attack, or conquer. For a few examples, see Hexagram 15, line 6 (征邑國); Hexagram 24, line 6 … 不克征); Hexagram 27, line 2 (征凶); or Hexagram 30, line 6 (王用出征). Those are just a few of dozens of instances that recur in the text.
71 Yang, "Shamanism and Spirit Possession," 55.
72 Arthur Waley, *The Nine Songs: A Study of Shamanism in Ancient China* (London: Allen & Unwin, 1955), 11.
73 Yang, "Shamanism and Spirit Possession," 55.
74 Zehou, *Origins of Chinese Thought,* 86.
75 Yang, "Shamanism and Spirit Possession," 56.
76 Gregory A. Plotnikoff et al., "Hmong Shamanism: Animist Spiritual Healing in Minnesota," *Clinical and Health Affairs* 85, no. 6 (June 2002): 31.
77 Across several East Asian cultures, including Japan, blindness is commonly associated with spiritual, psychic, or supernatural abilities.
78 Helen Hardacre, *Shinto: A History* (Oxford, UK: Oxford University Press, 2017), 184.
79 During the eighteenth century, a substantial source of the *miko*'s income came from selling talismans. Gerald Groemer, "Female Shamans in Eastern Japan during the Edo Period," *Asian Folklore Studies* 66 (2007): 38.
80 Training for *itako* involved ritual exposure to ice-cold water over a series of days for three years, memorization of sutras, and a spiritual marriage between the shaman and a patron *kami* or spirit. Groemer, "Female Shamans," 46.

81 In "On the Antiquity of Shamanism and Its Role in Human Religiosity," Homayun Sidky challenges the notion that Siberia and neighboring Uralic-Altaic Indigenous religions are the *locus classicus* of shamanism, surviving unchanged for millennia. For example, the form of South Asian shamanism practiced by the *jhākris* of Nepal is a dynamic and evolving practice. Shamanism is not "an ossified relic of an ancient and once universal religion. The idea that the belief systems of any people in any part of the world can persist unchanged over many millennia is simplistic and highly questionable. . . . There is an abundance of cross-cultural evidence demonstrating the fact that nowhere do magico-religious traditions remain unchanged." Homayun Sidky, "On the Antiquity of Shamanism and Its Role in Human Religiosity," *Method and Theory in the Study of Religion* 22 (2010): 71–74.

82 "Xi Ci I or The Great Treatise I 繫辭上" from the Ten Wings: 精氣為物，遊魂為變，是故知鬼神之情狀。

83 One example of such shamanistic practices is necromancy. In *Haunted by the Archaic Shaman,* anthropologist and ethnographer Homayun Sidky recounts a Nepalese shamanic ritual for raising the dead: The *jhākri* disciple began the ritual at midnight, playing thighbone and tiger bone trumpets to raise a *masān,* a spirit of the dead. A cock is sacrificed to raise a male spirit from the dead, and a hen would be used to raise a female spirit from the dead. Blood is a required sacrifice. The *jhākri* must also be naked, smeared with ashes from a crematory. A ghost mantra is repeated and the bone trumpets are played. Once the spirit of the dead has risen, it can be controlled by the *jhākri,* and questions can be asked of it. Sidky, *Haunted,* 70.

84 *Jun Shi* 君奭 from the *Shangshu* 尚書, noting: "在祖乙時，則有若巫賢。可知巫賢是商王祖乙時期擔任上帝與商王之間媒介任務的大巫。"

85 Pranee Liamputtong Rice and Pranee Liamputtong, *Hmong Women and Reproduction* (Westport, CT: Bergin & Garvey, 2000), 47.

86 Homayun Sidky, "On the Antiquity," 72.

87 陳夢家 [Chen Mengjia], 古文字中的商周祭祀 ["The ancient writings of the Shang and Zhou"], *Yenjing Journal* 19 (June 1936): 125–29.

88 My correspondences for Tiāndì (Shangdi) to Heaven, Shè to Earth, Fēng to Wind, Hé to Water, and Yuè to Mountain are self-explanatory, as the associations are rather literal. I associate Dōng Mǔ with Thunder due to the eastern direction and the trigram's connections to Wood in the Wu Xing cycle and Xī Mǔ to Lake through the directional and trigram connection to Metal. Morever, the western direction, Lake, and Metal correspond with the planet Venus, and in Taoist mysticism, Xī Wáng Mǔ, the Queen Mother of the West, would come to be associated with Venus.

89  陳夢家 [Chen Mengjia], 商代的神話與巫術 ["Myths and Wū Shamanism,"] 518–19. The concept of human sacrifice to appease the gods continued long after the Shang and even the Zhou. According to popular lore, in response to a seven-year drought, Emperor Shang 唐殤帝 or 少帝 (AD 695–714) of the Tang dynasty purportedly suggested offering himself to be burned as a sacrificial offering for the gods to bring rain. Although the emperor did not act on his suggestion, the offer moved the gods so much that immediately it began to rain. Historically accurate or not, the underpinning rationale of the lore exposes the enduring superstition that burning or drowning people as offerings can alleviate natural disasters.

90  In addition to ancestor veneration and tutelary gods, worship of the Mother Goddess has maintained an important position in the folk practices of the Vietnamese. The Mother Goddess is a triple goddess, or a union of Mother Goddesses, of the Three Realms: (1) a mother goddess of heaven or the skies, (2) a mother goddess of water, and (3) a mother goddess of mountains and forests. Worship of the Mother Goddess was also closely linked to shamanism among the ethnic groups of Vietnam. Vu Hong Van, "Origin of Worshipping the Mother Goddess in Vietnam," *Asian Research Journal of Arts and Social Sciences* 10, no. 2 (February 2020): 19–29.

91  From Shuo Gua 說卦 in the Ten Wings: "神也者、妙萬物而為言者也。" James Legge translates that line to: "When we speak of Spirit we mean the subtle (presence and operation of God) with all things."

92  Rice and Liamputtong, *Hmong Women*, 51.

93  Paja Thao, Lorne Dwight Conquergood, and Xa Thao, *I Am a Shaman: A Hmong Life Story with Ethnographic Commentary* (Minneapolis: Center for Urban and Regional Affairs, 1989), 51.

94  Sarangerel, *Riding Windhorses: A Journey into the Heart of Mongolian Shamanism* (Rochester, NY: Inner Traditions, 2000).

95  Plotnikoff et al., "Hmong Shamanism," 29–34.

96  Just to clarify, for simplicity and continuity of wording, I'm referring to many shamanistic practices as "soul retrieval" where some of those practices should be categorized as exorcisms. Southern Taiwanese and Fujianese practices that are equivalent in objective to soul retrieval are premised on the belief that a demon spirit has attached to part of a person's soul, causing decay or modifying the characteristics of that soul, so the purpose of ritual is to eradicate that demon spirit attachment to the soul. Thus, technically not all traditions of Asian shamanism include soul retrieval, but they *do* all include some form of practice *similar* in concept to soul retrieval.

97  Matsu was a tenth-century shaman and sorceress from the Fujian province of southern China, a Hokkein-speaking region of the mainland. She was spiritually trained under the tutelage of the bodhisattva Kuan Yin. In one legend about her,

during a severe storm that occurred while many of her village's fishermen were still out at sea, Matsu set her own house on fire so the flames could provide light for the fishermen to find their way back home. Matsu died at the age of twenty-eight in an act of self-sacrifice, taken by the seas after she saved a crew from a shipwreck. Upon her early death, Matsu was deified, and temples were built along the coast of southern China, the island of Taiwan, and other southeast Asian islander countries in her honor. When Hokkien migrants left the mainland in search of new homes across Asia, they brought statues and icons of Matsu with them to protect their travels and guide them on their journey across the seas. Where there is a presence of a Hokkien diaspora, there will be Matsu. She is particularly venerated by Hokkien Taiwanese islanders. Some of Matsu's most ardent devotees are fishing families whose livelihoods depend on the South China Sea. Since Matsu was a shaman and sorceress, in the present day she is often the goddess invoked by the *tâng ki* (the Taiwanese/Hokkien term for the Mandarin *jitong*), who are spirit mediums that channel Matsu. The twenty-third day of the third lunar month in the Chinese calendar is Matsu's birthday, and for seven days prior, those who venerate Matsu will take off work and go on a pilgrimage to the main Matsu temple. Incense is burned at sunrise and sunset as a ceremonial call to Matsu, inviting her presence for the celebrations that will be held in her honor. Then on the twenty-third, the spirit of Matsu will enter a local *tâng ki* or spirit medium and speak through the medium to bestow blessings upon the pilgrims. There is a vibrant traditional subculture in Asia for the veneration of Matsu, so distinct and independent in its own right that not even other fellow Asians fully understand the subculture. During the annual weeklong pilgrimage in Matsu's honor, pilgrims will walk the entire way, for seven days straight, loudly reciting mantras, channeling Matsu, purporting to be possessed by spirits, and they will get their fortunes read by priests or priestesses of Matsu. Devotees will swear to having paranormal or miraculous experiences during the pilgrimage, in addition to passionate testimonies of Matsu sightings. Matsu is of great cultural importance to me as a Taiwanese. I'm Hokkien (though we say "Minnan") on my mother's side, and southern Taiwan, where we're from, is mostly Hokkien. The myths and legends of Matsu are beautiful examples of how Buddhism, Taoism, and regional folk religions get syncretized. As a shamanic healer, Matsu was in effect practicing Taoist magic, but then she was said to be a disciple of Kuan Yin, a Buddhist bodhisattva. She's also region-specific to the Hokkien and to fishing or southern coastal and islander communities. She was also renowned as her community's local shaman. Until you've physically been to the South China Sea, Matsu can feel theoretical. Once you're there, it's hard not to be convinced that she's real. There are countless stories of Westerners who find themselves in the region and in a moment of jeopardy encounter Matsu, and who later swear up and down that a divine goddess of the seas saved them. An entire body of urban legends with that theme are dated to the World War II era.

98  The two most common invocation calls to deity are "召請" *(zhào qǐng)* as used here to invoke Kuan Yin and Matsu, and the one we worked with earlier for invoking the Lady of Mystery (the Lady of the Nine Heavens), which was "拜請" *(bài qǐng).* The two can be used interchangeably. That said, *zhào qǐng* makes more sense when invoking a god, celestial, buddha, or bodhisattva for inner alchemical cultivation practices, or in meditation. Alternatively, *bài qǐng,* as used here, makes more sense when you're asking that divinity to endow you with a blessing or perform a particular miracle. In short, in general devotionals to deity, *zhào qǐng* works. If you are hoping the deity will do something for you, go with the more formal *bài qǐng.*

99  Turner, *Sky Shamans,* 92.

100  Turner.

101  Turner, 115.

102  Can you perform a soul retrieval ritual on yourself? The efficacy of having the ritual performed by someone whose authority we trust is precisely because of that perceived authority. When we are afflicted, we distrust ourselves. We lack confidence. It feels good to push ownership and responsibility onto someone else. We want to lean back, close our eyes, and have someone else do all the work. The comforting feeling of being handled with care is a significant part of the magic. But if you are willing to achieve magic by the harder route and take ownership of your own health, then yes, you can absolutely perform a soul (fragment) retrieval ritual on yourself.

103  Suzanne Elizabeth Cahill, *Transcendence and Divine Passion: The Queen Mother of the West in Medieval China* (Stanford, CA: Stanford University Press, 1993), 11–12.

104  The 1956 text 殷墟卜辭綜述 *(Yīn xū bǔ cí zòng shù)* by Chen Mengjia 陈梦家 remains one of the most comprehensive texts on Shang oracle bones, deciphering over seven hundred thousand words of oracle bone inscriptions. Chen noted that the most common structure of a divination record was: the name of the god or ancestor called upon, the dates when sacrifices and offerings were made to that god or ancestor, what the sacrifices or offerings were (usually the number of animals and what types of animals), and a record of the weather on that day (e.g., rain, wind, astrological alignments, moon phases, etc.).

105  Cahill, *Transcendence,* 12.

106  *The Travels of Zhou Mu Wang* 穆天子傳 *(Mù tiānzǐ chuán)*, a biographical travelogue written between 976 and 922 BC, described a king of Zhou's encounter with the Western Mother. The text was intended to serve as a factual historical chronicle but is colored by fanciful encounters with gods, goddesses, and mythical creatures. The king writes about meeting Xī Wáng Mǔ in the west. (Present-day scholars theorize that he was in the Pamir Mountains near the Himalayas.) He describes her as graceful, sophisticated, and residing in a palace on Kunlun Mountain. In the *Biography of Mu Tianzi*, she's noted as the daughter of the Jade Emperor, though in other folktales she's married to the Jade Emperor. In Taoist metaphysics, she's often paired with the Grand Duke of the East 東王公 (Dōng Wáng Gōng). If you consider Xī Wáng Mǔ and the Xī Mǔ referenced in Shang oracle bones to be the same, then the Queen Mother's first counterpart was Dōng Mǔ, Eastern Mother.

107  As described in *Songs of the Eminent Ones* 大人賦 *(Dà Rén Fù)* by Sima Xiangru 司馬相如 (179–117 BC).

108  Jade Maidens 玉女 (Yùnǔ) are celestials who also have powers that a mystic can call upon. They're invoked as patron protectors over homes, shrines, or altars, and they can also serve as psychopomps, or guides through the underworld. Their roles in the celestial realm range from handmaidens to warriors. For instance, the Jade Maidens that attend to the Lady of the Nine Heavens are usually depicted as warrior spirits (depicted in figure 8.1 in chapter 8), while the Jade Maidens that attend to the Queen Mother of the West are depicted as handmaidens.

109  The fourth century BC text *Classic of Mountains and Seas* 山海經 *(Shān hǎi jīng)* describes a realm atop the mountain called the kingdom of Wu Xian 巫咸國, named after the great Ancestor Wu Xian, forefather of shamans, who lived during the Shang dynasty. This astral realm of the shamans is where a mythical yellow bird 黃鳥 *(huáng niǎo)* is native, along with a mysterious black/indigo snake 玄蛇 *(xuán shé)*. "山海經 [Classic of mountains and seas]," Chinese Text Project, ed. Donald Sturgeon, accessed July 7, 2022, https://ctext.org/shan-hai-jing/zh.

110  From the Western Mountain Sutra 西山經 *(Xī Shān Jīng)* from the *Classic of Mountains and Seas* 山海經 (475–220 BC), 49: 又西三百五十里，曰玉山，是西王母所居也。西王母其狀如人，豹尾虎齒而善嘯，蓬髮戴勝，是司天之厲及五殘。 Three hundred and fifty *li* to the west is Jade Mountain, where Xi Wang Mu dwells. Xi Wang Mu (Queen Mother of the West) resembles a human, with a leopard tail and the teeth of a tiger, a good howl, long and wild ragged hair, and a crown of colorful bird feathers. "西山經," Chinese Text Project, ed. Donald Sturgeon, accessed June 26, 2022, https://ctext.org/shan-hai-jing/xi-shan-jing.

111 Paintings on Majiayao 馬家窯文化 (3000–2000 BC) pottery featured human figures with zoomorphic components, such as leopard prints and tiger stripes. Sandrine Larrivé-Bass, "Embodied Materials: The Emergence of Figural Imagery in Prehistoric China" (PhD thesis, Columbia University, 2015), 105.

112 The 太玄數 *("Tài xuán shù")* is a chapter from the Eastern Han (2 BC) text *Canon of Supreme Mystery* 太玄經 *(Tài xuán jīng)* by Yang Xiong (53 BC–AD 18). The text names the nine heavens: "九天：一為中天 (Zhongtian), 二為羨天 (Xiantian), 三為從天 (Congtian), 四為更天 (Gengtian), 五為睟天 (Guantian), 六為廓天 (Kuotian), 七為減天 (Jiantian), 八為沈天 (Shentian), 九為成天 (Chengtian)." The Tài Xuán Jīng is a divinatory system inspired by the I Ching, whereby a solid line – represents Heaven 天, a broken line -- is Earth 地, and a twice-broken line ⋯ is Humanity 人. "太玄數," Chinese Text Project, ed. Donald Sturgeon, accessed July 9, 2022, https://ctext.org/taixuanjing/tai-xuan-shu/zhs.

113 "大宗師 - The Great and Most Honored Master," from the Zhuangzi 莊子, also known as 南華真經 *(nán huá zhēn jīng)*, Chinese Text Project, ed. Donald Sturgeon, accessed June 26, 2022, https://ctext.org/zhuangzi.

114 "大宗師 - The Great and Most Honored Master," Chinese Text Project.

115 The word "厲" in reference to the Five Destructions constellation or Demon Star (Algol) appears several dozen times throughout the Zhouyi. For example, "貞厲" *(zhēn lì)* appears several times, e.g., Hexagram 6, line 3; Hexagram 9, line 6; Hexagram 10, line 5; Hexagram 21, line 5; Hexagram 34, line 3; Hexagram 35, line 4 (noting how the Queen Mother was referenced earlier in Hexagram 35); Hexagram 49, line 3; and Hexagram 56, line 3. The phrase can be used in hexes and curses. Recite the name of the target and then "貞厲" *(zhēn lì)*. Alternatively, the phrase can be recited first, followed by utterance of the target's name.

116 The Living Sutra of the Queen Mother of the West, 洞真西王母寶神起居經.

117 Cahill, *Transcendence,* 11–12.

118 The Yaochidao 瑤池道 was a Taoist secret society that organized underground during the Qing dynasty and early Maoist era in China. The religion is heavily rooted in mystical practices, such as thaumaturgy, Fu talisman crafting, channeling spirits, shamanistic practices, speaking in tongues, faith healing, and divination. Many became political refugees in Taiwan and now continue to have a significant minority presence on the island. The Yaochidao is an offshoot lineage of a more prominent Taoist religious sect, the Tiandao 天道, or Way of Heaven, founded during the Yuan dynasty (AD 1271–1368). Groups such as the White Lotus, Tiandao, and Yaochidao are considered subversive, rebel, heterodox groups and are often politically active against authoritarian regimes.

119  The *Yì wěi* 易緯 (127–200 AD) instructs on using Hexagram 63 in exorcism spells to vanquish demons. The line being referenced is from the third line, "高宗伐鬼方" *(Gāozōng fá guǐ fāng),* translating to "Gaozong [Ancestor Wu Ding] vanquishes the demons." The line can be modified to invoke the Queen Mother of the West to punish and curse someone who has gravely wronged you and who has not received due punishment for the transgression. Using a ritual dagger, sharpen the tip of a tree branch until it is a deadly spike. Write the target's full name and as many personal identifiers as you can onto a piece of parchment, or alternatively, use a photograph of the target. With red ink, write the following character over the perpetrator's name or photograph: 鬼. Pierce the parchment or photograph (or both) with the spike. Set it up at the tip of a mound atop a campfire outdoors in the remote woods. Perform this ritual late at night under a waning crescent or dark moon. Pour a hard liquor of at least 100 proof on the branch, and light the campfire from its base, so that the fire does not start with your spike or the target's identifier. In front of the campfire on a makeshift altar, light three sticks of incense, and pour a tall chalice of the hard liquor as an offering. As the fire begins, call upon the dark and feral goddess, Queen Mother of the West. Invoke her by reciting "Bài qǐng Xi Wang Mu" (拜請西王母) seven times. (Translation: "I call upon Queen Mother of the West.") Kneel on the ground before the fire and state your case: who you are, who the perpetrator is, what happened, and why the perpetrator needs to be punished. When the fire has grown tall enough to reach your spike, begin the recitation modified from Hexagram 63: 王母伐鬼 (Wáng Mǔ fá guǐ), meaning "the Queen Mother defeats and vanquishes the demon." When you recite such an exorcism incantation, it must be done with the tone and display of authority of judge, jury, and executioner. The reference Wáng Mǔ 王母 becomes both a reference to your ancestors and to Queen Mother of the West (Xi Wang Mu, 西王母). The maternal instincts of your ancestors who are listening—and, of course, the Queen Mother of the West—are triggered, and they'll come to your assistance. After the campfire is extinguished, pour out the liquor offering onto the earth in a counterclockwise circle.

120  "八正神明論" [The eightfold gods], in the 黃帝內經 *(Huángdì nèi jīng)* [Yellow Emperor's classic of internal medicine], Chinese Text Project, ed. Donald Sturgeon, accessed July 7, 2022, https://ctext.org/huangdi-neijing/zh.

121  The original text in "The Eightfold Gods" reads: "帝曰：何謂神?"

122  Translation of "岐伯曰：請言神，神乎神，耳不聞，目明，心開而志先，慧然獨悟，口弗能言，俱視獨見，適若昏，昭然獨明，若風吹雲，故曰神。三部九候為之原，九針之論，不必存也。" "八正神明論" [The eightfold gods], Chinese Text Project.

## 11. Returning Full Circle

1. Yang Li, *Book of Changes and Traditional Chinese Medicine* (Beijing: Beijing Science and Technology Press, 1998), 30.
2. Trian Nguyen, "Provisions for the Soul: The Yao Objects in the Museum of International Folk Art's *Sacred Realm* Exhibition," *El Palacio* (winter 2016): 68–75; Trian Nguyen, *How to Make the Universe Right: The Art of the Shaman from Vietnam and Southern China* (Santa Barbara, CA: Art, Design & Architecture Museum, UC Santa Barbara, 2015).
3. The Book of Documents 書經 (Shūjīng), one of the Five Classics of Chinese literature, notes the three virtues as follows: "乂用三德：正直、剛克、柔克" (integrity, fortitude, and tenderness). The line is found in the "洪范" *(Hóng fàn)* from the Book of Zhou 周書 (dynasty).

## 12. Appendices

1. "二十四節氣與八卦的對應關係" [Twenty-four solar terms correspondences and the Ba Gua], 故宮歷史網 the Palace Museum History Network, last modified August 25, 2021, accessed July 11, 2022, https://www.gugong.net/wenhua/27278.html.
2. Xú Chè 徐彻 and Lǐ Yànzhe 李焱著, *Hundred Buddhas of the Buddha Realm* 佛界百佛 (Shanghai: 上海三聯書店 Shanghai Sanlian Publishing, 2019), 50.
3. "商朝" [(Historical maps of the) Shang dynasty], 歷史地圖網 Historical Map Network, accessed July 12, 2022, https://www.historical-map.com/mpcn/shangchao-1.html.
4. "西周" [(Historical maps of the) Zhou dynasty], 歷史地圖網 Historical Map Network, accessed July 12, 2022, https://www.historical-map.com/mpcn/xizhou-1.html.
5. [(Historical maps of the) Zhou dynasty].
6. Historian and scholar Wang Guowei 王國維 (1877–1927) is credited as being the first to propose this theory.
7. Maotao Wen, "The Creation of the Qiang Ethnicity, Its Relation to the Rme People and the Preservation of Rme Language" (master's thesis, Duke University, 2005), 56–57.
8. Anthony R. Walker, *Merit and the Millennium: Routine and Crisis in the Ritual Lives of the Lahu People* (Delhi: Hindustan Publishing, 2003), 59, 754.
9. "Xióng 熊 ('bear') was the totem and royal clan name of the ancient south central state of Chu (704–223 BC)." Shuheng Zhang, "Three Ancient Words for Bear," *Sino-Platonic Papers* no. 294 (November 2019): 3.

10 When the kingdoms of Wu and Yue fell during the Warring States period (403–222 BC), the ruling families fled to Japan. These ruling families were the descendants of a Xia king who founded the kingdom of Yue. Wai-ming Ng, *Imagining China in Tokugawa Japan: Legends, Classics, and Historical Terms* (Albany: State University of New York Press, 2019), 50–52.
11 Ward Hunt Goodenough, ed., *Prehistoric Settlement of the Pacific* (Philadelphia: American Philosophical Society, 1996), 48. Thus, the Taiwanese are descendants of the kingdom of Yue.
12 Nam C. Kim, "Sinicization and Barbarization: Ancient State Formation at the Southern Edge of Sinitic Civlization," in *Imperial China and Its Southern Neighbors*, ed. Victor H. Mair and Liam C. Kelley (Singapore: Institute of Southeast Asian Studies, 2016).
13 Thich Nhat Hanh, *Master Tang Hôi: First Zen Teacher in Vietnam and China* (Berkeley, CA: Parallax Press, 2001), 2.
14 Hanh, *Master Tang Hôi*, 2.
15 Hanh.

# INDEX

## A

The Abyss. Kǎn (Hexagram 29), 537–42
Accolades. Dà Yǒu (Hexagram 14), 460–64
Adler, Joseph, 124
adornments, 500, 501–2
Advancement. Jìn (Hexagram 35), 571–77
After the Ending. Jì Jì (Hexagram 63), 738–45, 747, 750
Agents, Five. *See* Wu Xing
Agni, 195
Akashagarbha, 840
alchemy
    cosmological trinities in, 351
    cycles of creation and destruction, 245–46
    Gua Qi school, 52
    inner, 87, 220–22, 230
    main rules of, 245–46
    six keys of Eudoxus, 351, 352
Algol, 807
Alliance. Bǐ (Hexagram 8), 428–33
altar
    definition of, 760
    setting up, 760–63
Amitabha, 271
ancestor veneration, 3, 755–71
Archetypes of the Mystic, Eight, 167, 241, 242, 793–94
The Army. Shī (Hexagram 7), 424–28
Arts of Taoist Metaphysics, Five. *See* Mystical Arts, Five
Ascent to Heaven spirit body journeying technique, 174–78
Assembly. Cuì (Hexagram 45), 628–32
astral journeying, 174–77, 221, 259–60, 668, 782, 784, 821
astrology
    horary, 324–39
    natal, 240
    Wu Xing and, 235–36
Âu Lạc, 845
auspicious vs. inauspicious, 380
Avalokiteshvara, 841

## B

Ba Gua (Eight Trigrams)
    arrangements of, 163–67
    constructing hexagrams with, xx–xxi
    Early Heaven (Fuxi's), 12, 17, 135, 161, 163–64, 167
    Earth (Kūn), 222–25
    Eight Bodhisattvas and, 840–41
    Eight Immortals and, 155, 167–69
    feng shui and, 839
    Fire (Lí), 188–91
    Five Mystical Arts and, 791
    Four Faces of God and, 153, 157–60
    gods corresponding to, 793–94
    Heaven (Qián), 172–74
    Lake (Duì), 179–82
    Later Heaven (King Wen's), 17, 163–67
    Lo Shu magic square and, 104–5, 164
    Mountain (Gěn), 218–20
    numerical assignments for, 132
    origins of, 11–12
    Plum Blossom, 135
    standardized correspondences for, 166–67

Ba Gua (Eight Trigrams) *(continued)*
   stems, branches, and, 837–38
   Taiji and, 164
   tarot and, 347, 357–58
   thaumaturgical order of, 55
   Thunder (Zhèn), 196–99
   Water (Kǎn), 212–14
   Western elements and, 153
   Wind (Xùn), 203–6
   Wu Xing and, 170, 242–43, 245–47
   yin and yang in, 12, 13, 96, 132, 133, 155–60
   Zodiac and, 171
Basic Classic. *See* Zhouyi
Baynes, Cary F., 386
Ba Zi (Eight Terms), 235–36
Beidi, 794
Benyi, 40
*bhumisparsha* mudra, 225–26
Bǐ. Alliance (Hexagram 8), 428–33
Biànyì, 102
bibliomancy, 137–40
Big Dipper, 690, 691, 694
*bigu*, 581
Bì. Luminosity (Hexagram 22), 499–506
binding spell, 563
birth date, Mystical Art associated with, 243–44
birth month, hexagrams ruling, 52–56
Bite Through. Shih Hé (Hexagram 21), 420, 493–98
black, symbolism of, 275
blackbirds, 453
Black Tortoise, 257, 611, 635, 694, 762, 764–67, 770, 805, 839
Blockade. Kùn (Hexagram 47), 637–43
Bodhisattvas, Eight, 840–41
book divination method. *See* bibliomancy
Book of Documents, 228, 232, 265, 774, 787
Book of Rites, 31, 33, 608, 744, 773
Book of the River Maps, 12, 160–62, 826
Bō. Partition (Hexagram 23), 506–12

Boundaries. Jié (Hexagram 60), 718–23
Bouvet, Joachim, 62, 63, 74–75
Boxer Rebellion, 65
Bo Yikao, 21
Buddha, 225–26, 485, 765, 801, 840, 842
Buddhism, 4, 8, 31, 57, 65, 137, 141, 153, 194, 229, 239, 267, 345, 668, 672, 762, 778, 798, 841
Buddhist hexagram interpretation, 140–45
Burgeoning. Yì (Hexagram 42), 612–17
Burning of the Books and Burying of the Confucian Scholars, 34–35
Bùyì, 102

C

Cai Yuanding, 95
cangue, 498
Caodaism, 57
Cao Guo Jiu, 168, 169, 197–202, 794
Cao Xinyi, 345
Carus, Paul, 13, 757
Castro-Chavez, Fernando, 80
The Cauldron. Dǐng (Hexagram 50), 653–61
cauldrons, 118–19, 655
Celestial Stars, Three, 279, 350
Chang-Er, 175, 454, 682
changing lines, 111–12, 116–20, 129–30, 138, 231, 261, 289–92, 296, 298–306, 308–9, 312, 318–19, 321–22, 326, 334–35, 338, 340, 359–61, 364–68
channeled divination method, 125–30, 341–45
Cheng Yi, 113–15, 477
Chen Mengjia, 774
Chen Shu, 2, 29, 92
Chu, kingdom of, 754, 844
civil suits, omen of, 420
clarity, fire ritual for, 191–94
Cleary, Thomas, 124, 129
Clymer, Reuben Swinburne, 69
coin toss divination method, 89–90, 216, 267, 296–309

Index 915

Confucianism, 6, 27, 34, 37, 42, 45, 57, 61, 64, 239, 383, 604, 782, 783, 784
Confucius, 26–27, 34, 36–37, 40, 50, 51, 87, 373, 496, 580
cowrie shell divination method, 310–12, 764–71
Creative Power. Qián (Hexagram 1), 389–94
criminal suits, omen of, 494
"crossing the great stream," 387–88
Crowley, Aleister, 69–74, 75, 123, 147, 267, 305–6, 346, 347, 353
crows, 415, 453, 781
crystal lotus, 207–9
Cuì. Assembly (Hexagram 45), 628–32
Cultivate Gently. Xiǎo Chù (Hexagram 9), 433–38
Cultivate the Supreme. Dà Chù (Hexagram 26), 523–26
Cultural Revolution, 60

## D

Dà Chù. Cultivate the Supreme (Hexagram 26), 523–26
Dà Guò. Undertake the Great (Hexagram 28), 532–36
Daji, 19–21, 25, 29, 584, 623, 627, 798
dance
    I Ching divination by, 776–77
    shamanism and, 775, 782
*daren* (eminent one), 383–84
Darkening of the Light. Míng Yí (Hexagram 36), 577–86
Dà Yǒu. Accolades (Hexagram 14), 460–64
Dà Zhuàng. Great Power (Hexagram 34), 566–71
Debilitation. Sǔn (Hexagram 41), 607–12
Decay. Gǔ (Hexagram 18), 478–83
Decisive Action. Guài (Hexagram 43), 617–21
depth psychology, 66
Destructions, Five, 807
Dharma Fan, 184–88
Dǐng. The Cauldron (Hexagram 50), 653–61

divination. *See also* hexagram interpretation
    as art, 292
    channeled method, 125–30, 341–45
    coin toss method, 89–90, 216, 267, 296–309
    as conversation, 88
    cowrie shell method, 310–12, 764–71
    by dance, 776–77
    to find lost objects, 364–67
    fortune-telling vs., 145–46
    history of, 97, 267
    horary astrology method, 324–39
    invoking Divinity and presenting the question, 270–73
    numerological method, 131–38, 339–41
    oracle bone, 16, 25, 33–34, 381
    Originalist approach to, 40, 41
    Personality Profile reading, 367–71
    Plum Blossom methods, 267, 313–45
    preparations before, 268–70
    psychic health readings, 261–64
    Rationalist approach to, 39
    rice grains method, 314–24
    space for, 269
    tarot card method, 267, 345–58, 362–65
    wind, 209–11
    Wu Xing and, 239
    yarrow stalk method, 97, 267, 270, 273–95, 811–17
Di Yi of Shang, Emperor, 150–51, 448, 683, 686, 687, 694
DNA, 76–80, 82
Dōng Mǔ, 792, 793, 794, 805
Dong Wang Gong, 794
Dongyue, Emperor, 401, 672, 794
Dong Zhongshu, 139, 238, 249, 250, 252, 254, 256
dreamwork, 782
Duì (Lake), 179–82
Duì. Joyous Exchange (Hexagram 58), 706–10

Du Jiyuan, 152
Duke of Zhou, 23, 24–25, 27, 40, 64, 99–100, 108, 228, 359, 565, 572, 683, 744, 774, 782, 783, 815, 826
Dùn. Withdraw (Hexagram 33), 560–66, 568

## E

Earth (Kūn), 222–25
Earth (Tǔ), 232, 252–53
Earth Goddess, calling upon, 223–27
Eastern Mother, 792, 794, 805
Eclectism, 58
eclipses, 694
Edmond, Magus, 356
"endeavor for corrective measures," 386
Enthusiasm. Yù (Hexagram 16), 468–72
The Eternal. Héng (Hexagram 32), 555–60
Eudoxus of Cnidus, 351, 352
exorcism rituals, 743, 797

## F

Faces of God, Four, 153, 157–60, 234–35
Faith Within. Zhōng Fú (Hexagram 61), 724–30
The Family. Jiā Rén (Hexagram 37), 586–91
Fangfeng, 430
Fǎn Hún Xiāng, 803
Faraday, Michael, 353
fasting, 580–81
Fellowship. Tóng Rén (Hexagram 13), 455–59
Fēng, 792, 793, 794
Fengbo, 794
*fenghuang*, 204–5
*fēng jiǎo*, 209–11
Fēng. Opulence (Hexagram 55), 688–94
Fēng Pópo, 706, 794
feng shui, 191, 207, 211, 239, 269, 839
Fire (Huǒ), 231, 250–51
Fire (Lí), 188–91
fire ritual for clarity and advancement, 191–94
fish drum, 220

fortune-telling vs. divination, 145–46
Fountainhead. Jǐng (Hexagram 48), 643–48
Fǒu. Stalemate (Hexagram 12), 449–55
Fu Hao, 24–25, 310, 552, 741, 781
Fù. Repose (Hexagram 24), 513–17
Fu talismans, 83, 84, 483, 743, 784
Fuxi, 11–12, 13, 17, 27, 68–69, 75, 135, 158–59, 163–64, 167, 178, 810
Fuxi order, 375, 379

## G

Gan Bao, 59
Gao, duke of Bi, 525, 573
Gaozong. *See* Wu Ding of Shang, King
geese, wild, 675, 677
Gěn (Mountain), 218–20
Gěn. Listen to the Wind (Hexagram 52), 666–72
Gé. Revolution (Hexagram 49), 649–53, 655
Ghost Festival, 759
Ghost Month, 759
Gija (Jizi), 583, 584, 585, 845
gods of Shang shamanism, 792–95
Gòu. Improper Meeting (Hexagram 44), 622–27
Goujian of Yue, King, 93, 547–48, 845
gourd, healing, 215–17
Grand Duke of the East, 810
Great Compassion Mantra, 798
Great Power. Dà Zhuàng (Hexagram 34), 566–71
Guà Biàn, 111–12
Guài. Decisive Action (Hexagram 43), 617–21
Guān. Observation (Hexagram 20), 488–92
Gua Qi school, 45–52, 56
Guarding of the One meditation, 258–60
Gu Dao, 482
Gǔ. Decay (Hexagram 18), 478–83
Guifang devils, 740, 742, 743, 749–50, 844
Guī Mèi. The Marrying Maiden (Hexagram 54), 454, 680–87

Guo Kuntao, 265
Guo Xu, 12
*Guo yu*, 774
Gu Quan, 177

# H

Hai, Prince. *See* Wang Hai
Haindl, Hermann, 346–47
Hǎi Ruò, 549
Hànbá, 781
Hangonkō, 803
Han Kangbo, 45
Han Xiangzi, 168, 169, 173–74, 793
Harmony. Tài (Hexagram 11), 443–49
Harrington, L. Michael, 123, 129
Hé, 792, 793, 794
Heaven (Qián), 172–74
Héng. The Eternal (Hexagram 32), 555–60
Hermetic Order of the Golden Dawn, 72, 74
Hé Tú, 161–62, 163
hexagram interpretation. *See also* divination
    auspicious vs. inauspicious, 380
    Buddhist, 140–45
    "crossing the great stream," 387–88
    cultivating objective, 150–52
    "endeavor for corrective measures," 386
    general insights on, 145–50
    Image and Number tradition (Xiàng Shù), 95, 98, 99, 103–12, 131, 166, 248, 262, 267, 296, 297, 298, 324, 365, 366
    locked hexagrams, 292, 302, 308–9, 312–13, 361
    Meaning and Principle tradition (Yì Lǐ), 95, 98–99, 112–30, 156, 169, 296, 297, 298, 312
    to offer sacrifice and to divine, 380–82
    summary outline of, 358–61
    "there is no blame," 385–86
    Three Meanings of Change, 102–3
hexagrams (general)
    birth month ruled by, 52–56
    constructing, with trigrams, xx–xxi

feudal hierarchy of lines, 115–16, 313
first sequence, 375–76
implied secret, 827–28
locked, 292, 302, 308–9, 312–13, 361
numbering sequences for, 60–61, 375, 379
number of, 348
principle of, 116
*qi* of, 44, 67–68, 83–84, 96, 105–6, 148
rulers, 109, 115
second sequence, 377–78
Solomonic, 349, 350
transformations, 111–12
hexagrams (specific)
    1: Qián. Creative Power, 389–94
    2: Kūn. Supportive Power, 395–401
    3: Tún. Initial Challenge, 402–7
    4: Méng. Naiveté, 407–13
    5: Xū. Patience, 414–19
    6: Sòng. The Trial, 419–23, 494
    7: Shī. The Army, 424–28
    8: Bǐ. Alliance, 428–33
    9: Xiǎo Chù. Cultivate Gently, 433–38
    10: Lǚ. Treading, 438–43
    11: Tài. Harmony, 443–49
    12: Fǒu. Stalemate, 449–55
    13: Tóng Rén. Fellowship, 455–59
    14: Dà Yǒu. Accolades, 460–64
    15: Qiān. Modesty, 464–68
    16: Yù. Enthusiasm, 468–72
    17: Suí. Inspiring Followers, 473–77
    18: Gǔ. Decay, 478–83
    19: Lín. Spring Is Coming, 484–88
    20: Guān. Observation, 488–92
    21: Shih Hé. Bite Through, 420, 493–98
    22: Bì. Luminosity, 499–506
    23: Bō. Partition, 506–12
    24: Fù. Repose, 513–17
    25: Wú Wàng. Without Folly, 518–22
    26: Dà Chù. Cultivate the Supreme, 523–26
    27: Yí. Receive Nourishment, 526–32

hexagrams (specific) *(continued)*
    28: Dà Guò. Undertake the Great, 532–36
    29: Kǎn. The Abyss, 537–42
    30: Lí. The Spark, 542–49
    31: Xián. Mutual Accord, 550–54
    32: Héng. The Eternal, 555–60
    33: Dùn. Withdraw, 560–66, 568
    34: Dà Zhuàng. Great Power, 566–71
    35: Jìn. Advancement, 571–77
    36: Míng Yí. Darkening of the Light, 577–86
    37: Jiā Rén. The Family, 586–91
    38: Kuí. Opposition, 591–96
    39: Jiǎn. An Impasse, 597–601
    40: Jiě. Release of Tension, 602–7
    41: Sǔn. Debilitation, 607–12
    42: Yì. Burgeoning, 612–17
    43: Guài. Decisive Action, 617–21
    44: Gòu. Improper Meeting, 622–27
    45: Cuì. Assembly, 628–32
    46: Shēng. Hoist, 633–37
    47: Kùn. Blockade, 637–43
    48: Jǐng. Fountainhead, 643–48
    49: Gé. Revolution, 649–53, 655
    50: Dǐng. The Cauldron, 653–61
    51: Zhèn. Jolt, 661–66, 667
    52: Gěn. Listen to the Wind, 666–72
    53: Jiàn. Steadfast, 673–79
    54: Guī Mèi. The Marrying Maiden, 454, 680–87
    55: Fēng. Opulence, 688–94
    56: Lǚ. The Wanderer, 695–700
    57: Xùn. Use Gentle Force, 701–6
    58: Duì. Joyous Exchange, 706–10
    59: Huàn. Making Waves, 710–18
    60: Jié. Boundaries, 718–23
    61: Zhōng Fú. Faith Within, 724–30
    62: Xiǎo Guò. Pay Attention to Details, 121–24, 730–37
    63: Jì Jì. After the Ending, 738–45, 747, 750
    64: Wèi Jì. Toward an End, 745–53

He Xian Gu, 167–68, 169, 204–7, 786, 794
Hinduism, 194–95, 229
Hirata Atsutane, 58
Hoist. Shēng (Hexagram 46), 633–37
horary astrology, 324–39
horses, white, 503–4
Hou Ji, 843
Houtu, 401, 794
Houyi, 453, 454, 682
Huang, Alfred, 124
Huang, Kerson, 1, 70–71, 123, 128, 129, 574, 749
Huang Di. *See* Yellow Emperor
Huang Tao (Yellow Path), 48, 50, 54, 56
Huang Zongxi, 58
Huàn. Making Waves (Hexagram 59), 710–18
*hún*, 758
Huǒ (Fire), 231, 250–51

# I

I Ching. *See also* Ba Gua (Eight Trigrams); divination; hexagram interpretation; hexagrams; Wu Xing (Five Phases of Change); Yì Xué (I Ching scholarship)
    benefits of studying, 229, 230, 825
    circular pattern of, 823
    DNA and, 78–80
    etymology of, 7–8
    evolution of, 32
    as fundamental cornerstone, 3–4
    history of, 4–5, 26–27, 30, 31, 824
    Jesuit missionaries and, 61–65
    King Wen's revealed sequence, 60–61, 375, 379
    as mandala, 79, 81, 228–30, 823
    as mirror, 5, 30
    morality and, 34–35
    origins of, 9–10, 17–18, 29, 63, 773–75
    politics and, 58, 60
    shamanism and, 773–75
    square representation of, 79, 81
    tarot and, 72–73, 267, 345–58, 362–64

translations of, 62, 64–65, 70–71, 122–24, 374
universality of, 230
Western occultism and, 68–74
Zhouyi (Basic Classic), 24, 373–75
Image and Number tradition (Xiàng Shù), 95, 98, 99, 103–12, 131, 166, 248, 262, 267, 296, 297, 298, 324, 365, 366
Immortals, Eight, 155, 167–69, 227. *See also individual immortals*
An Impasse. Jiǎn (Hexagram 39), 597–601
Improper Meeting. Gòu (Hexagram 44), 622–27
Initial Challenge. Tún (Hexagram 3), 402–7
Inoue Kinga, 59
Inspiring Followers. Suí (Hexagram 17), 473–77
intermarriages, between different clans, 504

## J

jade, 178–79
Jade Emperor, 394, 810
Jesuit missionaries, 61–65
*jhākri*, 194, 787
Jiǎn. An Impasse (Hexagram 39), 597–601
Jiang Ziya (Grand Duke Jiang), 579–80, 627
Jiàn. Steadfast (Hexagram 53), 673–79
Jiao Bingzhen, 17, 829
Jiā Rén. The Family (Hexagram 37), 586–91
Jié. Boundaries (Hexagram 60), 718–23
Jiě. Release of Tension (Hexagram 40), 602–7
Jì Jì. After the Ending (Hexagram 63), 738–45, 747, 750
Jīn (Metal), 232, 254–55
Jìn. Advancement (Hexagram 35), 571–77
Jing Fang, 46, 58
Jǐng. Fountainhead (Hexagram 48), 643–48
Jing Guang hand mudra, 199, 200
Ji of Zhou, 753
Ji Shi, 228
Jiǔ Tiān Xuán Nǚ. *See* Mysterious Lady of the Nine Heavens

Jizi (Gija), 583, 584, 585, 845
Jolt. Zhèn (Hexagram 51), 661–66, 667
Joyous Exchange. Duì (Hexagram 58), 706–10
Jung, Carl Gustav, 33, 65–68, 69, 74, 88, 136
*junzi* (sage), 27, 74, 87, 382–83, 384

## K

*kalpas*, 137
Kǎn (Water), 212–14
Kanō Sansetsu, 10, 23
Kǎn. The Abyss (Hexagram 29), 537–42
Katen, 195
Keishu Takeuchi, 809
Kepler, Johannes, 134
King Wen's revealed sequence, 60–61, 166, 375, 379
*kirin*. *See qilin*
Krauth, Charles Porterfield, 62
Kshitigarbha, 841
Kuan Yin, 198, 271–72, 796, 798–802, 841
Kuí. Opposition (Hexagram 38), 591–96
Kūn (Earth), 222–25
Kùn. Blockade (Hexagram 47), 637–43
kundalini serpent, 533, 535–36
Kunlun, Mount, 735, 805–6, 810, 821
Kūn. Supportive Power (Hexagram 2), 395–401
*kut* rituals, 782–83

## L

LaCouperie, Albert Étienne Terrien de, 62–63
Lady of the Nine Heavens. *See* Mysterious Lady of the Nine Heavens
Lady Queen Mother, 805
Lake (Duì), 179–82
Lan Cai He, 168, 169, 198, 202, 204, 223–25, 241, 794
Lao Naixuan, 65
Lao Tzu, 8, 258, 554, 557
Legalism, 34–35

Legge, James, 64, 69, 109, 123, 216, 386
Lèi, 115
Leibniz, Gottfried Wilhelm von, 75–76, 135
Lei Gong, 200, 615
Lê Quý Đôn, 4
Levi, Eliphas, 68, 346, 349
Lévi-Strauss, Claude, 415
Lí (Fire), 188–91
light, meanings of, 579
*lìn*, 386
Ling Bao tradition, 260
Lín. Spring Is Coming (Hexagram 19), 484–88
Listen to the Wind. Gěn (Hexagram 52), 666–72
Lí. The Spark (Hexagram 30), 542–49
Li Tie Guai, 168–69, 204, 213–15, 240, 794
*liubo*, 753
Liu Xin, 37
Li Zehou, 773–74
locked hexagrams, 292, 302, 308–9, 312–13, 361
Longnu, 174
Lo Shu magic square, 12–13, 16, 17, 43, 104–5, 160–62, 164, 247, 832
lost objects, finding, 364–67
love and romance hexagrams, 551, 556, 674, 681
Lü Dong Bin, 167, 168, 169, 190–91, 199, 751, 793
Luminosity. Bì (Hexagram 22), 499–506
Lunar New Year, 756, 758
Luò Shū. *See* Lo Shu magic square
Lǚ. The Wanderer (Hexagram 56), 695–700
Lǚ. Treading (Hexagram 10), 438–43

# M

Madame of the Winds, 706
Mahādev, 787
Ma Hezhi, 27
Maitreya, 485, 840
Making Waves. Huàn (Hexagram 59), 710–18

Ma Lin, 14
mandalas, 79, 81, 228–30, 823
Mandate of Heaven, 13, 18, 22–24, 29, 37, 428, 622, 623, 650, 652, 655
Mañjushri, 840
mantras
 definition of, 195
 Great Compassion Mantra, 798
 Pavamāna Mantra, 194–96
 to reverse misfortune, 538–39
 Small Victories, Gain by Gain Mantra, 435
Mao Zedong, 60
Mara, 223
marquis of Kang, 119, 572–73
marriage
 by abduction, 595, 596
 between different clans, 504
The Marrying Maiden. Guī Mèi (Hexagram 54), 454, 680–87
Matsu, 787, 792, 794, 796
Mawangdui order, 60–61, 375, 379
McClatchie, Canon Thomas, 62–64, 123
McDonald, Michael, 367–69
Meaning and Principle tradition (Yì Lǐ), 95, 98–99, 112–30, 156, 169, 296, 297, 298, 312
Meanings of Change, Three, 102–3
Méng. Naiveté (Hexagram 4), 407–13
Meng Xi, 46
messianism, Buddhist, 485
Metal (Jīn), 232, 254–55
Mianshen, King, 512
Milky Way, 161, 445
Míng Yí. Darkening of the Light (Hexagram 36), 577–86
Modesty. Qiān (Hexagram 15), 464–68
Mountain (Gěn), 218–20
Mozi, 246
Mù (Wood), 231, 248–49
mudras
 *bhumisparsha*, 225–26
 Jing Guang, 199, 200

mulberry trees, 453
muskmelon, white, 626, 627
Mutual Accord. Xián (Hexagram 31), 550–54
Muye, Battle of, 22–24, 579–80, 582, 694, 735
Mysterious Heavenly Bird of Destiny, 415, 845
Mysterious Lady of the Nine Heavens (Jiŭ Tiān Xuán Nǚ), 91–93, 125, 175, 176, 178, 271–73, 342, 343–45, 348, 349, 353, 400, 415, 547–48, 743, 807, 810–11, 818, 824, 826, 845
Mystical Arts, Five, 238–44, 790–91
mystical cultivation, guiding principles for, 413
mysticism, Taoist, 82–86

## N

Naiveté. Méng (Hexagram 4), 407–13
Needles, Nine, 818
Nemoto Michiaki, 58, 59
Neo-Confucianism, 57
New Culture Movement, 60
new moon purification ritual, 194–96
New Text vs. Old Text schools, 36–37
Newton, Isaac, 353
Nezha, 796
Nirenberg, Marshall, 79
numerological divination method, 131–38, 339–41
Nǚwā, 11, 19, 20, 137, 273, 694, 807, 810, 824

## O

Observation. Guān (Hexagram 20), 488–92
occultism, Western, 68–74
*okubi,* 582
Old Text vs. New Text schools, 36–37
Opposition: Kuí (Hexagram 38), 591–96
Opulence. Fēng (Hexagram 55), 688–94
oracle bone divination, 16, 26, 33–34, 381
Oracle school, 59

Originalists vs. Rationalists, 38–42
ouroboros, 160
Ouyi Zhi-xu, 141

## P

Partition. Bō (Hexagram 23), 506–12
Patience. Xū (Hexagram 5), 414–19
Pavamāna Mantra, 194–96
Pay Attention to Details. Xiăo Guò (Hexagram 62), 121–24, 730–37
Perfected Hexagrams, Four, 48–50
Personality Profile reading, 367–71
Phases of Change, Five. *See* Wu Xing
phoenix
  *fenghuang,* 204–5
  flaming, 737
  imperial, 601
  nine-headed, 754, 844
Pillars of Destiny, Four, 236
Plum Blossom methods, 131–40, 243, 267, 313–45
*pò,* 758
poison magic, 82–83, 482–83
prosperity talisman, 182–84
protection
  jade amulet for, 178–79
  knotted red string bracelet for, 802
psychic health readings, 261–64
Pure Land Mahayana Buddhism, 65, 140, 141
Pure Ones, Three, 350–51, 394, 798

## Q

Qabalah, 32, 70, 72–74, 75, 346
*qi*
  of hexagrams, 44, 67–68, 83–84, 96, 105–6, 148
  Wu Xing and, 231, 232, 236–37
  yin and yang, 95–96, 231
Qi, state of, 845
Qián (Heaven), 172–74
Qián. Creative Power (Hexagram 1), 389–94
Qiang, 844

Qianlong, Emperor, 388
Qiān. Modesty (Hexagram 15), 464–68
Qibo, 817, 818
*qilin,* 396, 465, 508, 668
Qin Shi Huang, Emperor, 35
Qishan (Mount Qi), 477, 636
Queen Mother of the West (Xī Wáng Mǔ), 91, 173, 175–78, 271, 516, 574, 735, 792, 793, 796, 804–17, 818, 824, 826
questioning, repeated, 408, 409

# R

Ranks of Nobility, Five (Wǔ Jué), 109–10, 307, 313
Rationalists vs. Originalists, 38–42
rats, 575–76
realgar wine, 482
Receive Nourishment. Yí (Hexagram 27), 526–32
*Records of the Grand Historian,* 87, 627, 753
Regardie, Israel, 351
Release of Tension. Jiě (Hexagram 40), 602–7
Repose. Fù (Hexagram 24), 513–17
retributive justice magic, 201–3
Revolution. Gé (Hexagram 49), 649–53, 655
Ricci, Matteo, 61–62
rice grains divination method, 314–24
River Maps, Book of the, 12, 160–62, 826
RNA, 77

# S

Sacred Tortoise, 528
sacrificial offerings, 26, 380–82, 744
Samantabhadra, 820, 841
Sarvanivaranavishkambhin, 841
School of Mystery, 45
Schrödinger, Erwin, 354
The Scriptures of the Great Peace, 258
Seiōbo, 809, 810
Seowangmo, 810

*Seven Signs of Yunji,* 92
sexagenary cycle, 132–34
Shakti, 533
shamanism
 astral journeying and, 782
 by culture, 777–79, 783–86
 dance and, 775, 782
 definition of, 786
 dreamwork and, 782
 etymology of, 777–79
 gods of Shang, 792–95
 historical traditions of, 780–86
 I Ching's origins and, 773–75
 soul retrieval, 795–803
Shangdi, 61–62, 64, 394, 614, 694, 712–13, 753, 792, 793
Shang dynasty, map of, 843
Shangqing school, 260
Shanshin, 794
Shao Yong (Shao Kangjie), 67, 131, 134–37, 229, 267, 268, 313, 314, 316, 324, 335, 336, 339, 343, 349, 375, 379, 764
Shè, 792, 793, 794
*shén*
 healing inner, 817–21
 meaning of, 795, 817–18
Shēng. Hoist (Hexagram 46), 633–37
Shih Hé. Bite Through (Hexagram 21), 420, 493–98
Shī. The Army (Hexagram 7), 424–28
Shizuki Tadao, 75
*shou jing,* 796–98
shrine
 definition of, 760
 setting up, 760–63
Shuǐ (Water), 232, 256–57
Sima Qian, 26, 87, 627, 753
Sima Tan, 753
Sima Xiangru, 807
*Six Keys of Eudoxus,* 351, 352
Small Victories, Gain by Gain Mantra, 435
Smith, Pamela Colman, 355

social change, 650
solar terms, 42–43, 49–50, 325, 831–36
Solomonic hexagram, 349, 350
Sòng. The Trial (Hexagram 6), 419–23, 494
Son of Heaven, Twelve Hexagrams of, 47
soul dualism, 758
soul retrieval, 795–803
Sovereign Hexagrams, Twelve, 47
The Spark. Lí (Hexagram 30), 542–49
spirit body journeying, 174–78
Spirit Helpers, Eight, 84–85, 120, 186–87, 351–52, 354, 355, 356, 363, 820
*Spirit Keeper's Tarot,* 362, 363, 364
spiritual cultivation, visualization technique for, 220–22
Spring Is Coming. Lín (Hexagram 19), 484–88
Stalemate. Fǒu (Hexagram 12), 449–55
statecraft, divining on, 307–9
State Functions, Five, 238
Steadfast. Jiàn (Hexagram 53), 673–79
Su Daji. *See* Daji
Suí. Inspiring Followers (Hexagram 17), 473–77
Sǔn. Debilitation (Hexagram 41), 607–12
Sun Tzu, 191, 684, 844
Sù Nǚ, 353
Supportive Power. Kūn (Hexagram 2), 395–401
swans, 675, 677, 678, 679
sword grass, 534
synchronicity, 33, 65–68

T

Tài. Harmony (Hexagram 11), 443–49
Taiji, 132, 159–60, 164, 270–71, 353, 355, 807
Taijitu, 160
Tai, Mount, 672, 845
Tai of Zhou, King, 477
Tai Ren, 17, 19, 25
Tai Si, 18–19, 24, 25, 150, 151, 448, 683, 686, 687

Tai Sui, 458, 611, 639, 679
Takashima Donsho, 60
Taoism, 6, 28, 31, 34, 40, 57, 82–86, 160, 239, 345, 668, 782, 784, 785, 798, 808
Tao Te Ching, 4, 8, 39, 139, 258
tarot, 69, 72–73, 267, 345–58, 362–64
temple names, cultural practice of, 742
Tengrism, 778–79
Ten Wings
    authorship of, 26, 27, 34
    image statements from, 374
    preparations prior to divination, 268
    yarrow stalk method, 97, 273, 274, 278–92
Thelema, 72, 74
"there is no blame," 385–86
Thunder (Zhèn), 196–99
thunder magic, bottling, 199–201
Thunder Rites, 56, 83, 200, 277, 342, 615, 662–63, 743, 750, 751
Tiāndì, 792, 793
Tian Shi tradition, 260
time, nine categories of, 136
Tomb-Sweeping Day, 759
*tongji,* 412
Tóng Rén. Fellowship (Hexagram 13), 455–59
Toriyama Sekien, 803
totemism, 415
Toward an End. Wèi Jì (Hexagram 64), 745–53
Treading. Lǚ (Hexagram 10), 438–43
Tree of Life, 70, 71, 267, 346
The Trial. Sòng (Hexagram 6), 419–23, 494
Tria Prima, 349, 350, 351
trigrams. *See* Ba Gua
Trinity of Lucks, 279, 281
Tǔ (Earth), 232, 252–53
Tudigong, 794
Tún. Initial Challenge (Hexagram 3), 402–7
Turning Points, Five, 234
turtle shells, 780

## U

*ua neeb khu*, 795–96
Undertake the Great. Dà Guò (Hexagram 28), 532–36
Use Gentle Force. Xùn (Hexagram 57), 701–6

## V

Vajrapani, 840, 841
Văn Lang, 845

## W

Waite, A. E., 355
Wajin, 844
The Wanderer. Lǚ (Hexagram 56), 695–700
Wang Bi, 38–42, 45, 67, 100, 116, 117, 275
Wang Hai (Prince Hai), 509, 510, 512, 567–68, 570, 696, 700, 709, 712
Wáng Mǔ, 574
Water (Kǎn), 212–14
Water (Shuǐ), 232, 256–57
Way of Heaven and Man, 43
Way of the Sages, 87–88
Wèi Jì. Toward an End (Hexagram 64), 745–53
Wen of Han, Emperor, 401
Wen of Zhou, King, 9–11, 17–18, 21–22, 25, 26, 27, 64, 99, 150–51, 163–67, 229, 292, 359, 477, 579, 582, 627, 636, 683, 686, 687, 753, 774, 826. See also King Wen's revealed sequence
Western Mother, 178, 792, 793, 804–5. See also Queen Mother of the West
White Lotus, 65, 808
Wilhelm, Bettina, 65
Wilhelm, Richard, 64–65, 68, 88, 123, 128, 176, 346–47, 386
Wind (Xùn), 203–6
wind divination, 209–11
Wind spirit, bottling, 207–9
Withdraw. Dùn (Hexagram 33), 560–66, 568
Without Folly. Wú Wàng (Hexagram 25), 518–22

Wood (Mù), 231, 248–49
*wū*, 774–75, 779, 780–81, 783–84, 786. See also shamanism
Wu Ding of Shang, King (Ancestor Wu Ding, Ancestor Gaozong), 24, 740–42, 750, 843
Wuji, 160, 270–71, 353, 355, 807, 810, 811
*wú jiù*, 385–86
Wǔ Jué (Five Ranks of Nobility), 109–10, 307, 313
Wu of Han, Emperor, 401, 803
Wu of Zhou, King, 18, 19, 21–24, 25, 387, 445, 565, 572, 573, 579–80, 584, 627, 683, 694, 774
Wú Wàng. Without Folly (Hexagram 25), 518–22
*wu wei*, 275, 569
Wuxian, 787–90, 792, 806
Wu Xing (Five Phases of Change)
   astrology and, 235–36
   Ba Gua and, 170, 242–43, 245–47
   concept of, 231–32
   cycles of creation and destruction, 245–46
   days of the week and, 235
   diet and, 237–38
   Earth (Tǔ), 232, 252–53
   Fire (Huǒ), 231, 250–51
   Five Mystical Arts and, 238–44
   Five State Functions and, 238
   Four Faces of God and, 234–35
   history of, 232
   human functions and, 236–37
   importance of, 235
   Metal (Jīn), 232, 254–55
   *qi* and, 231, 232, 236–37
   ruler of a book, 139–40
   translation of, 231
   Water (Shuǐ), 232, 256–57
   Wood (Mù), 231, 248–49
   yin and yang, 231, 232–34
Wu Yi of Shang, King, 753
Wu Zetian, Empress, 19

## X

Xiàng Shù. *See* Image and Number tradition
Xián. Mutual Accord (Hexagram 31), 550–54
Xiǎo Chù. Cultivate Gently (Hexagram 9), 433–38
Xiǎo Guò. Pay Attention to Details (Hexagram 62), 121–24, 730–37
Xī Mǔ, 792, 793, 804
*xiaoren* (adversary), 383–84
Xī Wáng Mǔ. *See* Queen Mother of the West
*xuán,* 348–50, 356–57
Xuanwu, 794
Xuan Xue (School of Mystery), 45
Xún, 792, 793, 794
Xùn (Wind), 203–6
Xùn. Use Gentle Force (Hexagram 57), 701–6
Xū. Patience (Hexagram 5), 414–19
Xu Shen, 445
Xu Zhonglin, 21, 22

## Y

Yan, Johnson F., 78, 82
yang. *See* yin and yang
Yang Li, 78–79
*yao,* 117, 373
yarrow stalk divination method, 97, 267, 270, 273–95, 811–17
Yellow Emperor, 87, 91–92, 93, 178, 271, 272, 349, 400, 544, 655, 787, 817–18, 826, 844
Yellow Path. *See* Huang Tao
Yellow River, 25, 161, 387, 445, 453, 549, 780
Yellow Sea, 549
Yetts, Walter Perceval, 223
Yì. Burgeoning (Hexagram 42), 612–17
Yi Hwang, 57
Yìjiǎn, 102
Yi Jiang, 25
Yì Lǐ. *See* Meaning and Principle tradition

yin and yang
  combinations of, 157–58
  DNA and, 78–79
  in the eight trigrams, 12, 13, 96, 132, 133, 155–60
  elder and younger, 78–79, 96, 157–58, 234–35
  at equilibrium, 233–34
  Gua Qi school and, 45–52
  phase changes of, 232–33
  principles of, 156–57
  *qi* and, 95–96, 231
  symbol (Taijitu), 160
  Tao and, 157
Yí. Receive Nourishment (Hexagram 27), 526–32
Yi River, 114
*Yì wěi,* 42–44
Yì Xué (I Ching scholarship)
  diversity of, 31–32, 42
  early, 33–36, 60
  Gua Qi school, 45–52, 56
  New Text vs. Old Text schools, 36–37
  Oracle school, 59
  other Asian influences on, 57–61
  Rationalists vs. Originalists, 38–42
  School of Mystery, 45
  shifting definitions and, 35–36
  Way of the Sages, 87–88
  Western perspectives on, 61–82
*Yì wěi,* 42–44
*yomi,* 647
Yuè, 792, 793, 794
Yue, kingdom of, 845
Yù. Enthusiasm (Hexagram 16), 468–72
Yuenü, 93, 547–48
Yun Shouping, 32
Yu the Great, 12–15, 17, 18, 161, 178, 401, 430, 655, 826

## Z

Zhang Guangzhi, 774
Zhang Guo Lao, 168, 169, 219–20, 221, 794

Zhao Mengfu, 799
Zhèn (Thunder), 196–99
Zheng Yi lineage, 260
Zhèn. Jolt (Hexagram 51), 661–66, 667
Zhen Yang Zi, 345
Zhōng Fú. Faith Within (Hexagram 61), 724–30
Zhong Li Quan, 168, 169, 180–82, 184, 190, 793
Zhou dynasty, map of, 843
Zhou of Shang, King, 9, 18–23, 29, 387, 477, 623, 683, 694

Zhouyi (Basic Classic), 24, 373–75
Zhuang Zhi, 232
Zhurong, 793
Zhu Xi, 38, 40–42, 57, 59, 95, 100, 112, 117, 162, 273
Zodiac
    Eight Trigrams and, 171
    numerology of, 337
    spirit helpers and, 186
Zou Yan, 232
*zouyu*, 6, 405, 628, 629, 725–26
Zu Yi of Shang, King, 787

# ACKNOWLEDGMENTS

I am grateful to Gillian Hamel for overseeing the production of this book—your expertise, tireless support, kindness, and adept management made everything possible. To be part of the North Atlantic Books family of authors is a privilege; their team of editors take such good care of us and are fearless when it comes to standing up for equity and justice.

Brent Winter greatly improved the readability of this manuscript. Many thanks to the proofreaders Karen Davis and Zhui Ning Chang (@witchywonderer). The typesetting and layout can be credited to the magnificent efforts of Maureen Forys and Jeff Lytle, with creative input from Jasmine Hromjak. Thank you to Mimi Bark for the cover design. And this type of book would not be as accessible without an index, so for that I am grateful to Ken DellaPenta. Bevin Donahue, who I have worked with on several books, thank you for all that you do.

To my inspiring polymath cousin Yu-fen Chen 陳玉芬, who is a preeminent vessel for the Oracle in her own right—you have been formative in my work with the I Ching. Ah Ma 陳駱品, Ah Gong 陳生枝, I feel you ever present in my bones. Ah Po 溫詹綢妹, every day you showed me what it means to be Buddhist. Ah Gong 溫喜財, I honor the trail you blazed. All my reverence to 張民壽 and 許曉明, who have welcomed me into the 張 and 許 families.

I am grateful to have connected with the late Prof. Kerson Huang 黃克孫, whose translation of the I Ching introduced me to Eastern philosophy. To my AAPI witchy fam: the charismatic occult author and thought leader Chaweon Koo (@chaweonkoo), powerful conjurer and diviner Ryan Trinh (@ryantheconjureman), and the brilliant journalist and advocate Fei Lu (@thisisfeilu), I lean on you, I am inspired by you, I'm always cheering for you.

To the pillars of my tradition who sidestep the limelight because the real work, the hard work, that bearing the more profound influence and the service that matters the most occupies so much of you that you do not seek splendor: I honor you.

# ABOUT THE AUTHOR

benebell wen is neither a multigenerational lineaged Taoist master nor an Ivy League university professor. She's a daughter, wife, and sister, living a pleasantly moderate life. She enjoys posting food and garden photos on Instagram @bellwen, travel, and cheap wine.

Her previous publications include *The Tao of Craft: Fu Talismans and Casting Sigils in the Eastern Esoteric Tradition* (2016) and *Holistic Tarot: An Integrative Approach to Using Tarot for Personal Growth* (2015). For multimedia supplements and addenda to this book, please visit www.benebellwen.com.

## *About North Atlantic Books*

North Atlantic Books (NAB) is a 501(c)(3) nonprofit publisher committed to a bold exploration of the relationships between mind, body, spirit, culture, and nature. Founded in 1974, NAB aims to nurture a holistic view of the arts, sciences, humanities, and healing. To make a donation or to learn more about our books, authors, events, and newsletter, please visit www.northatlanticbooks.com.